The Colonial Problem

The Colonial Problem: An Indigenous Perspective on Crime and Injustice in Canada

LISA MONCHALIN

UNIVERSITY OF TORONTO PRESS

LIBRARY AND ARCHIVES CANADA CATALOGUING IN PUBLICATION

Monchalin, Lisa, 1981–, author
The colonial problem : an Indigenous perspective on crime and injustice in Canada / Lisa Monchalin.

Includes bibliographical references and index.

Issued in print and electronic formats.

ISBN 978-1-4426-0805-4 (bound).—ISBN 978-1-4426-0662-3 (paperback).—
ISBN 978-1-4426-0663-0 (pdf).—ISBN 978-1-4426-0664-7 (html).

1. Native peoples—Cultural assimilation—Canada. 2. Native peoples—Colonization—Canada. 3. Native peoples—Canada—Social conditions. 4. Native peoples—Crimes against—Canada. 5. Native peoples—Legal status, laws, etc.—Canada. 6. Native peoples—Canada—Government relations. 7. Criminal justice, Administration of—Canada. I. Title.

E78.C2M59 2015 305.897'071 C2015-903725-5
C2015-903726-3

We welcome comments and suggestions regarding any aspect of our publications—please feel free to contact us at news@utphighereducation.com or visit our Internet site at www.utppublishing.com.

North America
5201 Dufferin Street
North York, Ontario, Canada, M3H 5T8

2250 Military Road
Tonawanda, New York, USA, 14150

ORDERS PHONE: 1-800-565-9523
ORDERS FAX: 1-800-221-9985
ORDERS E-MAIL: utpbooks@utpress.utoronto.ca

UK, Ireland, and continental Europe
NBN International
Estover Road, Plymouth, PL6 7PY, UK
ORDERS PHONE: 44 (0) 1752 202301
ORDERS FAX: 44 (0) 1752 202333
ORDERS E-MAIL: enquiries@nbninternational.com

This book is printed on paper containing 100% post-consumer fibre.

The University of Toronto Press acknowledges the financial support for its publishing activities of the Government of Canada through the Canada Book Fund.

Printed in the United States of America

For Grandma Monchalin. She explained that, upon her first sight of me when I was born, she felt that I would make a difference for our peoples. This is one of my attempts, so I dedicate this book to her, as part of trying to walk this path.

Contents

Illustrations

Figures

Images

Table

Acknowledgements

KWEY KWEY. LISA MONCHALIN NIDIJINIKÀZ. NIAGARA NIDONJABÀ. I am grateful to the land in which I live, work, and play and to which I wrote this book. The majority of the writing took place in the shared traditional unceded territories of Kwantlen, Katzie, Semiahmoo, and Tsawwassen, where I currently reside. Some parts were also written while I was living on unceded Algonquin territory.

The completion of this book would not have been possible without the unwavering support of several friends, family members, and colleagues. My sister Renée Monchalin was always a phone call away, ready at any time to talk through ideas or concepts. Rex Turna proofread an early draft. Nadine Pluzak spent countless hours of her time proofreading and providing many thoughtful comments. I am extremely thankful for all of this wonderful help, love, and support.

Another big thank you goes to Sino General, Shelly Hill, Melinda Bige, Shylo Pruyn and Jerilynn Snuxyaltwa Webster who all continued to provide their words of encouragement throughout the writing phase. I wish to also thank to my PhD supervisor and mentor Irvin Waller, who provided invaluable guidance and support. I want to acknowledge also the outstanding reviewers Greg Younging, Wenona Victor, Jennifer Dalton, and Rob Nestor, as well as the blind reviewers, who provided exceptional and helpful feedback that shaped this book. The time and energy you gave are much appreciated, and your thought-provoking comments and suggestions were extremely valuable.

I am grateful for the time, experiences, opinions, and stories shared by Darrell Bob, Robert Shintah, Kim Baird, Dan General, Ian Campeau, and Bear Witness, which helped shape parts of this book. I am also appreciative of the time and comments provided by Jeff Corntassel and Taiaiake Alfred. They graciously had me out to the University of Victoria, where they provided outstanding comments, feedback, conversation, and support for which I am forever grateful.

A special thanks goes to my friends and colleagues at Kwantlen Polytechnic University. Jeff Shantz, Chuck Reasons, Michael Ma, Hisham Ramadan, Seema Ahluwalia, Mike Larsen, Wade Deisman, Jane Miller-Ashton, and Dave Lyon warrant notable mention, as they provided intellectual guidance and keen support throughout the project. A special thank you goes to

Darlene Willier who has provided guidance, advice, and insightful conversation. I would also like to express gratitude to my previous colleague Stephen Dooley, who has been a great friend and mentor during this process.

Thank you to Jackie Traverse for her amazing artwork that is on the cover of this book. I would also like to thank Karen Taylor who did an outstanding job copyediting this book. Thank you to Jesse Thistle for his outstanding advice on certain historical terminology.

A big thank you is also deserved for the Pow Wow community. Dancing helped carry me through this project. The laughter, friendship, and healing in the Pow Wow circle has been key to this books completion. When I needed a break, I would dance, laugh, and socialize with this amazing circle of friends and family. Finally, a big *meegwetch* to my ancestors who have been with me every step of the way as I danced to heal, listened and watched to learn, and taught and wrote to try to make a difference for our future generations.

Note to Instructors

I am of mixed descent, a combination of Algonquin, Métis, Huron, and Scottish. I feel just as much Algonquin as I do Métis, and just as much Huron as I do Scottish, and just as much Métis as I do Huron, and so on. I was born in St. Catharines, Ontario, and grew up in the Niagara Region of that province (having been raised mainly in Haudenosaunee and Neutral traditional territory there). I received a rowing scholarship in 2001 to attend Eastern Michigan University on Chippewa, Ottawa, Potawatomi, and Wyandot shared territories (Ypsilanti, Michigan) where I did my bachelor's and master's degrees in criminology. In 2006, I moved to Algonquin territory (Ottawa, Ontario) where I did my PhD in criminology at the University of Ottawa. I now live in Kwantlen, Katzie, Semiahmoo, and Tsawwassen shared territories (Surrey, British Columbia) and teach at Kwantlen Polytechnic University in the Criminology Department. I am subject to my own experiences, teachings, and research.

Whether Indigenous, non-Indigenous, mixed, or undefined, everyone is welcome to use and read this book to pursue education and learning; exclusion has never been part of Indigenous cultures. If one attempts to teach or learn about cultures and knowledges other than one's own, situating oneself is a first step. This step includes self-reflecting on personal standpoints and acknowledging bias. However, a person trying to "learn" Indigenous cultures or realities from a book will have an incomplete knowledge of them. These cultures and realities must be lived and experienced. Good intentions are useful when one learns and teaches outside of the context of lived experience, but many horrible atrocities throughout the world were done with the "best of intentions." Consequently, an acknowledgement of difference and of limitation is due when someone is teaching about or informing others on another group's culture or realities. And those not from Indigenous cultures must consult people with lived experience of those cultures.

This is not to say that non-Indigenous peoples cannot teach courses on Indigenous justice or on related matters, but a caution is in order. Students must be told who instructors are, where they come from, and any biases they might hold. This presentation of the instructor as a subjective self is important and must not be glossed over, given the colonial past and present.

Any scholar or professor today understands the need to acknowledge perspective and bias. But doing so consistently and comprehensively throughout our interactions with colleagues and students is crucial when we research and teach about peoples who have faced injustice, subjugation, assimilation, and even extermination at the hands of colonial powers—whose ideologies still inform contemporary judicial, political, and societal structures.

How, then, should we teach? Indigenous education scholar Susan Dion (Lenape and Potawatomi) suggests being conscious of and working from your own position. She encourages non-Indigenous educators to follow Indigenous peoples' lead and stand with us as "a settler in solidarity, an Indigenous ally, and tell your story of learning."[1] Algonquin Anishinaabe-kwe scholar Lynn Gehl has developed an "Ally Bill of Responsibilities" that outlines 16 different settler responsibilities. The first is that responsible allies should not "act out of guilt, but rather out of a genuine interest in challenging the larger oppressive power structures."[2] South Asian activist and author Harsha Walia contends that, for non-Indigenous peoples to ally with Indigenous peoples, they must be "accountable and responsive to the experiences, voices, needs and political perspectives of Indigenous peoples themselves."[3]

Sociology professor Seema Ahluwalia who teaches and researches in areas of Indigenous justice, describes herself as "a Canadian settler of Punjabi ancestry."[4] She explains that she deliberately uses the term "settler" as a way of foregrounding her understanding of ongoing colonial occupation and to "out" herself to Indigenous scholars as someone consciously engaged in the process of decolonization. Political science professor Rita Dhamoon (who is from Punjab, India) explains that the use of the term "settler" definitely remains contentious.[5] One point of argument involves distinguishing between white settlers and settlers of colour because settlers of colour, like Indigenous peoples, experience racism, and many have experienced colonialism in their countries of origin. As Dhamoon further clarifies, the term "settler" situates non-Indigenous peoples "in a structural relationship to dispossession of Indigenous land and within imperialistic nation-building projects that require ongoing settlement."[6]

Indigenous governance professor and Tsalagi scholar Jeff Corntassel suggests looking to Indigenous words for "settler" in order to put the focus on what this term means from an Indigenous perspective and from Indigenous lived experience.[7] As he explains, *yonega* is a Tsalagi (Cherokee) term for white settlers, which means "foam of the water; moved by wind and without its own direction; clings to everything that's solid." *Wasicu* is a Dakota term for settlers, which means "taker of fat." In the northwest, *hwunitum* is a Hul'qumi'num and SENĆOŦEN word for settler, that some have described as meaning "the hungry people."

These words give insight into Indigenous understandings of and perspectives on settlers, which might not be understood fully if we relied only on colonial languages. We must acknowledge that where one stands in the world affects one's view. So inviting into the classroom the languages and perspectives of those about whom one is teaching is crucial.

Teaching Material that Challenges

In all of my classes, I ask students, "Who has heard of residential schools?" Often, only a few raise their hands. Many have never heard about residential schools. This reality reflects the presence and operation of the colonial mindset in the education system. A 2008 national benchmark survey reveals that, although 80 per cent of Indigenous peoples are aware of residential schools, only 51 per cent of Canadians have heard of them.[8] The survey also found that just over one-third (36 per cent) of Canadians reported being somewhat familiar with the issues surrounding residential schools, and only 1 in 20 (6 per cent) reported being very familiar.[9] According to the same survey, Canadians are somewhat but not strongly aware of current Indigenous issues in Canada. When asked, one-third (33 per cent) of Canadians were unable to say what they thought the most important issue facing Indigenous peoples was.[10] The point is that many students could be unaware of unjust Canadian policies.

Students could also have very different views of Canadian and Indigenous history and politics, depending upon their heritage. In interviews conducted with 70 First Nations and Métis peoples (including 14 residential school survivors) and 70 white, Euro-Canadian residents in northwestern Ontario in 2008–09, Indigenous peoples and Euro-Canadians framed issues regarding residential schools—such as the national apology, the associated monetary settlement, and reconciliation and healing—in incompatible ways.[11] For instance, although most did agree that monetary compensation cannot remove the survivors' pain, many Indigenous peoples felt that monetary compensation was insufficient, whereas many Euro-Canadians felt that it was excessive. When asked about follow-up actions, the majority of Euro-Canadians (56 per cent) felt that Indigenous peoples needed to "just move on." A typical response was this: "Look, we've apologized. It's over and done. What more do they want? Move on!"[12] On the other hand, when Indigenous peoples were asked about follow-up actions, most provided practical healing suggestions, with 82 per cent of respondents citing specific actions that could be taken by governments, churches, and local residents.

To address the general lack of knowledge about Indigenous issues, some professors and educators have incorporated the study of Indigenous history and Indigenous peoples in their courses when the opportunity arises. Recent conversations, writings, and conferences involving Indigenous educators and allies have pointed to a need to "indigenize the academy." Discussions focus on how to make universities welcoming for Indigenous cultures, knowledge, students, staff, and faculty.[13] Also explored are new ways of integrating Indigenous peoples and knowledge in academic institutions and how to make these a central focus in university operations and curriculum.

Many universities and colleges across Canada have included Indigenous education in their strategic plans or priorities.[14] Memorial University of Newfoundland's strategic plan has a goal of partnering with Indigenous peoples and communities, which includes promoting "research on issues affecting aboriginal peoples, their culture and heritage."[15] The University of Regina's 2009–14 strategic plan is titled *mâmawohkamâtowin: Our Work, Our People, Our Communities*. It borrows the Cree word *mâmawohkamâtowin*, which means "co-operation; working together towards common goals."[16] Educators at the university note their continued commitment to learn from Indigenous peoples, as well as from their colleagues at the First Nation University of Canada, to assure that First Nations and Métis cultures are reflected across their programs and campus life. The university's 2015–20 plan is entitled *peyak aski kikawinaw: Together We Are Stronger*; the borrowed Cree words can be translated as "We are one with Mother Earth." [17] Since 2009, the University of British Columbia has a specific section on Aboriginal engagement in all strategic plans; this section includes expanding curriculum offerings for courses containing significant Aboriginal content, as well as increasing service learning opportunities with Aboriginal organizations and schools.[18] Although these attempts to "indigenize the academy" show improved "effort," at its root, the purpose is flawed. The "academy" is a colonial institution, so "indigenizing" it misses the real structural change that must happen in order for Indigenous knowledge, peoples, and research to become more than a piece of the colonial construct. Rather, we must carve out our own space where authentic work can be done by and for Indigenous peoples.

The task is difficult because "white" culture dominates in Canada. This culture is rooted in early European philosophies that were formed out of European colonial expansion and constructed by white people in their own image.[19] It is "defined by several strong features including capitalistic market society structure; belief in progress and science; possession of modern concepts of family[;] and societal group structures based on individualism, competition, social mobility, and belief in Eurocentric cultural, philosophical, and economic superiority."[20] These features remain entrenched in and dominate Western thought. This culture of "whiteness" remains hidden within early Euro-Canadian inherited "grand narratives" of "Western Enlightenment," including Eurocentric rationality and histories, religious bodies, media and technologies, and Western systems of education.[21] It operates at an invisible level, producing, spreading, and preserving racism in Canadian society throughout its numerous institutions.

Historical knowledge has been, and continues to be, dominated by white people. They have put into writing how events will be remembered, and these events have usually been told from a Eurocentric perspective and not in their entirety. For instance, history books present accounts of white "battles" while describing "massacres" by Indigenous peoples.[22] White history has attributed the practice of "scalping" solely to "barbarous" Indigenous behaviour while, in truth, this practice was often used and encouraged by Europeans as a way of exterminating Indigenous peoples resisting settler encroachment.[23] General Canadian history has typically minimized or rationalized the realities of colonization, and most Canadians will distance themselves from the wrongful acts perpetrated by their European forebears.[24] Many also fail to acknowledge that all remain accomplices through contributing to a society that perpetuates continued injustices.

Because of the "whiteness" of Canadian culture, many misconceptions and stereotypes about Indigenous peoples remain. These are entrenched in the dominant discourse, and, because of these believed stereotypes, people find it difficult to admit they have prejudices. Olga Marques and I conducted a research project that brought to light some people's prejudices about Indigenous peoples.[25] We did a content analysis of 657 story comments posted in response to an initial article from the CBC regarding the Akwesasne border dispute of 2009. To post a comment to a news story, a person needs to register with the CBC but need not use a real name, so a commentator can hide behind a fake identity. Many comments were racist, implying that Indigenous peoples were "lesser" human beings and indicating a mind-set that viewed Indigenous peoples as "the other." Some comments suggested Indigenous peoples were a threat to dominant Canadian governance structures. In general, the study showed that denial of colonialism continues, as does the mentality that Indigenous peoples need to "just get over it" and assimilate. It made clear that colonial assaults on Indigenous peoples still exist and frame everyday reality for many.

The view that the general public has of Indigenous peoples is largely based on mass media descriptions, which often characterize them as militant and radical when they try to protect their land or water. In particular, by associating warrior societies, "the most visible face of . . . resistance," with organized crime and violence, the media criminalizes Indigenous protest, "adhering to several themes that build upon the colonial mythology and serve to demonize indigenous people," according to Mohawk scholar Taiaiake Alfred and Lana Lowe (from Fort Nelson First Nation).[26] The media spin that casts protesting Indigenous peoples as criminal and violent and stages them as people who are only participating in violence for violence sake could not be further from the truth. Rather, Indigenous movements and their associated organizations, such as warrior societies, are premised on connecting to land and asserting nationhood.

Stó:lō scholar Wenona Victor points out that "the brutality of the colonial process has been denied and kept from the general population," and "it remains largely unknown and has yet to be fully written let alone acknowledged."[27] Consider as evidence of this denial and ignorance a book found at a popular mall in Surrey, British Columbia, published in 2012. It is entitled *We Are Canada: A Very, Very Short History of Canada*, and here is what it has to say about land claims: "The First Nations agreed to surrender all rights to the land, forever, in exchange for exclusive reserves of land, cash payments to each band member, and continued royalties."[28] These inaccurate ideas, understandings, and opinions are still published, used, and accepted by many, and they are pervasive.

Given this discourse on Indigenous peoples and Canadian history, students will likely arrive at college and university classes with understandings and opinions informed by inaccurate information, or by a lack of information.[29] Indeed, a 2002 national Canadian survey of 519 first-year college and university students—who were graduates of Canadian public education—found that 67 per cent of respondents never discussed issues of concern to Indigenous peoples in their elementary or secondary classrooms.[30] Eighty per cent of students surveyed also indicated that they were dissatisfied or strongly dissatisfied with Indigenous studies curriculum in their elementary and secondary school experience. One respondent from Ontario noted, "I was barely taught ANYTHING regarding Aboriginal peoples in school. I am absolutely clueless with regard to these issues. I am uneducated on these matters and as such feel ill equipped to even have an opinion much less come to an understanding."[31]

This situation may not improve quickly. A 2012 research study examining Métis and Indigenous content in Ontario university faculties of education found "overwhelming evidence of ongoing and deeply embedded resistance to engaging with Aboriginal Education by students in Teacher Education Programs."[32] In interviews, 18 recent graduates of Ontario teacher education programs "reported learning 'not much' or 'very little' about teaching Aboriginal content, and 'absolutely nothing' about teaching Métis specific content."[33]

So let us consider, for a moment, all the challenges that face a person teaching about Indigenous peoples and contemporary circumstances. People lack an understanding of Indigenous peoples' struggles, survival, and traditions. Historically, education has been delivered in a way that validates colonialism. Postsecondary educational institutions are notably reflective of white Euro-Canadian content, values, and perspectives. Eurocentrism has become naturalized in Canadian institutions and is now assumed to be the *only* world view to embrace in order to arrive at knowledge and "truths."[34] Correct depictions of history weaken or threaten European hegemony, power, and culture on this land, so they will be resisted. Canadian school curriculum has historically ignored Indigenous accomplishments, complexities, and even the existence of various Indigenous peoples and cultures.[35]

Teaching about Indigenous peoples and justice, then, will not be easy. Probably, you will face resistance, and sometimes you might be confronted with racist or emotionally difficult opposition. I have experienced all of these things. For instance, on the very first day of the first class I taught about Indigenous justice, a student raised his hand to comment. "I'm disgusted at how many are addicted to solvents," he said, noting that this "gas sniffing" happens because Indigenous peoples are "weaker" than others. The comment made me sick, physically sick. But I was able to use it to introduce the topic of stereotypical assumptions and their role in continuing colonialism. As the class continued and students introduced themselves, one woman identified herself as Métis. I had an immediate sense of relief. The earlier racist comment had made me feel isolated, but now I felt that I would have an Indigenous sister with me throughout the course for support. At the same time, I felt a big responsibility to her, a duty to reinforce that our peoples are strong and that our ways are valid. After class, another woman let me know privately that she was Indigenous. She did not want to disclose this heritage to the class because she did not want to be dismissed as simply "another Indian" when she voiced opinions. This story gives a simplified version of the deeply felt and sometimes hostile emotions that can emerge in classes focusing on systemic injustice.

After this first class, I knew that teaching about Indigenous justice would require me to include Indigenous ways of coming to know and learn—and to legitimize these ways of knowing and learning as valid forms of understanding. Yet, at the same time, I needed to present material in a way that would capture students used to the dominant Western methods of arriving at knowledge and "truth." Achieving this balance takes effort, as one must draw on a large array of sources, including statistical data, academic literature from across disciplines, scientific reason, and, at the same time, traditional knowledge, voices from the Indigenous community, elder knowledge, and other non-Western resources.

Being an Indigenous woman teaching in the academy also brings many challenges. I will tell some of these challenges to highlight the fact that we are teaching in an environment that tolerates (some would say perpetuates) injustices.

During the first course on criminal justice administration that I taught as a full-time faculty member, I was harassed throughout the term. I was brought to my office door by loud knocks, only to find no one there; I received heavy breathing and hang ups on my personal cell phone or text messages calling me names; and hostile messages were left for me to find on the chalkboard and on my office door. I stayed silent about this harassment, not wanting to be viewed by my new colleagues as "the problem Indian" and fearful of losing my position.

An atrocious and degrading letter threatening me with rape and giving details, including sick drawings and personal information about my residence and referencing my birthday, changed my mind. I called the RCMP and campus security to notify them of the letter. My interaction with these authority figures was also humiliating. I was brought into the security office, seated between a male security guard and a male RCMP officer, and asked to read the letter out loud for a recording device.

A handwriting analysis comparing the letter to the final exam of one of my students confirmed the identity of the culprit. I was encouraged not to press charges because the student was sorry and the charges would lead nowhere—except they might damage the student's future. He wanted to become a police officer.

I tried to put this incident behind me and move on with my teaching, but, a year or so later, I started to receive sexualized emails at work. After consulting a colleague I could trust, I notified the university judicial affairs office, asking for a resolution that addressed the student sending me emails and my previous stalker, who remained a student at the university. The formal processes of complaint required me to retell all stories and provide evidence. In the end, all the students involved remained in the criminology program, where I continued to teach.

I tell a softened version of this story here only to show how violently people can resist messages that threaten their perspectives and how difficult it is, in an atmosphere geared to credit those perspectives, to maintain one's own view calmly, in the face of opposition, while treating others with openness.

In addition to these experiences, racially charged student papers and appraisals of my teaching have been the norm. For instance, one student appraisal said I taught "propaganda." Another student constantly interrupted my class, challenging the material on colonialism and arguing that racism does not exist. Reflective journal assignments would contain all sorts of racially charged statements about Indigenous peoples being "lazy" or "drunk" or getting "everything for free." Ultimately, to teach against these attempts to silence the voices, histories, and cultures of Indigenous peoples—and in institutions that continue to uphold racism and patriarchy—one must reach out to other Indigenous faculty, friends, and allies for support.

Mohawk scholar and law professor Patricia Monture-Angus taught law from a perspective that acknowledges the true history of Indigenous peoples in Canada, and she has noted how her teaching has been devalued and attacked within the university environment.[36] She, too, experienced students turning in blatantly racist papers and claiming that she was teaching "propaganda, not law." She notes the "air of European superiority" present in student exams, which were difficult to grade given that she was forced to subject herself to this hostility and racism in students' work.[37] Evaluations of her teaching sometimes seemed based on racist fantasies: a student wrote that she wore "too many beads and feathers to class" although she never wore any because, as she explains the situation, she was trying to "find individual ways to protect (some might say hide)" her difference.[38] For Monture-Angus, the monolithic white (and male) voice remains sanctioned within education in Canada, and it will continue to exclude and silence "those of us who speak in a different voice."[39]

In the words of Paulette Regan, "Indigenous peoples must speak with their own voices about their histories, cultures, and experiences as people who continue to resist the onslaught of colonial structures, policies, and practices."[40] When the knowledge systems of Indigenous peoples are heard, honoured, and respected, that will be a step toward walking a path to healing.

For non-Indigenous peoples, learning about injustices can produce feelings of guilt, anger, and shame. Some people will resist learning about the violent, brutal, and heinous policies and practices of the cultural annihilation, European domination, subjugation, and exploitation of Indigenous peoples. This story challenges the Canadian identity, the country's view of itself "as a nation of benevolent peacemakers."[41] Learning about these aforementioned realties not only brings students' conceptual understandings into dispute but also challenges students at an emotional level. According to Professors Megan Boler and Michalinos Zembylas, this teaching "often means asking students to radically reevaluate their worldviews," which "emphasizes the need for both educator and student to move outside their comfort zones."[42] Yet as Paulette Regan notes, stepping outside of one's comfort zone can serve "as a catalyst for engaging in constructive critical dialogue."[43]

The goal of educating students on Indigenous injustices is not to shame and blame but to join people from all backgrounds together as brothers and sisters on this healing and educational journey. Such a journey will involve truth telling, challenging world views, and taking action to address historical wrongs. Canadian settler of Punjabi ancestry Seema Ahluwalia notes that reflecting on this shameful history will be painful for Canadians, yet continuing down the "path of denial, hypocrisy and historical amnesia" will serve no one—"not the students who demand relevant and responsive education, and not the educational institutions that will continue to alienate non-Western students and students from the Western world who live as minorities in white settler nation-states."[44] It is my hope that this book will further the goal of achieving Indigenous justice *and* contribute to dismantling colonial narratives (what Ahluwalia calls "the fantasies of Eurocentrism"), as these histories are no longer credible in Canada.

In the Classroom

Teaching this material in a Euro-Canadian classroom is neither traditional nor ideal.[45] There are some ways to work around this problem. One is to get out of the classroom and learn from the natural world. Another is to focus on the oral transmission of knowledge: include storytelling in your class, share lived experiences, and incorporate non-textual material. I bring drumming and singing into the classroom and share traditional songs (where permission is given) and social songs. Each song has a story, teaching, or meaning associated with it. I also invite guests to the class to share songs, stories, and teachings, and I honour these guests or elders in customary ways (e.g., with offerings of tobacco and water). I also give each an honorarium to cover expenses. Additionally, it is important to acknowledge the guest's gift of time and experience and to prepare the class to receive teachings with an open heart and spirit. Smudging or other ceremonies might be used, under the direction of elders or those who practice the cultures, to prepare students to learn.

Bringing in others who are a part of the cultures students are learning about and who can share lived experience is essential. Thinking of oneself as a facilitator of knowledge transmission, rather than as an "expert," is one effective way to deliver material. Incorporating terms, concepts, or words in an Indigenous language connects learners to the teachings of the lands. Draw on local language to honour the land on which one is situated. If the world is depicted only through the English language, then people are limited to seeing and understanding only what the English language conveys. Language embodies traditional knowledges; it can open the door to a culture; it allows for the interpretation of the world through Indigenous concepts and understandings. As Nêhíyaw and Saulteaux scholar Margaret Kovach explains, "Language matters because it holds within it a people's worldview."[46] Also, because English is the language of the settler and of the nation responsible for colonizing most of Canada, its words can have connotations that are unfriendly to Indigenous cultures. As Mohawk scholar Patricia Monture-Angus explains, it is an insufficient language for fully expressing Indigenous people's experiences, as it is the language of our colonization.[47] According to Nishnaabeg scholar Leanne Simpson "learning through the language" can provide those who are not familiar with an Indigenous language a window through which they can learn "the complexities and depth" of Indigenous cultures.[48]

For some concepts, such as connection to the natural environment and feelings of Indigenous identity as these relate to the land, Indigenous languages are essential. As anthropologist W. E. H. Stanner notes, "No English words are good enough to give a sense of the links between an Aboriginal group and its homeland."[49] I find singing traditional songs helps to solidify the language as I learn it. Through the singing of traditional songs, I continue to learn and honour my language. Of course, one does not have to know an Indigenous language fully in order to teach a class on Indigenous justice, but it is beneficial to be able to incorporate concepts from Indigenous languages. Doing so actively engages students in a small, but important, process of decolonization.

Using Indigenous teaching methods, such as storytelling and sharing circles, is also an act of decolonization. These help students become active participants in the process of learning cultures. Additionally, incorporating these approaches validates them as acceptable, correct, and essential ways to exchange and learn. When I share songs with my students in class, I also pass on the teaching I have received from the song. This approach lets me share both content, the story that coincides with the song, cultural processes, and Indigenous ways of knowledge sharing.

Other useful activities involve helping students understand the history of the land on which they currently reside. Who lived on this land before Europeans arrived in Canada? How did they live? How do we know about them? These questions will lead to discussions about oral history and cultural items. Indigenous research methods and ways of coming to know can be incorporated into research assignments.[50] Encourage students to seek out material written by Indigenous peoples and to acquaint themselves with the extensive body of Indigenous works. Instruct students to visit the Indigenous centre on campus to gain access to resources. Advise them to consult Indigenous academic journals and newspapers. Have students explore the Indigenous studies section in libraries. Some libraries, such as the Edmonton Public Library, have an Aboriginal collection that focuses on resources written, performed, or produced by Indigenous peoples. In addition to written materials, knowledge acquired through dreams and from the natural environment can be cited and used for assignments, research, and class discussions. It is my hope that expanding students' ways of knowing will broaden what they understand to be true.

Introduction and Purpose: Understanding and Reducing Injustice

THE BROAD GOAL OF THIS BOOK is to provide an expansive consideration and in-depth examination of the injustice affecting Indigenous peoples. Injustice is defined as a lack of harmony and balance.[1] This book seeks to illuminate this lack of harmony and balance in an effort to seek justice for Indigenous peoples. It does not seek to outline or apply the dominant Western conception of justice, which pursues an individualist and materialistic sameness. Rather, it seeks Indigenous justice, which Mohawk scholar Taiaiake Alfred describes as "the achievement of respectful coexistence—restoration of harmony to the network of relationships and renewed commitment to ensuring the integrity and physical, emotional, and spiritual health of all individuals and communities."[2] Thus, to seek justice is to strive for harmony, balance, and peaceful coexistence.

By drawing on and bringing together various literatures, voices, histories, and interpretations, as well as by interjecting my own personal understandings of such works, I hope to shed light on the injustices affecting Indigenous peoples. However, so many injustices face Indigenous peoples today that they cannot be outlined in the small confines of one book. Nevertheless, the purpose of this book is to illuminate as much as it can of the past, current, and ongoing injustices affecting Indigenous peoples, so as to further the aim of seeking harmony and balance.

As a criminologist using an Indigenous justice lens, I define the injustice affecting Indigenous peoples as a "crime." I do not rely on state definitions of what a "crime" is, as it is my belief that the Canadian state itself has been built on crime. In my definition, then, crime is a dysfunction that upsets harmony and balance, a definition that parallels my view of injustice. Thus, the focus of this book is not on the Canadian criminal justice system. Portions of the book do focus on criminal justice, but I do not seek for or expect to find justice through such a system, which is foreign and does not strive to treat Indigenous peoples with respect and even-handedness. This book seeks to reduce harm and advance harmony through education. It aims to teach Canadians about their own colonial history; to educate university students on issues pertinent to Indigenous peoples; to encourage good relations between cultures; to challenge the stereotypes, misconceptions, and outright lies regarding Indigenous peoples; and to share important Indigenous teachings, philosophies, and values so as to help pave the way for a better future for all.

My inner drive moves me to speak out about the injustices facing Indigenous peoples. I do this because I am united with my Indigenous sisters and brothers across Turtle Island. I do this because I feel an inner duty as an Indigenous woman to reclaim our voices. Like many Indigenous peoples, I am connected through personal relations and history to the injustices I discuss. This injustice is more than a curious question to examine. Studying it and writing a book about it is about making a difference.

I share the vision of activist Charles Eisenstein, who wants to create "the better world our hearts know is possible, a world that works for everyone."[3]

Being educated about and aware of Indigenous injustice are the first steps Canadians need to take in order to reduce this injustice. According to Taiaiake Alfred, one way to effect change is through higher education. He states that "education holds the best promise for positive change, because it creates awareness of the inconsistencies between the world as it is and as it should be."[4] Education is a crucial starting point for rectifying injustices. The need to educate is one of the reasons I chose to write a textbook because, as Dakota Sioux scholar, visionary, and activist Vine Deloria Jr. says, the "problems" affecting Indigenous peoples "have always been ideological," so it is vitally important that Indigenous peoples choose the ideological arena as the one in which to make a difference. Therefore, in order to reduce injustices and crime affecting Indigenous peoples, I follow the teachings of Vine Deloria Jr. and attempt change by using "ideological leverage."[5]

The Canadian government has continually imposed its colonial "truths" on institutional structures. This imposition has caused a disruption, one that has led to many injustices. Western world views and the oppressive power structures they uphold have to be dissected to establish what can be useful and what should be left behind. In the words of the Dalai Lama, what our world needs to solve its problems is "critical thinking, followed by action."[6] We must achieve change, as Brazilian liberatory educator Paulo Freire suggests, through praxis, "that is, with *reflection* and *action* directed at the structures to be transformed.[7]

This book presents one Indigenous woman's truths and views—one Indigenous woman's voice. My purpose is to help readers hear, see, engage with, and share in this interconnected and Indigenous perspective. If ideas are only presented from the dominant colonial perspective, a real understanding of why Indigenous peoples face injustice will not be revealed fully. If material is presented through a colonial lens, it will simply reinforce the very perspective that plays a large part in contributing to the various injustices

Indigenous peoples face. Colonial interpretations include incorrect, inaccurate, and glossed-over versions of Indigenous history. They also ignore or discount Indigenous voices and perspectives.

Yet I speak for myself. I cannot speculate as to what other Indigenous peoples might think. I do not speak for all Indigenous women or people. One cannot homogenize Indigenous peoples, assuming we all have the same view on injustice and crime. I refuse to bolster this incorrect assumption rooted in colonial misrepresentations and fuelled by inaccurate stereotypes.

This book challenges readers to see beyond these misrepresentations rooted in and upheld by colonialism. According to professor of ethnic studies Mario Barrera, colonialism "is a structured relationship of domination and subordination, where the dominant and subordinate groups are defined along ethnic and/or racial lines, and where the relationship is established and maintained to serve the interests of all or part of the dominate group."[8] As First Nations political leader Arthur Manuel (Secwepemc) sees it, "colonialism has basically three parts, dispossession, dependency and oppression."[9] Indigenous peoples became dispossessed of their land base, were forced to live under a Canadian system of law and governance, and, because dispossessed, were compelled to become dependent on a foreign colonial system. Under this colonial system, Indigenous peoples as a whole became problematized—the "Indian problem." Colonizers then used irrational notions of racial and cultural superiority to subjugate Indigenous peoples—to solve the "problem" by taking their land and suppressing their rights and cultures.

This book might present some readers with discomforting realities. I write from a political standpoint. In Canada, many dance around politics with politeness, avoiding the fact that dispossession and colonialism are at the root of Indigenous injustice. These unpleasant facts are not debatable. Taiaiake Alfred explains that Indigenous peoples are still thought of as "the problem" today, as those "who need to reconcile with the modern day reality of what Canada is—as opposed to Canadians having to reconcile that their country is built on crime, and that their country has been built on injustices."[10] Māori scholar Linda Tuhiwai Smith notes the Western obsession with problematizing Indigenous peoples. By the 1960s, she argues, this "indigenous problem" had become part of academic discourse and research. As Smith states, "The belief in the 'indigenous problem' is still present in the Western psyche" and "is a recurrent theme in all imperial and colonial attempts to deal with indigenous peoples."[11] It stems from the widespread discourses of sexism and racism, and through other methods of positioning "the other." To Taiaiake Alfred, the "problem" needs to be reframed. We need to ask, "What is wrong with Canada?" rather than "What is the problem with Indians?"[12]

One problem with Canada is that its accepted history is inaccurate. In his address for the launch of the report of the Royal Commission on Aboriginal Peoples in 1996, George Erasmus (Dene) stated that "the roots of injustice lie in history."[13] To address the subject of injustice and crime, we need, as a first step, to look at where we are and where we have come from. We need to look back and see what went wrong. Canadians must have an accurate representation of history, one that includes Indigenous world views, information about Indigenous governance structures and cultures, and Indigenous perspectives concerning the initial agreements made with European colonists.

With historical amnesia, Canadians cannot understand why Indigenous peoples face injustice; it gets glossed over or told incorrectly. How can one understand the injustice and crimes perpetrated against Indigenous peoples when a discourse exists upholding Indigenous peoples as savages or as a contemporary problem, when one thinks that no pre-contact Indigenous governance structures existed or that colonial North America was a "discovered" wilderness almost empty of people, when one doesn't know that Indigenous peoples had—and still have—the Indian Act to constrain them, or when one doesn't know the full extent of what happened in residential schools (and the intergenerational effects of this trauma)? These are all, in themselves, injustices, and they substantially explain the lack of harmony and balance present today. Often, however, these are the very things peoples and governments fail to acknowledge—which contributes to increasing the injustice affecting Indigenous peoples.

I want the reader to consider the historical underpinnings that have shaped the current reality for Indigenous peoples in Canada. Students often want to "cut to the chase" and look for solutions, but they do not realize that the challenges faced by Indigenous peoples in Canada are a result of a colonial relationship, so the only way to approach solutions is through understanding the historical relationship. A colleague told me that I teach and write like a Quentin Tarantino film, presenting first the key issue (in this case injustice affecting Indigenous peoples), then slowly illuminating the pieces that lead up to the whole picture. There is no other way to present this material. We live in a society that demands instant answers and ignores the power in seeing the emergence and build-up that can reveal history. Glossing over history is a hasty approach. We miss the whole picture and fall back on colonial assumptions, the untruth, for example, that Indigenous peoples had no value systems or governance structures and "surrendered" their land, lured by the desire to "modernize."

The primary intended audiences for this book are students in criminology, sociology, and victimology programs in Canada. The purpose is to reach students who might get jobs working for the government and in the criminal justice, victim services, or other service provider fields. Chapter 1 sets the stage by offering some basics, such as who Indigenous peoples are, and by debunking some common stereotypes. I outline why Indigenous peoples are not going to "just get over" history, which is a common inaccurate discourse perpetrated by colonialism. This lack of correct information is itself an injustice facing Indigenous peoples today. The fact that many Canadians have inaccurate knowledge about Indigenous peoples (and assume, for example, that they don't pay taxes or get free education) all interconnects with why we face injustice and crime today. Chapter 1 serves to make visible these inaccuracies, which are substantiated by colonialism and the dominant Western ideology.

Chapter 2 draws on various resources to outline an Indigenous person's perspective of the world—a world view that, in many ways, differs from that held in mainstream society. I draw on various teachings, readings, and traditions I am familiar with. This chapter shares some Indigenous nations' ancient ways of acquiring knowledge and interpreting the world. Although these vary from nation to nation, many are rooted in a world view that acknowledges the land and the importance of maintaining balance within an intricate environment. This chapter also shows that Indigenous peoples have diverse and complex cultures and belief systems rooted in respect and equality. Demonstrating this complexity debunks false assumptions, for example, that Indigenous peoples had no or only "primitive" value systems pre-contact and that Indigenous peoples had to be raised up to a level of civility. Furthermore, we need a clear idea of just what the laws and policies that tried to eradicate Indigenous peoples were trying to erase. It is crucial that people understand how deeply held the inaccurate and misleading notions, beliefs, and ideas about Indigenous peoples were (and still are).

Chapter 3 shares Indigenous nations' various complex governance structures, ways of organizing peoples, and methods of addressing crime. Indigenous peoples did not need "enlightening," which is a common misrepresentation. Nations had their own various systems of governance in place, rooted in their respective world views, which sought to maintain balance, peace, and equilibrium based upon the connection to the land.

Chapters 4 and 5 provide a backdrop against which it is possible to understand initial Indigenous and European relations—a framework for comprehending how relations unfolded between and among nations. Colonialism is outlined and explored as a past and present reality, but readers are cautioned against accepting the idea of conquest, the assumption that

Indigenous nations were "overtaken" or conquered. This notion is untrue and springs from European misconceptions. Chapter 5 provides the real history of the foundation of Canada. It outlines original treaty agreements and looks at how those treaties have been dishonoured.

Chapters 6 and 7 further elucidate Canadian governments' disregard of treaties and describe Euro-Canadian attempts to eradicate and assimilate Indigenous peoples. These include the creation of "Indian"-specific laws and forcing children into foreign educational systems and residential schools, which attempted to "kill the Indian in the child." These are essential pieces of history that are all too often glossed over.

Chapter 8 looks at the aftermath of these policies—their historical and present impact on Indigenous peoples. More specifically, it examines risk factors related to victimization and offending resulting from the histories of trauma that assimilationist and racist policies induced, such as family violence, addictions, and low levels of educational attainment and employment. Chapter 9 analyses the violence and victimization affecting Indigenous women. It outlines their sexualization and describes the historical and enduring paternalistic attacks they experience. This violent objectification has ongoing impacts, not the least of which is the large number of Indigenous women who are sexually violated and who go missing and are murdered.

Chapter 10 considers who, in fact, the actual criminals in this country may be. Many times, Indigenous peoples are quickly framed as criminal, yet governments, corporations, and big businesses continue to commit major crimes against Indigenous peoples. The colonial forefathers'[14] legacies continue. Euro-Canadian priorities such as resource development and extraction, and the persistent desire for economic and geographic expansion, continue to trump the treaty relationship.

Chapter 11 examines how Indigenous peoples today still struggle to achieve recognition of their title over land. It looks at "modern" land claim processes, which, on the surface, may seem like positive steps forward. However, after closer examination of these processes, one begins to recognize that not much has changed. Such processes are an advanced form of government-attempted assimilation and manipulation; we see new words, yet it is the same agenda.

Chapter 12 examines the Canadian criminal justice system. This system operates by positioning wealthy and mainly white people so they can benefit while pushing the poor—and many Indigenous peoples—into deeper poverty and, in many cases, into prison. The chapter contends that the structure of justice in Canada, which primarily encompasses police, courts, and corrections systems, does little to reduce injustice. Rather, in many ways, the criminal justice system, which is rooted in Euro-Canadian colonialism, fuels injustice that is directed specifically against Indigenous peoples.

Finally, Chapter 13 discusses various solutions for reducing the injustice facing Indigenous peoples in Canada. It explores possibilities for decolonization, reconciliation, acts of resurgence, and prevention programming, and it also discusses next steps forward toward a positive future for all.

1
Introduction to Indigenous Peoples in Canada

For too long Canadian educational systems, including curriculum and textbooks, have denied, ignored, or deprecated Indigenous peoples' history, knowledges, and ways of coming to interpret and understand the world. Canada is still very much predicated on an existence, and an understanding of that existence, based on colonial and colonizing mind-sets. Canada's colonial past and present must be brought to the forefront. People's understanding of Canadian history (or Canada as an entity) needs to be examined, challenged, and held accountable. This place many have come to know and understand as "Canada" is a place known to many Indigenous peoples as "Turtle Island" (with Turtle Island encompassing both Canada and the United States).

All of North America is Indigenous land. Indigenous peoples have occupied and lived on this land for thousands and thousands of years, and their histories begin before concepts of time. It is important to acknowledge the original keepers of the land where one resides or visits. This book acknowledges that Indigenous peoples were, and still are, the original inhabitants and stewards of Turtle Island and presents material from this perspective. It thereby reframes incorrect assumptions and twisted or "careful" interpretations of history.

By Way of a Definition: Who Is Indigenous

For the purposes of this book, the word "Indigenous" is used to describe a large and very diverse group of peoples in Canada. Indigenous is a colonial term. To talk about the colonial system using the English language, I draw on the term. The problems with the term are numerous. First, Indigenous peoples encompass a wide range of diverse cultural groups and practice a wide variety of traditions. Numerous unique Indigenous cultural groups live in Canada, which all have some related yet diverse cultural traditions. In Canada alone, there are 86 different Indigenous languages still spoken today.[1] These languages are reflective of unique histories, cultures, and identities linked to family, community, the land, and traditional knowledge. Languages are fundamental to identity, so considering as one group Indigenous peoples who speak distinct languages is not only very restrictive but also a very inaccurate depiction of who these peoples and nations are and how they should be represented. This approach is sometimes referred to as a "pan-Indian" means of defining Indigenous peoples.

The term "Indigenous" is a word recognized in the seventeenth century that stems from the Latin root "*indigena*,"meaning "sprung from the land." [2] As the Latin language evolved, the meaning came to be defined as "born in a country, native." "Indigenous" has been used in the international and United Nations context to define peoples in relation to their colonizers.[3]

The term Aboriginal is used generally "in reference to inhabitants of lands colonized by Europeans."[4] Some do not like the all-inclusive "Aboriginal" term used in Canada. As Lynda Gray (member of the Tsimshian Nation) states, "I personally do not like the word, as most words starting with 'ab' mean 'not.'"[5] Such is the case with the term "abnormal," which means not normal. In Latin, "*ab*" literally means "from" and is used in law frequently in the phrase "*ab initio*" or "from the beginning"; however, the word-forming element of "*ab*" means "off, away from."[6] Thus, as Gray explains, she started using the term "*AN*original."[7]

Aboriginal is also a constitutional term, found in the Constitution Act, 1982, which defines Aboriginal peoples as "the Indian, Inuit, and Métis peoples of Canada."[8] When using an all-encompassing term, some prefer "Native." However, in the mid-fifteenth century, this term was used to describe a "person born in bondage." In the sixteenth century, "native" was used to describe a "person who has always lived in a place."[9] We see the meaning change again in the seventeenth century with the growth of colonialism; the vernacular came to mean "home-born slave" and its definitional meaning "original inhabitants of non-European nations where Europeans hold political power." Therefore, all of these terms connote a political identity and define us in relation to the colonizers.

Some terms used to refer to "Aboriginals" carry even more disparaging and inaccurate judgments. Marriage records from my great-grandparents, for example, identify their origins as "*sauvagesse*" and "*Indien*," which translate from French as a female form of "savage" and, of course, "Indian." The term "Indian" is still widely used today, as in the "Indian Act" and "Indian status." The word "Indian" exemplifies a historical farce. When Christopher Columbus encountered Taíno people in 1492, he incorrectly labelled them "Indians," thinking he was in the Indies.[10] Incidentally, although Columbus claimed to have "discovered" a "new world," the Americas were already home to 112 million Indigenous peoples.[11]

The term "Indian" has since been considered derogatory, especially because Euro-Canadian government systems used it throughout many racist documents, policies, and acts. However, at the same time, some have used it as a term of resistance, reclaiming it. As Mohawk scholar Patricia Monture-Angus states, "I want to re-claim that word, Indian, once forced upon us and make it feel mine."[12] No matter which term listed above is used, one is still left with a "pan-Indian" approach to defining Indigenous peoples, one that groups everyone into one big category. Many Indigenous peoples identify with their specific nation, treaty, or ancestral heritage or background: "Mohawk from Tyendinaga" or "Cree from Treaty Eight" or "Cayuga," "Assiniboine," "Sioux," "Algonquin," "Métis," or "Nisga'a."

In 2008, the 42 member communities of the Anishinabek Nation endorsed a resolution at their Grand Council Assembly to stop using the term "Aboriginal." They noted that it was a word that represented assimilation through the displacement of First Nation–specific inherent treaty rights. The use of the term "Aboriginal," lumps all First Nations, Métis, and Inuit peoples together, and, as Grand Council Chief John Beaucage states, although "[w]e respect the cultures and traditions of our Metis and Inuit brothers and sisters . . . their issues are different from ours."[13]

An additional problem with using these all-encompassing terms is that they label and define the continent's first peoples according to the cultures, perceptions, and languages of the European colonizers, a form of identity control that angers many. As Patricia Monture-Angus has expressed, "not being in control of the process of naming, that is, defining who you are, serves as one of the most express examples of silencing I can think of."[14]

Even less-general terms used by Europeans to name the people they encountered in the Americas are problematic. "Naskapi" and "Montagnais" were used by colonizers to define Innu people from Québec and Labrador.[15] "Naskapi" is a derogatory term meaning "uncivilized," and "Montagnais" comes from French meaning "mountain people." These people called themselves "Innu," which means "human being" and is now the more commonly preferred name.[16] The term "Huron" was used by colonizers to define the Wendat people. "Wendat" means "Dwellers of the Island."[17] Wendat people called their country "Wendake"; the French renamed it "Huronia" and then called the Wendat people "Hurons." Some Wendat people today will refer to themselves as Huron, Wendat, or, sometimes, Huron-Wendat.

What's in a Name?

Because the people of Turtle Island have been named and renamed by others over centuries, I make an effort in this book to let individuals name themselves. I try to use the same names and spellings to describe the people I mention in this book as those people use to describe themselves. This policy makes for a bit of inconsistency, so you may find Anishinaabe, Anishinabek, Anishnabe, or Nishnaabeg used to name people with similar heritages. However, the very complexity of the task of naming the descendants of the original inhabitants of Turtle Island speaks to the variety of cultures and histories these descendants have inherited. Also, recognizing that naming can be used as a tool of both social control and resistance—and putting this tool in the right hands—is more important than adhering to technical correctness.

Sometimes, people reclaim the right of naming themselves and their lands. In 2009, the Haida peoples replaced the colonial name "Queen Charlotte Islands" with "Haida Gwaii," which means "Islands of the People" in Haida. This archipelago of 150 islands off British Columbia's north coast was given the name "Queen Charlotte Islands" by British explorer Captain George Dixon in 1787, after one of his ships, the *Queen Charlotte* (named after the wife of King George III of the United Kingdom), surveyed the islands.

Canadian Definitions of Indigenous Peoples

On April 17, 1982, section 35 of the Constitution Act defined Aboriginal peoples in Canada as inclusive of "the Indian, Inuit, and Métis peoples."[18] For some Indigenous peoples, this definition was an important step forward in Canadian history, as all three groups were recognized officially in Canada's Constitution. The Constitution also affirmed existing Aboriginal treaty rights and declared these rights as being guaranteed to both males and females equally. Some Métis peoples also considered the Constitution to be significant, as Métis were now officially recognized as a distinct Aboriginal group in Canada.

In Canada, Aboriginal peoples have been mainly classified into four major groupings: status Indians, non-status Indians, Métis, and Inuit.[19] Status "Indians" are registered under the Indian Act of Canada. Persons who are registered under this act and can confirm their affiliation to a band that signed a treaty are also considered "treaty Indians."[20] Non-status Indians have

Indigenous ancestry but have lost the status of "Indian" granted under the Indian Act or have never received this status.

"Indian" is the word used under the Indian Act, but First Nations is a more acceptable term for this word. The term "First Nations," a political neologism, is used both for status and non-status "Indians."[21] This name came into widespread usage during the 1970s, and, for the most part, has replaced the words "Indian" and "band" (terms that reflect colonialism but are nevertheless still used in the Indian Act to refer to First Nations peoples and Indigenous communities). The term "First Nations" is not synonymous with "Aboriginal peoples," as it does not include Inuit and Métis people.

Describing the Métis is more complex because those claiming this identity have a variety of statuses, histories, and cultural and racial backgrounds. All Métis have ancestry stemming from both Indigenous and non-Indigenous origins, but they are distinct from individuals claiming some Indigenous ancestry. Both the Métis Nation of Saskatchewan and Alberta define a Métis person as one who "self-identifies as Métis, is distinct from other Aboriginal Peoples, is of historic Métis Nation ancestry, and is accepted by the Métis Nation."[22] The Métis Nation of Alberta also notes that the Métis people were born originally from the marriages of "Cree, Ojibwa, and Salteaux women" with French and Scottish fur traders, commencing in the mid-1600s, but that Scandinavian, Irish, and English men also intermarried with Indigenous women and their descendants became recognized as Métis later.[23]

According to the Manitoba Metis Federation, "Manitoba is the birthplace of the Metis Nation."[24] It makes this statement because the Métis of Red River and their leader Louis Riel became a strong political force and contributed substantially to Métis resistance and to Manitoba's history and governance.

A Brief History of the Métis Nation, the Birth of Manitoba, and the North-West Uprising

After the Dominion of Canada purchased Rupert's Land from the Hudson's Bay Company in 1869, the Métis of the Red River set up a national committee to stop this land transfer, as they were never consulted about it.[25] Louis Riel led a resistance, which became known as the Red River Resistance. As a consequence, the Canadian government did not assume control of the territory in December 1869 as scheduled, and the colonists held two conventions, eventually agreeing to form a representative provisional government to negotiate terms for entering into Confederation. In particular, the Métis wanted self-governing rights in their territory and the preservation of "all privileges, customs and usage existing at the time of the [land] transfer." These were issued in a bill of rights, delivered from the "Provisional Governing Council of the Métis Nation," and were the basis of negotiations between the Canadian government and a Métis delegation sent to Ottawa.

As negotiations continued over the winter so too did the fighting. Agitators made various attempts to overthrow the Métis government. One was a Canadian surveyor named Thomas Scott who was executed for treason on March 4, 1870. Vilified in eastern Canada for this execution, Riel fled to the United States to avoid lynching.[26] Even in the face of impediments and upheaval, however, negotiations did lead to the Manitoba Act, 1870, and to Manitoba's entry into Canadian Confederation.

In 1884, Riel was sought to help Saskatchewan Métis and other prairie Métis peoples resist exploitation and dispossession by the Canadian government and to help negotiate the provincial status of three territorial districts: Saskatchewan, Assiniboia, and Alberta.[27] Seeing an opportunity to create a Métis homeland, Riel accepted and led another uprising against the government, the North-West Uprising, but it lasted fewer than three months. Riel was declared guilty of high treason by the government and executed in Regina on November 16, 1885.

Indeed, many people see Manitoba as the epicentre for the origin of the Métis people because of the Red River Resistance. Yet this unbalanced focus on the Red River Métis has left other Métis, who do not have roots in the Red River, largely unrecognized.[28] Who the "original Métis" were is contested. For some, Métis people have a distinctive connection to their Métis communities and can trace their lineage to certain Métis families or settlements that arose during the early years of European settlement or during the fur trade. Métis identity is also embraced by some non-status First Nations peoples, those without a connection to a Métis community but who have Indigenous and European roots. These might include people who have mixed heritage not stemming from a specific era, for example, the offspring of more recent unions between Indigenous and European couples. Some argue that the latter are not "true Métis" people and that the word "Métis" has simply become a catch-all for anyone with some Indigenous lineage. Strong proponents of this view suggest using the term "Michif" to describe their identity rather than "Métis."[29] Michif is the language of the Métis people. It combines Plains Cree (an Algonquian language) and French.[30]

For Native studies professor and Michif scholar Chris Andersen, to understand the "Métis," one must not focus on "mixedness."[31] He explains that the identifier "is not a catch-all term for anyone who is Indigenous but-not-First-Nation-or-Inuit." He uses "Métis" "to refer to the history, events, leaders, territories, language, and culture associated with the growth of the buffalo hunting and trading Métis of the northern Plains, in particular during the period between the beginning of the Métis buffalo brigades in the early nineteenth century and the 1885 North West Uprising." He contends that, although many might argue that his definition omits large numbers of Indigenous peoples and communities, "Métis" must not be "a soup kitchen for Indigenous peoples and communities who have become disenfranchised by the Canadian state."[32]

In 2003, *R. v. Powley* provided a legal definition for who is entitled to Métis rights. This case involved a father and son, Steve and Roddy Powley, who killed a moose just outside of Sault Ste. Marie, Ontario. They were charged with unlawfully hunting a moose without a hunting licence and with knowingly possessing game hunted in violation of ss. 46 and 47(1) of Ontario's Game and Fish Act. The case made it all the way to the Supreme Court, and judges, reaching a unanimous decision, ruled that the Powleys—as Sault Ste. Marie Métis community members—could exercise their Métis right to hunt, which is protected under section 35 of the Constitution Act, 1982. Furthermore, the ruling offered a definition of the term "Métis" as it was used in that act: "it refers to distinctive peoples who, in addition to their mixed ancestry, developed their own customs, and recognizable group identity separate from their Indian or Inuit and European forebears."[33] The case outlined three other factors that must be met for an individual to have rights as a Métis person: self-identification as Métis, an ancestral connection to a historic Métis community, and acceptance by a Métis community. Even after the *Powley* case, however, who can be considered a "true" Métis is contentious and confusing.

On January 8, 2013, the Federal Court in *Daniels v. Canada* deemed Métis and those Indigenous peoples without status as "Indians" under the Constitution Act of 1867, deciding that both groups fall under federal jurisdiction.[34] This ruling came after a 13-year court battle. In 1999, the Congress of Aboriginal Peoples and several Métis and non-status First Nation peoples took the government to court because of discrimination. Although considered "Aboriginal" in section 35 of the Constitution Act, 1982, they did not fall under the definition of "Indians" under section 91(24) of the Constitution Act, 1867,[35] which left them in a sort of jurisdictional limbo and without the same rights as those afforded "Indian" status under the Indian Act.

Although the *Daniels* case did not put Métis and non-status first peoples under the Indian Act, it did place them under federal jurisdiction, which could assist them in future negotiations with the federal government over specific needs and rights. Being clearly under federal jurisdiction prevents the federal or the provincial government from using jurisdictional ambiguity to shift responsibility from one level of government to the other. The *Daniels* case, then, was about attaining recognition under federal jurisdiction so as to open the door to discussions at that level of government, discussions on the issues, concerns, and needs of Métis and non-status peoples that could now take place on a nation-to-nation basis.

On February 6, 2013, the federal government appealed the ruling in the *Daniels* case. On April 17, 2014, this appeal was heard. The court ruled that Métis peoples would remain as "Indians" under the Constitution, but recognition to "non-status Indians" was considered a separate issue, one that was to be handled on a case-by-case basis. If the federal government appeals again, the case would then be heard in the Supreme Court of Canada.[36] Clearly, arriving at legal definitions regarding who is considered Métis, "Indian," or even "Aboriginal" and what that means in terms of rights and governmental responsibilities is complex and disputed.

The federal government's relationship with the Inuit was also ambiguous for a good part of the twentieth century. In 1939, the Supreme Court of Canada decided that Inuit were included under section 91(24); however, the Indian Act was amended to reject its application to Inuit so as to keep them distinct from those considered "Indians."[37] Inuit are the original inhabitants of Canada's Arctic and sub-Arctic areas including parts of Yukon, the Northwest Territories, Nunavut, and northern Québec and Labrador. The word Inuit means "the people" in the Inuit language of Inuktitut. Inuk is the singular form of Inuit. According to Inuit Tapiriit Kanatami (ITK)—the national voice of Inuit peoples in Canada—Inuit have occupied "the Arctic land and waters from the Mackenzie Delta in the west, to the Labrador coast in the east and from the Hudson's Bay Coast, to the islands of the High Arctic" for "more than four thousand years." The ITK note four Inuit regions in Canada: the Inuvialuit Settlement Region (Northwest Territories), Nunavut, Nunavik (Northern Québec), and Nunatsiavut (Northern Labrador). These are collectively known as "Inuit Nunangat," a term used to reference the "land, water, and ice" so integral to Inuit cultures and ways of life.[38]

How Many Indigenous Peoples Are in Canada?

Statistics Canada has identified the continuing growth of Indigenous peoples in Canada. The numbers of people reporting "Aboriginal identity" on the

Canadian census has risen from 799,010 in 1996, to 976,305 in 2001, and 1,172,790 in 2006.[39] Since the mandatory long-form census was replaced in 2011 by a voluntary National Household Survey (NHS) sent randomly to approximately 4.5 million dwellings in Canada, more recent statistics are less reliable.[40] Even Statistics Canada noted that new procedures will not "provide a level of quality that would have been achieved through a mandatory long-form census."[41] One problem is that voluntary data collection methods have a lower response rate, and overrepresented among those who tend not to respond are Indigenous peoples, new immigrants, people living in rural areas or small communities, and those with low incomes. Thus, these people, who are often in need of services, are underrepresented in the data, creating what is referred to as "non-response bias." Additionally, the first report of 2011 NHS statistics on Indigenous peoples attached notes explaining that some First Nation communities did not participate in the survey because "enumeration was either not permitted, it was interrupted before completion, or because of natural events."[42]

Nevertheless, the report estimated that 1,400,685 people had Indigenous identity in 2011, comprising 4.3 per cent of the total Canadian population. This statistic represents a 20.1 per cent population increase for Indigenous people between 2006 and 2011, when the non-Indigenous population increased by only 5.2 per cent. Actually, the Indigenous population has been growing much faster than the non-Indigenous population for some time. From 1996 to 2006, the Indigenous population increased by a staggering 45 per cent compared to the non-Indigenous population, which increased only 8 per cent over that same time period.[43]

These drastic increases in persons reporting Aboriginal identity are not simply a result of births, deaths, and migration, although these are factors. (Fertility rates for Indigenous women, for example, are higher than those for Canadian women in general.[44]) Changes in self-reporting continually affect estimates of the size and growth of Indigenous populations. This phenomenon of people changing their ethnic affiliation, say from non-Aboriginal to Aboriginal, from one census to the next is referred to as "ethnic mobility."[45] Several factors underlie this phenomenon, including legislative changes as well as a variety of social factors. The legislative amendment to the Indian Act of Canada in 1985 (known as Bill C-31) is a prime example of how legislative changes have influenced people to change their self-reported ethnic identity. It redefined who was entitled to legal Indian status; before 1985, the act had held that a registered Indian woman and her children would lose their legal status if she married a non-status man. By allowing these women and their children to regain "Indian" status, this amendment led to an increase of over 110,000 persons in the total status population between 1985 and 2001.[46]

Even after Bill C-31, the Indian Act still contains discriminatory aspects denying "status" to Indigenous peoples. This legal denial of status might play a role in people underreporting "Aboriginal identity." A notable discrimination is the "second generation cut-off rule" specifying that, after two successive generations of an "Indian" having children with a non-Indian, descendants will no longer have "Indian" status.

In her book *Beyond Blood: Rethinking Indigenous Identity*, Mi'kmaq professor, lawyer, and activist Pamela D. Palmater notes how imposed government definitions of who is "Indian" have affected identity in her family.[47] Palmater experienced "cousins" discrimination, meaning that, because of various sections of the Indian Act, she was denied status based on the fact that her grandmother, Margaret, married a "non-Indian." As Palmater explains it,

> My grandmother Margaret married a non-Indian man. As a result, her children, including my father, were registered as section 6(2) Indians. Had Margaret been a man who married a non-Indian woman, both the non-Indian woman and the children would have been section 6(1)(a) Indians. The grandchildren of Indian women who married out do not have status, whereas the grandchildren of Indian men who married out do.[48]

Basically, the Indian Act discriminates between the offspring of men and women who "marry out": "section 6(2) Indians"—the children of "Indian" women and men without "Indian" status—have status themselves but cannot pass it on to their children whereas "section 6(1)(a) Indians"—the children of "Indian" men and women without "Indian" status—are considered "status Indians," leading to a situation in which one cousin is denied status and another is not.

Although Bill C-3, assented to in December 2010, responded to the gender discrimination with which "Indian" status was assigned, it did not override the second-generation cut-off rule. So, in spite of decades of legal battle by women such as Sharon McIvor (see Chapter 6), as of 2015, although some have been able to reclaim *legal* status as an "Indian," grandchildren of "section 6(2) Indians" cannot claim that status.

These legal definitions and challenges might influence some people who have not identified themselves as having "Aboriginal identity" to change their stance. Indeed, as Palmater explains, registration as an "Indian" has turned out to be "a significant part of Indigenous identity on an individual and communal level."[49] If people are denied this "Indian" status through the government, they might not be allowed to live in their First Nation community, participate in governance activities, or run for elected office in their First Nation community, for example.

On the other hand, some people will continue to deny their Indigenous background, heritage, or ancestry and want no part of being "Indian." Blatant and systemic racism has led to some Indigenous people passing themselves off as having another ethnicity. Justice Murray Sinclair explains that some of his family members and friends spent their lives trying to hide their own identities by passing as French or Spanish.[50] The shame society has associated with being an "Indian," or what was derogatively termed a "half-breed," has no doubt kept many from self-identifying as "Aboriginal."

So how might racism, the ambiguities of identity, and the newest legislation on "Indian status" affect the number of people identifying as "Aboriginal"? Indigenous and Northern Affairs Canada estimated that the status Indian population would increase by 45,000 members as a result of Bill C-3, which is a 6 per cent increase.[51] The department also projects a significant natural increase in the "registered Indian" population living on reserve and a more modest one in this population living off reserve, although both will increase by a higher percentage than will the Canadian population in general.[52] With a significant and growing population of Indigenous peoples, Canada must address issues of Indigenous injustice.

Debunking Stereotypes and Assumptions

There are many stereotypes, assumptions, and common misrepresentations of Indigenous peoples. Some of the most notable will be addressed, such as the assumption that all Indigenous peoples have the same defining physical characteristics and the misconception that all Indigenous peoples get free education or don't have to pay taxes. These misconceptions continue to frame Indigenous peoples incorrectly and to perpetuate stereotypes, providing leeway for others to blame Indigenous people for misfortunes or other struggles. In many ways, these incorrect assumptions shift blame to and lower Indigenous peoples down to a level of inferiority, thereby making it easier for others to avoid involvement or culpability and claim, "They are different than us," "They do it to themselves," or "They have so many resources." It is important to confront these misconceptions directly.

Not All Indigenous Peoples Look the Same

All Indigenous peoples do not have the same general physical features and characteristics. Of course, people from the same family often look the same, and there may be distinct features among peoples of specific First Nations. Cayuga elder Carol Jacobs told my younger sister that she inherited the Algonquin nose, for example. Yet a misconception exists that every single

Indigenous person must have dark hair, either brown or black; brown eyes with a certain shape; and, in some cases, high cheekbones, among other features. As mentioned, there are many different First Nations. There are also Indigenous peoples of mixed race. Thus, especially given the circumstances of history by which the first peoples of a continent were categorized as one racial entity called "Indian," the argument that race is a social construct and not rooted in biological differences is salient. Professor Ian Haney-López, one of the leading thinkers on race and racism, agrees:

> Evidence shows that those features usually coded to race, for example, stature, skin color, hair texture, and facial structure, do not correlate strongly with genetic variation. Populations that resemble each other might be genetically quite distinct. . . . Conversely, . . . [p]eople who look alike do not necessarily share a common genetic heritage, and people who share a similar genetic background do not necessarily look alike.[53]

He goes on to note, however, that Western society still seems wedded to the notion of biological race. This Western idea of race and of the significance of "blood" status is not traditional to Indigenous peoples. Nor are other "European concepts that separated people into a distinct hierarchy based upon birth, colour, race, lineage, religion, profession, wealth, politics and other criteria," argues Mi'kmaq elder, author, and human rights activist Daniel N. Paul. For him, this lack of bias "is one of the best indicators of how far advanced their cultures were in the development of human relations."[54]

Indigenous peoples acknowledged and knew of other peoples of the earth. Yet they did not consider blood heritage or race to make one people better or worse than another. And the European concept of race, stemming as it did from the medieval idea that the three known continents were inhabited by three separate races—"Caucasoid," "Negroid," and "Mongoloid"—was definitely a foreign construct.[55] Traditional Indigenous ideologies acknowledge that humans carry the earth in us, and we are all connected. According to Ojibeway Elder Pat Bellanger, "We are all people of the earth, the Mother Earth."[56]

An indicator of this more open perspective is that Europeans or people of other First Nations could be adopted by a "foreign" clan or nation, and racial characteristics such as skin or hair colour or physical features would not matter. What mattered was the honour and respect with which an "adopted" person treated others. Huron-Wendat historian and philosopher Georges Sioui confirms that the Wendat people adopted Europeans in the past.[57] At the same time, however, First Nations had their own sophisticated and complex family structures in place to acknowledge who was related, mostly to assure that relatives did not intermarry.[58] These distinctions were not in place as a form of exclusion, however.

What, then, do Indigenous people look like today? As is obvious from the previous section on who was considered "Indian," which demonstrates that people with the same grandparents were often ascribed different statuses, this question is somewhat ridiculous. Indigenous people can have hair that is straight or curly and red, blonde, or light brown as well as black. Some have green, hazel, or blue eyes. Of course, many Indigenous peoples do have the physical characteristics that people would typically assign to them. The caution here, though, is that definitions of identity based on stereotypical physical characteristics spring from racist colonial conceptions and history. A repugnant variation was the definition in the United States that became known as the "one-drop rule" (anyone with a single drop of "coloured" blood was given that label). As professor and expert in race and ethnic relations G. Reginald Daniel explains, "the one-drop rule is racist . . . it was historically implemented to create as many slaves as possible."[59] It is well to remember that definitions of identity based on appearance or blood heritage are often more about gaining power and maintaining control than about actual genetics.

This point is driven home by Canada's long-followed policy of Indigenous assimilation, which was also supported by arguments based on biological heritage. In this instance, having "one drop" of Indigenous blood was not always enough to be considered an "Indian" because the government wanted Indigenous peoples to be "absorbed into the body politic."[60] In 1885, Prime Minister John A. Macdonald stated that intermarriage would be one tool of absorption: "If they are Indians, they go with the tribe; if they are half-breeds they are whites."[61] In this case, too much "white" blood would eliminate governmental treaty responsibilities.

In other words, the Indian Act excludes those not "Indian" enough according to the government's definitions of race so as to avoid honouring the limited amount of "rights" allotted to Indigenous peoples. The Euro-Canadian government defines who is and who is not an Indian based on a system of registration that has its roots in a racist, archaic blood quantum concept, meaning that the amount of "Indian blood" is what determines whether one is a "true Indian."[62] The government set rules that will eliminate many from being "Indian" because doing so limits its obligations. It is actually harder to get an "Indian status" card in Canada than a Canadian passport, or any other legal government document for that matter, as Canada still wants to eliminate the "Indian," which will be further discussed in Chapter 6.

Indigenous Peoples Still Exist

Another misconception commonly held echoes the blood quantum and race-based theories used as a colonial tool to try to eliminate "Indians." It goes something like this: after centuries of intermarriage, education, cultural exchange, and common history, no real Indigenous peoples or nations exist, and we are all just "Canadians." This idea, which focuses mostly on "blood" makeup, is false. It serves the colonial purpose of attempting to assimilate all Indigenous peoples into Euro-Canadian society. Indigenous peoples exist even after decades of legislation regulating "Indians" in a way that purposely unravels social connections and severs the ties between Indigenous peoples and the land base. Professor of equity studies Bonita Lawrence (Mi'kmaw) explains the effects of this legislation:

> In Canada, . . . direct colonial control exerted by a settler state maintained by a global imperial power enabled Canada to create the Indian Act's legal status system and its highly divisive manner of externalizing "half breeds" and creating patriarchal divisions within Native communities, which automatically and continuously "bled off" people from their communities without the need for other policies of removal.[63]

If the desired outcome of assimilation is achieved, then the argument made by Euro-Canadian society calls for all peoples to be "equal" Canadians, with no one getting more benefits than the other. Yet missing from this argument is any acknowledgement that "Canada" is created off the resources, lands, and at the continual expense of Indigenous peoples. With this point forgotten, people will argue that they are being "progressive" when they state that they want "equality for all." But there cannot be "equality for all" when Indigenous peoples, lands, and resources continue to be taken without consent or recognition. Furthermore, equal access to oppressive, colonial, and foreign laws and governance structures is not "progress" for Indigenous people, and neither is any goal of equality predicated on being "the same as" Euro-Canadians. Indeed, equality within Western society today is typically envisioned as achieving a white, middle-class, and male ideal of "sameness." As Cree lawyer and scholar Harold Cardinal notes, "Indians have aspirations, hopes, and dreams, but becoming white men is not one of them."[64]

It seems, however, that some Euro-Canadians claim to be "Indian." It is not uncommon to find non-Indigenous peoples who will argue that they are "Indian too" or that they have a "great-great-grandmother who was an Indian princess." Whether consciously or not, non-Indigenous peoples who make these claims serve the colonial purpose of eliminating "Indians."

Although these claims of "sameness" equality might appear benign, they have the effect of denying the existence of Indigenous peoples and distancing Euro-Canadians from both Canada's racist colonial history and their legal and moral obligations to First Nations.

Tsalagi scholar Jeff Corntassel experienced one of these claims first hand. He was approached by another professor after he gave a presentation on Indian mascots, who asked him "how much Indian are you?" Corntassel went on to tell his questioner "in some detail that this was an inappropriate question given the colonial history of blood quantum measurements and that this question of pedigree is not posed to any other cultural group in the United States." As Corntassel further explained, "undaunted, the professor flouted his ignorance even further by stating 'I'll bet I'm even more Indian than you are.'"[65]

Reliance on such a claim and on the blood quantum definition of Indigenous peoples only serves a colonial agenda, which tries to argue that Indigenous peoples have been conquered and eliminated and that the only "Indians" who are still here are those whose blood is "mixed" or "diluted." These arguments and definitions attempt to erase Indigenous peoples—to continue the colonial agenda of their silent surrender.

The Misconception of Free Education

There is a common misconception that all Indigenous peoples get free education, that all have easy access to fully funded postsecondary education. The truth is that status "Indians" can access funds for education. Yet it is not as simple as money just being handed over. A potential student must apply to the education department of her or his First Nation, and there are typically more applications than funds.[66]

One must also take into consideration the obstacles to higher education these students face. There is the high cost of tuition and the distances many Indigenous peoples living in remote regions have to travel to attend school (some students' home communities are only accessible by helicopter or small planes). Also consider other barriers such as the high levels of poverty in many First Nation communities, the hurdles facing young mothers, and, in many cases, the sheer culture shock of moving to a big city.[67]

Those Indigenous peoples without status do not fall under the jurisdiction of the federal government and thus do not have access to the limited funds available from the education department of their First Nation community. These students can apply to various scholarships set up for Indigenous peoples, such as the Indspire Scholarship (previously the Aboriginal Achievement Foundation Scholarship). However, these scholarships have application processes and guidelines that are similar to those of the scholarships available to other groups and peoples (e.g., non-Indigenous Canadians, women, or those interested in particular fields of study). Applicants are required to fill out forms and, in some cases, write essays or offer other proofs of academic readiness or financial need. The Indspire Scholarship, for example, requires recipients to provide receipts to show that the money they received was spent on school and school-related costs. In other words, these scholarships do not provide "free" money that can be spent on anything.

Furthermore, Indigenous peoples have paid for their education, and continue to pay, over and over again. In the 1870s, representatives of the Crown and First Nations negotiated treaties 1 to 7, and, in the late 1800s and early 1900s, they negotiated treaties 8 to 11; each of these treaties included provision or discussion of education.[68] Not only have these treaties not been honoured but the fulfilment promised by education has been illusory.

These treaties were negotiated with First Nations from western Ontario to the foothills of the Rocky Mountains. Treaties 1 to 7 have only a little variation in regards to educational rights, and all treaties give similar meanings to education: schools for instruction and teachers to instruct. For example, in Treaties 1 and 2, the article relating to education is the same: "Her Majesty agrees to maintain a school on each reserve hereby made whenever the Indians of the reserve should desire it."[69] In both Treaties 3 and 5, the article relating to education reads as follows: "Her Majesty agrees to maintain schools for instruction in such reserves hereby made as to Her Government of Her Dominion of Canada may seem advisable whenever the Indians of the reserve shall desire it."

These treaties give First Nations peoples not only the right to education but also the responsibility for its implementation and control, stating that services are to be provided whenever "Indians" would "desire" such services. During treaty negotiations, both First Nations and the Crown made reference to the fact that education would be provided for the future prosperity of First Nations.[70] Although brief, each of Treaties 1 through 6 clearly outlines the Crown's responsibility to provide a physical "school." Treaties 7, 8, 9, and 11 all state, "Her Majesty agrees to pay the salaries of teachers to instruct children of said Indians." Treaty 9 adds that the Crown also agrees "to provide . . . school buildings and educational equipment." Treaty 10 does not have a specific article about education, as do all the other numbered treaties. However, as the *Report of the First Commission for Treaty No. 10* states, "There was evidenced a marked desire to secure educational privileges for their children . . . The chief of the Canoe Lake band asked that a day school be established at Canoe Lake for their benefit and that it be put under the management of a woman teacher."[71]

There is no question, then, that Indigenous peoples have a fundamental right to education. The United Nations Declaration on the Rights of

Indigenous Peoples (2008) affirms not only this basic right but also the right of Indigenous people to control their education: "Indigenous peoples have the right to establish and control their educational systems and institutions providing education in their own languages, in a manner appropriate to their cultural methods of teaching and learning."[72] Because the Constitution Act of 1867 vested all legislative authority for "Indians" and "Indian Lands" with the Crown, however, First Nations education was defined in Canada as a responsibility of the federal government.[73] This right to education was to be forever. As the Crown's chief negotiator stated in reference to Treaty 4, "You are the subjects of the Queen . . . what she promises never changes."[74] These agreements were not limited by time—"the promises we make will be carried out as long as the sun shines above and the water flows in the ocean"—and they were in exchange for the peaceful sharing of land, and for services that would enable Indigenous peoples to participate fully in the new economy.[75] With the passage of time, the Crown's commitment to the treaty right to education waned.

The Crown's choice to dishonour these treaties can be witnessed first with the enactment of the Indian Act in 1876, which was after the negotiation of Treaties 1 through 5. This act did not mention the treaty commitments, education, or schools, except in reference to the authority of the chiefs and councils to establish policies for "the construction and repair of school houses."[76] Rather, the Indian Act produced a standardized approach for the control and management of First Nations communities, lands, moneys, and properties.[77] It amended and consolidated previous laws concerning "Indians" and turned "Indians" into wards of the state.

With the Indian Act, the Crown assumed control over First Nations education and could then choose to provide limited educational services, yet not as a treaty right but instead as an assimilationist mechanism in line with the underlying goal of the act itself.[78] Thus, residential schools were created in the 1880s, four short years later, with the intent to assimilate Indigenous peoples. These schools and the many travesties of them will be further outlined in Chapter 7.

The federal government's various treaty promises to provide education "whenever the Indians . . . shall desire it" has not been honoured. Yet in 1982, the Constitution Act purported to ensure that "The existing Aboriginal and treaty rights of the Aboriginal peoples of Canada are hereby recognized and affirmed."[79] But, in spite of these constitutional and treaty rights, Indigenous students still continue to struggle to attain education.

Schools located in First Nation communities for Indigenous children are the only ones in the country that do not have a guaranteed funding base. They are funded under an obsolete formula developed over three decades ago. This funding was further restricted when placed under a 2 per cent cap in 1996, and it does not include funding for sports or recreation, school libraries, technology, or Indigenous languages. Schools teaching Indigenous children living on reserves receive an average of $3,500 less per student, per year, as compared to off-reserve schools located in the provinces and territories. The off-reserve schools in the comparison include Catholic or French schools, as well as public schools in Canada. This shortfall means fewer learning resources, fewer teachers, and little or no funding for things such as books and other essential equipment. The result: fewer educational and employment opportunities available for Indigenous children living on a reserve.[80] In October 2015, a majority Liberal government was elected in Canada, led by Prime Minister Justin Trudeau. On November 4, 2015, Trudeau assumed office. On December 8, 2015, Prime Minister Justin Trudeau made a promise at the Assembly of First Nation's Special Chiefs Assembly to lift the 2 percent cap for First Nations education programs "immediately," as part of their first budget. Thus, many are hopeful for the changes to come.[81]

Without this basic right to elementary and secondary education being fulfilled, the chances for postsecondary education opportunities become out of reach. If one is not afforded the same opportunities for advancement from the outset, it is much more difficult to advance as compared to someone who is. Finally, treaty negotiations made regarding education were ignored. What was supposed to be allocated to First Nations peoples "as long as the sun shines above and the water flows in the ocean"[81] is a constant struggle to attain. On top of this, Indigenous peoples have to face the incorrect assumption that Indigenous peoples have free and easy access to education, as well as having to educate Canadians constantly on the truth of history.

Ultimately, holding on to this assumption serves the colonial purpose of asserting power and control over Indigenous peoples and their lands and resources. It presses a false narrative, one that keeps people blindly believing that Euro-Canadians were the "first" Canadians who rightfully own this land called "Canada." Recognition is not given to the fact that Canada is built on the lands and resources of Indigenous peoples—and at their continual expense. The false assumption of "free education" flips the true narrative; it keeps the settler society at the top of the colonial hierarchy that this society imposed, and it places Indigenous peoples in a subordinate position—so as to continue the colonial agenda of Indigenous assimilation. But the true narrative is not forgotten in Indigenous people's history.

The Tax Free Myth

In August 2012, Canadian pop icon Justin Bieber made the following comments to *Rolling Stone* magazine: "I'm actually part Indian . . . I think Inuit or something? I'm enough per cent that in Canada I can get free gas."[82] This upset many Indigenous people; not only did he use the term "Indian" but he perpetuated the stereotype that Indigenous peoples receive things for "free." Maybe Justin is Indigenous. Maybe not. The Congress of Aboriginal Peoples said it would help him trace his ancestry. Whether he is Indigenous or not is not the major issue; the problem is that he reinforced a racist stereotype, which is upsetting because he has so many fans and is a role model to many.

The reality is that no Indigenous person gets free gas. First Nations people in Ontario who have a "Certificate of Exemption" (gas card) issued by the Ministry of Finance are exempt from the provincial gas tax of 14.7 cents per litre, but they must have this card, and the exemption applies only if they are buying gas for their own use and on a reserve. Furthermore, to get such a card one has to have an "Indian" status card issued by Indigenous and Northern Affairs Canada, and not all Indigenous peoples have this card, which will be explained in more depth in Chapter 6.

A coinciding myth assumes that Indigenous peoples essentially get a "free ride" and never have to pay taxes. This is also not true. Indigenous people pay taxes. There are exemptions under the Indian Act; section 87 stipulates that "personal property of an Indian or a band situated on a reserve" is tax exempt. However, Indigenous peoples without status, Métis, and Inuit are not eligible for this exemption. In fact, the tax exemption applies only in limited cases and circumstances. Every year Indigenous peoples pay significant amounts of tax.

Those with "Indian" status who are working on a reserve are exempt from income taxes. But a convoluted formula comes into play that factors in the location of the work and the residences of both the employee and employer, making some with status ineligible for the exemption. For example, First Nations people working off a reserve have to pay income tax, even if they live on a reserve and commute to a job, which could be down the street but is not located on what is considered "reserve" land.

The Indian Act does allow some Indigenous peoples with status cards to get some sales tax exemptions. However, these exemptions apply automatically only to purchases made on a reserve or delivered to one. It is possible to claim a tax exemption for a purchase not made on a reserve, but the administrative costs and hoops faced by those making the claim discourage many people from even beginning the process, so many just end up paying the taxes.

As with education, tax exemption is part of the minimal rights First Nations people have. It is a statutory obligation set out in the Indian Act, 1985, yet the government makes it difficult for many to have access to this right. The exemptions laid out in section 87 of the Indian Act, 1985, have existed prior to Confederation.[83] They are in place in recognition of the unique historic and constitutional place of First Nations people in this country.

Another related misunderstanding is that the federal government simply hands over taxpayers' money to Indigenous peoples. Anishinaabe hip-hop artist, journalist, and educator Wab Kinew explains this misconception quite simply. He estimates that the amount of money allocated to Indigenous and Northern Affairs Canada each year is $7 billion.[84] As Kinew explains, this money has to pay for services delivered to a population the same size as that of New Brunswick, and New Brunswick spends $8 billion on its population. Yet we never hear Canadians saying, "Hey New Brunswick, what are you doing with your 8 billion dollars?" Finally, we must also acknowledge the fact that more than a third of this money (an estimated 41 per cent) goes to the federal government bureaucracy and never actually reaches First Nations communities, with an estimated 11 per cent spent on departmental overhead alone.[85]

Why We Won't Just "Get Over It"

A permeating conception held by some Canadians questions why Indigenous peoples won't just "get over it," referring to Canada's oppressive colonial history. The argument is that history is just history, and we should move on and forget it because it is "a thing of the past." Many times people hold these views because they are misinformed. Also, some non-Indigenous peoples might not want to face up to the discomforting reality that they are living on stolen land or to the other consequences resulting from their colonial forefathers'[86] legacies—not the least of which are the many horrible atrocities committed against Indigenous peoples for colonial benefit. I say this neither to blame any specific group for the actions of their ancestors nor to make people feel bad, but to educate. Through education and the recognition of past and present injustice, a greater nation-to-nation relationship will emerge and persist. Often, people just don't know about history. They may encounter a protest or roadblock and be upset with Indigenous peoples for interrupting their drive. Later, they might read a news article that omits pertinent information, leaving them angry and misinformed. Simply put, people who do not live someone else's reality may be dubious about it.

The reasons we will not just "get over it" are numerous, and different people will list different reasons. First, Indigenous peoples are not going to just "get over" things that still greatly affect them today. If we don't recognize our past history, how do we make sense of the legacies left behind from it? All Canadians must recognize and understand true history to be able to move forward from it and heal its lingering harms.

So here is some of that history. Canadian land is Indigenous land, always has been, always will be, since time immemorial. The colonial project is not natural and has asserted itself with deceit and false promises. Ongoing assimilationist acts, laws, and policies were forced upon peoples and dismantled communities and governance structures.[87] Indigenous women, who used to hold positions of leadership and value in communities, were displaced and subjugated upon the imposition of patriarchal systems and laws. For many years, Indigenous spiritual and cultural practices were legally prohibited. And Indigenous children were stolen away from their homes and abused, emotionally and mentally, and often sexually and physically as well. The travesty and horror of residential schools cannot be forgotten and is just one of many interrelated wrongs perpetrated against Indigenous peoples. Wab Kinew shares that his father is a survivor of the residential schools. In response to people who ask "why won't you just get over it?" he explains, "You know what, I am over it. My Dad was raped in a residential school by a nun, I'm over it. But it doesn't mean that we should forget it."[88] He echoes a sentiment of George Santayana's: "Those who cannot remember the past are condemned to repeat it."[89] Canadians cannot forget the atrocities of the past, especially because these events didn't happen very long ago and because colonization is still ongoing. The problems that have resulted from these atrocities must be addressed actively and rectified.

The last residential school was closed in 1996; the first ones opened in the 1880s. Many generations are still living with the residential school's legacy of atrocity. I tell my classes that, not long ago, an Indigenous woman teaching university would have been unheard of and that, just over 60 years ago, I would have been arrested for wearing my regalia on campus. The ban on various First Nation ceremonial activities and dress was lifted only in 1951, in the time of not only my grandparents but also my parents.

In addition to this list of past wrongs, what is also disheartening is that, because people today unfortunately do not know certain parts of history, we are, in fact, repeating it in various ways. For example, although Indigenous children are no longer being taken from their homes and put into residential schools, they are being taken in large numbers from their homes and put into foster care. There are three times the number of Indigenous children in the child welfare system than there were in residential schools at the height of their operation in the 1940s. Data suggest that there are about 27,000 children in First Nation and provincial agency care.[90] Essentially, this different strategy has the same result. Children are being removed from their families, leading to family breakdown. The policy basically chastises Indigenous peoples for the loss of parenting skills and the family disruption caused originally by residential schools. And the harmful cycle repeats.

Furthermore, as Lynda Gray (member of the Tsimshian Nation) explains, for far too long history has been written from a colonial perspective and distributed via assimilationist educational projects. Indigenous peoples have been struggling for decades to bring to light the truth about our shared histories. Recognizing this truth and being heard is especially essential to us, because as Gray states, "we cannot just carry on as if nothing has happened."[91] In order for all people to move forward and start on a healing path, the painful national wound needs to be revealed and understood by every one. We must acknowledge the shared history of Indigenous and non-Indigenous peoples in Canada, and the impacts—past and present—of this history on Indigenous peoples.

Discussion Questions

1) Consider the stereotypes and assumptions imposed on Indigenous peoples. What are they, and where have you witnessed these stereotypes?
2) Can you think of any stereotypes that affect you personally? How might these stereotypes affect your day-to-day living and interactions?

Activities

1) Watch the first episode of CBC's 2012 documentary series *The 8th Fire*, "Indigenous in the City" (available online at cbc.ca/8thfire). Reflect on what has been taught to you over the course of your life about Indigenous peoples. Where have you learned this information? To what degree were Indigenous peoples discussed throughout your elementary, secondary, and postsecondary educational experiences? How would you describe or characterize what you have been taught?
2) Follow at least two Indigenous news sources (e.g., *APTN National News* or *Two Row Times*) and two general Canadian news sources (e.g., *CBC News* and the *National Post*) for one week. Make note of what is being covered and what is not being covered. What stories are making headlines, and which stories are not? How are Indigenous peoples being portrayed within the various news sources?
3) Watch the short YouTube video "Justice for Aboriginal Peoples—It's Time" (available online at www.youtube.com). In this video, various Indigenous peoples answer the question of why they won't "just get over it." Outline and discuss the reasons that they provide.

Recommended Readings

Gray, Lynda. *First Nations 101: Tons of Stuff You Need to Know about First Nations People.* Vancouver: Adaawx Publishing, 2011.

Lawrence, Bonita. *"Real" Indians and Others: Mixed Blood Urban Native Peoples and Indigenous Nationhood.* Lincoln: University of Nebraska Press, 2004.

2
Introduction to an Indigenous Perspective: Ideology and Teachings

THE DOMINANT KNOWLEDGE SYSTEMS IN CANADA are those derived from European colonizers. These ways of knowing tend toward a hierarchal way of thinking that is rooted within individualistic value systems and centred on greed, rising to the top, and economic achievement. These values are in stark contrast to Indigenous value systems, which are framed by respect, harmony, and balance. They guide our way of knowing the land, the environment, and our place in it.

Indigenous cultures hold knowledge, and knowledge holds cultures.[1] This chapter highlights some selected aspects of Indigenous knowledges and cultures, an important project of reclamation because these have been largely devalued, undermined, appropriated, and diminished by colonizers. Given the European attempts to eradicate Indigenous cultures, we must work diligently to understand what colonization has tried so hard to erase.

Indigenous World Views

This book places Indigenous knowledge, perspectives, and ways of coming to know at the foundation of its analysis, as the perspective chosen to examine all topics and not as a topic in itself. Ojibwa journalist and professor Duncan McCue said it well when he stated, "Teach us as Indians, not about Indians."[2]

Bearing in mind that Indigenous peoples are not simply one cultural group, we realize that neither is there one Indigenous world view or ideology. For example, the world view and ideology presented in this book will be influenced by and reflective of me, the author, who has a mixed heritage, a combination of Algonquin, Métis, Huron, and Scottish descent. I recognize I am subject to my own experiences, teachings, and research. Clearly, as with all peoples in the world, everyone has a unique perspective on the world and how it operates. Common threads about living in balance with the land, and with spirit, however, shape the world view of diverse Indigenous cultures. Yet for each of these diverse Indigenous groups, the land is unique, so each has a unique way of life, depending on where various peoples live on Turtle Island. Okanagan scholar Jeannette Armstrong shares one perspective:

> The way we survived is to speak the language that the land offered us as its teachings. To know the plants, animals, seasons, geography is to construct

> language for them. We also refer to the land and our bodies with the same root syllable. This means that the flesh that is our body is pieces of the land that came to us through the things that this land is. The soil, the water, the air, and all other life forms contributed parts to be our flesh. We are our land/place.[3]

Languages hold within them knowledge of our place and space in this world. They reflect and incorporate world views. The distinctive structure of Indigenous languages reflects the unique flow of Indigenous knowledges.[4] According to Professor Leroy Little Bear (Blood Tribe of the Blackfoot Confederacy), most Indigenous languages "are generally aimed at describing 'happenings' rather than objects":

> The languages of Aboriginal peoples allow for the transcendence of boundaries . . . Aboriginal languages allow for talking to trees and rocks, an allowance not accorded in English. If everything is animate, then everything has spirit and knowledge. If everything has spirit and knowledge, then all are like me. If all are like me, then all are my relations.[5]

Peoples are the land, the language comes from the land, and thus teachings reflect place, connection, and way of life with the land and, most important, depend on where peoples are from. The health of the land is the health of the people; "what we do to the land, we do to ourselves."[6] Our environment shapes our world views.

Walking the Red Road: Following "Traditional" Teachings

Some people who aim to live their lives according to ancestral teachings might identify as being "on the Red Road." Among Anishnabe peoples, to be "walking the Good Red Road" means to walk gently on Mother Earth, and have a deep respect for all creation.[7] When walking the Red Road, they acknowledge that all is interconnected and one thing is not more important than another. Thanks are given to the male and female aspects of life, to the two-legged, four-legged, the creepy crawlers, the winged, finned, and the root and mineral aspects of creation. All beings are acknowledged as part of the circle of life and are referred to as "all my relations." Humans are a sum total of their relationships. Everything coexists equally. Each has its own purpose for being placed on Mother Earth. Thus, humans are to "go gently" upon Mother Earth, learn from other beings, be non-judgemental, and recognize the implications of our own actions for Mother Earth and our relatives.

According to Jack D. Forbes (Powhatan-Renape, Delaware-Lenape),

> On the whole, history of the Americas (prior to European conquest) reveals a land where most human groups followed, or tried to follow, the "pollen path" (as the Navajo people call it) or the "good red road" (as the Lakota call it). The pollen path and the red road lead to living life in a sacred manner with continual awareness of the inter-relationships of all forms of life.[8]

Lakota storyteller and historian Joseph M. Marshall III explains the Red Road in the Lakota way by juxtaposing it with the Black Road. Marshall tells a story of a man who travelled the Black Road throughout his life, which was a road of greed, but as his final days grew near he realized this was a very sad and lonely road. On the advice of the oldest wise woman in the village, he changed to a road of generosity, the Red Road. He held a feast for the people, and gave away all of his belongings, even his lodge. Although he had no place to sleep, only left with the clothes on his back, every night from that day forward he was invited to sleep in another person's lodge and was never alone or without friends for all days left in his life. Thus, as Marshall explains, the Red Road is the narrow road fraught with dangers and obstacles and extremely hard to travel, but it is "the good way, the good side, and the right choice." The Black Road is a wide road and easy to travel, but it is "the bad way, the bad side, the wrong choice."[9]

The word "traditionalist" is a term sometimes used to describe those who follow the "Red Road," their ancestral ways of living, or in reference to those who practice the ancestral cultures of their peoples. However, a caution is in order because when we use terms such as "traditionalist" or "traditional," we keep Indigenous peoples frozen in time. When the Europeans who form the dominant culture follow their ancestral teachings, they are not referred to as "traditional" or as a "traditionalist." The word "traditional" is a colonial term stemming from the British; it came to be used by institutional and academic scholars as a way to frame Indigenous cultures under one all-encompassing term.[10] Many Indigenous peoples use terms in their own various languages for their teachings and perspectives, which include a complex set of beliefs and practices. Stó:lō scholar Wenona Victor explains that she follows her Stó:lō culture, traditions, and ways of knowing.[11] She would not refer to doing so as following "traditional" teachings nor would she identify herself as being a "traditionalist"; doing either would incorrectly assume that Stó:lō teachings and culture are stagnant, which is incorrect. Indigenous peoples and cultures are still here and alive. Assuming otherwise is an incorrect assumption, rooted in a Eurocentric colonial mentality.

Elders

Among many Indigenous peoples today, the term "elder" represents an older wise person who is well respected in the community. Not all elders are elderly, but they are usually older and have a rich life experience.[12] Elders frequently come to be identified by the community over time, although no set criteria or time frame must be met for a person to become an elder. Rather, a person's knowledge and community recognition and respect are what usually play a part in being acknowledged as an elder.

The term "elder" was not used in pre-colonial times, as this word is English. Instead, various Indigenous languages had specific names for older, wiser people before colonization.[13] The terms originally used recognized the distinct and unique roles that these wise people held in communities, as keepers of great knowledge, educators, culture carriers, individuals involved in ceremonies and medicine, and people who kept our communities and cultures flourishing and alive.[14] According to Blackfoot elders Reg Crowshoe and Geoff Crow Eagle, in Piikani Blackfoot society, "an elder is somebody who has looked after a bundle that helped the community." Their sacred bundles represent their sources of authority and legislation in the community. Elders "passed on that bundle and became a ceremonial grandparent. The ceremonial grandparent can be called back to conduct or oversee ceremonies. And you look to them for guidance, and consult with them."[15]

Their wisdom may be gained through lived experience, oral transmission, or staying in touch with and practicing ancestral ways. Elders were and still are both teachers and healers. Elders are sometimes sought for their knowledge of ancestral ways, teachings, stories, and ceremonies.[16] They are role models for future generations. Walter Lightning explains that, when elders "teach others they very often begin by quoting the authority of Elders who have gone before. They do not state the authority as coming from themselves. They will say things like 'This is what they used to say,' or 'This is what they said.'"[17]

You can find elders in various roles today. For example, they provide teachings to children, youth, families, and the community. In urban settings, they might contribute to advisory committees, assist in programming and policy, and act as an elder in residence at universities, colleges, correctional institutions, and community organizations. Elders can be found everywhere, living spiritually connected to the land, helping communities.

Circular Thinking

Much of the knowledge and teachings that have been passed down through generations encompass a way of thinking that has been called "circular."

As Huron-Wendat scholar and historian Georges Sioui explains, ancestral Huron-Wendat social principles regard the universe as a great wheel of relationship; the position of humans in this relationship is not more or less important than that of any other life form.[18] This circular way of thinking, then, acknowledges the sacred link among all things in the universe and views the land, people, animals, insects, plants, and rocks (all things, both human and non-human) as equal, interconnected, mutually dependent, and embracing a sacred relationship in this world. All of these things are revered as gifts. They are provided by Mother Earth and are sacred.

In contrast to this circular thinking is what has been termed "linear" thinking.[19] Linear thinking is hierarchical, often seeing the world as organized in a progressive ladder of worth and time as a movement toward ever-better states of reality. This linear thought process is widely held to comprise much of current Western society's thinking.[20] As Professor Leroy Little Bear (Blood Tribe of the Blackfoot Confederacy) explains, "In contrast to Aboriginal value systems, one can summarize the value systems of Western Europeans as being linear and singular, static, and objective."[21] According to Sioui, those holding a linear world view have "the incapacity to see and feel the sacred relation that exists between all beings in the universe."[22] Rather, those holding this world view put humans above all else, including the land, animals, insects, plants, and rocks, and deem humans (usually "man" specifically) as the highest form of intelligence. This viewpoint also positions material and economic growth above anything non-human, such as the land or water or trees. At the extreme end of this ideology, all beings, human and non-human, are considered matter to be transformed into material wealth and power for the gain of "mankind." Humans are seen as having a "right" to take control of nature—and to use and exploit anything assumed to be "found" in nature.

A similar sentiment is expressed by Blackfoot elders Reg Crowshoe and Geoff Crow Eagle, who ask, "What is a white man thinker?" The elders that answer remember the Western saying "God gives dominion to man."[23] As Crowshoe and Crow Eagle explain, "We were taught in residential school that this dominion gives man the right to be superior over all Creation: over the plants, animals, rocks, even the skies. This type of thinking was new to our elders; because if you're superior to everything, then the power to make decisions and build credibility is given to man; it's not in Creator's hands anymore." They further explain that this word "dominion" used to be written in all government documents. Rather than song and ceremony, the written word is authority in this "white man's" way of thinking.[24] The type of written documents one has comes to identify and define one's leadership. Products become "owned" through dominion; they become "authorized by the written word, and controlled by a hierarchy that places man at the top of all creation."[25]

In contrast, all ancestral teachings consider Mother Earth and nature as sacred. As Chief Arvol Looking Horse (Lakota Sioux Nation) states, "Every human being has had Ancestors in their lineage that understood their umbilical cord to the Earth, understanding the need to always protect and thank her."[26] Much can be learned from Mother Earth, the land, and Father Sky, the cosmos. They communicate the natural order of things. For instance, we can be guided by water, wind, plants, and animals. They all are interconnected with us, teach important lessons, and have a spiritual bond. Ojibway scholar Basil H. Johnston echoes these sentiments when he says, "by observing the relationship of plants, animals, and themselves to Earth, the Anishinaubae people deduced that every eagle, bear, or blade of grass had its own place and time on Mother Earth and in the order of creation and the cosmos. From the order of dependence on other beings, the Anishinaubaek determined and accepted their place in relation to the natural order of Mother Earth."[27]

Knowledge Creation and Interpretation

Given this world view, Indigenous perspectives do not restrict understanding to only reason or science. Alternatively, all of the senses are used in coming to know and learn. This perspective is much more interdisciplinary. It takes into consideration numerous ways to explore, analyse, and learn. It is a way of learning that considers mind, body, and spirit as equally important in achieving and interpreting knowledge.[28] According to Indigenous studies

Figure 2.1 Indigenous Circular Thinking and Western Linear Thinking

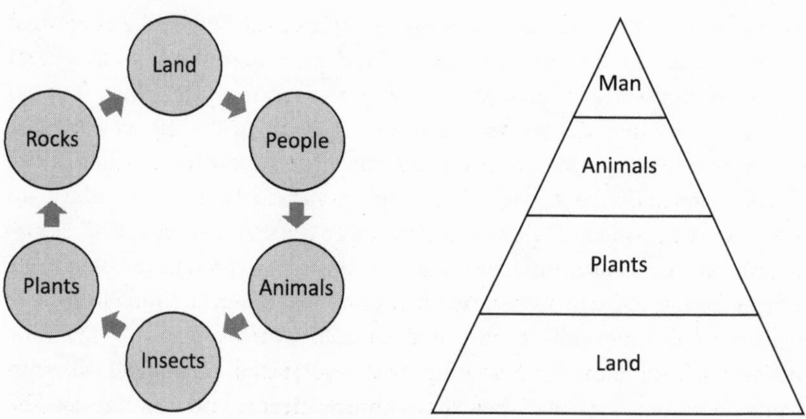

professor David Newhouse (Onondaga), Indigenous knowledge is grounded in the spiritual: it "consists of more than a collection of observations that are then packed into a set of theories that tell us how things work. The spiritual reminds us of a universe that is alive everywhere, that we are intimately connected to all living things and that we have a set of relationships that need to be maintained in order to live well in the universe."[29]

Newhouse further points out that there "is a sense in which Indigenous knowledge is also still viewed as inferior to scientific or western knowledge, that it must still, first of all, be checked and validated by western science before it is accepted as valid."[30] In Western society, scientific knowledge makes an authoritative claim to holding "truth." Answers derived from science are commonly viewed as absolute. In today's public education systems, scientific method and reason are ranked above all other systems of knowledge and ways of coming to know and interpret the world around us.

Kenneth Robinson, an English author and international advisor on education, notes that the whole public education system around the world was invented during the nineteenth century "to meet the needs of industrialism," and, as a consequence, it does not match today's needs:

> Our education system has mined our minds in the way that we strip-mine the earth: for a particular commodity. And for the future, it won't serve us.[31]

He argues that the way children are educated in the Western world is "disembodied," meaning that this education lacks spiritual substance and a human element. The goal of education in the Western world is largely centred on preparing students to secure a "job" that typically contributes to the market economy. It is an education not grounded in values of balance, harmony, and respect. It forgets human's relationship to the land. Rather, Western education contributes to and upholds Western value systems, which, in turn, support notions of the benefits of the "market," "economic development," and "corporate globalism." These types of values typically fuel competition, getting to the top, greed, and materialism.

Indigenous knowledges are explained by theoretical physicist David Peat, who works with Professor Leroy Little Bear (Blood Tribe of the Blackfoot Confederacy), as being "alive" and as having "spirit." He describes Indigenous knowledges as coming about "through watching and listening, not in the passive way that schools demand but through direct experience of songs and ceremonies, through the activities of hunting and daily life, from trees and animals and in dreams and visions. Coming to know means entering into a relationship with the spirits of knowledge, with plants and animals, with beings that animate dreams and visions with the spirit of people."[32] According to Mohawk scholar Marlene Brant Castellano, Indigenous knowledges can be oral, personal, experimental, or holistic.[33] They can be gained through observation of the natural symmetry and repetitious configurations of the world, through dreams, intuitions, or visions. Nêhíyaw and Saulteaux scholar Margaret Kovach also notes that Indigenous knowledges can be arrived at through various paths, such as intuition or dream knowledge.[34] Given the interconnection humans have with all aspects of life and creation, gaining information is reciprocal opposed to extractive, she continues. Consequently, knowledge gained through Indigenous ways of coming to know uphold the cosmological and ecological balance. Different Indigenous cultures will all have their own multifaceted and unique practices used to gain knowledge, as all these methods are relative to place and person, and part of the reciprocal relationship.[35]

Newhouse explains that Indigenous perspectives consider the relationship between things and their influences on the system as a whole rather than focusing on just the measurement of results or trying to identify cause and effect.[36] These perspectives do not reject or disregard quantitative or other modes of scientific data collection, he continues; rather, science is seen as an added way of seeing and understanding the complex social reality of the world we inhabit. Knowledges created by Westernized modes of exploration are then accepted or rejected on the basis of their usefulness.[37] Thus, Indigenous modes of reasoning and perspectives might work together with Westernized modes of exploration. Yet, what Western science can learn from Indigenous perspectives is the need to educate the spirit and to acknowledge the intelligence of creation, which is what Indigenous peoples have been living and practicing since time immemorial. Furthermore, the Indigenous perspective teaches us to recognize that science cannot improve what is already perfect—nature.

Teachings

Teaching and learning are embedded in Indigenous ways of life and culture. Spiritual or intellectual wisdom shared by elders and other ancestral knowledge keepers is commonly referred to as "teachings" of a First Nation. Jo-ann Archibald (from the Stó:lō River People and the Xaxli'p First Nation) uses "the term 'teachings' to mean cultural values, beliefs, lessons, and understandings that are passed from generation to generation."[38] They are philosophies of life—and instructions to live by.

In the past, as well as in the current day, these teachings have been shared for educational, spiritual, and cultural growth to instil balance, harmony, and a way of life. Teachings are typically conveyed through narrative or metaphorical communication.[39] Prior to colonization, a large majority of, if not all, Indigenous peoples in Canada, would gain knowledge through the oral tradition, passed down from one generation to the next.

Today's educational institutions have rendered many people dependant on the written word, and this type of learning and coming to know is being used to a larger degree in order to communicate and distribute Indigenous teachings and knowledge.[40] Indigenous peoples today are using various forms of written knowledge and teachings, including interactive media such as websites and smartphone applications, to preserve their cultures. For example, the website Omàmiwininì Pimàdjwowin (http://thealgonquinway.ca/) provides an online English/Algonquin language translator, as well as audio and lesson workbooks. Similarly, the website FirstVoices (http://www.firstvoices.com) provides Indigenous language translation for various Indigenous languages in Canada. It also includes language games that assist in language learning (e.g., sentence scramble and word searches). It also provides links to traditional songs and stories. The website Four Directions Teachings (http://www.fourdirectionsteachings.com) provides traditional stories and teachings from elders. These are just some of the websites that are attempting to relay "teachings" to today's generations.

Various iPhone and smartphone applications (apps) also teach Indigenous languages, such as Ojibwa, Yati, Oneida, Kwak'wala, Nisga'a, and Cree, among others. However, from an app one does not get the same lived experience or the language connecting to that experience. Language must be learned fully through lived experience; we must be careful not to think that technology is an adequate source for learning something that must be lived.

Recently, young people from Kahnawà:ke created a video game entitled *Skahiòn:hati: Rise of the Kanien'kehá:ka Legends*. Its main story centres on a man journeying to become a warrior. This story unfolds as one goes through the game, and, along the way, players are exposed to and learn about Mohawk culture. For example, players learn about the longhouse, pottery, corn, and the corn masher, among other elements of traditions and culture. Elders, community people, and others who know the stories were brought together to assist in the creation of this game, which aims to relay and teach a positive portrayal of Mohawk culture.[41]

Although these new ways of dispersing and preserving Indigenous knowledges, cultures, and languages use Western technology and are not a substitute for lived experience, they have a place in communicating Indigenous wisdom. Furthermore, there is an Anishnabe prophecy that contends that a time will come to share Indigenous knowledge with all peoples of the Earth.[42] That time may be now or fast approaching as books and other resources that teach the philosophical understandings of Indigenous peoples have become more popular in recent years. Although one should be mindful of who wrote these books (as some might be written by non-Indigenous peoples for monetary gain and others could be exploiting or providing incorrect interpretations of knowledge), they can often teach aspects of traditions and culture. Many books written by elders or other knowledge keepers are designed for Indigenous peoples who may not have had exposure to their own culture, as well as for non-Indigenous peoples who wish to learn about Indigenous cultures.[43]

Borrowing this Euro-Canadian approach that values the written word, we now turn to some teachings recorded in writing. There are far too many Indigenous teachings to outline in one chapter, however, especially given the great vastness of the lifelong learning of Indigenous cultures and peoples. Also, some are not to be written down in order to respect the oral tradition. Therefore, for the purposes of this book, some of the concepts, teachings, and practices with which the author is familiar and that have been put into writing by others or shared more widely will be explained and outlined as an introduction.[44]

Seven Sacred Grandfather Teachings

According to Ojibway Grand Chief Edward Benton-Banai, "Ojibway tradition tells us that there were Seven Grandfathers who were given the responsibility by the Creator to watch over the Earth's people."[45] The Grandfathers sent a helper to the Earth to find a person to provide their teachings on how to live in harmony with Creation. A baby boy was selected, as "children are born with fully-developed senses," and "they can even communicate with the Spirit World" because they are not as far removed from this world as are adults. The helper was instructed to show this boy all "Four Quarters of the Universe," which took seven years. Once they returned, the boy went to the Grandfathers who gave him teachings, seven gifts, and a bundle to take to his people. The bundle was big, so along his journey he had to stop seven times. Each time he stopped a spirit came and explained the meaning behind one of the seven gifts that were given to the boy from the Grandfathers. These teachings were wisdom, love, respect, bravery, honesty, humility, and truth. The boy continued on his journey to take these teachings to his people, during which time he grew into an old man. Upon making it to his village, he was greeted by his parents who still awaited him. He came with the teachings, instructing his people in the right way to use each gift.

Other teachings use the words "courage" or "generosity" to describe one of the seven gifts; one will always find variations in the stories. But the central teaching remains embedded in each story and is the same. These teachings of the Seven Sacred Grandfathers all incorporate notions of respect, harmony, equality, and peace between all of Mother Earth's creations. They act as a guide to maintaining balance within ourselves and with the world around us. They are a reminder to take care of Mother Earth. They provide direction in people's lives and for people in the world.

Many elders and other traditional knowledge keepers have passed these teachings on throughout generations. The seven concepts can have their own corresponding teachings and subteachings, as well as supplementary material that clarifies and describes each of them further.[46] Sometimes, teachings that coincide with each of the concepts are told in a story that provides a lesson. Also, as with many stories, the ones related to the seven concepts can be interpreted and explained in a variety of different ways. Regardless of this variation, however, the Seven Sacred Grandfather teachings are foundational in terms of the ethics of behaviour and conduct in relation to the world.

The Circle

Blackfoot Elders Reg Crowshoe and Geoff Crow Eagle explain that many elders believe there is an oral circle, or a system that includes all First Nations across Turtle Island.[47] For example, their Piikani Blackfoot systems make up part of this greater circle. In 1930, teacher and visionary Black Elk (Oglala Lakota) explained this idea of the circle:

> You have noticed that everything an Indian does is in a circle, and that is because the Power of the World always works in circles, and everything tries to be round. In the old days when we were a strong and happy people, all our power came to us from the sacred hoop of the nation, and so long as the hoop was unbroken, the people flourished. . . . Everything the Power of the World does is done in a circle. The sky is round, and I have heard the earth is round like a ball, and so are all the stars. The wind, in its greatest power, whirls. Birds make their nests in circles, for theirs is the same religion as ours. The sun comes forth and goes down again in a circle. The moon does the same, and both are round. Even the seasons form a great circle in their changing, and always come back again to where they were. The life of man is a circle from childhood to childhood, and so it is in everything where power moves.[48]

According to scholar Jo-ann Archibald (Stó:lō and Xaxli'p First Nations), "The image of a circle is used by many First Nations peoples to symbolize wholeness, completeness, and ultimately wellness. . . . Each Indigenous group has developed its own cultural content for the holistic circle symbol; however, a common goal has been to attain a mutual balance and harmony among animals, people, elements of nature, and the Spirit World."[49] For Georges Sioui (Huron-Wendat), the circle is the "sacred circle of life" wherein a relationship exists between all beings in the universe.[50]

Maintaining holism involves sustaining balance with the world around us and within us. Holism refers to our interconnectedness to everything in the world, and to living in harmony with all of creation. The "concept of First Nations holism" relates to the symbolism of the medicine wheel; however, not all Indigenous peoples draw on the medicine wheel to explain the circle, and "there is not one absolute version of the wheel."[51] Cree (Nehiyawak) Elder Mary Lee has the medicine wheel in her teachings. She explains that Cree people were called "Nehiyawak," which means "being balanced in the four parts that are found in the four directions of the Medicine Wheel." These parts are the "spiritual, physical, emotional, and mental aspects of the self." She explains that the "Medicine Wheel represents the life journey of people" and that "the old people will tell you it is life itself":

> Look at the four seasons and follow the sun. Spring in the east, summer in the south, fall in the west and winter in the north. It tells the whole story of how all life came into being abundantly bright, rising in the east and then fading away as it moves west and north. All life rises and sets like the sun.[52]

Ojibwe and Potawatomi Elder Lillian Pitawanakwat also has the medicine wheel in her teachings. She explains that the teachings are vast and that there are seven teachings within each of the four directions on the "Ojibwe wheel," which all have subteachings to them. The teachings are reminders for many things, such as the "need for balance in the world, and the balance we must strive for everyday within ourselves."[53]

According to Algonquin Anishinaabe-kwe scholar Lynn Gehl, "many Indigenous Nations have adopted its [the wheel's] basic structure to organize sacred and essential features of their world view and culture."[54] Sharilyn Calliou (Michel First Nation) uses the medicine wheel as a pedagogical tool for teaching and learning, explaining that "it is a pedagogical device designed to assist contemplation of the continuity and interconnectedness of events and conditions of all beings." She further explains that "various cultural communities associate different aspects of their humanness, seasons, colours, animals, plants, minerals, etc., with each of the four directions."[55] As these descriptions show, the wheel is many things to many people and has various purposes. Often, it is divided into four with each part of the wheel rendered in a different colour: white, yellow, red, and black (or blue).

For Georges Sioui (Huron-Wendat), these divisions represent "four sacred directions, four sacred colours, four races of humans, each with its own sacred vision, as well as four ages in human life (childhood, adulthood, old age, then childhood again), four seasons, and four times of the day which are also sacred."[56] Thus, for Sioui, the operation of the circle is through four. In Ojibway teachings, as told by Grand Chief Edward Benton-Banai, the four points encompassed in the circle represent the four directions, south, west, north, and east, and these directions are represented by the colours red, black, white, and yellow, respectively. These four colours also represent the four races of people Creator placed on Earth.[57]

The Smudging Ceremony

Four is an important number in other ways too. Four sacred medicines—tobacco, sweetgrass, sage, and cedar—are used in everyday life as well as in various ceremonies by numerous Indigenous peoples (and others). These medicines are also typically used in smudging ceremonies. This ceremony is frequently referred to as a "smudge," and it is commonly practiced in Indigenous cultures to cleanse oneself and restore balance.

A smudge can take place at any time, such as before sleep or after sleep, but it is also a protocol used before people gather. When used to begin a meeting of peoples, it signifies cleansing oneself so that one approaches with

Figure 2.2 Four Directions

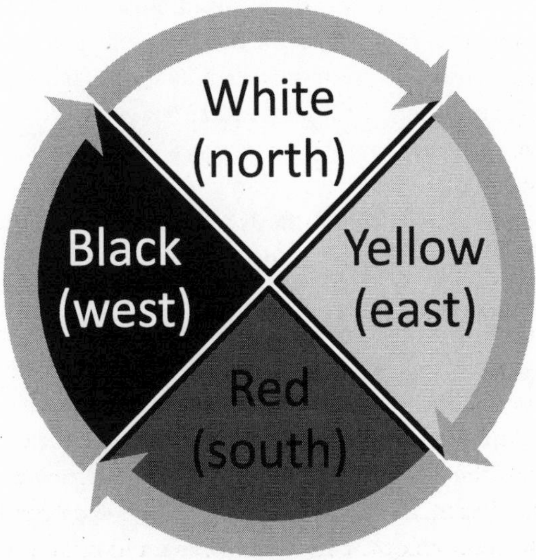

a humbled spirit and listens with an open heart. Smudging, then, involves the cleansing and purification of objects, oneself, or places. One or all of the four sacred medicines can be used to smudge. A teaching that I learned during times spent at Minwaashin Lodge in Ottawa was that sage is known as the women's medicine, and it is typically used in a circle of all women. The medicines are dried and typically put into bundles. Pieces are taken from these bundles and put into a smudge bowl, which can be of clay, stone, or ceramic. Many people have also been using large abalone shells recently, although, in the past, only coastal peoples used these shells. The medicines are then burned in the containers. The smoke will rise up from the medicines, and a feather (typically an eagle or wild turkey feather) will be used to fan the smoke toward what is to be cleansed.

The smoke purifies and restores balance and drives away negative energies. One by one, people will rub their hands over the smoke, in an action similar to how we would wash our hands. Then, each person would cup her or his hands to catch the smoke, putting it over the head, ears, eyes, heart, and down the arms and legs, the small of the back, and the feet. Yet there is no right or wrong way to do this act of purification; rather, the intention behind the act is what is important. Once a smudge is completed, one becomes more grounded and back into a state of balance. Smudging a room or object also helps to purify it, to offer it protection, and to rid the area or object of any negative energy.

Protocols and Learning More

Protocols are about respect.[58] The various Indigenous communities and peoples across Turtle Island follow different protocols because these vary depending on the nation and culture. For instance, for Cree peoples, the Sun Dance ceremony must not be filmed or photographed. Other First Nations and peoples also object to having pictures taken or to filming during certain ceremonies.

No authenticated photograph exists of the renowned Oglala Lakota leader Crazy Horse, for example, as it has been said that being photographed went against his beliefs.[59] Among those who knew him best, he is remembered as one of the most humble people who practiced and lived the Lakota virtue of humility.[60] In response to those who tried taking photos, he asked, "Why should you wish to shorten my life by taking from me my shadow?"[61] Many peoples (and not only Indigenous peoples) feel that photographing them or their cultural events is invasive. Today, and historically, there are also many Indigenous peoples who do not object to photographs or film, as we can see from the videos and pictures taken during Pow Wows, for example, and uploaded to YouTube and Facebook. Yet, at some times, these are not to be taken, such as during flag songs. At most gatherings, a master of ceremonies will typically let everyone know when it is not appropriate to take photographs or videos. However, one should always ask any dancer or drum group before taking photographs or filming.

At Pow Wows and other ceremonial events, touching people's regalia or drums without asking permission first is also inappropriate. Regalia is never to be referred to as a "costume"; people are not playing "dress up" but are wearing outfits that are tied to meanings, stories, and their cultures. Sometimes these outfits are passed down over generations through families.

One of the reasons some people object to photographs when they are wearing regalia is that they might not want their family design or sacred outfit being copied and recreated in an inappropriate fashion or reproduced for profit. Doing so is cultural appropriation, whereby elements from oppressed peoples are taken by members of the dominant society for their own self-interest. When cultural appropriation takes place, the sacred meanings, stories, or cultural significance tied to the design, symbol, or outfit are completely disregarded. Cultural appropriation encourages the dominant culture to continue its agenda of colonialism. Take, for example, Urban Outfitters, which sexualized and trivialized the Navajo people's name and symbols for its own monetary benefit. In this case, the Navajo Nation sued after Urban Outfitters released its "Navajo" inspired line, which included a low-rise "Navajo hipster panty" and a "Navajo flask." The inappropriate and sexualized depiction of Indigenous peoples in popular culture is further discussed in Chapter 9.

If you are unfamiliar with the ancestral teachings of the territory where you live or are visiting, seek to connect to these and to discover the protocol that guides respectful interaction with regional First Nations. Get involved in local Indigenous organizations such as friendship centres. Attend gatherings and activities. Seek out books written by Indigenous elders and knowledge keepers.[62] Humbly sit and listen to an elder. Some universities and colleges have an elder-in-residence program through which you can meet these wise individuals. When approaching an elder for guidance or stories, people customarily offer tobacco or a gift. Nêhíyaw and Saulteaux scholar Margaret Kovach explains that, for Cree peoples, the acceptance of tobacco is an acknowledgement that they will tell the truth and speak from the heart.[63]

Kovach also explains the importance of reciprocity: when you ask another to share her or his story, it is customary to share your own. This process starts with locating yourself by providing your own cultural identification and where you are from. For many Indigenous peoples, sharing our ancestry and where we are from is intuitive. According to Kovach, following the protocols of introductions shows respect to the ancestors. It allows people to be located, which is consistent with the belief that "we can only interpret the world from the place of our experience."[64]

Look into your own ancestral teachings. Let me emphasize how important it is to be grounded in your own history. And from this position, proceed with humble curiosity about the various cultures and ways of the land in Turtle Island. Mohawk scholar Patricia Monture-Angus shares a teaching that "explains that you must know where you have been in order to know where you are going."[65] If you want to learn more, try connecting to nature and to the teachings of the land. Remember to learn the protocol of the territory where you are with humility and respect, to approach ceremony with decorum, to watch, listen, and learn with propriety. As stated by The Circle of Turtle Lodge, "Everyone is equal in the circle."[66]

Discussion Questions

1) What are teachings? What do they tell us? How and in what ways might these teachings be useful for both Indigenous and non-Indigenous peoples?
2) Why is it important for criminal justice personnel to know the cultural protocols of the land on which they work?

Activities

1) Listen to the elders teachings on the Four Directions Teachings website (http://www.fourdirectionsteachings.com/). Have a sharing circle discussion on how and in what ways people might apply this knowledge to their lives.
2) Split into seven groups. Each group is to be assigned one of the Seven Grandfather Teachings from the book *Seven Sacred Teachings Niizhwaaswi gagiikwewin* by David Bouchard and Dr. Joseph Martin (available online at http://www.davidbouchard.com). Each group reads the teaching together and reflects on and discusses the teaching being shared. Consider the animal discussed in each teaching and how and in what ways this animal provides insight related to the teaching. Each of the seven groups then shares its teaching with the rest of the class.
3) Invite to the class a local Indigenous elder to share her or his wisdom or ancestral teachings.

Recommended Readings

Benton-Banai, Edward. *The Mishomis Book: The Voice of the Ojibway*. Minneapolis: University of Minnesota Press, 2010.

Bopp, Judie, Michael Bopp, Lee Brown, and Phil Lane, Jr. *The Sacred Tree: Reflections on Native American Spirituality*. Twin Lakes, WI: Lotus Light Press, 1992.

3

Indigenous Governance and Methods of Addressing Crime

PRIOR TO **E**UROPEAN CONTACT, Indigenous peoples had sophisticated systems of governance and social control in their communities. This chapter examines some of these customary Indigenous structures and systems of governance, including the longest standing governance structure in North America. It provides a look into kinship and social control systems as well as intertribal relations.

This chapter will also touch on some traditional methods of addressing crime, drawing on examples from Inuit, Mi'kmaq, Ojibwa, Huron, Blackfoot, Cree, Tsilhqot'in peoples, and others. It will be demonstrated that methods of incarceration and the use of written laws were not part of Indigenous justice systems. Among all of the Indigenous cultures within the northern part of the Northern Hemisphere, no First Nations practiced methods of incarceration and no communities used holding cells for punishment.[1] Across various Indigenous communities and cultures, Indigenous laws emphasize social harmony, restoring balance, and re-establishing peace rather than retribution or punishment.[2]

Turtle Island

The name "Turtle Island" stems from various nations' creation stories.[3] Many of these stories are shared by elders who maintain the responsibility to do so. It is not ethically appropriate to share these stories here because elders are the great keepers of this knowledge. However, elders and other knowledge keepers have provided sketches of these stories in print, and it is possible to share these versions. We must remember, though, that particular stories (creation stories, for example) can take several hours or, in some cases, days to tell.[4] And no written description of any story is as comprehensive or as authentic as its telling would be.

The Haudenosaunee creation story speaks of Skywoman, who fell from the sky onto the back of a turtle.[5] Thomas King (Cherokee) tells an archetypal story of creation that includes a woman who fell from the sky, whereby birds placed her onto the back of a turtle.[6] Creation stories typically speak of peace, harmony, and inclusion. Depending on the story, various participants will play equal roles in creation; sometimes animals, people, plants, and mud, among other things, are named as equally responsible in the development of Turtle Island. Creation stories provide a framework for understanding how Indigenous peoples govern themselves because their governing structures are rooted in this world view, which is inclusive of equality and balance. According to Blackfoot Elders Reg Crowshoe and Geoff Crow Eagle, when they asked elders what their creation stories said, they were told that many stories conveyed this idea of the people being equal to and in balance with the other aspects of creation:

> And a lot of our stories said that humans were created as equal to all creation. And the concept of being equal defined our thinking and understanding. So I was equal to the animals and plants, the air and the water; the stars were equal to me, and I was equal to all human beings, and even to bugs.
>
> Now the concept of being created equally was the basis of all our practices—our forms of governance, and social relations. We are all created together, and all are sacred. So our Piikani Blackfoot language and oral system are based in ceremonial practices; a ceremonial circle structure was our way of communicating and working in a group.[7]

This idea that all elements of creation, and not just all peoples, are created as equals and should remain in balance is essential to an understanding of Indigenous concepts of justice. It sustains a view that justice is rooted in relationship, with the land and animals and plants, with the Creator, and with others, whether they are offenders or victims. Thus, restoring balance and healing relationships are central factors in Indigenous justice systems.

Traditional Governance and Governance Structures

For thousands and thousands of years, Indigenous peoples across Turtle Island had governance structures in place that assured all in the community had their needs met.[8] One of the most important things was the welfare of the community as a whole because, as Professor Leroy Little Bear (Blood Tribe of the Blackfoot Confederacy) explains, "If the 'whole' is maintained, then beauty, harmony, and balance result."[9] Daniel N. Paul (Mi'kmaq elder, author, and human rights activist) notes that, in traditional Mi'kmaq societies, this concern for the whole resulted in health and lack of poverty:

> Because of the communal nature of the society and the abundance of food, poverty among the People was virtually unknown. Material things, other than clothing and household goods, were equally shared. Thus, the old, sick, infirm and otherwise were all protected from destitution. Endowed with a

> high level of personal security, the People had a relatively low level of stress in their lives. This, combined with a healthy diet, blessed them with unusually long lifespans; centenarians were not rare.[10]

Indigenous communities shared common egalitarian characteristics, but each First Nation lived according to original instructions from Creator and in a way consistent with the teachings of the land. Through democratic and self-government systems, pre-colonial Indigenous societies maintained their thriving communities.

According to Mohawk scholar Taiaiake Alfred, before colonial influence, the majority of Indigenous societies "achieved true civilization: They did not abuse the earth; they promoted communal responsibility; they practiced equality in gender relations; and they respected individual freedom."[11] He further explains that the vast majority of pre-contact societies were egalitarian, had no forced authority structures, and sustained no major distance between those in leadership roles and others.

Some communities had hierarchies in place and a governing leader.[12] But these hierarchies were not structured according to Euro-Canadian understandings of hierarchies, with power at the top and certain people having less importance. Rather, in Indigenous hierarchies, everyone had her or his own unique role to play. Social structures existed, but there was no "wealth hierarchy."[13] For example, Nuu-chah-nulth societies recognized different social classes of people, yet necessities were shared generously.[14] A template for their social and political organization can be described through a depiction of the "whale," which was both symbolically and materially important for Nuu-chah-nulth peoples. The whale's "functionally related parts map the relation of classes in society. The mass and boundedness of the whale's body can be seen to represent the holism of the polity. Finally, the qualitative distinctions made among nutritionally similar pieces of whale meat are a useful representation of the mediation of hierarchy and solidarity in society."[15] Thus, the whale's body reflects the togetherness of the whole society. Necessities were apportioned according to need although certain parts within the whole played particular roles.

The different way that leadership is understood in Indigenous and Euro-Canadian society is apparent when one considers the following example. A leader in many traditional Indigenous societies does not ask "what can I control?" but "what am I responsible for?"; a leader does not ask "what do I get?" but "what can I contribute?"[16] So people in positions of leadership in Indigenous societies were typically seen as assuring the ongoing circulation of resources, so the whole community could thrive.[17] For example, in Mi'kmaq societies, "Chiefs provided subsistence for all connected to them and did not accumulate individual wealth." They had "tremendous generosity and kindheartedness towards others, values highly regarded among the Mi'kmaq."[18] In Cree societies, "a chief had to give freely of his possessions to needy tribesmen, and usually set the pace on the occasions for ceremonial gift-giving."[19] In Cree language, "*okimow*" translates to "chief" and "derives from the verbal form of 'give away.'"[20] In Nuu-chah-nulth societies, "generosity is proof of chiefly essence," and a leader is "defined by his respect, both for himself and others."[21] Their leader would head up the whale hunt, but, once a whale was caught, its meat was shared generously among community members, with the leader taking only very little for themselves.

Some of the most common systems of Indigenous governance are called clans, houses, councils, and confederacies. The Wendat Nation was a confederacy of five nations: Attignawantan (Bear), Attigneenongnahac (Cord), Arendahronon (Rock), Tahontaenrat (Deer), and Ataronchronon (Swamp or Mud).[22] Traditional Huron-Wendat governance consisted of four levels: lineage (a clan segment within the village), village, nation, and confederacy councils.[23] "Chiefs" were selected from a certain number of individuals with hereditary rights.[24] Lineage councils were composed of chiefs who were selected by the older women members of the lineage.[25] Women chose them based on intellect, oral proficiency, inclination to work, acceptance by the community, and, most notably, courage. The women could also dismiss an insufficient chief. Village councils were composed of chiefs of civil affairs from each lineage, chiefs of defence from each lineage, and elders. Nation councils were comprised of chiefs from all clan segments, from all villages. The confederacy council was made up of civil chiefs who met each spring for several weeks to deal with all matters relating to the life of Wendat peoples as a whole; this council was motivated by "an ideal of peace." Matters dealt with included unifying the five Wendat nations, welcoming newcomers, and discussing "topics such as political developments, trade, village resettlement and subdivision, new subsistence strategies, diplomatic missions, important feasts, major expeditions (fishing, hunting, trading), the development of new routes, and 'raising fallen trees'—that is, replacing dead chiefs. Emergency confederacy councils could also be called and these were held in the village of the chief who convened the meeting."[26]

The Blackfoot Nation is a confederacy of three nations: the Siksika (meaning "'black foot,' from a legend of walking across burned prairie") in the north, the Blood or Kainai (meaning "many chiefs") in the central region, and the Peigan or Piikani (meaning "'scabby robes,' from a legend in which the women had not properly prepared the hides") in the southerly portion of their shared territory in the Prairies. The Tsuut'ina joined later, in the beginning of the nineteenth century.[27] Although these nations shared the same language and customs and often intermarried, they had separate political units. Nations "were sub-divided into clans, each governed by an elected Chief."[28] Clan chiefs chose a head chief for their nation. To become a leader of the people, a person had to display bravery, generosity, and compassion. The Blackfoot Nation also had "All Comrades" societies that had leadership over the affairs in clans and whose function was to preserve order and protect the people.[29]

The foundations and organization of Gitksan and Wet'suwet'en peoples emerge directly from "the most basic of human relationships—those of the family."[30] The "House" is their main political unit, its name stemming from their "Long Houses" where community members lived. Common ancestry is shared by all of the house members. Oral histories are captured in their crests and songs and shown on blankets and poles. The responsibilities of community members are passed on orally from each House's head chief through the people. Succession to leadership is matrilineal, coming from the mother's side, as "a person is born into his or her mother's House."[31] The head chief is accountable for the members of the House and their activities, but this leader also has help, including from the "wings" of the head chief and from elders, both of whom are consulted. Chiefs of other houses are also consulted when larger matters arise. Finally, clans are the broadest group of related houses. The Gitksan have four clans and the Wet'suwet'en have five. Neighbouring societies have people originally from the same clans, who are historically related; thus, clan identity is central in marriage law, as no one of the same clan is permitted to marry.

Many original forms of Indigenous governance still exist; however, many systems have been disrupted as a result of colonization.[32] These disruptions have included oppressive measures of varying degrees. Indigenous peoples were dispossessed of their land, relocated, and forced to follow imposed definitions of citizenship and leadership (e.g., the chief and council systems) and "foreign" laws, many of which tore at the hearts of communities (e.g., the anti-potlatch law). Stó:lō scholar Wenona Victor points out the devastating impacts colonial governance had on Stó:lō governance and leadership.[33] Among these was the severe displacement of their women-centred society and social organization: "Stó:lō were/are matriarchal with respect to cultural property, and egalitarian with respect to decision making and familial and communal contributions."[34] In matriarchal societies, women hold leadership roles within the social organization of the community, and ancestral names are predominately passed through the matrilineal line (the female line).

Victor notes how the prominent, crucial, and vital roles that the Sí:le (Grandmothers) held within their communities were displaced through colonial legislation.[35] From 1869 to 1951, the Indian Act prohibited Stó:lō women from voting and from holding leadership roles. Yet within Stó:lō custom, both women and men make decisions. Responsibilities were decided in a "fluid and flexible" way, and gender alone was never the sole factor in determining who would carry out certain responsibilities or roles.[36]

As explained in Chapter 1, the Indian Act stripped women who married a "non-status" man of "Indian status"; the children of these women were also stripped of status, and this law was applied equally to any children of these women born previously with a "status" father. The artificial designations of "status" and "non-status" that disinherited women impacted Stó:lō governance and leadership, as the names, ceremonies, songs, and cultural property of this nation were "owned" by the Sí:le, and the Sí:le were the ones who decided which family members carried on the cultural property. According to custom, then, the men carry the masks and dances, and the women own the songs and determine which men carry the masks. Thus, removing women from their communities severely displaced them from essential roles and responsibilities related to the interlinked cultural, leadership, and governance practices of the Stó:lō.

Also, upon marrying a status man, a woman was forced by the Indian Act to be registered under her husband's "band," which directly affected the passing on of Sí:le ancestral names. Many ancestral names—and material property associated with those ancestral names—are passed predominately through the matrilineal line. As a result of this imposed patriarchal "band" structure, kinship ties became severed, and vital cultural knowledge and property became displaced.

Colonial legislation did more than disrupt matrilineal lines of culture and kinship. These laws attempted to impose a fundamentally foreign view of governance, one that was more about bowing to authority than contributing to community. As Wenona Victor notes, Indigenous forms of governance were not about power and control. In fact, she could not find one word in her Halq'eméylem language that relates to "'government' or 'controlling' the masses or 'exerting ones power over others' or directing the 'affairs of the state.'"[37] She identifies a central aspect of Indigenous governance missing in colonial governance—the role of spirituality. For Indigenous leaders, "their connection to spirituality was the key to their ability to lead and govern."[38] Mohawk scholar Taiaiake Alfred points out that Western systems of governance separate land, culture, and governance, which are inseparable in Indigenous governance.[39]

Forcibly imposed Western governance structures continue to have damaging impacts on Indigenous peoples. The colonial project has disconnected Indigenous peoples from our lands, cultures, and spirituality. As Alfred explains, it has bound Indigenous peoples to the colonial power order and created a dependency on the state, which has been used as a tool of compliance.[40] Some Indigenous peoples and communities have become co-opted into complying with a foreign European-style governance structure. This compliance involves conducting interactions through the use of the English language and cooperating with this imposed system of "Canadian" governance and social organization. "Band" council governments and elected "chiefs" are part of these colonial impositions, forced through Euro-Canadian laws. Indeed, these types of First Nation "governments" have been largely shaped by the Euro-Canadian state, and thus serve its interests, not the interests of Indigenous peoples.[41]

At the same time, Alfred also notes that Indigenous peoples have survived this colonial disease. We have resisted and are recovering. Despite the attacks on Indigenous systems of governance, frameworks that form Indigenous value systems still remain intact. Alfred contends that these traditional forms of governance, and their values of "harmony, autonomy, and respect," will provide a "lasting solution to the political, economic, and social problems that beset our people."[42] While being careful not to "romanticize the past," he asserts that traditional methods of Indigenous governance will need to be revived and regenerated, as they hold "the antidote to the colonial disease."[43]

The Haudenosaunee Great Law of Peace

Much has been written on Haudenosaunee systems of governance, in part because the Haudenosaunee have been able, largely, to preserve the values of their traditional systems and to keep these values and systems alive amidst colonization.[44] In a report prepared for Canada's solicitor general, Christie Jefferson wrote, "During the 150 years of European presence, the peace created within the Six Nations was never broken, even in the face of murder. The constitution and laws of the confederacy were so effective that they maintained harmony between their member nations."[45] The Haudenosaunee—meaning "People of the Longhouse"—formed the Haudenosaunee Confederacy (also referred to as the Six Nations Confederacy). It consists of six nations (originally five): Mohawk, Oneida, Onondaga, Cayuga, Seneca, and Tuscarora (with the Tuscarora Nation joining later, in 1722). The Great Law of Peace formed an alliance between these member nations.

The Great Law of Peace is the founding constitution of the Haudenosaunee Confederacy.[46] It is an oral tradition codified in a series of wampum belts currently retained by the Onondaga Nation. Wampum belts are made from sacred shells and clam beads, and these belts were typically used by the ancestors of the peoples of the Eastern Woodlands to symbolize or commemorate important events and agreements. According to Mohawk scholar

Patricia Monture-Angus, a literal translation of the Great Law of Peace from Mohawk to English is "the great big nice."[47] One of Mohawk scholar Taiaiake Alfred's elders told him it meant "the great good way."[48] In discussion with Atsenhaienton, who is Kanien'kehaka, a member of the bear clan, and a respected voice on Indigenous government among the Haudenosaunee Confederacy, Alfred discovered that the term the "Great Law" is a mistake. Atsenhaienton explains that this is not what it says in his language. A better translation would be something along the lines of "the big warmth" or "the big harmony." In other words, this "big warmth" is not "law" in the way a constitutional lawyer would view legislation but rather provides "guidelines to help people get to harmony and coexistence."[49]

Haudenosaunee history is an oral history, and these oral histories have kept the peace among Indigenous nations for thousands of years. Stories, such as how the Great Law of Peace formed, have been passed on from generation to generation using the wampum belts.[50] Oral history preserves and retains cultural traditions. It unifies generations of the past, present, and future. Instructions on how to live are embedded in its stories.

Many versions of the Great Law of Peace have been recorded in writing. The Haudenosaunee Confederacy notes that one specific account of this story is not preferred over another, as all themes in the accounts are similar and all highlight the story's key values. The National Museum of the American Indian has digested various versions of this story to provide an abbreviated one, which has been reviewed by five different Haudenosaunee peoples, including a Mohawk editor.[51] In this version of the story, a man called "Peacemaker" was on a journey to spread peace throughout Haudenosaunee territory because, at this time, the Haudenosaunee Nations were at war with one another. While on his journey, Peacemaker came to the home of Hayo'wetha (hi-an-WEN-ta), an Onondaga leader. Hayo'wetha wanted to spread the message of peace as well, especially as his wife and daughters had been previously killed by Tadadaho, the leader of the Onondaga.

The Peacemaker supported Hayo'wetha through the loss of his wife and daughters. Hayo'wetha decided to travel with the Peacemaker to spread the word of peace among the Haudenosaunee peoples. The Peacemaker wanted to show people the strength of unity. As a way to demonstrate this idea, he took a single arrow and snapped it into two pieces. Then he took five arrows, tied them together and tried to snap this bundle. He demonstrated that these arrows could not be broken easily, as the single arrow could. A single arrow is weaker than five tied together, which the Peacemaker used to symbolize the strength of a unifying confederacy.

This message of peace was received and undertaken by the Mohawk, Oneida, Cayuga, Seneca, and Onondaga Nations. Once these nations united,

Hayo'wetha, along with the Peacemaker, sought out Tadadaho, the leader who had killed Hayo'wetha's family, and invited him to join the confederacy. At first he was reluctant, but then they promised Tadadaho that, if he joined, the Onondaga would be the capital of the "Grand Council."[52] Tadadaho ultimately accepted.

The unified nations then emerged as the Haudenosaunee Confederacy. The message of peace was spread. According to Cayuga Nation Sub-Chief (Bear Clan) Leroy (Jock) Hill, the values of peace that form the basis of the Great Law are benevolence, good mind, and caring.[53] According to Seneca historian and scholar Sotsisowah (John C. Mohawk), this message of peace is not simply defined as the nonexistence of conflict or war but as humans actively striving to achieve universal justice.[54] He further notes that power, reason, and righteousness are what the people must strive to achieve under the Great Law. "Righteousness" refers to a shared ideology of the people, one that is pure and unselfish. It happens when people synchronize their thoughts and feelings with the flow of the universe and have the intentions of the "Good Mind." All judgements of privilege, superiority, or prejudice are cleared. Instead, acknowledgement is given to the equality among all things in the universe, recognizing that humans do not own the world but rather that all of creation is intended for everything to benefit equally, including animals, plants, insects, humans, and all that is. Not even human labour or skill is owned by an individual or people; these too are gifts of the "Great Creator." The things required for human survival—protection, shelter, clothing, and food—are gifts. So no one, regardless of ability, should be deprived of these necessities. No one has any right to deprive others of any of earth's gifts.

"Reason" is the power of the human mind to arrive at righteous decisions regarding complex questions or concerns. The Peacemaker began by sharing the teaching that human beings were gifted with of the power of reason. This power was given to them so they could resolve differences without the use of force, which was to be used only as a last resort. The Peacemaker taught that everyone who has a healthy mind desires peace; all human beings have the ability to understand and grasp the main principles of righteousness; and the skill of reason is needed in order for the objectives of justice to be reached so no one's rights are abused.

"Power" is next described by the Peacemaker: the "power to enact a true peace is the product of a unified people on the path of righteousness, and reason is the ability to enact the principles of peace through education, public opinion, and political, and when necessary, military unity."[55] Power is having the ability to call on fighting parties to lay down their weapons of war and arrive at an agreement. It involves the power of reason and persuasion, the power of the intrinsic good will of human beings, and the power of a unified and devoted people.

The Haudenosaunee Nations all joined together in a celebration embracing this message of peace.[56] They gathered weapons, dug a hole, and put the weapons into it. They then replanted a white pine tree over the place of the hole. This tree was named "The Tree of Peace." And this tree continues to act as a symbol for the Great Law of Peace by which the nations live. The tree has four main long roots, which signify the four directions and pathways of peace that lead to the centre of Haudenosaunee territory. These roots are representative of a path to which all are welcome. An eagle sits at the top of the tree. This eagle is the people's messenger to the Creator and a protector of the Haudenosaunee.

Once the nations had joined together, the Peacemaker asked each one to select men to be leaders. Laws were given to the Haudenosaunee men who formed the Grand Council, which was made up of 50 leaders who would take decisions that coincided with the Great Law of Peace. Each leader in the Grand Council was called a "*hoyaneh*"(ho-YA-ne), which means a "caretaker of peace."[57] Each leader's role was to represent his clan in the Haudenosaunee government. Over time, the selection process for new members became the responsibility of clan mothers, who would closely observe children as they grew up and decide whom they felt had the nation's best interests at heart. According to Doug George-Kanentiio (Mohawk from Akwesasne), clan mothers would ensure that candidates had no motive for greed, envy, or malice.[58] Candidates also had to embody the ability to see beyond their time and to have the wisdom and fortitude to enact laws and policies that would safeguard the rights of people for the next seven generations. Clan mothers not only selected who would serve as a *hoyaneh* but also decided upon the removal of any leaders whom they felt did not have the best interests of the nations as their focal point.[59] Indeed, clan mothers played a central role in the Grand Council.

Chosen leaders representing the people would gather together as a Grand Council to discuss things such as peace treaties or trade agreements. All council members had to agree on decisions, and all laws had to be passed by consensus. Although united, each nation was permitted to make independent choices concerning its own internal matters. This idea of independence within a confederacy of nations was borrowed by the United States years later when the colonies united.

Indeed, the United States Constitution was influenced by several aspects of the Great Law.[60] Benjamin Franklin, who is known for his role in helping to draft the Declaration of Independence and the Constitution of the United States, was influenced by the Haudenosaunee governance structure and by Haudenosaunee notions of peaceful respect among nations unified under one council. In reference to this structure, Franklin wrote, "it would be strange if [the Haudenosaunee] could execute a union that persisted ages and appears indissoluble; yet a like union is impractical for twelve colonies to whom it is more necessary and greatly advantageous."[61] To a large extent, what had influence was the idea of the arrows, of strength in unity. Through a resolution passed on October 4, 1988, the United States Congress formally acknowledged the influence of the Haudenosaunee Confederacy on the United States Constitution, stating the following purpose in the resolution's first paragraph: "To acknowledge the contribution of the Iroquois Confederacy of Nations to the development of the United States Constitution and to reaffirm the continuing government-to-government relationship between Indian tribes and the United States established in the Constitution."[62]

Yet, as Lynda Gray notes, a vital part of the governance system of the Haudenosaunee Confederacy—the role of clan mothers—was not included in the United States Constitution.[63] These women held key roles that maintained cohesion, accountability, peace, and equality among all. As mentioned, they could not only nominate the men who would be in positions of leadership but also impeach leaders.[64] Women, then, play an essential part in the Haudenosaunee Confederacy, but interpreters and Western observers of Haudenosaunee culture have never articulated fully the true powers of women within this culture or government.[65]

Neither has Euro-Canadian society consistently acknowledged the age and significance of this form of Indigenous governance. Within all of Turtle Island, the Haudenosaunee Grand Council is the oldest governance system that has been able to maintain its original form.[66] The Peacemaker came to remind people how to live according to the laws of the land. The ancestors hold the vision and knowing that maintain this democratic tradition.

Clan Systems

The Haudenosaunee also have clan systems, and these have played a large role in the maintenance of "the social, political, economic, and spiritual cohesion of the people for centuries," according to Professor Theresa McCarthy (Onondaga Nation, Beaver Clan).[67] In order to understand Haudenosaunee clan systems fully, one has to acknowledge the language and stories from which clans stem, McCarthy continues, because the translation of words from traditional languages shows clearly that land relationships actually form the basis of the clans. Drawing on the work of Deborah Doxtator, she notes that the word "*otara*" in Mohawk "means land, clay, or earth as well as clan."[68]

So when you ask a person to identify his or her clan ("*oh nisen'taroten*"), you are literally asking, "What is the outline or contour of your clay?"[69]

This land relationship is echoed within the creation story as well. To make this point McCarthy draws on the words of Snipe Clan Confederacy Chief Jake Thomas: "If you go back to the time of Creation, when the Creator made mankind, he made them by molding them from the earth—that's why we call it *Q:gwehǫ́ Q:weh. Q:gweh* is what we are from. . . . *Qg:weh* means the real thing from mother earth—that's what we are."[70]

Haudenosaunee clans are also said to be ingrained in "patterns of activity," rooted in place, territory and ecology. This idea is also supported in the language of the people. The way one would ask a person to identify her or his clan in the Cayuga language, "*De'ni:s nisa'sgao'de?*" translates to, "What family or animal grouping do you belong to?"[71] Being part of a clan, then, is something that is rooted within everyday life and being. Clan membership incorporates lived reciprocal relationships with other clan members. Clan membership also involves having reciprocal responsibilities to the clan.

Teachings on the origins of the clans also bring to light further understandings of what they are. To make this point, McCarthy draws on a story by Chief Thomas about the origins of the Haudenosaunee clan system.[72] This story flows from the time of creation. As told by Chief Thomas, this was a time when people were being created and being birthed from women. During this time, people were multiplying, and they gave their gratitude to the Creator for providing them with the joys of these new lives.

On the other side of this joy was death. After a certain amount of time, people would also die. People had a hard time dealing with death. So even when a new person was born, sometimes they would still be left struggling with trying to get over a death, and the sorrows were more consuming than the celebrations of births. The people struggled with how to cope with such grief. It was causing depression and sickness. Furthermore, as people multiplied and branched out into various settlements, they started to forget about the ceremonies. They also started to forget how they were related to one another. Because of this forgetfulness, they would start to wage war on one another.

A young man then thought he knew of a way to deal with this problem, so he took people out on a journey. On this journey, they all had to cross a grapevine to get from one side of a river to another. While the people were trying to cross, the vine breaks. The result was that people were divided in half, with each separate group on an opposite shore. The fact of this physical separation was part of the teaching. As the storyteller explained, the division of the peoples is reality; sometimes people will get separated from one another, and this separation will continue to happen for generations to come, yet this fact does not mean that we will be actually *separate* from one another.[73]

The following morning, people were told to go out from their camps and take note of the first thing they saw. When they returned to camp, they shared what it was that they had seen. People reported the different animals they had seen, saying "I saw a beaver" or "I saw a wolf" or "I saw a turtle." Then, in response to these reports, the young man told the people that what they had seen would be their clan. Every person was to pass this clan information on through the generations to come, and the clans would continue through the matrilineal line.

It was further explained that, any time one feels discomfort or stress, one can look for comfort in the clans. So, for example, the bear will comfort the wolf or vice versa. Also, all of the clans within the clan system will support one another. The specific clan that one is a part of will come to serve as one's identity. This clan is where a person can go for comfort when needing help to get his or her spirits back up. The teachings of the clan help people walk the good path.

According to McCarthy, teachings on the origins of clans reveal their true purpose. Clan systems support kinship, and clans are places where people get help to repair personal and interpersonal detachment caused by anguish, loss, or grief.[74]

Clans are rooted in creation, and they are also affirmed and reaffirmed in ceremonies. Both the story of the origin of the clans and the Great Law of Peace remind us that we are all united; the clan system helps us remember not to wage war on our brothers and sisters because we are united in peace. The clans maintain the interconnectedness of the people despite the vastness of geographical distance that might separate us. In the Great Law of Peace, clans are the building blocks for the confederacy's government. Clans establish and re-establish relatives, responsibilities, economic activities, and political voices. They create and recreate the bonds and ties between families of the past and future.

According to the Haudenosaunee Confederacy, the clan system is still followed among those Haudenosaunee peoples who follow ancestral ways.[75] Regardless of what nation an Indigenous person might belong to, if that person is in the same clan as another, they consider each other familial relatives. Thus, a wolf clan member of the Seneca Nation and a wolf clan member of the Cayuga Nation would still consider one another relatives. Given that all in a clan are considered relatives, intermarriage within the same clan is not allowed, although some clans allow marriage between the members of different subgroups (or species) within a clan. Turtle clans, for example, can be comprised of three different species of turtles. Marriage would therefore be allowed between members of different species group. When a marriage takes place, the husband moves into the wife's longhouse.[76] Families of the same clan live together in a longhouse, including extended family members, such as grandparents, cousins, uncles, aunts, brothers, sisters, fathers, and mothers. The clan system, then, supported strong, cohesive family units.

Although clans were made up of extended family members, people could also be adopted into a clan.[77] Sometimes adoptions would take place in order to keep a clan large and strong. People could be adopted from other First Nations because of sickness or war. After the Europeans arrived, they were also adopted into clans. Typically, women or children were adopted. Men were sometimes also adopted, but they would usually have to undergo endurance and bravery tests. Ultimately the women of the clan would decide who was allowed to join the clan through adoption. If someone were to be adopted, she or he would take on the name of a clan member, for example, the name of a deceased relative.

Clans were also very helpful when a person travelled, as visitors from the same clan were treated exactly the same as resident clan members.[78] They would be provided with shelter and food and taken care of as if they were members of the family. According to Sino General (Cayuga Nation, Wolf Clan), each clan of the Haudenosaunee has a specific role to play within the confederacy. For example, the wolf clan protects; the turtle clan carries knowledge, so its members are known as the wise ones; and the bear clan symbolizes medicines and has the natural role of healing.[79] This quality of unified diversity, which is embodied in the clan system, is significant for understanding not only Indigenous governance but also Indigenous justice and methods of addressing crime.

Traditional Methods of Addressing Crime

Chief Justice Emeritus of the Navajo Nation Robert Yazzie shares his perspective on why Indigenous methods of justice and law were not recognized by the colonizers:

> European explorers often said, "Indians have no law." Why? They couldn't see police; they didn't find courts; they didn't see uniforms, jails and all the trappings of power. But they also couldn't see the clan mothers, who are so important to our Native legal institutions.[80]

Upon arrival, then, Europeans made the colonial assumption that there were no laws on Turtle Island. Eurocentric scholarship and religious teachings have also often incorrectly assumed that Indigenous peoples lacked justice systems, laws, culture, and religion. In fact, Indigenous peoples had very advanced laws and spiritual practices, which comprised many unique systems of justice and culture. Each nation had its own laws, as well as its own ways of healing harms and solving conflicts in its communities. Given that many of these systems were different from European ways, Europeans overlooked them; but they were wrong in their perceptions of justice practices as underdeveloped or non-existent.[81]

Indigenous people's ways of addressing victimization and offending tend to be rooted in their own respective world views, and these typically emphasize concepts such as respect, harmony, and the maintenance of balance. For many traditional communities, concepts such as these framed their laws and their methods of governing crime. As Professor Leroy Little Bear explains, "Aboriginal traditions, laws, and customs are the practical application of the philosophy and values of the group."[82] For example, Gitksan and Wet'suwet'en societies "recognize a commonality of the spirit among humans and all living things including the land. This spirituality is the basis of the laws governing the peoples' relationship with the rest of the world."[83]

An overarching spirituality that honours the Earth and all in it as equal creations is often the bedrock of Indigenous concepts of justice and social harmony. According to Daniel N. Paul, the culture of the Mi'kmaq people is founded on "three principles: the supremacy of the Great Spirit, respect for Mother Earth, and people power. This instilled in them a deep respect for the laws of the Creator, the powers of Mother Earth, and the democratic principles of their society. As a result they enjoyed the benefits of living in a harmonious, healthy, prosperous, and peaceful social environment."[84]

According to Mohawk scholar Taiaiake Alfred, sanctions, solutions, or actions taken to address crimes were based on collective agreements among community members.[85] It would be up to the community to decide what to do. Depending on the crime and the seriousness of the crime, responses would vary, especially among the many diverse Indigenous communities and peoples across Turtle Island.

Alfred further explains that many communities used consensus-based decision making.[86] Ojibwa and Cree decisions, for example, involved "the participation and consent of the community at large."[87] In traditional Navajo societies, decisions were made "by the agreement and consensus of everyone involved in a problem."[88] Historically, Mi'kmaq societies resolved conflicts by bringing together "disputing parties . . . for mediation and reconciliation by community members, who would then assist them to reach an agreement based on justice and fairness."[89] Once a final agreement was made, it addressed all main "concerns of the individuals, groups or governments involved. After the opposing parties accepted an agreement, it was understood, and supported by the will of the people, that they would live by its provisions."[90]

Cree peoples also abided by the decisions of the community when it came to resolving disputes or delivering justice. As sociologist John G. Hansen (member of the Opaskwayak Cree Nation) explains, "Cree practiced a justice system that was able to meet the needs of the people. When a member of the community did something wrong, the people came together to deal with it."[91] He further explains that collaboration and cooperation are at the core of survival in tribal societies and that these qualities are reflected in the restorative approach to addressing crime followed by many First Nations. Importance was placed on restoring to health those who had been harmed and those who had done harm, which allowed people to concentrate on healing. This approach contradicts the pursuit of justice in the Western world—whereby the goal is typically to find who is "guilty" and successfully convict that person in a court of law and then punish or reform that individual.[92]

Hansen did interviews with six Omushkegowuk (Swampy Cree) elders originally from Manitoba and investigated the ideas, practices, and principles of traditional Swampy Cree justice. According to Hansen, the elders all explained justice "in terms of healing rather than punishing."[93] It is vital to hold the offender accountable and to restore health after any harm caused. As Hansen notes, this is a restorative approach, one that elders explain as seeking "understanding of the wrongdoing . . . to learn the impact of the harm and thereby take measures in order to prevent the wrongdoing from happening again."[94] Holding the wrongdoer accountable and repairing the harm supports healing for the victim, offender, and community. A harm done to anyone, then, is viewed as affecting the entire community.

An important part of holding the wrongdoer accountable is educating that person regarding the feelings of his or her victim. As the former chief of the Opaskwayak Cree Nation, William G. Lathlin, states, offenders "were sent to the people who they harmed to find out how those people felt."[95] The purpose of this visit was not to punish but rather to focus on repairing the harm done and on making sure the offender understood the consequences of her or his behaviour. Sometimes banishment was used in the case of a serious crime. But the elders explained that the Omushkegowuk peoples did not see even banishment as a form of punishment; rather, elders took this decision as a way of helping the individual who had done harm reclaim spiritual health. Banishment was also a means of protecting communities, in that a wrongdoer was kept away from community members until that individual was healed enough to take responsibility.[96]

Preventative measures were also emphasized in controlling misbehaviour leading to crime. Omushkegowuk elders explain that traditional education, delivered through stories and lessons, was used "to ensure continuation of life in the community" and to encourage thankfulness for the land, and that these lessons "extended into the development of appropriate behaviour."[97] Similarly, Ojibwa First Nations maintained peaceful coexistence through the exemplary "behaviour of their leaders," through "established tradition taught by elders," and because these elders undertook the "regular teaching of community values."[98] In the Carrier Nation, laws "were ingrained in youth so they would carry on the wisdom of their ancestors."[99]

Historically, Indigenous communities did not have laws written out.[100] The idea to write laws down was a concept brought from Europe. Instead, Indigenous communities in North America had various injunctions and rules that were passed down by word of mouth for centuries. In many Indigenous societies, these injunctions and rules were passed on through oral exchange and interpreted by elders for the peace of all.[101] As Leroy Little Bear explains, knowledge and the behavioural code would be internalized by members of the community.[102]

For Inuit communities, any response to crime was not to cause more problems for the community than the original crime.[103] Rather, the focus was on maintaining the well-being and strength of the community in accordance with the highest societal values. Given the significance of kinship in many Indigenous communities, the sanctions of shame, avoidance, or ridicule were effective methods of social control and order in some societies.[104] Among Blackfoot people, a person who thieved or who was a major nuisance faced ridicule and scornful laughter.[105] In small, tight-knit communities such as the Inuit communities in Canada's North, for example, where most people knew each other, all were susceptible to public opinion and quite sensitive to these informal means of addressing crime.[106]

Ridicule and scorn seem to have been used quite frequently in crimes of sexual assault. Two examples come to mind. The first happened among the Kiowa and was recorded by Jane Richardson:

> The Kiowas inflicted such embarrassment and ridicule on a criminal that he reportedly soon died. The man was a chronic rapist who was finally taught the error of his ways by the women; they laid an ambush and baited the trap with a beautiful young girl. When he took the bait, they suddenly appeared and overpowered him. As others held him helpless on the ground, each woman in turn raised her skirt and sat on his face. The experience was not in itself fatal, but the loss of status stemming from the derision it inspired was.[107]

The second example, a sanction of ridicule for rape described by a Moses-Columbia woman, emphasizes how the people most harmed in the community were allowed to decide upon and carry out punishment:

> The chief asked the people, what should we do with this man? The women wanted to punish him themselves. The chief agreed. The women took the man away somewhere. They held him down while one older woman rubbed her bottom on his face, asking him, wasn't this what he wanted? She was so mad at him that she threatened to pee on him, but he begged for mercy, so she didn't. The chief then told the man he must leave the village.[108]

The fact that shaming and banishment were sometimes applied to crimes as serious as rape does not imply that traditional Indigenous communities never invoked physical punishment. Some Indigenous communities used physical force when arbitrating disputes, for example, to discipline those who committed infractions that put the welfare of the community at risk or that went against a group's moral code.

The Aboriginal Justice Implementation Commission contends that some Indigenous societies applied the death penalty, but only in extreme situations.[109] In some communities, banishment was tantamount to a death penalty because, without the connection and support of others, an individual struggling on his or her own had little chance of survival, especially in harsh climates.[110]

The death penalty was usually reserved for crimes against the community. The Tsilhqot'in peoples in the interior of British Columbia faced death as a sanction from their community if a person were to do anything that would threaten the waterways, on which the communities rely for their livelihood.[111] Without fresh water and fish, a Tsilhqot'in community could not survive and live its traditional life. Water is sacred; water is life.

For the Indigenous communities along the Atlantic seaboard, referred to by some historians as the "New England Indians," rape was punishable by death because of the significance of women.[112] Teachings I learned during times spent at Minwaashin Women's Lodge in Ottawa promoted women as being sacred. A woman is respected because she carries the world inside of her. Women are the strongest because they have the ability to carry two heartbeats. In Blackfoot societies, women were regarded as very powerful because of their life-giving ability.[113] They were so powerful that only women could unwrap and rewrap sacred medicine bundles; men were unable to handle these bundles without the intersession of women.[114]

Because women are at the centre of these communities, which would break down without women, crimes against women were considered especially grave. Traditional teacher and visionary Black Elk (Oglala Lakota) acknowledged the significance of women to Indigenous communities when he said, "when the women are defeated then we as a nation are truly defeated."[115] Thus, crimes against women in Indigenous communities were not tolerated. In reference to the Plateau peoples, ethnographer Lillian A. Ackerman notes that violence against women was considered to be "shameful and illegitimate," and rape was an "uncommon crime and in no way condoned."[116]

Children are very sacred in Indigenous societies, as they are closer to the spirit world than are adults. Consequently, the people of the Seneca Nation will not tolerate hitting a child, as Tehanetorens explains: "some of you have been among white people and have seen their peculiar way of punishing a child. The Creator loves children [so instead] blow water into a child's face. If the child still does not mind, threaten to throw him into the river."[117] Among Blackfoot peoples, "children were never punished by striking them"; rather, "kind words and good examples" were used.[118]

As in other Indigenous communities, in Cheyenne communities, murder is a serious offence. The Cheyenne deny murderers participation in national activities for up to 10 years.[119] Lakota and Crow people regarded murder as a private affair to be dealt with among the parties involved, encouraging the accused family to offer reparation to the victim's family.[120] In Blackfoot societies, murder was resolved either by compensation or by taking the life of the murderer or of a member of the murderer's family. If it was settled through compensation, a third party would do the negotiating, and the offender would be stripped of all possessions. The victim's family had to be accommodated up to the point at which family members felt they had reached satisfaction enough to allow their loved one's soul to rest.[121]

For Haudenosaunee Nations, reaching a settlement among the involved parities was encouraged.[122] The clan councils urged the guilty person to admit to the murder and provide an offering of six white wampum (the customary number for a life) as a humble appeal for forgiveness. It would be up to the head woman of the clan and her council to come to a decision on the murderer's fate. If the offender sent in his or her offering before someone was chosen to punish the murder, the parties might come to an agreement. But if the offender did not make this recompense in time and the victim's clan had already come to an agreement on punishment, then it was too late to offer the customary wampum. The person in some cases could face death. Sometimes, the head women of the family adopted the murderer as a replacement for the lost victim. If this option were chosen, the offender had to "run the gauntlet" of stick brandishing. If the individual survived, that person would be accepted into the family to replace the victim.

When people dealt with crimes committed between different communities, they would employ various methods given the variations in cultural views on justice and in kinship ties. In some cases, nations might instigate a type of war against one another. Yet "war" had different meanings in the past. As Peter Hessel explains, Algonquian nations historically had wars or disputes that could be described as "skirmishes, random raids and sporadic war parties," in which the number of casualties seemed to have been low, with small numbers dying in battles and others at the stake.[123] When Europeans interfered with the customary order of Indigenous life, more wars and disputes between nations began to occur, he continues.

In fact, contrary to what was taught in the Canadian school system for decades, 70 per cent of Indigenous nations did not practice war at all, and those that did practiced a type of war not found in current society.[124] Often, Indigenous wars were more similar to what could be deemed a "noble sport," the point of which was not to eliminate the enemy but rather to achieve honour by a show of bravery.[125] Native American studies professor Tom Holm (Creek/Cherokee) explains:

> [T]raditional Indian warfare had much more in common with Euroamerican contact sports like football, boxing, and hockey than with wars fought in the European manner. This, of course, is not to say that nobody was ever killed. . . . They were—just as they are in modern contact sports—but the point of the exercise was *not* as a rule purposefully lethal.[126]

According to Georges Sioui, coercion and war were virtually absent in traditional Huron-Wendat societies. He explains that they never inflicted great harm on one another during "wars" between other nations or communities.[127] At the same time however, they were not always at peace with others. Conflicts did exist, and, at times, enemies would treat each other with extreme cruelty. As Daniel N. Paul explains, all people of Mother Earth have those among them who are capable of committing horrible crimes.[128] Yet, in most traditional Indigenous societies, he argues, cruelty was not a practice organized, endorsed, or supported by the governing structures or leaders, as it was in European societies. One need only go to see museums full of torture equipment and instruments of death to understand that European leaders used to intimidate people intentionally with violence or the threat of violence to maintain social control, according to Paul. In reference to traditional Mi'kmaq societies, Paul notes that no instruments or tools of this nature were ever developed or used—nor would they have been tolerated. The same point can be made for most other Indigenous societies as well.

Ultimately, Sioui contends that it is certain that the majority of pre-contact Indigenous societies did not live in perfect continuous harmony. However, archaeological evidence has proven that many Indigenous peoples did not have substantial conflicts, likely because they had the collective and ideological means to sustain peace.[129] Given the relative peace among Indigenous peoples, when Europeans arrived, they were accepted as fellow human beings. Reparation and restoration of health to that which was harmed were used to overcome many disputes with the newcomers. Yet not all newcomers responded with mutual integrity, as Seneca Chief Red Jacket explained (in his response to a white preacher of Christianity):

> Your forefathers crossed the great water and landed on this island. Their numbers were small. They found friends and not enemies. They told us they had fled from their own country for fear of wicked men, and had come here to enjoy their religion. They asked for a small seat. We took pity on them; granted their request; and they sat down amongst us. We gave them corn and meat; they gave us poison in return. The white people, Brother, had now found our country. Tidings were carried back, and more came amongst us. Yet we did not fear them. We took them as friends. They called us brothers. We believed them, and gave them a larger seat. At length their numbers had greatly increased. They wanted more land; they wanted our country. . . . Wars took place . . . many of our people were destroyed . . . You have got our country, but are not satisfied; you want to force your religion upon us . . . Brother: We do not wish to destroy your religion, or take it from you. We only want to enjoy our own . . . [130]

Discussion Questions

1) What types of stories are used in various Indigenous traditions, history, or cultures? How and in what ways are they used as reminders or teachers?
2) How did Indigenous societies contribute to colonial governing structures?

Activities

1) Invite to the class a local Indigenous elder, knowledge keeper, or storyteller to share insight into the traditional governance, laws, and clan systems in that person's community.
2) Attend a local museum or cultural centre that has various Indigenous arts and artifacts on display, such as the Cultural Centre at Kitigan Zibi, Québec; the Canadian Museum of Civilization in Gatineau, Québec; the UBC Museum of Anthropology in Vancouver, British Columbia; or the Squamish Lil'wat Cultural Centre in Whistler, British Columbia. Consider the

role the artifacts play in traditional governance and clan structures. What do these artifacts tell us about traditional Indigenous societies?

Recommended Readings

Alfred, Taiaiake. *Peace, Power, Righteousness: An Indigenous Manifesto*. 2nd edition. Don Mills, ON: Oxford University Press, 2009.

Simpson, Leanne. *Dancing on Our Turtle's Back: Stories of Nishnaabeg Re-Creation, Resurgence, and a New Emergence*. Winnipeg: Arbeiter Ring Publishing, 2011.

4
Historical and Contemporary Colonialism

Although Indigenous peoples across Canada have many differences, we do have a shared colonial history in common. Also shared across the country are our efforts to survive as distinctive peoples in the face of encroaching colonialism. These efforts are based on the foundations established in traditional ways of being, distinctive customs and traditions, and deep connections to traditional territories.

When the British Empire expanded itself into Turtle Island, Europeans forced Indigenous peoples into imperialist power structures as a way to try to attain and serve Eurocentric interests and goals. Preconceived notions of cultural, social, and racial superiority on part of the Europeans are what affirmed their colonization efforts. This presumption of dominance also included their religious world views, which positioned white, Western men as having a "God-given" right to rule over others. Eurocentric ideology justified the harsh treatment Europeans meted out to Indigenous peoples, including the outlawing of Indigenous beliefs and traditions, a reorganization of Indigenous societies, and the subjection of North America's original inhabitants to extensive regulation.[1]

This chapter examines some of the roots of colonialism by exploring its origin in Turtle Island and how it continues. To begin, we examine the doctrines of discovery and conquest, which provide a framework for understanding Europeans' justifications for their colonization efforts.

Doctrines of Discovery and Conquest

Forty years before Europeans even set sail for the Americas, theological and legal rulings avowed them a right to dominate any non-Christian people and to take ownership and control over any "uninhabited" or "seized" land.[2] One ruling, a papal document that Pope Nicolas V issued to King Alfonso V of Portugal in 1452, stated that Europeans possessed "the right to attack, conquer, and subjugate Saracens, pagans, and other enemies of Christ wherever they were to be found," and it "recognized title over any lands and possessions" gained in these forays.[3] So Christopher Columbus was practicing an ingrained custom of discovery and conquest when he landed in the Americas in 1492. He arrived with an understanding that he had a right to take over any land occupied by non-Christian peoples.[4] Yet the American continent was home to 112 million Indigenous peoples, and 18 million lived in North America alone.[5]

Upon Columbus's return to Spain after this so-called "discovery," other European countries—particularly Portugal—became apprehensive, not because they had concern for Indigenous peoples but because they, too, wanted a stake in the resources and land of the "New World." Spain's rulers, Queen Isabella and King Ferdinand, appealed to the pope to confirm Spanish title in the Americas, and, in 1493, Pope Alexander VI issued the Spanish papal bull known as the *Inter caetera divinai*.[6] The document approved Spain's efforts to spread Catholicism in the Americas and stated that the lands there "not hitherto discovered by others" and not "in the actual possession of any Christian king or prince" as of 1493 would be considered Spanish possessions.[7] The papal bull not only gave Spain the legal right to the lands Columbus claimed to have "discovered" but also legitimized for the Europeans colonization of Native America. It and other papal bulls set the precedence for the next 500 years: "The pope could place non-Christian peoples under the tutelage and guardianship of the first Christian nation discovering their lands, as long as those peoples were reported by the discovering Christian nation to be 'well disposed to embrace the Christian faith.'"[8]

These papal bulls were enacted without any consultation with Indigenous peoples. These papal rulings and other international legal documents, collectively known as "the doctrine of discovery," are what Europeans used to gain authority over lands. This doctrine became the principle by which imperialists rationalized their authority and presence. It was applied later by all of the other European states that moved into the Americas to declare their control and dominion over the land. No European states contested these tenets and beliefs, although they were developed primarily by Spain, Portugal, England, France, and the Roman Catholic Church, and used as a mechanism to steal the land and declare war against all non-Christians. They were created and justified by religious, cultural, ethnocentric, and racially based ideas of European superiority over others.[9]

Under this established international law, Europeans gained automatic property rights in Indigenous lands. They used this body of law to gain commercial, political, and governmental rights over the peoples living in the Americas without Indigenous consent. The laws recognized the concept of "*terra nullius*," meaning a "territory without people . . . one that was either previously unoccupied or not recognized as belonging to another political entity."[10] *Terra nullius* is often translated from Latin to mean "the land is empty."[11] These doctrines endorsed that, if any land were "empty" according to the European definition, Europeans could claim it as theirs.

What they usually considered "empty" was sparsely settled or "underutilized" land, according to their standards, regardless of whether that land had been occupied by Indigenous peoples and used in its entirety according to tribal custom and the Indigenous economy.[12] When Europeans planted flags, they were taking part in what they viewed as a ritual of discovery, what they considered to be a well-recognized legal procedure designed to exhibit and validate their legal claim over "newly discovered" lands and people.[13]

Therefore, when Europeans travelled to the Americas in 1492, they brought with them pre-existing and ingrained ideas regarding ownership, property, and people. Using the Catholic faith as their principle rationalization for conquest, they advanced their authority over Indigenous peoples (and lands) by dehumanizing them, casting the first inhabitants of the Americas as "the other" and demonizing the people—calling them "beasts," "savages," and "infidels."[14]

Through a historical recounting of constitutional documents and treaties, Indigenous studies professor Tracey Lindberg (Cree and Métis) demonstrates how the doctrine of discovery is firmly entrenched in Canada's legal history.[15] She argues that Canadian law still applies the doctrine of discovery today, and that this doctrine and associated assumptions of European superiority and Indigenous inferiority have shaped how Indigenous peoples were perceived from the beginning of contact. Most important, these ways of thinking enabled Europeans to consider Indigenous peoples as conquered subjects without rights.

These international legal doctrines disregard Indigenous self-determination in that they do not consider Indigenous peoples to equate to "nations" or even to unique "peoples" with specific customs, languages, and histories. In 1960, the United Nations General Assembly ratified a resolution that restricted the right of self-determination to colonies in which the colonizing immigrant populations did not become numerically dominant. As it stated, "Any attempt at the partial or total disruption of the national unity and the territorial integrity of a country is incompatible with the Purposes and Principles of the Charter of the United Nations."[16] The limits of self-determination were further narrowed through the implementation of what came to be known as the "salt-water thesis." This thesis stipulates that "only territories separated by water or that were geographically separate from the colonizing power could invoke self-determinism."[17] Thus, in order to be considered a truly self-governing entity (or one eligible for self-government through decolonization), a territory must be geographically separated from the colonial power by a substantial body of water, preferably an ocean. Essentially, a colony not separated by a substantial body of water, such as an ocean, from the state that had colonized it was considered to have been subsumed by that state—to have ceased to exist.

Severe limitations are put on Indigenous peoples through ad hoc restrictions such as the "salt-water thesis." In their attempts to secure land, colonizers adjust policies to suit their agenda. Yet, in some cases, countries such as Canada will even break or bend their own laws in their quest for Indigenous lands and resources. Still, Canada participates in the system of English law, under which, as Brian Slattery has pointed out, a state can acquire land through conquest, cession, settlement, or annexation.[18] He explained that the conquest of land involves military subjugation whereby a ruler states an outright demand for permanent sovereignty. Cession usually entails an official transfer of territory (through a treaty, for example) from one autonomous political entity to another. Settlement involves attaining land that was formerly unused, uninhabited, and not belonging to another political unit and occupying it; the process is considered legitimate providing "the Sovereign authorized the settlement or subsequently sanctioned it, and so doing clearly expressed the intention to gain sovereignty."[19] Annexation or the affirmation of sovereignty involves the Crown simply annexing a territory in a unilateral act. According to Slattery, acquiring land using these various modes results in differences in regards to the legal responsibilities and rights of the Crown:

> In territories acquired by conquest, cession, or annexation, the Crown initially holds full prerogative powers of legislation and may alter any existing laws or abrogate them entirely and introduce new ones, subject to overriding legislative authority of Parliament and perhaps to certain fundamental principles. However in the absence of such acts the original laws of the place remain in force, except to the extent that they are unconscionable or inconsistent with the change of sovereignty itself. By contrast, in colonies acquired by settlement English law is introduced *ipso facto* [as a resultant effect], insofar as it is applicable to local circumstances. The Crown has no greater prerogative powers of legislation in a settled colony than it possesses in the mother country, and so may not legislate there apart from Parliament.[20]

Mainly, European governments justified their claims to sovereignty in North America, at least in regards to Indigenous peoples and lands, by invoking the settlement claim. Treaties were arranged between Britain and various First Nations, of course, and wars of conquest were fought in North America, although these were seen generally as taking place between the various colonial powers vying for power in the continent. Yet settlers occupying land was a main justification for European sovereignty. Anthropology professor Michael Asch, who analysed various court decisions in cases related to Aboriginal rights and the Canadian Constitution, agrees. He concludes that

Canada relies on the "settlement thesis" to validate and rationalize its acquisition of sovereignty. This thesis categorizes the land claimed by colonists as *terra nullius*, a claim that Asch argues might be reasonable in regards to Antarctica but can unmistakably not be made in regards to Canada's presently claimed territory. Canada's reliance on the settlement thesis has therefore "required a certain elasticity of logic."[21] The logic relied upon presumes that the colonized land was not considered to be belonging to another political unit.

The Underpinnings of the Rights of Property

When the explorers arrived in Indigenous lands (in the fifteenth century), they justified their governmental and property claims over those lands and peoples by developing the "discovery doctrine," which was embodied in various documents issued under the authority of the pope.[22] With the rise of rationalism and the decline of religious authority following the Protestant Reformation (in the sixteenth and seventeenth centuries), colonizers needed additional and new legal and political doctrines to follow in order to justify their colonization of Native America.[23] Two related theorists, Thomas Hobbes and John Locke, posited views on the natural state of human beings and on the origins of government that provided a rationale for colonization.

In his famous book *Leviathan or the Matter, Forme, and Power of a Commonwealth, Ecclesiastical and Civil*, published in 1651, Thomas Hobbes argues that there is no such thing as natural order or any justice in nature, so humans need to create a government, which Hobbes describes as an artificial man-state called Leviathan. For Hobbes, if people were left in nature to their own devices, they would engage in war, "man against every man."[24] He referenced Indigenous peoples of North America as "evidence" of this natural state of warfare, explaining that those in America had "no government at all, and live at this day in that brutish manner."[25] For Hobbes, the artificial man-state was the only solution to creating a "civil" society and putting a stop to the "savage" state of nature.

Rebellion against this artificial man-state would break society's basic contract. Thus, to maintain peace and order, the sovereign would put "fear and terror" into potential law breakers, using any penalty deemed necessary in order to assure there would be no return to the original state of nature.[26] "Sovereigns" of the "non-state" could use what Hobbes called "positive laws" (man-made laws) to maintain order and the state's power, and only the sovereign of the man-state could command and make valid laws. Hobbes's state of nature then became the starting point of Eurocentric discussions of government and politics. Indigenous peoples were deemed as being "in a state of nature and an antithetical civilized society."[27]

Hobbes's immediate successor was John Locke, a senior official in the British Colonial Office and the principal author of the philosophical underpinnings of colonialism.[28] Like Hobbes, Locke used the state of nature as a philosophical starting point. Yet he had a different view. Hobbes described the state of nature as being "solitary, poore, nasty, brutish, and short,"[29] but Locke considered humans in their natural state to be tolerant, joyful, free, and equal. By the same token, humans in this state of nature are "insecure and dangerous in their freedom,"[30] so they must join with others in society and put themselves under a government, giving up some of their natural rights for mutual security and, in particular, for the preservation of their right to property enforced by human law.

In defence of England's colonial interests in the Americas, Locke develops a concept of agrarian labour, its fundamental premise being that the right to claim land as property was the result of agricultural labour.[31] This definition of property effectively dispossessed Indigenous peoples of their land. Thus, even though Locke and Hobbes differed regarding the state of nature itself, both men's theories were used to substantiate and validate European colonization in America. Locke provided Europeans a proclaimed "right" to instigate war against Indigenous peoples whom they considered would be "dangerous" to their freedom and property rights.[32]

Locke also argues that humans in a state of nature lack "positive laws." This theory, which was applied to Indigenous nations, had self-serving implications for European powers because, if Indigenous peoples had nothing resembling European laws, they were deemed as having no government. If they had no government, then their only option was seen as having to ally themselves with a European state, which would protect them and offer them governance and rule of law. The British looked to their own laws as the most rational, effective, and impeccable; thus, proposals from settlers or colonial governments asking for the imposition of British laws on Indigenous nations were accepted.[33]

In his *Two Treatises of Government*, Locke drew on Hugo Grotius's 1625 book *De Jure Belli ac Pacis* (*On the Law of War and Peace*), which is regarded as one of the foundational writings on international law. Locke largely agrees with Grotius's concept of natural law, which views the state as "a complete association of free men, joined together for the enjoyment of rights and for their common interest."[34] The two also agree that the earth was given to men "in common" as a gift from God. Thus, both Locke and Grotius used God and natural law as their points of departure and viewed natural law as a universal concept, providing the foundation for all human social order. However, on the issue of property rights, their viewpoints diverged. For Grotius, gaining ownership of land required an agreement that included obtaining social consent. He also argued for a system of law that would be binding on all peoples through consent regardless of custom. As identified by Indigenous studies professor Gregory Younging (Opaskwayak Cree Nation), Grotius acknowledged Indigenous rights to the land.[35]

Although agreeing with Grotius on natural law, Locke defines property rights more narrowly, as mentioned. Locke views Indigenous territory as part of the "great tracts of ground, which lie waste and are more than the people who dwell on it . . . or can make use of, and so still lie in common."[36] This concept became a very influential ideological tool for the colonizers because land that was considered as being wasted or at an earlier, communal stage of ownership became "free" to usurp.

Locke introduces his theory of property rights in Chapter Five of his *Second Treatises of Government* (this was seventeenth-century liberalism's Lockian doctrine on property). He claims that it is a natural right of mankind to preserve itself by drinking, eating, and taking things from nature. As he states, "God, who hath given the world to men in common, hath also given them reason to make use of it to the best advantage of life, and convenience." According to Locke, the earth should be considered the property of people, and it should be used for their benefit and survival: "the earth, and all that is therein, is given to men for the support and comfort of their being."[37] His stance is that an individual or group acquires property by adding labour to it: "as much land as a man tills, plants, improves, cultivates, and can use the product of, so much is his property."[38] According to this "labour theory of value," one is entitled to appropriate and enclose land if one adds labour to it and improves it or, similarly, if one employs the labour of another to do this work.[39] His labour theory of value was developed alongside his notions of productivity—notions tied to the growth of market economy. It was his belief that productivity stems from profit, which would be produced through naval commerce and colonial exploitation.[40]

Political science professor Barbara Arneil notes that embedded in Locke's theory of property is a vigorous defence of England's colonial activities in North America.[41] Essentially, he argues that England should colonize North America so as to encourage economic and social development. He makes this case by comparing what he refers to as the impoverished, "vacant" lands of Indigenous peoples and the wealthy, settled lands of Europe. And he criticizes Indigenous peoples for being "rich in land, and poor in all the comforts of life,"[42] arguing that America would be a hundred times more valuable if "Devonshire farmers" were to labour on it rather than leaving it to Indigenous peoples.[43]

Mary L. Caldbick examines the details of Locke's views on acquiring ownership and rights of territory through labour by considering how these views were used as a justification for displacing the Passamaquoddy people and taking their lands.[44] The Passamaquoddy are indigenous to the Maine-Maritime region. Drawing largely on Passamaquoddy world views, Caldbick compares Indigenous conceptions with respect to the land and the Lockian doctrine of property. She explains that lands inhabited were seen not as property to be "improved," cultivated, or acquired but as "a gift from the Creator, given to sustain," so lands must be held in "trust for future generations."[45] To the Passamaquoddy people, then, humans are intimately connected to the land, and, just as humans have a soul, so does the land.

The Loyalist settlers who arrived in the Passamaquoddy Bay region after the American Revolution and dispossessed the Passamaquoddy people of their territory at Gunasquamcook, however, had different attitudes about the land. These settlers came with the idea that land had to be cultivated in order to be owned, a Lockian concept. Upon arrival they disregarded the Passamaquoddy people's way of life and their sacred connections to the land. Instead, they surveyed it and planned their townships.

James Tully, professor of political science, law, Indigenous governance, and philosophy at the University of Victoria, contends that Locke intentionally created his idea of property specifically to contrast with Indigenous customs related to the land in order to refute the latter and to rationalize the appropriation of Indigenous lands in America by English settlers.[46] Tully notes that Locke's library was full of European accounts of colonization and of the exploration of Indigenous lands and that it also contained many books on Indigenous people's ways of life. For Locke, land ownership and governance systems are not comparable or equivalent to contemporary European political formations. He declares that Indigenous peoples are in the late stages of "the state of nature," one that is historically less developed when compared with European political organization. At this stage, neither nationhood nor territorial jurisdiction exists.[47] These conceptions were then used to justify European appropriation of Indigenous land without colonizers having to get Indigenous consent.

Given that Locke declared Indigenous peoples as being outside of civil society, Europeans assumed that Indigenous political formations and property rights were negligible and that, therefore, Indigenous people should be subjected to the "sovereignty of European notions of property and politics."[48] Locke's concepts and writings justified and upheld the presumed superiority of European and, specifically, of English forms of property and political society.

Locke's concepts and notions, then, were used as ideological weapons. He was intervening in one of the major political and conceptual challenges in the seventeenth century. The long-term consequence of this intervention is that Locke's theories of political society and property became widely accepted and circulated in the eighteenth century.[49] They became laced into models of growth, expansion, and statehood and were the building blocks of the conceptual framework of property ownership still in existence today. According to Caldbick, many of Locke's ideas continue to inform modern legal thought, a statement most notably true in regards to Locke's justification of colonialism on the basis that private property is acquired through labour.[50]

Colonialism

According to professor of Native American studies Jack D. Forbes (Powhatan-Renape, Delaware-Lenape), when Columbus arrived in the Americas, he carried with him a terribly contagious psychological disease, which Forbes calls the *wétiko* psychosis.[51] "*Wétiko*" is a Cree term meaning "cannibal." For Forbes, this psychosis does not involve directly eating the flesh of another but rather eating the life of another. It is a disease of aggression against other living things, a disease that consumes other creatures' lives and possessions. In essence, it is the sickness of exploitation. He explains that imperialism and exploitation are the most diabolical and malicious forms of cannibalism. This *wétiko* psychosis, he argues, is the most profound epidemic of illness ever known—and is extremely contagious.

Academic and United Nations human rights expert Erica-Irene Daes draws on a handy expression to explain the blindness of Europeans to the wrongs of imperialism and exploitation: "You cannot be the doctor if you are the disease." She argues that Europeans have suffered the "disease of the oppressed consciousness for centuries," so the attitudes supporting colonialism have now become normalized. Indigenous people, on the other hand "are much closer in time to the experience of spiritual independence and therefore are generally far more aware of the extent to which symptoms of the disease persist."[52] Ronnie Martin (Mi'kmaq) shared a teaching with me that he had received from an elder; it also explains why European peoples are blind to the ills of colonialism. The teaching is that the people of Europe all used to be connected to the land and to their ceremonies, but they have left their drums behind much longer ago than have Indigenous peoples, so Europeans forget.[53]

Barbara-Helen Hill (from Six Nations of the Grand River Territory) explains that "the Europeans came to the Americas escaping the Renaissance period in Europe where they were under religious persecution, political degradation and darkness." When they arrived they were "filled with fear . . . they were running from fear and from their oppressors who had taken over their lives and their lands. In coming to the Americas, they only had to fear the unknown."[54] Unfortunately, as Chief Dan George (Tsleil-Waututh Nation) says, fear of the unknown is a powerful motivator of violence: "what you do not know, you will fear. What one fears, one destroys."[55]

Thus, sometimes direct methods were planned to eradicate Indigenous peoples. In the 1700s in North America, colonizers planned to give Indigenous peoples blankets infected with small pox.[56] As Sir Jeffery Amherst, overall commander of the British in North America, wrote in July 1763 to Colonel Henri Bouquet of the 60th Royal American Regiment of Foot, "Could it not be contrived to Send the Small Pox among those Disaffected Tribes of Indians? We must, on this occasion, Use Every Stratagem in our power to Reduce them."[57] Bouquet replied, "I will try to inoculate the [illegible] with Some Blankets that may fall in their Hands, and take Care not to get the disease myself."[58]

During this same time, John Hughes of Pennsylvania set out elaborate plans to use dogs to kill Indigenous peoples resisting British colonialism.[59] These plans involved the release of packs of dogs as a way to force Indigenous peoples into positions of self-defence, thus making them easier to fire at. As Hughes explains, "Let loose all the dogs, which will rush at the concealed Indians, and force them in self-defence to expose themselves."[60] He goes on to say that the dogs could be trained in this act of terror if Bouquet got "one or two Indians kill[d] & the Dogs put at them to tear them to pieces." "You wou[d] Soon See the Good Effects of it," Hughes predicts.[61]

These stories show the extreme face of colonialism, which social work Professor Michael Yellow Bird defines as "a system in which one people claim sovereignty over another and assert social, political, economic, and spiritual domination over the colonized."[62] Yellow Bird, who is a citizen of the Arikara (Sahnish) and Hidatsa nations in North Dakota, also posits that colonial efforts are motivated by the perspective that the colonizers' beliefs and values are superior to those of the colonized. He outlines three types of colonialism: internal, external or exploitation, and settler. Internal colonialism is the biopolitical and geopolitical management of people—in this case, of Indigenous peoples and their land, territory, vegetation, and wildlife—all within the borders of the imperial nation. It involves particularized modes of control that manage populations through imperial political and economic systems and through institutions such as prisons, schools, and policing agencies.

Exploitation colonialism refers to "the expropriation of fragments of Indigenous worlds, animals, plants, and human beings"; these are exploited for the benefit of the colonizers—"to build wealth . . . and privilege . . . or feed the appetites of . . . the colonizers who get marked as the first world." Resource extraction is an example of exploitation colonialism, in that big multinational corporations reap profits by extracting resources from Indigenous territory.

Settler colonialism happens when "foreign family units move into a place and reproduce" and "an imperial power oversees the immigration of these settlers." Eventually, settlers take over lands and attempt to destroy the people who live there. This form of colonialism involves master narratives framing the settlers as "superior" and as representative of so-called progress and civilization. It also involves ignoring or stripping away the identity of the land's first inhabitants, as was done to Indigenous people through the attempted and forced removal of unique identities, histories (including traditions), cultures, and voices. In Canada, it involves the disconnection and dislocation of Indigenous peoples from traditional territories and forcing these peoples under the governing influence and control of European settlers.

All forms of colonialism, then, involve external aggression and domination, which are both intimately tied to internal control, repression, and violence.[63] As Barbara-Helen Hill notes, "Europeans used many methods to conquer and 'civilize' the people whom they called the 'Devil's children.' Today we call these methods racism, genocide, acculturation, assimilation, and integration."[64] Thus, "Canada was not created in the smooth, flowing seasons of Aboriginal thought; it was created in the jagged path of colonialism and empire."[65]

Erica-Irene Daes explains that a deliberate strategy of colonialism is to break down the opposition of those who are being colonized. These people are influenced to think that they are not only helpless to resist but also naïve to think they could even make any effort to try. A central purpose of colonialism is to ingrain in colonized people the impression that they are "out of step" with everyone else in the world; "that they have no friends"; and that their thoughts of "resentment and resistance" are irrational, crazy, and unjustifiable, and merely serve to prove how "savage" and "ignorant" they must be.[66] As Jack D. Forbes notes, "a colonial system almost always assigns low status to all Native customs and, if racial differences are apparent, also assigns low status to the physical characteristics of the conquered population. The conquered people are made to feel inferior and this inferiority is used as a weapon of psychological warfare to control them."[67]

Daes further states that a vital weapon most colonizers use against colonized peoples is isolation from all external foundations of knowledge and information. The colonized are then bombarded with propaganda meticulously designed to try to persuade them that they are ignorant, weak, unimportant, backward, and extremely privileged to have been colonized.[68] According to legal expert James (Sákéj) Youngblood Henderson (from the Chickasaw Nation and the Cheyenne Tribe in Oklahoma), modern

European political thought is built on the notion that "terror" is a valid basis of sovereign power and law. Yet modern European political thought hides "the effects of such terror on those who suffer under the rule of law."[69]

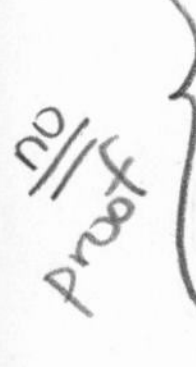

The Eurocentric political and legal thought of seventeenth- and eighteenth-century Europe shaped colonial reasoning, as we have seen in the discussion concerning Hobbes and Locke's conceptual underpinning of colonialism. Yet neither Hobbes nor Locke had proof of their theories, and no "historical or social evidence validated its assumptions."[70] Nevertheless, British settlers relied on this philosophical and legal thought as a rationale for the colonization of North America.

Colonialism was a conscious choice taken by the settlers. There were alternative relationships possible between Indigenous and European nations. Hobbes conceived that the law of nature allowed for peace and friendship treaties with Indigenous peoples (an idea that Locke took up when he described his "treaty commonwealth").[71] Thus, colonialism was not something inescapable, inexorable, or preordained by European philosophical thinking about the state of nature. Europeans could have followed the notion of the treaty commonwealth and entered into limited contractual alliances with Indigenous peoples. However, they choose to create "new hierarches, governments, and legal systems that believed in the absolute superiority of Europeans over the colonized, the masculine over the feminine, the adult over the child, the historical over the ahistorical, and the modern or 'progressive' over the traditional or 'savage.'"[72]

When Europeans started to arrive in larger numbers, they not only moved on to Indigenous lands but also framed Indigenous peoples as lesser beings and as obstacles to the creation of a Euro-Canadian civilization.[73] Given this view, settlers developed many laws, policies, and procedures to keep a desired hierarchal system operating, one that favoured the colonizers and European principles. This legislation, much of it enacted in the 1800s specifically to eradicate Indigenous peoples, will be addressed in Chapter 6.

As important as understanding colonialism is to pursuing justice for Indigenous peoples, we must remember that this concept is itself a Western construct typically used to describe encounters between Indigenous peoples and imperial powers, encounters involving exploration, conquest, settlement, and exploitation. As Mohawk scholar Taiaiake Alfred and Tsalagi (Cherokee) scholar Jeff Corntassel argue, we must be careful not to allow colonialism to be the only story we use to describe Indigenous people's lives: "colonialism is a narrative in which the Settler's power is the fundamental reference and assumption, inherently limiting Indigenous freedom and imposing a view of the world that is but an outcome or perspective on that power."[74] Legal experts James (Sákéj) Youngblood Henderson, Marjorie L. Benson, and Isobel M. Findlay agree, stating that "colonialism is an artificial construct of European elites using political ideology and human made legal rules."[75]

If we invoke only colonialism as the standpoint from which to frame Indigenous people's existence in Canada, we are privileging the perspective of the assimilators, as doing so legitimizes their discourse, which claims to have overcome and overtaken Indigenous peoples. This is not the reality. As mentioned, Indigenous peoples have their own unique histories and cultures, their own narratives and world views, which continue to exist. Neither Indigenous peoples nor their teachings were eradicated, although colonizers made strong attempts; rather both were interrupted and disrupted by the colonizing West. Many still fight strongly against the mechanisms of colonialism today. Despite relentless attempts at annihilating Indigenous peoples and cultures, we remain; we were never destroyed.

Orientalism

Another concept related to the colonial and imperial enterprises of the West is orientalism. According to Edward Said, a key contributor to post-colonial studies, orientalism is a Western way of seeing "the East" that patronizes and fictionalizes its societies and peoples and assumes European superiority.[76] He suggests that an inherent hegemony embedded in European, Westernized ways of thinking represents anything non-European as backwardness to the West, which is perceived as an "advanced" civilization. The roots of this embedded colonial discourse can be traced to the same ideals supporting the doctrine of discovery, ideals that presuppose Western superiority, which then fuel power leading to the presumption of Europe's dominance.

In other words, orientalism posits a "progressive civilization," the West, and a "backwards civilization," the East, but it is also, according to Said, a method of "normalized" research, writings, and study, dominated by imperatives, perceptions, and ideological preconceptions presumably suited to those being colonized.

A comparable Western discourse produces fictionalized representations of North American "Indians" as inferior. Mi'kmaq elder, author, and human rights activist Daniel N. Paul explains the potentially long-term effects of these representations:

> Because of their belief that European civilizations were superior, and therefore all others were inferior or savage, these writers reported the superior human rights practices of Amerindian civilization as if they were abnormal. Later, using these biased records as gospel, many Caucasian authors have written works about Mi'kmaq civilization that doesn't present a true picture.[77]

Similarly, Oglala Lakota chief, author, and educator Luther Standing Bear notes that "irreparable damage" has been done by some white authors and that "books have been written about Aboriginal peoples which are so 'distorting' that they 'scarcely resemble' a real person."[78]

Romanticized depictions as well as demonic ones came into being when explorers and colonists studied, examined, and then classified and interpreted Indigenous peoples through a Western lens. Sometimes, "the Indian" was portrayed as a "Noble Savage" and sometimes as a "bloodthirsty redskin."[79] Whichever portrait was drawn, both deemed Indigenous peoples as inferior in comparison to European Christian civilizations.

Consequently, the West could rationalize European colonialism based on a self-serving history that deemed those being colonized as in need of "rescue" from their "inferior," "savage," or possibly "dangerous" ways. Furthermore, the colonizers, in attempting to "save" or "improve" these "other" peoples, created for them a new history and culture, which, they argued, would provide a future full of "potential" but which was actually suited solely to fuelling European superiority. Thus, by creating this false knowledge about "Indians" and their histories, Europeans forged a tool to gain power. Both the obfuscation and distortion of the true identities of Indigenous peoples were used as ideological weapons to further subjugate us.

Contemporary Colonialism

Contemporary colonialism is a method of postmodern colonization in which domination is still based on settler rules and priorities but settlers calculate and perform more indirect or crafty ways of achieving their goals.[80] The attitudes of the original European settlers regarding the inferiority of Indigenous peoples live on and have become systemic. The legacies of earlier forms of colonialism become entrenched and embedded within society's dominant discourses and institutions. These include governmental, educational, political, and religious institutions, among others. Colonialism is then sustained through an intimate relationship between education, imperialism, and capitalism.[81]

Scholarship on contemporary colonialism has parallels within the academic literature on systemic racism, which expert researchers define as the broad "laws, rules, and norms woven into the social system that result in an unequal distribution of economic, political, and social resources and rewards among various racial groups."[82] Systemic racism rejects the idea that certain racial groups should have equity, for example, equal access to and involvement in services such as housing, education, and employment. It manifests itself in the media's negative representations of certain racial groups, in the erasure of that group's experiences and voices, and in the repetition of racist imagery and discourse.[83] In a famous quotation, human rights activist Malcolm X comments on the power of these racist messages: "If you aren't careful, the newspapers will have you hating the people who are being oppressed, and loving the people who are doing the oppressing."[84]

The same oppressive messages, attitudes, and objectives that existed in the early years of settlement exist today. As noted by Thomas King (Cherokee), although this Euro-Canadian sense of superiority is more hidden than it was, attitudes toward Indigenous peoples today are curiously analogous to those of the past.[85] The views of European colonial forefathers toward Indigenous peoples prevail and permeate Euro-Canadian institutions and political systems and discourses. Although we no longer have colonizers trying to kill off Indigenous peoples with infected blankets, we do have a government system in place that has been formed by the ancestors of the original colonizers. This government system allows and supports policies that keep Indigenous peoples living in third world and impoverished conditions, making peoples more susceptible to disease and death.

In 2011, Canada ranked sixth on the United Nations Human Development Index (HDI), which takes into consideration educational attainment, average annual income, and health. This ranking placed Canada among the top 10 countries in the world.[86] However, if Indigenous peoples in Canada formed a country, that nation would be in thirty-second place (calculated using the 2001 HDI scores and the same dimensions).[87] Many Indigenous communities have no running water, no sanitation, and have deplorable housing. Many Indigenous communities lack education and employment opportunities. Policies exist today that maintains these discrepancies. The Indian Act of 1985 is the most notable.

This federal act still regulates "Indians" in Canada, and, consequently, First Nation communities fall under federal jurisdiction. The result is that the federal government allocates less to First Nations communities for things such as water, housing, and education than do the provincial, territorial, and municipal governments responsible for funding these things in non–First Nation communities. For example, the amount allocated to First Nations for education has not kept pace with either inflation or the growth rate of the First Nation population, which is unlike the situation in provincial schools. Also, the type of infrastructure usually provided by the provinces, territories, and municipalities to non-Indigenous citizens is often superior to that provided in First Nation communities because these communities do not fall under provincial or municipal legislative frameworks that guarantee minimum standards in areas such as housing, water quality, and education. Such disparities are demonstrative of systemic racism and continuing colonialism.

Colonization has been an ongoing process, especially as the process relates to assimilation. In 1869, Canada passed the Gradual Enfranchisement Act, and, for the first time, a blood quantum requirement was added to define who was and who was not a legal "Indian."[88] Only individuals with at least one-quarter Indian blood were eligible. As Canada expanded into the western regions of the continent and government officials encountered and negotiated treaties with additional First Nations, the government wanted more stringent controls on who would be recognized as "Indian."[89] With the Indian Act of 1876, which consolidated legislation related to First Nations peoples, these controls were made clear. A provision of this act excluded from "Indian" status any person who was not considered to be a "pure Indian": "... no half-breed head of a family (except the widow of an Indian, or a half-breed who has already been admitted into a treaty) shall ... be accounted an Indian, or entitled to be admitted into any Indian treaty."[90]

The Indian Act of 1985, which is in effect today, still categorizes who is an "Indian" and who is not based on a racist and sexist system of registration. Professor of equity studies Bonita Lawrence (Mi'kmaw) points out that, in order to be recognized under this federal categorization, a person has to meet very specific standards of government regulation. She explains the long-lasting and pervasive impact of these attempts at colonial control:

> The effect of these regulatory regimes might be best understood in terms of a discourse, in the sense that Foucault used the term—as a way of seeing life that is produced and reproduced by various rules, systems and procedures—forming an entire conceptual territory on which knowledge is produced and shaped.... The Indian Act in Canada, in this respect, is much more than a body of laws that for over a century have controlled every aspect of Indian life. As a regulatory regime, the Indian Act provides ways of understanding Native identity, organizing a conceptual framework that has shaped contemporary Native life in ways that are now so familiar as to almost seem "natural."[91]

Clearly, the Indian Act frames the identity of First Nations people according to colonial definitions and purposes. Even the terms "Indigenous" and "Aboriginal" are problematic, as Chapter 1 explains. Although this book uses these terms in order to discuss the colonial system using the English language, we must note and remember that they are inaccurate and erroneous classifications. As Bonita Lawrence points out, "for Indigenous peoples, to be defined as a race is synonymous with having our Nations dismembered. And yet, the reality is that Native people in Canada and the United States for over a century now have been classified by race and subjected to colonization processes that reduced diverse nations to common experiences of subjugation."[92]

According to Taiaiake Alfred and Jeff Corntassel, this racial labelling, which has been ongoing, reached a climax when the definition of who was "Aboriginal" was written into the Canadian Constitution Act of 1982. Using such all-encompassing terms provides to Indigenous peoples a false sense of inclusion, although, really, these labels are another colonization mechanism and a powerful assault on Indigenous identities.[93] The assumption that all Indigenous cultures are the same is part and parcel of the Euro-Canadian political, legal, and cultural discourse designed to serve an agenda of the silent surrender of the original peoples of North America.

Places, spaces, and cultures have been shaped by Euro-Canadian discourse and structures, which attempt to "fit" pieces of Indigenous cultures into boxes and slot them neatly into existing Euro-Canadian institutions so as not to disrupt Euro-Canadian processes or goals. As we have seen, this work of social construction even extends to Indigenous identities themselves, which have been confined to Euro-Canadian political and legal definitions. If people internalize these classifications, they more readily copy and follow the practices of the dominant Euro-Canadian political and legal institutions. According to Alfred and Corntassel, this internalization leads to the "compartmentalization of community values" and a "politics of distraction" that deflects and reroutes energies and momenta away from the decolonization and regeneration of communities because community relationships are depicted in state-centric terms.[94]

This is not to say that teams of government officials are trying to tick off the agenda item "eradicate Indigenous peoples." I am not implying that there is a conspiracy against Indigenous peoples. Rather, Canadian governments and agencies are operating within and fuelling a system that first defined "Indians" as a category and then set out to destroy Indigenous peoples. Canada's officials are following the same processes, functions, and ways of thinking passed down to them by their colonial forefathers.[95] Consequently, Indigenous voices are often ignored and trumped by Euro-Canadian priorities, as a policy maker admitted to me during my PhD research in Winnipeg in 2009: "As a mainstream government worker . . . I sometimes think we're replicating the very same [colonialist] policies; maybe we're politer, maybe we're more understanding, but we are still making decisions for another group in society, and, if we really listened to First Nations people and what they're asking us for, we very rarely ever deliver that."[96] As Chief Justice Emeritus of the Navajo Nation Robert Yazzie contends, "Colonialism remains when national legislatures and policy makers make decisions for Indigenous peoples, tell them what they can and cannot do, refuse to support them, or effectively shut them out of the process."[97] The entire parliamentary and legal system used in Canada is a foreign system imported by European settlers. It was created to produce the results it has been producing. And those operating within this system have made decisions for Indigenous peoples without Indigenous peoples' consent.

White Privilege

Part of the reason a discourse becomes dominant is that it is collectively relied on and held up as "truth." So the power of a discourse rests upon people believing, internalizing, and acting on it. When people begin to perform these actions unquestioningly, a discourse becomes an understanding of "the way things are." But are things really this way? Should they be? Considering the accuracy, validity, or fairness of these "truths" is often uncomfortable, especially for those who come from a position of privilege. Some whom society privileges might not recognize or believe that they are afforded more access than others to the necessities and luxuries of life. They might go about their lives enjoying "how things are."

Like most invisible privileges, white privilege is afforded to those who are Caucasian. Often, these people live their lives according to traditional middle- or upper-class Euro-Canadian values. Sociology professor James Frideres defines white privilege as "an institutional set of benefits granted to those who, by colour, resemble the people who dominate the powerful positions in our institutions and organizations."[98] Unearned racial privileges afforded to white people are so entrenched that they do not intrude on our conscious minds; they are not thought about and often go unrecognized. In Canadian society today, white people are not racially named as they signify the dominant societal "norm" by which other identities come to be recognized and marked.[99] Thus, white people are free from being categorized in a racial group. Ask yourself, for instance, if you have ever read a newspaper article in which the writer made reference to a "white community."

Considering invisible privileges prompts people to reflect on their own social position by contemplating what life would be like if they were living in a society that was not created or built around their cultures, traditions, or governance structures but rather around a model designed to effect their silent surrender to a foreign heritage. Unfortunately, some non-Indigenous Canadians continue to rely on misrepresentation as a mechanism to defend against attending to the post-contact experiences of Indigenous peoples, to the history that led to white privilege and the current circumstances that sustain it. Some people simply do not want to acknowledge their privileged positions because doing so could necessitate learning a history they do not want to admit. According to Indigenous education scholar Susan Dion (Lenape/Potawatomi), this failure to listen and attend to the post-contact experiences of Indigenous peoples is sustained through numerous mechanisms:

- Challenging the relevance of the narrative for one's life in the present
- Locking the events in a history that has no present
- Dehumanizing Aboriginal people
- Claiming "there is nothing I can do, therefore I don't have to listen"
- Claiming the stories are too hard to listen to[100]

The refusal to acknowledge, know, and understand is comforting to some, yet it creates a barrier that continues to enable a denial of the past. And what are the options if one does not acknowledge how Indigenous peoples in this country came to be disenfranchised on almost every social and economic indicator as compared to non-Indigenous peoples? There are only two: deny current reality, including white privilege, or blame Indigenous peoples for the societal positions they currently hold. Either attitude basically repeats the early colonizers tactics of blame, denial, or assumed superiority. Dion feels that there is something repulsive about having to ask Canadians why it is too difficult for them to look at reality and to hear Indigenous people's stories. In response to those who declare that the "stories are too hard to listen to," she asserts, "Hard to listen to—try surviving them."[101]

Discussion Questions

1) Discuss how and in what ways ideologies of land and the doctrines of discovery and conquest still influence systems and ways of thinking today.
2) What is colonialism? Identify how and in what ways colonialism is still ongoing. Provide and discuss examples.
3) Why is it important to consider history and historical contexts? Identify and discuss aspects of history that have affected the generations of your family, both positively and negatively.

Activities

1) Locate a blank map of Turtle Island and, to the best of your knowledge, fill in all of the traditional territories of Indigenous peoples. Also consider the places where you were born, have lived, currently live, and spend a lot of your time. What traditional territories are these places located in? Find out about and gain knowledge of the traditional territory you are on, and take the next step and learn about this territory's original peoples.
2) Locate old non-Indigenous writings about or images of Indigenous peoples. How are Indigenous people being framed? What types of language or

visual representations are used? Also locate current non-Indigenous writings or visuals depicting Indigenous peoples. Has much changed? Discuss.

3) Compile a list of invisible privileges. Then locate, discuss, and compare and contrast your list with that compiled by Peggy McIntosh in *White Privilege: Unpacking the Invisible Knapsack* (various condensed versions available online).

Recommended Readings

Forbes, Jack D. *Columbus and Other Cannibals: The* Wétiko *Disease of Exploitation, Imperialism, and Terrorism*. Revised edition. New York: Seven Stories Press, 2008.

Paul, Daniel N. *First Nations History: We Were Not the Savages—Collision between European and Native American Civilizations*. 3rd edition. Halifax: Fernwood, 2006.

5
Canadian Legal History: The Interpretation of Indigenous Treaties and Rights

IN THE EARLY YEARS OF EUROPEAN ARRIVAL, agreements were made between European settlers and Indigenous nations. These agreements were mutual arrangements of peace and friendship, which included the sharing of lands.

This chapter will provide a historical outline of some of the major treaty agreements essential to understanding Indigenous people's rights, land title, and sovereignty. Some initial agreements actually laid out positive frameworks for future negotiating. So, although Europeans were migrating to Turtle Island and many viewed "Indians" as subhuman, Indigenous peoples never relinquished rights, sovereignty, or title but bargained in good faith with the newcomers, nation to nation. Yet European governments did not hold up their end of the agreements. Rather their approach after such agreements was to continue their colonization efforts. They tried to supersede agreements through forced legislation and through what can essentially be described as a coerced takeover.

Treaty Overview

Long before the arrival of Europeans, Indigenous peoples had already been engaged in the process of making treaties amongst themselves.[1] These treaties were about peace and friendship, and they were recorded orally and represented through the exchange of sacred items. One of the earliest treaties on record, which has since been written down, is the "Great Law of Peace" of 1142, an agreement that led to the forming of the Haudenosaunee Confederacy (discussed in Chapter 3).[2] However, these treaties between First Nations are usually ignored by the Canadian government.

The agreements and sacred covenants made between Indigenous peoples and the Crown after the arrival of the Europeans have come to be known as the "Indian treaties." These are mutual agreements that set the parameters of the relationship between the Indigenous and non-Indigenous parties and how that relationship will be conducted. These agreements were negotiated on a nation-to-nation basis. As was spoken at negotiations, the Crown will honour these treaties "as long as the sun goes round and the water flows."[3]

Within the territory covered by a treaty, agreements were made between the signatory nations. Consequently, all within these territories are provided the ability to share the land, govern themselves, and conduct their economic activities in the ways they choose. Everyone has these rights. On the other side of these rights are obligations that must be acknowledged. For example, European governments became obliged by some treaties to ensure that Indigenous peoples have exclusive use of lands designated as "reserves." In territories not covered by specific treaties, there is no settled constitutional structure. Settlers exist, live, and do business there. However, they are operating in a sort of legal limbo, as no official understanding of how lands are shared or can be used has been worked out in these areas.

Treaties between European and Indigenous nations date back to the early 1600s.[4] Throughout the 1700s, various peace and friendship treaties were made. Many were about peaceful coexistence, so they define the respective rights allocated to Indigenous peoples and settlers to enjoy and use lands. They outlined various other rights and responsibilities as well, including recognizing Indigenous people's original title to lands.

Some treaties exchanged the use of land for money given as a one-time payment, a perpetual annuity, or a combination of both payment methods. In the areas surrounding Lake Huron and Lake Superior, for example, the Robinson treaties were signed in 1850. One, between the "Ojibewa Indians" and the Crown, involved a large tract of land from the eastern and northern shores of Lake Huron to the northern shore of Lake Superior. This treaty also included deals that went beyond title to land or monetary compensation: for example, it set aside an area "for the exclusive use of the Anishinabe," and, so their economy would remain unaffected by European settlement, it guaranteed the people "full and free privilege" to hunt and fish on territory set aside for this purpose.[5] During this time, then, other components started to be added to agreements that extended additional rights to First Nations. From 1871 to 1921, 11 numbered treaties were signed, which will be further outlined later in the chapter. First, however, we must consider the treaty that is viewed by the Crown as having established the basic principles of treaty making: the Royal Proclamation of 1763.

The Royal Proclamation of 1763

In 1763, King George III issued the Royal Proclamation after Britain won the Seven Years' War.[6] By way of this document, Britain proclaimed its sovereignty over "the extensive and valuable Acquisitions in America, secured to our Crown by . . . the Treaty of Paris." In other words, because Britain beat France in war, the British monarch claimed land that had been taken from

Indigenous peoples by the French. Although Britain did lay claim to North America as British territory in this manner, it reserved a large area in the interior for the exclusive use of Indigenous peoples, which was to be kept under protection as their hunting grounds. At the same time, the proclamation clearly recognized Indigenous title of the "reserved" land not ceded by or purchased from them. All this land was Indigenous land until ceded by treaty. It also outlined that only the Crown could enter into land negotiations with Indigenous occupants.

Settlers were prohibited from acquiring land from Indigenous inhabitants directly; Indigenous land had to be first purchased from First Nations by the Crown and then sold to the colonists.[7] This Royal Proclamation has been referred to as the "Indian Bill of Rights," the "Indian Charter," or, sometimes, the "Indian Magna Carta" because it established the constitutional framework for the future negotiation of treaties. Even though treaties between colonists and Indigenous peoples had already been established before the Royal Proclamation, this document set the groundwork for future treaty making.

There are different viewpoints regarding what this proclamation meant for Indigenous peoples. One can argue that the document essentially took away Indigenous people's land without any consultation and without their knowing. The British wrote the document that, ultimately, confirmed North America as a land under the dominion of King George III. According to sociology professor Menno Boldt, the Royal Proclamation actually grew out of the villainous doctrine of discovery and turned the peoples of self-governing Indigenous nations in North America into wards of the Crown.[8] Those that follow this interpretation of the proclamation note that it was written by British colonists without any Indigenous consultation or input and that it laid the foundation for the creation of a monopoly over Indigenous territory.

On a similar note, the documentary film *The Invisible Nation* argues that Britain had economic motives for issuing this proclamation. At first, according to the film, many Indigenous peoples were happy about the Royal Proclamation because it gave Indigenous peoples control over their land as well as a degree of political autonomy. Ultimately, however, Indigenous peoples realized that the proclamation wasn't intended to protect them but rather to protect the beavers.[9] In essence, it was protecting the beaver habitats, so Europe could continue to acquire the pelts through the fur trade.

These interpretations all hold some truth. However, we must be cautious of how we come to interpret the Royal Proclamation and also of what we hold up as a "truth." A view espoused by an Anishinaabe law professor, John Borrows, gives us a different interpretation. According to Borrows, Indigenous peoples were "active participants, in the formulation and ratification of the Royal Proclamation."[10] He argues that, in these early negotiations with the Crown, Indigenous peoples had their "own power and a range of choices to which they could bring their own alternatives and considerations." Consequently, he states, the Royal Proclamation should not be looked upon as a document that undercuts Indigenous people's rights.[11] Doing so, he cautions would be taking a colonial interpretation of it.

According to Borrows, the Royal Proclamation was an attempt to convince Indigenous peoples that the British would respect their existing territorial jurisdiction and political rights. The British demonstrated this respect by incorporating Indigenous understandings into the document, such as ensuring "the several Nations or Tribes of Indians" that they "should not be molested or disturbed in the Possession" of their lands and implying that no lands would be taken from Indigenous peoples without their consent.[12] At the same time, however, to consolidate the Crown's position in North America, the British claimed "sovereignty" and "dominion" over Indigenous lands. Borrows argues that the British were trying to meet the expectations of both sides and ended up with a document that awkwardly straddles the conflicting objectives of Indigenous peoples and the Crown. The British knew they needed Indigenous lands for the expansion of their colonial enterprise. So perhaps, at heart, governments did want to protect the beavers over Indigenous peoples—colonialists did have a capitalist demand for expansion as a focal point. However, Indigenous peoples did want their territory and jurisdictions protected. Unfortunately, although the Royal Proclamation seemingly protected Indigenous people's lands and cultures from European settlement or imposition, it simultaneously opened the door to the loss of both. Indigenous title was recognized until ceded by a treaty between Indigenous peoples and the Crown, so colonial governments were not allowed to grant or survey any unceded lands. On the other hand, although the proclamation limited European rights to unceded land and made conditions for the future surrender of Indigenous territory, it didn't specifically set out whether Indigenous peoples would have the political power needed in order to exert "autonomy through their own sovereignty or under British jurisdiction."[13]

Nevertheless, according to Borrows, the Royal Proclamation is a positive guarantee of Indigenous self-government. He further argues that, if we look at the Treaty of Niagara of 1764 and its associated conditions, we get a better picture of just what the Royal Proclamation attempted to do and stand for.

The Treaty of Niagara of 1764

Given the Royal Proclamation's lack of clarity regarding the interplay between Indigenous "possession" and British "sovereignty," Borrows argues that the intent and true spirit of this document can be better understood by referencing the Treaty of Niagara of 1764. At the meeting held to arrange this treaty, a nation-to-nation rapport between Indigenous peoples and settlers was put forth and renewed. According to Lynn Gehl, an Algonquin Anishinaabe-kwe Indigenous human rights researcher and activist, this event served to ratify the 1763 Royal Proclamation.[14] Or as public intellectual John Ralston Saul explains, this great gathering at Niagara was organized to "cement" the Royal Proclamation.[15] A multination alliance, often referred to as the Covenant Chain of Friendship was declared, wherein no participant renounced sovereignty.[16] The colonists presented the Royal Proclamation during the meeting at the Treaty of Niagara; Indigenous peoples then accepted and affirmed it.[17] Also, parties came to a mutual agreement through means beyond a written treaty. They made oral declarations and presentations and exchanged wampum belts. These beaded belts, like paper treaties, are symbols of the agreements made, and they were given and received by both British and Indigenous representatives.[18] The superintendent of Indian Affairs, Sir William Johnson, himself engaged in the giving and receiving of belts of wampum.[19]

Indeed, Johnson was instrumental in organizing the meeting at Fort Niagara that resulted in the treaty. The winter after the British issued the Royal Proclamation, Johnson invited Indigenous leaders to a conference, which was to be held at Niagara the next summer. Johnson commissioned the Algonquin and Nipissing Anishinaabe nations as runners for the 1764 conference.[20] Constitutional delegates from these nations travelled throughout the surrounding waterscapes and territory to invite other nations to attend. They carried with them white wampum strings as a sign of peace, in addition to a printed copy of the Royal Proclamation.

The conference resulted in a discussion that was to formulate the governing principles of the Indigenous-Crown relationship. Its intended function, though, was to agree to a "Treaty of Offensive and Defensive Alliance." Johnson stated that this treaty would include a promise by the Crown to Indigenous peoples that would "Assure them of a Free Fair & open trade, at principle Posts & a free intercourse, & passage into our Country, That we will make no Settlements or Encroachments contrary to Treaty, or without their permission. That we will bring to justice any persons who commit Robberys or Murders on them & that we will protect and aid them against their & our Enemys, & duly observe our Engagements with them."[21]

Because William Johnson wanted to signal his intention to engage in meaningful negotiations at Niagara, he set out to invite and interact with Indigenous peoples in accordance with their preferred customs.[22] These included the practice of "wampum diplomacy and its inherent forms of symbolic literacy."[23] Thus, wampum belts were to be used as a way to codify this historic event and to ensure clear understanding.

The eventual negotiators of the Treaty of Niagara came together in July and August 1764. The conference was held at what was referred to as the "crooked place" on the Niagara River.[24] The delegates commissioned by Johnson to invite Indigenous delegates were successful. People travelled months and weeks to be able to attend.[25] Over 24 nations and about 2,000 leaders attended the negotiations, some coming from as far north as Hudson's Bay, as far west as Mississippi, and as far east as Nova Scotia.[26] There is further documentation to suggest that even the Cree and Lakota (Sioux) nations were in attendance.[27] The conference has long been regarded as the most widely representative gathering of Indigenous peoples ever brought together for a treaty agreement.[28]

Once the meeting began, Johnson read the terms of the Royal Proclamation to Indigenous representatives, with whom he made a shared agreement of non-interference. Indigenous nations gave a promise of peace, and, as a sign of good faith, gifts were exchanged between the parties according to Indigenous custom. Johnson then offered two wampum belts and delivered a speech. These two belts are referred to as "The British and Great Lakes Covenant Chain Confederacy Wampum Belt" and "The Twenty-Four Nations Wampum Belt."[29] The first belt represented a strong relationship among equal allies, a relationship that would be as strong as chain links. Yet this relationship could also tarnish, just as silver tarnishes, implying that it might need regular polishing and repolishing.

The other belt depicts a chain secured around a rock, which ran through the hands of the 24 other Indigenous nations at the conference and was attached to a British ship. It served to represent the negotiated promise that Britain and Indigenous nations would share North America's resources and bounty. The British ship contains bounty reaching across the Atlantic and anchored to North America; this wealth is connected to a rope in the hands of representatives of the 24 Indigenous nations. If the British ever forgot their responsibility of providing the agreed upon gifts to Indigenous nations, Indigenous peoples are to pull the rope as a reminder to get the British back on track.

William Johnson's speech told of renewed and strengthened engagements. It recognized Indigenous peoples' promises of friendship and attachment to the British. It explained that "there now remains for us only to exchange the great Belt of the Covenant Chain that we may not forget our mutual Engagements."[30] Once Johnson finished his speech, Indigenous peoples presented him with the Gus Wen Tah, or the "Two-Row Wampum Belt," as a way to demonstrate their understanding of the Royal Proclamation and the Treaty of Niagara.[31] This belt had been presented previously by Indigenous peoples to Europeans. Indeed, the Haudenosaunee people were the first to give it as ratification of the oldest treaty between them and Europeans, dating back to the 1600s.[32]

The Two-Row Wampum Belt "codified a nation-to-nation relationship rooted in the philosophy and practice of non-interference mediated by peace, friendship, and respect."[33] It is made of white and purple wampum beads. It has two parallel purple lines, one line representing the canoe of Indigenous peoples—their customs, ways, and laws—and the other a European ship that carries the laws, traditions, and customs of that world. Each vessel travels down the river of life in tandem, and that river is symbolized by the white wampum background, which also represents the purity of the agreement. Each party will travel down the river side by side, but in their respective boats, the one never interfering with the other and never trying to steer the other's boat. There are also three rows of white wampum beads separating the two purple rows; these represent respect, friendship, and peace. As much as the three rows keep the two worlds separate and independent, they also bind them together. Through symbolic literacy, this wampum belt states that Indigenous nations lived in solidarity with Britain—and no nation was subjugated to the other.

Through this exchange of wampum belts, the British entered into a nation-to-nation relationship with Indigenous peoples, one embedded in an agreement of non-interference. As Gehl contends, these three wampum belts make it clear that Indigenous nations are not subjects of the British.[34] For Borrows, these belts undoubtedly show Indigenous nations to be sovereign.

The agreements decided on at Niagara and intimated in the Royal Proclamation have never been rendered nugatory. Nor have they been overruled by any Canadian laws or abridged or curtailed. Also, once the Royal Proclamation is understood in light of the Treaty of Niagara—as not a "unilateral decision of the Crown" but rather as something entered into, something about which Indigenous peoples had significant say—the need for the proclamation to be interpreted as it would have been "naturally understood" by the peoples of that time is clear. An understanding of the Royal Proclamation that takes into consideration the agreements made at Niagara, including the synchronous speeches and physical symbols, therefore includes the recognition of Indigenous sovereignty. It requires an acknowledgement of two related facts: an alliance between Britain and Indigenous nations and Indigenous sovereignty.[35] These two things require the Crown to seek Indigenous consent for settlement on Indigenous land, as well as the creation of open free trade and passage between Indigenous peoples and the Crown and an alliance between the two.

Indigenous peoples have continued to reflect on and reiterate promises made. The strong tradition of oral knowledge transmission kept these agreements alive amongst Indigenous peoples, and future generations have kept to them. According to Cayuga Chief Jake Thomas, elders have taught children how to memorize stories thoroughly and in great detail, so the same interpretations and understandings of the past can be passed on to descendants.[36] Ethnohistorian Kathryn V. Muller, biographer of the Two-Row Wampum Belt, explains that, although written documents provide a valuable source exemplifying European understandings of events, they must be considered alongside oral tradition and wampum belts if we are to grasp the intricacies of post-contact diplomacy fully.[37]

Not only is the true meaning of the Royal Proclamation well documented in oral history, wampum belts, and the speeches given at the Treaty of Niagara, but the nation-to-nation agreements are also international legal contracts. According to Borrows, legally, Canadian "Indian" treaties would be classified as *sui generis*, meaning unique, a contract, or law, of its own kind or in its own class. Thus, these treaties are most analogous to contracts.[38] Put another way, Canadian jurists make fundamental comparisons between treaties and legal contracts because both are similar in law. Borrows further outlines that the contents of a contract must include not only what appears on its face but also the terms implied in subsequent agreements, terms that might not have been included due to pure inadvertence. Thus, evidence of customs and subsequent agreements must be considered when we interpret Indigenous-European treaties.

There are many Indigenous peoples who continue to interpret the Royal Proclamation from this perspective—from the understanding that they are sovereign—hence contradicting the claim laid out in writing in the proclamation itself, which names the Crown as having "sovereignty" in North America.[39] This interpretation, derived from the Treaty of Niagara, is held not only by Indigenous peoples. Burrows highlights the fact that William Johnson expressed a similar view when he commented on a problematic treaty in 1765:

> These people had subscribed to a Treaty with me at Niagara in August last, but by the present Treaty I find, they make expressions of subjection, which must either have arisen from the ignorance of the Interpreter, or from some mistake; for I am well convinced, they never mean or intend anything like it, and that they can not be brought under our laws, for some Centuries, neither have they any word which can convey the most distant idea of subjection, and should it be fully explained to them, and the nature of subordination punishment ettc [sic], defined, it might produce infinite harm . . . and I dread its consequences, as I recollect that some attempts towards Sovereignty not long ago, was one of the principle causes of all our troubles.[40]

Clearly, Johnson did not view the Royal Proclamation and the Treaty of Niagara to be declarations of British sovereignty over Indigenous peoples. Johnson's comment provides evidence that there was indeed consensus between the parties in regards to the agreements made at the Treaty of Niagara meeting, a consensus that provides for a particular interpretation of the Royal Proclamation and for mutual acceptance of Indigenous sovereignty. As David T. McNab writes in his examination of treaty processes, "Johnson understood the significance of Aboriginal sovereignty [and] . . . moreover, was aware of the solemnity and the ceremony involved in the treaty-making process."[41]

Finally, I agree with the sentiments expressed by both Borrows and Gehl: 1) viewing the Royal Proclamation as a one-sided action by the British Crown to impose sovereignty over Indigenous nations is a colonial interpretation, and 2) a transfer of sovereignty from Indigenous peoples to the Crown has never been agreed to, so legitimate British sovereignty in North America ceases to exist. However, it must be noted that even this notion of "sovereignty" is a colonial and foreign concept. As Taiaiake Alfred explains, "Indigenous peoples are by definition the original inhabitants of the land. . . . And they never gave consent to European ownership of territory or the establishment of European sovereignty over them."[42] He further notes that the concept of "sovereignty" is contrary to traditional Indigenous notions of power, citing it as an "inappropriate concept" because their societies recognized no absolute authority, no coercive types of hierarchy, and no outside ruling entity.[43] Just the acceptance of this concept, then, reinforces the imposed foreign authority and, thus, legitimizes its associated structure of colonial hierarchy. A caution is in order: if Indigenous peoples frame their understanding within this state-constructed concept of "sovereignty" and try to achieve it as a goal, they accept—without really meaning to—this colonial construct and the "state" as their model of governance.[44]

In summary, for Borrows, the wampum belts described previously undoubtedly show Indigenous nations to be sovereign; but, for Alfred, "sovereignty" is not the language of Indigenous liberation as this term has "no relevance to Indigenous values" and, by adopting it, Indigenous peoples merely legitimize the foreign state's hierarchy.[45] Alfred explains that the *Kanien'kehaka Kaswentha* (Two-Row Wampum Belt) did not symbolize power relations in which one nation would be subjugated by another nation but rather a "negotiated and lasting peace based on coexistence of power in a context of respect for the autonomy and distinctive nature of each partner." It shows that "interference with the other partner's autonomy, freedom, or powers was expressly forbidden." As long "as these principles were respected, the relationship would be peaceful, harmonious, and just."[46]

An Organized Takeover: The Conspiracy of Legislation

It is clear. Indigenous peoples never gave up their "sovereignty." But, ultimately, Europeans pushed forward their priorities and goals, which involved achieving power in North America, and they did so in a systematic way that bypassed many of the promises made. One unsettling fact contributing to Europe's increasing power on the continent was that many Indigenous peoples suffered incredible losses due to the diseases that accompanied the massive immigration of European peoples. An estimated 50 to 90 per cent of Indigenous peoples (depending on the peoples considered) died of diseases brought from Europe, diseases against which Indigenous peoples had no immunity.[47] In the face of such losses, nations had to rely on the integrity of the Europeans to maintain and uphold the negotiated relationship of peace and mutual rights. Unfortunately, Indigenous peoples came to be viewed as "the vanishing race" rather than as partners.[48] Treaty promises were reinterpreted and relationships shifted, as did the goals of the British towards the end of the 1700s. The procurement of Indigenous land and the displacement of Indigenous peoples became policy drivers; there were even attempts at eradication, through wars and violence.[49]

As Europeans continued to colonize Turtle Island, in vast areas of Canada—including most of British Columbia and Québec and parts of the Maritimes—numerous Indigenous nations never received any type of compensation for being dispossessed of rights in their original homelands.[50] The Crown's explanation for its failure to follow the treaty-making agreements and processes in parts of the Maritimes and in Québec involve claims that Britain received title to these regions from France. In other words, the British chose to recognize only that the French passed to Britain control and "ownership" of the land in North America claimed by France but not that the French never really properly acquired this land in the first place.

In British Columbia between 1850 and 1854, acting on behalf of the Crown, James Douglas negotiated 14 land agreements with Indigenous peoples on Vancouver Island.[51] Today, these are known as the Douglas treaties. James Douglas's superiors in London left him in charge of negotiations, assuming that he would continue to make more treaties with Indigenous peoples in British Columbia, but Douglas began creating "reserves." Under Douglas, both individual Indigenous peoples and settlers could come to land agreements with the Crown to take up farming, mining, or other economic activity on land outside of these reserves.

After Douglas retired, the colonial government took away the right of Indigenous peoples to make agreements regarding rights to their land, reduced the size of their "reserves," paid no compensation for the loss of their lands and resources, and denied that Indigenous peoples ever owned the land.[52] When British Columbia joined Confederation in 1871, the federal government made an effort to negotiate a more standard approach to Aboriginal title. However, the province refused to cooperate, avowing that the Royal Proclamation was not applicable in British Columbia.[53] Because the Province of British Columbia was not yet colonized by the British in 1763—when the Royal Proclamation was issued—the argument went, the province did not have to recognize Aboriginal title to the land. As no recognition of Aboriginal title existed, there was no need for treaties to extinguish it. Basically, the province was saying, "Laws written before I was born do not apply to me."

By the 1860s, Indigenous peoples were no longer viewed as allies that the Crown had an obligation to respect and protect. In earlier years, for example, during the Seven Years' War (1756–63) and the War of 1812 (1812–14), "Indian" policy was relatively straight forward—"maintain the various tribes as military allies."[54] Once the threat of war started to recede, Indigenous peoples were no longer needed as allies and began to be seen as in the way of European colonization efforts.

The signs of this changed relationship with Indigenous peoples were pervasive. Canada's parliament buildings finished construction in 1866, just in time for Confederation in 1867. They cost $4.5 million to build, were modelled on the Palace of Westminster that houses the Parliament of the United Kingdom, and were built right over an ancient Algonquin burial site.[55] In an effort to boost European colonization, the colonial and provincial governments established a policy of land pre-emption or grants in 1870 that disregarded Aboriginal title. Any European male 18 or over could simply occupy from 160 to 320 acres of land and ultimately claim legal title to it, regardless of any pre-existing Indigenous rights to this land. No compensation was outlined for the taking of Indigenous peoples' land.[56] The policy stated only that "reserve" lands could not be acquired on this basis, but, basically, other land was up for the taking. Here is the section of the Colonial Land Ordinance (1870) legalizing this method of acquiring land:

> 3. From and after the date of proclamation in this Colony of Her Majesty's assent to this Ordinance, and male person being a British Subject, of the age of eighteen years or over, may acquire the right to pre-empt any tract of unoccupied, unsurveyed, and unreserved Crown Lands (not being an Indian settlement) not exceeding three hundred and twenty acres in extent in that portion of the Colony situate to the northward and eastward of the Cascade or Coast Range of Mountains, and one hundred and sixty acres in extent in the rest of the Colony. Provided that such right of pre-emption shall not be held to any of the Aborigines of this Continent, except to such

> as shall have obtained the Governor's special permission in writing to that effect.[57]

Since the second half of the nineteenth century, an array of federal and provincial legislation specifically designed to eliminate Indigenous people's rights has been put into place. The diminishing of Indigenous land rights was compounded by federal legislation that denied Indigenous peoples access to the courts to oppose this policy objective. In 1927, the federal government amended the Indian Act to make it illegal for First Nations peoples to obtain a lawyer to advance their claims over land.[58] It was even made illegal for anyone (Indigenous or otherwise) to solicit funds with the intention of obtaining a lawyer in support of Indigenous land claims. Anyone found guilty of such an offence could face imprisonment. Indigenous peoples were therefore denied the right to their original homelands and to a just hearing. In many ways, "Indian" land policy was an organized takeover that was quite systematic.

In 1951, the restriction on negotiating land claims agreements was lifted. Slowly, we have witnessed small steps in positive directions. But often a step forward is followed by a step or two back. Chapter 6 will look more specifically at government policies that continue, through legal manipulation, to ignore Indigenous rights, most notably, the Indian Act.

The Numbered Treaties

The numbered treaties, or what are also referred to as the post-Confederation treaties, were signed from 1871 to 1921 in parts of Ontario; all of Manitoba, Saskatchewan, and Alberta; portions of Yukon; a small part of northeastern British Columbia; and the western part of the Northwest Territories.[59] They were not monolithic, as each was created in relation to people's own specific geographies and social conditions;[60] however, they were alike, as all were designed to allow Canadian governments to pursue settlement and resource extraction. Thus, although the treaties do vary, their provisions are similar. In exchange for land or its use, Indigenous peoples were to receive reserve lands, monetary payments, educational allowances, and agricultural supplies and other tools or various items that would assist in their transition to participating fully in this new economy.

Sir John A. Macdonald helped inaugurate these numbered treaties, which the government viewed, in part, as a means to eliminate the uniqueness and distinctiveness of Indigenous peoples, whom he planned to absorb into Euro-Canadian culture and ways of life.[61] Macdonald also aimed to achieve his "national dream," the creation of a country connected by a sea-to-sea railway. Gaining title of Indigenous territory was necessary to achieve this goal and to other economic aims, such as bringing land under cultivation, so the land rights of Indigenous peoples began to be seen as obstacles to settlement and "development."[62]

Even though Canadian governments had their specific agendas, these treaty negotiations were not completely one-sided. Many strong Indigenous leaders were vocal in asserting the terms of their respective treaties. Given the decline of the buffalo and other natural food sources, an increase in European diseases, and the continued expansion of European settlement and economic interests, many Indigenous peoples viewed these treaties as a means to secure the well-being of their peoples and future generations. Consequently, they were active and creative agents throughout negotiations. Recognizing this changing environment and the inevitability of Euro-Canadian settlement on Indigenous land and interaction with Indigenous peoples, with or without treaties, those who entered into negotiations also did so to protect their cultures and peoples from the government's goal of Indigenous assimilation.[63]

Treaties 1 and 2 were both signed in August of 1871. They were made between the treaty commissioners representing the federal government and Chippewa and Cree nations. Treaty 1 covers areas referred to today as southeastern Manitoba. Treaty 2 covers areas in what is now known as southwestern Manitoba, as well as a small area in southeastern Saskatchewan. Not wanting to be dispossessed of their lands, on which their livelihoods relied, the Indigenous parties involved decided to negotiate these treaties with the government. Both treaties had similar but not identical provisions.[64] Indigenous peoples would receive smaller pieces of reserve land to live on, agricultural tools, a school on each reserve (whenever people on the reserve desired one), an annuity of $3 a person or $15 per family (in either goods or cash), and a census to track members of First Nations for financial purposes. In return, Treaty 1 (the written document) states that Indigenous peoples "cede, release, surrender and yield up" their lands included within the specified limits of the treaty. They also promise to "maintain perpetual peace" and not to "molest the persons of Her Majesty's white or other subjects." Additionally, the treaty prohibits the possession or sale of liquor on their reserves.[65]

However, as with many of these numbered treaties, what came to be written in the treaty documents did not reflect what was spoken at negotiations.[66] Both of these treaties had to be renegotiated only four years later, as the oral promises made when they were originally negotiated were not included in the written terms of either agreement.[67] As a result, more agricultural tools were provided, and the government increased annuity amounts from $3 to $5 a person.[68] However, in return for this "correction," the government stipulated that any First Nations person who received this increased annuity had to relinquish any claims against the government in regards to any other "outside" oral promise.[69]

In a detailed analysis of Treaty 1, Anishinabe lawyer Aimée Craft explains that, in order to understand what was negotiated and agreed to, we must consider the true spirit and intent of the treaties by acknowledging what all parties contemplated during negotiations.[70] From the perspective of the Crown, this treaty was a complete surrender of Indigenous peoples' land. But for Anishinabe peoples, the treaty was not a sale of land but a promise to share in the bounty of the land. Craft shows how Anishinabe laws (*inaakonigewin*), which are founded on a relationship with the land that has nothing to do with ownership, defined the negotiations leading up to Treaty 1. Thus, the agreements are about the use of resources and land alongside settlers rather than outright ownership. To the Anishinabe peoples, whose views were "rooted in an attachment to the land, based on use assigned by the Creator," this treaty was an agreement to secure a good life for future generations.[71] They also felt that they had an underlying responsibility "to share in the bounty of the earth with other brothers and sisters," which, as Craft indicates, also helps to clarify the willingness of the Anishinabe peoples to enter into a shared agreement.[72]

Treaty 3 was negotiated in October 1873 between the treaty commissioners representing the Crown and various Anishinaabe (Ojibwa and Saulteaux) nations. It covers the areas referred to today as northwestern Ontario, as well as a smaller area in eastern Manitoba. The federal government viewed the signing of Treaty 1 and 2 as a "success," one it was hoping to repeat with the various Anishinaabe nations in Treaty 3 territory. Initially, however, there were four unsuccessful attempts to get this treaty negotiated before it came to be signed. This difficulty in coming to an agreement was not uncommon. As happened during the negotiation of other numbered treaties, during Treaty 3 talks, the government commissioners and official sources contended that Indigenous negotiators were requesting "extravagant demands."[73] But, in reality, the demands considered "extravagant" were forward-looking provisions set forth by Indigenous negotiators to ensure the future social and economic well-being of their peoples.[74] This treaty included provisions similar to those in the first two numbered treaties, but, in addition, it included a $1,500 annum for ammunition and fishing net twine and a right to hunt and fish on unoccupied Crown land—although only until such time as the government deemed that the land was needed for forestry, mining, settlement, lumbering, or other purposes.[75]

As happened during the making of Treaties 1 and 2, what was spoken during Treaty 3 negotiations was not fully included in the written terms of the treaty. For instance, during negotiations, representatives of the Saulteaux peoples stipulated that they would be compensated if mineral resources were extracted from their reserve land or paid if "Indians" found minerals off reserve.[76] Yet this stipulation was never put into the printed version of Treaty 3. For Saulteaux peoples, the true version of what was decided during Treaty 3 negotiations is the "Paypom" treaty, which is a written record of the oral agreements negotiated. This record was made by Joseph Nolin, a prominent Métis whom the Saulteaux people had hired to provide a transcript on their behalf. Governor Morris gave Chief Powassan a copy of the Nolin notes when the treaty was signed.

Treaty 4 was negotiated in September 1874 between various Cree and Anishinaabe nations and the treaty commissioners representing the Crown. It covers the area referred to today as southern Saskatchewan as well as small areas of western Manitoba and southeastern Alberta. This treaty's provisions are similar to those of Treaty 3, but one notable addition was that "trapping" was added to the provision of hunting and fishing rights.

The terms of Treaty 5 were first established in September 1875 between the government and Swampy Cree, Pimicikamak Cree, Norway House Cree, and Saulteaux peoples. Today, this treaty covers northern and central Manitoba, as well as some smaller areas in Ontario and Saskatchewan. The terms set out in the original, written version of Treaty 5 are similar to those of earlier treaties, although there are some notable differences. One is the much smaller size of the reserves it allows, which was raised as a major problem by First Nations peoples on several occasions. Instead of the 2.5 square kilometres for each family of five, which Treaties 3 and 4 provide, Treaty 5 limits reserved land to only 600 square metres for each family of five. In part, this decreased allotment resulted from the government's view that the land in these regions was not suitable for agriculture and therefore unfit for use. In other words, the government contended that Indigenous peoples only needed small tracts of land because they could not farm on it.

Treaty 5 was added to after 1875, with the last adhesion signed in 1910. Given the decline of fur-bearing animals, increased development, and European encroachment, additional First Nations petitioned the government to be included in the agreement in order to receive benefits.[77] By 1878, most of the nations within the initial boundaries of Treaty 5 had negotiated into the agreement. As the government became more serious about supporting the building of a railway between Winnipeg and Churchill, Manitoba, northern adhesions to Treaty 5 also began to occur.[78] Five more nations signed on in 1908, three more in 1909, and the final two in June and August of 1910.

The first signing of Treaty 6 was in 1876. This treaty was negotiated between the treaty commissioners representing the Crown and the peoples of the Plains Cree, Woodland Cree, Assiniboine, Saulteaux, and Chipewyan nations. It covers most of the central portions of present-day Alberta and Saskatchewan. Many of the Indigenous peoples in this region were concerned about their future: they feared increased settlement now that the Canadian government claimed to have taken over sovereignty from the Hudson's Bay Company, and they worried about European diseases and starvation decimating their populations as white settlers became plentiful and the buffalo scarce. Consequently, some leaders felt pressure to negotiate before the situation deteriorated.

Acknowledging Indigenous concern about the diminishing supply of game in the 1870s and 1880s is key to understanding Treaty 6. After all, a central way the woodland peoples in this area maintained their livelihoods was through hunting forest game, including fish and fur animals, and the prairie peoples in this region relied largely on the buffalo.[79] By the late 1870s, however, the buffalo were on the brink of extinction. Before Europeans arrived, there were an estimated 60 million buffalo in North America; by 1890, there were fewer than 100 buffalo left.[80] Many Euro-Canadian and Euro-American hunters shot countless buffalo with their rifles, grossly overhunting them and making profit from their hides.[81] American military authorities, too, killed massive numbers of buffalo—sometimes as a matter of policy designed to starve "Indians" into submission. "Kill every buffalo you can!" exclaimed Colonel Richard Dodge of the US Army. "Every buffalo dead is an Indian gone."[82] Buffalo bones and skulls soon blanketed major areas of the plains, so much so that settlers even complained that they could hardly plough the land.[83]

After the major decline of the buffalo, settler hunters turned to hunting wolves, which had begun to prey on livestock. Wolves were also hunted for their thick winter fur, which received high prices on the European market.[84] The preferred method was to bait wolves with pieces of buffalo, sheep, or cattle meat that was laced with a poison called strychnine. Thousands of trappers came to be engaged in what has been described as a "frenzy of poisoning."[85] This strychnine-laced bait killed anything that ate it, in a painful death, including killing thousands of birds. Poisoned wolves would go into convulsions, drooling and vomiting in the grass, inadvertently killing more buffalo and many Indigenous people's horses that consumed the grass.[86]

Concerned over the depletion of the buffalo and the destruction that seemed to accompany European settlement, Indigenous peoples in the Treaty 6 territory recognized that they needed to negotiate a treaty in order to safeguard their culture from being devastated by the inevitable incursion of settlers. Some of the local nations requested that negotiations begin a full five years before they actually did, as they were anxious to safeguard their

Image 5.1 Buffalo Bones Gathered from the Prairies

Credit: Library and Archives Canada / PA-066544

peoples and territories.[87] Yet not everyone was on board with negotiating this treaty. Speaking to those opposed, Chief Ahtahkakoop, one of the main negotiators, outlined the pressures pushing Indigenous peoples toward accepting the treaty:

> [T]he buffalo will be gone forever before many snows. What then will be left us with which to bargain? With the buffalo gone we will have only the vacant prairie which none of us have learned to use. Can we stop the power of the white man from spreading over the land like the grasshoppers that cloud the sky and then fall to consume every blade of grass and every leaf on the trees in their path? I think not. Before this happens, let us ponder carefully our choice of roads.[88]

The provisions that ended up in the written treaty are similar to those of the previous numbered treaties. Notable additions include a promise to keep a medicine chest at the house of each chief or Indian agent. Treaty 6 is the only numbered treaty containing this provision, which was arranged at the request of Indigenous negotiators in response to the many European diseases that had swept across the plains, and continued to do so.[89] As Cree lawyer Sharon Venne explains, the Indigenous negotiators of this treaty were well aware that European diseases were destroying their populations and that they needed non-Indigenous medicine to fight off these diseases.[90] Another notable provision is a guarantee that the Queen will care for Indigenous peoples in the event of a famine.[91] In Treaty 6, Indigenous peoples also agreed to share the topsoil of their lands "to the depth of a plough" (six inches deep), thus allowing settlers to farm.[92]

Only three years after the signing of Treaty 6, the buffalo herds disappeared.[93] But treaty terms that guaranteed assistance in the event of a famine were not held to by the government. As Venne explains, instead, the most horrible rations, hard dark biscuits known as "dog biscuits," were provided to Indigenous peoples: "As the settlers grew rich and prosperous from the lands of Indigenous peoples, these dog biscuits replaced buffalo, moose, deer, ducks, geese, roots, and berries."[94] There were other treaty violations. Euro-Canadians drilling deep into the land (rather than keeping to the depth of a plow) extracted minerals without Indigenous consent, and, only two years after signing the original treaty, the government reduced the agreed upon $15 per person annual cash provision to only $5, where it remains to this day. The Indigenous peoples who negotiated this treaty were told that the money from this reduction would be "set aside for them in Ottawa for their future use," but their descendants have yet to see this money.[95]

In the surrounding territories, First Nations that did not originally sign Treaty 6 ended up negotiating as the buffalo disappeared. After the three original signings in 1876, 11 more took place between 1877 and 1898 and 5 more in the 1940s and 1950s, with the last occurring in May of 1956. Like many other numbered treaties, Treaty 6, in its original written form, has long been disputed. Words that were never discussed or negotiated ended up in this written document, such as the declaration that Indigenous signatories agree to "cede, release, surrender and yield up . . . forever, all their rights, titles and privileges whatsoever, to the lands."[96] As Venne states, "The Elders maintain that these words were not included in the original treaty."[97]

Treaty 7 was made in September 1877 and covers what is referred to today as southern Alberta. Settlers rather than Indigenous peoples pressured the government to get this treaty negotiated.[98] Traders and missionaries added their voices, telling the government that they were afraid they would be faced with violence if they were to venture into these Indigenous territories without a treaty being in place.[99] For instance, missionary Father Constantine Scollen reported that, during this time, settlers were "anxious that a treaty be made as soon as possible, so that they may know what portions of land they can hold without fear of being molested."[100] This treaty was also needed if the transcontinental Canadian Pacific Railway (CPR) were to be finished.[101]

The peoples in the Treaty 7 territories are from the Blood, Piikani (Peigan), Siksika, Stoney Nakoda, and Tsuut'ina nations. Again, this treaty contained provisions similar to those of earlier numbered treaties, but one notable difference was that it increased the supplies to be allocated to First Nations peoples. As with official versions of Treaties 1 through 6, the government's written Treaty 7 document is considered inaccurate. A study that gathered the testimony of over 80 elders from the five First Nations involved in Treaty 7 found a consensus among them: "there is a fundamental problem with the written treaty because it does not represent the 'spirit and intent' of the agreement" that was verbally negotiated.[102] A most significant problem is that this treaty was supposed to be a peace treaty, primarily, and elders do not remember Indigenous negotiators ever having been told that it was about surrendering land, as is stipulated in the government's treaty document. All of the elders surveyed agree: their people never gave up their territories.

These elders also explain that, in their languages, there is no translation for the terms "surrender" or "cede." Instead, their languages reflect the view that "we are one with the land." Given this view, they ask, "Is it possible to give or relinquish part of oneself?"[103] As was stipulated in Treaty 6, settlers were granted by the Indigenous negotiators of Treaty 7 the use of the land's topsoil to farm.[104] There was absolutely no conversation or dialogue relating to land surrender.

How did these different views of what was agreed upon come to be? Problems of interpretation during treaty talks have been identified as one culprit. Reverend John McDougall, an adviser to the Stoney chiefs during negotiations, spoke Cree but not Nakoda (Stoney). Jerry Potts, the Blackfoot translator, was fluent; his mother was from the Blood Nation. However, he was not an effective translator for the Tsuu T'ina peoples—he was remembered as speaking in Blackfoot to their negotiators—and he was not able to understand the formal and legal English well enough to translate it into the Blackfoot dialects.[105]

Elders also noted that the promise of food rations was simply an empty promise. The government provided rations, but, over time, these became less and less, until they were stopped. People were extremely hungry. Some men were so weak they were unable to work, and babies died of malnutrition. The withholding of food was even used to convince Indigenous peoples to give up their lands. The people of the Siksika First Nation were told they would receive their flour rations only if they allowed the CPR to cut through their reserve lands.[106]

As well, tensions over supplying food according to treaty specifications arose, in part, because of different views of the future. The government's aim was to assimilate the "Indians," so they would eventually give up hunting and start farming, thus reducing the support the government was required to give them. The Indigenous negotiators aimed to secure the survival of their way of life by allowing settlers to farm the land in return for direct financial support. In this context, Prime Minister Sir John A. Macdonald assured critics of his policy of provisioning "treaty Indians" that government agents were "doing all they can, by refusing food until the Indians are on the verge of starvation, to reduce the expense."[107]

Treaty commissioners representing the Crown negotiated Treaty 8 in June 1899 with people of the Woodland Cree, Dane-zaa (Beaver), and Chipewyan (Dene) nations. It covers the areas now known as northern Alberta, northeastern British Columbia, and northwestern Saskatchewan, as well as the southernmost part of the Northwest Territories. It contains provisions similar to those of previous treaties, with one notable difference: the option for an individual family to have its own small reserve. This provision was intended to meet the different demographic situation in these territories, where small family groupings lived by hunting and other individual efforts.[108] The government was eager to negotiate Treaty 8 because the Klondike gold rush was drawing non-Indigenous prospectors and settlers toward these territories, so it wanted to get this treaty secured to avoid conflict and obtain land. Indigenous peoples aimed both to establish a peace and friendship agreement and to secure their livelihoods for future generations.[109]

For Indigenous negotiators, Treaty 8 was intended to cement friendly relations and peaceful coexistence between Indigenous and non-Indigenous peoples. Sheldon Cardinal, who is from Treaty 8 territory and a direct descendant of an original signatory of the treaty, explains it this way: "The Creator owns the land and we cannot sell what is not ours. As a result, our forefathers would have only agreed to share the land with non-Native settlers."[110] Besides, "Elders are adamant" that they never agreed to "cede" or "yield up" their territories, and these words are "culturally nonsensical" when used in relation to land.[111] As happened during earlier treaty talks, Indigenous negotiators were told they would always have enough land to accommodate their hunting, fishing, and trapping, and that their access to land would increase as their population increased.[112] Indigenous negotiators were so adamant about retaining their right to hunt, fish, and trap in traditional territories that they stated there would be no treaty if this condition were not met.[113] The written treaty, however, put severe limitations on this right, making it "subject to regulations as may from time to time be made by the Government of the country, acting under the authority of Her

Majesty, and saving and excepting such tracts as may be required or taken up from time to time for settlement, mining, lumbering, trading or other purposes."[114] It also limited the size of the reserves the government had agreed to set aside as "bands" desired them, and it said nothing about increasing the land held in reserve in the event of population growth.

As they did in other numbered treaty talks, Indigenous negotiators stressed education as an essential provision.[115] In response, the treaty commissioners agreed that education would be provided with no interference with religious beliefs. Although this oral assertion was put into the report of the commissioners, it was not part of the final treaty document.[116] A blatant breaking of this promise was the provision of residential schools, where the Christian religion was forced on Indigenous peoples (see Chapter 7).

Treaties 9 through 11 are the final numbered treaties. These treaties were signed in the 1900s. Treaty 9, which is also known as the James Bay Treaty, was first made in 1905, with adhesions continuing until 1930. This original agreement was between the treaty commissioners representing the Crown and the peoples from Ojibwa and Cree nations. It covers a large area in what is now referred to as northern Ontario. Treaty 10 was signed in 1906; the Government of Canada wanted to negotiate for what it considered the unceded districts of the newly formed Province of Saskatchewan, so the territory covered by the treaty includes a large area in what is now northern Saskatchewan and a smaller part of eastern Alberta. It was negotiated between the treaty commissioners representing the Crown and the Cree and Chipewyan (Dene) Nation. Treaty 11, the last of the numbered treaties, was first signed in 1921; signatories were added throughout that year, and the final one was added in 1922. Treaty 11 was entered into with various peoples from several different Métis, Inuit, Gwich'in, and Dene nations (including many Tłı̨chǫ peoples). Its territory includes a large area in what is referred to today as the Northwest Territories, as well as a smaller part of Yukon.

These later numbered treaties, which covered the more northern areas, came about much slower than the earlier numbered treaties because the government initially saw little use for the land they covered. Treaty 11, which Indigenous peoples in the area wanted, was especially slow in coming because the government saw this land as unsuitable for agriculture, so there was no hurry to get a treaty signed. However, as soon as oil was discovered at Norman Wells in 1920, the government was quick to get going with negotiations.[117]

Treaties 9 through 11 are not exceptional with regards to the obvious inconsistencies between their written texts and the oral agreements made during negotiations.[118] They also contain provisions similar to those of the numbered treaties negotiated near the end of the nineteenth century: smaller pieces of reserve land to live on; annuity payments; educational allowances; the right to hunt, fish, and trap (except on land that might be taken up for mining, forestry, or other government purposes); and the provision of supplies such as fishing net twine and ammunition. All this was to be given in exchange for Indigenous peoples sharing the bounty of their lands—never for outright ownership.

Discussion Questions

1) Consider the land on which you currently reside. Has a treaty been signed related to it? If so, what agreements were made, and are they being followed? If no treaty has been signed, consider this land in light of this chapter's discussion on the Royal Proclamation and the Treaty of Niagara, which states that a transfer of "sovereignty" from Indigenous peoples to the Crown has never existed. What does this mean for you and your neighbours? Do you believe that it is important to live in a country that has legitimacy to it? Discuss.
2) If the true "spirit and intent" of all treaties were honoured and followed, how and in what ways would Canada be different today?

Activities

1) Without treaties we wouldn't have Canada. Everyone in Canada is a treaty person. Treaties, which are nation-to-nation agreements, constitute our country. Each person has these rights tied to him or her. On the other side of these rights are obligations. Get into groups and compile lists of what these obligations are. Then come together in a larger group and share and discuss your lists of obligations.
2) Watch the music video by Charlie Angus (NDP member of Parliament) titled "Four Horses: official music video" (available online at www.youtube.com) regarding the broken treaties on the plains. Listen to and read the lyrics (available below the video if you click "Show More"). What does he mean when he states, that "to break a people you need a bureaucrat man"?

Recommended Readings

Craft, Aimée. *Breathing Life into the Stone Fort Treaty: An Anishinabe Understanding of Treaty One*. Saskatoon, SK: Purich Publishing, 2013.

Daschuck, James. *Clearing the Plains: Disease, Politics of Starvation, and the Loss of Aboriginal Life*. Regina: University of Regina Press, 2013.

6
Indigenous Peoples and the State: Legal Manipulation and Indian Legislation

Indigenous peoples and communities have been systematically interrupted by the colonizing West. Under colonial influence, Indigenous ways and cultures have been devalued. Many of these travesties are rooted in colonial laws and policies, most notably, the Indian Act. Some Indigenous peoples were also moved to pockets of land called "Indian reserves" to which they never retained official ownership. Then, assimilationist policies were put in place to regulate Indigenous peoples on those "reserves."

Throughout the centuries, people from various European nations enacted laws and policies to establish their authority and decree a self-proclaimed "right" to their settlement on Indigenous land. This chapter outlines the policies and laws that served to uproot and dismantle our peoples and that, at some points, tried to eradicate us altogether.

"Indian Reserves," "Indian Agents," and the "Indian Pass System"

"Indian reserves" are small tracts of land—especially in comparison to traditional Indigenous landscapes—onto which Indigenous peoples were pushed after they signed treaties or entered into other agreements with non-Indigenous settlers and governments. Thus, "reserves" were created over time and through various negotiations and agreements. For example, the Robinson treaties made with the Ojibwa of the northern Great Lakes region in 1850 included a provision for the creation of "reserves."

"Reserves" were later defined in the Indian Act of 1876 as lands "reserved" for Indian use.[1] Note the word "use." Most Indigenous peoples assumed they could keep these lands for their children in perpetuity, but, in fact, according to this piece of legislation, the reserved lands were still considered owned by the Crown, which left Indigenous peoples with no actual land. Instead, they were allowed to live on and use reserved lands, presumably so they would be out of the way of settlers and their colonization efforts.

During land negotiations—such as the Treaty 6 talks—elders assumed that the bargain was for Indigenous peoples to live independently on reserved lands and not be interfered with by the settlers.[2] These lands were not *borrowed* from the Crown for Indigenous peoples to use—as the

Crown declared. This concept did not make sense to elders: How could reserved lands be *borrowed* from the Crown when all land was given by the Creator for Indigenous peoples to use? At the signing of Treaty 6, the elders understood that they could reserve as much land as they wished for "as long as the sun shines." "Here on earth [there's] no two-legged person that's going to break those reserves once you select the site," officials assured them. Yet, just years after Treaty 6 was signed, surveyors came to establish boundaries for "reserves," limiting them to only 160 acres per person (a bit more than the "one square mile for each family of five" that had made its way into the written treaty but less than was expected).[3] And many nations that eventually signed Treaty 6 were resistant to the very idea of reserves.

Pitikwahanapiwiyin (Poundmaker) spoke against reserves at the Treaty 6 negotiations held at Fort Carlton: "The governor mentions how much land is to be given us. . . . This is our land! It isn't a piece of pemmican to be cut off and given in little pieces back to us. It is ours and we will take what we want."[4] Big Bear was also against signing the treaty, and he wanted nothing to do with any kind of reserve. He finally signed in 1882, but didn't chose a reserve until 1885.

Throughout the years, Indigenous peoples were displaced from their original lands to smaller "reserved" tracts of land, which shrunk if non-Indigenous peoples thought these lands were valuable. For example, the Papaschase and Michel nations no longer have the reserves in the Edmonton area that they negotiated under Treaty 6. Euro-Canadian governments and settlers thought that they could simply push Indigenous peoples out of the way, confining them to small tracts of land in the hope that they would be assimilated eventually or die off.

For example, in the early 1900s, European colonists decided they wanted the lush lands in Vancouver's Kitsilano area, yet Salish peoples were residing there and had been for centuries.[5] Colonists did not consider this de facto occupation significant, and the Salish peoples were prompted to move. In fact, the *Salish peoples* were deemed to be *encroaching* on an emerging Euro-Canadian suburban neighbourhood. Indigenous people were moved off their lands to "make room" for colonists' priorities. Another example is the relocation of the Fort St. John Beaver Band after World War II to make the group's land, Indian Reserve 172 (IR 172), available for returning non-Indigenous veterans. After they were relocated, conveniently, oil just happened to be discovered on IR 172.

Usually, Indigenous peoples were pushed onto less desirable pieces of land, as the Europeans hastily snatched up and laid claim to land that was resource rich, lush, productive, and abundant. And even if Indigenous peoples did end up on land with economic potential, they were still at a disadvantage because investors were reluctant to supply capital for projects on land that was not actually owned and therefore could not be pledged as security.

Often colonial agents would maintain that their principal objective for instituting reserves was to urge Indigenous peoples to implement agriculture. However, many Indigenous peoples were moved to lands that were covered in rocks or that had slopes far too sharp for cultivation or soil too poor to grow any crops.[6] In addition, restrictions were put on "Indians'" right to sell agricultural products. These began in the 1880s. For example, a provision in 1888 prohibited the sale of agricultural products by the Indians of the West without the consent of an Indian agent.[7] A statutory amendment of this kind was passed in 1930. Another similar prohibition, applying to all "Indians," was enacted in 1941 and included restrictions on the sale of wild animals and furs. These provisions limiting the sale of "Indian-grown" agricultural products remained unchanged until 1951, hindering the ability of Indigenous peoples to engage fully in agricultural trade.

With the aggressive pursuance of the federal government's nation-building strategy in the late 1870s, Indian policy and administration started to emphasize the social conversion of Indigenous peoples and their communities.[8] Indian agents, first mandated by the Indian Act of 1876, were seen as a mechanism to help move these priorities along. Agents were white, male government officials (with one female exception during World War II) whose duty was to administer the delivery of treaty provisions.[9] Yet they were also given a variety of other powers and responsibilities, including the power to recommend that a chief or council be removed, the authority to impose residential school attendance, the responsibility of limiting traditional customs or practices deemed by the state as "uncivilized," the duty of dispensing rations to individuals defined as in need, the ability to stand in as a justice of the peace when First Nations people violated laws, and the power of asserting control over First Nations people's movement on and off reserves.[10]

The controlling of Indigenous peoples' movement on and off reserve was a policy implemented in certain areas of the Prairies.[11] It was called the "pass system" because First Nations people could not leave the reserve without a pass issued by an Indian agent. The pass system was originally devised for the reserves in Upper Canada after 1828 and was part of the assimilationist schemes at that time. Yet it wasn't until the fear occasioned by the Riel resistance in the Prairies that this system came into its full functioning. In some places, it remained in place as late as the 1930s.

Where this system was in effect, a First Nations person wishing to leave the reserve had to obtain a pass stipulating the duration and purpose of his or her absence and signed by an Indian agent. If a First Nations person was found without a pass or was found to have overstepped the conditions of the pass, she or he would be put into police custody and brought back to the reserve. This system was a direct assault on Indigenous mobility and autonomy. Its aim was racial segregation. Indeed, South African representatives visited western Canada in 1902 to study this pass system, and, eventually, the country created its own version in 1905 as a method of social control for black peoples and a precursor of apartheid.

As this brief history shows, the reserved lands promised to Indigenous peoples, lands that they thought would ensure future generations the ability to maintain cultural, economic, and political autonomy, eventually became prison-like enclosures used to keep "Indians" controlled by and separate from non-Indigenous Canadians. How did this ironic story unfold? A more general understanding of "Indian legislation" is needed if we are to answer this question.

The Origins and Development of Indian Legislation

When the Royal Proclamation and the Treaty of Niagara were entered into in 1763 and 1764, British imperial authorities were assuming ministerial responsibility in Canada. In other words, according to British constitutional tradition, Britain put ministers in place in its territories to advise the sovereign, and these ministers were deemed constitutionally responsible for the conduct and provision of government. So British imperial authorities entered into the 1763 and 1764 agreements. Gradually, however, British colonies in Canada developed their own parliamentary governments and constitutions. In 1841, the Province of Canada was formed from a merger of Lower Canada and Upper Canada, two colonies that had seen legislative councils and assemblies established in 1791. Although still considered a British colony, Nova Scotia, which had established a legislative assembly in 1758, was granted ministerial responsibility in 1848. This responsibility was extended to the Province of Canada the same year and to the colonies of Prince Edward Island in 1851, New Brunswick in 1854, and Newfoundland in 1855.[12] In this way, responsibility for "Indian" affairs started to be transferred from British officials, for example, governors, to representatives of the Canadian British colonies themselves throughout the mid-1800s.

In 1850 and 1851, the first pieces of "Indian" legislation were enacted by a Canadian legislature operating with ministerial responsibility.[13] These acts were passed by the Province of Canada: An Act for the Protection of Indians in Upper Canada from Imposition, and the Property Occupied or Enjoyed by Them from Trespass and Injury (1850) and An Act for the

Better Protection of the Lands and Property of Indians in Lower Canada (1851).[14]

The legislation pertaining to Lower Canada vested all Indian land and property in a commissioner of Indian lands. This commissioner had full control over property, including leasing and the gathering of rents. This statute also offered the first definition of an "Indian." No Indigenous person had input into the creation of this definition, which described as an Indian someone of Indian blood who belonged to a specific band or body of "Indians." First Nations spouses and children, including adopted children, were considered "Indian" by this definition. The following year, this definition was amended (again without any Indigenous input) because the government felt it was too inclusive. The revised law excluded "non-Indian" males married to "Indian" women and "non-Indian" people living among First Nations people.

So began the legislative process of governments classifying and defining Indigenous peoples according to Euro-Canadian interests and cultural judgements. Defining "Indians" meant excluding Métis and Inuit peoples. Definitions were created so as to make it easier for Euro-Canadian governments to attain and achieve power, reach their goals of expansion, and expedite colonization. Essentially "Indians" were not considered real "persons" but rather wards of the government. They could not vote in federal elections and were barred from sitting on juries. It wasn't until 1960 that the right to vote was extended to all Indigenous individuals.

The 1850 legislation pertaining to Upper Canada prohibited anyone but the Crown from dealing with Indian lands. Consent to sell or buy these lands had to be obtained from the Crown. The act also declared that "Indians" were not liable to taxation and exempt from the payment of debts under certain conditions. Though these measures offered a degree of protection, this security, or tutelage (in effect), was considered temporary, a protection of First Nations peoples and lands from abuse until the "Indians" were assimilated, or, as government officials also called it, "civilized."[15]

To forward this "civilizing" mission, the Province of Canada legislated a mechanism by which qualifying "Indians" were able to get full citizenship—if they left being an "Indian" behind. In 1857, the Act to Encourage the Gradual Civilization of the Indian Tribes in the Canadas was passed. This act specified that an adult male "Indian" who was free of debt, of good moral character (as determined by a commission of non-Indigenous examiners), and fluent in either English or French could qualify for enfranchisement.[16] Enfranchisement meant foregoing "Indian status" and becoming part of the larger colonial society, in other words, giving up being "Indian" to become a "person." Any "Indian" man deemed worthy would receive full colonial citizenship as a British subject (including the right to vote), up to 50 acres of land from his reserve, a per capita share of treaty annuities, as well as other band money.

Enfranchisement was to be completely voluntary. At the same time, however, the wife and children of any enfranchised "Indian" man would lose their status and become colonial citizens whether they wanted to or not. Many First Nations peoples strongly opposed this legislation, which they saw as a threat to the integrity of their lands. From 1857 to 1867, only a few First Nations peoples applied for enfranchisement; just *one* person was accepted. To account for the failure of the enfranchisement measure, authorities accused tribal councils of coordinating opposition to it.

In 1860, the Province of Canada (still at that time a British colony) passed the Indian Lands Act by which it assumed responsibility for all Indian affairs from the imperial government.[17] A chief superintendent then became designated as the single official for managing all Indian affairs in the colony. However, after Confederation, when the Province of Canada united with Nova Scotia and New Brunswick to form the new Dominion of Canada, responsibility for the management of "Indians and Indian lands" came under federal control and was completely removed from provincial jurisdiction.[18] This transfer of responsibility was outlined in the 1867 Constitution Act (originally enacted as the British North America Act) under section 91(24).[19] This section affords the federal government absolute jurisdiction and power over "Indians and Lands Reserved for Indians."[20]

In 1869, the Canadian government passed An Act for the Gradual Enfranchisement of Indians, the Better Management of Indian Affairs, and to Extend the Provisions of the Act 31st Victoria.[21] A significant provision in this act made it illegal to sell intoxicating liquors to any First Nations man, woman, or child.

This act also instituted a compulsory enfranchisement provision for First Nations women. Any "Indian" woman who married any "non-Indian" man would "cease to be Indian." The children of such unions would also no longer be considered "Indians." Further assimilationist provisions were also in this act. For example, the act states that no person with "less than one-fourth Indian blood, born after the passing of this Act," would be eligible for or entitled to any share of "Indian" annuities, interests, or rents, once "the Chief or Chiefs of the band or tribe in Council" so specified.[22]

Also significant is that this act was the first to introduce provisions for the election of chiefs and councils. Women were excluded from running for positions and from voting. Chiefs were to be elected by the male members from each "Indian settlement," who were aged 21 and over, and "in such a manner as the Superintendent General of Indian Affairs may direct."

They were to be elected for three years, "unless deposed by the Governor for dishonesty, intemperance, or immorality."[23] These provisions not only put First Nations peoples under the control of Indian Affairs in regards to the administration of their lands but also forced them to take on a foreign system of governance that did not necessarily fit or coincide with their existing ones. Most important, the act did not give any consideration to First Nations people's desires. Rather, it served the interests of the state. Not surprisingly, First Nations peoples were reluctant to obey these new rules. Two years after this new system of electing band councils was put in place, Deputy Superintendent of Indian Affairs William Spragge wrote that this reluctance could be "accounted for from the fact that the Indian mind is in general slow to accept improvements."[24]

The Philosophy and Intent of the Indian Act

In 1876, the Parliament of Canada enacted the Indian Act. This act consolidated all prior federal legislation related to First Nations peoples and centralized the administration of "Indian" lands and laws, placing it under the authority of the "Superintendent of Indian Affairs."[25]

Ultimately, assimilation and control were the main purposes and philosophical underpinnings of the Indian Act. It was initially intended to be a temporary set of laws, in effect only until "Indians" came to be assimilated fully into the body politic. According to sociology professor Cora Voyageur (member of the Athabasca Chipewyan First Nation), the Canadian government enacted the law to fulfil three main functions: "to define who was and was not an Indian, to civilize the Indian, and to manage the Indian people and their lands."[26]

Fixed in paternalism and colonialism, the Indian Act positions First Nations peoples as persons in need of specific regulation. This attitude toward "Indians" is evidenced by the very existence of one set of laws that applies only to First Nations peoples and to no other Canadians. Other evidence exists that Indigenous peoples were viewed as an incompetent population that must be "civilized" through assimilation. Consider the following from the 1876 annual report of the Department of the Interior:

> [O]ur Indian legislation generally rests on the principle, that the aborigines are to be kept in a condition of tutelage and treated as wards or children of the State. The soundness of this principle I cannot admit. On the contrary, I am firmly persuaded that the true interests of the aborigines and of the State alike require that every effort should be made to aid the red man in lifting himself out of his condition of tutelage and dependence, and that is

> clearly our wisdom and our duty, through education and every other means, to prepare him for a higher civilization by encouraging him to assume the privileges and responsibilities of full citizenship.[27]

The Indian Act has undergone several revisions and amendments since its inception in 1876. Between 1878 and World War II, key amendments essentially reinforced assimilation. For example, 1920 amendments required First Nations peoples to seek permits to appear in traditional dress and instituted compulsory enfranchisement at the discretion of a board of examiners and with two years' notice.[28]

In 1951, a series of amendments to the Indian Act lifted some of its most coercive restrictions. At the same time, however, the act retained much of its regulatory demand for assimilation and for the expansion of Euro-Canadian goals. Some of its most egregious provisions can be categorized under the following headings:

- Defining "Indians" out of existence or assimilation through a system of enfranchisement
- Implementing a non-traditional chief and council governance structure and regulating Indigenous lands and reserves
- Implementing "Indian"-specific liquor laws and regulating "Indians'" access to pool halls
- Outlawing "Indian" culture, dancing, and ceremonies

Although the Indian Act expands beyond these listed points, provisions in these categories have been identified as some of the most restrictive and regulatory. They are summarized in the following sections.

Defining "Indians" out of Existence and the System of Enfranchisement

The Indian Act of 1876 continued in the tradition of earlier legislation to use the concept of "Indian status" in defining who was legally an Indian and who was not. It placed a greater weight on patrilineal lineage, including as "Indian" any male with Indian blood who is a member of a specific band. It also specified that any child or wife of that person would also be considered an "Indian." What's more, the act refuted "Indian" status to Métis peoples because such status was only "given" to those who met a certain blood quantum.

The 1876 act also broadened the system of enfranchisement. At various times, the act was amended so First Nations peoples who received a university degree, served in the military, or became a clergyman, lawyer, or doctor were vulnerable to compulsory enfranchisement and the concomitant loss of their status.[29] First Nations women and their children would also still lose their "Indian" status upon marrying a non-status man. Every effort was made by the government to compel "Indians" to give up their status. Those "Indians" who would not be enfranchised were ruled with an iron fist.[30] Between the 1920s and 1940s, some First Nations peoples did, in fact, renounce their status. Typically, they would do so in order to receive the right to attend university, to vote, to receive equal access to veterans' benefits after fighting in a war, to own property, or, in some cases, to be able to simply have a beer after work without being guilty of an offence.

The 1951 revisions to the Indian Act still upheld the government's authority to define who was legally an "Indian" and who was not. However, the criterion of having "Indian blood" was removed and replaced by a system of registration, although a glaring bias toward patrilineal lineage remained. Today, the government still defines who is legally an "Indian" and who is not based on system of registration.

The 1951 revisions also kept enfranchisement in the act. Those who got a university degree or who became a lawyer, doctor, or clergyman would still lose their status. Women with "Indian" status who married a non-status man (including a man who was Métis, a non-status "Indian," Inuit, Native American, or non-Indigenous) would have their status removed. This loss of status extended to any children resultant of such unions. A new compulsory enfranchisement rule was also introduced. Referred to as the "double-mother" rule, it stated that a child with "Indian" status would become automatically enfranchised if that child's mother and grandmother had obtained their status through marriage to a status man.

The compulsory enfranchisement provisions for men remained in the act up until 1961. Changes for women happened in 1985, with the passing of a major set of revisions to the act: Bill C-31, or A Bill to Amend the Indian Act. Several actions led up to this bill, including the *Bédard* and *Lavell* cases brought to the Supreme Court in 1973. Originally, these were separate cases, but they were heard together. In both instances, First Nations women had lost their status through marriage: Jeannette Corbiere Lavell from Wikwemikong on Manitoulin Island and Yvonne Bédard from Six Nations. After a joint appeal, heard in the Supreme Court of Canada and initiated by the Federal Court, the final judgement ruled that Lavell and Bédard were not discriminated against—the marrying out rule in the Indian Act was upheld.[31] However, even though they lost their case, their legal challenge played a role in influencing women's lobby groups to combat sex discrimination under the law.

Another significant action leading up to Bill C-31 was the United Nations Human Rights case brought forth by Maliseet woman Sandra Lovelace. In 1970, Lovelace married a non-Indigenous American man and moved with him to the United States. A few years later, their marriage ended, and she moved back to her home community—the Tobique First Nation. Upon her return, she learned that, because she was a woman, her name had been removed from the Indian Register after she married a non-Indian, and, thus, she was denied her right to education, housing, and health care in her community. Her United Nations Human Rights case was heard by the UN Human Rights Committee in 1981, which decided that Canada was in violation of the International Covenant on Civil and Political Rights. Then, in 1982, the Canadian Charter of Rights and Freedoms was passed, and Bill C-31 came about largely because of its introduction. The Charter stipulated under section 15, that people could no longer be discriminated against because of race, colour, ethnicity, mental or physical disability, or sex. Thus, Bill C-31 was intended to bring the Indian Act in line with the Charter.[32]

In 1985, the Indian Act removed the compulsory enfranchisement of status "Indian" women who married non-status men (status "Indian" men who married non-status women could already maintain their status so were not mentioned in Bill C-31). The double-mother rule was eliminated. Women would no longer gain or lose status resulting from a marriage. Moreover, those who had lost their status in the past due to automatic enfranchisement were allowed to regain it, including children who had lost status as a result of their mother's automatic enfranchisement, as well as those persons who had lost their status as a result of the previous double-mother rule.

Under the 1985 amendment, there is what is called a "two-generation cut-off clause." Status "Indians" are registered within section 6 of the Indian Act. A person must prove that she or he has two parents who have Indian status, and then that person would be registered under section 6 (1).[33] If an individual has only one parent with Indian status, he or she would be registered under section 6 (2). Those individuals registered under section 6 (2) must marry a status "Indian" to pass this status to their children. Even with this amendment, however, the grandchildren of women registered under Bill C-31 face unequal treatment. If an Indigenous woman who had Indian status through Bill C-31 married a non-status man, their children will be registered as having "Indian" status but their grandchildren would not. On the other hand, if an Indigenous man with status married a non-status woman, both their children and their grandchildren would be entitled to status. The law works this way because the children of Bill C-31 women were registered under section 6 (2), so they are only be able to pass their status on if they parented with another status "Indian." But the children of status "Indian" men were registered under section 6 (1), so they can pass their status on no matter with whom they have children. Thus, the second-generation cut-off clause forced those grandchildren from status females who married and had children with non-Indians to give up their status one generation sooner than the grandchildren of male "Indians" who married and had children with non-Indians.

In response to this unequal treatment, Sharon McIvor fought a long court battle. As a result, Bill C-3, or the Gender Equity in Indian Registration Act, was introduced. Bill C-3 received Royal Assent on December 15, 2010, and, on January 21, 2011, it was made law. This bill reinstated status to those denied it on the basis of gender discrimination. However, it was still insufficient, because the legislation is "a patchwork solution to the fundamentally flawed provisions dealing with status and citizenship in Indigenous communities."[34] Given this incomplete remedy, McIvor applied to have her case heard in the Supreme Court of Canada. She was denied this request and has since approached the United Nations.[35]

Although Canada has made changes to address sex discrimination, Indigenous women and their descendants are still assigned to inferior categories of status by the Indian Act. Furthermore, although there has also been a shift from blood quantum definitions of "Indian" status to a system of registration, this system is still rooted in the sexist and racist values of the past, which consider paternal lineage and the quantity of Indigenous blood to be the main determiners of "Indian" status. There is no reference to any other aspect of identity to make this distinction.

The system of registration still operates so as to define Indigenous peoples out of existence. According to Thomas King, about 50 per cent of status "Indians" are marrying peoples without status.[36] Citing two leading Indigenous scholars, John Borrows and Leroy Little Bear, King asserts that, if such a rate holds steady, in 50 to 75 years, status "Indians" will cease to exist in Canada—meaning that there will be a dilution of status over time. The treaties will still be there, and so will treaty land, which is to be "held in trust for status Indians by the government." Yet, as King contends "We just won't have any Indians . . . legally, that is."[37]

Similarly, Mi'kmaq lawyer and professor Pamela Palmater explains, "eventually, according to current demographic studies, all Indians will be legislated out of existence, as will their communities. Bill C-3 will only delay this process by one generation, and only for a limited group of reinstatees."[38] According to Palmater, the goal of government policy has always been the same:

> What is happening now is a legislated form of population reduction based on the previous goal of assimilation . . . [and it aims] to reduce the number

> of people the government must be accountable to in terms of protection, treaty obligations, land rights, self-government, and other Aboriginal rights, including a whole series of culturally specific programs and services that are provided today. . . . [The] historical record shows clearly that cost reduction is the ultimate objective.[39]

Thus, the Indian Act was specifically set up by governments in an attempt to eliminate Indigenous peoples in Canada, detach women from communities, and acquire Indigenous land. These policies and strategies were not implemented by accident but rather as a way to advance the Euro-Canadian government's continuing colonial agenda.

Chief and Band Council Structure: The Prohibition of Hereditary Leadership and an Assault on Indigenous Lands

The 1876 Indian Act maintained the elected chief and council structure that had replaced traditional forms of governance with government-imposed ones. Furthermore, the superintendent general could order a reserve to be surveyed and divided up into lots. Individual band members would then be obligated to get tickets for separate sections of the land. The purpose of this provision was to force First Nations peoples to operate according to a system of individual property ownership, thus coercing First Nations away from communal ways of sharing lands.

What constituted a "band" or a "reserve" was also defined.[40] According to the act, a band is a body of Indians for whose use and benefit in common lands and legal title to them are vested in the Crown. A reserve was defined as a tract of land—the legal title of which is vested in the Crown—that "Indians" had the right to use. This 1876 Indian Act also included some protections. No First Nation property could be seized for debt or have a lien placed on it. There was no taxation on real estate or of individual personal property on reserves. Only an "Indian" of the band having a right to an Indian reserve was allowed to live on it without obtaining a licence from the superintendent general.

Yet the Indian Act was used continually to terminate traditional Indigenous ways of living. In the early 1900s, policymakers started to think that living on reserves might discourage enfranchisement and promote traditional ways of life that the government was trying so hard to eradicate. Thus, essentially, an "assault" on reserve lands arose.

In 1905, an amendment allowed First Nation peoples to be removed from reserves that were next to or partially within a town having more than 8,000 residents. In 1911, a further amendment permitted municipalities and companies to seize portions of reserves—expropriate them without First Nation surrender—to be used for railway construction, road construction, or other public works. Another 1911 amendment allowed judges to move whole reserves away from municipalities without band consent, if doing so was considered in the best interest and practical. Of course, questions of what was in the best interest were determined according to Euro-Canadian definitions of growth and economic development.[41]

In 1918, an amendment allowed for the superintendent general to lease out uncultivated reserve land to non-Indigenous peoples, so they could gain revenue through farming or pasture.[42] All of these measures eroded (and sometimes eliminated) First Nation control over the reserved lands. They were also all justified in terms of progress, as being in the best interest of the country. Officials argued that such provisions were good for the advancement of economic growth.[43]

In 1920, the Indian Act was amended to permit the Department of Indian Affairs to prohibit "Indian bands" from following traditional hereditary leadership. In 1936, an amendment permitted Indian agents to lead band council meetings and to cast the deciding vote in the case of a tie. Because of these provisions, band councils no longer had full authority, even over their own internal political affairs. Power ultimately rested with Euro-Canadian governments, as all band council judgements, rulings, or changes put through were subject to a final authorization from the government department charged with overseeing Indian affairs.[44] The authority of band councils was superficial; they had no sizeable or significant power.

With the 1951 Indian Act amendments, First Nation peoples were finally considered citizens and gained the ability to pursue land claims. Women, who had never been allowed to vote in band elections before, gained this right (if they had status). However, the general (and non-traditional) governance structure on reserves remained the same after 1951, although band councils have acquired more powers of self-government over the years. Today, they enact their own by-laws (as long as these are consistent with the Indian Act). But First Nations peoples have not used this power to make by-laws to any large extent (with the exception of taxation by-laws, which are being passed more frequently today).[45] There are numerous explanations for First Nations reluctance to pass by-laws:

- First Nations must submit the by-laws to the federal minister, who can disallow a by-law.
- The by-law making power is formalistic and derived from the Indian Act, making it unpalatable for First Nation use.

- Most First Nation communities do not have any way of enforcing the by-laws.
- Perhaps most significantly, many First Nations have politically rejected the Indian Act as a tool for effective self-governance.[46]

Ultimately, by-law powers do not represent true self-government because they are based on the forms of governance compelled by the Indian Act rather than on the inherent rights of First Nations peoples. A number of First Nation communities strongly oppose the "governing structure imposed by the Indian Act." For example, many people of the Six Nations of the Grand River "refuse to vote in Indian Act elections, and the traditional Haudenosaunee Confederacy has a strong following."[47]

"Indian"-Specific Liquor Laws and Regulating Pool Hall Entry

The 1876 act also consolidated all laws regarding "Indians" and liquor. So, after its passage, nobody ("Indian" or otherwise) was permitted to sell liquor to a status "Indian."[48] Any "Indian" found in a state of intoxication would be imprisoned until sober and, if convicted of the offence of being intoxicated, liable to be locked up for a period not exceeding a month. Another 14 days could be added to this sentence if the convicted individual did not tell who had provided the liquor. The act also came to ban the simple possession of liquor by an "Indian" on a reserve.

In 1930, the Indian Act was amended to forbid pool hall owners from permitting entrance to an "Indian" who "by inordinate frequenting of a pool room either on or off an Indian reserve misspends or wastes his time or means to the detriment of himself, his family or household." An owner caught allowing these excesses could face a fine or a one-month jail term.

In 1951, amendments to the Indian Act finally allowed status "Indians" to enter pool halls, and there were also changes to laws relating to "Indians" and liquor. Status "Indians" were now given permission to drink in licenced bars in accordance with provincial laws, but no one was allowed to take liquor on to a reserve. However, a stipulation was added that "Indians" were not allowed to have intoxicants in their possession or be "intoxicated" off of a reserve.

The stipulation against being "intoxicated" off-reserve finally fell into disuse as a result of a 1970 case known as the "*Drybones* case." In 1969, Joseph Drybones was arrested for being intoxicated in a Yellowknife hotel lobby—off of a reserve. Yet, at this time, there were no reserves in the Northwest Territories. Drybones fought this case through to the Supreme Court of Canada, where he won. The judge found the police discriminated against him because of his race under the Canadian Bill of Rights (enacted in 1960). With the passing of Bill C-31 in 1985, any substantive provisions in the Indian Act relating to liquor were finally repealed (now it rests with the band councils to set by-laws relevant to this issue).

Outlawing "Indian" Culture, Dancing, and Ceremonies

From 1884 to 1951, the Indian Act outlawed the ceremony known as the "potlatch" and the traditional sacred dance known as the "Tamanawas."[49] Those found to be engaging in these ceremonies or dances would be liable to imprisonment. By banning the potlatch, the government eliminated a cultural practice central to the identity of some West Coast peoples. Elaborate and multifaceted, it was, and still is, a significant ceremony that utilizes traditional longhouses and validates the heritage, value systems, and social organization of many West Coast Indigenous peoples.[50] After the potlatch became illegal, First Nation peoples were forced to take its practice underground. On more than one instance, elders were arrested and imprisoned for partaking in a potlatch. Without a doubt, this legislation attacked the cultural foundations of many First Nations and disrupted their customs and laws. One reason the government outlawed the potlatch was that it involved generous gift giving. Governments viewed this ceremonial gift giving as too radical, perhaps even communist, and thus in contradiction to the Euro-Canadian principles of private property that they were trying to encourage at the time.[51]

In 1914, an amendment made it mandatory for "Indians" living in the West to obtain authorization before appearing in what the government declared was a "costume" (more properly called regalia) or taking part in any "dance, show, expedition, stampede or pageant." Indeed, Euro-Canadians of the early twentieth century seemed to approach the sacred and significant ceremonies of Indigenous peoples with either disdain or paternalistic indulgence. In 1921, for example, Duncan Campbell Scott, deputy superintendent of the Department of Indian Affairs from 1913–32, showed his contempt for Indigenous cultural practices. As he wrote to Indian Commissioner William Morris Graham, "It has always been clear to me that the Indians must have some sort of recreation, and if our agents would endeavor to substitute reasonable amusements for this senseless drumming and dancing, it would be a great assistance."[52]

In 1927, the Indian Act became even more restrictive in its exclusion of Indigenous traditions and dances, as outlined in section 140(3): "Any Indian in the province of Manitoba, Saskatchewan, Alberta, or British Columbia, or in the Territories who participates in any Indian dance outside the bounds of his own reserve, or who participates in any show, expedition, performance, stampede or pageant in aboriginal costume without the consent of the Superintendent General or his authorized agent, and any person who induces or employs any Indian to take part in such dance, show, exhibition, performance, stampede or pageant, or induces any Indian to leave his reserve or employs any Indian for such a purpose, whether the dance, show, expedition, stampede or pageant has taken place or not, shall on summary conviction be liable to a penalty not exceeding twenty-five dollars, or to imprisonment for one month, or to both penalty and imprisonment."[53]

Once again, after the 1951 revisions to the Indian Act, potlatches and other Indigenous ceremonies were no longer illegal. First Nation peoples were also now allowed to wear traditional "costumes" (regalia) at public dances, exhibitions, and stampedes.

Scrap the Act?: The White and Red Papers

We still have the Indian Act today. It still gives to the federal government (the Crown) final legislative authority over all reserve land. It still defines who is legally "Indian" according to a convoluted formula papering over the cracks that continue to arise from the legislation's sexist and racist origins. Having this separate set of laws to govern a specific group of peoples sends powerful ideological messages. For example, it implies that Indigenous peoples are inferior because they must be regulated by special laws. It implies that they might be morally insufficient or flawed and thus in need of special regulation.

There is no doubt that the Indian Act remains a very controversial piece of legislation. Today, the law is predominantly the version that emerged after the 1951 revisions, although amendments are still enacted. Amnesty International, the United Nations, and the Canadian Human Rights Commission have all continued to criticize the Indian Act for infringing on human rights. However, despite the controversy surrounding this act, it is historically and legally significant. It is a piece of legislation affirming that First Nation peoples do have some rights. The present act and its predecessors are also markers of a discriminatory history—a reminder of the unequal treatment Indigenous peoples faced and still face today.

In 1969, Prime Minister Pierre Trudeau's government issued a "White Paper" on "Indian" policy that advocated putting those with Indian status on an equal footing with other Canadian citizens and, over a short time, abandoning the Indian Act and all the First Nation rights it guaranteed. For Trudeau's Liberal government of the late 1960s and, undeniably, for many Canadians, the 1969 White Paper embodied a just political vision of Canada and a practical resolution to the century-old "Indian problem." [54] However, this infamous policy initiative reveals itself as a low point in the political relationship between Indigenous peoples and the Canadian state.

Operating from the principle that rights accrue to individuals rather than to communities or nations, Indian Affairs Minister Jean Chrétien and his deputy John MacDonald sought to convince Canadians to consider the White Paper's proposals, which they purported would make Canada an improved and fairer nation for all citizens. It was obvious that something had to be done to address the inequities that continued to exist, they argued. The two-volume Hawthorn Report published in 1966–67, which surveyed the circumstances of "Indians" in Canada, revealed them to be the country's most disadvantaged and marginalized population. The government's answer was, basically, to repeal what it called "discriminatory" legislation and stop regulating "Indians" and "Indian" affairs. To this end, Trudeau and his government argued that Canada should eliminate Indian status, disband the Department of Indian Affairs within five years, convert reserve land to private property, integrate services provided to First Nation peoples with those provided to other Canadian citizens, and address existing land claims but no longer negotiate further treaties. Treaties were considered to be agreements between two sovereign nations, and, according to Trudeau and other government officials of the time, Indigenous peoples no longer comprised their own sovereign nations.

Yet for many Indigenous peoples, First Nations were and would remain sovereign, and this White Paper was an additional display of Euro-Canadian colonialism. Its plans were a deliberate effort by the federal government to "get out of the Indian business" and close the political landscape by unilaterally enacting Indigenous peoples out of existence—it was extermination as an act of so-called justice. These conflicting interpretations require closer scrutiny.

The 1969 White Paper was written primarily by Minister of Indian Affairs Jean Chrétien. It was 13 pages in total. As mentioned, its main tenant was assimilation. How interesting, then, that its introduction focuses so strongly on difference. Here is how it reads: "To be Indian is to be a man, with all a man's needs and abilities. To be an Indian is also to be different. It is to speak different languages, draw different pictures, tell different tales and to rely on a set of values developed in a different world."[55] Professor of government and Native American studies Dale Turner (member of the Temagami First Nation) argues that the term "different" is stressed so as to imply that, although "Indians" are part of humanity, they are different, separate from it in significant ways.[56]

After this initial emphasis on difference, the White Paper turns to how to effect sameness, in other words, how to assimilate First Nation peoples.

Its answer is to repeal the Indian Act and to have the governments of the provinces take over responsibility for "Indians" from the federal government: "Services must . . . come through the same channels and from the same government agencies for all Canadians."[57] This transfer of responsibility away from the federal government was not only an assimilationist mechanism but also an attempt to offset the increasing costs of running the Department of Indian Affairs.

Treaty agreements were largely under-acknowledged in the White Paper. Consider the following, for example: "The terms and effects of the treaties between the Indian people and the Government are widely misunderstood. A plain reading of the words used in the treaties reveals the limited and minimal promises which were included in them."[58] Clearly, the document takes a very literal "plain reading" and interpretation of the treaties. Wampum belts and oral traditions, indeed, Indigenous perspectives and interpretations in general, are not even acknowledged in the White Paper.

In terms of the reserve system, the White Paper proposes to grant ownership of these lands to bands yet explains that "full ownership implies many things," including the obligation to "accept taxation the way other Canadians do" and to "pay for certain services. Essentially, the White Paper contends that "Indians" should be "welcomed" into mainstream Canadian society (and celebrated) and that people recognized as having "Indian status" should be offered the full benefits and responsibilities that come with citizenship.[59]

Yet what would come with these "full benefits"? It was nothing less than a revoking of any Indian rights and status.[60]

Indigenous people and organizations and supporters overwhelmingly rejected the White Paper. Indeed, the policy document became an important stimulus of Indigenous activism. The newly formed National Indian Brotherhood (the Assembly of First Nations today) became a very vocal proponent of First Nation rights. Indigenous women and their organizations started to speak out publicly against the discriminatory aspects of the Indian Act.[61] Harold Cardinal, a Cree lawyer and scholar who headed up the Indian Association of Alberta, published a book in 1969 entitled *The Unjust Society*, which countered Prime Minister Trudeau's claim that Canada was a "just society."[62] Cardinal also helped draft the "Red Paper" entitled *Citizens Plus*, which was a direct response to the White Paper.

The title *Citizens Plus* came from the Hawthorn Report, which was commissioned by the federal government in 1963 and, upon publication in 1966–67, officially called *A Survey of the Contemporary Indians of Canada: Economic, Political, Educational Needs and Policies*. In it, University of British Columbia anthropologist Harry B. Hawthorn, who directed the survey, outlined how "Indian" peoples in Canada were among the most marginalized, deprived, and poorest peoples in the country. He explained that they were essentially "citizens minus," due to failed government policy; he highlighted in particular the disastrous residential schools policy.[63] Thus, Hawthorn recommended that "Indians" be considered "citizens plus" and provided with resources, opportunities, and authority over their own lives and affairs. The report stated that, as "citizens plus," "Indians" have "in addition to the normal rights and duties of citizenship, . . . certain additional rights as charter members of the Canadian community."[64] Alan Cairns, one of the authors of the first volume of the Hawthorn Report, explained the meaning of "citizens plus" in this way:

> By "plus" we referred to ongoing entitlements, some of which flowed from existing treaties, while others were to be worked out in the political processes of the future, which would identify Indian peoples as deserving possessors of an additional category of rights based on historical priority. In other words, we sought to preserve "difference" while simultaneously supporting a common citizenship as a basis for empathy and solidarity between the Indian people and the majority population.[65]

The document *Citizens Plus* prepared under Cardinal's leadership was presented by the Indian Chiefs of Alberta to the federal government in 1970. More widely referred to as the Red Paper, it countered all the proposals of the White Paper. Its authors state their overall view of the White Paper in the first paragraph of the preamble:

> We have studied carefully the contents of the Government White Paper on Indians and we have concluded that it offers despair instead of hope. Under the guise of land ownership, the government has devised a scheme whereby within a generation or shortly after the proposed Indian Lands Act expires our people would be left with no land and consequently the future generation would be condemned to the despair and ugly spectre of urban poverty in ghettos.[66]

Ultimately, citing widespread protest, the government officially withdrew the White Paper in the spring of 1970. The attitude of Prime Minister Trudeau and his government did not shift, however, until after the Supreme Court gave support to the concept of Aboriginal title in its ruling on the *Calder* case in 1973. In 1969, Trudeau famously stated the view that the Nisga'a's claims to Aboriginal title were little more than make-believe because they were not based on treaties: "We can't recognize Aboriginal rights because no society can be built on historical 'might have beens.'"[67] In a television interview in March 1970, he responded to the Red Paper by saying, "We'll keep them in the ghetto as long as they want."[68] It was not until the Supreme Court divided evenly on the question of whether Aboriginal title had been extinguished prior to Confederation that Trudeau observed to Nisga'a representatives, "Maybe you have more rights than we thought you did."[69] In 2014, at its biennial convention in Montreal, the Liberal Party of Canada finally acknowledged the White Paper of 1969 as the mistake it was.

Discussion Questions

1) How and in what ways have Indigenous peoples been racially segregated in Canada?
2) Consider race-based crimes. How and in what ways have Canadian governments committed race-based crimes against Indigenous peoples?
3) Why was the potlatch so threatening to the government? What does the potlatch encourage, and, in contrast, what does private property ownership encourage?
4) Consider the "Indian"-specific laws and policies put in place in Canada. How might these regulatory and restrictive types of laws negatively affect Indigenous peoples?

Activities

1) Watch the second episode of CBC's 2012 documentary series *The 8th Fire*, "It's Time" (available online at cbc.ca/8thfire). Reflect on the policies and restrictions placed on First Nations peoples through the Indian Act. Why might it be important to be aware of such policies? Why do you think it is that not everyone in Canada is aware of the Indian Act? Compare the before and after reactions and viewpoints of the non-Indigenous people shown in the video who took the Indigenous awareness training in Saskatoon (the steel worker and farmer). Do you think if Canadians are taught true history, viewpoints might possibly change?
2) Examine the current Indian Act as it stands today (available online at http://laws-lois.justice.gc.ca). Create art visuals that seek to expose the racism, realities, and various discriminatory aspects of the act.

Recommended Readings

Cardinal, Harold. *The Unjust Society*. Vancouver: Douglas & McIntyre, 1999.

Palmater, Pamela D. *Beyond Blood: Rethinking Indigenous Identity*. Saskatoon, SK: Purich Publishing, 2011.

7

The Impact of Assimilation: Residential Schools and Intergenerational Trauma

MANY GOVERNMENT POLICIES SOUGHT to maintain or extend control and domination over Indigenous peoples, not only by taking land but also by subjugating Indigenous peoples to European Christian religions and culture. Perhaps the most devastating of these measures of forced assimilation, however, was the policy of taking children away from their parents and First Nation communities and putting children in residential schools. This chapter outlines the beginnings, function, purpose, realties, and aftermath of residential schools.

The Davin Report

On January 28, 1879, Prime Minister Sir John A. Macdonald, one of the "Fathers of Confederation," commissioned Nicholas Flood Davin (a conservative MP from Regina) to investigate the industrial schools established for Indigenous peoples in the United States and to write a report on what Macdonald saw as a problem—"Indians."[1] In 1879, the "Davin Report," officially entitled *Report on Industrial Schools for Indians and Half-Breeds*, was complete. The report's solution to what the government viewed as the "Indian problem" was to focus on training Indigenous children in boarding schools; as it stated, children were to be taken away "from the influence of the wigwam."[2] The report declared that not much could be done in terms of "civilizing" Indigenous adults, as, according to Davin, they were incapable of learning and had traditions of their own, "which make civilization a puzzle of despair."[3] Indigenous children, however, could be schooled and trained to become like non-Indians. As Davin states, ". . . if anything is to be done with the Indian, we must catch him very young."[4] Residential schools, then, were seen as the way of "catching Indians" when they were young enough to "civilize."

Davin looked to the United States for his ideas, especially to the policy of "aggressive civilization," which was intended to encourage Indigenous peoples to take up American citizenship and abandon their tribal affiliations.[5] The industrial boarding school was a principle feature of this policy because it forced total immersion in what was considered "civilizing" education, which was thought more effective than more usual schooling: "The experience of the United States is the same as our own as far as the Indian is concerned. . . . The child . . . who goes to a day school learns little, and what little he learns is soon forgotten, while his tastes are fashioned at home, and his inherited aversion to toil is in no way combated."[6] Davin was particularly impressed by the total assimilation approach being practiced at the United States Indian Industrial School in Carlisle, Pennsylvania, which was the first residential school for "Indians" in the United States.[7]

The architect of the American residential school system was Richard Henry Pratt, an officer in the United States Army.[8] In 1875, Pratt was given responsibility for transporting a group of Indigenous prisoners, who had been captured during the Plains Wars, to Fort Marion in St. Augustine, Florida.[9] Upon arriving at the fort, which had been turned into a jail earlier that year, Pratt supervised these prisoners of war. Pratt's objective at Fort Marion "was to encourage the rapid assimilation of the Indians."[10]

The Fort Marion prisoners were released in 1878, but Pratt persuaded the Indian Office to allow him to send 17 of his former Indigenous prisoners to the Hampton Normal and Agricultural Institute in Virginia, established after the Civil War to provide education to former black slaves.[11] Here "Pratt began his educational career."[12] Arguing that the 200 years of contact between "the negro" and "Anglo-Saxons" had made the African American "fitted as a fellow citizen," he undertook to transform Indigenous peoples in a similar fashion. As Pratt stated,

> If millions of black savages can become so transformed and assimilated, and, if annually hundreds of thousands of foreign emigrants from all lands can also become Anglicized, Americanized, assimilated, and absorbed through association, there is but one plain duty resting on us with regard to Indians, and that is to relieve them of their savagery.[13]

It was Pratt's belief that Indigenous peoples could become progressive members of the population through the kind of education that removed them from their communities and transplanted them into an "Anglo-Saxon" environment, which would work to "civilize" them. They would have to be torn from their cultural roots and forced to learn English.[14] Under Pratt's influence, the stated objective of the United States government became this: "Kill the Indian. Save the Man."[15]

Non-Indigenous peoples looked to Pratt as a visionary because his idea of assimilation, as opposed to extermination, seemed more benign.[16] In 1879, Pratt petitioned the federal government for a separate school for "Indians" because he was concerned that educating "Indians" and African American peoples together would link "Indians" and blacks together in the public mind, and he did not want this to happen as his goal was for "Indians" to be assimilated into white society.[17] After Pratt's successful petition, the first American residential school opened in Carlisle, Pennsylvania, in November 1879.[18] Indigenous children sent to this school endured assimilative measures instantly upon arrival. They were bathed and deloused like new recruits to the army; their Indigenous clothing and blankets were replaced. Children were allowed to speak only English. Children's long hair was cut.[19] Obedience to the rules was strictly enforced, and punishment was used for any violations. Those who followed these rules would be given rank and be promoted.[20]

Homesickness and serious illnesses were also problems at Carlisle. Today there are more than 175 children's tombstones in the school's cemetery. In addition, many children's bodies were sent home for burial. Indigenous students were ravaged by disease at the government boarding schools; tuberculosis, pneumonia, and trachoma were the greatest threats. Today, Carlisle and the "Indian" boarding school policy it initiated are seen as part of an attempt to eliminate all that is uniquely Indigenous—as genocide.

Nevertheless, the US model of the industrial Indian residential boarding school was adopted under Prime Minister Macdonald, following the advice of Davin. And the Canadian residential schools copied some of the most damaging and cruellest parts of this American model, including severe punishment and correction, the obliteration of Indigenous children's identities, and the denigration of Indigenous languages and cultures.[21] Although not part of the official model, another crime was reproduced in practice—routine sexual and physical abuse.

Residential Schools

Residential schools were in operation in Canada from 1831 until the close of the final federally run school in 1996.[22] The first school was the Mohawk Institute, which began operating as a boarding school for boys from Six Nations in 1831 in Brantford, Ontario.[23]

Over the nineteenth century, these early church-supported and run boarding schools became incorporated into the broader residential school system that was part of Canadian federal policy. The federal government, which had opened its own residential schools in the 1850s, officially entered into a partnership with the churches running schools and formalized the funding of the whole system through an order in council in 1892. After this agreement, the number of schools grew substantially. Located from coast to coast, these schools affected, and still affect, the lives of First Nations, Métis, and Inuit people throughout Canada. In 1931, the schools reached their peak with over 80 in operation throughout Canada.[24] Seven generations of children attended these schools.[25]

In 1920, the federal government made it mandatory for all Indigenous children between the ages of 7 and 15 to attend school; although this new amendment to the Indian Act did not mean compulsory attendance at residential schools—because more First Nations children attended day schools than residential schools until the 1944–45 school year, when the pattern was reversed—it did mean that authorities could compel attendance at residential schools when there were no other educational options.[26] Parents who refused to send their children to school were threatened with fines or imprisonment.[27] Given that "Indians" were not "persons" under the law but wards of the government until the 1960s, Indigenous parents had no rights to challenge the orders given to their families and communities when their children were being taken. Indeed, Indigenous adults had legal rights comparable to those of children themselves and were not even considered to be Canadian citizens.[28]

The immensity of the atrocities that took places in these schools is too big to be explained in the small confines of a book. Authorities took children by force from families and put them in residential schools where they were forced to stay for about 10 months of every year.[29] During their stay, they were denied communication with their families, so as not to be influenced by their traditional culture. Many schools were far from student's homes, so students could not travel back to their families or have any access to their traditional practices. For example, the annual report of the Department of Indian Affairs for the year ending 1889 documents that authorities thought it was a "danger" to have Indigenous children "under the influence of their homes," and, quoting an earlier report, R. E. Robillard, Indian agent for Manitoba and the North-West Territories, reiterates his promise of "making strong efforts, without, of course, being too precipitate, to stop pupils visiting reserves during their course of training, and to discourage parents and relatives from going to see the pupils at the schools too frequently."[30] On March 9, 1893, Minister of the Interior Thomas Mayne Daly reported that the schools are located by design at places far from the reserves "because it is found in practice, that unless these children are taken from the reserve a sufficient distance to remove them from the influence of their parents, the work of the schools will go for nothing."[31]

The alleged function of these schools was to provide education to Indigenous children. Other functions and purposes have been now revealed. All of the schools mandated the learning and adoption of the Christian religion. Many Indigenous pupils were falsely taught that their culture was the way of the devil. Some were threatened with going to hell if they continued to practice their traditional culture. Barbara-Helen Hill (from Six Nations of the Grand River Territory) uses the term "churchianity" to reference this forced indoctrination of Christian values because, as she explains, Christian teachings are not necessarily wrong but the church's interpretation of these teachings was destructive, as was the imposition of them.[32] English and French language was also forced upon children, and speaking in one's traditional language was forbidden. Most other "educational" activities were centred on industrial education aimed at preparing students for life in the "lower fringes of the dominant society."[33]

Immediately upon attending the schools, children would be assigned a number and their traditional names would be replaced by English or French names.[34] Traditional long hair or braids would be cut short or shaved off. Traditional clothing was confiscated and replaced by standard issued uniforms. Sacred regalia and objects were burned.

Many children suffered emotional, physical, and sexual abuses. Indeed, sexual abuse in residential schools has been found to have reached epidemic levels.[35] For example, in 1990, Special Advisor to the Minister of National Health and Welfare on Child Sexual Abuse Rix Rogers declared that ". . . closer scrutiny of past treatment of Native children at Indian residential schools would show 100% of children at some schools were sexually abused."[36] Suzanne Fournier and Ernie Crey (Sisaqiweltel) describe the experience of Emily Rice, who had left Kuper Island Residential School at the age of 11 in 1959:

> She had been repeatedly assaulted and sexually abused by Father Jackson and three other priests, one of whom plied her with alcohol before raping her. A nun, Sister Mary Margaret, known for peeping at girls in the shower and grabbing their breasts, was infuriated when Emily resisted her advances. "She took a big stick with bark on it, and rammed it right inside my vagina," recalls Rice . . . in the years that followed, Emily would have to twice undergo reconstructive vaginal surgery, and she suffered permanent hearing loss.[37]

Children also faced severe sanctions for breaking the strict rules imposed upon them.[38]

For example, if children spoke their Indigenous language, they could be whipped publically, given lashes or beaten, or forcibly confined for days. Another torture for this infraction was to have needles stuck through children's tongues; the needles were often left in place for extended periods. For wetting the bed, a child could be forced to take his or her pants down in front of peers so as to receive a vicious lashing. Other punishments for bedwetting included forcing children to wear diapers or their soiled clothing.

Some children would be shamed continually and called names such as "heathen" and "savage." Some children were beaten into unconsciousness and to the point of receiving serious permanent injuries, including broken limbs, fractured skulls, and shattered eardrums. Indigenous parents complained officially about the injuries their children received at Rupert's Land Industrial School near Selkirk, Manitoba, for instance, as Fournier and Crey explain:

> Young girls of eight or nine still bore bruises on their bodies several weeks after being strapped, they said. During an investigation, the Anglican principle admitted he fed the children rancid butter and crept into the dormitories at night to kiss the little girls, but he was reprimanded, not removed.[39]

Even further atrocities were forced upon other children in residential schools. Some were used in pedophile rings organized by the clergy, police, and business and government officials.[40] Female children who had been impregnated by men in authority were forced to have abortions, and some were also involuntarily sterilized. Former students revealed that some of the schools had unmarked graveyards where murdered babies were buried, babies that had been born to Indigenous girls raped by priests and other church officials. To date, thousands of survivors have given testimony about these atrocities.[41] For example, in a CBC interview in July 2008, survivor Irene Favel explains how she witnessed a baby being murdered by the staff at the Muskowekwan Indian Residential School in Lestock, Saskatchewan. The baby was put into an oven and burned to death.

Even residential schools that tried to offer what was considered at the time to be a good education for "Indians" could end up harming Indigenous children physically. Tensions always arose between keeping up standards and keeping costs down. Consequently, school buildings were often in poor condition, having been built with the cheapest materials and designs. There were reports of poor ventilation and overcrowding and unmet safety regulations, such as having inadequate safety equipment and fire escapes.[42] Government inspectors of these schools repeatedly recommended improvements and, often times, closures. For example, an inspector in 1953 described raw sewage seeping into the boys' recreation room and almost to the level of the floor in the girls' recreation room. His letter states that "the smell in the building was unbearable and no human being should be asked to live under such conditions." His conclusion was that the "school should be closed."[43]

The poor sanitary conditions of many of the schools fuelled the high rates of disease that also plagued the schools.[44] Overcrowding worsened the problem and often led to tuberculosis (TB) epidemics. For example, in File Hills Industrial School in Saskatchewan, 69 per cent of students died of TB in one decade at the turn of the century. At Upker Island, Indian Affairs' own files revealed that an estimated 40 per cent of children died before they were able to make it back home.

A 1907 report by Peter Henderson Bryce, chief medical officer for the Department of Indian Affairs, outlines the conditions he found at the 35 different residential schools in the Prairies that he inspected.[45] He reports "the defective sanitary condition of many schools, especially in the matter of ventilation, have been the *foci* from which disease, especially tubercular, has spread, whether through direct infection, from person to person, or indirectly through the infected dust of floors, school-rooms and dormitories."[46] The report further indicated the large number of deaths due to tuberculosis. For instance, he cites that, out of the 1,537 students he reported upon, "nearly 25 per cent are dead," and "of one school with an absolutely accurate statement, 69 per cent of ex-pupils are dead," indicating "that everywhere the almost invariable cause of death given is tuberculosis."[47] He also documents the experiences of students kept in dormitory rooms without proper ventilation during winter months "in order to save fuel and maintain warmth"; sometimes they remained in these rooms for 10 continuous hours, whereby they would be exposed to polluted air that was "extremely inadequate."[48] As a result of these findings, Bryce sent a number of recommendations to the Canadian government calling for immediate action to address these health concerns, which were causing the deaths of many children. Yet the Canadian government largely ignored Bryce's calls for action; his report was shelved, and children continued to die. The government failed to implement his recommendations, dismissed him from federal service in 1921, and undermined his credibility.[49]

Many children also went hungry in residential schools, which contributed to the death toll. A young boy attending Onion Lake Residential School wrote to his parents about the problem during Christmas of 1953: "I am always hungry. We only get two slices of bread and one plate of porridge." John Milloy's extensive research on residential schools identified hunger as a "continual and systemic problem."[50]

In the 1940s and 1950s, nutritional experiments were conducted on Indigenous peoples by various "experts," scientists, and government bureaucrats "who exploited their 'discovery' of malnutrition in Indigenous communities and residential schools."[51] Historian Ian Mosby documents the most ambitious and well known of these nutritional experiments—the James Bay survey of peoples from the Attawapiskat and Rupert's House Cree First Nations conducted from 1947 to 1948—but he also outlines experiments that received practically no attention until his 2013 article. These include two separate long-term studies undertaken on peoples of the Norway House and Cross Lake First Nations in northern Manitoba, as well as experiments conducted over a five-year period at six residential schools across Canada: "the Alberni School in Port Alberni, British Columbia; the St. Mary's and Cecilia Jeffrey schools in Kenora, Ontario; the Shubenacadie school in Shubenacadie, Nova Scotia; and the St. Paul's and Blood schools in Southern Alberta near Lethbridge."[52]

Framed as "benevolent administration" and "charity" by government administrators and scientists, these nutritional experiments were often conducted without the informed consent or knowledge of those involved.[53] Mosby argues that "during the war and early postwar period" people "increasingly came to view Aboriginal bodies as 'experimental materials' and residential schools and Aboriginal communities as kinds of 'laboratories.'" Many experiments involved dividing research "subjects" into experimental and control groups and keeping the control group at a normal diet, which meant underfed or malnourished, while giving the experimental group vitamins or certain foods or flour enriched with vitamins or minerals. All the children at St. Paul's school were selected as a "control" group, and no changes were made to the food children received, the initial investigation of this school having shown that students were inadequately fed and in need of vitamins. In other words, each child at this school was deliberately kept malnourished for the purpose of the experiment, as happened with those in the control groups at other residential schools or First Nations communities.

At the residential schools under study, students were not provided with dental care and were denied the use of sodium fluoride because scientists worried that providing adequate dental care would interfere with study results. Regular physical examinations were conducted on students in the study, which Mosby notes as being possibly "confusing, painful, and potentially traumatic."[54] Mosby concludes that the risks to the children's health, for example the risk of developing anaemia, far outweighed any benefits gained from these studies. These callous experiments show a disregard for Indigenous people and children that highlights the racist colonial ideology at the centre of "Indian" policy.

Genocide

Through the implementation and operation of residential schools, Canadian governments, churches, and citizens all played a major part in the commission of genocide upon Indigenous peoples.[55] Although all did not play a first-hand role in these schools, many obsequiously condoned their existence and are thus complicit in their operations. As South African social rights activist

Desmond Tutu states, "If you are neutral in situations of injustice, you have chosen the side of the oppressor."[56]

Scholar Roland Chrisjohn, member of the Oneida Nation of the Haudenosaunee Confederacy, has studied and published works detailing this genocide of Indigenous peoples in Canada.[57] As Chrisjohn explains, genocide is the systematic and deliberate annihilation and elimination of a racial, political, or cultural group. Although policies related to "Indian" education did not state directly the intention to murder Indigenous children, many Indigenous children did die, some of whom were murdered. Additionally, to commit an act of genocide does not require direct killing; rather, it is about the destruction and eradication of a people. In 1944, Raphael Lemkin coined the term "genocide" during discussions leading up to the United Nations Genocide Convention:

> Generally speaking, genocide does not necessarily mean the immediate destruction of a nation, *except* when accomplished by mass killings of all members of a nation. It is intended rather to signify a coordinated plan of different actions aiming at the destruction of essential foundations of the life of national groups, with the aim of annihilating the groups themselves. The objectives of such a plan would be disintegration of the political and social institutions, of culture, language, national feelings, religion, and the economic existence of national groups, and the destruction of the personal security, liberty, health, dignity, and even the lives of the individuals belonging to such groups ... Genocide has two phases: one, destruction of the national pattern of the oppressed group; the other, the imposition of the national pattern of the oppressor.[58]

According to this definition, residential schools were in place to commit genocide, to completely eradicate Indigenous peoples in Canada, be it through forced sickness, "accidental" killings, assimilation, or cultural and linguistic destruction. The intent of the Canadian government was made very clear in numerous documents and public statements. Consider, for example, a 1920 statement by Duncan Campbell Scott concerning Bill 14, which introduced to parliament an amendment to the Indian Act that would allow the federal government to enfranchise "Indians," even against their will, and to compel "Indian" children to attend school:

> I want to get rid of the Indian problem. I do not think as a matter of fact, that this country ought to continuously protect a class of people who are able to stand alone. That is my whole point. Our objective is to continue until there is not a single Indian in Canada that has not been absorbed into the body politic, and there is no Indian question, and no Indian department and that is the whole object of this Bill.[59]

Residential schools practiced this brand of extermination over generations. Photographs of young Thomas Moore, taken before and after tuition at the Regina Indian Industrial School, document this "imposition of the national pattern of the oppressor."[60] They were published in 1897, in the preface to the 1896 annual report of the Department of Indian Affairs, which is available in the *Sessional Papers of the Dominion of Canada*.[61] As John Milloy explains, these photos represent a telling image of what federal policy has been since Confederation and what it would continue to be for decades.[62]

Image 7.1 Thomas Moore Before and After Tuition

Legal Challenges, Residential School Settlement Agreements, and Apologies

In the 1990s, residential school survivors started legal challenges against the churches and governments for their crimes against children.[63] For example, in 1995, the administrator of Port Alberni Indian Residential School, Arthur Henry Plint, was convicted of indecent assault against 18 of the school's students; the victims were from 6 to 13 years of age. Plint, who had worked at the school from 1947 to 1968, was sentenced to 11 years in prison for his

Image 7.1 Thomas Moore Before and After Tuition (continued)

Source: Saskatchewan Archives Board: R-A8223(1) & R-A8223(2)

rape of both young girls and boys.[64] This trial brought to light many horrible abuses, including how Plint made a young boy perform oral sex on him before handing over a letter from the boy's mother.

Trial witnesses included a member of the Gitxsan First Nation, Willy Blackwater, who was the first Indigenous person in Canada to sue and win a case against the federal government for post-traumatic stress disorder resulting from residential school abuses. At the Plint trial, Blackwater gave testimony, which he later repeated to Suzanne Fournier and Ernie Crey for their book:

> Arthur Henry Plint was the dorm supervisor for the younger boys, boys my age. My first week there, he woke me up in the middle of the night. He told me to come into his office because there was an emergency phone call from my father. . . . He had a door from his office right into his bedroom. He took me there and dropped his robe and faced me, naked. . . . [After forced oral sex,] I started to get sick and tried to puke. He laughed and told me that if I puked on his bed, I'd get hurt. . . . After that, Plint raped me anally about once a month for the next three years. I finally got up my nerve to tell Mr. Butler what Plint was doing to me. . . . Butler gave me a severe strapping and called me a dirty, lying Indian.[65]

At the sentencing, BC Supreme Court Justice Douglas Hogarth called Plint a "sexual terrorist," and further explained, "As far as the victims were concerned, the Indian residential school system was nothing more than institutionalized pedophilia."[66]

On November 6, 2013, Paul Leroux was found guilty in a Battleford court in Saskatchewan of eight counts of indecent assault and two counts of gross indecency; he assaulted eight boys while he was employed as a supervisor at the Beauval Indian Residential School in the 1960s.[67] Justice Murray Acton sentenced Leroux to three years in prison, but he received parole after serving 13 months. In May 2015, Leroux was sent back to prison after the Saskatchewan Court of Appeal found the original sentence "wholly unfit in the circumstances" and increased it to eight years.[68] Leroux's abuses included repeatedly going into boys' beds at night and fondling them and beckoning boys to his office after dark to further molest them.

This was also not the first time Leroux was found guilty of molesting children in a residential school. In 1998, Leroux was sentenced to 10 years in prison for abusing 14 boys at Grollier Hall, a residential school in Inuvik. His convictions were for gross indecency, indecent assault, and attempted buggery, which took place between 1967 and 1979 while he was working as an activities supervisor and guidance counsellor at the school.

Residential school abuses were reported across Canada. Countless survivors from coast to coast to coast have come forward and shared their stories of abuse. This outpouring of testimony could no longer be ignored by the government, which really had no choice but to acknowledge these atrocities and reach an agreement or settlement with survivors. On May 10, 2006, in a landmark event, this agreement, which came to be known as The Indian Residential Schools Settlement Agreement (IRSSA), was finally approved.[69] The IRSSA was signed by the Government of Canada, legal representatives for residential school survivors, the Assembly of First Nations, Inuit representatives, and legal representatives from the various churches that had operated residential schools. This agreement confirmed that a comprehensive resolution to the legacy of residential schools would be set into motion. It represents the largest out-of-court class action settlement in Canadian history. The IRSSA came into effect on September 19, 2007.

One of its measures is the "Common Experience Payment" (CEP), a $1.9 billion amount to be supplied as lump sum payments to former residential school survivors. Upon verification, survivors who applied could receive $10,000 for their first year of attendance at the school and $3,000 for each year thereafter. Another component of the agreement included an "Independent Assessment Process" (IAP). The IAP would evaluate whether a payment in addition to the CEP should be made. It was set up to compensate survivors who experienced physical, sexual, and other forms of abuse suffered during their attendance at a residential school. One problem has since been noted with this compensation process: it forced survivors to retell their horrible experiences in order to receive compensation money. For some people, this retelling is like being wounded again and amounts to a form of double victimization at the hands of the Canadian state. According to Justice Murray Sinclair (chair of the Truth and Reconciliation Commission), whenever possible, commissioners tried to spare survivors this retelling, and it was avoided if their stories had been previously documented.[70]

The Truth and Reconciliation Commission (TRC) is another established component of the IRSSA. It was allocated a budget of $60 million over five years.[71] The commission was mandated to promote public awareness; to provide a culturally safe place for survivors, their families, and communities to come together and share their stories about residential schools; and to acknowledge residential school experiences and the consequences of these experiences. The TRC was also mandated to create as complete a record as possible about residential schools and their impacts, from the information gathered throughout the commission's work, and to set up a permanent archive of all relevant documents and material. Two reports, one about the truth of what happened in the schools and one about reconciliation, were also required of the TRC. This report writing involved gathering statements from survivors (only those who wanted to participate).

Unfortunately, the TRC got off to a rocky start in its first year with the resignation of its first chair and commissioners.[72] Formally commencing in June of 2008, the TRC did not get underway practically until the following summer, when the new chair, Justice Murray Sinclair, and commissioners Chief Wilton Littlechild and Marie Wilson were appointed. An unfortunate consequence of this delay was a reduced timeframe for completion. The TRC faced other difficulties too, including problems obtaining from governments the documents necessary to complete its final report. The government tactlessly disagreed with commissioners over which documents were "relevant" and required from government files and archives. The TRC had to turn to the courts for assistance, which was especially difficult given the TRC's huge mandate, the deadline of July 1, 2014, for issuing its final report (which was extended to June 30, 2015), and its time-limited funds.

The TRC held its closing events in Ottawa from May 31 to June 3, 2015. On June 2, 2015, commissioners released their summary report and calls to action. There were a total of 94 calls to action, created based on over 6,750 survivor and witness statements collected by the commission over a six-year period. The final report was released December 15, 2015. It has six volumes, and contains over two million words.[73] On December 8, 2015, Prime Minister Justin Trudeau made a promise at the Assembly of First Nations' Special Chiefs Assembly to implement all calls to action outlined by this commission. Thus, many are hopeful for changes to come.[74]

Another measure of the IRSSA was the allocation of a further $125 million to the Aboriginal Healing Foundation (AHF).[75] These monies were designated to fund healing projects that would address the legacies of residential schools. An additional $100 million was also contributed by the involved churches to support healing initiatives. A sum of $20 million was allocated to commemoration—to national and regional commemorative initiatives that honour, remember, memorialize, and pay tribute to the survivors of the schools, their families, and the wider Indigenous community. These memorials also aimed to educate all Canadians about this shameful part of Canadian history.

Beyond the monetary compensation packages, research, and other related healing initiatives agreed to as part of the IRSSA, various church and government officials have offered public apologies to those directly and indirectly harmed by the residential schools. All Christian churches that had a role in the running of residential schools offered public apologies with one exception. The Catholic Church, which administered up to 60 per cent of Canada's residential schools between the 1880s and 1970s, did not offer an official apology.[76] Rather than an apology, Pope Benedict XVI offered an "expression of regret" on behalf of the Catholic Church.[77] The Canadian Catholic Bishops and the Missionary Oblates of Mary Immaculate in Canada, a Catholic order, did offer separate direct apologies to the First Nations of Canada in 1991.[78]

All the other churches involved did apologize. In 1986, the United Church of Canada apologized in general terms for the harm its missionary work had done to Indigenous peoples. In 1998, the Right Reverend Bill Phipps offered the church's direct apology: "To those individuals who were physically, sexually, and mentally abused as students of the Indian residential schools in which The United Church of Canada was involved, I offer you our most sincere apology. You did nothing wrong. You were and are the victims of evil acts that cannot under any circumstances be justified or excused."[79]

Archbishop Michael Peer expressed a similar apology to Indigenous leaders on behalf of the Anglican Church: "I am sorry, more than I can say, that we were a part of a system which took your children from home and family. I am sorry, more than I can say, that we tried to remake you in our image, taking from you your language and the signs of your identity. I am sorry, more than I can say, that in our schools so many were abused physically, sexually, culturally and emotionally. On behalf of the Anglican Church of Canada, I present our apology."[80]

Finally, on June 11, 2008, then-Prime Minister Stephen Harper made a formal apology on behalf of Canadians for the residential school system. His speech, delivered from the House of Commons, outlined the wrongs committed against students, the fact that Indigenous cultures and languages were denied to them, and the great harms caused by forcibly removing children from their homes and from their nurturing and caring families. He acknowledged that children were inadequately fed and clothed and that some children died before they were able to return home. Although he mentioned that "some former students have spoken positively about their experiences at residential schools," he admitted that "these stories are far overshadowed by tragic accounts of the emotional, physical and sexual abuse and neglect of helpless children." He also recognized the culpability of the involved churches and the federal government. "We are sorry," he declared, "on behalf of the government of Canada and all Canadians, I stand before you . . . to apologize to Aboriginal peoples for Canada's role in the Indian residential schools system."[81]

Ultimately, these apologies do acknowledge responsibility for some of the major atrocities suffered at the schools.[82] The financial packages, healing initiatives, apologies, and expressions of regret offered by churches and government officials were much needed, and long awaited. They finally gave recognition to the wrongs. Unfortunately, the horrible reality is that the damage has been done. Nothing can help the children who died as a consequence of attending residential schools. No compensation seems adequate for those who suffered abuse. Besides, the program of genocide carried out at these schools affected not only the children who attended them but also their children and their children's children. No amount of money or "regret" will undo the intergenerational legacies that continue to affect Indigenous peoples so greatly today.

Intergenerational Legacies and Trauma

Upon leaving schools, some people denied their identity as a consequence of the severe program of cultural replacement and because they had been raised in an environment that had little or no respect for Indigenous peoples. Many had trouble admitting their identity not only to others but also to themselves.[83]

The residential school experience had broken the crucial tie between a child and parents at a critical time in child development. Also, children were not raised within their culture or according to the teachings of the elders. They were denied a traditional, nurturing family environment. Indigenous communities, too, suffered. The loss of these children dismantled family social organization and structure and affected parenting. Given the overt racism children experienced at the schools and in the broader Euro-Canadian world, many educated there were unable to fit into society easily, feeling alienated from their communities because of broken ties and unwanted elsewhere. According to Fournier and Crey, by the late 1940s, four or five generations of Indigenous peoples had come out of residential schools as angry, poorly educated, abused strangers "who had no experience in parenting."[84] Deborah Chansonneuve contends that some residential school survivors and their descendants found it hard to establish trusting or supportive attachments with family members, including their spouses, children, and grandchildren.[85]

Tragically, some students learned from the behaviour they had endured and, as a result, began abusing others.[86] The Royal Commission on Aboriginal Peoples—which completed over 2,000 consultations and public hearings with Indigenous communities across Canada—reports that this "learning" may have been one of the most damaging legacies of the residential schools.[87] The testimony given to this commission, which was provided by Indigenous peoples themselves as well as by professional consultants representing their interests, identified social maladjustment, family breakdown, suicide, alcoholism, domestic violence, and loss of parenting skills as among the traumatic effects of residential school experiences. The commission's report also describes how many of the abuses experienced in the residential schools have now become intergenerational. So even after the schools were closed, the after-effects echoed through the lives of following generations. As one consultant's report explains,

> The survivors of the Indian residential school system have, in many cases, continued to have their lives shaped by the experiences in these schools. Persons who attended these schools continue to struggle with their identity after years of being taught to hate themselves and their culture. The residential schools led to a disruption in the transference of parenting skills from one generation to the next. Without these skills, many survivors have had difficulty in raising their own children. In residential schools, they learned that adults often exert power and control through abuse. The lessons learned in childhood are often repeated in adulthood with the result that many survivors of the residential school system often inflict abuse on their own children. These children in turn use the same tools on their children.[88]

Amy Bombay (Ojibway from Rainy River) is an expert in the neurological and intergenerational impacts of residential schools. The research she and her colleagues have conducted provides empirical evidence that residential schools have caused intergenerational impacts on future generations. A survey of 143 First Nation adults between the ages of 18 to 64 revealed that depressive symptoms are elevated among First Nations adults who had at least one parent who attended residential schools compared to those whose parents did not attend. In other words, second-generation residential school survivors were "at increased risk for depression, likely owing to greater sensitivity to and experiences of childhood adversity, adult traumas, and perceived discrimination."[89]

Researcher and expert in Indigenous trauma Deborah Chansonneuve, who studied addictive behaviours among Indigenous peoples by examining the experiences of her clients and by consulting 18 key informants from the addictions field, explains that some residential school survivors express their grief as lateral violence directed toward family and community members. This violence creates intergenerational cycles of abuse—abuse that resembles the mistreatment experienced at the residential schools.[90] Given the abundance of research concluding that negative experiences in childhood and youth are linked to crime and its associated risk factors,[91] it is no surprise that the resulting after-effects of these schools might play a part in causing many former students to be re-victimized, or to become victimizers themselves.[92]

Criminologists Raymond Corrado and Irwin Cohen, in an analysis of 127 case files of Indigenous residential school survivors who had undergone clinical assessment, showed that almost half (49 per cent) had been convicted of charges, including murder, theft, arson, possession of a weapon, robbery, major driving offences, drug offences, and sex offences. (In total, 62 people were convicted of 150 charges.)[93] Slightly more than half (51.6 per cent) were convicted of at least one sexual offence, and 55 per cent were convicted of assault. The authors argue that neither the type nor the rate of offense is unexpected given the extensive cases of abuse experienced by those in their research sample, with 100 per cent of the case files indicating that offenders suffered sexual abuse while attending a residential school and nearly 90 per cent indicating physical abuse.

Expert in trauma and violence Judy Atkinson provides an account of the trauma suffered by Indigenous peoples in Australia, outlining what she terms "trauma trails." Atkinson contends that traumatic symptoms, such as turning to alcohol to cope or acting out violently, must be viewed not as "signs of personal weakness, or mental illness"[94] but rather as a natural human consequence in response to a tragedy or disaster. These traumatic symptoms, she argues, are "the natural and predictable reactions of normal people . . . to abnormal experiences."[95] Trauma trails disrupted and reorganized Indigenous peoples and communities, which affected future generations. As Atkinson states, "When physical, structural or psychological violence is used to achieve the objective of domination, the outcomes may not only produce acute trauma, but may set in place chronic conditions of ongoing victimization and traumatisation at different levels, compounding the traumatisation across generations."[96]

Maria Yellow Horse Brave Heart (Hunkpapa and Oglala Lakota), who is a professor and an expert in Native American collective trauma and mental health, explains that, for over 500 years, Indigenous peoples have "endured physical, emotional, social, and spiritual genocide" from colonialist policy.[97] She describes how, over these years, Indigenous peoples went through immensely traumatic experiences, including residential schools; starvation and displacement; the tuberculosis epidemic; forced assimilation; and the cumulative loss across generations of language, culture, and spirituality. All of this trauma has influenced the breakdown of social structures and disrupted traditional family kinship ties and organization. She contends that this historical legacy continues to contribute to ongoing intergenerational trauma today.[98]

Yellow Horse Brave Heart explains this situation as the experience of historical trauma (HT), which she defines as a "cumulative emotional and psychological wounding over the lifespan and across generations, emanating from massive group trauma experiences."[99] She explains that people display a historical trauma response (HTR), a collection of behaviours and conditions that are a reaction to this trauma. These include "self-destructive behaviour, suicidal thoughts and gestures, depression, anxiety, low self-esteem, anger, and difficulty recognizing and expressing emotions," as well as substance abuse, which is used to try to numb the pain of trauma. Furthermore, continuing oppression, low socioeconomic status, and high mortality rates, not to mention racism, put Indigenous peoples at a higher risk of experiencing continued traumatic loss and exposure—which also act to perpetuate the cycle of trauma.

The tragic legacy of "Indian residential schools" is still with us, as is seen in the accumulating responses to this immensely traumatic historical policy.[100] Commonly identified responses include depression, mental illness, post-traumatic stress disorders, addictions to alcohol and drugs, powerlessness, dependency, low self-esteem, suicide, prostitution, homelessness, gambling, sexual abuse, and violence—both interfamilial and extrafamilial.[101] Many of these responses are interrelated, and they are also known risk factors predictive of crime. The issue of crime is further explored in the next chapter.

Discussion Questions

1) The term genocide has been used to describe what the Canadian government and churches did by setting up and implementing the residential school policy. Explain how and in what ways these actions constitute genocide.
2) How have experiences from residential schools become intergenerational? Explain some of the continuing impacts of historical traumas.

Activities

1) Watch the documentary *Unrepentant: Kevin Annett and Canada's Genocide* (available online at www.youtube.com). What types of abuses did the survivors report? Before reading this chapter or watching this film, were you aware of the residential schools or of the extent of the horrible abuses that took place in them? What happened to Kevin after he told the church what he had learned about the residential schools?
2) Examine the Project of Heart website (http://www.projectofheart.ca/). How do you rate this project, or another similar one, as a way to examine the history of residential schools, seek truth, commemorate those children who never made it home, and call Canadians to action? Figure out the total number of students at your school, and divide that number in half. Create commemorative painted tiles, sewn quilt pieces, or drawn puzzle pieces totalling that number. Then join these together to create a visual representation of how many students would not have returned home from your school had it been a residential school. Have students organize and run a symposium to teach others about residential schools through displaying and explaining the commemorative art piece. Arrange to have this art piece

brought to local high schools and other postsecondary schools, then have it hung in a high traffic area in your school.

3) Watch the music video "Indigenous Holocaust" by Wahwahtay Benais (available online at www.youtube.com), which is about the "Indian" boarding schools in the United States. Listen to and read the lyrics (available below the video by clicking on the "Show More" tab), and consider the situation facing Indigenous peoples in the United States and Canada. What are the similarities? Are there differences? Can you also draw similarities to other countries and peoples?

Recommended Readings

Metatawabin, Edmund, with Alexandra Shimo. *Up Ghost River: A Chief's Journey through the Turbulent Waters of Native History.* Toronto: Knopf Canada, 2014.

Sellars, Bev. *They Called Me Number One: Secrets and Survival at an Indian Residential School.* Vancouver: Talonbooks, 2012.

8
Crime Affecting Indigenous Peoples: Over-Representation, Explanations, and Risk Factors

INDIGENOUS PEOPLES ARE NOTABLY over-represented in the criminal justice system, both as victims and as those incarcerated.[1] This development is not new. It has been well documented for decades. What has been termed "over-representation," however, is clear evidence of a major injustice, one resulting from the centuries of subjugation and mistreatment Indigenous peoples have experienced in this country, from the devastating consequences of having been, and of continuing to be, targets of colonization. We must acknowledge, consequently, that a large portion of the over-representation of Indigenous peoples in the criminal justice system is due to systemic issues of racism and discrimination and not because actual crimes have been committed.

A continuing Eurocentric belief in "white" racial superiority is what fuels the ongoing oppression of Indigenous peoples in Canada. When we add to this systemic racism the traumatic symptoms some Indigenous peoples exhibit as a consequence of living under oppression and genocide for prolonged periods, we see the root causes of the crime and victimization affecting Indigenous peoples. These traumatic symptoms are many of the same factors that crime prevention literature refers to as "risk factors." And many of the "real" crimes committed by or against Indigenous peoples can be explained in part by way of these risk factors. This chapter provides an overview of the many risk factors that affect Indigenous peoples.

The Criminalization of Indigenous Peoples

Earlier chapters have made clear that many crimes have been committed against Indigenous peoples, crimes ranging from stealing their land to their physical, sexual, and emotional abuse in residential schools. But now Indigenous peoples are facing yet another form of injustice and crime. They are being criminalized by a system that is supposedly set up to achieve justice for all. Indigenous peoples are grossly over-represented in jails, as compared to non-Indigenous peoples.[2] In 2011, Indigenous peoples made up 4.3 per cent of Canada's total population, yet Indigenous adults (over 18 years of age) accounted for 28 per cent of admissions to sentenced custody, 25 per cent of admissions to remand, and 21 per cent of admissions to probation and conditional sentences in 2011–12.[3] In specific institutions across Canada, most notably in the Prairies, numbers reach even more acute levels. For example, in 2005, Indigenous peoples represented 14.9 per cent of Saskatchewan's total population yet accounted for 81 per cent of those admitted to provincial custody. Certain prisons in the Prairie region also reveal critical levels of Indigenous over-representation, such as the Stony Mountain Penitentiary in Manitoba (about 11 kilometres from Winnipeg), where more than 60 per cent of those incarcerated are Indigenous.[4] Between 2005–06 and 2012–13, the Indigenous incarcerated population increased by over 40 per cent.[5] From March 2005 to 2014–15, it increased by 47.4 per cent.[6]

It is clear that Indigenous peoples are being disproportionately criminalized by the criminal justice system—from arrest to incarceration. After all, is it really logical to assume that Indigenous peoples are committing such a disproportionate amount of crime? Scholars argue that more reasonable explanations include racial discrimination in charging, judging, and sentencing Indigenous peoples who do commit crime, as well as the socioeconomic and cultural differences that make Indigenous peoples more vulnerable to having crimes brought to the attention of authorities.[7] Others point to the strained relations between the authorities and First Nations. This tension is often the result of Indigenous peoples' legitimate distrust of the police, who have been used to further the objectives of various governments in terms of arresting those exercising their rights in land disputes or enforcing assimilationist educational or child welfare policies.[8] The criminal justice system operates to uphold existing power structures, and these were initially set up to eliminate Indigenous peoples. Racism against Indigenous peoples runs deep—in society and in the criminal justice system.

The Canadian criminal justice system is structurally racist, meaning that its policies and practices, either overtly or subtly, advantage one racial group over another.[9] Indigenous peoples are systematically excluded and marginalized, as this system facilitates racially disparate policies. Many policies are not as overtly racist as they were in the recent past, but racism remains embedded in the regular practice of the criminal justice process in Canada. For instance, policies that seem race neutral result in the unequal treatment of Indigenous peoples. Take, for example, an offence such as driving with your licence suspended. Although this policy does not seem directly racist, it disadvantages Indigenous peoples, who have higher rates of poverty and so are less likely to be able to pay a fine and more likely to end up in jail. Poverty and unemployment also affect Indigenous people at other stages of the criminal justice process. For example, unemployed individuals are less likely to get a good attorney or to get their sentences reduced.

Overt racism also remains. Consider the recent finding that Indigenous as opposed to non-Indigenous incarcerated peoples are sentenced to longer terms, spend more time in segregation and maximum security, and are less likely to be granted parole and more likely to have parole revoked for minor infractions.[10] These are all forms of structural racism, which normalizes and perpetuates violence against Indigenous peoples. This violence is structural violence, frozen within the structure of the criminal justice process and, consequently, legitimized by the dominant colonizing culture.

What should be done? If Canadian responses to crime affecting Indigenous peoples still frame the problem of Indigenous over-representation in the criminal justice system within a narrow colonial perspective—as being an "Indian problem"—then people will only understand it through a colonial lens and, thus, only attempt solutions that fit within the parameters of colonialism. These are not real solutions. Crime affecting Indigenous peoples is not a "problem" with Indigenous peoples but rather a colonial problem.

Because Canadian society gives only a cursory acknowledgement of true colonial histories, many Canadians cannot come to understand, or *see*, why Indigenous peoples are so over-represented in jails and as victims of crime. The reason people cannot see the causes of this over-representation is that they fail to recognize history and the ongoing colonialism *in which they are directly implicated*. The reality is that Indigenous peoples are being processed in and out of the colonial criminal justice machinery and bureaucracy as the government continues to try to reach its goal—Indigenous peoples' silent surrender. As Mohawk scholar Patricia Monture-Angus writes, "the state is fully implicated in the violence that exists in Indian communities today."[11]

The Victimization of Indigenous Peoples

The reality is that crime hurts—and it has always hurt. It hurt when it was committed against Indigenous peoples in the residential schools, and it hurts now because ongoing colonialism and oppression and the legacies from these experiences compound and make Indigenous peoples even more susceptible to victimization. This susceptibility is well documented. As compared to non-Indigenous groups, Indigenous peoples were,

- twice as likely to report being the victim of violent assault (i.e., physical or sexual assault or robbery) in 2009;[12]
- about six times more likely to be the victims of homicide in 2014; and[13]
- at a higher risk of being victimized multiple times.[14]

The General Social Survey undertaken in 2009 by Statistics Canada shows that 37 per cent of Indigenous peoples (aged 15 years or older) reported being a victim of a crime compared to 26 per cent of non-Indigenous peoples.[15] This is equivalent to almost 322,000 Indigenous peoples aged 15 years or older being victimized annually, an average of about 882 victimizations every day.

Indigenous women experience violence at a higher rate than any other group of women in Canada. Monture-Angus explains that, for many Indigenous women, violence began in childhood and is a result of generationally layered violence. As she states, "Violence is not just a mere incident in the lives of Aboriginal women. Violence does not just span a given number of years. It is our lives. And it is in our histories. For most Aboriginal women, violence has not been escapable."[16] Violence affecting Indigenous women is discussed further in Chapter 9.

Resilience and Risk Factors

The previous chapter outlined much of the intergenerational trauma experienced by today's Indigenous generations. Non-Indigenous peoples were not subject to this deplorable colonial history and treatment. The ordeal of residential schools, the effects of colonization on traditional values and culture, and abusive governmental practices and laws inflicted on Indigenous peoples (e.g., the Indian Act) are major causes of risk factors related to the victimization and incarceration affecting Indigenous peoples. These risk factors have been cited by many research studies in recent years and have been highlighted in Statistics Canada surveys.[17] The factors include, but are not limited to, high levels of unemployment; low incomes; poverty; overcrowded, disorganized, and substandard living conditions; social exclusion and marginalization; racism and discrimination; lack of cultural identity and pride; alcohol and drug addictions or misuse; low education and poor school access and involvement; and poor child rearing and supervision, as well as dysfunctional, disorganized, and disconnected families.[18] These factors are all direct results of living under prolonged periods of oppression and genocide—they are consequences of the massive traumatic group experiences Indigenous peoples have endured for 500 years.

Given history and current circumstances, Indigenous peoples have had to be strong to survive. They have had to be and are very resilient. Many have overcome the historical traumas that can predispose people to the previously mentioned risk factors. "Resilience" is defined as "patterns of positive adaptation during or following significant adversity or risk."[19] For Indigenous peoples who have suffered intergenerational traumas, these patterns of adaptation can involve drawing from Indigenous cultures or various intervention or support programs. For example, many residential school survivors found support from elders, drug and alcohol abstinence programs, and healing circles.[20] Others have sought higher education, relearned Indigenous languages and culture, or taken their own spiritual paths in order to regain and reinforce their Indigenous identity.

Two concepts to strengthen resilience are discussed in the literature: addressing risk factors and enhancing protective factors. Risk factors are defined as factors that increase the probability of a negative outcome, such as being exposed to crime or victimization. For example, poverty or parental alcoholism would be considered a risk factor for a child's future delinquency or victimization. Protective factors aid in counteracting risk factors by decreasing vulnerability to conditions such as crime or victimization and by increasing durable resiliency. The presence of nurturing parents in a home, for example would be considered a protective factor.

Risk factors are frequently categorized according to whether they originate at the individual, relationship, community, or societal level.[21] Figure 8.1 illustrates how risk factors can exist at these four levels. An individual's risk of being involved in crime, whether as a perpetrator or victim, may be elevated when the risk factors at various levels interact with one another.

Increased effects also result from the coexistence of numerous risk factors, at whatever level. If the presence of one risk factor increases the chances

Figure 8.1 The Four-Category Risk Factors Model

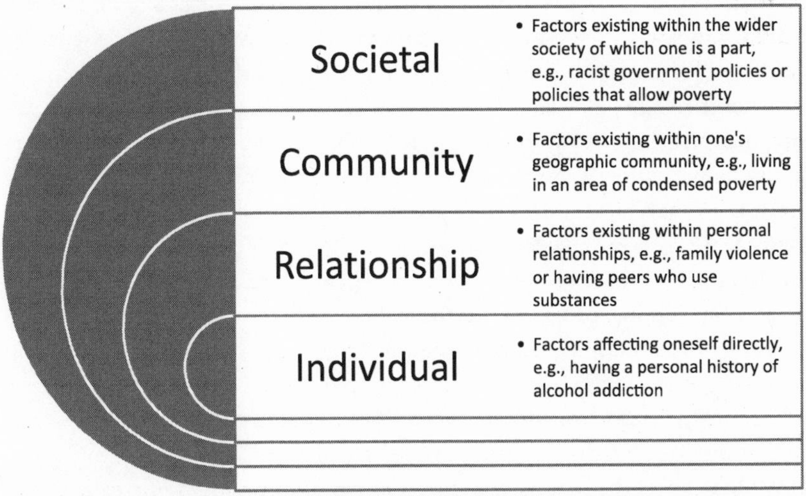

Source: Adapted from the World Health Organization, *Preventing Violence: A Guide to Implementing the Recommendations of the World Report on Violence and Health* (Geneva: WHO, 2004), Figure 2.

of offending or victimization, then multiple risk factors will produce an even greater increase. Crime, however, is not a direct result of the presence of risk factors. An individual with multiple risk factors related to crime will not necessarily become an offender or a victim. Risk factors are not totally independent from the dynamics of individual development or from relationships within a community or society, so they can undergo transformations with changing conditions.

Research has shown that protective environmental factors can often counter the effects of some risk factors on vulnerable populations. This research stems from the social development model (SDM) posited by Richard F. Catalano and J. David Hawkins (both are experts in violence prevention and social development research).[22] The model suggests that risk and protective factors operate reciprocally across five social domains—individual, family, school, peer group, and community—and that increasing positive relationships within these domains will reduce delinquency, crime, and substance abuse. For example, Catalano, Hawkins, and their colleagues examined the long-term effects of an intervention that strengthened protection during childhood.[23] This intervention combined teacher training, parent education, and social competence training and targeted children at the public elementary schools serving high-crime areas in Seattle, Washington, in 1985. A total of 643 students were split into three groups: one group was exposed to the full set of interventions from grades one through three and five through six. The second group was exposed to the interventions only during grades five through six. And the third group, a control group, received no intervention. In 1993, when these students reached 18 years of age, 598 of them were interviewed. Results showed fewer reports of violent delinquent acts and heavy drinking by those students who received the full intervention, as compared to the control group students. The full intervention group was also found to have more commitment and attachment to school, have better academic achievement, and less school misbehaviour as compared to the control group.

What this study and others like it tell us is that it is possible that protective factors can to reduce the presence and effects of risk factors that increase a person's likelihood of becoming the victim or perpetrator of crime. Let us examine some of these risk factors more fully.

High Residential Mobility and Poor Living Conditions

Research shows that residential mobility—meaning moving from dwelling to dwelling on a frequent basis—is linked to higher rates of crime.[24] Many times, people and families move because of their poor socioeconomic status and limited access to proper housing, so poverty and low income are risk factors related to residential mobility. Physical environments, such as poor living conditions and crowded housing, can put stress on people and families, who are forced to live in close quarters and who struggle to make ends meet with seemingly no hope for a better future.[25] Some might turn to substance abuse to alleviate the stress that accompanies this lack of resources or hope, or just the discomfort of sharing poor conditions and cramped living quarters. Regardless, living in a state of perpetual stress affects even an individual's body chemistry.

In 1992, the US National Institutes of Health defined stress "as a state of disharmony or threatened homeostasis" and defined a stressor as "a threat, real or perceived, that tends to disturb homeostasis."[26] According to Gabor Maté, who has worked as a palliative care physician with addicted peoples in Vancouver's Downtown Eastside, "What . . . all stressors have in common [is] . . . the absence of something that the organism perceives as necessary for survival—or its threatened loss." He continues, "The threat itself can be real or perceived."[27] For example, lack of access or threatened access to adequate shelter, food, or water is a stressor. For human beings, the loss of love is also a stressor. Gabor further explains that "addiction is a deeply ingrained response to stress, an attempt to cope with it through self-soothing."[28] Using alcohol or other drugs in this way lowers inhibitions and impulse control, and these disinhibiting effects can make it more likely for someone who is experiencing stress or frustration to act out their feelings. This path, from stress because of the threatening absence of life's necessities to self-soothing through intoxication, can lead to increased vulnerability to crime.

Studies have also identified the links between overcrowded living conditions, youth substance abuse, violence, and increased aggression in children.[29] Children who move from dwelling to dwelling on a frequent basis face a host of challenges while trying to adjust to new communities and schools and to rebuild social support systems. This "rebuilding" often includes an imposed reorganization of peer networks and adult social support networks. According to child social behaviour experts Maria E. Parente and Joseph L. Mahoney, these adjustment processes can harm the socialization process and manifest in aggressive behaviours.[30] According to crime prevention experts Robert J. Sampson and Stephen W. Raudenbush, with the absence of residential stability, opportunities to build a foundation in one's community are lost.[31]

Sampson and Raudenbush further explain that neighbourhood crime and disorder stem from concentrated poverty and the associated lack of social resources. Using geocoded crime incident data, as well as census data from the City of Winnipeg in 2001, criminologists Robin Fitzgerald and

Peter Carrington conducted a neighbourhood level ecological analysis of crime affecting urban Indigenous peoples.[32] They concluded that the high rates of Indigenous representation in the criminal justice system are due to the structural characteristics of the neighbourhoods in which Indigenous peoples live. Specifically, large numbers of those who are involved in the criminal justice system also suffer from a high degree of socioeconomic disparity and more residential mobility. Criminologists such as Jeffrey Reiman note that people who face high degrees of economic disparity and poverty come to be more involved in the criminal justice system because laws are created to serve the interests of the wealthy.[33] The wealthy have the power to make the laws, and the poor have little to no power to challenge or change them. As we will see in Chapter 12, society ignores this biased use of coercive power by the wealthy while incorrectly problematizing the behaviour of the poor as being due to inherent "moral shortcomings."[34]

Indigenous peoples are more likely to be poor, to live in inadequate housing, and to have high rates of residential mobility as compared to non-Indigenous peoples. According to the 2001 census, over a 12-month period, one in five Indigenous peoples moved compared to one in seven for the general Canadian population.[35] Throughout the 1990s and 2000s, Indigenous peoples moved to cities from First Nation communities in increasing numbers, and now the majority live in urban areas (54 per cent in 2006).[36] When relocating from First Nation communities or remote communities to the city, many Indigenous people move to inner cities, as is the case in Winnipeg or Toronto, typically attracted there by lower housing prices and the presence of members of their family and community.[37] Unfortunately, moving to the inner city is usually a move from one marginalized community into another.[38] In Winnipeg for example, Indigenous peoples are disproportionately located in the inner-city area, with approximately 44 per cent of Winnipeg's Indigenous peoples residing there. The Winnipeg inner city has approximately 120,000 people in total, and Indigenous peoples constitute 20 per cent of this total, compared to a concentration of only 6 per cent in the remainder of the city.[39]

Furthermore, although the size of the disparity is declining,[40] Indigenous peoples are more likely than non-Indigenous peoples to live in crowded living conditions. In 2006, Indigenous peoples were almost four times as likely compared to non-Indigenous peoples to live in a crowded dwelling. They were also three times more likely than non-Indigenous peoples to live in a dwelling requiring major repairs, a rate unchanged since 1996.[41]

Some northern or remote Indigenous communities, and some Indigenous accommodations in inner cities, offer what can be described as third-world living conditions.[42] On October 28, 2011, the First Nation community of

Attawapiskat declared a state of emergency because of a housing crisis. At the time, this community had just over 1,500 residents. After declaring a state of emergency, Attawapiskat received support from the Canadian Red Cross Society, which flew in various emergency supplies. Aid workers found community members living in makeshift tents, sheds, or shacks with plywood walls, or in condemned houses with fire and water damage.[43] Many of these places had black mould and no running water, electricity, insulation, or proper heating. Many families living in these poor conditions had children. In at least one case, a single mother with multiple children was living in a shed with no heat. With winter fast approaching in October of 2011, the community needed to get people into adequate accommodations quickly, so they could survive the cold season. In Attawapiskat, average lows reach below freezing from October through April.

Then-Prime Minister Harper's first reaction to this crisis was to send a third-party manager to the community and order an audit. He assumed that Attawapiskat's governing council was mismanaging funds. To the government's embarrassment, a federal court ruled in 2012 that this response was "unreasonable," stating that "despite the comments about management, the Respondent has not produced evidence of mismanagement or incorrect spending."[44]

In December of 2011, the government announced that it would finally send Attawapiskat 22 modular homes, as well as some toilets and wood stoves. After waiting for the ice roads to freeze and become useable, the community finally received their homes in February 2012. Today, people have moved into these homes and some conditions have improved. Unfortunately, some in the community still live in mould-filled, condemned homes and sleep on cots in the healing lodge. As well, many people live in a dangerously overcrowded construction trailer (acquired from the nearby diamond mine after the company no longer had use for it). No long-term plan is in place to address the housing problem in Attawapiskat.

Attawapiskat is only one example. There are numerous communities in Canada facing similar issues. For instance, in December of 2012, just one year after Attawapiskat declared a housing crisis, Kashechewan, a neighbouring First Nation community, also declared a state of emergency. This community had 21 houses that were unfit for people to live in and survive a winter. Kashechewan was also running out of fuel, so it could no longer provide heat to homes and other buildings. In November 2011, the community had to shut down two schools, the power-generation station, the fire hall, and a health clinic because they could no longer be heated and safely operated. Fortunately, just in time, the government released funds for emergency supplies to fix the 21 houses and for fuel. Yet this First Nation community, like

Attawapiskat and many others across the country, has no long-term, sustainable plan to address the linked crises of inadequate housing and poverty. In December 2012, NDP MP Charlie Angus stated that First Nation communities in his riding alone declared 13 emergencies in just 7 years, the majority of which were associated with poor infrastructure. He went on to state, "We're always putting Band-Aids on septic wounds."[45]

Previously, in 2005, the Kashechewan community had to evacuate its people after their water supply was found to have very high levels of E. coli; as a result, the water was shock-treated with chlorine, which in turn caused impetigo, scabies, and skin rashes.[46] Attawapiskat and Kashechewan are also 2 of the 118 First Nation communities in Canada where boil-water advisories were in effect in 2013.[47] Communities under these advisories must not only suffer the injustice and stress of being denied access to one of life's basic essentials but also endure the practical difficulty of boiling their tap water in order to be able to safely use it for drinking or brushing teeth.

Sometimes, getting clean water is an added expense that stretches already limited community resources very thin. For example, the Pikangikum First Nation in Ontario is a remote community of about 2,300 residents. In April of 2011, it issued a state of emergency because community members had no access to clean drinking water. The community was left with no choice but to ship in more than 21,000 litres of bottled water.[48]

Six case studies on the Indigenous water crisis were published in a 2008 report from the Polaris Institute. The report also provides information about the state of the Pikangikum First Nation. Ronda Potts, a teacher there for two years gave this evidence: "A lot of the buildings are very outdated, very overcrowded. You have families living all together in one home, no indoor plumbing, problems with the water and old pipes. . . . I would say it's Third World conditions."[49] This same report described Pikangikum resident Juliette Turtle's situation. Turtle is a 58-year-old woman who has seven of her children buried in her back yard. She lost all seven to suicide. She shares a 65-square-metre home with eight other relatives. In this house, children sleep in rooms with several mattresses covering one floor. There is no running water and no toilet.[50] People have to use an outhouse in the backyard. Once it fills up, they dig another hole and move the outhouse. The inconvenience and insecurity of having an outhouse at a distance that doesn't lock or keep insects and animals out is nothing compared to the indignity of having to avoid the graves of one's children when determining where to dig a new receptacle for one's waste.

In 2006, the Northwestern Health Unit conducted a study on the drinking water and sewage in this community.[51] The report found that the water situation in Pikangikum is a serious hazard to the community's health. Rates of gastrointestinal and skin infections; lice infestations; and eye, ear, and urinary tract infections are higher as compared to those experienced by other communities in the surrounding region. Lack of access to a safe and clean water supply was found to be the most likely cause.

In effect, Pikangikum has been under a boil-water advisory since 2000 (these are periodically lifted and reinstated). In 2012, Pikangikum Chief Johan Strang recalled the following, in relation to his community's water situation: "Since I remember, I haven't had any water."[52] Chief Strang further explained that he does not expect that residences in his community will be able to get piped water until at least 2015. Indeed, as of February 2015, the Pikangikum Working Group had installed water systems in 10 of the 450 homes, but efforts have been hampered by an inadequate electrical power system.[53]

Although many of these boil-water advisories occur in remote First Nation communities, some happen in communities positioned right next to urban centres, where clean water flows from taps. Such is the case with the Semiahmoo First Nation, which, in 2013, had been on a permanent boil-water advisory since 2005 and had suffered intermittent advisories since 1996.[54] This community is in the metropolitan Vancouver area, adjacent to the wealthy community of White Rock where million-dollar homes line the beach. In the Kitigan Zibi First Nation, located in Québec, about a two-hour drive north of Ottawa, some residents still use wells contaminated with traces of uranium.[55] In 2006, the community's residents who were using well water reportedly had to spend a total of $200,000 a year on bottled water.[56] Of course, boil-water advisories happen in non-Indigenous communities, but not at the same rate or for the same length of time.[57] In May 2015, there were 127 drinking water advisories in effect in 88 First Nation communities across Canada, excluding British Columbia. In that province, the First Nations Health Authority reported 25 drinking water advisories affecting 21 First Nation communities as of June 2015.[58]

What relationship do these often appalling conditions have to crime? Aside from the fact that poverty is a risk factor related to crime, imagine the difficulty, when living in these conditions, of deferring to the "way things are" and the structures and authorities that seem to keep them from changing. Imagine how hard it might be to keep even one's self-respect strong. Then imagine the temptation of escape, perhaps by breaking rules or through drug and alcohol use. As we have already seen, the consequences of yielding to these temptations, even a few times, can be more serious for Indigenous peoples than for others in terms of their relation to the criminal justice system.

Poor Health, Suicide, and Addictions

Given the abject poverty in which many Indigenous peoples live today, it is no surprise that, over the past several decades, diseases that were once rare have now become increasingly common.[59] For example, the prevalence of diabetes among Indigenous peoples who do not live in their First Nation communities is double that of non-Indigenous peoples. And residents of First Nation communities have an even higher rate of diabetes—one that is three to five times greater than other peoples in Canada.[60] Reportedly, this rise of "new" diseases affecting Indigenous peoples, such as cardiovascular disease and diabetes, is partly linked to communities' quickly transformed lifestyles, social conditions, and dietary habits.[61] These health inequalities can also be explained, in part, by Indigenous peoples' lower socioeconomic status, as compared to the status enjoyed by other peoples in Canada.[62] Lower socioeconomic status is commonly recognized as being correlated to poorer health, given that those with less education, less income, and less stable or no employment will have limited access to nutrient-rich food as compared to those with high levels of education, high incomes, and stable employment. Indigenous peoples are also denied access to their own food sources, such as wild game, fish, roots, and berries, which affects their health.

Living in and trying to survive conditions of such poverty and despair has sadly led some Indigenous peoples down the road of suicide, heavy drinking, or addictions. Some of the remote First Nation communities described previously have the highest rates of suicide in Canada. In fact, the community of Pikangikum was described by sociologist Colin Samson as having one of the highest rates of suicide in the world, when its 2000 rate soared to 470 deaths per 100,000 people.[63] Suicide rates in First Nations communities have been recorded at twice the general Canadian rates. Among Inuit, the rate is even higher, being 6 to 11 times greater than that of the general population.[64]

Psychology professor Michael J. Kral, who conducted research on suicide among the Inuit in Nunavut for 17 years, contends that suicide is a learned behaviour, finding that it is common for Inuit youth to talk about and copy other suicides.[65] He explains that killing one's self has become a normative option, with a social logic to it, whereby older Inuit will talk about the suicide contagion and copying. As Kral explains, suicide is a current reality because of the perturbation resulting from colonialism, which has "dramatically altered their family and romantic relationships including [causing] a serious intergeneration segregation for a kinship-based culture."[66] Suicide, being now available, has become an option for youth in response to this perturbation of colonialism.

Psychology professors Michael J. Chandler and Christopher E. Lalonde suggest that Indigenous youth and young adults whose identities are weakened or challenged by essential or drastic individual or cultural change are put at an exceptional risk of suicide because they lose vital guarantees that are essential to their security and welfare.[67] They explain this lack of assurance as being a lapse in what they refer to as "cultural continuity." Any challenge to personal or cultural identity poses such a threat; for example, limited access to traditional lands or the loss of an Indigenous language upsets cultural continuity.[68] Chandler and Lalonde state that youth and young adults who are living through instants of this particularly dramatic change (i.e., the interruption of their cultural continuity) experience high rates of suicide.

Looking at patterns of suicide among Indigenous people outside of Canada, Laurence J. Kirmayer and his colleagues note that high rates are also found among those who have encountered colonization or other forms of marginalization or cultural oppression.[69] They further note that various interrelated risk factors "interact with each other to amplify the risk of suicide," such as being a victim or perpetrator of violence or physical abuse, bullying, school problems, poor family environment, poverty, social isolation, alcohol use, and inhalant or solvent use, among others. In effect, the authors describe a cycle of increasing despair:

> For example, lack of meaningful activities in the community for youth will increase hopelessness and pessimism. Hopelessness and lack of a vision of the future, in turn, will make individuals less able to engage in potentially meaningful activities (e.g. persisting in school with the thought of eventually finding interesting work). Poor interpersonal skills may increase the likelihood that youth will experience negative life events like conflict with peers or adults, or the breakup of a relationship, and also make it more difficult for them to cope with the subsequent distress.[70]

The authors also note that these youth often lack the protective factors that decrease the risk of suicide because their communities and peoples have been affected by rapid cultural change and the repression of their cultural traditions, as well as by racism and marginalization.

Research has also shown heavy drinking to be linked with suicidal behaviour and to suicide and deaths from unintentional injury.[71] As Kirmayer and his colleagues note, "Alcohol or drug intoxication may disinhibit the behaviour of individuals, contributing to the risk of suicide."[72] Yet, contrary to the horrible "drunken Indian" stereotype, many Indigenous peoples refrain from drinking alcohol. In fact, research has shown that abstinence was actually almost two times more frequent among Indigenous peoples than among non-Indigenous peoples in 1991.[73] Statistics Canada surveys have shown alcohol consumption to be lower for Indigenous peoples living in their First Nation communities as compared to the general Canadian population (in 2002–03).[74] Furthermore Statistics Canada reports for 2011, for example, indicate that 34 per cent of Inuit and 29 per cent of First Nations people living off reserve did not drink as compared to 24 per cent of non-Indigenous peoples.[75] The same report indicates that Indigenous peoples not living in a First Nation community are also less likely to be weekly drinkers as compared to the general Canadian population (in 2000–01).

However, 22.6 per cent of Indigenous peoples not living in a First Nation community were identified as being heavy drinkers compared to 16.1 per cent of non-Indigenous peoples (in 2000–01).[76] And, in 2002–03, the proportion of Indigenous peoples living in their First Nation community who reported heavy drinking on a weekly basis (16.0 per cent) was double that of the general Canadian population (7.9 per cent).[77] More recent statistics (2007–10) indicate that between 26 and 27 per cent of First Nations people living off reserves, Inuit, and Métis report being heavy drinkers as opposed to 19 per cent of the non-Indigenous population.[78] Heavy drinking is defined as having five or more drinks on one occasion.[79]

A study examining 10 years of Santé Québec surveys found a similar pattern: alcohol consumption was less frequent among Indigenous women in northern Québec as compared to among other women in the province but the quantity consumed was higher.[80] Thus, research shows that fewer Indigenous people drink, as compared to non-Indigenous people, yet, when Indigenous peoples do drink, they tend to drink more heavily.

Unfortunately, heavy drinking and violence are correlated. The World Health Organization (WHO) outlines the strong links between alcohol and violence.[81] In a review of research studies, the WHO found that individuals who begin to consume alcohol at an early age, consume it more frequently, in large quantities, and to the point of intoxication, have much higher risks of violence as compared to those who do not consume alcohol early in life. Likewise, those who are living in a culture characterized by heavy alcohol consumption, and in circumstances where alcohol is readily available, experience higher levels of violence. This finding suggests that people who drink alcohol heavily are more likely to be not only violent offenders but also victims of violence. Heavy drinking can even be a response to this violence, as the same report concludes: the "problematic use of alcohol can even develop as a coping mechanism among victims of violence."[82]

Some Indigenous peoples have indeed turned to alcohol or other substances as a way to cope with current situations of poverty and despair. According to a 2007 study, alcohol and drug abuse are cited as the most dominant types of addictive behaviours faced by Indigenous peoples in Canada.[83] For example, in some northern Innu communities, addiction to huffing solvents has been a major worry for decades. Left with no hope and living in despair, some Innu youth sniff gas or turn to suicide to escape their realities. In 2012, estimates from the RCMP suggest that about 40 to 50 per cent of Innu *children* living in the community of Natuashish are addicted to sniffing gas.[84]

This finding suggests that the people of Natuashish may have experienced trauma during their recent history. And, indeed, they have. The Mushuau Innu currently residing in Natuashish have undergone three forced government relocations—in 1948, 1967, and 2002.[85] The people are traditionally nomadic, and they continued their migratory and semi-nomadic existence for over 2,000 years and well into the twentieth century.[86] As social work professor Myriam Denov and criminology professor Kathryn Campbell explain, by the 1940s, Innu peoples were living semi-permanently in their coastal settlements near Davis Inlet because their traditional way of life was no longer sustainable due to colonization.

In 1948, they were torn from these traditional settlements—places that were a small part of the land on which they had once thrived and that provided a link of central importance to their identity, culture, and well-being—and moved to Nutak. As mentioned, the Mushuau Innu were relocated again in 1967, when they gave up the remnants of their nomadic culture to move to poor quality "modern" houses on Iluikoyak Island. With this move came forced assimilation through "education," which attempted to dramatically alter their world views from Innu values (e.g., respect for all things and living in balance with the environment) to Canadian values (e.g., Judeo-Christian teachings and economic development). Families who stayed in the village all year round and sent their children to schools would get government allowance cheques, and people who chose to hunt and remain in the bush would not. As Denov and Campbell explain, this and similar policies created dependence on government assistance.[87]

The government not only destroyed the Innu people's traditional economies by these policies but also displaced them from their land, which was then used without their consent for economic development that did not benefit them. Indeed, profits from the hydroelectric plants, mines, and pulp and paper mills built on Innu land went to governments and multinational corporations and harmed Innu peoples by reducing the land they could use for things such as food, clothing, tools, and trading with others. For example, one of the largest hydroelectric generating stations in the world was set up on their land at Churchill Falls; billions of dollars have been made from this project, with 8 per cent going to Hydro-Québec and the rest going to Newfoundland and other investors. Not only did the Innu receive no compensation, but they lost resources when, in 1973, this project dammed Churchill Falls and flooded 1,300 square kilometres of their ancestral territory, destroying sacred Innu grave sites in the process. According to Denov and Campbell, experiencing such severe cultural displacement and disruption has resulted in stress, self-destructive behaviours, substance abuse, and suicide as ways to cope with these government-imposed disasters.

According to psychology professor Bruce Alexander, people who are chronically and severely dislocated are vulnerable to addictions. As he says, "the historical correlation between severe dislocation and addiction is strong."[88] He further points out that no anthropological research shows Indigenous peoples to have had addictions before the arrival of Europeans in Canada. He contends that the dislocation of Indigenous peoples by Europeans is the ultimate precursor of addiction for Indigenous peoples. Research has shown that addictive behaviours and substance abuse have taken a terrible toll on Indigenous peoples and contribute significantly to instances of accidents, death, disease, and illness, as well as to violence.[89]

According to Gabor Maté, addictions cannot be understood without acknowledging the pain and hurt that people have gone through in their lives.[90] He explains that not all addictions are rooted in trauma or abuse; however, they can all be traced back to painful experience because at the root of all addictions is hurt. The psychology and neurobiology of the brain becomes affected by stress or adversity that happens early in one's life. In his review of research studies on addictions, he finds that "studies of drug addicts repeatedly find extraordinarily high percentages of childhood trauma of various sorts, including physical, sexual and emotional abuse."[91] Drawing on his personal experiences of treating patients, he explains these conclusions:

> The hardcore drug addicts that I treat (but according to all studies in the States, as well) are, without exception, people who have had extraordinarily difficult lives. And the commonality is childhood abuse. In other words, these people all enter life under extremely adverse circumstances. Not only did they not get what they need for healthy development, they actually got negative circumstances of neglect. I don't have a single female patient in the Downtown Eastside who wasn't sexually abused, for example, as were many of the men, or abused, neglected, and abandoned serially, over and over again.
>
> And that's what sets up the brain biology of addiction. In other words, the addiction is related both psychologically, in terms of emotional pain relief, and neurobiological development to early adversity.[92]

In sum, the challenges facing some Indigenous peoples today—challenges related to poor health, suicide, and substance abuse—can be addressed effectively only by acknowledging the destructive legacies of colonialism and racism and by applying what we now know about the origins of addiction in trauma and of the connection between substance abuse and violence.

Education and Academic Advancement

Research shows that those who advance educationally and occupationally are much less likely to be engaged in crime and much less likely to be arrested as compared to those who do not.[93] But not all people have or are able to take advantage of opportunities for advancement, and unequal access affects people early in life. When children and youth have limited opportunities for academic advancement (such as when they live in poverty or despair), their academic ambitions can decrease. When opportunities for educational advancement are available and are supported, students are opened up to more options for a viable future.

The value of providing this access and support has been demonstrated in various randomized controlled trials and educational interventions. One is the Quantum Opportunities Program, a demonstration project begun in 1989 and delivered to 50 teens in each of the five participating US cities; families of the teens were receiving public assistance.[94] Each participating site randomly selected a group of grade eight students, assigning 25 of them to a group that received developmental programming and 25 to a control group that received no programming.[95] Programming was structured around educational activities and provided up to 250 hours of education, 250 hours of development activities, and 250 hours of service every full year from grade nine through high school graduation. Educational activities included tutoring, computer skills training, and life and family skills training, as well as guidance activities such as planning for postsecondary education.[96] For their participation in the program, the teens from the program groups received small cash and scholarship incentives.

An evaluation comparing the program and control groups in 1990, 1991, and 1992 found that, at all study sites, the teens that received the programming were more likely to graduate from high school, enrol in postsecondary education, or receive an honour or award; and they were less likely to get pregnant, drop out of high school, or get involved in crime.[97] Furthermore, the number of participating teens arrested was 70 per cent lower than the number arrested from the control group.[98] These results suggest that supporting educational achievement is an effective crime prevention measure. So what are the educational outcomes for Indigenous peoples in Canada?

Even though Indigenous peoples have had rapidly increasing levels of educational attainment, they still lag behind the general Canadian population.

In 2006, 32 per cent of Indigenous peoples in Canada were without a secondary school diploma while non-Indigenous peoples without a diploma made up only 15 per cent of the population.[99] According to a 2007–10 survey, the high-school dropout rate among Indigenous peoples aged 20 to 24, who were not living in their First Nation community, was 22.6 per cent, compared to 8.5 per cent for non-Indigenous peoples.[100] In June 2011, the Assembly of First Nations reported that Indigenous students living in First Nation communities have a kindergarten to grade 12 completion rate of 49 per cent. In fact, the group declared, it is statistically more likely that students from First Nation communities will go to jail than graduate from high school.[101]

Data from 2006 shows that non-Indigenous Canadians are still much more likely to complete high school and get a university degree as compared to an Indigenous person, with this gap between the groups actually growing over the 10 previous years.[102] The same study shows that non-Indigenous women obtain university degrees or higher at a rate double that of Indigenous women and that fewer than a third of Indigenous men receive a university degree or higher.[103] More recent statistics are similar; only 9.8 per cent of those reporting Indigenous identity on the National Household Survey questionnaire of 2011 had a university degree compared with 26.5 per cent of non-Indigenous Canadians.[104]

Unfortunately, as mentioned in Chapter 1, not all Indigenous children and youth in this country are afforded the same educational opportunities as others. Many schools in First Nation communities are chronically underfunded and, in some cases, structurally falling apart. The conditions are so bad in some instances that children and youth themselves have protested, demanding fair treatment and equal access to education.

Such is the case with 15-year-old Shannen Koostachin (koo-staj-IN). This courageous youth led a social media campaign, calling on the government to create a proper school in her community and to provide equal access to culturally based education for Indigenous children, as well as to fund infrastructure, libraries, computers, and extracurricular activities. She was from the community of Attawapiskat and was attending classes in a series of trailers. She and other youths organized the younger children to write a letter to the prime minister asking for a school. As Shannen argues, "School is a time for dreams and every kid deserves this."[105] The government's response to the letter indicated there was not enough money to build them a new school. Thus, the grade eight students all agreed to cancel its graduation trip to Niagara Falls and use those funds to go down to Ottawa and confront Indian Affairs directly. Shannen and two other youths met with Indian Affairs Minister Chuck Strahl, but they were told that the government could not afford the school. Shannen replied that she did not believe him and would continue to fight until every child in Canada received equal education and "safe and comfy schools."[106] Sadly, Shannen died in a car accident in 2010 before her dream was realized. She was in Thunder Bay when she died. She was there because, like many other youths living in northern First Nations communities, she had to fly over 700 kilometres away from her home and board with a family in order to attend high school.[107]

The elementary school that Shannen would have attended in Attawapiskat was closed in 2000–01 because it was located on a contaminated brownfield. The contamination dated from 1979, when a diesel-oil spill of 30,000 gallons (the largest in northern Ontario) leaked under the school and eventually forced its closure.[108] The ongoing health problems of children forced the government to investigate—in 2000—and to provide the community with portable trailers as a temporary measure.[109]

Ten years later, those temporary portables were still in use and extremely run down. Other problems were evident too: attendance dropped; contamination leaked under the portables causing the ground to shift, which triggered windows to wedge shut and doorways to become unsymmetrical, so doors could not be closed; cold air drafted into open classrooms during winter months, forcing children to wear coats in school because portables had no heat to cope with –40-degree temperatures; and community members reported seeing mice entering the school.[110] More important, children reported headaches, nausea, and nosebleeds resulting from the toxicity.[111] Finally, in June 2012, after much fighting to continue Shannen's dream, this community received the government's promise to build an elementary school. The Kattawapiskak Elementary School opened for the 2014–15 school year: "If you look at the contamination of the school grounds that have existed, it's been pretty much 30 years since the children have been educated in a safe environment," remarked Timmins-James Bay MP Charlie Angus.[112] This story uncovers some of the reasons that Indigenous educational attainments lag behind those of others in Canada. And remember, this story received attention because of Shannen's campaign and because her family and community continued to fight for her dream. Other stories of inequity take place in obscurity.

Many First Nation schools in Canada today are in a deplorable condition, and their students continue to be plagued by serious health concerns. For example, a 2011 report written by Gitxsan activist and academic Cindy Blackstock describes a First Nation school in Manitoba that had to be closed and replaced with portable trailers because it was "infested with snakes." The water system at this particular school had become overrun with the snakes, so "when children turned on the taps, baby snakes would come out."[113]

This situation sounds like a nightmare come to life. This same report tells of another First Nations school in Manitoba that began its 2009 school year in tents because no building was available in the community.

Even when school buildings exist, they are sometimes so overcrowded that children have to go to school in shifts. It is also routine for many children living in First Nation communities to be sent away from their families and homes to attend school. This circumstance echoes the traumas of residential schools. In 2011, the Assembly of First Nations reported that 40 First Nation communities had no schools and that, in some First Nation communities, children had not been to school in more than two years.[114]

In 2009, the Office of the Parliamentary Budget Officer reported that, according to the internal database used by Indian Affairs (the Integrated Capital Management System), only 49 per cent of First Nation schools were in good condition and close to 21 per cent of the schools were listed as "not inspected."[115] In Alberta and British Columbia, the situation was worse: 76 per cent of First Nation schools were listed as in "poor condition."

Clearly, Indigenous children living in their First Nation communities face major educational challenges, but the situation for Indigenous peoples living outside their First Nation communities is also a struggle. For example, Winnipeg, which has the highest percentage of urban Indigenous peoples in Canada as well as the largest total number of Indigenous peoples of any major city in Canada, has educational attainment rates that are much lower for Indigenous peoples as compared to non-Indigenous peoples.[116] In 2006, about 30 per cent of Indigenous peoples in Winnipeg between the ages of 25 and 64 did not have a certificate, diploma, or degree, compared to only 13 per cent of the non-Indigenous population in the same age group. Also in 2006, Indigenous youth aged 15 to 24 living in Winnipeg were found to have lower school attendance rates compared to non-Indigenous peoples, with a 58 per cent attendance rate for Indigenous youth compared to 66 per cent for non-Indigenous youth.

In 2002, a study investigating the educational circumstances of Indigenous students in Winnipeg's inner-city high schools provided a clear explanation of why the Winnipeg school system seemed to be failing Indigenous peoples. Interviews were conducted with 47 Indigenous students in the inner-city high schools, 50 Indigenous school leavers, 25 adult members of the Indigenous community, and 10 teachers, 7 of whom were Indigenous. The study concluded that the school system marginalizes Winnipeg's Indigenous students, as it does not adequately reflect their cultural values or their daily realities and feels alien to many Indigenous peoples.[117] Furthermore, the prevalence of institutional forms of racism as well as evident, direct racist actions and attitudes, including name-calling and stereotyping, was very high. The school system was described as non-Indigenous, overly Eurocentric, and colonial. For example, there were very few Indigenous teachers and very little Indigenous content in the curriculum. Some textbooks still explained history in terms of the West being settled by persons of non-Indigenous ancestry, referred to as "we," thus placing Indigenous students in the less desirable "other" category.

The study also found that the schools still operated according to dated, ineffective, and inaccurate ideas similar to those that formed the basis of education in the residential schools: for example, the assumption that Indigenous culture is inferior and that Indigenous students must be "raised" to the level of the superior culture. This approach, the researchers declared, had obviously not worked. Given these findings, they argued, Indigenous students will continue to resist education as it means resisting racist assumptions and the associated actions seen in Winnipeg's inner-city school system.

A national Canadian survey conducted in 2002 with 519 first-year university and college students, who had all graduated from the Canadian public education system, found that 67 per cent of these students had never discussed issues of concern to Indigenous peoples in their elementary or secondary classrooms.[118] As a respondent from the Prairies notes, "I don't have a clue about what's going on and don't know where to get the truth."[119]

Eighty per cent of students surveyed indicated that they were dissatisfied or strongly dissatisfied with the Indigenous studies curriculum in their elementary and secondary schools.[120] As this student from the Atlantic region of Canada states, "We did not learn anything about indigenous people in school! Absolutely nothing (except for historical facts). . . . It would be good for young people to be more informed on the culture and history of First Nation people; that would prevent useless prejudice."[121]

The Canadian school curriculum has historically disregarded Indigenous achievements, complexities, and even the existence of numerous Indigenous cultures and peoples.[122] We cannot forget that Canadian schools themselves were once part of the government's strategy of Indigenous assimilation and have been central institutions through which Indigenous peoples have been oppressed and colonized.[123] Curriculum in Canadian classrooms has historically been delivered in a way that strengthens and validates colonialism.[124] Even today, the system of education "remains a tool of colonialism" and still subtly perpetrates the colonial philosophy of Indigenous inferiority.[125]

First Nation communities, Indigenous educators, and their allies have been working to address the clear gaps in curriculum across the country, for example, by developing improved curriculum, promoting the certification of more Indigenous teachers, increasing cross-cultural awareness among students and teachers, and sharing resources and supports to improve educational outcomes for Indigenous students.[126] New Indigenous-focused schools have opened in urban areas, such as the one in Vancouver's Sir William Macdonald Elementary School. In 2011, this school opened to both Indigenous and non-Indigenous students from kindergarten to grade three. The curriculum is explained as being "respectful of local First Nations and the shared values, experiences and histories of all Aboriginal peoples. It is respectful of the shared history between Aboriginal peoples and Canada and about a shared world view between Aboriginal people and environmentalists."[127] In December 2015, the Winnipeg School Division announced that they would be establishing Cree and Ojibway bilingual language programs at their Isaac Brock School in Winnipeg, set to begin in September 2016.[128]

However, too few schools in Canada have been proactive in finding ways to improve curriculum, to prioritize Indigenous education, or to implement new polices and guidelines.[129] Both Indigenous and non-Indigenous students are still largely experiencing "the same limited and narrow curriculum." Seeds of racism are sown very early when the school curriculum is not reflective of the realities and cultures of all students, and this stereotyping in education "contributes to the lack of Canadian understanding of Aboriginal rights, culture, and traditions." More related to the point of this chapter is that Indigenous children who experience this racism and are made to feel inferior or like outsiders are more likely to become disengaged and to drop out of school, which puts them at more risk when it comes to poverty and crime.

Employment and Income

Research shows that unemployment is associated with physical and mental health problems such as stress, anxiety, depression, and increased suicide rates.[130] And it just makes sense that an employed person with an income sufficient to sustain self and family has less stress. Being employed also correlates to having a good education and to being less likely to engage in criminal activity. Studies show that people with access to quality education in their elementary and high school years and who graduate are less likely to commit crimes, as they are more likely to have stable families and to achieve employment.[131] According to the 2012 Aboriginal Peoples Survey, Indigenous adults (aged 18 to 44) who graduated from high school were more likely to be employed than those who did not.[132] Obviously, the education gap between Indigenous people and non-Indigenous people has long-term implications for earning sufficient income. Indeed, Indigenous peoples in Canada have high rates of unemployment as compared to non-Indigenous peoples. In 2006, the census showed that the unemployment rate for Indigenous people (aged 25 to 64) remained almost three times the rate for non-Indigenous people, with unemployment for Indigenous peoples at 13 per cent compared to 5 per cent for non-Indigenous peoples.[133]

Employment is directly tied to income. The median income for Indigenous peoples in 2006 was $18,962, which was 30 per cent lower than the $27,097 median income for the general Canadian population.[134] This disparity exists for Indigenous peoples no matter where they live. Non-Indigenous people who work in urban First Nation communities earn 34 per cent more than other First Nation peoples. In rural First Nation communities, non-Indigenous Canadians make 88 per cent more than First Nation peoples. On top of this disparity, Indigenous peoples can have difficulty getting one of the few jobs existing in rural First Nation communities. In some cases, the only jobs might be with the local band office, grocery store, nurse station, or gas station.

Outside of First Nation communities, different barriers face Indigenous peoples. A study conducted by the Canadian Council on Social Development found that racism has a major impact on some people's ability to obtain employment.[135] If someone from a visible minority does gain employment, racism hinders his or her ability to receive equitable earnings or treatment. A few Indigenous people reported seeking work with Indigenous-owned businesses or organizations to avoid these inequities or people's lack of understanding of their culture. The council further identified that Indigenous peoples with a university education are less likely to hold managerial or professional jobs as compared to those from non-racialized groups. It concluded that racial discrimination in the workplace is a "hidden thing" but nonetheless adversely affects people's career possibilities.

It must also be recognized that this demand for "jobs" and "employment" is a result of the empire- and nation-building desires of the Canadian colonial state. Before colonization, traditional Indigenous communities thrived in Turtle Island; they enjoyed holistic relationships with one another and the land, as evinced in the clan systems, rites of passage, and ceremonies that acknowledged the intricate balance and equality between all things. In comparison, the current Canadian social structure is very individualized and competitive; it creates greed and the fear of not having enough—and it creates scarcity for some. This competitive drive leads to people being out of balance with the natural cycles and rhythms of life, as well as to a reliance on the artificial "man-state" and its system of money.

Ultimately, as mentioned, the criminological research proves that lack of employment and income are risk factors for crime. And Indigenous peoples are placed at a disadvantage when it comes to getting and keeping work and receiving equitable wages. In part, this disadvantage stems from the educational gap between them and non-Indigenous peoples, but racism is also a significant factor. At an even deeper level, Indigenous people may feel that the whole system of employment and education—indeed, the complete structure of Euro-Canadian society—is culturally foreign, or even criminal, based as it is upon competitive production and consumption that discounts their ancestral teachings.

Family Environment and Child Welfare

Indigenous children are also less likely than non-Indigenous children to live with both parents. In 2001, twice as many Indigenous children lived with a lone parent compared to non-Indigenous children.[136] We know from countless research studies that the presence of two nurturing parents in the home serves as a protective factor against crime.[137] Thus, the chances of becoming involved with crime, as either victim or offender, are lower if one grows up with two nurturing parents in the home as opposed to one. As we learned in Chapter 3, children are considered sacred within Indigenous cultures. Before colonization, Indigenous children grew up surrounded by love and supported by families, extended families, the community, or all three (depending on the structure and organization of the nation, which varied from small, nomadic families to multinational confederacies).

According to Gabor Maté, the environment that a child grows up in has direct impacts on brain development.[138] He explains that paternal nurturing determines the levels of key brain chemicals, and maternal deprivation is directly linked to a "permanent decrease in the production of oxytocin" (which he explains as being our "love" chemical in the brain).[139] Without experiencing loving attachments as children, people have difficulty forming intimate relationships later in life. They are thus at a higher risk for addiction because they sometimes turn to drugs as "social lubricants" to ease the pain resulting from their difficulty in attaining "emotionally supportive relationships."[140]

Early childhood deprivations are linked not only to a deficiency of "good" brain chemicals but also to dangerous and "chronically high levels of the stress hormone cortisol."[141] And people who begin their life under extremely stressful conditions become quickly triggered into a stress reaction. These stress reactions, once emotionally triggered, can challenge a person's ability to think rationally. Difficulty forming attachments, high levels of stress, problems coping with stress through rational thinking, and a tendency toward substance abuse: this person seems to fit the profile of someone at a high risk for engaging in crime.

Research has also shown that, when young at-risk mothers are provided maternal supports and are connected to services to help strengthen their resiliency and adversity to risk, they are less likely to turn to substance abuse to deal with the stress, and, as significant, their children are less likely to be involved in crime later in life. These were the findings of a randomized, controlled trial undertaken using a sample of 400 women in the region of Elmira, New York, who had low income (85 per cent), were unmarried, or were younger than 19 years of age.[142] The women were split into two groups, with 200 receiving home visits and the other 200 relying on the standard services being offered in the area at the time. The home visits consisted of public health nurses visiting the high-risk mothers for 75 to 90 minutes on a weekly or monthly basis.[143] A mother would typically be enrolled at the end of her first trimester of pregnancy and continue in the program until her child was two years old. The nurses provided mothers with information on the health and development of the children and helped the mothers cultivate supportive relationships with friends and family and link to essential health and human services.

Outcomes of program effectiveness were measured using data derived from interviews, observations of parenting, conditions in the homes, and reviews of medical and social service records from pregnancy until the children reached 15 years.[144] Final analysis showed that the children of the mothers who received nurse visits had 56 per cent fewer arrests than the control group by age 15.[145] Mothers visited by nurses were also found to be more likely to avoid substance abuse and other criminal behaviours that were exhibited by those in the control group.[146] Additionally, the mothers visited by nurses were less likely to abuse and neglect their children, achieving an 80 per cent reduction in verified cases of child abuse and neglect as compared to the control group.[147]

What might this research teach us? First, it shows that a stable family environment serves as a protective factor against crime. Second, it suggests that a supportive environment can reduce their children's risk of suffering early childhood trauma, which could increase susceptibility to crime. Given this research, the government's response to the effects of residential schools on Indigenous children and parenting is very disappointing.[148] As discussed, residential schools disrupted Indigenous people's families, taking children away from parents during critical times in their development. In 1951, around the time these schools started to close, a new section was added to the Indian Act entitled "General provincial laws applicable to Indians." That section (s. 88) states that "all laws of general application from time to time in force in any province are applicable to and in respect of Indians in the province, except to the extent that those laws are inconsistent with this Act" or with other similar legislation.[149] This new section cleared the way for provincial laws to apply to Indigenous peoples living in First Nation communities.

Following this change, provinces began to take Indigenous children from their homes in abominable numbers—by applying provincial child welfare laws in First Nation communities.[150] According to Lynda Gray (member of the Tsimshian Nation), these laws were not in line with Indigenous values but rather with Eurocentric beliefs and customs. When there were real safety issues in the home, she states, Indigenous families were given no support to help them deal with the intergenerational impacts of neglect and abuse resultant from residential schools.

From the 1960s through to the mid-1980s, thousands of Indigenous children were taken from their families and put into the child welfare system.[151] Many were either put into foster care or put up for adoption during what has come to be known as the "sixties scoop."[152] Patrick Johnston first coined this term in a 1983 report he wrote for the Canadian Council on Social Development.[153] Johnston recalled that he got the term from a British Columbian social worker, who told him " . . . with tears in her eyes—that it was common practice in BC in the mid-sixties to 'scoop' from their mothers on reserves almost all newly born children."[154] Many times, children were fostered or adopted out to other provinces. In some cases, children were adopted out to the United States or overseas. Approximately 70 per cent of the adopted children were placed with non-Indigenous families. Furthermore, there was often inadequate to no screening of families to ensure their suitability, and, although money was exchanged during adoption, especially when cases involved private American adoption agencies, no record exists of any money reaching the children's families.[155]

There are even some reports of foster or adoptive parents sexually and physically abusing children in their care.[156] Christine Smith (McFarlane), a woman of Saulteaux background from the Peguis First Nation, suffered abuse after she and her three siblings were removed from their mother's care as part of the sixties scoop. Her traumatic experience started in the early 1970s in Winnipeg:

> For the first couple of years, our situation seemed okay: there were no outright displays of abuse towards us, or none that I can recall. But once we started school, the emotional and physical abuse began. We were separated from our culture, kept from knowing our own language or traditions.
>
> Our adoptive parents believed that because we were First Nations we were genetically predisposed to obesity. Their obsession with fat led them to withhold adequate food from us. They would lock me in the backyard, crying from hunger, with the family pets. When I was allowed to eat, I was given bland foods or small portions. My sister would convince me to go down to the kitchen late at night and sneak us some food even though it meant getting beaten if I was caught.

> Physical and emotional abuse were a part of my daily life. I was called insulting and degrading names and, toward the end of my time with my adoptive family, I was locked in my bedroom and only allowed out to go to school. I reacted to this abuse by acting out and running away from home.[157]

Many Indigenous children are still under the authority of the child welfare system. Indeed, Cree scholar Lauri Gilchrist of Lakehead University has described a recent "scoop" of Indigenous children as the "millennium scoop."[158] It is a scoop driven by systemic discrimination coupled with the federal government's severe underfunding of First Nations child welfare agencies.[159] As briefly mentioned in Chapter 1, about 27,000 Indigenous children were in state care as of 2006; the Assembly of First Nations estimates that the number had not changed substantially as of 2010.[160] In 2008, Canada's auditor general estimated that First Nations children were six to eight times more likely to be put into foster care than other children, citing neglect as the key reason for these children's overrepresentation in care. Often, this neglect is driven by substance abuse or by influences typically beyond parents' control, such as poor housing and poverty.[161]

Though this problem is well known, the current government has done little to make essential changes to the existing child welfare system. Data from fiscal year 2009–10 show that First Nations Child and Family Service agencies receive approximately 22 per cent less funding than provincial agencies.[162] Also, an evaluation of the antiquated formula used to fund First Nations child and family services (Directive 20–1) shows that it currently steers agencies toward the most disruptive and expensive care options—foster care, group homes, and institutional care—because only these agency costs are fully reimbursed.[163] A result is that most Indigenous children are placed in non-Indigenous settings, where it is difficult to be exposed to and learn about Indigenous teachings and to develop a cultural identity.[164] Recent longitudinal research from the United States has proven that those who grow up in the foster care system are highly likely to become involved in crime later in life given their lack of a strong and stable nurturing family environment.[165] Given the instability in their lives, many also struggle to find jobs and adequate housing and find it hard to complete their education.

In February of 2007, Gitxsan activist and academic Cindy Blackstock, the First Nations Child and Family Caring Society of Canada, and the Assembly of First Nations launched a human rights complaint with the Canadian Human Rights Tribunal against the Canadian government.[166] The complaint was in response to the continued discriminatory treatment facing the over 160,000 First Nations children who are in the child welfare system and who receive inequitable funding of child welfare services, as compared to all other Canadian children. A campaign entitled "I am a witness" was initiated to publicize the issue, educate the public, and invite people to support and follow the tribunal proceedings. These proceedings have been among the most watched in Canadian history; over 6,300 people and organizations have been physically present to watch—to be a witness.[167] The final ruling from the tribunal was issued on January 26, 2016, and ruled that Canada discriminates against children living in First Nations communities.[168] Thus, there are champions, like Cindy Blackstock, who continue to fight for justice to change the discriminatory treatment—and to ameliorate the trauma that past and present assimilationist initiatives have wreaked on Indigenous families and communities, damage that leaves Indigenous peoples at a higher risk of being involved with the criminal justice system.

Indigenous Peoples: Young and Growing

As a result of the disruptions of colonialism, not to mention the attempts to eradicate "Indians," the numbers of Indigenous peoples diminished for a time. But now, Indigenous peoples are gaining in numbers and momentum. The Indigenous population, however, is not only growing but also young. As mentioned, the median age of Indigenous peoples was 27.7 years in 2011, compared to 40.6 years for non-Indigenous peoples.[169] Consider the relative youth of the Indigenous population in light of the fact that the age range for the highest rate of offending is from about 16 to 21.[170] The median age of federal incarcerated persons is 32.[171] Overall, police-reported offending rates tend to be higher among youth and young adults, with rates increasing incrementally for youths aged 12 to 17, peaking at age 18, and decreasing with age after that.[172] Based on these statistics alone, Indigenous peoples are more likely to be incarcerated at higher rates than non-Indigenous people.

Research in the field of juvenile justice has shown that youth involvement in crime is due to the interaction of various risk factors related to crime that then have a "multiplicative effect."[173] One of those factors is engaging in risk-taking behaviours. Laurence Steinberg, a professor of psychology and a leading expert on adolescent behaviour, argues that risk-taking increases between childhood and adolescence due to changes in the brain's socio-emotional system that take place during puberty.[174] These changes lead to amplified reward-seeking behaviour, which is heightened when youths are in the company of their peers and which is driven largely by a notable remodelling of the brain's neural pathways. He notes that risk-taking declines between adolescence and adulthood because the brain's cognitive control system changes. These changes increase people's ability to self-regulate their behaviours.

As Indigenous peoples experienced a 20.1 per cent increase in population between 2006 and 2011, and an Indigenous woman, from 1996 to 2001, was estimated to have an average of 2.6 births throughout her life course, as opposed to 1.5 for a non-Indigenous woman, we can expect the percentage of youths in the Indigenous population to grow, especially in comparison to the overall demographic trend of aging within the general population of Canada.[175] Indeed, Indigenous children and youth under the age of 24 made up almost one-half (48 per cent) of all Indigenous peoples in 2006. Compare this to the non-Indigenous population under 24, which was 31 per cent of the overall population.[176] Population projections show that, by 2017, Indigenous peoples between the ages of 20 to 29 could comprise 24 per cent of Indigenous peoples in Manitoba, 30 per cent in Saskatchewan, and 58 per cent in the Northwest Territories.[177]

Canada's North has been termed "the territory of the young" because of these statistics.[178] Indigenous peoples between the ages of 20 to 29 comprise more than 80 per cent of Nunavut's population, and this proportion is projected to increase.[179] Of the 2,000 or so residents of Attawapiskat, more than a third are under 19 years of age, and those under the age of 35 make up three-quarters of the community.[180]

Based on these demographics alone, Indigenous peoples have a higher chance of having contact with the criminal justice system. Given the Indigenous birth rate and the number of Indigenous people who will soon be in their child-bearing years, many more, in years to come, will enter the age ranges associated with a higher risk of offending and incarceration.[181] Furthermore, according to criminologists Julian Roberts and Ronald Melchers, Indigenous peoples experienced their "baby boom" 10 years after the rest of Canada, so its effects are also abating more slowly.[182] Over time, these various demographic factors could cause the number of Indigenous peoples incarcerated to rise even higher.[183]

The Cycle of Crime Affecting Indigenous Peoples

The Pauktuutit Inuit Women of Canada outline a cycle of abuse—in other words, a cycle of crime against children—and explain that, in the Inuit context, the cycle can be traced back to two root causes.[184] The first is a loss of culture and tradition, and the second is loss of control over individual and collective destiny. These lead to psychological trauma, the breakdown of families, alcohol and drug addiction, and increased feelings of powerlessness. Then fear, mistrust, abuse, and denial become involved, creating a cycle of abuse in which individuals can be both victim and abuser. As an Inuk elder and healer explains, "It is all about your upbringing. If a child was abused at a very early age, sexually or physically, then that's all they know, and they will continue to abuse. And it's up to the community to stop that abuse with education and awareness. The root causes come from shame, guilt and what you've learned from a young age."[185] Other crimes are also related to an experience of or a proximity to this cycle of abuse.

Through life history interviews of Indigenous males imprisoned at federal and provincial facilities in Manitoba and Saskatchewan, James Waldram found that many of the men had experienced long-term trauma and considerable violence, including physical and sexual abuse and alcoholism.[186] A survey of 249 of these men showed that 66 per cent had physical violence in their families when they were growing up; 80 per cent said that at least one parent (or foster or adoptive parent) had a problem with alcohol or drugs. Familial disruption was also a significant finding, as 35 per cent of the men interviewed had spent time in foster homes, 30 per cent had attended residential schools, and 5 per cent were adopted.

In a study on violence and street gangs in Winnipeg, researchers met with six Indigenous gang members living in the city's north end; the researchers adopted an approach intended to " . . . learn from the wisdom of street gangsters."[187] Ultimately, the gang members demonstrated that street gangs and gun violence are products of poverty, systemic racism, and the associated consequences and conditions of these two afflictions, that is, addictions, violence, family disintegration, neglect, drugs, and abuse. All were conditions that these men experienced while they were young. The men indicated that, to them, such conditions were normal "everyday events."[188]

Research has shown that exposure to traumatic factors such as violence and abuse will carry on within families and communities, causing the next generation to suffer the same or similar effects or to resort to dangerous coping mechanisms, such as substance abuse, to "bury the pain." It is not an absolute that these traumas, in one form or another, will be passed down; nor is crime the only response to experiencing trauma. However, the chances of being involved in crime increase dramatically if a person is exposed to violence or abuse or to the other traumatic events or circumstances outlined previously. This cycle of crime is sketched out in Figure 8.2.

Figure 8.2 The Cycle of Crime Affecting Indigenous Peoples

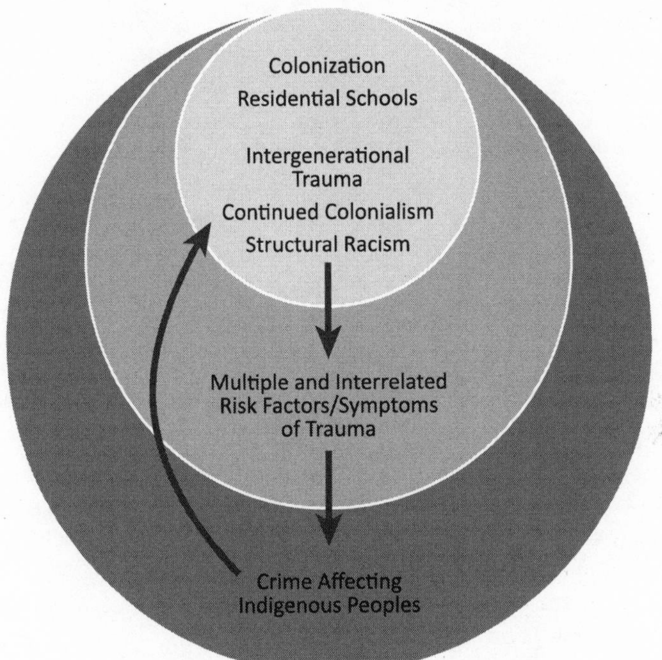

Only by addressing all that fuels the cycle of crime affecting Indigenous peoples—past and current trauma, racism, continuing colonialism, inequality, and Eurocentric ideologies that commodify the land and its inhabitants—can we hope to break this cycle.

Discussion Questions

1) What is the sixties scoop, and what are its impacts?
2) What are risk factors? How can the cycle of abuse affecting Indigenous peoples be explained?
3) If Indigenous children living in their First Nation communities were allocated the same amount of money to attend school as is currently allocated to other children living in Canada, if First Nations child and welfare agencies were allocated the same amount of money for children as is currently allocated to provincial agencies with the same function, and if there were no longer various inequalities such as these, what do you think would be different in this country? Furthermore, if non-Indigenous Canadians were all educated on Indigenous people's true histories—including the history of Indigenous oppression and the histories of the various Indigenous peoples,

cultures, traditions, and original homelands—what do you think would be different? What would be required for such a consciousness raising?

Activities

1) Watch the 2012 National Film Board of Canada documentary by Alanis Obomsawin *The People of the Kattawapiskak River* (available for free streaming at most universities and colleges in Canada and, at a cost, from www.nfb.ca). The film shows that some in Canada are living in what can be described as third-world conditions. Considering history, explain why this might be the case. Further explain why the Canadian government fails to take immediate action on the major catastrophic circumstances facing Indigenous peoples, such as the housing crisis and the poor living conditions documented by the film.
2) Watch the 2007 National Film Board of Canada documentary by Richard Desjardins and Robert Monderie *The Invisible Nation* (available online at www.nfb.ca). What access to education do the Algonquin children in the film have? What are some of the living conditions in the communities? What differences between communities does the film document, and how can these differences be explained?

Recommended Readings

Blackstock, Cindy. "The Canadian Human Rights Tribunal on First Nations Child Welfare: Why If Canada Wins, Equality and Justice Lose." *Child and Youth Services Review* 33, no. 1 (2011): 187–94.

Monture, Patricia A. "The Need for Radical Change in the Canadian Criminal Justice System: Applying a Human Rights Framework." In *Visions of the Heart: Canadian Aboriginal Issues*, 3rd ed., edited by David Long and Olive Patricia Dickason, 238–57. Don Mills, ON: Oxford University Press, 2011.

9
Violence Affecting Indigenous Women: Struggle, Sexualization, and Subjugation

INDIGENOUS WOMEN SUFFER FROM HIGH RATES of victimization in many forms; they also go missing and are murdered in large numbers. Additionally, Indigenous women are victims of racism and sexism and experience excessive levels of violence when compared to other women in Canada. The Canadian criminal justice system has done little to protect Indigenous women from these major social injustices. This chapter outlines the historical and continuing paternalistic assault on Indigenous women, an ongoing violence that continues to have dire implications.

The Challenge: Violence Affecting Indigenous Women

Indigenous women are almost three times more likely than non-Indigenous women to become a victim of a violent crime in Canada. Statistics Canada reported that 13 per cent of all Indigenous women aged 15 years or older, living in the provinces, had been violently victimized during 2009. This is close to 67,000 Indigenous women who were violently victimized in one year alone. Of those women who reported being victimized, more than a third reported repeat victimization, meaning that they had experienced victimization on two or more occasions.[1]

Furthermore, Indigenous women are also more likely to be victims of spousal violence than are non-Indigenous women. Statistics Canada reported that, in the five years preceding its 2009 survey, 15 per cent of Indigenous women reported spousal violence, compared to 6 per cent of non-Indigenous women. Indigenous women who experienced spousal violence were also more likely than non-Indigenous women to report being injured as a result of such violence. Further, close to half (48 per cent) of these Indigenous women reported the most severe forms of violence, which included being sexually assaulted, choked, beaten, or threatened with a gun or knife. In addition to suffering more injuries, these women were also more likely to state that they feared for their lives as compared to non-Indigenous women.[2]

Overall, Indigenous women and girls are much more likely to experience violence, and to die as a result, as compared to other Canadian women and girls.[3] Amnesty International reports that Indigenous women in Canada aged 25 to 44 are five times more likely than non-Indigenous Canadians in the same age group to die of violence.[4] In 2014, the rate of homicide committed against Indigenous women was 3.64 per 100,000, compared to the rate for non-Indigenous women of 0.65 per 100,000—a rate that is six times higher for Indigenous women.[5] The Native Women's Association of Canada reports that Indigenous women are almost three times more likely than non-Indigenous women to be killed by a stranger.[6]

Indigenous women are also more likely than non-Indigenous females to be incarcerated, and the number of Indigenous women admitted to correctional facilities continues to rise. What's more, Indigenous females are more commonly represented among the female correctional population than are Indigenous males within the male correctional population.[7] In 2011–12, federally incarcerated Indigenous women represented 34 per cent of all incarcerated women in Canada while Indigenous incarcerated men represented 21.5 per cent of all incarcerated men.[8] During the same period, Indigenous females accounted for 43 per cent of female admissions to provincial or territorial sentenced custody and 37 per cent of female admissions to remand, while men accounted for 27 per cent and 23 per cent of these admissions.[9] These troubling statistics suggest gross inequities for Indigenous women within the criminal justice system.

Traditional Indigenous Societies' Treatment of Women: Valued, Honoured, and Respected

All of this violence and crime affecting Indigenous women is not traditional. Many pre-contact Indigenous societies had an equitable division of labour between men and women, as well as women leaders. Indigenous women held unique roles and responsibilities in their communities, and, though these would vary from nation to nation, a common thread was that women were valued, honoured, respected, and viewed as sacred human beings.[10]

Before the arrival of the Europeans, some Indigenous societies and communities were matriarchal, which means that women headed the social organization of the community.[11] Even in those that were not matriarchal, Indigenous women still had significant roles, including taking part in politics, decision making, family life, marriage, and ceremonial life.[12] Women were often in charge of key decisions—in some Indigenous societies, women would even select which men would be in positions of leadership.[13] When European religion, customs, and laws were forced on Indigenous peoples, however, women's roles began to be devalued.[14] Indeed, the patriarchal and competitive nature of European societies often contrasted strikingly with the nature of Indigenous societies, many of which were egalitarian, communal, and peaceful.

This peacefulness frequently extended to gender relations in traditional Indigenous societies. In the early years of colonization, Europeans remarked on this tendency, noting that Indigenous peoples rarely committed sexual violence and that, in all the colonial records of "Indian barbarity," it was difficult to find evidence of Indigenous peoples violating women.[15] Indeed, evidence exists of Indigenous *respect* for women in the instructions that General James Clinton gave to his soldiers, who were on their way to burn and destroy a village, castle, and sundry "cattle and effects" belonging to the Onondaga Nation in 1779: "Bad as the savages are, they never violate the chastity of any women."[16]

Records also indicate that the men of traditional Indigenous societies would not tolerate any sexual assaults or advances against women. For example, when French men made unwelcomed advances toward some Mi'kmaq women, they were warned off. The Mi'kmaq men told the French captain in charge to watch out for his men because anyone who made an attempt to do that again "would not stand much of a chance, that they would kill him on the spot."[17]

Of course, I do not present this evidence as a way of suggesting that acts of violence against women never took place in Indigenous societies. However, before European contact, these were rare, and when they did happen they were not accepted or tolerated. Indigenous communities often dealt with these offences through sanctions (e.g., embarrassment, ridicule, or shunning); in some cases, even death was the punishment.[18] Not until colonization efforts had systematically interrupted Indigenous societies, cultures, and identities—the structures that framed and supported people's lives—did the prevalence of violence increase dramatically, notably against women.

Euro-Canadian Treatment of Indigenous Women: "Rapable" Sexual Objects

Native American studies professor Jack D. Forbes (Powhatan Renape and Delaware Lenape) points out that Miguel Cuneo—who accompanied Christopher Columbus on his second expedition to the Americas—was given a Carib woman as a slave from Columbus. Cuneo attempted to rape this woman, who resisted with all of her might, "but Cuneo, in his own words, thrashed her mercilessly and raped her."[19] As Forbes contends, "no wonder the successors of Columbus in the Americas, the mercenaries of the CIA and the fiends of the various military dictatorships rape and abuse women today almost as an act of normal routine!"—especially, he notes, targeting Indigenous women.[20]

In contrast to how Indigenous men traditionally treated women, European men have historically viewed women as subordinates who were the property of men.[21] As Barbara-Helen Hill (from Six Nations of the Grand River) explains, "The European came with the belief that everything was chattel, property to be purchased, stolen, or owned, including the women and the children."[22] These colonial notions shaped and changed Indigenous norms. Indeed, the displacement of Indigenous women from the positions of leadership and influence they had enjoyed within some First Nations began during the early days of contact with Europeans. For example, some nations initially sent their women forward to confront early explorers or to enter into negotiations and make decisions about agreements. However, many British and French representatives refused even to communicate with the women and demanded that Indigenous peoples send their men forward to speak and make decisions.

Other effects of colonization also contribute to the high degree of violence many Indigenous women face today. Now, many families are struggling not only with multiple risk factors resulting from the legacies of abuse in residential schools but also with the fact that their traditional ways of recognizing women as equal and sacred have been undermined and damaged. Another related factor that perpetuates violence against Indigenous women is stereotyping caused by discrimination. These prejudices also date back to the colonial period, when European colonizers considered Indigenous peoples to be less than human. Native studies professor and Métis scholar Emma LaRocque explains that Indigenous women were considered to be "squaws," which is the female counterpart of the male Indigenous "savage."[23] This depiction as a "squaw" is extremely dehumanizing in that it represents a female who "has no human face; she is lustful, immoral, unfeeling and dirty."[24] LaRocque contends that this grotesque dehumanization has rendered Indigenous women and girls more susceptible to physical, psychological, and sexual violence and abuse.[25] Because the negative connotations of these appalling racist and sexist stereotypes have become ingrained, some men, even today, consider Indigenous women to be less than people and, thus, "rapable" sexual objects.[26] These racist notions, which are derived from the historical labelling of Indigenous peoples as being more animal than human, have seriously damaged the Indigenous image—and still permeate Euro-Canadian society.

Popular Culture Depictions: The Sexualization of Indigenous Women

Indigenous women in Canada are hypersexualized within Western media and culture, a circumstance stemming from imperialism and the preconceptions of European settlers, which have permeated institutions and become embedded in today's value systems. Indigenous women have been portrayed as highly sexual "squaws" in numerous writings, films, and products of popular culture, and they continue to be depicted this way today. There are numerous examples to draw on. A glaring one is the imagined Pocahontas, who, in reality, was a 12-year-old child, yet who has been portrayed in story and on film as a sexy, slim, young woman with curves, long legs, a tiny waist, and breasts. Her story, which has since been turned into a Disney film, romanticizes Indigenous women as "Indian princesses." In Disney's film, Pocahontas is also a friend to non-domesticated animals, which further plays on this idea that Indigenous peoples are more animal than human.[27]

Similar romanticized constructions are seen elsewhere. Consider Princess Tiger Lily in *Peter Pan* or even the Land O'Lakes woman on butter boxes.[28] These sexualized depictions of Indigenous women are frequently "whitened" to make them more palatable to North American audiences. So "Indian" women are given features such as lighter-than-usual skin or Playboy or Barbie bodies. Otherwise, all are very stereotypical representations of women. They have long dark hair, lightly tanned skin, and high cheekbones; they wear feathers and fringes and show skin. In many ways, they look like exotic Barbie dolls.[29]

Certainly, the word "exotic" is often used to describe Indigenous women (and other non-white women as well). Here, we are again shown a sexualized woman, an "Indian princess" who is an "exotic" or "erotic" other. In the Disney film *Peter Pan* (first released in 1953 but re-released in high definition in the spring of 2013), Indigenous women are depicted in two ways: as a temptress "Indian princess" or as an overweight, ogre-like "squaw." (The term "squaw" is actually used in the film.) Tiger Lily is the "princess," a sexy tease who tries to tempt Peter Pan by dancing erotically on a drum. The overweight "squaw" is depicted as unintelligent, ugly, and mean. She tells Wendy about woman's place using simple statements and broken English: "Squaw no dance! Squaw gettum firewood." White Wendy replies in a simplified, "dumbed-down" fashion: "Squaw no gettum firewood! Squaw go home." Apparently, only these simplistic replies will "get through" to the unintelligent ogre created by Disney.

These sexist and racist portrayals of Indigenous women are still with us. For example, a comic book published in 2005 entitled *Gunpowder Girl and the Outlaw Squaw* can be purchased from Amazon.com for only $12.95. This comic book is about an orphan girl with no home and a deviant Indigenous woman who refuses to live on her reservation (where she apparently belongs). Both seek their fortune as outlaws, wearing tight denim or buckskin pants (in the case of the "squaw") and showing a lot of cleavage.

In 2012, as part of the Aboriginal Gathering Place Lecture Series at Kwantlen Polytechnic University, I presented a content analysis of depictions of Indigenous women in popular culture. My purpose was to demystify this reality of their sexualization and subjugation.[30] As a way to explore this topic, I chose to look at people dressing up as "Indians" during the widely celebrated holiday, and uniquely constructive space, of Halloween. During Halloween, many different professions, cultures, celebrities, and religious figures, symbols, or clothing are used as part of the charade—for jokes, fun, or to present something sexy. Indigenous themed costumes are no exception. In fact, as Adrienne Keene (Cherokee Nation and EdD graduate from Harvard University) points out, costumes of Indigenous peoples are common at Halloween, and many people think dressing up as an "Indian" is something sexy and fun that doesn't harm anyone.[31] However, this view fails to acknowledge what these costumes really signify given the statistics on violence against Indigenous women and on the numbers of them who have gone missing or have been murdered.

To begin my study on popular representations of Indigenous women at Halloween, I chose three major Halloween costume websites. Websites were chosen based on four factors:

1) Popularity—websites had to come up on the front page of a Google search for "Halloween costumes" to ensure these sites were the most "popular" and were frequently accessed.
2) North American—websites had to cater to both Canada and the United States.
3) Searchable—websites had to allow me to search the term "Indian" in order to facilitate a consistent mode of accessing data.
4) Linked to social media—each site had to be linked to Facebook and provide the number of costume "likes"; these factors enabled an additional and consistent mode of examining the popularity of sites and costumes.

Data analyzed included costume descriptions, customer reviews (available on two of the three sites assessed), as well as the number of Facebook "likes" for individual costumes. Descriptive statistics were gathered on the number of Facebook likes, and themes were derived from costume descriptions and reviews. Thus, what emerged from the data (after successive waves of reading) was a very distorted, sexualized depiction of Indigenous women, which, in many ways, reinforced white male dominance over them. Five major themes were identified, and these included referring to Indigenous women as sexual objects and in racist sexualized terms, such as "temptress," "trouble," "squaw," "sexy," and "exotic."

For example, the "Temptress Indian Costume" found on Halloween-costumes.com had 100 Facebook likes. Here is how the site describes this costume: "Tempt those cowboys to stay for a little longer when you wear this temptress Indian costume." This idea of an Indigenous woman as a temptress is very dangerous because a temptress is "a woman who sets out to lure or seduce a man or men"; she is a "seductress."[32] Defining Indigenous women in this way shifts accountability for men's actions to her, making her seem like the aggressor or, at the very least, like someone who wants to be seduced—someone who is asking for it.

Write-ups on Halloween costume websites drew on many sacred items, reducing both them and Indigenous women to something trivial. For example, on the spirithalloween.com website, the following description received 523 Facebook "likes": "Put the wow back in pow-wow when you go native in this very sexy Tribal Trouble Indian adult women's costume. They may need to break out the peace pipe because the other squaws will want to torch your teepee when their menfolk see you in this foxy costume!" This description draws on Pow Wow, a ceremonial celebration. It draws on the peace pipe, which is another sacred ceremony. It also suggests that all Indigenous peoples used to live in tepees, which is inaccurate and continues to frame Indigenous peoples in one cookie-cutter description. In fact, Indigenous peoples had all sorts of traditional living accommodations. For example, my Algonquin ancestors used wigwams, and my Huron ancestors had longhouses.

What's more, the description uses the word "trouble" to depict this "sexy" costume, which is pictured next to the write-up. Again, the Indigenous woman is labelled as being the "problem" in the first place; the dangerous inference is that Indigenous women are deserving of sexual advances. This idea reinforces stereotypes and perpetuates the sexual violence that affects Indigenous women.

Some of the other costumes available from these websites are labelled "Pocahottie" or "Sexy Cherokee Warrior," again playing on the idea that an Indigenous woman is some sort of sex-goddess Pocahontas or sexy fantasy warrior. These types of portrayals are seen beyond Halloween as well. In the 2012 Victoria's Secret fashion show, for example, white model Karlie Kloss was dressed to depict a "sexy warrior"; she wore a headdress and turquoise jewellery, coupled with a leopard-print bra and underwear set and clear high-heeled stilettoes fringed with leather. Similarly, in 2008, the model representing Canada at the Miss Universe pageant wore a headdress and a leather-fringed, bikini-like outfit and high heels, of course.

Outfits such as these fuel an inaccurate stereotype that makes it easier to objectify and sexually violate Indigenous women. Also, using regalia and sacred objects or other props (e.g., axes, bow and arrows, or other weapons) in these sexualized and girly-girly ways trivializes Indigenous cultures and women. At the same time, the wisecracks made about Indigenous peoples sitting around fires or everyone living in tepees reduce all Indigenous heritage to one cookie-cutter, stereotypical facet, suggesting that Indigenous cultures are inconsequential or, in some cases, a joke.

Many times, non-Indigenous women will use these sexualized "temptress" representations of Indigenous women to seem sexier or more "exotic." Popular singer Kesha, whose albums have reached number one on Billboard charts in both Canada and the United States, often does so. In 2010, on the popular show *American Idol*, she danced in sultry movements on stage while singing "Think you'll be gettin' this [while pointing to her body] / Nah nah nah / Not in the back of my / Car, car, car / If you keep talkin' that Blah, blah, blah," implying that men should get straight to it (sex) and cut the talk. She does this while wearing an Indigenous headdress and with war paint on her cheeks.

White women who use Indigenous people's sacred objects, such as the headdress, while representing themselves as not much more than highly sexed bodies play a part in normalizing the rape and sexual assault of Indigenous women by buttressing the idea that Indigenous women are sexual objects to be used at others' disposal. It incorrectly frames Indigenous peoples and cultures as being okay with disrespecting women. Further, these white women are appropriating sacred objects from cultures that they maintain their "white privilege" over and, moreover, that their settler ancestors attempted to destroy. Headdresses have real meaning to the particular Indigenous peoples who wear them. They are usually used only for certain ceremonies or for official addresses. Also, headdresses or certain feathers (e.g., eagle feathers) are just as sacred to certain Indigenous cultures and peoples as the Bible or images of Jesus on the cross are to many Christians. If sacred Indigenous objects are used in such an inappropriate fashion, they are desecrated and belittled.

Sometimes, sacred objects and "sexy squaws" are presented in popular culture along with other stereotypical representations of Indigenous peoples. In October 2012, for example, popular American singer Lana Del Rey released her music video *Ride*, which shows her wearing a feathered headdress and putting a gun to her head while, at the same time, moving about and striking sultry poses. Now direct violence is added to the picture, but worse is yet to come. During this headdress scene, the video cuts to frames of whiskey bottles with booze being sprayed everywhere. (The people drinking are on motorcycles around a huge campfire.) These scenes not only fuel the inaccurate stereotype of the "drunken Indian" but also show a complete disregard and disrespect for the Indigenous people who do struggle with alcohol.

Popular culture's distorted representations of Indigenous women make their sexual exploitation easier by objectifying and dehumanizing them, clearing the path for the real sexual violence perpetrated against Indigenous women. Research shows that, in the absence of any moral justification for violence, both routinization and dehumanization make violence easier. In other words, the strength of the restraining forces against violence are weakened if the violence is seen as routine and both the victim and the victimizer are deprived of identity and community—dehumanized.[33] Once this dehumanization becomes normalized by wider society, it is even more dangerous. The normalized practices of Western society, which include objectifying and dehumanizing Indigenous women and appropriating and devaluing Indigenous identity through dressing-up as "Indians," has led to further threats. Indigenous identity has become a cipher to be bought and sold in the same market as "Indian" costumes and "Indian-paraphernalia."[34]

I am not suggesting here that Kesha or model Karlie Kloss or others who have assumed these costumes are maliciously or purposefully trying to promote sexual violence against Indigenous women. Rather, they too have been blinded by colonial ideologies, by the dominant values, beliefs, and prejudices of this colonized world. The answer is not condemning or blaming individual people who have yet to *see* the realities stemming from the legacies of Canada's colonial history but rather to educate. If we only villainize people who engage in these colonial misrepresentations, we will never be able to move forward. Education and understanding are key. Once aware that their actions objectify Indigenous women, some will change and some will choose to turn a blind eye. But we must first give people an honest chance to acknowledge, understand, and change behaviours, to join in the quest to eliminate the misrepresentations of Indigenous women in popular culture.

Finally, as Adrienne Keene explains, although some purport that presenting these inaccurate, stereotypical, and sexualized representations of Indigenous women is simply "harmless fun," they are "hurtful and dangerous because they present a false and stereotyped image"—one that puts "Indians . . . in the same category as pirates, princesses, and cartoon characters."[35] So people need to start asking, "Harmless to whom?" These representations open the door to violence against Indigenous women by reasserting the historical labels once applied—by characterizing Indigenous women as less than human and, thus, as "rapable" sexual objects.

The National Crisis of Missing and Murdered Indigenous Women

The view that Indigenous women are "rapable" is further supported by the way the Canadian criminal justice system chooses to deal with the cases of those who are missing or murdered. Indigenous women have become easier targets for abduction and abuse not only because of ingrained notions that they are lesser beings but also because of the deficient reactions the police and other government officials have to these incidents.

As of March 2010, the Sisters in Spirit initiative estimated that 582 Indigenous women in Canada had gone missing or had been murdered over the past 30 years. Of the cases identified, 39 per cent were found to have occurred between 2000 and 2010 and 17 per cent in the 1990s. The majority of these cases, regardless of when they took place, involved young women and girls; just over half of the cases in which the age of the victim was known involved women under 31 years of age, and 17 per cent of these cases involved females 18 years of age and under. What's more, many of these women had become mothers, which speaks to the intergenerational impacts that this crisis will have. Of the cases in which family information was known, which included just over one-third of the cases (206), 88 per cent were mothers.[36]

In September 2013, Maryanne Pearce created a database of missing and murdered women in Canada as part of her PhD thesis at the University of Ottawa. Information was gathered from "websites, police files on the Internet, print and electronic newspaper articles, books, journals, theses, government and non-governmental reports, missing women posters and other publicly available information."[37] Cases from 1946 to 2013 were documented, and the database eventually contained the details of 3,329 missing and murdered women, 824 of whom were Indigenous.

In 2014, the RCMP documented 1,181 cases of missing or murdered Indigenous women between 1980 and 2013; 1,017 had been murdered and 164 were still listed as missing.[38] These data show that, although they represent only 4.3 per cent of the total female population in Canada, Indigenous women represent 16 per cent of the female homicides in Canada.

This situation is being referred to as a "crisis"—and rightly so, as Indigenous women comprise only about 2 per cent of the Canadian population. But this crisis has not been given the same attention as others in Canada. If women from the general Canadian population had gone missing or were murdered at the same rate as Indigenous women, Canada would have lost 18,000 women since the late 1970s.[39] This statistic would have most definitely triggered a national call to action as it would have represented 61 per cent of all the murders committed between 1970 and 2013.

Thus, Indigenous women face not only extreme levels of violence in their communities and are being targeted for abduction, rape, and murder but also face the social injustice of the lack of adequate response to the high rates of victimization they experience. Ignoring this major crisis essentially means re-victimizing Indigenous women. After concluding his visit to Canada in October 2013, James Anaya, the UN special rapporteur on the rights of Indigenous peoples, noted the "disturbing phenomenon" of the missing and murdered Indigenous women.[40] Amnesty International has noted the utter failure of police and other government officials to investigate these cases, or even take them seriously.[41] Almost half of the murder cases documented by the Sisters in Spirit initiative remain unsolved.[42]

For example, in Kitigan Zibi First Nation in Québec, just north of Ottawa, Ontario, two young Indigenous women, Maisy Odjick and Shannon Alexander, have been missing since September 2008. Their families have received little support or help from the police, as is evident from a letter one of the mothers wrote to politicians in March 2009: "Since my daughter's disappearance, September 6, 2008, to present day, very little to nil support and communication has been provided by these police services. The lack of police services and support from the onset has been a long, frustrating and exhausting six months for me and my family."[43]

The families were told that the girls had probably run away, and the cases were not given any media coverage until Maisy and Shannon had been missing for two weeks. However, when a baby lion cub that someone was keeping as a pet got loose in the area in April 2008, the cub, "Boomer," received far more media attention than did the two missing girls. In addition, police brought in helicopters and a team of 20 officers to search an area of 20 square kilometres to help locate the animal.[44] No such measures were taken for the two young women. These unequal responses demonstrate an unsettling attitude and send an ideological message that a lion cub is more important than two Indigenous women.[45]

In former Prime Minister Stephen Harper's Speech from the Throne on March 3, 2010, he finally called real public attention to the crisis of missing and murdered Indigenous women. "Our Government will take additional action to address the disturbing number of unsolved cases of murdered and missing Aboriginal women," he promised. "The Sisters in Spirit initiative has drawn particular attention to this pressing criminal justice priority."[46] The federal government then pledged $10 million in funding over two years to address the high rates of missing and murdered Indigenous women.[47] Far from supporting the work done by Sisters in Spirit, however, the government, after this announcement, initially excluded the group from the ongoing development of policy related to missing or murdered Indigenous women and then, in effect, defunded Sisters in Spirit, eliminating support for the group's database completely and substantially redirecting money to government departments.[48] Liberal MP Anita Neville called the government's proclamation of action on this issue "a duplicitous announcement": "Sisters in Spirit was told to shut down, told not to collect stats or advocate, but still they were used as a poster program. It's all smoke and mirrors and it's disrespectful."[49] Unfortunately, responses to this crisis from the provinces have been inadequate as well.

The Highway of Tears and Abuse and Fear in Northern British Columbia

Sadly, the dehumanizing treatment of Indigenous women is also symbolized by a stretch of road dubbed the "Highway of Tears." Over a period of 40 years, between 18 and 40 women and girls have gone missing along or in the vicinity of Highway 16, which stretches for 724 kilometres between Prince Rupert and Prince George in northern British Columbia. The vast majority are young Indigenous women.[50]

Between 1988 and 1995, at least five young Indigenous women went missing along this highway. Despite protests by Indigenous communities, however, the police did not take these disappearances seriously, nor did the media give them any real attention. This situation did not change until June 2002, when a non-Indigenous woman disappeared along Highway 16.[51]

Some women have been found dead along or near this highway, and others are still listed as missing.[52] Consequently, in the fall of 2005, the RCMP established Project E-PANA, an initiative specifically designated to investigate the Highway of Tears cases.[53] The project investigates cases of missing or murdered women dating from 1969 to 2006 that took place along or near three BC highways (16, 97, and 5). By 2012, the RCMP had investigated 1,413 cases since the project started; it had also conducted 2,500 interviews, administered 100 polygraphs, and taken 750 DNA samples.[54] In September of 2012, using DNA evidence, police finally linked a now-deceased Oregon convict to the 1974 Highway of Tears murder of 16-year-old Colleen MacMillen. More of these highway murders are believed to be linked to this suspect.[55] However, the majority of these cases remain unsolved, or suspects remain uncharged because of lack of evidence.

In February of 2013, the Human Rights Watch released a report documenting the lack of police accountability, abusive policing, and the failure of police and the government to protect Indigenous women and girls in northern British Columbia. This report was based on five weeks of field research conducted between July and August 2012. In total, 87 interviews were conducted; researchers interviewed 42 Indigenous women and 8 Indigenous girls (all females were aged from 15 and to their late 60s) and 19 community service providers, including transition house and homeless shelter workers and youth outreach workers. The victims' family members and 7 current and former RCMP members who policed these areas were also interviewed. More Indigenous women and girls initially expressed an interest in being interviewed for this study; however, some withdrew because they feared retaliation from the police.[56]

The final report, entitled *Those Who Take Us Away: Abusive Policing and Failures in Protection of Indigenous Women and Girls in Northern British Columbia, Canada*, highlights how people in authority not only have ignored their responsibility to protect Indigenous women and girls but also have taken advantage of them. For example, the case of former British Columbia provincial court judge David Ramsay is discussed. In 2004, Ramsay was convicted of breach of trust by a public officer, sexual assault causing bodily harm, and two counts of obtaining sexual services from a child. The offences took place while he was a sitting provincial court judge (between 1992 and 2001), when he habitually sought out girls on the streets for prostitution and raped them.[57] His victims were Indigenous girls between the ages of 12 and 17, some of whom had appeared before him in court.

Evidence showed that Ramsay once raped a young girl in his car, slamming her head into the dashboard until she bled, assaulted her, and left her naked by the roadside; she was forced to hitchhike back to the town without clothes. Human Rights Watch researchers spoke to the father of one of Ramsay's 13-year-old victims. This father also described his daughter being sexually abused by police officers in the area when she was in her late teens: "For sexual favors [the police] would stop her on the road and put their hands down her pants saying they were searching her [for drugs]."[58]

Indeed, when the *Ramsay* case broke, various Indigenous women alleged that the police had been involved or complicit in their sexual exploitation. Many times these allegations were dismissed because of various delays. In one instance reported by Human Rights Watch, a police officer was alleged to have paid $60 for oral sex from a child and then struck her across the face after she asked for a condom to be used. Disciplinary action against this officer was dismissed, as the incident had reportedly taken place more than one year before the accused became aware of the allegations.[59]

Of the 10 towns visited by Human Rights Watch researchers, 5 alleged their women had been sexually assaulted or raped by police officers. For example, a homeless woman interviewed explained how she was taken to a remote location in July 2012, where she was raped by four police officers. This same woman described similar incidents that happened earlier. In one, police officers had taken her underwear after the rape. For the Indigenous women in these areas who report being assaulted, having their underwear taken seems to be a recurring issue, so much so that a community worker in one of the towns keeps packages of underwear to distribute to women living on the street, who report similar abuses at the hands of police.[60]

The breach of trust and abuse of power by men in authority was further highlighted by one Indigenous woman who had spent time in various group homes for children. When she accompanied another Indigenous group home member to that person's court appearance, she noted how long it took for that woman to say her goodbyes and leave the courthouse after her appearance:

> I asked, "How do you know these people?" "They're my regulars," she said. Judges, lawyers, police . . . She killed herself a month before her 19th birthday.[61]

Those Who Take Us Away revealed other very serious incidents of police abuse, many dating back decades that have yet to be brought to justice. Here is the story of one woman who is still hoping for justice:

> When I was 16, I was raped by a police officer and became pregnant. I got an abortion because otherwise I would have done it to myself with a coat hanger. . . . I was working for a police officer who had a pizza joint. Some of his young officers would come in to eat and one night one offered me a ride home. That was the first time he raped me. The second time he caught me. I didn't ask for a ride, but he got me. . . . I'm looking at filing an application to the Attorney General about the rape. He [the perpetrator] is still on the force . . . how many other young girls has he hurt, as he hurt me.[62]

In another incident, a police officer is said to have stalked an Indigenous woman for a year and a half. She described him parking outside of her home, following her to the bank and the grocery store (indeed, wherever she went), and phoning her. She said it got so bad that she could not go anywhere without him popping up. He would even abuse his authority by pulling her over with his police car. Because of this behaviour, the woman (who was also a mother) became too afraid to leave her house. She reported the stalking to the Commission for Public Complaints Against the RCMP, but her complaint was dismissed, and the commission failed to take action.[63]

The Human Rights Watch researchers noted how struck they were during the course of their research by how much the women they interviewed feared the police. The level of fear they witnessed, stated researchers, is typically found in post-conflict communities or post-transition countries. They cited Iraq as an example.[64]

Women also reported calling the police for assistance but, instead of being helped, being shamed (e.g., for alcohol or drug use), blamed, abused, or arrested themselves. In 2012, for example, one mother, Lena, reported that her 15-year-old daughter's arm was broken by a police officer when Lena called for help to deal with a domestic dispute between her daughter and her daughter's 22-year-old boyfriend. Another incident reportedly occurred in 2011. A 17-year-old who was being chased by gang members yelled to a woman on a balcony to call the police. When the police arrived they put the girl who had been running away into the police car where an officer repeatedly punched her in the face. She was later taken to city cells for the night and then released. Her face was so badly beaten that she lost her job at a restaurant. In this case, the officer was charged with criminal assault, which is pending.[65]

The Human Rights Watch study also expressed concern about the number of women reporting experiences of abuse in city cells. Some of the women interviewed claimed they were jailed for public intoxication, held for extended periods without food, and left unprotected against other incarcerated individuals, who were allowed to attack them (while officials watched rather than intervening). Others reported being sexually assaulted and abused while in city cells. Indigenous women and girls, acquaintances, and advocacy organizations reported similar incidents—of Indigenous female prisoners being sexually assaulted while passed out. On some occasions, the women woke to find their pants and underwear missing.[66]

That sexism and racism exist in law enforcement is supported by evidence from within policing organizations as well. In a personal communication from a currently employed female RCMP officer working in the lower mainland of British Columbia—who wishes to remain nameless because she fears retaliation—the force is described as "an old boys club." The officer reports hearing sexist comments in her workplace and being made fun of by colleagues for expressions of Indigenous culture.[67]

Currently, a class action lawsuit is underway against the RCMP, instigated by former Nanaimo RCMP police officer Janet Merlo.[68] Merlo claims she was a victim of "persistent and ongoing gender-based discrimination and harassment" by male RCMP police officers and that the RCMP did not do anything to put a stop to it.[69] One of Merlo's lawyers, Jason Murray, notes that more than 200 additional women—current and former RCMP officers—have come forward to join this case. A recent survey of 426 RCMP officers identified that women officers have little confidence in the processes in place to address sexual harassment.[70] Many of these women do not feel harassers will be held accountable or face consequences, and many fear retaliation. The Human Rights Watch researchers interviewed an Indigenous male RCMP officer from BC who explained that he had witnessed the misogynist attitudes of his fellow officers: "They used to fax racist and sexist jokes around and wonder why I didn't laugh—I'm First Nations and I have sisters."[71]

The report also reveals that women have very limited recourse against police abuse. A complaint can be lodged with the Commission for Public Complaints Against the RCMP; however, the process is not seamless and does not inspire confidence. Rather, it is time consuming, and, because investigation of the complaint will likely fall to the RCMP itself or to another external police force, fear of retaliation is very high in these small northern BC communities. The Human Rights Watch chose to name its report in order to highlight this fear. *Those Who Take Us Away*, the report's title, is a literal translation of the word for "police" in the Carrier language, which is spoken by a number of Indigenous communities in northern British Columbia.[72]

In September 2012, British Columbia tried to address the problem of police investigating complaints against police by opening a civilian-led investigatory body called the Independent Investigations Office (IIO). However, much of what Indigenous women are experiencing is outside of the mandate of this office. The IIO is limited to investigating only certain types of serious bodily injury or death, and rape and sexual abuse are excluded from its mandate. As the Human Rights Watch report contends, this exclusion is a major mistake and an injustice to Indigenous women; it "sends a loud message that assaults on women are not important."[73]

At the national level, Canada does have some strong legal protections for women experiencing violence. Various inquiries and reports have also addressed issues related to violence against women. For example, in response to the failure of the police to investigate properly and fully the women who had gone missing from or were murdered in the Downtown Eastside of Vancouver, the government put in place a provincial Missing Women Commission of Inquiry in 2010. This commission, headed by Wally Oppal, released its final report in December of 2012.

Missing and Murdered Women in Downtown Eastside Vancouver

In the late 1990s, women in Downtown Eastside Vancouver started to go missing in alarming numbers; many were Indigenous (an estimated 58 per cent according to some).[74] Initially, it was thought that about 27 women were missing, but this number continued to increase.[75] The police were doing very little to discover why these women were going missing. When the families and friends of these missing women made reports, police and staff at the Vancouver Police Department (VPD) suggested that the women were transient drug addicts and not in any danger.[76] Media stories painted these women with a single stereotypical brush, fuelling the prejudiced assumption that all of these missing women were "drug-addicted sex workers" and noting that "'many' of the women were Aboriginal."[77] Community members and advocacy organizations pointed to the fact that society—the media, police, and others in authority—basically thought of these women as "disposable." Given that some were working the streets or were poor and marginalized, the police didn't take reports seriously, nor did they care to dedicate their time fully to try to get to the bottom of this growing epidemic.

During the same time that these women were going missing, a "garage burglar" was on the loose in the municipality of West Vancouver, where, in three months, there were 28 garage burglaries involving expensive houses. In response to this, Vancouver Mayor Philip Owen offered a $100,000 reward for any information leading to the capture of this "garage burglar."[78] This reward helped in locating and charging the thief.

Not surprisingly, women's organizations working with the missing women's families were shocked at the skewed priorities shown by the city responding to the "garage burglar" and not to the crisis involving missing women in the Downtown Eastside. After experiencing intense lobbying and being offered support from BC Attorney General Dosanjh (to the tune of $70,000), the Vancouver Police Board okayed a $100,000 reward to aid in the investigation of the missing women in April 1999. A poster featuring the 31 missing women was prepared in June and made public in July. Meanwhile, attracted by the mystery and by reports of a possible serial killer at large, *America's Most Wanted* arrived in Vancouver in late July to film a segment dedicated to the missing women, which aired July 31, 1999. It was highly sensationalized and focused on the prostitution angle: "Tonight there is fear in Vancouver's Downtown Eastside, fear among many of the women working the street, that they could be the next victim of a *mysterious* killer."[79] Four women were found; two were alive and two had died (one of a heart condition and one of an overdose). This discovery caused police to question the media's suggestion that a serial killer was at work—"no bodies equals no murder," was the attitude of some.[80]

One Vancouver police officer consistently maintained, however, that a serial killer was probably responsible for the disappearances. Detective Kim Rossmo—who was actually the first police officer in Canada to hold a PhD in criminology—was using geographical profiling to understand criminal behaviour patterns.[81] As early as September 4, 1998, Rossmo presented a report to the upper management of the Vancouver Police Department (VPD); he proposed that a press release be issued as a warning to the community of the possibility that there was a serial killer at work. The VPD rejected this idea, and, reportedly, considerable interdepartmental strife hampered the investigation of the missing women over the next few years.[82] In 2000, Rossmo's five-year contract as a geographic profiler was not renewed, and he was asked to return to the position of constable with the VPD, a lower rank with less salary.[83] Not surprisingly, Rossmo declined and left the department. Some officers of the VPD, now retired, think that taking Rossmo's various reports seriously earlier could have saved lives, as suburban pig farmer Robert Pickton had been arrested as recently as 1997 on a charge of attempting to murder a woman working in the sex trade.

The attitude of the police to women working in the sex trade or struggling with addictions in Downtown Eastside Vancouver was also complicit in the murder and unexplained disappearances of these women. Criminologist and leading expert on prostitution in Canada John Lowman describes how the police attitude of stamping out prostitution and drug use worked against proper investigation:

> The police and the politicians actively created the problem they are now trying to fix. The rhetoric of the '80s and early '90s was "We'll get rid of the prostitutes." The idea of eliminating prostitution in Vancouver has translated tragically into REALLY getting rid of prostitutes. We chase them from one area to another. They find themselves in dark streets in defenceless situations.[84]

To the families and friends of the missing women, police seemed to be doing little and not to care. Given this perception, families were taking matters into their own hands, going to the Downtown Eastside and asking around for information with photos of their loved ones. The story of Lynn Frey (mother to Marnie Frey, whose body would later be found on Pickton's farm) shows how frustrated the families became with the investigation. Lynn Frey testified that she reported her daughter as missing in August 1997. Because Marnie was living away from home and an adult, Lynn says her reports were not accepted until December 1997. Indeed, the first official record of the case is the Campbell River RCMP's missing person's file opened that month, which lists Marnie as having had no contact with her family since August. Because Marnie was living in Vancouver working in the sex trade when she went missing, a copy of her file was forwarded to the VPD, which did investigate, but not until a delay of about nine months. Meanwhile, Lynn travelled to Vancouver multiple times to look for Marnie. On one trip, she reportedly discovered information about the Pickton farm and visited there herself, telling her suspicions to the VPD; the Vancouver detective investigating Marnie's case reports no record of Lynn Frey informing the VPD about Pickton. The detailed log of Marnie's case ends in the summer of 1999, although a few notes were added through 2001. Lynn Frey thinks the case was treated as if Marnie were still alive. Marnie's remains were found on Pickton's farm in 2002.[85]

During this time, the number of women missing from Downtown Eastside Vancouver continued to rise, to 61 in 2003 after 30 more were reported missing.[86] Finally, in January 2001, the RCMP and VPD created a special taskforce on missing women called "Project Evenhanded."[87] It replaced the VPD-based Missing Women Review Team that wound down in the fall of 2000. Neither investigative group was "suspect based" as they were both instigated to track down the women, although Project Evenhanded finally indicated in May 2001 that it "generally suspected" the actions of a serial killer were connected to the disappearances.[88]

Still, Project Evenhanded was found to have made various mistakes, such as incorrect risk assessments and wrong assumptions that the serial killing had stopped. The project investigated the cases of 68 women missing from Downtown Eastside Vancouver and surrounding areas; the DNA of 33 of those women was found on Robert Pickton's farm. Of those 33 women, 12 were Indigenous.[89]

Taken as a whole, the investigations into the fates of these missing women were not without their various critical police failures. According to the Missing Women's Inquiry, these failures included a lack of prevention strategies to address the known vulnerability of the women being targeted, the failure of the VPD and Project Evenhanded to provide warnings to vulnerable women because of paternalistic and prejudiced attitudes toward these women, the failure to employ a full range of investigative strategies (e.g., surveillance, undercover operations, proper interview and interrogative techniques, search warrants, and the use of forensic evidence), the failure to implement an Indigenous-specific investigation strategy, a lack of collaboration with the families and communities of the women, the restricted involvement of unofficial parties (e.g., family members or non-profit organizations) in the investigations, and ineffective strategies to engage and collaborate with the media, among other problems.[90]

On February 5, 2002, Pickton was finally arrested. Police were acting on a warrant for a firearm violation and came across the personal belongings of a woman who had been missing. It has since been revealed that Pickton brutalized these women. He raped them and butchered them as if they were animals at his slaughterhouse. He also fed their remains to pigs on his farm. Some women's bodies he dumped at an animal waste-rendering facility in Vancouver (West Coast Reduction).

In January 2006, Pickton pled not guilty in the deaths of 27 women (one charge was rejected for lack of evidence in March), and what has come to be called "the largest-known serial-murder case in Canada" got underway.[91] The 26 charges were split into two groups, one including 6 counts and the other 20. He was tried for the murder of 6 women, 3 of whom were Indigenous, in January 2007 and found guilty of second-degree murder in December of that year. The Crown then decided that, as long as the 6 convictions were upheld on appeal, it would not pursue the next trial, for the deaths of 20 women, reasoning that Pickton had already received the maximum sentence one was able to get in Canada—life with no possibility of parole for 25 years. This decision, of course, was very upsetting to many of the victims' families, who never received their day in court and thus were denied closure.[92]

The final report by the Missing Women Commission of Inquiry highlighted the systematic bias of the police. At the release of the inquiry's findings, Oppal was quoted as saying that these women were "treated as throwaways."[93] The report also noted the cross-jurisdictional problems that significantly contributed to the failures of the investigations. For example, even though the VPD thought Robert Pickton was a top suspect, the department did not pursue him because he was located in the RCMP's jurisdiction.

The report evaluated the investigations into the women's disappearances that were conducted by all the police forces in British Columbia, investigations that occurred between January 23, 1997, and February 5, 2002. It also examined the decision not to proceed with Pickton's second trial. As part of the research process, the commission held evidentiary hearings in which it heard from family members and friends of victims, witnesses, 911 operators, police, and other government officials and experts (e.g., John Lowman). The hearings took place from October 2011 to June 2012. In May 2012, it also held a series of public policy forums during which various community members, professors (myself and my colleagues included), police, 911 operators, and others were asked to speak. Of course, the commission also examined various expert reports, evidence, photographs, affidavits by officers, letters, and other related documents.

The report noted two measures as needing immediate attention: the allocation of funding to existing centres that provide emergency services to women in the sex trade and the development and implementation of an enhanced public transit system in northern BC communities (most notably along Highway 16). Highlights from the other formal recommendations include the implementation of various restorative measures that would include Indigenous elders, as well as a compensation fund for the children of the missing and murdered women.[94] Additionally, equality-promoting measures, policies, and guidelines were called for, including equality audits of police forces in BC, which would focus specifically on the duty to protect marginalized and Indigenous women. Mandatory, experiential police-officer training offered in cooperation with vulnerable community members and funding for law reform research projects were also suggested.

A significant recommendation of the report was to put in place measures to enhance the safety of vulnerable women. Initially, these would involve conducting evaluations of current programming and developing new protocols to measure high-risk offenders. The prevention of violence against Indigenous women and rural women was specifically highlighted as an aim. Measures were to include more consultative processes, a Highway of Tears symposium, and additional funding for violence programs in First Nations communities. Improved missing person policies and practices, enhanced police investigations and accountability, a regional police force for the greater Vancouver area, and more effective multi-jurisdictional policing were also recommended. Finally, the report suggested measures to assure that these missing and murdered women's legacies were honoured: for example, it recommended the appointment of both a provincial advisor to champion the implementation of the report's other recommendations and an independent advisor to work collaboratively with the families during implementation.

Some were happy with the report because it highlighted police and government failures and legitimized previous criticisms of the authorities' attempts to respond to the crisis. Also, the report provided to the families and friends of the victims some additional closure. However, many have called this report inadequate. Some note that the voices and experiences of Downtown Eastside women, families, women's groups, and Indigenous organizations were shut out of the processes. Rather, the testimony of police and their evidence were favoured over those of groups, organizations, and community peoples. These organizations and groups were only invited participants and had no official voice on the commission. Also, they were offered no funding to participate in the processes, yet the province paid for 25 lawyers for police agencies and individual police officers.[95] Furthermore, the inquiry was not led or headed by an Indigenous woman or women but rather by a non-Indigenous male.

Calls for a National Public Inquiry

Many individuals and advocacy groups called attention to the urgent need for a national public inquiry into the missing and murdered Indigenous women in Canada. In October 2013, James Anaya, the UN special rapporteur on the rights of Indigenous peoples, documented this support for a national inquiry:

> I have heard a consistent call for a national level inquiry into the extent of the problem and appropriate solutions moving forward with the participation of victims' families and others deeply affected. I concur that a comprehensive and nation-wide inquiry into the issue could help ensure a coordinated response and the opportunity for the loved ones of victims to be heard, and would demonstrate a responsiveness to the concerns raised by the families and communities affected by this epidemic.[96]

One day after the release of the Human Rights Watch report *Those Who Take Us Away* (on February 15, 2013), Liberal MP Carolyn Bennett called for the launch of a missing and murdered women's committee. A unanimous vote on February 27, 2013, approved it. This committee is not the same as a national commission, for which many Indigenous supporters had hoped; however, it did represent a positive move forward. The mandate of the committee was to study violence affecting Indigenous women. Members travelled across the country to collect evidence. Their report, entitled *Invisible Women: A Call to Action—A Report on Missing and Murdered Indigenous Women in Canada*, was tabled in parliament on March 7, 2014.[97]

For many, this report was a massive disappointment. Carolyn Bennett called it "hugely disappointing" and "a total travesty of Parliamentary process."[98] The Native Women's Association of Canada (NWAC) expressed its "disappointment and frustration" in a press release responding to the report.[99] Then Assembly of First Nations (AFN) National Chief Shawn A-in-chut Atleo stated that the report "disappoints victims and families"[100]

One reason for the expressed disappointment was that the report's final 16 recommendations did not reflect the witnesses' testimony. Notably missing was the recommendation that a national public inquiry into the missing and murdered Indigenous women in Canada be established, along with a national action plan to address this crisis. The report itself acknowledged that many witnesses called for a nation-wide public inquiry: "Several witnesses called for the establishment of an independent public inquiry into the issue of missing or murdered Aboriginal women in Canada, adding their voices to those of leaders of national Aboriginal organizations, premiers and leaders of provinces and territories and several international organizations."[101] In spite of these calls for action, the report failed to include recommendations "to hold a National Public Inquiry and to implement a National Action Plan."[102]

Rather, in many ways, the report seemed to support the federal Conservatives' own agenda. (Harper's Conservatives had a majority government at the time.) For example, the second recommendation of the report reads, "That the federal government continue strengthening the criminal justice system to ensure, among other things, that violent and repeat offenders serve appropriate sentences."[103] This upheld the Conservative government's tough-on-crime agenda but did not reflect the witness testimony outlined in the body of the report.[104] Ultimately, the fact that an inquiry was not recommended remains at the heart of disappointment for many.

Furthermore, NWAC was originally offered the role of special advisor and expert witness to the Parliamentary committee, which could have proved very beneficial given the organization's extensive knowledge on the subject of Indigenous women. However, the NWAC was not included in a major way. Indeed, as NWAC President Michèle Taïna Audette explains, "It truly is unfortunate that this opportunity has been lost; on paper it looks like we are the special advisor and expert witness, but what we received was tokenism and no real engagement."[105]

Right before this final report was tabled, the murder of a 26-year-old Inuk woman, Loretta Saunders (who was working on her honours thesis proposal at St. Mary's University in Halifax), sparked many Indigenous peoples and groups to renew their call for a national inquiry.[106] Among them were President of the Nova Scotia Native Women's Association Cheryl Maloney and Holly Jarret, one of Loretta Saunders's family members.[107] On March 5, they organized a rally on Parliament Hill in Ottawa; it served as both a memorial to Loretta and the call for a national inquiry. Loretta Saunders was found murdered on February 26, 2014. Two of her roommates were charged with her murder. In her honours thesis, she planned to study the murders of three Indigenous women who were from Nova Scotia: Nora Bernard, Anna Mae Pictou Aquash, and Tanya Brooks.[108]

On February 13, 2014, NWAC presented the federal government with a petition calling for an inquiry; it was signed by 23,000 people.[109] On March 2, 2014, Mohawk people from Tyendinaga blocked a road, then later a railway crossing, calling for a national inquiry into missing and murdered Indigenous women and girls.

Then, on March 6, 2014, when Conservative Justice Minister Peter MacKay responded to calls for an inquiry by asking to table "the 40 initiatives" that the Conservatives had taken to address the issue of murdered and missing women, he got agitated by Opposition members and threw the documents he wanted to table onto the floor of the House of Commons (he has since apologized).[110] This action upset many Indigenous peoples, but even more upsetting was MacKay's implication that the federal government's anti-crime initiatives were sufficient to address this problem. Defending against initiating a national inquiry into the disproportionate murder and disappearance of Indigenous women was the continual response of the Conservative government. For example, in May 2014, then-Prime Minister Stephen Harper offered his opinion of such an inquiry: "I remain very skeptical of commissions of inquiry generally. My experience has been they almost always run way over time, way over budget, and often the recommendations prove to be of limited utility."[111]

The Conservative government stuck by its decision not to initiate an inquiry; Indigenous women continued to go missing and to be murdered. In 2014, the bodies of seven Indigenous women were found in the Red River that runs through Winnipeg, Manitoba.[112] After 15-year-old Tina Fontaine's body was found wrapped in a bag in the river in August 2014, a group of volunteers organized to dredge the river to look for bodies or any other related evidence. Bernadette Smith—whose sister Claudette Osborne went missing in July of 2008—organized this team of volunteers. Thus, in the face of government inaction, community peoples and families started doing the best they could to cope with the disappearance or murder of loved ones. The Conservative government made excuses *not* to act and *not* to fulfil the request made by so many. As Stan Beardy, previous Ontario regional chief with the Assembly of First Nations, explains, "I am not sure who else besides the Conservative government doesn't want a national inquiry. First Nations leaders and the premiers of the provinces unanimously back this call and the United Nations has called Canada to support an inquiry. Why are Harper and the Conservatives not listening?"[113]

In October 2015, a majority Liberal government was elected in Canada, led by new Prime Minister Justin Trudeau. On November 4, 2015, Trudeau assumed office. In the election platform, the Liberal government committed to "immediately" launching a national public inquiry into missing and murdered Indigenous women and girls, promising to spend $40 million over two years on this inquiry.[114] In his mandate letter to the newly appointed Minister of Indigenous and Northern Affairs, Carolyn Bennett, Trudeau listed "an inquiry into murdered and missing Indigenous women and girls in Canada" as a top priority. He also noted that this was to be developed "in collaboration with the Minister of Justice." For the first time in Canadian history, this Minister of Justice is an Indigenous person, Jody Wilson-Raybould, who is a "descendant of the Musgamagw Tsawataineuk and Laich-Kwil-Tach peoples, which are part of the Kwakwaka'wakw."

In November of 2015, Carolyn Bennett started pre-inquiry consultations with families of missing and murdered Indigenous women and girls.

On December 8, 2015, Prime Minister Justin Trudeau made a promise at the Assembly of First Nations' Special Chiefs Assembly that he would move forward with this inquiry.[115] The same day, Jody Wilson-Raybould, Carolyn Bennett, and Status of Women Minister Patty Hajdu made the announcement that the first phase of this inquiry will begin, taking place over next two months. These three ministers will begin by meeting with families across Canada; then they will meet with Indigenous leaders, organizations, and provinces. They will also have a have an online survey and discussion. After these consultations, they will develop the scope of the inquiry, which the three ministers planned to announce in the spring of 2016.

Discussion Questions

1) Compare the traditions of Indigenous and Western societies related to the treatment and depiction of women. How are Indigenous women depicted by each cultural group?
2) What contributes to violence affecting Indigenous women?

Activities

1) Watch the 2004 live performance by OutKast of "Hey Ya" at the Grammy Awards (available on www.youtube.com). Identify how and in what ways this performance contributes to a misrepresentation of Indigenous women. How might this type of portrayal exacerbate the violence affecting Indigenous girls and women? Do you know of other popular culture depictions that misrepresent Indigenous women? What are they, and what are their characteristics?
2) Invite a local Indigenous person to come and share the "Strong Women's Song" and the "Women's Warrior Song," as well as their associated teachings. Or locate an Indigenous drum group and arrange a visit.
3) Watch the 2006 National Film Board of Canada documentary by Christine Welsh *Finding Dawn* (available online at www.nfb.ca). What do you think contributes to the epidemic of missing and murdered women in Canada? Why is it important to put a human face and name to each missing and murdered woman? The film notes that these women are mothers, aunties, daughters, and friends. Explain the importance of this view.
4) On March 18, 2011, I attended the Empty Shoe Vigil hosted by McGill University on the steps of Parliament Hill in Ottawa to honour missing and murdered Indigenous women. To serve as a symbolic representation of these women, people were asked to bring shoes. The goal was to place at least 500 pairs of shoes on the steps of parliament to represent the

Image 9.1 Shoes on the Steps of Parliament Hill: A Symbolic Representation of the Missing and Murdered Indigenous Women

women who could no longer speak for themselves. The shoes were later donated to shelters. Hold a vigil at your school for the missing and murdered Indigenous women. Ask people to bring gently used or new shoes, and display them where the vigil is held; later donate them to women's shelters.

Recommended Readings

Acoose, Janice. *Iskwewak-Kah'Ki Yan Ni Nahkomakanak: Neither Indian Princesses Nor Easy Squaws*. Toronto: Women's Press, 1995.

Anderson, Kim. *A Recognition of Being: Reconstructing Native Womanhood*. Toronto: Canadian Scholars Press, 2001.

10
The Real Criminals: Governments and Their Corporate Priorities and Failed Agreements

DURING THE EARLY DAYS OF EUROPEAN and First Nations contact, Indigenous peoples were living in harmony with their environment—mostly as hunters, gatherers, and fishers, but also in agricultural communities. Their ways of life made few demands on the environment, which remained undamaged for centuries. On the other hand, Europeans were continually developing their technology to achieve control over nature.[1] In this Euro-Canadian ideological system, everything became the possession of man, including the air, water, plants, animals, earth, and rocks. This chapter examines how these priorities of destruction and expansion and systematic takeover have been executed through broken treaties and false promises. It begins by outlining some significant Supreme Court cases in which Indigenous peoples have resisted colonial destruction and sought recognition of their rights.

Next, the chapter examines attempts by government and big businesses to follow capitalistic policies of constant growth in production and consumption through breaking or not fully acknowledging the original agreements made with Indigenous peoples. It will also outline resistance to such attempts. Ultimately, Euro-Canadian priorities tend to trump Indigenous rights and the historic promises made to Indigenous peoples, while the government still continues down the same profitable path of colonialism and theft.

Constitutional Rights Recognition

For over 80 years, the leading case concerning Aboriginal title was *St. Catherines Milling and Lumber Co. v. The Queen*, decided in 1888. This case was part of a dispute between Ontario and Canada over rights to land for timber. It asserted that land title in Canada remains with the Crown and that Aboriginal rights to the land are allowed only at the Crown's pleasure and can be revoked by the Crown at any time. An argument made by Ontario's attorney general in this case disputed Indigenous land claims on the basis that the Indigenous peoples who entered into the various treaties were not nations: "to maintain their position the appellants must assume that the Indians have a regular form of government, whereas nothing is more clear than that they have no government and no organization, and cannot be regarded as a nation capable of holding lands. . . . The Indians had no rules or regulations which could be considered laws."[2]

That unceded lands are not recognized as Indigenous and that treaties and the treaty relationship are not honoured demonstrates continuing colonialism. Although treaties between First Nations and colonizing nations are different across the country, they are generally inclusive of an agreement to share lands, resources, and wealth. They outline an agreement that we would all live in prosperity together as partners. So far, the general population of Canada has reaped the benefits of Indigenous land and resources while Indigenous peoples have been disrupted from thriving.

In 1982, the Royal Proclamation itself actually came to be included within the Canadian Charter of Rights and Freedoms under section 25:

> 25. The guarantee in this Charter of certain rights and freedoms shall not be construed so as to abrogate or derogate from any aboriginal, treaty or other rights or freedoms that pertain to the aboriginal peoples of Canada including
>
> (a) any rights or freedoms that have been recognized by the Royal Proclamation of October 7, 1763; and
> (b) any rights or freedoms that now exist by way of land claims agreements or may be so acquired.[3]

Despite the fact that the Royal Proclamation is constitutionally protected, Indigenous peoples today fight through legal hoops to substantiate Aboriginal title to the land. This struggle is especially notable in British Columbia, where most of the territory now claimed by the province has never been ceded by its Indigenous peoples.

In British Columbia and elsewhere, Indigenous peoples assert their inherent rights as the original stewards of the land since time immemorial. The Euro-Canadian legal system, however, often discounts these rights and recognizes only the written treaties and other government documents of colonial institutions. In some instances, Indigenous peoples have turned to this colonial legal system as a way of trying to retain or regain their inherent rights. When the Constitution Act was set for a redrafting in the 1980s, for example, Prime Minister Pierre Trudeau's government had no plans to include Indigenous peoples.[4] In response, Indigenous peoples held protests in an effort to get their rights protected and enshrined in the Constitution. The result was section 35 of the Canadian Constitution Act of 1982:

> 35. (1) The existing aboriginal and treaty rights of the aboriginal peoples of Canada are hereby recognized and affirmed.

> (2) In this Act, "aboriginal peoples of Canada" includes the Indian, Inuit and Métis peoples of Canada.
>
> (3) For greater certainty, in subsection (1) "treaty rights" includes rights that now exist by way of land claims agreements or may be so acquired.
>
> (4) Notwithstanding any other provision of this Act, the aboriginal and treaty rights referred to in subsection (1) are guaranteed equally to male and female persons.[5]

Although Aboriginal rights did become recognized and protected with the patriation of the Constitution in 1982, the inherent rights of Indigenous peoples to all unceded land was not, and neither was this land returned outright. Rather, the colonial system expected these rights to be defined on a case-by-case basis in the courts. As the following Supreme Court cases show, defining rights in this way means that limits become set simultaneously.

There have been a series of court judgements dealing with Aboriginal rights and title. A notable one is the Supreme Court decision in 1973 referred to as the *Calder* decision.[6] The *Calder* case really laid the foundation for "modern" land claims and the rectification of treaty breaches. It was the first court case to recognize Aboriginal title of the land at the Supreme Court level. In it, Frank Calder and other elders from the Nisga'a Nation declared that Aboriginal title and rights to their land had never been extinguished, and they wanted this fact to be recognized. The judges were split on whether Nisga'a Aboriginal title existed or had been extinguished. Although Frank Calder and the other Nisga'a elders did not win this case, it is considered to have paved the way in Canada for acceptance of the idea that Aboriginal title pre-existed treaties and other colonial documents acknowledging it. Six of the seven judges confirmed that Aboriginal title is "a legal right derived from the Indians' historic . . . possession of their tribal lands" and that this right existed whether or not governments recognized it.[7] In other words, this case recognized and affirmed that Aboriginal title did indeed exist previous to and at the time of the Royal Proclamation in 1763.

Aboriginal Rights: The *Sparrow* Decision and the *Van der Peet* Trilogy

One of the major cases dealing with Aboriginal rights is the 1990 Supreme Court case known as the *Sparrow* case, which was also the first case at the Supreme Court of Canada that tested section 35 of the Constitution Act of 1982.[8] In *R. v. Sparrow*, member of the Musqueam First Nation Ronald Sparrow was arrested and charged under section 61(1) of the federal Fisheries Act for fishing with a drift net that was longer than was permitted by his licence.

He did concede that the net was larger than was permitted by the food fishing licence; however, he argued that he was exercising an existing Aboriginal right to fish, so the restriction in the food fishing licence was void because it was inconsistent with section 35(1) of the Constitution Act, 1982.[9]

The court ruled in favour of Sparrow, declaring that Musqueam peoples have a right to fish that had not been extinguished prior to the 1982 Constitution. Thus, Sparrow was exercising his inherent Indigenous right to fish when he was arrested on May 25, 1984. The ruling by the court resulted in what's known today as the "Sparrow test," or the "justification of infringement test." This test sets out a list of conditions to determine whether a right exists. If a right is found to exist, it outlines how the government may be justified in breaching or limiting that right.

Determining whether a right has been infringed upon is the first part of the test. A law or regulation might be infringing upon an Aboriginal right if

- it is considered "unreasonable" by the court;
- it imposes an "undue hardship" on First Nations;
- it denies right holders their "preferred means of exercising that right."[10]

This test then outlines what justifies the infringement of an Aboriginal right. Infringing upon an Aboriginal right may be justified if

- there is "a valid legislative objective," such as "conserving and managing a natural resource";
- there is "as little infringement as possible in order to effect the desired result";
- the situation is one of expropriation, and "fair compensation" is provided;
- the "aboriginal group in question has been consulted with respect to the conservation measures being implemented."[11]

Another major case dealing with Aboriginal rights is the 1996 *Van der Peet* case. This case was the first of three that became known as the "*Van der Peet* Trilogy," which also included the *Gladstone* and *N.T.C. Smokehouse* cases. In *R. v. Van der Peet*, member of the Stó:lō First Nation Dorothy Van der Peet was charged with selling 10 salmon caught under a food fish licence, contrary to section 27(5) of the British Columbia Fishery (General) Regulations. Under this type of licence, First Nations people were permitted to fish only for the purpose of getting food or conducting ceremonies, so the law prohibited the sale of the fish.

Van der Peet did not win her case. The Supreme Court of Canada upheld the Court of Appeal's ruling, which stipulated that, although fishing constitutes an Aboriginal right, the sale of fish for exchange of money or other goods does not. To be considered an Aboriginal right, "an activity must be an element of a practice, custom or tradition integral to the distinctive culture of the aboriginal group claiming the right." And the "practices, customs and traditions which constitute aboriginal rights are those which have continuity with the practices, customs and traditions that existed prior to contact with European society."[12]

The "integral to a distinctive culture" test, otherwise known as the "*Van der Peet* test" came out of this case. The test outlined 10 criteria that must be met in order for a practice to be affirmed and protected as an Aboriginal right under section 35 of the Constitution Act:

1) Courts must take into account the perspective of aboriginal peoples themselves.
2) Courts must identify precisely the nature of the claim being made in determining whether an aboriginal claimant has demonstrated the existence of an aboriginal right.
3) In order to be integral a practice, custom or tradition must be of central significance to the aboriginal society in question.
4) The practices, customs and traditions which constitute aboriginal rights are those which have continuity with the practices, customs and traditions that existed prior to contact.
5) Courts must approach the rules of evidence in light of the evidentiary difficulties inherent in adjudicating aboriginal claims.
6) Claims to aboriginal rights must be adjudicated on a specific rather than general basis.
7) For a practice, custom or tradition to constitute an aboriginal right it must be of independent significance to the aboriginal culture in which it exists.
8) The integral to a distinctive culture test requires that a practice, custom or tradition be distinctive; it does not require that that practice, custom or tradition be distinct.
9) The influence of European culture will only be relevant to the inquiry if it is demonstrated that the practice, custom or tradition is only integral because of that influence.
10) Courts must take into account both the relationship of aboriginal peoples to the land and the distinctive societies and cultures of aboriginal peoples.[13]

In *R. v. Gladstone* and *R. v. N.T.C. Smokehose Ltd.*, the additional two cases in the *Van der Peet* trilogy, both of which took place in 1996, the court applied this "*Van der Peet* test." In *Gladstone*, the court decided that there was an Aboriginal right to exchange or trade herring spawn on kelp, according to the *Van der Peet* test. Charges were dropped against the two Heiltsuk brothers William and Donald Gladstone, who had been accused of attempting to sell herring spawn on kelp without a J-licence, which is contrary to section 20(3) of the Pacific Herring Fishery Regulation.[14] The Supreme Court recognized that they had an unextinguished Aboriginal right to sell herring spawn on kelp and that the J-licencing scheme infringed on their Aboriginal right.[15] Historical evidence proved that the commercial fish trade was an integral to Heiltsuk culture and "a central and defining feature of Heiltsuk society."[16]

In the *N.T.C. Smokehouse* case, members from the Sheshaht and Opetchesaht First Nations (members of the Nuu-chah-nulth Tribal Council) caught chinook salmon under the authority of food fishing licences. They then sold the surplus of their food fishing quotas to the First Nations–owned business N.T.C. Smokehouse Ltd, which then sold the salmon its employees caught to non-Aboriginal fish-processing companies.[17] N.T.C. Smokehouse Ltd. was charged with the selling and purchasing of fish caught under the Indian food fish licence, contrary to sections 4(5) and 27(5) of the British Columbia Fishery (General) Regulations. These regulations prohibit the sale or barter of any fish caught under the Indian food fish licence, as well as the purchase of such fish. Through applying the *Van der Peet* test, the Supreme Court determined that the sale of fish did not form an "integral" part of the distinctive cultures of the Sheshaht and Opetchesaht peoples. Rather, the court declared that, prior to contact, the sale of fish among the Sheshaht and Opetchesaht peoples was "few and far between" and while "Potlatches and other ceremonial occasions may well be integral features of the Sheshaht and Opetchesaht cultures and, as such, recognized and affirmed as aboriginal rights . . . the exchange of fish incidental to these occasions is not, itself, a significantly central, or significant or defining feature of these societies."[18] Thus, the appeal was dismissed.

Aboriginal Title: The *Delgamuukw* Decision

A foundational judgement regarding Aboriginal title happened during the 1997 Supreme Court case known as the *Delgamuukw* decision.[19] It confirmed that, when dealing with Crown land, the government must consult Aboriginal peoples and may have to compensate those of them whose rights might be affected.[20] In this case, the Hereditary Chiefs of the Gitksan and Wet'suwet'en wanted an assertion that their rights and jurisdiction over their land existed, remains, and had never been lawfully extinguished or surrendered. They were claiming jurisdiction over and ownership of 58,000 square kilometres of their traditional territory (in what is referred to today as northwestern British Columbia). The two First Nations had oral histories, stories, songs, crests, and names that justified their claims to these territories, claims dating back 12,000 years.[21]

A notable aspect of this case was the court's acknowledgement and acceptance of the oral histories of the Gitksan and Wet'suwet'en peoples as valid. Chief Justice Lamer recognized that oral histories both exemplify historical knowledge and convey cultural values; nevertheless, he saw some difficulty in considering this evidence under the stringent rules of tort law.[22] Lamer explains that the courts had to "come to terms with the oral histories of aboriginal societies, which, for many aboriginal nations, are the only record of their past." He adds, " . . . those histories play a crucial role in the litigation of aboriginal rights."[23]

The Gitksan and Wet'suwet'en both entered their oral histories as evidence, which are referred to as the "*adaawk*" and "*kungax*." The *adaawk* are the oral histories of the Gitksan houses. Each house, or *wilp*, has its own set of sacred oral traditions, territories for which it is responsible, histories, and ancestors—all of which are recorded and reaffirmed in the *adaawk*. The *kungax* is a spiritual song or dance tying the Wet'suwet'en people to their land.[24] The important point, though, is that, when the Gitksan presented their *adaawk* and the Wet'suwet'en presented their *kungax*, the court considered both as acceptable evidence of their claim to Aboriginal title.[25] As Chief Justice Lamer explained, the oral histories are "tangential to the ultimate purpose of the fact-finding process at trial—the determination of the historical truth."[26]

There was no final decision as to whether the Gitksan and Wet'suwet'en nations had Aboriginal title to the lands they claimed. This case did, however, set out how the courts would deal with Aboriginal title. It set out a test to determine whether Aboriginal title still existed, and, if it was found to exist, it outlined how the Crown could justify itself to breach this title. To establish proof of Aboriginal title, Justice Lamer outlined three standards that had to be reached; these were in addition to the 10 criteria previously listed in the *Van der Peet* test. First, the claimant had to demonstrate occupancy prior to Crown sovereignty being asserted. Second, the claimant had to demonstrate the continuity of present and pre-sovereignty occupation, thus, proving that present occupancy is rooted in the past. Continuity can be exhibited through either physical evidence, such as houses, cordoned-off fields, and consistent resource use, or through the continued use of Aboriginal laws governing the area. Finally, the test must prove that the site of the land is solely occupied by the group making the claim to the territory.[27]

Treaty Interpretation: The *Sioui* and *Marshall* Decisions

Indigenous peoples have turned to the court system to attempt to get governments to recognize and act upon treaty promises. Two Supreme Court of Canada cases, in particular, have transformed our understanding of treaty interpretation: *R. v. Sioui* (1990) and *R. v. Marshall* (1999).[28] Though supporting the idea that Indigenous interpretations of the original treaties remain valid, these cases set the precedent that interpretations of treaties must go beyond their straight and literal meanings.

In May of 1990, the *Sioui* case tested whether the federal government could apply a narrow, literal interpretation to define what treaty obligations must be fulfilled today. Four Huron-Wendat brothers—Regent, Conrad, Georges, and Hughes Sioui, from Wendaké in Québec—were charged with cutting down trees, making fires, and camping in undesignated places in Jacques-Cartier Park.[29] These were actions contrary to provincial regulations. The brothers explained that they were practicing their customs, which were part of a treaty negotiated between Huron people and the Crown in 1760.[30] The brothers referred to a document signed by General Murray that guaranteed Huron people the Crown's protection, as well as the free exercise of their religion, customs, and trade with the British. The Supreme Court held that the treaty was still in effect, and it gave the brothers the right to carry on their customs in the park.

In the *Sioui* case, the Supreme Court laid out conditions for what types of documents could be considered treaties.[31] The decision also stressed that the courts must take a "liberal and generous" interpretation of treaties.[32] As Justice Lamer wrote, "Finally, once a valid treaty is found to exist, that treaty must be given a just, broad and liberal construction." To elaborate on the correct approach to interpretation, Justice Lamer quotes a 1899 United States case, *Jones v. Meehan*, which notes that each treaty "must therefore be construed, not according to the technical meaning of its words by learned lawyers, but in the sense in which they would naturally be understood by the Indians."[33] He adds, "These considerations argue all the more strongly for courts to adopt a generous and liberal approach."[34]

In 1999, Donald Marshall Jr., member of the Membertou First Nation, was fishing for eels in Pomquet Harbour, Nova Scotia, when he was charged with fishing and selling eels without a licence and fishing out of season. As a result, he had his equipment seized. The Supreme Court of Canada confirmed that Donald Marshall Jr. had a treaty right to catch and sell fish. This treaty right had its origins in the "peace and friendship" treaties signed in 1760 and 1761 between the Crown and the Mi'kmaq and Maliseet peoples.

Ultimately, the *Marshall* case recognized that the oral histories of Aboriginal peoples, which often record their understandings of treaties, must be accorded equal weight alongside written records. The court was careful, however, to ensure that its decision did not mean that Indigenous views of treaty rights were to be recognized carte blanche. Yet this decision certainly did tip the scale toward Indigenous understandings of treaties, given that each treaty was to be interpreted according to its intent and spirit rather than to be taken literally. Quoting the *Sioui* case, Justice Binnie argued that Marshall should be acquitted on all charges: "The bottom line is [that] the Court's obligation is to 'choose from among the various possible interpretations of the *common* intention [at the time the treaty was made] the one which reconciles' the Mi'kmaq interests and those of the British Crown."[35] Binnie thus acknowledges that his conclusions about treaty rights in this case did not come completely from the written words of the treaty itself:

> It seems clear that the words of the March 10, 1760 document, standing in isolation, do not support the appellant's argument. The question is whether the underlying negotiations produced a broader agreement between the British and the Mi'kmaq, memorialized only in part by the Treaty of Peace and Friendship.[36]

Justice Binnie identified a broader interpretation of the treaty through an elaborate analysis of its wording and of its historical and cultural contexts. Extrinsic historical sources, such as earlier treaties between the Mi'kmaq and the British and the minutes of negotiating sessions between the British and the Maliseet (who had a comparable treaty with the British) were included in the analysis. Also included was expert evidence delivered at the trial. Based on this review, Justice Binnie concluded that the treaty was "partly oral and partly written."[37] The *Marshall* and the *Sioui* cases, then, recognize that Indigenous interpretations of treaties and of treaty rights deserve a place at the table. And, because the *Marshall* case involved a healthy majority of five to two and the *Sioui* case was unanimous, the Supreme Court strongly supported the need for more than a one-sided, technical interpretation of treaties.[38]

Shortly after this first *Marshall* decision, referred to as *R. v. Marshall (No 1)* [1999] 3 S.C.R. 456, the Supreme Court handed down a ruling in *Marshall II*, referred to as *R. v. Marshall (No 2)* [1999] 3 S.C.R. 533—which put significant limits on the first ruling. Acting on a motion put forward by the West Nova Fishermen's Coalition, the Supreme Court agreed to rehear the case, although the court did make explicit that this fisherman's coalition had no right to bring such a motion forward. The rulings from *R. v. Marshall (No 2)* added a "clarification". to the first *Marshall* decision, outlining that the Crown could limit the exercise of a treaty right if doing so "can be justified on conservation or other grounds."[39] So, although the Crown stipulated that it respected the Mi'kmaq peoples "limited commercial 'right to fish,'" it claimed the authority to limit that right with justifiable regulatory mechanisms: "The federal and provincial governments have the authority within their respective legislative fields to regulate the exercise of a treaty right where justified on conservation or other grounds."[40]

The Crown's Fiduciary Duty: *Haida Nation*, *Taku River Tlingit First Nation*, *Mikisew Cree*, and *Little Salmon/Carmacks First Nation* Decisions

The Canadian government has a fiduciary duty that was agreed to in the treaties. This "fiduciary duty requires the Crown to act honourably" due to its unique historical relationship with Aboriginal peoples.[41] This duty means that the Crown must not infringe on Aboriginal and treaty rights when passing laws. Various Supreme Court cases have ruled that the "honour of the Crown" is always at stake in all the Crown's dealings with Aboriginal peoples. Consider the 1996 *Badger* case (about treaty hunting rights), during which Justice Cory outlined as a second principle of treaty interpretation that "the honour of the Crown is always at stake in its dealings with Indian people."[42] The legal implications of this special duty to act honourably include the Crown's duty to consult and accommodate Aboriginal peoples when their interests and rights might be affected by a decision of the Crown.[43]

The Supreme Court of Canada has upheld this obligation as a constitutional duty. For instance, when the Crown wants to permit resource extraction on Indigenous peoples' territory—territory that was never ceded by treaty—it must consult the Aboriginal nation regarding impacts on that nation's rights and interests, and the Crown must address Aboriginal concerns. In addition, any legislation that the Crown wants to pass that might affect Aboriginal hunting and fishing rights, or any rights for that matter, must be developed in consultation with the Aboriginal peoples to be affected. The Crown must justify any negative impacts of the proposed legislation, and, in some cases, if the community is to be deprived in part or whole of its hunting and fishing rights, it should be compensated. Some of the Supreme Court of Canada cases that have confirmed the Crown's fiduciary duty to consult and accommodate Aboriginal peoples include *Haida Nation v. British Columbia* (Minister of Forests), *Taku River Tlingit First Nation v. British Columbia, Mikisew Cree First Nation v. Canada (Minister of Canadian Heritage)*, and *Beckman v. Little Salmon/Carmacks First Nation.*[44]

The Haida people have been the original stewards of their lands of Haida Gwaii since time immemorial.[45] Yet, in 1961, the Province of British

Columbia issued a "Tree Farm License" (TFL) to a large forestry firm authorizing tree harvesting on the Haida people's land. This TFL was renewed in 1981, 1995, and 2000. In 1999, it was transferred to a large forestry firm, Weyerhaeuser Co. No consent was obtained from the Haida Nation, nor was there consultation for any of these actions. The Haida Nation consequently challenged these renewed licences, as well as the transfer, because all these actions were taken without their consent and over their objections.

In 2004, in a unanimous decision, Chief Justice McLachlin found that "the government has a legal duty to consult with the Haida people about the harvest of timber from Block 6, including decisions to transfer or replace Tree Farm Licences"; she further stated that "consultation must be meaningful."[46] The decision also noted that third parties could not be held liable for failing to meet the Crown's duty to consult and accommodate. Thus, "the legal responsibility for consultation and accommodation rests with the Crown." But, at the same time, the court specified that its decision did not mean "third parties can never be liable to Aboriginal peoples."[47]

In 2004, the Supreme Court of Canada issued its decision in the *Taku River Tlingit First Nation v. British Columbia* case. A mining company, Redfern Resources Ltd., had been trying to get permission from the BC government since 1994 to get an old mine reopened. One aspect of the project, however, was the building of a 160-kilometre road, which would connect the mine to the town of Atlin. Members of the Taku River Tlingit First Nation (TRTFN)—who were project committee members of the environmental assessment process engaged in by the province under the Environmental Assessment Act—objected to the mining company's plan to build this road, as a portion of it would cut right through the heart of TRTFN traditional territory.[48] In 1998, the province granted Redfern Resources Ltd. approval for its project, even though the concerns expressed by TRTFN were not resolved. The conclusion from the Supreme Court of Canada was that the provincial government did satisfy its duty to consult and accommodate the interests of the TRTFN when it granted Redfern Resources Ltd. approval for its project in 1998.

The court also stated that certification of the project was only one stage in the development process and that some of the remaining TRTFN concerns could be "more effectively considered at the permit stage or at the broader stage of treaty negotiations or land use strategy planning." Thus, the court outlined additional steps that had to be taken after the project's approval ("certification"), which included more information from Redfern Resources Ltd. regarding baseline information, "which may lead to adjustments in the road's course," and "further socio-economic studies." The court also recommended the establishment of "a joint management authority."[49]

In 2005, the Supreme Court of Canada issued its decision in *Mikisew Cree First Nation v. Canada (Minister of Canadian Heritage)*. The Mikisew Cree First Nation is located within Treaty 8 territory. In 2000, the federal government approved a winter road without consulting the First Nation.[50] This road was planned to run straight through Mikisew territory. Concerned about the damaging affect this road would have on their traditional lifestyle, the Mikisew Cree people protested, and the road alignment was modified to run around the boundary of the nation. But, again, this decision was made without any consultation. So the Mikisew Cree First Nation turned to the courts.

In a unanimous decision, the Supreme Court found that the federal government was required to consult with the Mikisew Cree First Nation in "taking up" lands for a winter road in its section of the Treaty 8 territory; the court decided that "the duty of consultation, which flows from the honour of the Crown, was breached."[51] As Chief Justice Binnie writes,

> In this case, the relationship was not properly managed. Adequate consultation in advance of the Minister's approval did not take place. The government's approach did not advance the process of reconciliation but undermined it. The duty of consultation which flows from the honour of the Crown, and its obligation to respect the existing treaty rights of aboriginal peoples (now entrenched in s. 35 of the Constitution Act, 1982), was breached. The Mikisew appeal should be allowed, the Minister's approval quashed, and the matter returned to the Minister for further consultation and consideration.[52]

In 2010, the Supreme Court of Canada issued its decision in the *Beckman v. Little Salmon/Carmacks First Nation* case. In this case, the Crown's duty to consult and accommodate was being considered in relation to a "modern" land claim agreement. The Little Salmon Carmacks First Nation is located along the Yukon River, in the south part of central Yukon.[53] In 1997, after 20 years of negotiations, the Little Salmon Carmacks First Nation entered into a land claim agreement with the Canadian government.[54] Part of this treaty included a stated right for hunting and fishing within the nation's traditional territory, which includes a 65-hectare parcel of land.

In 2001, without consultation, the Yukon government transferred a parcel of land situated within the traditional territory of the Little Salmon Carmacks First Nation to a non-Aboriginal person. This parcel transferred by the government had been ceded to the Crown by the nation through its "Final Agreement" (treaty). However, that agreement also indicated that Little Salmon Carmacks First Nation members would have "the right of access for hunting and fishing for subsistence in their traditional territory, which includes a parcel of 65 hectares."[55] The land the government transferred was also within the trapline of one of the nation's members.

Ultimately, the court declared that "there is no legal basis for finding that the Crown breached its duty to consult" because negotiations leading to the Final Agreement had included a formal consultation process.[56] Given that the transfer of land was for the purposes of agricultural development, the Supreme Court identified that this type of project "was subject to Chapter 12 of the Final Agreement and that that chapter's transitional provisions established the applicable framework." (Chapter 12 describes the development assessment process that must be followed, and this process guarantees participation by "Yukon Indian People.")

These Supreme Court cases, it seems, not only prove the duty of Canadian governments to act honourably and to consult Indigenous peoples when taking decisions that affect their treaty rights but also suggest the extent to which such consultation will influence decisions when economic development is at stake. Although the story offers hope to Indigenous peoples attempting to use the courts to retain or regain their rights, it is also a cautionary tale. But what of more recent decisions? Do these present new opportunities and challenges?

Recent Aboriginal Title Decisions: Tsilhqot'n Nation and Grassy Narrows First Nation

In 2014, two more major cases regarding Aboriginal title were decided in the Supreme Court: *Tsilhqot'in Nation v. British Columbia* and *Grassy Narrows First Nation v. Ontario (Natural Resources)*.[57] Legal observers declared the *Tsilhqot'in Nation* case the most significant Supreme Court case on Aboriginal rights in Canadian history.[58] The decision furthered strengthened claims to Aboriginal title and rights and raised the standard of consultation required of governments engaged in dealings with First Nation communities.

The Tsilhqot'in Nation includes six bands that share a common culture and history and are located in central British Columbia.[59] In 1983, the provincial government granted a commercial logging licence to Carrier Lumber to cut trees on Tsilhqot'in traditional territory. The Tsilhqot'in Nation opposed this move, and set up a blockade to protect their land from logging.

On June 26, 2014, the Supreme Court of Canada unanimously declared that the Tsilhqot'in Nation had title to a 1,750-square-kilometre area of traditional territory and that the province had breached its duty to consult when it had granted logging licences on that territory. As Justice McLachlin wrote,

> I would allow the appeal and grant a declaration of Aboriginal title over the area at issue, as requested by the Tsilhqot'in. I further declare that British

> Columbia breached its duty to consult owed to the Tsilhqot'in through its land use planning and forestry authorizations.[60]

This case confirmed that the Tsilhqot'in Nation held underlying Aboriginal title to its traditional territory. It stated that "Aboriginal title confers ownership rights," which includes "the right to decide how the land will be used; the right of enjoyment and occupancy of the land; the right to possess the land; the right to the economic benefits of the land; and the right to proactively use and manage the land."[61] The decision also clarified that, without Aboriginal consent, governments had to have legal justifications for using Aboriginal land:

> The right to control the land conferred by Aboriginal title means that governments and others seeking to use the land must obtain the consent of the Aboriginal title holders. If the Aboriginal group does not consent to the use, the government's only recourse is to establish that the proposed incursion on the land it justified under s. 35 of the *Constitution Act, 1982*.[62]

Also in 2014, the Supreme Court of Canada issued its decision in the *Grassy Narrows First Nation v. Ontario* case.[63] In this case, treaty documents did not support the claims of the people of Grassy Narrows. Treaty 3 was signed in 1873 between Canada and Ojibwa chiefs; it related to what is now called northwestern Ontario and eastern Manitoba. In the written treaty, ownership was "ceded" to Canada, and certain lands within the territory were reserved for the exclusive of Ojibwa peoples. The treaty also granted to the Ojibwa the right to harvest on non-reserve lands until they were "taken up" for "settlement, mining, lumbering, or other purposes" by the Canadian government. When Treaty 3 was signed, an area known as Keewatin was under the complete control of Canada. In 1912, Ontario had taken it over and had begun issuing licences for land development.

In 2005, descendants of the original Treaty 3 signatories—who are from the Grassy Narrows First Nation—challenged a forestry licence that Ontario issued in 1997 to a large pulp and paper manufacturer. This licence granted permission for them to carry out clear-cutting forestry operations in the Keewatin area. Members of the Grassy Narrows First Nation challenged this licence, claiming it infringed upon their Treaty 3 harvesting rights. The central question in this case was whether the province of Ontario, under Treaty 3, needed federal authorization or had the authority to unilaterally "take up" lands in the Keewatin area and limit Aboriginal harvesting rights. In a unanimous decision, the Supreme Court determined that "Ontario has the power to take up lands in the Keewatin area under Treaty 3."[64]

Non-recognition of Aboriginal Rights, Title, and Self-Determination

Although we see the courts making some inroads toward the recognition of Aboriginal rights and the reaffirmation of Aboriginal title to the land, this legal process is slow, and just the fact of Indigenous peoples' participation in it entrenches Indigenous peoples further within a foreign imperial power and governance structure. Many times, inherent Indigenous title and rights, as well as original treaty agreements, are viewed disparagingly or skeptically by the non-Indigenous peoples writing policy.

Sparrow and *Van der Peet* are two foundational cases on Aboriginal "rights" in Canada. I use quotation marks around "rights" here because both cases actually took rights away from Indigenous peoples rather than granting them. In a strange twist, defining a right in law simultaneously limits it. The *Van der Peet* ruling was limiting because of its so-called "frozen rights approach," which ties Aboriginal rights to traditional practices and does not recognize that Aboriginal rights might change over time. As law professor Patrick Macklem explains, "*Van der Peet* unjustifiably excludes from constitutional protection practices that do not possess pre-contact referents but are integral to Aboriginal cultures."[65]

The *Van der Peet* case also emphasized reconciling Aboriginal rights with Crown sovereignty. It stressed that "the definition of an aboriginal right must, if it is truly to reconcile the prior occupation of Canadian territory by aboriginal peoples with the assertion of Crown sovereignty over that territory, take into account the aboriginal perspective, yet do so in terms which are cognizable to the non-aboriginal legal system."[66] Because of this emphasis on reconciliation, the fact of Crown sovereignty goes unchallenged, and the case fails to recognize inherent Indigenous rights and sovereignty.

Indeed, *Van der Peet* and both the *Delgamuukw* and *Haida Nation* cases want to achieve "the reconciliation of the pre-existence of aboriginal societies with the sovereignty of the Crown."[67] This perspective accepts as granted the sovereignty of the Crown and, consequently, puts Indigenous peoples at a lower level in the constitutional relationship. "I believe the legal notion of reconciliation is a soft sell for extinguishment," writes First Nations political leader Arthur Manuel (Secwepemc). To him, reconciliation should mean that "Canada and the provinces have to recognize and affirm our Aboriginal and Treaty Rights on the ground and a constitutional agreement on how this applies on the ground needs to be agreed to."[68]

In his analysis of the *Delgamuukw* case, Anishinaabe law professor John Borrows argues that, although it "somewhat positively changed the law to protect Aboriginal title, it has also simultaneously sustained a legal framework that undermines Aboriginal land rights. In particular, the decisions unreflective acceptance of Crown sovereignty places Aboriginal title in a subordinate position relative to other legal rights."[69] According to Mohawk legal scholar Patricia Monture-Angus "'Aboriginal Rights' is merely Canadian law wrapped up in a pretty red paper. Only on the surface does it appear to be 'Indian.' Once you carefully examine it, it is obvious that it is *not* about First Nations ways of 'doing law.'"[70]

According to Taiaiake Alfred, a Kahnawake Mohawk author and educator, the post-*Delgamuukw* conception of Aboriginal title is "fundamentally meaningless" to Indigenous peoples, as, in reality, it provides "no real protection."[71] As Alfred sees it, this *Delgamuukw* decision clearly stated that Canada itself may "infringe upon Aboriginal title for valid legislative objectives, including, but not limited to, settling foreign populations and instituting economic development projects."[72] So, although the *Delgamuukw* decision prevents individuals, corporations, municipalities, and provinces from infringing on Indigenous peoples' cultures within their traditional territories, it also serves to reinforce the "faulty logic" that assumes Aboriginal rights can be put aside when they conflict with economic development and settlement. These are the same excuses used for all of the "legalized" theft of Indigenous land, a theft on which colonial Canada was founded.[73]

Legal scholar Jennifer E. Dalton agrees that, even though many people have looked to *Delgamuukw* as furthering Aboriginal rights, in reality, it did the opposite.[74] Instead of furthering Aboriginal rights, the court wrote into law the ways in which these rights could be justly ignored. The court outlined that Aboriginal rights and title could be infringed upon if legislative objectives are "compelling and substantial." Thus, according to Dalton, *Delgamuukw* "provided little in the way of constitutional protection or recognition of Aboriginal self-government or self-determination."[75]

Jeff Corntassel, Tsalagi (Cherokee Nation), and Cheryl Bryce (Lekwammen) explain that Indigenous self-determination "entails unconditional freedom to live one's relational, place-based existence, and practice healthy relationships" and "is something that is asserted and acted upon, not negotiated or offered freely by the state."[76] Assuming that Aboriginal rights must be negotiated or given to Indigenous peoples by the courts is a state-centric point of view, they argue. Why would the state be in a position to give rights to Indigenous peoples, who have inherent rights and stewardship that were never given up? "Rights" are state constructions and do not reflect Indigenous peoples' inherent responsibilities to their traditional lands. Instead, they are conditional and, at any time, can be selectively enforced or revoked by the state. That Aboriginal rights are both conditional and selectively acknowledged or ignored is evidenced by the various justifications for their infringement outlined in the *Sparrow* and *Van der Peet* cases. Both of these cases set conditions on what constitutes a valid Aboriginal right—and then outline how governments can justifiably limit *all* Aboriginal rights.

Many hope that the much-celebrated *Tsilhqot'in* decision will lead governments, industry, and the general public toward recognizing Aboriginal title and rights in this country. According to senior lawyer Wayne Garnons-Williams from the Ottawa-based Garwill Law Professional Corporation (a firm noted for its expertise in Aboriginal law), the implications of the *Tsilhqot'in* decision include greater security for First Nations future control and ownership of their traditional resources and lands, a stronger relationship between First Nations and the business community, and a move toward First Nations environmental laws serving as requirements for businesses to achieve a harmonious and long-term business relationship with First Nations.[77]

On the other hand, some argue the *Tsilhqot'in* decision essentially tells the same story as other Canadian court cases dealing with Aboriginal title or rights and does nothing, really, to advance rights. The *Tsilhqot'in* judgement did not give the authority to First Nations to stop resource development projects outright. What this case did provide is a much clearer indication of what is needed to prove Aboriginal title for those First Nations not covered by a treaty. As stated by the court, these are the requirements for Aboriginal title: "sufficient pre-sovereignty occupation; continuous occupation (where present occupation is relied on); and exclusive historic occupation."[78] It is the claimant group that "bears the onus of establishing Aboriginal title."[79]

For Mohawk policy analyst Russell Diabo, there are "aspects of the *Tsilhqot'in* decision that are dangerous and a threat to First Nations and require a local, regional, national and international political response."[80] He outlines some of these dangerous aspects as follows:

- The SCC ruled that based upon the assertion of European sovereignty the Crown has "Radical or underlying title," thus keeping the racist Doctrine of Discovery alive in Canada;
- "The claimant group bears the onus of establishing Aboriginal title";
- "Governments can infringe Aboriginal rights conferred by Aboriginal title";
- "As a general proposition, provincial governments have the power to regulate land use within the province. This applies to all lands, whether held by the Crown, by private owners, or *by the holders of Aboriginal title*" (emphasis added [by Diabo]).
- "Provincial regulation of general application will apply to exercises of Aboriginal rights, including Aboriginal title land, subject to the s. 35 infringement and justification framework."[81]

Ultimately, the Supreme Court of Canada does little to advance "Aboriginal rights" or "title". It is a foreign entity that upholds the self-proclaimed "sovereignty" of the Crown. Many times, the courts rely on racist land doctrines, such as the doctrine of discovery and conquest. This reliance is evident when Crown sovereignty is used without question as a means to extinguish, infringe on, or limit existing Aboriginal rights and title. Indigenous engagement with Canadian law serves only to entrench Indigenous peoples deeper within a foreign colonial construct. Monture-Angus says it well when she states, "What I have come to understand through my last ten years of involvement with the law is that it is not the answer I am looking for. Every oppression that has been foisted on Aboriginal people in the history of Canada has been implemented through laws . . . Law is not the answer. It is the problem."[82]

As Corntassel and Bryce caution, Indigenous peoples should be careful not to become enmeshed within a state-centric rights discourse because doing so only serves to copy the functions of the state instead of honouring the balanced and spiritual relationship between First Nations and their traditional homelands.[83] This relationship and Indigenous people's resistance to Euro-Canadian attempts to discount it are exemplified in the Kanien'kéha:ka people's protection of their sacred burial grounds and pines in 1990 and the Musqueam people's protection of their sacred burial grounds in 2012—outlined in the following section.

Non-recognition of Indigenous Lands and Protection of Sacred Burial Grounds

In what the mainstream media called the "Oka Crisis," which took place in the summer of 1990, the Kanien'kéha:ka (or Mohawk) people of Kanehsatà:ke had to defend their sacred burial grounds and sacred pine trees from being taken over to allow for the extension of an 18-hole golf course.[84] In addition, 60 luxury townhouses that would back onto the golf course were scheduled for construction on the grounds where the sacred pines were located.[85] The people of Kanehsatà:ke had filed land claims in 1975 and 1977 but were told that these claims had been rejected.[86] Thus, the mayor of Oka, Jean Ouellette, did not consult the people of Kanehsatà:ke before setting out to expand the golf course and develop this sacred site.[87] At a March 1989 municipal council meeting, in response to a concerned townsperson's inquiry as to whether the mayor had consulted the people of Kanehsatà:ke, Ouellette responded, "You know you can't talk to the Indians."[88]

After this insulting non-recognition of their culture and their connection to these lands, the people of Kanehsatà:ke took action; members of the community set up a barricade and protested, leading to a confrontation lasting 78 days.[89] Mayor Ouellette was enraged with the protestors, and, on July 11, he called in the provincial police, the Sûreté du Québec (SQ). The SQ arrived early in the morning with three tactical intervention teams, each with five men, and with riot police who had shields, helmets, revolvers, and sticks.[90] There were also command and emergency units. This police activity caused the people of Kahnawà:ke to seize the Mercier Bridge in support of the Mohawk of Kanehsatà:ke and as a way to divert the police away from those protecting the sacred pines. This bridge is one of five that connect the south shore of the St. Lawrence to Montréal; in 1990 it carried about 70,000 cars a day.

During the next few hours, while the people of Kanehsatà:ke held a tobacco-burning ceremony, a police officer announced over a megaphone, "We want to talk to your leader. Have your leader approach the lines immediately." In response, the women of Kanehsatà:ke stepped forward with open hands to show they were unarmed. After they presented themselves, a police officer again demanded, over the megaphone, to see a leader, disregarding the women. The women then declared that there was not a single leader, that everyone was a leader. This was not the answer the police were looking for, so, again, they made their demand over the megaphone in a louder tone. Eventually, Kanehsatà:ke woman Ellen Gabriel, a central spokesperson during this crisis, stepped forward with faith-keeper John Cree.[91] They both explained the nature of democracy among the Mohawk people. Yet the police continued to make demands that completely disregarded the customs of the people of Kanehsatà:ke.

As time passed, the situation became more intense, and a gun battle erupted that lasted for about 15 minutes. The trigger was the police deployment of tear gas and flash-bang grenades, meant to confuse and frighten the people of Kanehsatà:ke. After police fired the first shot, the men of Kanehsatà:ke shot back.[92] Ultimately, this clash left SQ Corporal Marcel Lemay dead; whose bullet hit him is not known.

The Québec government eventually requested that the Canadian military be deployed, and the armed forces arrived in strength in August. (The total cost of the confrontation for the Québec and federal governments was "more than $150 million."[93]) The Fifth Brigade deployed 2,500 Canadian soldiers to stand by in areas near Kanehsatà:ke and Kahnawà:ke, and, on August 20, 400 troops moved into Kahnawà:ke and 385 into Kanehsatà:ke to replace the SQ officers.[94] Yet these police and soldiers were put in place to "deal with" villages whose population totalled between 1,800 and 2,100 people.[95]

One reason suggested for the disproportionate response was that the army knew it had to withstand assaults by angry and racist rioters, who were throwing rocks, bottles, and Molotov cocktails at the Mohawk people on the barricades or passing through them. By this time, the SQ had set up its own barricades, effectively sealing off the protesting communities, and, especially at the barricade near Chateauguay (a town of 40,000 residents), people would gather to shout racist remarks, burn effigies of Mohawk warriors, and threaten and engage in violence.[96] For example, when a woman was attempting to leave a barricaded Mohawk community because she had begun to haemorrhage after giving birth and needed to get to a hospital, a white mob surrounded her ambulance, and she was forced to "spread her legs" to prove she had actually delivered a baby. The police at the scene did not intervene.[97]

Although Corporal Marcel Lemay was the first victim to die because of the "Oka crisis," others suffered death or major injuries as well. An elderly Mohawk man died of heart failure, just a few days after he was subjected to one of the most shameful incidents of that summer. An angry mob that had gathered on the LaSalle side of the Mercier Bridge threw stones at the convoy of 70 or so cars carrying the Mohawk people leaving Kahnawà:ke. Another elderly man in Oka was poisoned by the tear gas that drifted down from "the Pines" (the sacred area being protected); he never fully recovered and died several months later. In addition to these three deaths, hundreds of Mohawk people, soldiers, police officers, and local residents were injured.[98]

After about three months of resistance, the Mohawks at the Oka barricade ended the protest. During the crisis, the federal government agreed to purchase the land in question to prevent the golf-course expansion and townhouse development, and it did spend $14 million from 1990 to 1995 to purchase properties that would create a contiguous land base for Kanehsatà:ke. "But 25 years later, the town of Oka still owns most of the forest at the heart of the standoff," according to a July 2015 report from *WC Native News*.[99]

A more recent example of the non-recognition and disrespect of Indigenous land rights is the Century Group's attempt to build a five-storey condo on the sacred land and burial site of the Musqueam people, who live near Vancouver, British Columbia. In January of 2011, the Musqueam people discovered that a 108-unit condo development was being planned on their unceded territory without any consultation. The Musqueam people have Aboriginal title and rights that they never relinquished. The land in question is ancestral land and contains a 4,000-year-old Musqueam burial ground, known as c̓əsnaʔəm.[100] This sacred place, c̓əsnaʔəm, is one of the largest ancient villages and burial sites in Vancouver. Under the name "Marpole Midden," it had been recognized as a National Historic Site of Canada in 1933. It is a place that contained countless cultural materials and undisturbed, intact burials, some of which were uncovered by local ethnographer Charles Hill-Tout in the 1920s and 1930s.

In May of 2011, the Musqueam people corresponded and met with the Archaeology Branch of the BC Ministry of Forests, Lands and Natural Resource Operations to ask it not to authorize permits for any more archaeological investigation of or alteration to this site under the Heritage and Conservation Act. Despite this request, permits were issued in December 2011 to a developer and an archaeological consulting firm. In 2012, the Musqueam people wrote to the provincial and federal governments, the City of Vancouver, and the developer, attempting to come to an agreement regarding their ancestral lands. No meaningful response was returned.

Developers went ahead with plans. During an archaeological excavation related to the proposed development, three intact burials, one of an adult Musqueam ancestor and two of babies, were discovered. In response, the Musqueam First Nation and supporters held a vigil that lasted more than 200 days. Imagine having to guard land—around the clock for over six months—so your ancestors' graves would not be dug up to profit a private corporation. Musqueam peoples wanted respect for their ancestors. Finally, British Columbia agreed to halt the condominium development at c̓əsnaʔəm on September 27, 2012. In a bittersweet victory, the Musqueam Nation paid millions of dollars in 2013 to buy back c̓əsnaʔəm, a two-acre parcel of land in South Vancouver containing the approximately 3,000-year-old village and burial site of their ancestors.[101]

The Resource Development Agenda Trumps Treaty Relationships

Not only has Canada failed to share lands and resources with Indigenous peoples but also Indigenous peoples have received a disproportionate share of the harmful and damaging impacts resulting from the government's hasty resource development agenda. As a result of this agenda, governments have made many Indigenous communities unfit to live in, left with polluted rivers, contaminated lands, and no clean drinking water.[102] The government ranks economic resource development over Indigenous peoples as a priority. As sociology professor Elizabeth Comack and her colleagues explain, "What the colonizers, the dominant society, call 'development' is experienced as devastation wrought by colonialism for those who are the colonized."[103] This development is largely non-sustainable and puts the health of Indigenous lands and community members at risk. It is also frequently attempted without governments upholding the fiduciary duty of the Crown to consult with Aboriginal peoples regarding the exploitation or "taking up" of lands, a duty of consultation flowing from the Crown's obligation to respect the existing treaty rights of Aboriginal peoples, which are entrenched under section 35(1) of the Constitution Act, 1982.[104] Thus, Canada seems to be breaking its own laws.

Consider Fort Chipewyan, Alberta, for example, where the Athabasca Chipewyan First Nation and the Mikisew Cree have relied on the Athabasca Lake for their water and livelihoods for centuries. The Mikisew Cree First Nation has nine reserves located adjacent to the municipality of Fort Chipewyan. These First Nation communities are about 200 kilometres away from Fort McMurray, which is at the centre of the Alberta tar sands. Many of the oil companies operating at these tar sands treat their toxic water and then filter it back into the Athabasca River. This river flows downstream into Lake Athabasca, the water supply for Indigenous peoples living in the Fort Chipewyan area.

The Canadian Association of Petroleum Producers declare that its members operating in the tar sands are in compliance with Alberta's environmental laws.[105] However, downstream in the Fort Chipewyan region people are becoming extremely ill. John O'Connor, the community's fly-in doctor, began calling for an official inquiry into the ill health of local residents when he discovered unusual rates of cancer among them, especially of cholangiocarcinoma, a very rare cancer of the bile ducts. He explained that he witnessed noticeable differences in the community members he was seeing in Fort Chipewyan as compared to his patients in Fort McMurray: "I began to realize I appeared to be seeing stuff here that I shouldn't be seeing in such numbers . . . various cancers, the autoimmune diseases, high number of people with diabetes, renal failure, hypertension, and then certain specific types of cancer—that really bothered me."[106] After O'Connor spoke out publicly, Health Canada tried to silence him, saying that his statements were causing local residents undue stress.[107]

In November 2007, however, a study published by ecologist Kevin Timoney on behalf of the Nunee Health Board Society of Fort Chipewyan, did yield troubling data concerning water and sediment quality in the Fort Chipewyan area.[108] This study examined water and sediment samples taken in May and June of 2007; water samples were taken from four sites and sediment samples from three sites. Given the "unacceptably high detection limits for total mercury in water," additional water samples were taken from the four sites again in August of 2007. Data were analysed by comparing the 2007 findings to pre-existing water and sediment quality data and to current pathological and the toxicological data gathered in the surrounding area. Findings were then examined against existing guidelines of water and sediment quality. In addition to these water and sediment samples and analyses, researchers conducted traditional knowledge interviews with local elders who had extensive knowledge of the area's waters.

One of the most notable results of the study was that downstream water in Fort Chipewyan had higher levels of contamination as compared to the water upstream. The main contaminants of concern were arsenic, mercury, and polycyclic aromatic hydrocarbons, and these pollutants were also shown to be rising. Concern was also expressed in regards to the level of contaminants in the fish used for human consumption. The study reported that, if US EPA standards were applied, all walleye (pickerel fish), all female whitefish, and 90 per cent of male whitefish surpassed subsistence fisher guidelines for mercury consumption. Mercury at these levels is said to affect the human fetus more than those in other age groups.

This study also re-evaluated an Alberta-funded study on lifetime exposure to arsenic and its links to cancer, finding that "questionable statistical methods" were used and that the government-supported study underestimated the levels of arsenic in water and sediment, as well as the fish ingestion rate of numerous residents of Fort Chipewyan.

After considering the scientific data and the information obtained from local elders' traditional knowledge of the waters, the Nunee Health Board Society study found that fish abnormalities could be higher than predicted or assumed by governments and others, might be increasing, and could even be linked to the drop in water quality.

In 2009, Kevin Timoney and Alberta researcher Peter Lee published the results of another related scientific study in the peer-reviewed journal *The Open Conservation Biology Journal*.[109] The main purpose of this study was to examine whether the Alberta tar sands industry causes pollution. This study analysed a series of environmental data on water and sediment chemistry. It examined contaminants in air emissions and wildlife, pollution incidents, traditional ecological observations, human health, as well as landscape changes, both upstream and downstream of the tar sands.

Results showed significant levels of air pollution in the local area and increases in contaminants in water, sediment, and fish downstream from the tar sands' industrial sources. For example, researchers noted that, in comparison to regional values, the levels of arsenic in water and sediment near Fort Chipewyan are high and might be rising. Citing health research, Timoney and Lee note that arsenic is a known carcinogen, found to be linked with human bile duct, liver, urinary tract, and skin cancers, in addition to vascular diseases and type II diabetes. Fort Chipewyan residents who depend on aquatic life as their main food supply are subjected to both arsenic and polycyclic aromatic hydrocarbons (PAHs).

In 2006, 22 people died in Fort Chipewyan, half due to cancer. This is in a community with a population of about 1,163. Compared to general Canadian rates, incidences of type II diabetes, lupus, renal failure, and hypertension are all elevated in Fort Chipewyan. Timoney and Lee cite a study from the Alberta Cancer Board that examined cancer incidence in Fort Chipewyan from 1995 to 2006. This study noted that the number of cancer cases was 30 per cent higher than had been hypothesized and included more than the usual number of bile duct cancers and cancers of the blood and lymphatic system.

Not long after Timoney and Lee published "Does the Alberta Tar Sands Industry Pollute?: The Scientific Evidence," a senior provincial government scientist, Preston McEachern, publicly accused them of intentionally manipulating and lying about their research findings. Timoney and Lee were appalled. They filed a lawsuit to defend their reputations but also to protect the scientific process and the research community and to avoid the undermining of their important scientific evidence (which required urgent action).

After Timoney and Lee threatened to file this lawsuit, the government scientist who made the claims officially retracted his statements, wrote a letter of apology to the two scientists, and paid up to $1,000 for their legal fees. Part of this letter of apology, dated June 11, 2010 (the deadline set by Timoney and Lee's lawyers) reads as follows: "The statements in my presentation . . . were false and I regret very much that I made these statements. I unequivocally retract them."[110] According to Mike Hudema from Greenpeace, this fiasco is an illustration of "the provincial government's preference of preserving the reputation of the oil sands over the environment—something the province denies."[111]

The Ring of Fire Project: Offering Economic Opportunities or Damaging the Environment?

Another development project that would affect First Nation communities is proposed for the area known as the "Ring of Fire." This large (5,120 square kilometres) mineral-rich region is located in the James

Bay lowlands of northern Ontario, where a major chromite mining and smelting development is being planned. Many First Nation communities are located close to the Ring of Fire, including Kasabonika Lake First Nation, Webequie First Nation, Attawapiskat First Nation, Nibinamik First Nation, Neskantaga First Nation, Eabametoong First Nation, Marten Falls First Nation, Kashechewan First Nation, Fort Albany First Nation, Mishkeegogamang First Nation, Aroland First Nation, Long Lake #58 First Nation, Constance Lake First Nation, and Ginoogaming First Nation. This Ring of Fire mining project promises to deliver the same economic potential as the oil sands and to bring economic benefits to First Nations. However, as Chief Peter Moonias of the Neskantaga First Nation states, "If the Ontario plan for the Ring of Fire is implemented it will bring limited economic benefits for First Nations, its social and environmental impacts would be devastating, and it would frustrate our longstanding belief that this is our land and we intend to decide what happens on our lands."[112]

Bill C-45 and the Idle No More Movement

In October 2012, the House of Commons introduced Bill C-45, also known as the Jobs and Growth Act.[113] Immediately after its introduction, the House of Commons passed a motion to limit how long this bill could be debated by members of parliament; the goal of the Conservative government was to "push the legislation through," a common practice for them. In an act of resistance and rights recognition, on December 4, 2012, First Nations chiefs tried to enter the parliament to offer their voices in regards to this bill. Anishinabek Nation Grand Council Chief Patrick Madahbee, Serpent River First Nation Chief Isadore Day, Onion Lake Cree Nation Chief Wallace Fox, and Grand Chief Derek Nepinak of the Assembly of Manitoba Chiefs all approached parliament with the goal of entering the House of Commons. Yet these Indigenous leaders were physically blocked and refused entry, in complete disregard of the promise made in the Treaty of Niagara in 1764, which established a nation-to-nation relationship between First Nations and Britain and her colonies (now called Canada). Thus, Indigenous leaders were denied an opportunity to deliver their messages in opposition to this bill.

On December 5, 2012, the Conservative Harper government passed Bill C-45, an omnibus bill of over 400 pages that contained more than 60 revisions and amendments to existing federal regulations. Among these amendments and revisions were changes to the Navigable Waters Protection Act, the Fisheries Act, the Canadian Environmental Assessment Act, and the

Indian Act, changes that, in many ways, attacked Indigenous treaty rights and made it easier to damage and exploit Indigenous peoples' land, water, and resources. This legislation also threatens Indigenous peoples' right to self-government.

The Navigable Waters Protection Act, which was a 130-year-old act in place to protect one of Canada's most precious resources—the waters—has been amended since the passing of Bill C-45.[114] The legislation is now called the Navigation Protection Act, and, indeed, protecting water is no longer the main emphasis of the legislation. The number of bodies of water in Canada protected under the new act has been reduced; only 97 lakes, portions of 62 rivers, and the 3 ocean coastal areas are protected.[115] Yet Canada has more than 2.25 million rivers and at least 32,000 lakes.[116] In other words, the legislation excludes over 99.9 per cent of Canada's rivers and 99.7 per cent of Canadian lakes from federal oversight.[117]

Essentially, the old act was an indirect tool protecting water and the environment from development because any project that might interfere with the right to navigate Canada's waters (logging, bridges, dams, pipelines, and such) had to go through an approval process that triggered a federal environmental assessment. This federal assessment activated the Crown's duty to consult and accommodate Aboriginal peoples. By only protecting bodies of water specifically listed in a schedule to the new act and by no longer requiring automatic federal environmental assessments, even for protected waters, Canada has opened the door for private companies such as Shell, Exxon, and BP to undertake projects that could more easily damage our most precious resource.

For many Indigenous peoples, both the water and the land are sacred. Many also rely on the water for their livelihoods and for connection to their culture. They see the protection of Mother Earth and of water, the blood of Mother Earth, as a sacred duty passed down from the ancestors. The new Navigation Protection Act limits the ability of First Nations to protect their lands and the water running through those lands because private companies have no duty to consult and accommodate Indigenous peoples when development projects could adversely affect Indigenous peoples and communities.

Bill C-45 also amended the Fisheries Act, the main federal statute in place to manage Canadian fish resources. One significant change is the new definition allotted to the term "Aboriginal": "'Aboriginal,' in relation to a fishery, means that fish is harvested by an Aboriginal organization or any of its members for the purpose of using the fish as food, for social or ceremonial purposes or for purposes set out in a land claims agreement entered into with the Aboriginal organization."[118] This definition does not recognize

Aboriginal peoples' already established (and constitutionally supported) right to harvest and sell fish for the purposes of maintaining a moderate livelihood.[119] Also, although the government's rationale behind adding this definition was to bring the legislation's language in line with that used in various land claim agreements, we must realize that, by applying this language, the government is defining the right to fish, a right that is *supposed to be* protected under section 35(1) of the Constitution Act, 1982.[120] As witnessed in the two *R. v. Marshall* cases, any definition of the "right" to fish also simultaneously sets the boundaries and limits of that right.

Changes to the Fisheries Act also have environmental consequences. In order for a species of fish to be subject to protection under the act, it now has to be part of or support a fishery, which the government defines as a commercial fishery, a recreational fishery, or an Aboriginal fishery. This change downgrades the protection of species that are not currently fished, and, more important, of their habitats, which are often the sparsely populated wilderness areas over which Indigenous people have title. Additionally, protecting only "fish of economic, cultural or ecological value" does not consider the whole ecosystem and endangers the delicate balance needed for the sustainability of Mother Earth.[121]

Changes were also made to the Canadian Environmental Assessment Act (CEAA). These included amending a "transitional provision," so new rules could be applied to development projects that had started earlier, when the CEAA would have required an environmental assessment.[122] These new rules had already changed substantially over the previous three years, since the first of the omnibus budget bills passed by the Conservative majority government in 2009. Essentially, over that period, the federal environment minister was given the power to exempt projects from thorough environmental assessment and to transfer some environmental reviews to other agencies. Also, the amount of technical information now needed for developers to move forward with projects that may impact the environment was reduced. These changes might limit Indigenous peoples' opportunities to examine and be part of environmental approval processes, which serves to circumvent the government's legal duty to consult Indigenous peoples on any matters that could impact their land and resources.

Bill C-45 also introduced changes to the Indian Act, 1985, changes relating to "surrendered and designated lands."[123] Bands can now lease reserve lands to third parties without the approval of the Governor in Council;[124] only the Minister of Indigenous and Northern Affairs Canada and the appropriate band council need to approve, and a band can do this through "simple majority" voting.[125] The problem is that only the votes of those community members attending a meeting or referendum are counted; the act does not require a majority of all on the eligible voter list to agree to surrendering land. Basically, according to a government official, this amendment makes it quicker and easier for First Nation communities to "take advantage of economic opportunities."[126] Although chiefs and councils may benefit from this change by being able to secure economic development opportunities faster, the result of this piecemeal and rapid approach to land leasing could be a "checkerboard" First Nation community, with bits and parcels of territory leased out and the community divided into various segments.

Another problem is that the government did not consult First Nations leaders or people before changing the Indian Act. By not consulting with First Nations leaders and communities, the government eschewed the Crown's obligations of consultation and accommodation. As Métis Elder Taz Bouchier comments about this mistake, "For too long in this country there has been no consultation with the Aboriginal community. We need to be consulted in every level of government."[127]

What's more, these changes to the Indian Act give the minister responsible for Indigenous affairs the authority to call a community band meeting or referendum so as to consider the surrender of the band's territory.[128] The minister is also given the power to accept or refuse the land designation after receiving a resolution from the band council. Ultimately, these changes seem to serve the government's resource development agenda rather than Indigenous peoples. Additionally, making changes to "Indian" legislation without consulting the Indigenous peoples themselves and giving government ministers increased authority in Indigenous matters act to undermine Indigenous peoples' rights to self-government.

Although the Harper government claimed that the purpose of Bill C-45 was to eliminate "red tape" and to rationalize government processes, many Indigenous peoples view it as legalizing ways for the government to circumvent its duty to consult, accommodate, and get the consent of Indigenous peoples in matters affecting their lands and resources.[129] Two strong underlying motives of the Conservative government, some suggest, were an agenda that emphasized economic development and an awareness that Aboriginal treaty rights—which are constitutionally protected—are the last best protection safeguarding resources and lands not yet "developed."[130]

These changes make it easier for pipeline developers (e.g., Enbridge and Kinder Morgan) and those supporting oil interests to advance their goals. And having fewer environmental protections makes it easier for governments and corporations to trump existing Aboriginal treaty rights—to cut across Indigenous lands from the tar sands in Alberta to the British Columbia coast, for example.

Indigenous opposition to pipeline projects has been strong. Between November 2010 and December 2011, over 130 First Nations with territories within the Fraser River watershed signed the "Save the Fraser Declaration," which expressed their adamant refusal to allow pipelines to go through their lands. "We have come together to defend these lands and waters from a grave threat," they declared. "Our laws require that we do this."[131] The "threat" in question is the Enbridge Northern Gateway Pipeline that would carry half a million barrels of oil a day from Alberta's tar sands to a port in Kitimat, British Columbia. From Kitimat, the oil would be shipped to Asian markets. In most of British Columbia, First Nations have not signed treaties with any government, so they continue to assert Indigenous title to their traditional lands, which the planned pipeline will cross. Consequently, First Nations leaders challenged the federal government's approval of the pipeline in 2014, arguing that this approval is a constitutional violation of their rights and citing the unanimous Supreme Court decision granting title to the Tsilhqot'in First Nation over its traditional and unceded territory.

There have been other, more direct responses to Bill C-45 and its predecessors, the earlier omnibus bills introduced by the Conservatives. One significant response is the grassroots movement called "Idle No More." Idle No More was first conceived by four women in Saskatchewan—Sylvia McAdam, Sheelah McLean, Jessica Gordon, and Nina Wilson—when they began sharing their concerns about Bill C-45. It turned into a global movement, expanding its focus beyond critiquing Bill C-45 and toward advocating for Indigenous human rights, for the equal treatment of Indigenous peoples, and for recognition of the treaty relationship.

Initially, though, the Idle No More movement protested against the environmental degradation, economic and social inequality, and abrogation of Indigenous rights that it claimed were furthered by Bill C-45 and the earlier Bill C-38, which became the Jobs, Growth and Long-Term Prosperity Act.[132] The numerous amendments in these omnibus bills "weaken Canada's capacity for environmental governance, threatening our land, climate and water," according to Idle No More supporters and environmentalists.[133]

Some Indigenous leaders and activists went on hunger strikes in support of the Idle No More movement and to protest the unequal treatment of Indigenous peoples in this country. Attawapiskat Chief Theresa Spence made headlines with her six-week hunger strike on Victoria Island (across the water from Ottawa's Parliament Hill). It started December 11, 2012, and ended January 23, 2013, and succeeded in drawing attention to many issues, including the failure of governments to honour treaty agreements, the Indigenous housing crisis, and Canada's negligence in implementing fully the United Nations Declaration on the Rights of Indigenous Peoples, which the government finally endorsed in 2010 (yet rather cryptically). During this time, she was on a fish-broth diet that included medicinal tea and some vitamins but no solid foods. According to Nishnaabeg writer and scholar Leanne Simpson, fish broth carries cultural meaning. It represents sacrifice and hardship, and, at the same time, it signifies the strength of the ancestors. It symbolizes survival because it sustained people through difficult circumstances, but it also holds an analogous understanding—fish broth cannot sustain a person forever.[134]

Chief Theresa Spence vowed not to eat until both Prime Minister Stephen Harper and Governor General David Johnston attended a meeting with First Nations leaders. She wanted everyone to be at the table at the same time, which never happened. She called for this meeting to highlight the special treaty relationships between Indigenous peoples and the government. As outlined in Chapter 5, these nation-to-nation agreements were established between First Nations and the British Crown.

At many of the Idle No More rallies, people reiterate the agreements made in original treaties and demand that they be honoured. For example, at the Idle No More rally I attended on December 23, 2012, on the steps of the Vancouver Art Gallery, Beverley Jacobs (Bear Clan), a Kanien'kehá:ka community representative from the Six Nations of the Grand River Territory, spoke with a beaded two-row wampum belt in hand, reiterating the treaty relationship first established in 1613.

Mi'kmaq lawyer and professor Pamela Palmater and many others involved in the Idle No More movement thought that Stephen Harper and the Conservative government were acting above the law "by pushing through" Bill C-45 and other omnibus bills using a timetable that did not allow for appropriate reflection or critique.[135] This view was one of the primary reasons that Indigenous leaders called for a meeting with not only Stephen Harper but also the governor general. Even though the governor general's position is symbolic, his or her role is to represent the British sovereign, the legal entity with whom First Nations signed treaties, and the governor general does have a few "reserve powers" that derive from the royal prerogative of the sovereign. As mentioned, this meeting did not occur.

More successful was the way the Idle No More movement united long-time Indigenous advocates with new generations of justice advocates. It brought Indigenous peoples together under a common vision. Using Twitter and other social media, such as Facebook, Indigenous peoples rallied, assembled flash mobs, and engaged in peaceful protests, some which garnered over 1,000 participants. This grassroots movement of the people and the oppressed has gone global—attracting supporters in the United States as

Image 10.1 Beverley Jacobs Speaking While Holding a Two-Row Wampum Belt

well as in various other countries, such as the Ukraine, Australia, and Egypt. These backers have also held demonstrations and posted photos and videos of support online.

As a demonstration of solidarity between the Indigenous nations in the United States and in Canada, protests have been organized along international borders. On January 5, 2013, my sister, father, uncle, and I were part of the peaceful rally at the Peace Bridge in Fort Erie, Ontario. At this rally, Indigenous peoples and other supporters from Canada did a peaceful march onto the bridge connecting Fort Erie, Ontario, and Buffalo, New York.

In the middle of the bridge, at the border dividing the two counties, we met with our Indigenous allies and supporters from the United States.

As protests spread, Indigenous hip-hop artists made songs in support of the movement, which not only added to its momentum but also served to educate through artistic expression. Such is the case with Ojibwe hip-hop artist Plex. In his song "No More," he catalogues the injustices facing Indigenous peoples and sings, "[We're] makin' our move; we ain't gonna Idle No More."[136] Or consider Saulteaux-Cree hip-hop artist Drezus who, in his song "Red Winter," sings that the government is "Making money off our land, and we ain't even on the guest-list." Still, he exclaims, now is the time for action: "You can lock us in jail and throw away the key, take away my rights but you ain't stopping me. 'Cause I've been quiet for too long, it's time to speak. We gotta stand for something to keep us free. I'm idle no more. I'm idle no more."[137]

Discussion Questions

1) What are some of the key court cases dealing with Aboriginal title, rights, and treaty interpretation? What do these cases mean for Indigenous peoples?
2) In what ways is it evident that the Canadian government has not fulfilled treaty agreements in relation to land and resources?
3) Provide and discuss examples of times when the Crown's obligations to consult and accommodate Indigenous peoples have not been met.

Activities

1) Watch the 1993 National Film Board of Canada documentary by Alanis Obomsawin, *Kanehsatake: 270 Years of Resistance* (available online at www.nfb.ca). What were the struggles faced by the people of Kanehsatà:ke?
2) Negotiated land claims are constitutionally protected, and the government is aware of that fact. However, in order to circumvent constitutional protection (afforded through section 35[3] of the Constitution Act, 1982) separate self-government agreements are being finalized. These do not classify as land claims and thus are not "modern" treaties under section 35. Without treaties, there is no settled constitutional structure, which results in a messy legal situation. For the next week, consider some of these ideas and watch *APTN National News* (available on basic cable and online at www.aptn.ca/news). Make a list of news stories that show the government ignoring Aboriginal rights and title to the land. A hint: some of these stories will probably involve resource development projects.
3) White peoples caused much of the destruction of traditional Indigenous homelands, society, and peoples. This history must be acknowledged, yet, at

the same time, we must remember that white people are not the enemy. The finger cannot be pointed at a single race of people. That would be counterproductive; the goal is peace and balance. European peoples once lived a life that acknowledged the land; they, too, used to have a balance. The white peoples across Europe were colonized long ago as well, long before their arrival in Turtle Island. The colonized becomes the colonizer. Research and discuss another nation of people in the world, nations that have also been colonized. How and in what ways did colonization affect them?

4) Cayuga hip-hop artist Chief Rock has a song entitled "The Colourless Hand." According to Chief Rock, this song title represents that no one specific race is behind the destruction of the environment or of inherent Indigenous rights, but what he calls "the colourless hand" is.[138] As he explains, although the European nations are the leaders behind the colonial agenda of resource extraction and land destruction, anyone who decides to follow the principles of colonial governance plays a role. Chief Rock urges Indigenous people not to become complacent about or enmeshed in Euro-Canadian institutions and systems of governance, which he believes hold Indigenous peoples back from breaking free of the colonial project. He explains that those who do nothing are giving away their authority every day, which, in some cases, causes people to be their own worst enemy. He calls on Indigenous peoples to resist the institutions and polices of colonialism and to assert their nationhood. Listen to his song, and identify further meanings and messages outlined by the artist (available online at www.youtube.com).

Recommended Readings

The Kino-nda-niimi Collective. *The Winter We Danced: Voices from the Past, the Future, and the Idle No More Movement.* Winnipeg: Arbeiter Ring Publishing, 2014.

Turpel, Aki-Kwe/Mary Ellen. "Aboriginal Peoples and the Canadian Charter of Rights and Freedoms: Contradictions and Challenges." *Canadian Women's Studies* 10, nos. 2 & 3 (1991): 149–57.

11
Modern Agreements and Land Claims: The Government's Desire for "Economic Certainty"

INDIGENOUS PEOPLES TODAY STILL STRUGGLE to achieve recognition of their full rights and of their title to ancestral and treaty land. They fight through the Euro-Canadian court system to regain or protect these rights and lands, as was discussed in Chapter 10. But agreements about Indigenous land and rights are negotiated outside of the courts as well. The federal government, for example, recognizes three types of Aboriginal land claim processes: one for comprehensive land claims in which Aboriginal title or land use rights have been continuous or unceded, a second for specific claims arising from treaties or other legal obligations, and a third for claims that do not fit into the other two categories (for example, a claim settled in the past by an agreement that did not meet reasonable standards for the time during which it was signed).

At first, having governments put processes in place to negotiate with Indigenous peoples over land and rights seems like a positive step. After all, it shows recognition on the part of governments that consultation and engagement need to take place. However, a close examination of the issue shows that governments put these processes in place mainly to expedite their own priorities and that, in many ways, these priorities are derived from a self-serving agenda rooted in colonialism. Such an agenda only serves to reinforce Indigenous injustice. This chapter, by examining the contemporary agreement processes and providing an overview of their procedures, intentions, and realities, will document how the economic priorities of governments affect modern-day negotiations.

Land Claims: Specific Claims and Comprehensive Claims

From 1927 to 1951, it was illegal under the Indian Act for "Indians" to raise money to advance land claims. In 1947, a joint committee of the Senate and House of Commons was created to examine the Indian Act and put forward a recommendation to establish a "Claims Commission," which would investigate the terms set out in Indian treaties and review, evaluate, and resolve any claims or grievances. Between 1959 and 1961, this joint committee also recommended the creation of an Indian Claims Commission to investigate land grievances in British Columbia and Kanehsatà:ke. The first legislative response to these recommendations was Bill C-123, introduced by the Liberals in 1969, but it died and went nowhere.[1]

The push for a contemporary means of conducting land negotiations with Indigenous peoples started to pick up in the 1960s and 1970s. In these decades, Indigenous peoples witnessed the federal and provincial governments' interest in industrial development and natural resource development and extraction. At the same time, many Indigenous peoples asserted the importance of protecting Mother Earth, as did others involved in the second wave of the environmental movement. Yet economic growth fuelled by industrial and resource development—and not the environment—was the top priority of governments during this time.

In order to move forward with this development agenda, governments sought to address the issue of Aboriginal title to the land and land-use rights. An important step was to put in place a policy for the settlement of Aboriginal land claims. As a result of the 1973 *Calder* decision—confirming that Aboriginal historic occupation of land conveyed rights despite European settlement—the federal government declared its new policy for negotiating Aboriginal land claims. In order to put this policy into motion, in 1974, the government created a special office within the federal Department of Indian and Northern Affairs (DIAND) called the Office of Native Claims (ONC). Through this office, Indigenous peoples could make two different types of claims: specific claims and comprehensive claims. Specific claims were those arising from unfulfilled treaty obligations. Comprehensive claims were those involving land never ceded by a treaty.[2]

In 1986, the ONC was replaced by several specialized units within DIAND (currently Indigenous and Northern Affairs Canada).[3] After the release of several policy papers in the 1980s and 1990s, provincial and territorial governments began to set up their own administrative structures to address Aboriginal claims.

After the "Oka Crisis" in 1990, Prime Minister Mulroney set up the Indian Claims Commission (ICC) with a mandate to review claims independently and provide mediation and facilitation services to help First Nations reach a settlement.[4] Yet this commission could only provide suggestions and advice, as it had no powers to make decisions that would be legally binding. In response to repeated recommendations from the Indian Claims Commission, made in its annual reports, as well as in response to the 2007 federal government's *Justice at Last* report, "an independent body with adjudicative powers" replaced the ICC.[5] In October of 2008, the Specific Claims Tribunal Act came into effect, and the Indian Claims Commission officially closed its doors in March of 2009.[6]

The Specific Claims Tribunal created by this act is a joint initiative between the federal government and the Assembly of First Nations; its purpose is to hear and resolve specific claims, those relating "to the non-fulfilment of an historic treaty or the mismanagement of First Nation land or other assets."[7] The government decided to create this tribunal because it felt something had to be done to address the hundreds of unsettled claims relating to Canada's failure to fulfil its treaty obligations. The tribunal was also set up as means of speeding up the specific claims process in order to provide "certainty" in relation to Indigenous territory. Many First Nations were hoping it would provide better transparency.[8]

Although defined as an "independent body," the tribunal is comprised of up to six judges who are appointed from the existing bench of superior court judges in the provinces. Although the tribunal officially began its operations only in 2011, Justice Harry Slade, the tribunal chair and its only full-time member, has stated that it is understaffed and overburdened. As he writes in September 2014, if things continue unchanged, "The Tribunal will fail" when his term expires in December 2015 because it will be unable to handle its caseload.[9] As of August 2015, 68 total claims were before the tribunal at various stages of decision, and it had ruled in 59 cases.[10] Many cases have been delayed, so the majority of open cases are listed as "ongoing."

In addition to specific claims, comprehensive claims are also piling up. These claims deal with Aboriginal rights and title to land not covered by a treaty or other legal agreements, and they are negotiated between the Aboriginal group, the federal government, and the relevant provincial or territorial government.[11] Since the 1970s, the comprehensive claims policy has undergone revision, with one of the most significant amendments announced in 1986.[12] This amendment eliminated the policy that required blanket "extinguishment" of Aboriginal rights in exchange for an agreement.[13] Another important change occurred on September 25, 1990, when the federal government announced that the process for negotiating comprehensive claims would no longer be limited to the consideration of six claims at one time.[14] In 1993, the government reiterated a main objective of the comprehensive claims process: "to negotiate modern treaties which provide clear, certain and long-lasting definition of rights to land and resources."[15]

Between 1986 and 1995, the issue of Aboriginal self-government grew in importance, which led to its increasing consideration in land claim agreements.[16] In 1995, the federal government stated that it recognized "the inherent right of self-government as an existing Aboriginal right under section 35 of the *Constitution Act, 1982*."[17] This federal recognition of the inherent right to self-government as an existing right under the Constitution means that negotiated self-government rights are constitutionally protected.[18]

In spite of these changes, the policy that guides the federal government in these negotiations, called the "comprehensive land claims policy," is still very similar in aim and effect to its 1973 predecessor, the Statement on Claims of Indian and Inuit People. This policy has never had the real aim of accepting Aboriginal title to lands not covered by treaty. Rather, its priority has been land surrender. It requires First Nations to extinguish their Aboriginal title by negotiating their land into private property.[19] Although 1986 called an end to "extinguishment" as a requirement, in reality, this option is frequently the only one for First Nations going through these negotiations. The term has just been reframed and expressed using new words, such as achieving "certainty" through "modification."

In order to negotiate a claim, the federal government typically puts together a team that consists of a chief federal negotiator, lawyers, and numerous other negotiators or analysts.[20] Other representatives from different orders of government also typically get involved in the process, by either joining the team or providing recommendations. These might include representatives from, say, Parks Canada, Environment Canada, Natural Resources Canada, or Canadian Heritage. A six-step process guides the negotiations. The first stage is called the "statement of claim"; this statement must include a clear outline of the claim, an indication of all First Nations involved, and a map of the geographic area being claimed. "Acceptance of claim" is second; at this stage a final decision is made by the government as to whether the claim will be accepted for negotiation. Third is the "preliminary negotiations" stage, during which the government makes a judgement on the likelihood of a successful negotiation. If it is high and the claim is deemed a priority, negotiations move toward the development of a framework. At this next stage, the "framework agreement" stage, the agreements forming the basis of the treaty are outlined. The fifth stage is called "agreement in principle"; at this point, the parties sign an agreement in principle that is not legally binding. At the final and sixth stage, the "final agreement" stage, all is complete: final approvals, formal ratification, and the passing of legislation to give effect to the agreements made.[21]

These six steps are outlined in the newly updated comprehensive land claims policy of September 2014, which was quietly released right after the decision on the *Tsilhqot'in* case (outlined in Chapter 10).[22] This new policy represents the first major revision of the comprehensive land claims policy since 1986, and, "*once finalized*," it will replace and supersede "*all previous versions of Canada's Comprehensive Land Claims Policy*" (original emphasis).[23] As explained in Chapter 10, the *Tsilhqot'in* case ruled that Aboriginal peoples hold title to their territorial lands and have the right to either benefit from or refuse development on that land.[24] According to researcher Shiri

Pasternak and Mohawk policy analyst Russell Diabo, the *Tsilhqot'in* case could have provided the opportunity for the federal government to rethink old and unsuccessful land claim negotiation processes and move toward land and resource co-management between the Crown and First Nations.[25] But, instead of exploring these options and engaging in honest discussion with Indigenous peoples, the Harper government opted to rewrite a policy that had failed Indigenous peoples since it began—the comprehensive land claims policy.

Indigenous and Northern Affairs Canada admits that this new policy was also a partial response to the 2013 Eyford report.[26] This report to the prime minister by Douglas R. Eyford, entitled *Forging Partnerships, Building Relationships: Aboriginal Canadians and Energy Development*, outlines the need to "capitalize" on the immediate oil and natural gas resource opportunities in Canada. To do so, it states, Canada needs "to construct pipelines and terminals to deliver oil and natural gas to tidewater."[27] Also, "Canada should continue to encourage industry and Aboriginal groups to develop flexible and innovative models to facilitate Aboriginal participation in economic development projects."[28] In other words, Canada must "encourage" Indigenous peoples to join resource development and extraction plans.

As Pasternak and Diabo point out, it is revealing that, right after the *Tsilhqot'in* decision was released, Eyford was appointed as the ministerial special representative to lead the reform of the comprehensive land claims policy.[29] Like the 2013 Eyford report, the new policy seeks to "advance reconciliation" as a central goal.[30] Why? According to the report, "Reconciliation promotes a secure climate for economic and resource development that can benefit all Canadians and balances Aboriginal rights with broader societal interests."[31]

The "renewed" policy also defines the Aboriginal rights affirmed in the Constitution as part of this reconciliation. In other words, these rights, it argues, should be understood as a way of reconciling that "prior to the arrival of Europeans in North America the land was already occupied by distinctive Aboriginal societies" with the "assertion of Crown sovereignty over Canadian territory."[32] This definition of reconciliation subordinates Aboriginal rights to Canadian sovereignty and to economic policies designed to benefit broader Euro-Canadian social interests.

This new policy also reasserts the government's right to infringe upon or limit Aboriginal rights as long as a rationale exists in law for doing so: "Canada acknowledges that any infringement of Aboriginal rights requires a justification in accordance with standards established by the Canadian courts."[33] As we saw in Chapter 10, any definition or "test" of an Aboriginal right, such as those outlined in the *Sparrow* and *Van der Peet* cases, not only sets conditions on what constitutes a valid Aboriginal right but also describes how governments can justifiably limit that right.[34]

The policy also has a section entitled "Certainty" in which that word is used to replace notions of "surrender," according to many First Nation critics. As the policy states, "The concept of certainty over lands and resources is central to the purpose of treaty negotiations, which provides a respectful framework for reconciliation."[35] In other words, the surrender of lands and resources is central to negotiating a treaty and provides the framework for Canada to achieve sovereignty over Indigenous peoples.

Additionally, the new policy makes it a First Nation responsibility to repay any money borrowed from government to pursue land claims research and negotiations: "Outstanding debts owed by the Aboriginal group to the federal Crown will be deducted from final settlements."[36] This definitely seems self-serving on the government's part.

The whole claims process can be very drawn out and lengthy and costly. Coming to a final agreement can take anywhere from about 5 to 20 years.[37] Since 1973, 26 comprehensive land claims and 3 self-government agreements have been signed. Of the 26 signed agreements, 18 have included provisions related to self-government.[38] These settlements have reaffirmed Aboriginal title to over 600,000 square kilometres of land and have provided capital transfers of over $3.2 billion. However, the average cost of negotiating a claim can vary from between $15 million and $50 million.[39] As a comparison, the Canadian government spent just over $730, 000 between 1875 and 1905 on costs related to the numbered treaties.[40]

Although a main motivator of government involvement in the modern negotiation process is to enable economic development of Indigenous lands and to expand Euro-Canadian systems of governance and economy, the land claims settlements do provide some mutual benefits. So although the process may be duplicitous, agreements are made that recognize the specific rights of Indigenous peoples. The fact of the negotiations themselves goes a long way toward recognizing Aboriginal title. However, the unfortunate reality is that these modern agreements are too often routinely broken after they are signed, as was the very first "modern treaty" signed.

Breaking the First "Modern Treaty": The James Bay and Northern Québec Agreement

The first "modern," comprehensive land claim settlement was the James Bay and Northern Québec Agreement signed in 1975. The Québec and federal governments wanted the surrender of Aboriginal title to northern Québec so a major hydroelectric development could go forward.[41] For Indigenous peoples, this negotiation was a chance to get compensation for their traditional ancestral land, which the development would use, while at the same time retaining certain rights to the land, such as the right to use the land to maintain their traditional lifestyles and the right to maintain a degree of control over their communities' livelihoods.

The province of Québec started development of these northern resources in the 1960s and, by 1971, had formed the James Bay Development Corporation to pursue development in the region, including of mining, forestry, and hydro resources.[42] This development began with the James Bay Project, a huge hydroelectric-power project opposed by many of the region's Cree and Inuit people, as they were never consulted. The water diversions, dammed reservoirs, and generating stations necessary to the project were to be undertaken on Cree and Inuit territory that had not yet been ceded and that the inhabitants still used for livelihood purposes, such as hunting, trapping, fishing, and harvesting.[43] Given the development plans, a group of Cree and Inuit peoples instituted legal proceedings against Québec and the James Bay Development Corporation. After Justice Malouf heard the testimony of Cree and Inuit hunters regarding their occupation and continuing use of the lands, the Québec Superior Court granted an interlocutory injunction against the hydroelectric development on November 15, 1973. This injunction blocked the project from furthering its development until an agreement was negotiated with the Cree and Inuit peoples in the surrounding areas.[44]

In reality, the injunction was ignored and work at the development site never stopped; it was continuing days after the injunction.[45] Also, the involved corporations and the Québec government immediately appealed the injunction and started a major media campaign against it, which attempted to convince the public that stopping this work would cost the people of Québec up to $500,000 daily. Just seven days after the injunction was given, it was overruled by the Québec Court of Appeal.[46]

Even though the injunction was overruled and construction was still ongoing, Justice Malouf persuaded the governments that they must arrive at a settlement with the local Cree and Inuit peoples.[47] Negotiations took place over the next year, and, one year exactly after the Superior Court decision, on November 15, 1974, an agreement in principle was signed between the federal and provincial governments, Hydro-Québec, the Grand Council of the Crees, and the Northern Québec Inuit Association. A year later, on November 11, 1975, the final agreement was completed and signed.[48]

About 10,000 Cree and Inuit people entered into this agreement. They had 13,696 square kilometres of land set aside for their exclusive use.

Fishing, hunting, and trapping rights were given exclusively to the Cree and Inuit people who signed this agreement, and they were awarded a measure of local control over education, health, and other matters. Also included was a "benefits package" totalling $226.3 million in additional programs and $267.5 million in cash. In return, Cree and Inuit people who entered this agreement had to "cede, release, surrender and convey all their Native claims, rights, titles and interests, whatever they may be, in and to land in the territory and in Québec, and Québec and Canada accept such surrender."[49]

Many view this agreement as inequitable and forced on the Cree and Inuit of the region.[50] According to the Grand Council of the Crees, they were really left with no choice but to come to an agreement because the construction of the hydroelectric project was already underway when negotiations began. So while they were in the process of negotiations, their land and waterways were already being threatened by construction. If they had continued to fight in the courts for better terms or to protect their lands, it would have been too late; construction on the project would have been complete by the time their case reached the Supreme Court.

It has also since been revealed that government negotiators came to the table with "surrender" and "extinguishment" as necessary conditions not up for deliberation or dialogue. Remember, too, that this agreement was being negotiated before Aboriginal rights were recognized in the Canadian Constitution, and the sentiments expressed by government at the time were reflective of the idea that Indigenous peoples had few rights. Governments brought "false and illegitimate arguments" to the negotiation table, according to the Grand Council of the Crees, "including that we had no aboriginal rights or title. We were told we were squatters."[51]

The governments also threatened to cut off funds that Cree and Inuit people depended upon in order to defend their rights. Additionally, both during and before negotiations, the government programs on which Indigenous peoples depended were being cut or frozen.[52] This circumstance led Justice A. C. Hamilton to conclude in a 1995 report entitled *Canada and Aboriginal Peoples* that, frequently, Indigenous negotiators signed modern treaties under duress: "Many signed because they needed the funding and other benefits for their impoverished people."[53]

At the same time, there was a tilted negotiation table. The Indigenous negotiators of the James Bay and Northern Québec Agreement had to face not only the federal and provincial governments as negotiators, but also Hydro-Québec. Thus, the Cree and Inuit people were compelled to negotiate land claims with a development corporation as well as two levels of government.

Today, many consider the James Bay and Northern Québec Agreement not only as Canada's first "modern" treaty but also as the first modern treaty to be broken.[54] Since its signing, the Cree and Inuit have repeatedly gone to court to try to force the parties involved to honour the agreement's terms, which were simply being ignored.[55] For instance, the treaty stipulated that Cree and Inuit would have priority in employment, in setting up tourist camps, and over hunting. A process for economic development was supposed to have been instituted, which would include training and education. None of these terms were met, initially, and, although court cases were won to achieve some of the things agreed to, these victories were brief. Only 10 years after signing the treaty, Cree people presented the government with a list of 65 broken promises. Six years down the road (in 1992) Grand Chief Matthew Coon Come estimated that not much had changed: "My people, the Crees of James Bay, signed a treaty only 16 years ago with Canada . . . but that treaty has become a shameful reminder of Canada's duplicity and ingratitude. That treaty has shown how greed triumphs over respect for the law, how politics supersedes constitutional responsibility. Our treaty has become infamous as Canada's first modern broken treaty."[56]

Land Claims in British Columbia: The Government's Self-Serving Agenda

In 1992, Indigenous representatives, British Columbia, and the federal government set up the British Columbia Treaty Commission (BCTC) in order to help facilitate and settle land questions and negotiate self-government agreements in the province. The process officially began in 1993. After the BCTC was established, the First Nations in British Columbia were left with the option of negotiating through the commission or going through the courts to settle land claims independently. Those are the two options. Ever since the 1973 *Calder* decision, the federal government has pushed to negotiate rather than litigate resolutions to Aboriginal land claims. In the *Delgamuukw* case, which was begun in 1984 but not settled until 1997, the Supreme Court of Canada also emphasized that negotiation is better than litigation.[57] The BCTC, then, was a response to this preference for negotiation.

The BCTC also provides funding for negotiations. Approximately 80 per cent of this funding is provided as loans from the federal government; the other 20 per cent is given in the form of grants from the federal government and the province.[58] Monies borrowed have to be repaid after the First Nation recipient reaches an agreement. Some nations have negotiated final agreements through the BCTC: for example, the Tsawwassen First Nation (implemented 2009), the five Maa-nulth First Nations (implemented 2011), the Yale First Nation (signed 2013), and the Tla'amin First Nation (signed 2014). Yet some critics argue that these settlements also came with consequences, including the extinguishment of Aboriginal title to parts of the traditional territory of the nations and the loss of certain Aboriginal rights in British Columbia. For example, some bands now operate akin to municipalities and face having tax exemptions eventually phased out.

According to Taiaiake Alfred, "behind the progressive facade, the BC treaty process represents an advanced form of control, manipulation, and assimilation."[59] It is operating on an incorrect notion—the assumption that Canada owns the land in the province—when, in fact, most of the land in British Columbia was never ceded by treaty. Consequently, Taiaiake Alfred argues, the BCTC process obliges Indigenous peoples to make a claim to land they have always possessed and never given up. He further asserts that the BC treaty process "is not about negotiating treaties at all" because a *treaty*, by definition, is "a formal agreement between two or more recognized sovereign nations operating in an international forum, negotiated by designated representatives and ratified by the governments of the signatories."[60] Really, these settlements are about the extinguishment of Indigenous people's nationhood, and pulling First Nations under Canada's own political and legal structures with "certainty and finality."[61]

As of 2014, more than 50 First Nations in British Columbia have borrowed $493 million in negotiation support through the BCTC; this money will have to be paid back.[62] Every community that has joined the BC treaty process has signed an agreement to borrow money.[63] As funds for negotiating land claims in British Columbia are administered by the BCTC, First Nations must participate in this "treaty" process to receive support. Currently, First Nations in British Columbia are divided on whether to enter into this negotiation. About 60 per cent of First Nations have decided that they will negotiate under the comprehensive land claims policy, and about 40 per cent have decided that they will not engage in this process, whose primary goal is to extinguish land rights.[64] For example, Honorary Chief Richard LeBourdais, a Secwepemc citizen of the Shuswap Nation, explained that the members of his nation "didn't enter into the treaty process" because they "saw through the smoke and mirrors."[65]

Two communities that initially engaged in the process but then withdrew were the Xaxl'ip Nation and the Ts'kw'aylaxw Nation. Xaxl'ip Chief Darrell Bob and Ts'kw'aylaxw Chief Robert Shintah said in a personal communication that their communities withdrew from the process because they decided that they didn't want to give up their Aboriginal title and rights.[66] Shintah explained that he sees no benefit because then governments would be "negotiating away our land right." Chiefs Shintah and Bob were involved in the BCTC process from the beginning and were present at its initial meetings.

In 1990, they were prime movers in the shutting down of the highway and railroad in Ts'kw'aylaxw territory. They did this because they wanted recognition as a people. Then-premier William Vander Zalm and two of his assistants came to meet with them right on the railway tracks near Seton Portage. They were told by the government officials that the blockade had to come down. Officials also said, "We can't recognize you as a people." According to Chief Bob, this was the response: "We're not taking it down ... if you can't recognize us as a people. We're not taking it down, and all these people here, you're going to have to take them to jail, and they did [take them to jail]."

According to Shintah, many of the chiefs in Ts'kw'aylaxw territory said the treaty process was born right there and at that moment, that the government was acting in response to Indigenous dissent and protest when it established the BC treaty process. Indeed, Indigenous peoples who wanted their rights and title recognized undoubtedly had an effect. In that same year, 1990, the Canadian government, the province of British Columbia, and Indigenous representatives established the BC Claims Task Force in order to establish how land claims negotiations could be set into motion, how they would operate, and what they should include. Within a few years, the province accepted the concept of Aboriginal rights as an official policy, which included the right for Aboriginal peoples to self-govern. The BC Claims Task Force made 19 recommendations and set up a six-stage process for treaty negotiation, which the BC Treaty Commission still follows. These six stages were designed to "assist the parties to progress rapidly" through the process:[67]

Stage 1: Statement of Intent to Negotiate
Stage 2: Readiness to Negotiate
Stage 3: Negotiation of a Framework Agreement
Stage 4: Negotiation of an Agreement In Principle
Stage 5: Negotiation to Finalize a Treaty
Stage 6: Implementation of the Treaty"[68]

Steps 3 to 6 are similar to those in the six-step Canadian policy outlined earlier in the chapter. The main difference is in the first two steps, which are much less formal. Instead of submitting a "statement of claim," in which the First Nation builds its case in the hopes that its claim will be accepted as worthy of a hearing, First Nations in BC do not need "supporting materials" or a "government review and acceptance of claim."[69] The claims of BC First Nations are considered able to go forward because the majority of land in British Columbia has never been ceded by a treaty. In other words, these are considered "unresolved claims" by governments.

As Darrell Bob explains, when the BC Treaty Commission was first created, chiefs were quite eager to participate. Some wanted to borrow money immediately to start negotiating a treaty. Chiefs Bob and Shintah, for example, both entered into this process thinking the results could be good for their communities. However, they soon realized that this settlement process might not be the best way forward. After borrowing an initial negotiating loan, they wanted out.

Both of their communities were able to pull out of this process because, in 2002, Premier Gordon Campbell[70] and the British Columbia Liberal Party, then in power, put into motion the BC Aboriginal Treaty Referendum. This referendum posed questions about policies outside of provincial jurisdiction, and it suggested that Aboriginal rights could be extinguished without negotiation. According to Darrell Bob, this referendum breached the 19 recommendations initially made by the BC Claims Task Force, which were to set the basis for the negotiating process in the province. As these principles informed the BC Treaty Commission's processes and purposes (to which the province had agreed), the referendum was a breach of faith, according to Darrell Bob: "He breached in our eyes; he breached the negotiation and that's what we stood on."

Robert Shintah explains how Gordon Campbell himself later admitted to his mistake. In 2007, at a First Nations Leadership Gathering at the Art Gallery in Vancouver, Shintah and Campbell were sitting at neighbouring tables, as they had a working relationship. This gathering had close to 2,000 people in attendance. Shintah was the first one to get up and speak at this event. In his speech, he called his friend Campbell the "worst redneck" in British Columbia for calling that referendum. Right after Shintah's talk, Campbell spoke, saying, "Yes, I am the worst redneck in BC for exactly what he said."[71]

After pulling out of the process, Darrell Bob was threatened by government officials. They sent a letter and called him on the phone and told him that if he and Shintah did not come back to the negotiating table or pay back the loan, remedial management would be hired to take over their band offices. According to both men, a main problem with these negotiations is this loan; the government sucks communities into the process and then keeps these communities stuck in it as the debt grows. As Bob explains, "Our community supposedly owes \$2.8 million dollars, which isn't true. . . . I told them it's just a down payment on what they robbed from us and there's no darn way we are paying it back." Shintah agrees, saying that when the government threatened his community and told it "to pay back the money, I told them to come and give me an invoice for the $2.8 million dollars; I'm giving them one for $16 billion annually."

The government does not want to change this land settlement process. Currently, the existence of these negotiations is the government's first line of defence when land title in British Columbia is discussed. The government uses as leverage the fact that some First Nations have entered into this comprehensive land claim settlement process, and it meets any criticism by saying that a process is in motion.[72] Many of these land claim agreements are still being negotiated today. Some of them are tabled, and have been for quite a few years, which means that negotiations are essentially delayed until the First Nations decide to resume bargaining. When this treaty process began in the early 1990s, the BC Treaty Commission expected it would be wrapped up by 1999, which clearly did not happen. It has actually come to be a very long, drawn out process.

In many ways, the process sets communities up for failure. Often, according to Darrell Bob, by the time a community actually negotiates its treaty, it will be very much in debt, and a considerable portion of the settlement money it has negotiated will go straight back into the hands of the government to pay off this debt, which was accumulated borrowing "negotiation funding" from the government. Given the length of negotiations and interest rates, $2.8 million borrowed in 2001 to pay for researchers and consultants to help a First Nation negotiate would probably mean a debt of at least $10 million 12 years later.[73]

Darrell Bob told me a story about this accumulating debt. He explained that one day he was walking through the Pacific Centre Mall in Vancouver, and, while he was walking, he saw a chief there crying. He didn't know who he was. But he was an older fellow standing there crying. So Chief Bob went over to him and said, "How are you doing?" The fellow chief responded, "I'm not doing good. I just got elected in as chief, and we owe so much money. I went to meet with the federal government today. They told me I might as well sign the treaty because the money they're going to give us isn't going to be enough to cover the amount of the loan."

Many Indigenous peoples (and others) believe that this process of negotiating comprehensive land claim agreements should be scrapped because, ultimately, the First Nations of British Columbia should not have to claim their lands from the government when most of the land claimed by the province has never been ceded by a treaty. As Robert Shintah contends, "We always say British Columbia is the biggest reserve in Canada; it's all ours."

In British Columbia, the government recognizes as "reserved land" only about 0.2 per cent of the province, which means the colonial government has just about complete control over 99.8 per cent of the land.[74] In many ways, then, the comprehensive land claims process demonstrates the government's reliance on the dated, racist conceptions of land ownership that stem from the doctrine of discovery.

As First Nations political leader Arthur Manuel (Secwepemc) explains, four white men *claimed* "discovery" of British Columbia: Captain James Cook, Simon Fraser, David Thompson, and Alexander Mackenzie.[75] But the land they claimed to have discovered was already the home of many First Nations, so the racist property concept stemming from the doctrine of discovery should not be used as Canada's claim to the territory known as "British Columbia." Settlers' only rights in this territory are based on their human rights, and both settlers and Indigenous peoples should recognize the human rights of both peoples. At the same time, settlers have to recognize Aboriginal title and that Indigenous peoples must be part of any decisions that have to do with the land. For example, First Nations should determine whether an Enbridge pipeline goes through these lands or whether a mining operation should be set up.[76] As Darrell Bob explains,

> We still own this land. Like one of our chiefs said to me—She says, "We can't kick everybody out; we just have to learn to live together . . . and have a common understanding of the law and of how we're going to live together and coexist."[77]

The Tsawwassen Final Agreement

The Tsawwassen First Nation is located in the lower mainland of British Columbia and is part of the Metro Vancouver area. It went through the BC treaty process and got an agreement, the first urban agreement signed in British Columbia. This First Nation submitted its statement of intent in 1993, and, in 2007, its agreement was ratified and received Royal Assent in the provincial legislature. This agreement entitled, the "Tsawwassen First Nation Final Agreement," came into effect in 2009.

Amidst the rapid development surrounding their community in the 1980s and 1990s, which was compounded by the Crown's continued denial of Indigenous sovereignty, the Tsawwassen people had three options for survival as a First Nation with inherent rights and title: "not recognize the Crown's sovereignty and do nothing; litigate; or enter treaty negotiations."[78] Consequently, the Tsawwassen Nation chose the treaty route. At the time, Tsawwassen Chief Kim Baird listed reasons for choosing this route, and these ranged from "improving economic opportunities" for the community, "resolving long-outstanding issues," "securing benefits" for the community, and "accommodating" Aboriginal rights.[79] In his master's thesis examining the Tsawwassen First Nation Final Agreement, Alan Hanna explained that "Chief Baird's statements reveal a determination to achieve economic stability in order to maintain or improve the way of life of her community, and her voice provides a human element, a war cry of sorts, to endure and succeed in the face of oppressive colonial forces occurring around the tiny Tsawwassen reserve in the early 1990s."[80]

In the year before Tsawwassen submitted its letter of intent, the community was faced with the potential expansion within the bounds of its traditional territory of a neighbouring shipping-container port. In April 1992, the Port of Vancouver announced that it would develop a new container facility at Roberts Bank and invest $200 million to expand this deep-sea terminal. This project was set to be "fast tracked" in order for the facility to be operative within only three years, which meant Tsawwassen land would be expropriated without any consultation or negotiation.

Only seven months later, local farmers got involved. They were upset that this terminal expansion would require 22 hectares of farmland (out of the original 360 hectares that the federal government had expropriated in the 1960s for the construction of a coal port). Their position was that this farmland should be given back to "the original owners," whom they considered to be themselves. However, what the farmers failed to recognize was that the true original owners were the Tsawwassen peoples. These incidents created an urgency to act for the Tsawwassen people, who faced not only the proposed expansion of a shipping-container terminal on their land but also the false claims of local farmers, who were publicly stating that this land belonged to them.

In a personal communication, Kim Baird (former chief of the Tsawwassen First Nation) shared her experience of invoking the treaty process as a way to better her community. These negotiations consumed a large piece of Baird's life, as she was involved from the very beginning to the very end of the negotiations. She started as a researcher and then moved into various roles, from administrator to junior negotiator to chief negotiator, and she was chief of the Tsawwassen First Nation for 13 years.[81]

Through entering into the Tsawwassen Final Agreement, the Tsawwassen people had to give up ownership rights within the full extent of their traditional lands in order to gain more say over their rights in a smaller, agreed upon area. The Tsawwassen First Nation is now operating under what is called a concurrent law model, which means that federal, provincial, and First Nation laws operate in their land. Notably, for Baird, this model means that the Tsawwassen First Nation is now out of the Indian Act. In spite of being outside the Indian Act, however, if the Tsawwassen people do not write their own law about a matter, then the relevant federal or provincial law will apply.

Baird describes herself as being very pragmatic and practical. She explains that she considers how to transfer theory into practice when dealing with real problems, such as alleviating poverty and improving education and obtaining the tools needed to do both. So, although at first during negotiations, she tried to wait for what she assessed was the "perfect agreement," she eventually decided, facing the looming possibility that another generation might have to suffer, to do what she thought would be best at that time to help her people. As she explains the situation, she and her community had to make some compromises in the treaty agreement.

She further explains that the federal government had failed the Tsawwassen people for "over a century." Thus, the treaty was a way to help the people get more certainty about their rights and to have less interaction with the federal government. For example, she says, after the agreement came into effect, Tsawwassen First Nation by-laws no longer had to be approved by a federal minister.

Indeed, after the treaty, the Tsawwassen First Nation created a new structure of government, which differs from the chief and council system it had before. Now, there is a legislature made up of 12 people, plus the chief, that meets at least twice a year to pass laws and budgets. An executive council, which is somewhat like the chief and council, oversees day-to-day governance rather than acting as administrators (its old role). An advisory council meets every two weeks to review each policy and law. Anyone can attend its meetings and raise concerns. A judicial council at arm's length from the government can rebuke any decision made and bring forth grievances. Overall, the nation has instituted a very participatory governance structure.

In order to reach its treaty agreement, the Tsawwassen First Nation borrowed from the government. This money went primarily to pay for staff and legal fees. Eighty per cent of the monies used to come to the agreement came from government loans while the remaining 20 per cent came from the Tsawwassen First Nation. The possibility of borrowing too much money and going into debt was high on the radar of Baird and her community. As she explains, referring to other First Nations, "Some people's cash proposal from the government is less than the money they've borrowed for the process." Not wanting to fall into this trap, her community gave her a mandate regarding how much she could borrow to participate in the negotiations; the limit was about $4 million. Community members thought negotiating a treaty was going to be a much shorter process than it turned out to be. Halfway through negotiations the borrowing limit was reached. When Tsawwassen negotiators told the government that the nation would not borrow any more money, the government "found" extra funds so they would reach a final agreement.[82]

The estimated total value of the final treaty was $120 million.[83] The total amount of land in the treaty settlement was 724 hectares. This land was said to be worth $66.7 million. There was also $34.6 million allocated to an "other" category, and $2.7 million to the provision of a guaranteed share of the Fraser River salmon run. In terms of cash dollars, the Tsawwassen First Nation received $16 million, which, to Baird, "wasn't that much money"; however, what she felt was really important was the amount of land retained.[84]

In terms of negotiating for this land, its exact borders had to be determined to fit within the government's parameters. The initial map of Tsawwassen traditional territory had no borders; rather, the people put arrows saying, "This is our winter village, and these are the areas we would travel" and such.[85] However, the treaty commission would not accept this sort of map. So negotiators had to draw lines and connect the dots, establishing boundaries, which became controversial in two ways. First, many people argued that Tsawwassen claimed too little of the nation's traditional territory. Second, neighbouring First Nations thought Tsawwassen claimed too much and that its claims were impacting their rights. When the Tsawwassen peoples were forced to draw lines on a map to delineate where their traditional territory was located, the Semiahmoo peoples worried that the Tsawwassen First Nation was claiming lands that fell within traditional Semiahmoo territory. In July 2007, the Semiahmoo First Nation filed a petition in the BC Supreme Court asking to have the Tsawwassen agreement put on hold until the matter could be investigated further.[86] "This is not an attack on Tsawwassen," said one of the lawyers for the Semiahmoo. "There wasn't any consultation with the Semiahmoo."[87] Yet in November 2007, their petition was dismissed.[88]

Engaging in this land negotiation process meant that Tsawwassen would no longer be a reserve under section 91 of the Canadian Constitution Act of 1867.[89] As part of the negotiations, all three parties agreed that Tsawwassen would no longer be under federal jurisdiction, but no formal agreement was reached concerning these jurisdictional matters. The Tsawwassen people, however, assert that they are under section 35 of the Constitution Act of 1982.[90]

One aspect of the Indian Act still applies to the Tsawwassen First Nation though. It still has community members who are registered as status

"Indians" under this federal act. The nation also has members who are non-status "Indians" because, according to Tsawwassen's policies, one has to have only one Tsawwassen parent to be considered a member of the community. Tsawwassen people who have "Indian" status under the federal government still retain their "Indian" status, and the nation still receives fiscal transfers to provide programs and services to its status people. However, once the Tsawwassen First Nation starts to develop its own economic base, the funding from the federal government will decrease. For every dollar the Tsawwassen First Nation makes, its funding from the federal government will decrease by 50 cents. So, as of 2015, some Tsawwassen people still receive the programs and services that other status "Indians" in Canada do, such as medical care and funds for postsecondary education. But, as the Tsawwassen First Nation develops its lands, various projects (such as the large mall set to open in the fall of 2016), and its own tax base, federal funding will be eliminated, including the tax exemption ensured by the Indian Act. In eight years from the effective date of the signed treaty, the nation's tax exemption for sales will be phased out, and, in twelve years, its income tax and property tax exemptions will be phased out.

According to Baird, before the treaty, the Tsawwassen people faced resistance and roadblocks when trying to engage in economic development on their territory. Such was the case when they tried to develop condominiums in the early 1990s. When the neighbouring municipality refused to provide water and sewer for the condominium project, they ended up having to provide independent services. Next, the Department of Fisheries and Oceans took them to court asserting that the sewage treatment plant the Tsawwassen First Nation had built impacted fish habitats. It was a "jurisdictional nightmare." Tsawwassen was essentially being "legislated out of the economy."[91] After the treaty, the Tsawwassen First Nation had powers similar to those of a municipality.

As the whole treaty process evolved, many different players and peoples had to sit around the negotiating table. According to Baird, it is hard for people to fathom what these negotiations are like in practice. For example, some days, 20 people would be around the table: 12 from the federal government, 6 from the provincial government, and perhaps 2 from Tsawwassen. The federal government always had the most resources, and the Tsawwassen people always had the least, so they were usually outnumbered at the negotiation table. At its core, the Tsawwassen team had four full-time Tsawwassen members and about five to ten advisors who were brought in as required (depending on the negotiations).

Every two weeks for two and a half years, 12 to 15 people met to develop the Tsawwassen constitution. Baird explains that they kept all facets of the negotiations open to the community. All ideas and agreements and all trade-offs were brought before their biggest critics in the community, as well as in the province. They even paid the members of their community who were opposed to the treaty to critique it so as to assure that negotiators would look at this process from many angles.

As Baird explains, the government clearly was not participating in the treaty-making process out of benevolence but rather out of a need to provide certainty, most notably, "economic certainty." According to her, some First Nations participate because they want a different sort of certainty—a certainty of rights. So different goals are always at play, a situation that makes the BC treaty process very controversial. Furthermore, not everyone will agree on how or whether to define "rights" because the minute you start defining your rights, you are limiting them. According to Baird, what the Tsawwassen First Nation did receive in its final agreement was more certainty over the "ownership" of a smaller area of land that belongs to their peoples.

Baird does admit that some Tsawwassen members feel that some parts of the agreement could have been better. Yet, as she says, "No one has been able to tell me a better way to do it." She further explains her pragmatic view of the treaty process and of her nation's final agreement:

> . . . there are lots of complaints about the treaty process and the federal policy positions. I completely agree. If they could change some of those positions, I think that would be great. I'm not going to sell the federal government position to anybody. We reached an agreement, but it took every comma, fish, and dollar within that agreement for it to be acceptable to us.[92]

After the ratification of the Tsawwassen Final Agreement, the Union of British Columbia Indian Chiefs (UBCIC), a coalition of BC chiefs formed in 1969 to oppose the White Paper, released a statement critiquing the BC treaty process and sent a letter to that effect to the prime minister, premier, and federal and provincial ministers of Aboriginal affairs.[93] The letter's press release quoted Grand Chief Stewart Phillip's view that "the ratification of the Tsawwassen Final Agreement is not a victory for the BC Treaty Process."[94] Chief Phillip holds this view because, at the end of the day, the fundamentally faulty treaty process remains in place. The UBCIC agrees and has always been strongly opposed to this treaty process. The letter, signed by President Chief Stewart Phillip, Vice President Chief Robert Shintah, and Secretary-Treasurer Chief Mike Retasket of the UBCIC states, "Canada's policy has moved from one of direct assimilation, to one of claims, but has otherwise changed little over the century."[95] It stresses this point by juxtaposing the current policy of "claims" to the previous policy of "assimilation," quoting Duncan Scott, who, in 1920, pledged to continue this earlier policy "until there is not a single Indian in Canada that is not been absorbed into the body politic."[96] Thus, the members of the UBCIC see new words yet the same agenda.

Grand Chief Stewart Phillip thinks that the Tsawwassen agreement suppressed Aboriginal rights, that it extinguished rather than recognized inherent rights.[97] The Tsawwassen Final Agreement is 212 pages long and has an exhaustive outline of Tsawwassen's rights; however, any rights not outlined and defined in the document are now extinguished. Alan Hanna notes that extinguishment is stated in section 16 of the agreement: "Tsawwassen First Nation releases Canada, British Columbia and all other Persons from all claims, demands, actions or proceedings, of whatever kind, whether known or unknown . . ."[98] Even though this section does not specifically use the word "extinguishment," the term "release," used in this context, means the same thing.

Chapter 9 of the agreement outlines rights in regards to "fisheries," and states that the Tsawwassen First Nation has the right "to harvest for Domestic Purposes" and "Trade and Barter Fish and Aquatic Plants . . . with other aboriginal people of Canada."[99] Alan Hanna points out that the inclusion of the word "Canada" effectively disallows trade with Indigenous nations in the United States, such as the nearby Lummi Nation whose peoples are also Coast Salish.[100]

Although the Tsawwassen First Nation is out of the Indian Act, it achieved through the agreement neither the status of a sovereign nation nor recognition of its peoples' inherent right to their lands. Rather, the Tsawwassen Final Agreement upheld the Crown's sovereignty, as is clear from the document's preamble: "The Parties are committed to the reconciliation of the prior presence of Tsawwassen First Nation and of the sovereignty of the Crown through the negotiation of this Agreement which will establish a new government to government relationship based on mutual respect."[101] Put another way, "reconciliation," as it is used here, does not amount to righting past wrongs but to the Tsawwassen people becoming reconciled to "the sovereignty of the Crown."

Thus, similar to the Supreme Court cases regarding Aboriginal rights outlined in Chapter 10, such as the *Van der Peet* case,[102] this agreement posits Crown sovereignty as an absolute and therefore fails to acknowledge inherent Indigenous rights and sovereignty, which were in place long before the Crown arrived. Because the Tsawwassen First Nation signed this agreement, the Crown's presumed sovereignty over Tsawwassen peoples not only remains in tact but is now agreed to in writing.

Given these problematic outcomes, why do Indigenous nations participate in colonial-centric legal discourses and procedures such as the BC treaty process? As described above, many factors pressure Indigenous peoples to copy or take part in the functions and methods of the state, in what some critiques call the "politics of distraction." Māori scholar Graham Hingangaroa Smith (of Ngati Apa, Ngati Kahungunu, Kai Tahu, and Ngati Porou tribal descent), explains the "politics of distraction" as follows:

> This is the colonizing process of being kept busy by the colonizer, of always being on the "back-foot," "responding," "engaging," "accounting," "following" and "explaining." These are typical strategies often used over indigenous people. The "logic" . . . seems to be that if the "natives" are kept busy doing "trivial pursuits" there will [be] little time left to complain, question or rebel against the "status quo" conditions.[103]

Through participation in the BC claims process, then, Indigenous peoples become pulled into these "politics of distraction" while momentum is directed away from finding solutions that lie beyond the boundaries of the colonial state.

The act of engaging in and relying on colonial laws, structures, and policies creates a situation in which the colonized contribute to colonizing themselves. People can become so distracted by and implicated in these systems, that they are unaware of participating in the very structures and processes that contribute to their oppression. Waziyatawin and Michael Yellow Bird argue that Indigenous peoples must stop thinking that it is in our best interest to take part in economic development or to join the "project of modernity," as both comprise a false path that does not lead to self-determination.[104] Taiaiake Alfred reveals that there is "not a shred of empirical evidence that increasing the material wealth of Indigenous people, or increasing the economic development of First Nation communities, in any way improves the mental or physical health or overall well-being of people in First Nation communities."[105] Jeff Corntassel states that Indigenous peoples "can decide the true motivations" behind terms such as "economic development" and can come up with much more sustainable approaches to counter the "politics of distraction" perpetrated by the state.[106]

The lure of economic resources, opportunity, and access is very appealing, especially when your land is being used without consent or consultation or when, as Baird explains, your community is dealing with real problems that need practical solutions *now*, such as alleviating poverty or improving education. This Tsawwassen community faced considerable upheaval because of the various economic development projects undertaken surrounding it.

In 1959, the Tsawwassen longhouse was bulldozed to clear the way for a causeway linking a new ferry terminal with the mainland.[107] This terminal has thousands of cars and trucks passing through it daily, and the causeway to it cuts right through the heart of the First Nation community. Yet this was only one of the large-scale development projects that disturbed the Tsawwassen people's way of life and benefited large corporations rather than the nation itself.

As well as the ferry terminal, Port Metro Vancouver's largest shipping-container terminal is located at the end of a long causeway just in front of Tsawwassen homes. Its 24/7 coal and container traffic leaves their homes coated with diesel particulate. Given Canada's oppressive colonial history, many First Nation communities are now in situations similar to that experienced by the Tsawwassen, and the BC treaty process might seem to these nations like the only viable option. However, as mentioned, once the process begins and the money borrowed to proceed with it grows, there is "great pressure on the community" to settle on an agreement with the government in order to avoid debt.[108]

For Grand Chief Stewart Phillip, this whole treaty process is flawed, as it does not recognize Indigenous peoples' inherent right to the land.[109] Engagement in such a process means tacit approval of a system fuelled by Euro-Canadian priorities that form the continuing and overarching agenda of assimilation, of the absorption of Indigenous peoples into "the body politic," an agenda reinforced by capitalist demands for expansion. Tsawwassen peoples should never have had to go through this claims process in the first place, as they are the original stewards of the lands in question, and have been since time immemorial. In 1879, Nez Perce Chief Joseph (Heinmot Tooyalakekt) explained this truth:

> If we ever owned the land, we own it still, for we never sold it. In the treaty councils, the commissioners have claimed that our country had been sold to the government. Suppose a white man should come to me and say, "Joseph, I like your horses, and I want to buy them." I say to him, "No my horses suit me, I will not sell them." Then he goes to my neighbor and says to him, "Joseph has some good horses. I want to buy them, but he refuses to sell." My neighbor answers, "Pay me the money and I will sell you Joseph's horses." The white man returns to me, and says, "Joseph, I have bought your horses, and you must let me have them." If we sold our lands to the government, this is the way they were bought.[110]

Grand Chief Stewart Phillip agrees that the "Tsawwassen settled for far less than they were entitled."[111] The land settlement of 724 hectares is very small compared to the 279,600 hectares of traditional territory they originally outlined.[112] These ancestral lands encompassed the whole Delta municipality and vast regions within the cities of Richmond and Surrey.[113] The Tsawwassen Final Agreement "released" much of this land to the Crown, which now has absolute jurisdiction over this territory. Alan Hanna calculates that, through the BC treaty process, the Province of British Columbia "bought" Tsawwassen's traditional lands for what amounted to only $69.80 per acre.[114] In 1742, Canassatego, chief of the Onondagas said, "We know our Lands have now become more valuable. The White People think we do not know their value; but we are sensible that the Land is everlasting, and the few Goods we receive for it are soon worn out and gone."[115]

Ultimately, as the UBCIC explains, having the BC treaty process in place demonstrates the Euro-Canadian refusal to deal with the land question in an honourable way.[116] These comprehensive claims agreements do not offer a model whereby reconciliation will be reached because Indigenous nations will continue to challenge the government's imposition of a "claims" process, given that there was never a transfer of sovereignty from Indigenous peoples to the Crown. Let us close with the UBCIC's guidance about how true reconciliation might come to pass:

> The goal to . . . achieve respectful resolution of the Land Question is a profoundly human one. It is the challenge of diverse peoples and cultures identifying ways to live together in harmony. It is the challenge of working to overcome the injustices of the past, by identifying new patterns of social, economic and political life for the future. This can be achieved only once Aboriginal Title is recognized, and the honour of the Crown is realized and reflected in Canada's policy and negotiation mandates. If governments approach us from a vision of recognition and ready to reconcile, perhaps justice could at long last be achieved.[117]

Discussion Questions

1) Compare and contrast "modern" land claims negotiations and processes with early treaty processes and negotiations, such as those used to arrive at the Treaty of Niagara in 1764. Do the colonizers have the same goals?
2) What are the pros and cons of the BC treaty process?

Activities

1) Watch the third episode of the CBC's 2012 documentary series *The 8th Fire*, "Whose Land Is It Anyway?" (available online at cbc.ca/8thfire). Reflect on and discuss the business relationships established between Indigenous and non-Indigenous peoples.

2) Visit a local First Nation that has established land agreements, economic development projects, entrepreneurial initiatives, or businesses, or invite an Indigenous person who was involved in the creation of such agreements or projects to discuss these with you. What positives and negatives can you discover about planning and negotiating these enterprises?

Recommended Readings

Ariss, Rachel, and John Cutfeet. *Keeping the Land: Kitchenuhmaykoosib Inninuwug, Reconciliation and Canadian Law*. Halifax: Fernwood Publishing, 2012.

Richardson, Boyce. *Strangers Devour the Land*. Revised edition. White River Junction, VT: Chelsea Green Publishing, 2008.

12
Euro-Canadian "Justice" Systems and Traditional Indigenous Justice

CHAPTER 3 EXAMINED VARIOUS TRADITIONAL Indigenous methods to address crime. These included approaches to crime arrived at through consensus and based on Indigenous peoples' respective world views, ones that tended to emphasize balance, harmony, and respect.

This chapter outlines the stark contrast between traditional Indigenous justice and the present Canadian criminal justice system. The Canadian system, which relies on incapacitation and other forms of deterrence, is largely driven by capitalism, greed, wealth addiction, and money. It relies heavily on the invocation of police, courts, and corrections systems; and, given the high rates of Indigenous people's victimization and incarceration, it has clearly not been successful.

Western Justice and Indigenous Justice

Although traditional Indigenous justice systems differed depending on the nation or community that developed them, they had some key aspects in common (see Chapter 3). These differ substantially when compared to the current Euro-Canadian, Westernized system of crime control. Consider the Tsilhqot'in people's sanction for damaging waterways, which was often death because damaging waterways threatened the entire community.[1] Compare this approach to the environment to the one taken by the current Euro-Canadian justice system, which might fine a person a few hundred dollars for throwing garbage into a lake. Indeed, many big corporations quite legally pollute our waterways and engage in mining operations that can contaminate groundwater and destroy the fish population of a vast region. Seepage from these operations can pollute waterways and destroy the natural habitat of animals and plants, affecting people's food sources and especially the economy of local Indigenous communities, which, in some cases, rely on these waterways for their livelihood.

Euro-Canadian governance structures and institutions are based on a different ideology than that informing Indigenous world views. An idea prevalent in many Indigenous world views is that human beings need to take care of the earth and respect its resources because all things human and non-human rely on the earth. As Chief Edward Moody (Nuxalk Nation) states, "We must protect the forests for our children, grandchildren, and children yet to be born. We must protect the forests for those who can't speak for themselves such as the birds, animals, fish and trees."[2]

On the other hand, Euro-Canadian structures and systems are fuelled by an economic and capitalist ideology in which the main goal is economic development. The people's role is to extract and consume resources and to operate, live, and sustain themselves for the purpose of monetary benefit. This ideology is clearly witnessed in the land negotiations outlined in the preceding chapter. It is also regularly expressed by governments. Here is an example from a speech by then-Prime Minister Stephen Harper given in Cartagena, Colombia, in 2012:

> Ladies and gentlemen, resource development has vast power to change the way a nation lives. . . . Today I want to talk to you briefly about how to maximize the value of this great industry for a country and its people . . . [t]o give a sense of what our resource industries mean to the Canadian economy. . . . We are already the world's number-one potash producer, second for uranium, and a major global producer of most mineral and energy products. . . . [W]e believe in Canada that we have found the way to transform resource assets into a sustainable foundation for equitable national development.[3]

The harmony, balance, and circular thinking integral to Indigenous teachings and knowledge is not internalized, grasped, or reflected within Canadian Westernized institutions, governance structures, or discourses. Rather, the country is predicated on capitalist ideals such as consumerism, competitive individualism, and disrespect for nature. This ideological underpinning is apparent in today's continuing overconsumption of energy, food, and many other of the world's limited resources.

This lack of harmonious living, devoid of balance among the components of nature, has led to a particular way of life, one that differs from the traditional ways of Indigenous peoples. Because so much emphasis is placed on self-interest in Euro-Canadian society, the current social and economic system and present conditions dictate a way of life that is highly individualized, divided, and centred on greed.[4] This system permits a small number of "elite" people to hold power, and they exploit the earth's resources for their benefit and profit while disregarding other people, beings, and nature in general. The system also creates institutions to maintain this hierarchal order by disciplining and incapacitating those who do not follow the rules. One of these institutions is the Euro-Canadian criminal justice system.

Some criminologists, such as Jeffrey Reiman, argue that the criminal justice system functions to allow wealthy, mainly white, people to enjoy enduring benefits while driving the poor—in large part racial minorities (including Indigenous peoples)—into deeper poverty and, in many cases, prison.[6] Such a system continually upholds the unequal, hierarchal status quo. Rather than actually trying to eliminate crime, the system is set up to fail because its main purpose is to deflect attention away from societal injustice, a root cause of crime, and toward the notion of the poor as a criminal class. Thus, the criminal justice system "serves the interests of the rich and powerful . . . the very ones who could change criminal justice policy if they were really unhappy with it."[7]

Reiman contends that the criminal justice system ignores or minimizes the damaging acts of the elite, so crime comes to be conceived of as "the work of the poor."[8] This view has powerful ideological implications. First, it communicates that any danger to society comes from the poor. Second, it implies that people are in poverty because of their own failings and not because of greater social wrongs or historical legacies. And third, it characterizes poorer people, especially those who break the rules, as somehow morally inadequate, unrestrained, or lazy.[9] This simplistic thinking compartmentalizes an entire group of people and encourages a conservative perspective that accepts a society with large disparities of wealth, power, and opportunity as just—it discourages demands for equality.[10] It also sustains the cycle of inequality and keeps the hierarchal order in place. So although the criminal justice system gives the appearance of equality, it actually does the opposite by allowing a small elite to maintain power over everyone else, and over all of Mother Earth's creations.

Three institutions—the police, courts, and corrections—are major components of this unequal system. If we consider these institutions as part of Canada's capitalist, class-based economy, then prisoners are the raw products required to keep the crime control industry operating and growing, and the criminal justice system itself functions in ways similar to big business: "This industry provides profit and work while at the same time producing control of those who otherwise might have disturbed the social process."[11] These institutions, then, continue to fuel the cycle of injustice.

Inequality, reinforced and intensified by capitalism, keeps those "othered" from the system near the lower end of the hierarchy and in danger of being criminalized. Indeed, Indigenous peoples have been both relegated to the bottom echelons of Canadian society and criminalized (see Chapter 8); at some points in our national history, governments even attempted to eliminate Indigenous peoples completely. The criminal justice system that maintains these large disparities in wealth and opportunity and functions to profit from individuals' and institutions' holding power puts Indigenous peoples into positions of constant struggle. As a result, they fight against and sometimes become victims of an unbalanced governance and criminal justice system that seems to be working against Indigenous interests.

Undeniably, we are living in a world that not only encourages inequality between people but also sustains inequality between all things, the land, peoples, animals, plants, rocks, and other parts of our world. A society that disrespects nature and people to such an extent commodifies every creation, turning all into power and material wealth. As Huron-Wendat scholar and historian Georges Sioui contends, these disrespectful interactions can result only in sexism, racism, violence, and the "destruction of life."[12] Steven Taylor, expert in transpersonal psychology, explains that Western society promotes such a strong association between wealth and happiness that people fail to realize the falsehood of this association and seek immediate gratification to fulfil the inner discontent that results from living in a society so disconnected and out of balance.[13] The drive for gratification can be so powerful that people go to any extent to become rich, even if it means harming the planet, human beings, or their own families.

Starlight Tours: Police Brutality against Indigenous Peoples

With Indigenous peoples "othered" to the lower rungs of society's ladder, agents of the criminal justice system operate in ways that keep this desired hierarchal order in place. Many times, Indigenous peoples are staged as the enemy or the troublemaker, which makes it much easier for authorities to treat Indigenous peoples differently and poorly. This poor treatment is apparent in a practice that has now been given its own name because of its severity and frequency: the "starlight tours," also known as the freezing deaths. These deaths are the result of police brutality, of the police picking up Indigenous peoples, who typically appear drunk or under the influence of drugs, and then driving them to the outskirts of town, leaving them to fend for themselves in freezing temperatures. Many of these Indigenous peoples have died from hypothermia or untreated beatings. Although this practice has been reported in various places throughout Canada, including Toronto, Halifax, Vancouver, and Winnipeg, starlight tours became infamous in Saskatoon, where the freezing deaths of Indigenous people drew attention to this cruelty in the 1990s and 2000s.

In November 1990, the frozen body of Cree teen Neil Stonechild was found beyond the northern outskirts of Saskatoon. Stonechild was only 17 years old. He was found wearing only one shoe, a light jacket, and jeans; there were parallel gashes across his face.[14] Stonechild was last seen alive on the night of November 24, 1990; he was in police custody in the back of a cruiser. It was suggested that Stonechild had been picked up because a complaint had been made against him of disorderly conduct at an apartment complex.[15] Stonechild's companion that night was Jason Roy. The two had become separated at some point, but, later that same evening, Roy was stopped by police officers and asked to identify Stonechild, whom they had in the back of their car. Fearful of being arrested himself, Roy told the police that he did not know Stonechild. During this interaction, Stonechild yelled to Roy, "Help me. These guys are going to kill me." Roy also reported seeing fresh blood across Stonechild's face.[16] Six days later, on the morning of November 29, 1990, two construction workers found the frozen body of Stonechild in a remote field. An autopsy concluded that he had died of hypothermia. On the date Stonechild was last seen alive, night-time temperatures dropped to –28.1 degrees Celsius.[17] Marks and lashes on his body also suggested that he might have been assaulted.[18] However, the original Saskatoon investigation into Stonechild's case concluded that he died while trying to walk to an adult jail to turn himself in—and that the police had no contact with Stonechild on the evening he went missing.[19]

In February 2003—partly because of publicity surrounding similar cases—an inquiry was called to investigate the death of Stonechild. This inquiry heard from 43 witnesses, including civilian witnesses, forensic and medical experts, memory experts, and a photogrammetric evidence expert, among others. It concluded on May 19, 2003.[20] Memory experts were "called to provide opinion evidence with regard to memory formation and retention."[21] Dr. John Richardson, one of these experts, was asked to give his opinion on blood alcohol concentration and its effects on the brain and memory in individuals of a similar size to Jason Roy and Neil Stonechild. Dr. John Charles Yuille, another expert in human memory and how it is developed, provided his opinion on eyewitness memory, memory formation, and interview techniques and their impact on memory, among other related issues. The photogrammetric evidence expert was Chief Medical Examiner for Alberta Gary Robertson, a forensic pathologist. He extrapolated measurements from the post-mortem photographs taken of Neil Stonechild and compared these to the measurements of the handcuffs used by Saskatoon Police Service.[22]

Evidence proved that Stonechild was in police custody the night he was last seen alive; Canadian Police Information Centre records confirmed this testimony from Roy.[23] In particular, the two Saskatoon police officers, Larry Hartwig and Brad Senger, who denied having Stonechild in custody, were identified as responding to a call mentioning the teen. Eventually, it was found that, indeed, he was last seen alive in their custody. Compelling evidence at the inquiry suggested, as well, that Stonechild had been struck in the face with the set of handcuffs that were on his wrists before his death.

The report also found that the officer in charge of the initial investigation, Sergeant Keith Jarvis, had dismissed important information about the original case, such as the fact that Roy reported seeing Stonechild in the back of the police cruiser the night he disappeared. Following the final report of this inquiry in November 2004, Saskatoon Police Chief Russell Sabo announced the dismissal of both Hartwig and Senger from the force.[24] However, neither of these police officers faced criminal charges, and, together, they appealed the findings of the coroner's inquest. In 2008, the Saskatchewan Court of Appeal upheld the decision of the inquest, and the officers remained dismissed from the force.

Ten years after the death of Stonechild, in January 2000, Darrel Night experienced a chillingly similar ordeal, but survived to tell his story.[25] On the evening of January 27, 2000, Night was at a party. He decided to leave the party after a fight broke out. In the early morning hours, he was walking back to his sister's house (where he was staying) while drunk.[26] A police car approached him. In it were two officers, Dan Hatchen and Ken Munson, who had been called to the party that Darrel Night had just left.[27] The last officers to arrive at the party's location, Hatchen and Munson were not needed there. As the officers approached him, Night shouted at them, gave them the middle finger, and lunged at their vehicle.[28] As a result, the officers called him a "drunken fucking Indian" and arrested him for causing a disturbance. He was handcuffed and put in the back of their car, and the police then drove him out of town rather than to the city drunk tank. They removed his handcuffs, abandoned him two kilometres away from the Queen Elizabeth II power plant, and shouted at him—"Get the fuck out of here, you fucking Indian."[29] He was wearing a denim jacket and the temperature with wind chill that night was –22 degrees Celsius.[30] Night walked to the power plant and was able to get the attention of the plant supervisor.[31]

Night did not report the abuse initially, as he felt the authorities would not listen to him.[32] Six days after the incident, however, he and his uncle, while pulled over for a seatbelt violation, heard on their radio that two frozen bodies had been found in locations close to where police had dropped Night off. They decided to speak to the sympathetic police officer who had pulled them over.[33]

The day after Darrel Night's starlight tour, a 25-year-old Cree man, Rodney Naistus, was found frozen near the same power plant.[34] Earlier in the evening, he had been out celebrating his recent reunion with his brother and cousin; Naistus had just been released from an urban work camp (a sanction he received for breaking and entering).[35] Only days later, another Cree man, Lawrence Kim Wegner, a 30-year-old who was a social work student at the

Federated College (now the First Nations University of Canada), was left for dead and died of hypothermia at the same power plant.[36] Both Naistus and Wegner were found close to the Queen Elizabeth II power plant, and both could not have survived the chilling temperatures of the northern Saskatoon nights in the clothes they were wearing.

Investigations ensued, and inquests into the deaths of Naistus and Wegner were held in 2001 and 2002, yet no one was ever charged with these deaths. On September 20, 2001, the police officers who dumped Night were fired by the Saskatoon Police Service because they faced charges of unlawful confinement. However, these officers were cleared of any assault charges and did not get charged with attempted murder, as would have been appropriate. Before their sentencing, these two officers actually requested an Indigenous sentencing circle (a practice that will be explained later in this chapter). Because, for such a circle to take place, all people involved have to accept responsibility for their actions and show that they have "deep roots" to the community in which the circle will be held, their request was denied.[37] Rather than admitting their culpability, the officers had pleaded not guilty and claimed they were not legally responsible for what happened. The Indigenous community actually felt its people were being mocked by the request for a sentencing circle. Ultimately, these two officers were sentenced to only 8 months in prison, when the maximum sentence for an unlawful confinement conviction was 10 years.[38] No officers in the other cases ever faced criminal charges.

Policing: Indigenization, Low Credibility, and Over- and Under-Policing

One of the major methods of controlling crime in Canada is policing. Indigenous peoples have been under the Euro-Canadian system of policing for decades, from when it was first used to control crime in Canada. Typically, policing of Indigenous peoples in Canada has been performed by non-Indigenous peoples, and this situation continues, particularly because Indigenous peoples are moving to urban areas in increasing numbers.

In response to this circumstance, which many of the Indigenous peoples being policed and the non-Indigenous officers doing the policing saw as unfavourable, the Department of Indian Affairs and Northern Development (DIAND), now Indigenous and Northern Affairs Canada, introduced the "Band Constable Program" in 1969.[39] Under this program, band councils hired band constables from the Indigenous community being policed to enforce band by-laws. In 1971, this program was expanded to include the hiring of "special constables" from Indigenous communities to supplement the senior police forces at the local level. However, these special constables had far less authority than police officers; they were not permitted to carry firearms and had very little money because they received a minimal salary. What's more, they were expected to provide their own vehicles and, in some cases, were not even provided with uniforms.

In 1973, Indian and Northern Affairs (yet another name for Indigenous and Northern Affairs Canada) issued its *Report of Task Force: Policing on Reserves*, which recommended three options for Indigenous policing: band council policing, municipal policing, and provincial policing. The third recommendation, provincial policing, became known as "Option 3b" and received the greatest attention from policy makers and police agencies. The report suggests two choices under this option:

> A separate Indian Provincial Force operating on its own under the authority of the provincial attorney-general and with some form of Police Commission. This force will not form part of the provincial police for the purpose of direction or control of administration. . . . [Or] Indian policing under the direction and control of the provincial police acting on its own responsibility to enforce general laws on Indian reserves, but mainly through the use of Indian special constables, who will comprise a special Indian police service as an integral part of the provincial police force.[40]

The RCMP's Native Special Constable Program was the major initiative under which Option 3b was implemented. Under this program, Indigenous peoples were recruited to police other Indigenous peoples in their own communities. The Indigenous officers received 16 weeks of training at the RCMP training headquarters in Regina before being posted in their home communities; non-Indigenous recruits received 25 weeks of training.[41] Furthermore, the Indigenous recruiting system had less rigorous entrance standards, and, upon completion of training, the Indigenous officers had peace officer status only and served as adjuncts to the RCMP. This program was criticized for a number of reasons: it lacked Indigenous peoples' input into the program and its operations, it failed to define the role of the participants adequately, and it provided lower salaries and less training to Indigenous special constables than to regular members of the RCMP.[42] Indigenous peoples were also reluctant to join the program, given community hostility to this police force and social isolation.[43]

In 1990, the Native Special Constable Program was terminated and replaced with the Aboriginal Constable Development Program, which was designed to increase the number of Indigenous peoples eligible to become regular RCMP members.[44] Many police initiatives have gone in this direction recently: attempting to get more Indigenous peoples to join the police service as both officers and civilian members. These programs to create "special" or Indigenous constables have been explained as attempts to "indigenize" or "indianize" the white policing system.[45] In other words, through these programs, Indigenous peoples are slotted into various roles in the criminal justice system, which makes room for them in the system without actually changing it. Doing this assumes that the system is fundamentally "good" and that only small, inconsequential reforms are needed in order to make it "good" for everyone.

Indigenization is still evident as the fundamental purpose of many current programs and policies, for example, the First Nations Policing Policy and the RCMP's many Aboriginal-focused programs and initiatives. From the 1980s to now, numerous cross-cultural and culturally sensitive policing programs based on this same fundamental concept have been launched across Canada. These programs generally seek to hire more Indigenous police officers and to provide cultural training for non-Indigenous officers; though this plan is not necessarily bad, relying so heavily on one concept restricts making larger changes that might contribute to a significant reduction in the high rates of over-representation of Indigenous peoples as both victims and those incarcerated within the system. In an investigation into the administration of justice within Indigenous communities, criminology professor Mylène Jaccoud explains that Canada attempts through these policies and programs to transfer Canadian strategies on matters such as judicial and police powers to Indigenous institutions, mistakenly assuming that the existing Indigenous systems will easily and readily incorporate these Canadian practices. According to Jaccoud, these strategies impose an unjust obligation on Indigenous peoples to adapt to approaches to justice that may not necessarily fit their sociocultural models and existing infrastructure.[46]

According to anthropology professor Rémi Savard, traditional Indigenous justice systems, organizational structures, and institutions have been systematically dismantled since the mid-nineteenth century.[47] Given this predicament, he argues that the Canadian criminal justice system lacks credibility in the eyes of many Indigenous peoples. A 1999 study by sociology professor Robynne Neugebauer reported similar findings in regards to criminal justice officials (in this study, the police) lacking credibility with Indigenous peoples.[48] She worked with an Indigenous community in metropolitan Toronto, interviewing and conducting focus groups with 35 community members and representatives of community-based organizations, as well as engaging in participant observation of community members at community functions and meetings. Participants in this study were found to lack confidence in the police. Community members conveyed that police mistreated them and were persistently disrespectful and offensive, maltreating Indigenous peoples through cruel spoken interactions, intimidating and aggressive acts, and a largely hostile demeanour. Furthermore, a 1994 study by researcher Carol La Prairie, who interviewed 621 inner-city Indigenous peoples in four Canadian cities, found that one-third of the respondents experienced rude or verbally abusive action by police.[49]

Related to this legitimate distrust of criminal justice officials is the debate over whether Indigenous peoples are "over-policed" or "under-policed." The "over-policing" side of the debate maintains that Indigenous peoples are singled out by police officers—who impose on Indigenous peoples "police control . . . at a level unlikely to occur in the dominant society."[50] The argument is that Indigenous peoples are stereotyped by police forces, charged with offences more than non-Indigenous peoples, and generally harassed. The report of the Aboriginal Justice Inquiry of Manitoba acknowledges the existence of over-policing: "We believe that many Aboriginal people are arrested and held in custody when a white person in the same circumstances either might not be arrested at all, or might not be held."[51]

The other side of the debate is the "under-policing" side. This side of the argument contends that the police tend to ignore Indigenous communities in the sense that officers are typically not present on a day-to-day basis to prevent crime or provide other police services to Indigenous peoples. The view is that, often, police only come to Indigenous communities to make an arrest.[52]

Ultimately, this over- and under-policing debate has been picked up numerous times by various reports and inquiries. The Aboriginal Justice Inquiry of Manitoba called them "simultaneous realities," for example. A research study of Native American experiences of policing, which conducted interviews with 278 Native American peoples across 7 US states, found that both are likely at play.[53] Respondents reported experiences ranging from the wilful blindness of police to extreme forms of police brutality.

The Court System: Tinkering with Laws, *Gladue* Reports, and Courts

All Canadian laws have been created by non-Indigenous peoples. Historical laws have been created mostly without any input from Indigenous peoples. There are a couple of Indigenous judges, yet no Indigenous person has been appointed to the Supreme Court. In fundamental ways, then, Indigenous peoples are outside of positions of power in the criminal justice system, appearing more frequently in prisons than as representatives of the court. One of the prime ways the government has tried to reduce Indigenous overincarceration has been through "tinkering" with this Canadian criminal justice system, for example, changing laws in an effort to divert Indigenous peoples from the prosecutorial process or modifying the system slightly to make it "fit" Indigenous peoples.

In 1996, the federal government decided to use law reform to address the high incidence of Indigenous peoples' incarceration. Its first action was to add a qualification to restrict the use of incarceration as a sanction. The courts declared that the stated intent of this measure was to decrease the incarceration of Aboriginal offenders. Section 718.2(e) of the Criminal Code outlines this qualification: "All available sanctions other than imprisonment that are reasonable in the circumstances, should be considered for all offenders, with particular attention to the circumstances of Aboriginal Offenders." This provision then became the focus of imperative ruling judgements from the Supreme Court of Canada. In 1999, in *R. v. Gladue*, the court presented an interpretation of this section, concluding that "the jail term for an Aboriginal offender may in some circumstances be less than the term imposed on a non-Aboriginal offender for the same offence." It went on to state, "Aboriginal offenders must always be sentenced in a manner which gives greatest weight to the principles of restorative justice, and less weight to goals such as deterrence, denunciation and separation."[54]

This case involved a young Indigenous woman named Jamie Gladue (who had a Cree mother and a Métis father). During a drunken argument, she had stabbed and killed her boyfriend while fighting over whether he had cheated with her sister. In the Supreme Court of British Columbia, she pled guilty to manslaughter. She was sentenced to three years in prison. Her appeal was heard in the Supreme Court of Canada, and, although her sentence was not actually changed, the ruling did provide a detailed statement on the operation of section 718.2(e) and on the duty of sentencing judges to find alternatives to incarceration for Indigenous defendants. The court recognized that systemic factors contribute to the overrepresentation of Indigenous peoples in the criminal justice system, explicitly named restorative justice as a solution, and called for creative criminal justice responses fitted to the circumstances of Indigenous peoples.

In March 2012, the Supreme Court of Canada cited *Gladue* in *R. v. Ipeelee*. This Supreme Court case released joint reasons for judgement in the criminal sentencing appeals of two Indigenous persons: Manasie Ipeelee, an Inuk man, and Frank Ralph Ladue, a member of the Kaska Nation from Ross River, Yukon.[55] Both men were long-term offenders and were sentenced for failing to comply with their long-term supervision orders (LTSOs).

Mr. Ipeelee and Mr. Ladue both struggled with substance abuse and had histories of committing crimes while intoxicated. Both men breached the no substance use provision of their LTSOs. Both men had been sentenced to three years imprisonment for this breach. However, Mr. Ladue, after his provincial court of appeal case, had his sentence reduced to one year, yet Mr. Ipeelee's sentence was not reduced. The Supreme Court of Canada granted Mr. Ipeelee's appeal and reduced his sentence to one year. Mr. Ladue's appeal was dismissed.

R. v. Ipeelee called on judges to use a different method of analysis when deciding on a fitting sentence for Indigenous offenders, one giving specific attention to the unique circumstances of those offenders. This time, the wording that describes the statutory duties of judges sentencing Aboriginal peoples is much more direct than in *Gladue*. Whereas *R v. Gladue* uses the term "may" in regards to considering alternatives to sentencing for Aboriginal peoples, *R v. Ipeelee* uses "must" and expresses this requirement strongly.[56] For example, not only does *R v. Ipeelee* direct judges "to consider the factors outlined in *R. v. Gladue*" when sentencing an Aboriginal offender, but it also details some of those factors: "When sentencing an Aboriginal offender, courts must take judicial notice of such matters as the history of colonialism, displacement, and residential schools and how that history continues to translate into lower educational attainment, lower incomes, higher unemployment, higher rates of substance abuse and suicide, and of course higher levels of incarceration for Aboriginal peoples."

This case also implied that judges were not applying *Gladue* principles consistently, and the Supreme Court justices stressed the importance of *Gladue* reports. These reports are done for Indigenous offenders and contain case-specific information. They are tailored to the specific circumstances of Indigenous offenders, providing detailed information about an individual's life history and unique circumstances, which are presented within the context of the systemic and historical factors faced by all Indigenous peoples. These *Gladue* reports can be done for any Indigenous offender in any court. They can be started after a guilty plea or upon a finding of guilt. They are used in sentencing to help judges take into consideration Indigenous peoples' circumstances. Depending on the services offered in the area, Indigenous court workers or probation officers might facilitate the writing of such a report. In places where more Indigenous court workers are available, they will usually write these reports. For example, the Aboriginal Legal Services of Toronto (ALST) has several specifically trained Indigenous court workers writing these reports for courts from Hamilton to Peterborough and north to Penetanguishene. The ALST also has *Gladue* Aboriginal Persons Courts.[57] These do not perform differently than other courts; however, they do offer all services in one place, including bail hearings, bail variations, remands, trials, and sentencing. What differentiates this type of court is that those working in it have specific knowledge of and expertise in the variety of services and programs available to Indigenous peoples.

The first Indigenous-specific court in Canada was the Tsuut'ina First Nation Court in Alberta, which opened in 2000. Toronto's *Gladue* court, which opened in 2001, was the first urban Aboriginal court in Canada. There are now five *Gladue* courts in operation in Toronto. Other Aboriginal courts are being opened, for example, the First Nations Court in New Westminster (2006) and the Cknúcwentn—First Nations Court in Kamloops (2013), both in British Columbia.[58] In Ontario, *Gladue* courts opened in London in 2012 and in Brantford in 2014; these courts also exist in other Ontario communities.

According to Kent Roach and Jonathan Rudin, judges frequently rely on *Gladue* as a justification for ordering a conditional sentence.[59] Conditional sentences can lead to net-widening if they begin to be ordered in cases in which less intrusive sanctions would typically have been ordered. The term "net-widening" describes a particular phenomenon that occurs when a program that is set up *to divert* people away from the criminal justice system—usually by preventing their incarceration—instead causes more people to enter the system, people who might not have entered it otherwise.

As Roach and Rudin state, in the majority of cases, "conditional sentences are being handed down where probations orders, fines, and suspended sentences would normally have been ordered." As compared to these sanctions, conditional sentences can be significantly more "coercive and intense."[60] Some people who might not have gone to prison consequently find themselves there. Research shows that Indigenous offenders who receive conditional sentences are disproportionately prosecuted for breaching conditions. As evidenced in research on Indigenous probation and parole, reasons for breaches include overt and systematic discrimination, as well as over-policing and the more intense surveillance of Indigenous as opposed to non-Indigenous peoples. When Indigenous people are found guilty of breaching the conditions of these sentences, they could be sent to jail. Furthermore, as the Supreme Court states in *R v. Proulx*,[61] conditional sentences are longer than actual prison sentences. So if a young Indigenous person, for example, is declared to have breached the conditions of her or his sentence, even near the beginning of that sentence, she or he could end up being imprisoned for even longer than if they had been sent straight to jail initially.[62]

Gladue-inspired conditional sentences might also be especially invasive if long "healing conditions" are imposed.[63] These might include attending intensive counselling, participating in substance abuse programming, or meeting reparation requirements. Trial judges might also be tempted to order a conditional sentence instead of probation, so they could require orders for treatment or medication or impose lengthier community service obligations. The longer and more arduous conditions become, the more likely that a breach will occur.

In sum, Roach and Rudin suggest that these problems related to conditional sentencing—combined with a young and growing Indigenous population, a shortage of community programs providing prison alternatives, and a hesitancy to stop ordering prison in serious cases—make it unlikely that *Gladue*-inspired sentencing innovations will have any major effect on lowering the high rates of Indigenous incarceration.[64]

The Correctional System: Indigenization and Traditional Healing in Prisons

Like the police services, Correctional Services Canada (CSC) implements programs and initiatives that attempt to incorporate traditional Indigenous methods or cultures in their design. CSC has developed a national healing program for Indigenous offenders in all federal prisons and facilities. The Corrections and Conditional Release Act contains sections 81 and 84, which have specific Indigenous provisions. Section 81 is intended to give capacity to CSC to enter into agreements with Indigenous communities for the care and custody of Indigenous offenders. This section also permits Indigenous communities to play a role in CSC Aboriginal program delivery. Section 84 permits Indigenous communities to propose parole conditions to the Parole Board of Canada for offenders wanting to be released to their communities.

Two types of healing lodges have been put in place under section 81, CSC-run healing lodges and section 81 healing lodges operated by Indigenous communities in agreement with CSC. The purpose of healing lodges is to assist in the successful reintegration of Indigenous offenders by using traditional healing approaches and holistic and culturally appropriate programming. As of 2013, Canada had four Indigenous-run healing lodges and four CSC-run healing lodges; all but Québec's Waseskun Healing Centre near Montreal were in the West.[65]

A report released by the Office of the Correctional Investigator in October of 2012 and tabled in parliament in March 2013 pointed out many of the problems with respect to implementing sections 81 and 84.[66] A key finding of the report was that, from 1992 to March of 2012, only 68 beds were arranged in 4 healing lodges in Indigenous communities under section 81. No section-81 agreements were in place in Ontario, British Columbia, or Atlantic Canada, or the North, and it was not until 2011 that spaces became available for women. The report also identified major funding discrepancies between section 81 healing lodges operated by Indigenous communities and those operated by CSC. For example, in 2009–10, the annual cost per offender at CSC-run healing lodges was about $113,450 whereas it was $70,845 for section-81 Indigenous-run lodges. Salaries for those employed at CSC-run facilities were also found to be about 50 per cent higher for similar work.

In regards to section 84, the report identified that, although this section was intended to enhance Indigenous community involvement, its implementation had become dominated by lengthy and onerous bureaucratic processes. Furthermore, of CSC's estimated 19,000 employees in 2012, only 12 were Aboriginal Community Development Officers mandated to help these processes run smoothly and to bridge the interests of incarcerated Indigenous people and the communities into which these people are released.

An additional key finding of the report was that CSC staff members, particularly the frontline staff at correctional facilities, had limited awareness and understanding of Indigenous peoples, cultures, and approaches to healing. Also, *Gladue* principles were not well understood nor were they applied in CSC correctional decision making. Another problem was that contractual and funding limitations impeded initiatives that put elders inside CSC institutions to provide support, guidance, and ceremonies. The report also found inadequate responses to urban Indigenous peoples; it was typically assumed that these incarcerated Indigenous individuals would be returning to a reserve after release, but many had no such plans. The number of interventions offered inside prison walls far outnumbered the number of community reintegration alternatives. Also, the validity of the community reintegration programs that were provided was determined by CSC and not by the Indigenous communities themselves, which many Indigenous peoples and communities found patronizing.[67]

Beyond all of the limitations documented by this 2012 report, entitled *Spirit Matters: Aboriginal People and the Corrections and Conditional Release Act*, the attempt to shift to more traditional healing and to the integration of Indigenous culture can be seen as positive. At the same time, incorporating traditional approaches or including Indigenous peoples, communities, and cultures in the correctional system is still trying to deliver "justice" within Euro-Canadian systems of governance and through Euro-Canadian institutions. It is yet another form of indigenizing the white system. The report itself, which reviewed and drew on many major Canadian conferences, task forces, studies, and commissions, notes that these plans to indigenize CSC have failed: "The findings from various task forces and commissions all point to the *failure to adapt* correctional systems to meet the needs of the growing Aboriginal offender population."[68]

Unfortunately, this report, like many others in Canada before it, does not question Euro-Canadian systems and structures. Instead, reports ask what more within the current system of corrections needs to be adapted or changed. For example, this report recommended more training of CSC staff; the creation of a new position, a deputy commissioner to enhance coordination between CSC, federal partners, and Indigenous communities; more funding for healing lodges and bed spaces; a resolution to fix service issues faced by elders working within prisons; and a reduction in the red tape limiting implementation of section 84. All of these recommendations involve changes within the current system rather than changes to the system itself.

I do not mean to suggest that culture should not be considered when implementing programming for Indigenous peoples, as many studies have revealed the importance of cultural relevance to the success of programs or other initiatives. For example, *The Aboriginal Offender Survey*, prepared for CSC in 1997, found that some Indigenous peoples who were incarcerated felt they would be most comfortable with an elder, spiritual leader, friend, or family member as their counsellor.[69] It also revealed that 69 per cent of the incarcerated Indigenous people surveyed wanted more institutional programs tailored specifically to their cultures and traditions. A study published in 2001 for CSC arrived at similar conclusions, finding that 72 per cent of the ex-incarcerated respondents surveyed felt that involvement with elders had a positive effect on turning their lives around.[70] As well, a research report prepared for the Department of Justice Canada found keen interest in Indigenous cultural and spiritual programming among Indigenous youth in the justice system.[71]

Some Indigenous prisoners are introduced for the first time to Indigenous culture, traditions, or spirituality while in prison. Various Indigenous practices are offered in correctional facilities and institutions. Many have at least one or two resident elders. Some institutions also have sweat lodges, which are part of a traditional ceremonial practice for some Indigenous peoples, a practice that involves rebalancing one's spirit, cleansing, and reconnecting to Mother Earth. For some, the sweat lodge ceremonies involve a type of rebirth. The sweat lodge is a circular dome-like structure into which hot rocks, typically referred to as "grandfathers," are brought in each round. As the number of grandfathers increases with each round, so does the heat. Inside the sweat lodge, the person facilitating the "sweat" will customarily use various medicines as part of the ceremony and will run it according to specific Indigenous teachings and customs, which can be different depending on the person, First Nation, and traditions being following.

A study conducted by James Waldram (identified in Chapter 7), interviewed 249 Indigenous males incarcerated at federal and provincial facilities in Manitoba and Saskatchewan. This study found that those who engaged in a "sweat" found it helpful for various reasons, such as helping them to make amends through prayer, encouraging spiritual renewal, enhancing the ability to cope with prison life, and removing a "bad" or "evil" type of essence.[72] Not all of these incarcerated Indigenous men, however, accepted having elders in prison. Some questioned the "true" purpose of these elders, and some simply did not want to reconnect with or practice Indigenous spirituality. However, Waldram did find that, of the 249 men he interviewed, 55 per cent, while incarcerated, had sought out an elder for consultation. When respondents were asked if they would prefer an elder or a Christian minister or chaplain, 78 per cent opted for an elder, and 14 per cent selected a Christian minister or chaplain.[73]

Cultural Misunderstanding within the Canadian Criminal Justice System

Opposite from traditional Indigenous systems of justice, the Canadian criminal justice system is founded on the ideas of deterrence and incapacitation—on theories about how to control or avert crime that are applied in capitalist societies seeking to uphold inequality and division. The concept of deterrence includes the idea that introducing harsh laws and penalties will deter potential lawbreakers from committing crimes by instilling fear in people that they will face excessive sanctions if caught. Incapacitation is the confinement in jails and prisons of people convicted of crimes, so they will be isolated from the rest of society and unable to offend while locked up.

The fundamentals of this Westernized system of justice have been explained by some as being different in some aspects from traditional Indigenous systems. For example, Table 12.1 outlines the Canadian Criminal Justice Association's comparison of Western justice and traditional Indigenous justice, as both function within the Euro-Canadian court system.

Rupert Ross, who worked previously as a Crown attorney with various Indigenous peoples in remote northwestern Ontario, describes in his book how Indigenous peoples might find the Euro-Canadian adversarial system foreign and inappropriate.[74] Through the help of Indigenous teachers, Ross learned to interpret and understand behaviours of Indigenous victims, witnesses, and those accused of crimes that he came into contact with in the courtroom. He learned that, frequently, cross-cultural misunderstandings had resulted in misplaced blame.

This sort of error is best illustrated with the example he uses to explain how a traditional Indigenous approach to showing respect works against fairness in the courtroom. As a sign of respect, an Indigenous person might

Table 12.1 Western Justice and Traditional Aboriginal Justice

	Western Justice	Traditional Aboriginal Justice
Justice System	Adversarial	Non-confrontational
Guilt	European concept of guilty/not guilty	No concept of guilty/not guilty
Pleading guilty	The accused has the right against self-incrimination. Thus, it is not seen as dishonest to plead not guilty when one has actually committed the offence (interference come[s] into play here)	It is dishonest to plead not guilty if one has committed the crime (values of honesty and non-interference come into play here)
Testifying	As part of the process, witnesses testify in front of accused	Reluctance to testify (it is confrontational to testify against the accused while in his/her presence)
Truth	Expectation to tell the "whole truth"	It is impossible to know the "whole truth" in any situation
Witnesses	Only certain people are called to testify in relation to specific subjects	Everyone is free to give their say Witnesses do not want to appear adversarial and often make every attempt to give answers that please counsel, thus often changing their testimony
Eye contact	Maintaining eye contact conveys that one is being truthful	In some Aboriginal cultures, maintaining eye contact with a person of authority is a sign of disrespect
Verdict	Accused is expected to show, during proceedings and upon a verdict of guilty, remorse and a desire for rehabilitation	Accused must accept what comes to him/her without a show of emotion
Incarceration/ probation	Means of punishing/ rehabilitating offender	Completely absolves Aboriginal offender of responsibility of restitution to victim
Function of justice	Ensure conformity, punish deviant behaviour and protect society	Heal the offender Restore peace and harmony to the community Reconcile the offender with victim/family that has been wronged Punishment is not the objective

Source: Canadian Criminal Justice Association, *Aboriginal Peoples and the Criminal Justice System* (Ottawa: Canadian Criminal Justice Association, 2000), 21–22.

not look an individual "in the eye" but rather stare off to the side when speaking to another. When Indigenous peoples on the stand try to show respect by doing this, they are regarded as being disrespectful or as possibly lying because of the way this gesture is considered in a Western or European social context.

Ross describes some key customs, tactics, cultural imperatives, or ethics that the Indigenous peoples he encountered in his courtroom lived by; in these descriptions, he draws heavily on Mohawk physician Clare Brant's leading paper "Native Ethics and Rules of Behaviour." For example, Ross explains that the Indigenous peoples he encountered followed "the ethic of non-interference." People living by this ethic consider interference in any form to be unacceptable. It would be rude to interfere with, comment on, or give advice about other people's behaviour unless called upon to do so. It would be considered very rude to criticize another's behaviour, talk about someone in a negative way, embarrass an individual, or do anything that might seem as if one were attempting to "show up" another person. Considering this ethic in the context of criminal justice processes, we can see that, to a person with this view, giving evidence would be seen as very confrontational. Someone following the ethic of non-interference might not be comfortable testifying against others in a public courtroom, or that person might even think testifying was a greater wrong than the crime that had been committed.[75]

Lying or minimizing one's behaviour is also considered very inappropriate and unethical for some Indigenous peoples. Rather, one must acknowledge fully all wrongs done and received. Truth telling is seen as the first step on the road to reconciliation; it allows for the rehabilitation of wrongdoers and for their reintegration into a community. Ross explains that, among all of the Indigenous groups with whom he worked, he found nothing akin to the Western concept that justice involves a "right to silence" or a right to refuse to incriminate oneself.[76] He suggests that this ethic of speaking truth and not remaining silent could be the reason for the high frequency of guilty pleas by Indigenous peoples accused of a crime; many Indigenous peoples might be uncomfortable entering a plea of "not guilty."

The Western justice system is set up so that a plea of "not guilty" requires the Crown to prove a charge under the law beyond a reasonable doubt. So "not guilty" is not an outright denial of guilt, although it seems to be given this wording. The plea could be interpreted as "prove it." Even if an Indigenous defendant understands this Western interpretation fully, Ross suspects that, for many Indigenous accused, putting the onus on the community by making witnesses testify would be seen as an immoral act, as the rule is not to lie to, burden, or embarrass people.[77]

This ethic of non-interference is also sometimes present in some Indigenous people's approaches to childrearing. Rather than withholding privileges or promising rewards, some Indigenous people caring for children model good behaviour. Unfortunately, judges and others working in the criminal justice system might see this modelling approach to parenting as an absence of parental control or discipline. For example, Ross describes the case of an Indigenous youth who pled guilty to breaking and entering into a school. The judge asked the youth what his parents had done in response to this behaviour, to which he replied, "Nothing." The same question was put to his father, who made the same reply. The then angry judge asked the father if he had responded in *any* way to his son's behaviour. The father explained that he would hide his son's shoes at night.[78]

The non-interference approach to parenting reminds me of a story my father told me several times. When I was about four years old, there was a creek in our backyard that was very muddy, like chocolate milk. When I was little, he told me *once* that I should only go near this creek when I was with adults, yet I wouldn't listen. I was just too curious and continually would go to the creek's edge. But I did not hear anything from my father on the matter again. Instead, he would watch me from the window. He said he had watched me numerous times getting really close to the creek's muddy edge, but he wouldn't say anything. Until finally one day I slipped in. But he was there, watching from the window, and he ran to the creek in time to pull me out. Now, of course, I never went that close to the creek's edge again without being with others. It taught me a good lesson. Yet consider a non-Indigenous onlooker and what he or she might have thought of that situation. My father's careful watching might have been taken out of context and seen as neglectful because, in many Euro-Canadian families, a child constantly wandering too close to a creek might be scolded, frequently corrected or reasoned with, or kept inside the house—and never afforded "safe" opportunities to learn from mistakes.

Ross also discusses the "ethic that anger not be shown." For example, one component of this value is controlling emotions when someone dies. In traditional times, you would not talk of a person's death and, in some cases, destroy anything that reminded you of that person. Ross gives examples of a building being demolished after a death and of some families destroying all photos or belongings of a deceased person. The idea here is to put sorrows out of your mind. This ethic is said to be related to traditional survival tactics; the restraint of anger, grief, or sorrow was important for the survival of the community. This tactic would be similar to those used for survival in wartime, when one has to remain collected to fight the common enemy.

According to some traditional Indigenous customs, when someone dies, people are not to speak that person's name for a full six months, and no one can retell stories about the deceased individual for a full year.[79] As Ross outlines, these customs can present difficulties within the context of the Euro-Canadian justice system, as court proceedings often require the names of the deceased to be mentioned several times. He gives an example from his own experience. Once he was questioning community members about a case that involved a deceased person, so he repeatedly said that person's name. He realized later that the interpreter translating his questions had gone through quite a difficult time rephrasing his words because of his frequent use of the deceased person's name.

Another traditional Indigenous ethic is not to burden people, especially when it comes to talking about self or feelings. It is not considered right to expect others to hear about your problems or comment on what you should be doing or feeling. This approach is quite the opposite of the one taken in many Westernized cultures, which can expect people to "put everything out on the table" or to "dig deep" and be assessed and "fixed" by experts, such as psychologists. Given this difference, some Indigenous peoples might be mistakenly viewed as "unresponsive," "undemonstrative," "uncommunicative," or possibly even "uncooperative" in psychological reports and assessments.[80] These assessments could very well impact their cases as well as their sentences.

In his study of Indigenous spirituality and healing in prisons, James Waldram quotes an incarcerated Northern Cree man who reflects on these cultural and ethical differences and how they can lead to misinterpretations and misunderstandings:

> I took a life and I regret that. When you take a life, up north, they're very forgiving. Before I came up to the courts, my people and the people I had injured had a meeting and they talked and they forgave one another for the healing. The Elders, I told them exactly what had happened. They took a message back and then I was forgiven, so they expected me back, but the court system is very different. They take you to a penitentiary . . . I made them [the Elders] look like liars because I didn't respect or accept their forgiveness for me to come back into the community, and I've never been able to get it back. It made them look bad. The healing hasn't begun at all. After the Elders forgave me, I was told by them never to talk about this crime again. It's over and done with and there's nothing you can do about it. Look to the future. So I said okay. I came to court, was convicted. And then I came into correctional services and they wanted to talk about the crime. But in my mind, I was told by the Elders to not talk about it anymore, because you'd be insulting the spirits and delaying all kinds of things.

> Delaying your healing too if you talk about it. So I never talked about my crime with a psychologist, because I wanted to respect what the Elders had said. And I was told that I refused to face my crime and I'm in denial and everything else. Unremorseful. I was deeply hurt by those comments . . . [81]

Waldram also notes that, sometimes, the comments in the case management files of Indigenous peoples who are incarcerated will be completely incorrect or very contradictory as a result of misinterpretation.[82] For instance, assessment files on an incarcerated Northern Cree man contained statements ranging from "not willing to speak in groups" to "somewhat shy." The assessment that this man "was somewhat shy and took a while to organize his thoughts when answering questions" also presented this explanation: "This could very well be a cultural factor and can be due to his educational background." And here is a completely opposite assessment of the same man: "appears to be mentally slow . . . Subject's mental stability is questionable." As Waldram points out, the diagnosis of a brain dysfunction, on the one hand, and of a "cultural factor" affecting communication, on the other, are drastically different, and it is very likely that others are also being labelled "slow" or "unresponsive" for erroneous reasons.

Waldram also describes the case of another incarcerated Indigenous man whose psychological assessment listed him as "indifferent or somewhat uncooperative."[83] An additional assessment stated that "he did not engage in any spontaneous speech, had poor eye contact, and spoke at a low volume." His deferential demeanour and quietness were then incorrectly framed as a "problem" by the prison staff. Yet, according to Waldram, these traits are not uncommon for northern Indigenous individuals from traditional backgrounds, and Ross identified similar behaviours among those Indigenous peoples who considered not making eye contact a signal of respect.

Another custom Ross outlines is the "conservation-withdrawal tactic." This behaviour is again reflective of traditional times, when actions were important because any hasty or ill-considered responses to certain situations could mean death. If a person out in the bush becomes lost in bad weather and acts in a frenzy, it can be fatal. Reacting in such a way, an individual could lose energy or presence of mind, and so make ill-informed decisions.[84] Some Indigenous peoples might still follow this rule and quietly turn inward when faced with a stressful situation. This withdrawal conserves both physical and psychic energy, so a person can make well-informed decisions before taking action. Ross notes that this behaviour can be misinterpreted. For example, he reports that some Indigenous peoples, especially the youth he encountered in remote communities, did not instantly try to dominate their surroundings when put into jail cells, as many of their white counterparts did. Given this difference, Indigenous youth were sometimes being recorded in jail reports as "passive," "sullen," or "unresponsive."[85] They were being misinterpreted negatively.

These ideas are indeed something to consider. At the same time, we have to be mindful that Ross is drawing on his own specific experiences as well as on the teachings he has received from various elders who come from certain backgrounds and have particular cultural beliefs. Therefore, we cannot assume that all Indigenous peoples follow these customs, tactics, cultural imperatives, or ethics. This note of caution is not meant to discredit his experiences and insights but rather to warn readers not to assume that *all* Indigenous peoples follow these ethics or customs.

The Restorative Justice Movement

Over the past 30 years or so, we have witnessed a movement toward restorative justice measures in Canada.[86] It is a movement that stems from the noticeable shortcomings of the current criminal justice system, most notably, from its ineffectiveness in reducing harm, bringing closure to victims, and providing a healing path for offenders.

Restorative justice is itself a theory of justice. This theory has been adapted to various restorative types of programming. It encompasses an approach designed to repair the harm caused by crime that affects victims, offenders, and communities. When executed in practice, it usually entails a process that brings together the offender, victim, and community to discuss the crime that has occurred. Given this approach, power is shifted to communities and individual victims and away from the state. Instead of relying on retribution, such as incarceration, probation, or another predetermined sanction, communities and other victims decide their response to the crime or conflict. The idea is that offenders, victims, and communities would partake together in developing and implementing solutions, which are decided upon in collaborative non-confrontational agreements. Thus, harms caused by crime or disputes are determined in a way that seeks to restore harmony in the community and between all of those affected by or involved in the crime or conflict.

For example, in a restorative justice proceeding, the victim might explain the harm and consequences resulting from a crime or conflict, and the offender or disputing party would have a chance to listen and learn and perhaps provide or explain his or her point of view or apologize. The process might also involve the victim and offender arriving at a collective solution to repair the harms caused, harms both emotional and material. It could also involve voices from the community; community members might explain the harms they have experienced and describe what they would like to see done.

This process typically confronts offenders with the consequences of their crimes, providing a place in which these can be explained to them in detail. At the same time, it helps the victims in the healing process. The restorative justice approach has been applied in many different programs and procedures, including victim-offender mediation, healing circles, sentencing circles, programs to reduce family violence, and various other initiatives.

The concept of restorative justice has been around for centuries and has been said to have roots in various Indigenous healing traditions, given its focus on restoring harmony and bringing back balance. At the same time, according to the Canadian Resource Centre for Victims of Crime, some of the earliest restorative justice pioneers were actually from faith communities such as the Mennonites. Drawing on the Bible and their faith's traditions, the Mennonites believed that justice could be achieved by making people whole again through healing. Justice was defined as making things right with each other and with God.[87]

Restorative justice has undoubtedly been promoted by various grassroots agencies, reformers, and some Indigenous peoples as an alternative to the ineffective Canadian criminal justice system. Indeed, mounting dissatisfaction with this system and the continuing over-representation of Indigenous peoples in it has led many to seek alternatives such as restorative justice. In a review of the literature on victims' experiences with restorative justice, Jo-Anne Wemmers and Marisa Canuto found that, although not all restorative justice programs are advantageous, most victims who participate in them feel they are beneficial. The authors also note a demand among victims for restorative justice programs.[88]

Some suggest that restorative justice approaches would go some way toward making the Canadian criminal justice system more acceptable to Indigenous peoples. Given Indigenous underrepresentation on juries and court benches, current legal proceedings do not seem welcoming. Indeed, an independent review by the Honourable Frank Iacobucci found that the underrepresentation of First Nations people on Ontario juries is actually a symptom of a much larger systemic crisis of the criminal justice system as a whole.[89] One of the major issues raised during his visits and meetings with First Nations communities and peoples was the conflict existing between, on the one hand, First Nations cultural laws, values, and ideologies regarding approaches to resolving conflict and, on the other, the values that underpin the Canadian system of justice. As he writes, "The objective of the traditional First Nations' approach to justice is to re-attain harmony, balance, and healing with respect to a particular offence, rather than seeking retribution and punishment."[90] The Canadian justice system is viewed by the First Nations people he met "as devoid of any reflection of their core principles or values," as "a foreign system that has been imposed upon them without their consent."[91]

Iacobucci also notes that, when community-based restorative justice initiatives were introduced, they were explained as being beneficial to First Nations because they were more culturally appropriate. Yet the restorative justice programs in First Nation communities had their funding cut by governments.[92] Leaders of the First Nation communities he met with made it clear that they wanted these programs back:

> First Nations leaders were unequivocal that re-introducing restorative justice programs would have multiple benefits at the community level. Such benefits include the delivery of justice in a culturally relevant manner, greater understanding of justice at the community level, increased community involvement in the implementation of justice and, finally, an opportunity to educate people about the justice system and their responsibility to become engaged on the juries when called upon to do so.[93]

Ultimately, he identified that First Nations want more control "of the justice system as it applies to their people and view the re-integration of restorative programs as one measure to achieve this goal."[94]

Other scholars warn of the dangers of thinking that Indigenous traditional justice and restorative justice are one and the same. The Accessing Justice and Reconciliation Project, a national initiative led by Val Napoleon at the University of Victoria, has as its goal to better understand Indigenous legal traditions and consider how they can be applied today. Project members analysed a number of published and oral stories relating to Indigenous legal traditions and presented these to elders and community partners, who shared further knowledge, opinions, and stories.[95] In their final report, they noted that "Aboriginal justice" is many times uncritically conflated with "restorative justice." Restorative justice is usually described idealistically as incorporating the values of "healing, reconciliation, harmony, and forgiveness." Although project researchers did find a strong emphasis on some of these principles in Indigenous legal traditions, they also note that these values are "not idealized, simple, or stand-alone responses to harms and conflicts."[96] Rather, all Indigenous legal traditions were identified as having their own distinct and vigorous interpretations of how these principles come to be implemented. An expansive range of responses and resolutions to conflict and harm are drawn on depending on each unique situation. For instance, Mi'kmaq peoples responses to harm included having offenders take responsibility for what they had done, perhaps by providing restitution to victims.[97] For Tsilhqot'in peoples, responses to harm included having the offender undergo separation and taking time to reflect. In some cases, a person might be put in a pit house in the mountains until his or her anger subsides, or an offender might be sent off alone to reflect on his or her actions.[98]

Traditional Approaches Incorporated into Non-traditional Social Structures

Although alternative strategies, such as restorative justice initiatives, have been suggested and promoted by those looking to do justice differently, one must take into consideration that the funding for the majority of Indigenous programs in Canada is through the Canadian government. The unfortunate implication of this is that the government invariably shapes and influences these processes and programs.

Native studies professor and Michif scholar Chris Andersen suggests that "traditional principles" are being incorporated into "non-traditional social structures."[99] He investigates the degree to which certain features or characteristics of Indigenous traditions have become tangled with recently emerging neoliberal discourses, which then results in a grafting of traditions onto non-traditional forms of social organization. He gives the example of Canadian judges having the authority to decide how and when Indigenous traditional approaches will be employed. For instance, Andersen mentions one case, *R. v. Alaku*, in which the judge disqualified the defendant from a sentencing circle by concluding he was not sufficiently remorseful or "sincere in his request" to participate in one.[100]

Although sentencing circles are said to be based on an Indigenous social structure, they have been reinvented to include officials representing the Canadian judicial system and to ensure that power rests in the hands of these representatives. Sentencing circles involve all the people associated with a court case: the offender, his or her friends, family, and neighbours, as well as the victim and the victim's associates. All involved parties sit in a circle for the hearing. The judge, the lawyers representing the Crown, the defence council, and involved probation or parole officers would also join the circle, and the case particulars would be heard by all these participants. The circles are sometimes joined by an Indigenous elder who often begins the hearing with a prayer. After the perspectives of the participants are heard, it is left to the *judge* to render a final verdict.[101] Although sentencing circles are not used to a large extent, it is important to note that they are typically considered an Indigenous initiative despite the fact that they are presided over by judges, which, in effect, makes the sentencing circle little more than a minor reorientation of a traditional court proceeding. The literature reveals that sentencing circles were actually developed by judges in the late 1980s and early 1990s in the Yukon Territory. Judge Barry Stuart used one in the case of *R. v. Moses*, for example.[102]

In September 2012, a sentencing circle was used for the first time in Kamloops, British Columbia. At this circle, people were dressed casually rather than formally. For example, Justice Ian Meiklem wore dress pants in place of his traditional black robes and an open-collared blue shirt. Defence lawyer Sheldon Tate wore a T-shirt, flip-flops, and chinos.[103] In the middle of the circle, a brown bearskin rug was laid down. Yet, at the same time, Circle Keeper Linda Thomas had to remind everyone that this circle was, indeed, a formal BC Supreme Court sitting and that all its proceedings would be recorded, as per official court process. Also, although the room did not resemble a traditional courtroom, judges would still have the final word in determining the appropriateness of the circle's recommendations and in the ruling. And judges would have already decided to convene a sentencing circle.[104]

Indigenous Traditions Reinvented in the Context of Colonization

Other literature points to the idea that some of the so-called Indigenous traditions being applied in the Canadian criminal justice system may have originated not from Indigenous peoples, as previously thought, but from their white colonizers. Native studies professor and Métis scholar Emma LaRocque, in her review of a collection of anthropological and historical sources, suggests that some things deemed Indigenous "traditions" may have been reinvented, possibly incorrectly, from amalgamated fragments of Indigenous and Western traditions. According to LaRocque, these reinvented Indigenous "traditions" have become highly politicized because they have been produced and shaped from a colonial perspective.[105]

Positioning herself against advocates of returning to the traditional Indigenous approach to justice that is conceived of as very *different* from the severe approach followed in Western society (see Table 12.1), LaRocque argues that truly traditional methods of dealing with serious crimes among Indigenous peoples were often harsh and matched the severity of these crimes. She asserts that the original purpose of holistic healing was to heal the illnesses caused by deviant actions and not to control deviance itself. As she states, "Traditionally, there was swift justice for transgressions such as murder, physical or psychic assault, theft, or personal injury, indicating that 'healing' was not the means of dealing with criminals."[106] Yet much of the contemporary literature on Indigenous crime intervention programming employs the term "healing" as an almost universal rehabilitative antidote for all modes of crime affecting Indigenous peoples. LaRocque states that it is historically incorrect to claim that all Indigenous cultures believed conflict was automatically two sided in every instance, and she suggests that restorative type programs and other supposedly culturally appropriate models of criminal justice may be incorrect in their assumptions about Indigenous culture.[107] It has simply not been established, she argues, that forcing mediation on victims is either helpful to the victim or in the rehabilitation of the offender.

LaRocque also takes on the claim made by some that Indigenous languages did not have a word for crime. Indigenous languages, she explains, may not have words that provide a direct translation for "crime." Yet various Indigenous languages have words referring to acts of wrongdoing. She gives the example of the Cree word "*My-yen-kewin*," which means "doing something wrong or bad, with the connotation of wilfulness."[108] She cautions that, to assume incorrectly that Indigenous peoples did not recognize crime is to suggest that our ancestors "were bereft of notions of justice and morality."[109]

Many agree that we need to bring back the vibrancy of our cultures and traditions. At the same time, we have to be careful of what we attempt to revive, especially given the effects of past and present colonialism. As LaRocque argues, caution is in order to assure we are returning to actual Indigenous traditions and not European reinventions of these traditions. As the Accessing Justice and Reconciliation Project identifies, Indigenous legal traditions include many methods to resolve conflict and respond to harm and wrongdoing. Given this adaptability of Indigenous responses to conflict and crime, the project recommended that Indigenous approaches be used to strengthen community justice and wellness initiatives and to provide the foundation for "practical justice reform rooted in mutual recognition and respect."[110] On a related note, Anishinaabe law professor John Borrows argues that, occasionally, Canadian law could be used successfully if Indigenous cultural traditions, values, and establishments were simultaneously part of the process.[111]

Indigenous justice, however, is not about trying to practice and implement certain aspects of Indigenous traditions under the umbrella of Euro-Canadian structures and systems. It has to go beyond this sort of effort. It is about drawing on our elders, attending ceremonies, and once again living our traditions. There are many who are. They are bringing new generations of youth down traditional paths and helping peoples toward balance, harmony, and reconnection with their cultures and land. Solutions to the injustice affecting Indigenous peoples will be further explored in the following chapter.

Discussion Questions

1) Discuss "pre-contact" crimes and contemporary crimes. What are the value systems that drive what were considered crimes in the "pre-contact" era? What are the value systems that drive what are deemed "crimes" today in Canada? How and in what ways might these value systems differ, and what role do value systems play in determining what a "crime" is and what is not a "crime"?
2) Compare traditional Indigenous methods of addressing crime with Euro-Canadian methods, and discuss differences and similarities. On what ideologies and goals are these two methods based?
3) What are the positive and negative aspects of making use of *Gladue* sentencing provisions?

Activities

1) Watch the 2004 National Film Board of Canada documentary by Tasha Hubbard, *Two Worlds Colliding* (available online at www.nfb.ca). Why do you think some Indigenous people fear reporting incidents to police? Where do you think this fear stems from? What do you think would drive a police officer to target Indigenous peoples or take them on starlight tours and leave them for dead? Where does this racism stem from?
2) Invite an Indigenous person working in the criminal justice system to discuss her or his job and the experience of working in the system as an Indigenous person.

Recommended Readings

Borrows, John. *Canada's Indigenous Constitution*. Toronto: University of Toronto Press, 2010.

Napoleon, Val, Jim Henshaw, Ken Steacey, Janine Johnston, and Simon Roy. *Mikomosis and the Wetiko*. University of Victoria: Indigenous Law Research Unit, 2013.

13
Moving Forward: Lighting the Eighth Fire

THERE IS LITTLE DOUBT THAT EURO-CANADIAN assimilationist policies, legal manipulation strategies, resource development priorities, disrespect of cultures, and retributive justice approaches contribute to the ongoing injustice impacting Indigenous peoples. This chapter describes how the invocation of traditional methods can form the basis of our healing journey. It explains how to move forward, how to light what some people call "the eighth fire," a prophecy that says, "Now is the time for all people to come together and build a new relationship."[1] Our people, including various Indigenous artists throughout Turtle Island, have been spearheading movements that take us forward—toward processes of decolonization. Many positive changes have drawn on various Indigenous traditional teachings as solutions to the injustices that have impacted us for generations. Today, Indigenous-specific preventative programming and educational initiatives, among other undertakings, may play a role in helping us toward a better future founded on our true history and traditions.

The Seven Fires Prophecy

There is an Anishinaabe prophecy known as the Prophecy of the Seven Fires. This prophecy is handed down orally through elders among the Anishinaabe peoples. Algonquin Elder Grandfather William Commanda, who was the Seven Fires Wampum Belt keeper from 1970 until his passing in 2011, handed down this prophecy, which was being passed down long before the arrival of Europeans. The prophecy tells the people of the eras in time that denote their past and future. Although the prophecy continues to be passed down orally, it has also been transferred into written word. The Circle of Turtle Lodge, for example, published teachings of the prophecy that drew on oral traditions and on the teachings by Grand Chief Edward Benton-Banai in *The Mishomis Book*.[2] According to the writings of the Circle of Turtle Lodge, many years ago, the original peoples on the northeastern coast of Turtle Island were given seven predictions from seven prophets. These predictions were each referred to as a "fire." Each fire referred to a particular time in the future.

The first fire speaks of a time when the Anishinaabe peoples are strong. During this time, the elders lead the peoples to an island shaped like a turtle;

this island will be associated with the earth's purification. Food will be growing on the waters of this island; and this will be a sign that the peoples have arrived at the correct place. This island is at both the start and finish of the journey, which will have seven stops along the way. As *The Mishomis Book* states, "You will know that the chosen ground has been reached when you come to a land where food grows on water. If you do not move, you will be destroyed."[3]

The second prophet explains that the second fire will be recognized because, during this time, people will be living by a big body of water. People will be lost, yet a boy will be born who will point them back in the correct direction. He will get them back on track with their traditional ways and direct them toward their future. The third fire is explained as a time during which people will continue on their correct path toward the place where the food grows on water (this food has later been identified by elders as wild rice).

The fourth fire speaks of the coming of a light-skinned race. Two prophets came forward to bring this fire. One of these prophets explained that, if these light-skinned people come with faces of brotherhood, then this will signal great changes to be had for the future generations. In this case, the light-skinned people would bring new knowledge that would be joined with the knowledge of the Anishinaabe peoples, and all peoples would be stronger together. Two more nations of people would also join our two nations, making us four strong nations of peoples. The first prophet foretold that the Anishinaabe peoples would know whether these light-skinned people were truly coming as brothers, if they arrive to offer only a handshake and information to share and if they come without weapons. The second prophet of the fourth fire warned the Anishinaabe peoples to beware if the light-skinned ones show the "face of death," as this face looks very similar to, and might be disguised with, the face of brotherhood.[4] If they arrive bearing weapons and appear to be suffering, the newcomers might be fooling the Anishinaabe peoples. In this case, the light-skinned people might be masking their greed for the riches of the land with the face of brotherhood. Eventually, it will be known if they came with the face of death because, if they did, they will turn the rivers into poison, causing the fish to become inedible.

The fifth prophet describes a struggle for our peoples, a struggle to decide between following traditional Anishinaabe teachings and giving them up for a false promise of "joy and salvation."[5] The people who accept this false promise will cause almost total destruction of the Anishinaabe peoples. Once this great struggle finally passes, the light-skinned people will fight fiercely, attacking the Anishinaabe peoples to take away their land and independence as free people.

The sixth prophet explains that it will become clear in this fire that the promise accepted during the era of the fifth fire came in a way that was false. Children will be taken away from the elders and their teachings, by those who were misled. Because the children become separated from the elders, many people will lose their purpose for living and their balance, get ill, and face death.

The prophet who brought the seventh fire was said to be different from the rest of the prophets; he had a light in his eyes and was younger than the others. He explained that, during this era, a "New People" (*Osh-ki-bi-ma-di-zeeg'*) will come into being. These people will start to retrace the paths taken and see what was left behind. While retracing these paths, they will turn to the elders for guidance but will come to find that the elders have fallen asleep because people had stopped asking them to share their wisdom and guidance. Some elders, however, "will be silent out of fear" and will choose to stay silent. Thus, the New People will have to approach the elders with care to ask for guidance and teachings; "The task of the New People will not be easy."[6] If the New People manage to stay strong and keep trying to find the true path, the Anishinaabe Nation could be reborn: old flames will be relit, and we could witness the sacred fire lit once again.

During this time, the light-skinned peoples will be faced with a decision. They will have to pick one of two paths. If they pick the correct path, it will light an eighth and last fire. This eighth and final fire would lead to an era of eternal sisterhood, brotherhood, peace, and love. Yet, if the light-skinned peoples choose the wrong path, the road to destruction, it will cause worldwide suffering for all peoples. Many will die as a result.

The Royal Commission on Aboriginal Peoples: Considering and Implementing Recommendations

Many people have noted this need to move forward and light "the eighth fire," to start on the path toward a new and strengthened relationship between all peoples on Mother Earth. A 2012 CBC television documentary hosted by Wab Kinew and titled *The 8th Fire* reiterates this theme of moving forward together after reaching a true alliance. Although many things may be needed to move forward, steps have been taken and inroads have been made toward this new and strengthened relationship.

In 1996, the report of the Royal Commission on Aboriginal Peoples was released. This report was the final one released by commission, which was formed in 1991 in response to high-profile incidents of Indigenous resistance to injustice, including the "Oka crisis" (see Chapter 10). The commission, which included many prominent Indigenous peoples, set out to examine the relationship between Indigenous peoples and the Canadian state at the time, and it offered recommendations for positive change. Commissioners travelled across Canada documenting the experiences and voices of Indigenous peoples. Their findings were brought together in the most comprehensive report ever done on Indigenous peoples in Canada.[7] Costing $58 million to produce, the final report is 5 volumes, 4,000 pages long, and has 440 recommendations. It notes the need for a renewed relationship between Indigenous and non-Indigenous peoples in Canada. This relationship, according to the report, should be based on the principles of mutual respect and recognition, sharing or reciprocity, and mutual responsibility. These principles served to underpin all of the commission's proposed recommendations. Fundamentally, the report recognizes that both Indigenous and non-Indigenous peoples need to acknowledge one another. It called on non-Indigenous peoples to recognize that Indigenous peoples are the original occupants of the land. At the same time, it notes the need for Indigenous peoples to accept non-Indigenous peoples because they now have ancestors who have lived on these lands and because they consider parts of Turtle Island home, by birth or adoption. The report, consequently, emphasizes the need for mutual respect—because we are all here to stay.

Among the report's recommendations are those addressing the critical social issues affecting Indigenous peoples, including child welfare, crime, education, and health disparities. Also recommended are improved prevention, treatment, and rehabilitation services. Other recommendations target some of the fundamental injustices in the relationship between the Canadian state and Indigenous peoples. For example, the report recommends the restoration of self-government, the restoration and control of an adequate land base, a restructuring of institutions according to Indigenous cultural values and organizing principles, and engagement with First Nations in interpreting or renewing treaties.

Commissioners also called for a new Royal Proclamation, coupled with companion legislation. The creation of this new Royal Proclamation was intended to demonstrate Canada's commitment to the treaty relationship. It would endorse and reaffirm the basic principles set out in the original Royal Proclamation of 1763 but also recognize the errors of the past and serve to commit governments to a new relationship.

The proposed companion legislation was to include various acts. One was the Aboriginal Nation Recognition and Government Act, which would officially recognize and legitimize Indigenous nations. It would also put in place new fiscal arrangements to support Indigenous activities. The companion legislation was also to include the Aboriginal Treaties Implementation Act, which would enable a recognized Indigenous nation to renew its existing treaties or create new treaties. An Aboriginal Lands and Treaty Tribunal Act was also proposed. This act would determine specific claims and safeguard treaty negotiations, making sure they are run, organized, and funded fairly.

Companion legislation also included the Aboriginal Parliament Act, which would establish a body to represent Indigenous peoples within federal governing institutions. Members of this advisory group would counsel and guide parliament on affairs involving Indigenous peoples. Eventually, the Indigenous counsellors would form a House of First Peoples, which would join parliament and govern alongside the House of Commons and the Senate. Another proposed law, the Aboriginal Relations Department and Indian and Inuit Services Department Act would replace the Department of Indian and Northern Affairs (now Indigenous and Northern Affairs Canada) with two departments. The first would implement the new relationship with Indigenous peoples, and the second would administer services to communities that had not yet selected self-government.

These recommendations are vast, covering almost every aspect of Indigenous peoples' lives. And some propositions could change the relationship between the Canadian state and Indigenous peoples in positive ways. The report set out a 20-year implementation plan during which all recommendations would be implemented.[8] Yet this document sits in Ottawa and collects dust. In 2013, Indigenous studies professor Gregory Younging (Opaskwayak Cree Nation) noted that, so far, less than 1 per cent of the recommendations have been implemented, and it is unlikely that the remaining 99 per cent will be implemented in the remaining three years.[9]

The United Nations Declaration on the Rights of Indigenous Peoples

In 2007, The United Nations General Assembly adopted the United Nations Declaration on the Rights of Indigenous Peoples (UNDRIP). This document set international standards for Indigenous rights. It specifies the need for rights to be recognized, which includes recognition of treaties. Some of its articles declare the right of Indigenous peoples not to be subjected to forced assimilation but rather to be able to retain "the right to determine their own identity or membership in accordance with their customs and traditions," as well as "to maintain, control, protect and develop their ... cultural heritage, traditional knowledge, and traditional cultural expressions."[10] It further sets out that Indigenous culture must not be destroyed, that children are not to be taken away from their families, and that all individuals, particularly children, have a right to education without discrimination. It states that all Indigenous peoples have a right to take part in decision making that would affect their rights, and it includes as rights the conservation and protection of Indigenous lands, territories, and resources; the determination of strategies and priorities that affect their lands and peoples; and other interrelated human, land, and cultural rights specific to Indigenous peoples.

Canada was originally involved in the creation of the text of UNDRIP, and the Liberal government supported it. Indeed, this declaration received almost universal backing from the international community. Four countries, however—Canada, the United States, Australia, and New Zealand—initially refused to sign it. These countries all later changed their positions and have now endorsed the declaration.

When it refused to sign UNDRIP, Canada's Conservative government at the time originally argued that some articles conflicted with Canadian constitutional laws and might put Aboriginal rights in a position that trumps those of other Canadians. These concerns of the Harper government were premised on fear and were largely due to a lack of understanding about what the recognition of Indigenous self-determination means. But finally, after much pressure and persuasion from the Indigenous and the international communities (both Australia and New Zealand endorsed UNDRIP in 2009), on November 12, 2010, Canada gave its official endorsement, and, one month later, the United States announced its decision to endorse the declaration as well.

Endorsing this declaration demonstrates the government's commitment to work in partnership with Indigenous communities and acknowledges Indigenous rights around the world. Since November 2010, however, nothing much has changed in Canada's relationship with Indigenous peoples, at least in practical terms. In many ways, since it endorsed the declaration, we witnessed the previous Conservative government trampling on many of the Indigenous rights UNDRIP asserts. A notable example is the passing of Bill C-45 (see Chapter 10), which contained certain provisions that amounted to a large-scale attack on Indigenous peoples' land and resources. These provisions were paternalistic and colonial and were imbedded in legislation that was pushed through parliament, in what Mi'kmaq lawyer and professor Pamela Palmater describes as "Prime Minister Harper's aggressive 'assimilatory' legislation plan meant to break up our communities and assimilate First Nations peoples."[11] With the Liberal majority government elected in October 2015, there has been a shift in the government's approach to UNDRIP. On December 8, 2015, Prime Minister Justin Trudeau made a promise at the Assembly of First Nations' Special Chiefs Assembly to implement UNDRIP. He also stated that his government will "conduct a full review of the legislation unilaterally imposed on Indigenous peoples by the previous government."[12] It must be remembered, however, that changes to *Canadian* legislation do not liberate Indigenous peoples from the veil of the colonial state. Until Indigenous lands are returned, these legislative changes keep Indigenous peoples entrenched within the Euro-Canadian colonial state.

Decolonization, Reconciliation, and Resurgence

Decolonization is a term used to describe the unlearning and undoing of colonialism. It is a process and a goal.[13] It is a reimagining of relationships with the land and peoples. It is about a conscious engagement with colonial structures, ideologies, and discourses. It is also about an active resurgence against these structures, ideologies, and discourses, which have come to be so dominant. For example, one major step to begin active decolonization in Canada would be to have all Canadians learn and acknowledge Indigenous histories from Indigenous perspectives, as opposed to from the colonial perspectives and understandings of history that dominate Canadian discourse and ideologies. This step would abolish the incorrect assumption that Indigenous peoples lacked a civilization prior to European arrival, an erroneous idea that is an excuse for the injustice still fuelled by mechanisms of colonialism. As we learned in Chapter 3, Indigenous peoples had complex and extensive civilizations already in place before European arrival. These accomplished civilizations had even discovered how to retain the delicate balance between the earth and all of its creatures—how to preserve the sustainability of the land. Decolonization means, as well, having all Canadians recognize and admit that this land called Canada is comprised of many traditional Indigenous territories. It means taking the time to learn and acknowledge the wisdom and teachings of the land—and to realize that the land is shared for living and being on.

As Indigenous peoples, specifically, to decolonize means to have the conviction and the courage to be who we are—to stand up and assert our place in our homelands. In practice, this decolonization process means that Indigenous peoples must continue to challenge Canada in a respectful way. The goal is not for Indigenous peoples to refuse to recognize the existence and human rights of non-Indigenous peoples but rather to encourage peaceful education and a growing awareness and understanding of true realities and histories. For Taiaiake Alfred, "decolonization starts becoming a reality when people collectively and consciously reject colonial identities and institutions that are the context of violence, dependency and discord in indigenous communities."[14] According to social work professor Michael Yellow Bird, citizen of the Arikara (Sahnish) and Hidatsa nations in North Dakota, decolonization involves the ". . . restoration of cultural practices, thinking, beliefs, and values that were taken away or abandoned (during the colonization period) but are relevant and/or necessary for survival and well being. It is the birth and use of new ideas, thinking, technologies and lifestyles that contribute to the advancement and empowerment of Indigenous Peoples."[15]

Yellow Bird also explains that we must use traditional teachings and ceremonies to change the mind, so the brain can heal from the traumas of colonialism: "In order for decolonization to be successful it must begin in our minds." He declares that we must free ourselves from post-colonial culture and thought, "from dependence on Western ideas, philosophies, beliefs, theories." For him, the mind (and brain) is Indigenous peoples' "most incredible ally." He uses the term "neurodecolonization" to encapsulate the work that must be done to free the mind from colonialism. The idea is that we can encourage the growth of new and beneficial brain networks that can enable us to train our attention, so we can "engage in optimistic thinking" and believe that colonialism can be overcome, "develop the courage to confront" colonialism, and "cultivate the creativity needed to use novel, effective approaches to change it."

The philosophy of neurodecolonization is based on neuroplasticity. Essentially, neuroplasticity is the ability of the brain to change with experience (to be able to develop new neuronal connections). For Yellow Bird, it is crucial to "create these healthy decolonized thinking patterns and actions" because "as we do that we positively shape and empower important neural networks in the brain." As he states, "Creative, healthy, decolonized thinking, actions, and feelings, positively shape and empower important neural circuits in our brain, which in turn provide us with the personal resources, strengths, [and] abilities we need to overcome colonialism." If we look at the flip side of this idea, we see peoples who have given into trauma and suffer the very "unconstructive, negative thinking, feelings, and behaviors [that] dampen and short-circuit our brain's creativity and optimistic networks, and increase our susceptibility to stress, failure, complacency, and fear." As Yellow Bird contends, we must follow the teachings of our ancestors—think positively, see the goal, see the vision, and the importance of ceremony—because we know now that "the more you have unconstructive negative thinking, feelings, and behaviors, the more you short-circuit and dampen those neural networks that are going to help liberate you from that oppression."

Many people have also spoken of the need for reconciliation between Indigenous peoples and non-Indigenous peoples in Canada. Reconciliation is not something new, as Indigenous peoples and settlers have tried to reconcile differences in countless treaty negotiations.[16] However, because of the settlers' lack of integrity and honour, the relationship did not solidify toward the envisioned peace. More recently, governments and others have been promoting reconciliation as an apology for Canada's historic mistreatment of Indigenous peoples, yet most fail to acknowledge the current role of Euro-Canadian governments, institutions, corporations, ideologies, and peoples in supporting and continuing colonialism.[17] The term "reconciliation" has resurfaced because of the establishment of the Truth and Reconciliation Commission of Canada (TRC), whose mandate explains the emerging and compelling desire to

> ... put the events of the past behind us so that we can work towards a stronger and healthier future. The truth telling and reconciliation process as part of an overall holistic and comprehensive response to the Indian Residential School legacy is a sincere indication and acknowledgement of the injustices and harms experienced by Aboriginal people and the need for continued healing. This is a profound commitment to establishing new relationships embedded in mutual recognition and respect that will forge a brighter future. The truth of our common experiences will help set our spirits free and pave the way to reconciliation.[18]

Some significant words are used to describe reconciliation in the TRC mandate. Truth telling and especially acknowledging injustices and "the truth of our common experiences" are what will enable reconciliation and a new and respectful relationship to emerge. Indeed, the mandate goes on to describe reconciliation as "an ongoing individual and collective process . . . [that] will require commitment from all those affected."[19]

Chair of the Truth and Reconciliation Commission of Canada Justice Murray Sinclair believes that, in order to move forward, we need reconciliation.[20] He explains that this is a process involving both Indigenous peoples and non-Indigenous peoples. For example, when Indigenous children were being taught in residential schools that they were inferior, non-Indigenous peoples were being taught these same racist attitudes—and that, consequently, what their European ancestors did was okay.

Indigenous rights and peoples are not going to disappear, so, according to Justice Sinclair, all peoples in Canada need to learn how to get along. He also explains that knowing where you came from and where you are going is an important part of reconciliation. For the process to work, all peoples need to establish a strong sense of identity, belonging, and self within the newly created relationship. Reconciliation is also about respect. Respect means the ability to tolerate differences between us. As mentioned, reconciliation requires the full truth to be told. Reconciliation, then, is a massive undertaking; it will not happen immediately; it takes time. According to Justice Sinclair, if we can agree on what reconciliation is now, maybe sometime beyond seven generations, we might have progress. Why seven generations? The residential schools did their damage over seven generations, and Sinclair thinks it takes a lot longer to rebuild a people's identity, cultures, and traditions than to break them down.[21]

At the same time, however, some people ask, "Why should Indigenous peoples reconcile?" Reconciliation implies that both parties have to forgive. As a residential school survivor explained to Justice Murray Sinclair, "How do you forgive something that doesn't have a soul, or an institution? It's about people." The Canadian government and various churches did apologize, yet to apologize can mean to provide an account of one's actions, which can be offered as a justification for or defence of these actions. Some think that the government uses the term "apology" in an ambiguous way—to pretend regret while justifying its actions. So are we to believe that the government is defending its actions against residential school survivors?[22]

The statements made by government officials after the apology in June 2008 seem to indicate this could be the case. Not long after the apology, on September 27, 2009, Prime Minister Stephen Harper announced to international community members at the G-20 summit that Canada is unique because it is not tarnished by a history of colonialism: "We . . . have no history of colonialism. So we have all of the things that many people admire about the great powers but none of the things that threaten or bother them."[23] Harper also suggests here that Indigenous efforts aiming to challenge and rive colonialism and dispossession can be thought of as simply a "bother." In many ways, these statements seem to contradict other announcements by the Harper government, which implied a respectful attitude toward both the survivors of residential schools and other members of the Indigenous community. In order to engage actively in the process of decolonization, colonialism must first be acknowledged and understood, not just given lip service. Then comes real action.

According to Tsalagi scholar Jeff Corntassel, reconciliation talk that is not followed by meaningful action simply reinscribes the status quo without holding anyone responsible or liable for continuing injustices.[24] He asserts that governments use the language of reconciliation to regulate the wrongs that have been committed. For example, the Truth and Reconciliation Commission, he argues, is really about the government telling Indigenous peoples to reconcile with the past and move on, to put it behind them and work toward the future. But will this future be one in which the Canadian government still operates according to the same old Euro-Canadian colonialist institutions, laws, and governance structures? What has happened since the TRC reports have been released? Have its reports and recommendations been largely shelved, like those of the Royal Commission on Aboriginal Peoples, which inspired no real action and thereby allowed the same old structures to dominate?

According to Nishnaabeg scholar Leanne Simpson, reconciliation will have to be given a much broader definition if it is to be meaningful to Indigenous peoples and useful as an actual decolonizing force. It will need to be grounded in political and cultural revival.[25] This reconciliation process would involve Indigenous nations being fully supported in regenerating languages, traditions, oral cultures, and traditional governance—all the things residential schools tried to eliminate. Language and cultural regeneration would be large scale and wide spread, for example, enabling whole communities to once again speak their traditional languages. This sort of reconciliation would also include the regeneration of conditions that would build and sustain Indigenous political systems and leadership, which would be rooted in Indigenous philosophies and values. It would also mean a large-scale re-education plan, so governments and citizens in Canada could engage with Indigenous peoples in an impartial, fair, and moral way. As it stands today, we are not on a level playing field, as Canada does not provide accurate education about Indigenous peoples. If this education and awareness were society wide, Indigenous peoples could engage with other Canadians and governments in a more just way.

Jeff Corntassel and others also note the need for Indigenous resurgence.[26] Resurgence means the ability to see life beyond the state. It involves connecting to homelands, communities, and cultures. In practice, the foundations of resurgence are everyday acts of renewal, such as making a personal attempt to revive, retain, or maintain one's culture (including language), homeland, ceremonies, and traditional sacred histories. For example, you could make a pact with yourself to eat only food native to your ancestors' homelands, to teach your children your traditional language, or to learn your ancestors' traditional crafts, medicines, or stories.

Decolonization in Practice: Artists Reversing the Gaze, Creating Conversation, and Reawakening Spirits

All peoples in Canada need to be on a path toward decolonization. Indigenous peoples need to "decolonize" just as non-Indigenous people need to "decolonizer" themselves. As mentioned, decolonizing means unravelling and reversing colonialism and its associated structures, institutions, and discourses. Many of our people today are working to do just that. The Indigenous DJ group A Tribe Called Red, for example, has dedicated itself to creating conversation and truth telling around contemporary colonialist discourses. The group is based in Algonquin territory (Ottawa, Ontario), and, until 2014, it included three DJs: Bear Witness (Cayuga), DJ Shub (Cayuga), and Dee Jay NDN (Anishnabe). In 2014, DJ Shub left the group, and 2oolman (Mohawk) became a new member. They have been travelling across Canada (as well as internationally), spreading their music through their "Electric Pow Wow" celebrations. They won Breakthrough Group of the Year at the 2014 Juno Awards for their blend of Pow Wow music and contemporary club sounds.

A Tribe Called Red also has tracks that draw from existing racist songs and media portrayals, which the DJs remix to change and make their own. In a sit-down discussion I had with the group, members explained this remixing as a way to indigenize and reclaim these images and songs.[27] To explain

Image 13.1 A Tribe Called Red

this process, they described their music video called "NDNs from All Directions," which includes the remixing of a song by Super Cat called "Scalp Dem" (Super Cat is a reggae dancehall MC originally from Jamaica). The original song and music video from Super Cat uses Westernized images of cowboys and Indians; its lyrics mention "scalping them" and "hanging them up high." Another part of the song tells of "Indians from all directions." A Tribe Called Red put these clips into its song as a way to reclaim and indigenize them. The DJs took the sample "Indians from all directions" and flipped it to be positive. As Bear Witness explained, they made "more of a unity song out of this."

In the video, they piece in clips of white people misappropriating Indigenous cultures. One shows dancers from a 1960s British variety show who are dancing and making a mockery of what they assume to be Indigenous culture. In fact, their dance is very misinformed and sexualized. They also include a clip from the television show *The Walking Dead*, in which one of the characters points a gun threateningly and says, "Let's have a Pow Wow." The members of A Tribe Called Red took these images, remixed the borrowed music with their own beats, and coupled all with visuals from real Pow Wow dancers, as well as with other graphic effects. They explain that, by doing these things, they are engaging in the process of decolonization. They are taking back these images and lyrics and actively decolonizing them. People do sometimes question them and ask whether they are actually re-appropriating these images and sound clips, but, as they explain, they are doing the exact opposite. They are remaking these audio and video fragments into their own art and undoing colonialist depictions by actively engaging in the processes of truth telling. They are making people aware that these pictures and words are colonial encroachments on our peoples, thereby resisting the inaccurate depictions and understandings that fuel colonialism.

Their music is empowering and has helped create a movement that communicates powerful coinciding messages. The group and its music reach out to both Indigenous and non-Indigenous peoples, encouraging conversations around these issues, even among people who otherwise might not have thought about colonialism and its effects. Dee Jay NDN explains that mainstream society seems to view as "completely okay" the really racist images and songs that permeate popular culture. He sees this acceptance as racial and cultural oppression. For him, music has the power to create conversations that can help change these attitudes; the shock of seeing racist depictions together with true ones might cause people to re-examine racism, to "see it and hear it and kind of see it in a new light, where like before you wouldn't have thought twice about seeing this . . . they're going to look differently and be like, oh wow yeah that's not okay, that guy shouldn't have done that in the first place."

The group also explained that bringing this music into club settings reaches audiences in places where people gather to have fun, thus bridging politics and entertainment. An additional goal behind bringing this music to the nightclub space was to create a place for Indigenous peoples within the club environment. Actually, creating this space was one of the reasons for starting the group. As Bear Witness explains, members of A Tribe Called Red see their Electric Pow Wow parties as, "A way of Indigenizing that space in the club environment and saying this is ours, you know, like as urban Aboriginal peoples we didn't have those spaces, those markers within the urban landscape to say this represents us. We were strangers in our own homeland."

These Electric Pow Wow parties create that space for our peoples. They create that space for Indigenous peoples to own. They also create meeting places. As Dee Jay NDN tells it, the first Electric Pow Wow party the group threw in Ottawa was sold out. There were about 400 people there, and, although he had grown up in the community where the Electric Pow Wow was held, he didn't know anyone there. The place was full of Indigenous peoples whom group members didn't actually know, he explains. It turned out that students from rural communities had come down for the party, as they had never before "had a space where they felt comfortable" in the city. That the group had created a space comfortable for Indigenous peoples who had grown up around only other Indigenous peoples was explained as one of A Tribe Called Red's first "uh-huh" moments in regards to the Electric Pow Wow; group members knew they were on to something different. What's more, although they have retained this important Indigenous space for Indigenous peoples, many non-Indigenous people also attend these Electric Pow Wows and learn about Indigenous culture and issues, as Dee Jay NDN explains:

> The conversation we are having with non-Aboriginal people is just as important as the representation we're giving to Aboriginal people. So it's a two-way street there. The same thing with the music; we're introducing a lot of non-Aboriginal people to Pow Wow music that they've never known, never been in touch with before, as well as bringing electronic music to Aboriginal peoples who maybe never experienced that as well.

Through creating spaces for Indigenous peoples, bringing both Indigenous and non-Indigenous peoples together in these spaces, and helping to fuse entertainment with political issues, A Tribe Called Red plays a role in creating conversation around truths, and thus contributes to the undoing of colonialist discourses. Other artists are raising our collective consciousness about colonialism and the injustices facing Indigenous peoples. Like A Tribe Called Red, these artists use their various art forms as mediums for decolonization and platforms for conversations. For example, Cree artist Kent Monkman, whose art forms include painting, film and video, and performance and installation art, reverses the gaze back onto Europeans through his creations. With his art, he reclaims some of the aspects of Indigenous cultures that have been suppressed. He also exposes the egotism, ignorance, and greediness of the colonizers. He sometimes paints as and depicts in his work his alter ego, "Miss Chief Ego Testickle." As Monkman explains, Miss Chief is a flamboyant, egomaniac artist who is in all of her own paintings.[28] She serves to reverse the gaze, so it becomes the Indigenous artist who is looking at Europeans. The videos and paintings of his alter ego tear down boundaries and break stereotypes.

Central themes in his work include sexuality and colonized sexuality. As Monkman explains, in our Indigenous cultures, "We used to have an openness to sexuality, which somehow got stamped out from the Europeans who didn't understand it." Using Miss Chief as his subject, Monkman takes the work of nineteenth century artists such as George Catlin, who idealized and romanticized Indigenous peoples in his paintings, and reverses these typified representations. His work incites conversation and plays a role in provoking Canadians and others to consider colonialist Eurocentric depictions of Indigenous peoples. Monkman looks to the history of art in North America, which, according to him, was really about wiping out Indigenous narratives through presenting false settler narratives about Indigenous peoples. He explains that these false narratives show a strong will to disappear us from places where we lived and were born, and he contends we must engage with these narratives to understand why we are where we are right now.

Another example of artistic resistance to colonialism was *The Indian Act Revisited*, an art exhibition produced by the Musée Huron-Wendat in Wendaké, Québec. It includes a collection of art pieces that challenge colonialism and its impacts and realities. In this case, the exhibit's central focus was the Indian Act. For this exhibition, several Indigenous artists were asked to produce a piece of art that comments on an article in the act. Contributing artists included Eruoma Awashish, France Gros-Louis Morin, Nadia Myre, Angela Sterritt, Jackie Traverse, Maria Hupfield, Teharihulen Michel Savard, and Louis-Karl Picard-Sioui. In fact, the cover of this book is from this exhibition, created by Anishinabe artist Jackie Traverse.

The artwork in this exhibition represents an artistic and political gust of resistance against the Indian Act. For example, to create the piece titled "Reciprocity," Wendat artist Teharihulen Michel Savard took a physical copy of the Indian Act into the woods and shot it with a gun, leaving a bullet hole through its front cover. The front cover is also splattered with red to symbolize blood, and wampum beads are pouring out of the hole, possibly signifying the government's broken treaty promises. A description of this piece explains its meaning further: "A printed copy of the Indian Act is exposed and perforated, deformed under the shock of an impact whose brutality leaves no place for imagination. Its wounds bleed 'red.' A light spray has delicately speckled the whole cover page. Mingled in this fluid reminding us of an open wound—of a wild animal or a human shot at blank point range—wampum beads appear to be coming out."[29]

Another artist who exposes realities through art is Cayuga hip-hop musician Chief Rock. His song "Rez Reppin" reveals the realities of reserves, tells of the policies that denied First Nations the ability to practice dances and other ceremonies, and describes other injustices. Mainly, though, it cautions Indigenous peoples to be careful of what he calls "reppin the rez," meaning, representing *only* the reserve. First Nations peoples were forced on these places, he explains, and were once put in jail for leaving them. So we must remember that all of this land in Turtle Island is Indigenous land, not just "reserve" land.

Chief Rock's music also merges traditional Haudenosaunee singing and drumming with contemporary beats, mixes, and raps. He explains his purpose in bridging traditional and contemporary music as bringing youth back to tradition.[30] Some young people might not be connected to their culture but might enjoy the contemporary hip-hop beats he uses. So, by mixing in traditional music, he hopes to draw back to Indigenous cultures people who might otherwise have been disinterested.

Chief Rock has also teamed up with Nuxalk and Onondaga hip-hop artist JB the First Lady, who is well known for her inspirational music. She is a role model to many, and, in her music and public presentations, she often speaks about Indigenous female empowerment. When Chief Rock and JB sing together, they are known as Enter-Tribal. In 2015, they released a powerful song titled "Sisterz" to raise awareness about the missing and murdered Indigenous women in this country. The song is an emotional, intense statement that speaks truths—it is a tribute to all of the missing and murdered Indigenous women and their families.

Stó:lō, Ojibway, and Métis artist Inez Jasper has been a very positive, inspirational, and motivational role model for youth. She blends hip hop, R&B, and pop music with traditional Native sounds.[31] She incites changes through her music and was recently featured on an MTV production called "Rebel Music". This show, which has been released on Facebook, documents the stories of artists across the world who are inspiring change through their music. In her segment, she draws attention to the crisis of the missing and murdered Indigenous women, notes how Indigenous women's sexuality has been threatened, and expresses the need for Indigenous women to reclaim our identities and sexuality in a safe way.[32] Also featured on this episode is her song "Dancin' on the Run," which praises the survival of Indigenous cultures despite policies that sought to destroy them—notably the potlatch ban enforced by the local "Indian Agent." The full official music video of this song includes enlightening captions and information related to these oppressive polices.[33] Thus, her music not only inspires but also teaches, and she seeks to reach out to all peoples. As she states, "Before, traditional indigenous music was limited to a niche audience. Now is the time for unity and change. It is not limited to indigenous people and this is an opportunity to learn together, share together, cry together, and come together."[34]

In a famous 1885 quotation, Louis Riel said, "My people will sleep for one hundred years, but when they awake, it will be the artists who give them their spirit back."[35] Various Indigenous artists seem to be doing just this. They are reclaiming, legitimizing, and indigenizing places and spaces, and, in some cases, reawakening these places, spaces, and discourses in a way that is both by and for Indigenous peoples. This resurgence of our peoples continues to get stronger and gain momentum. The Idle No More movement has sparked various artists to create songs of support, some of which have gone viral on YouTube (see Chapter 10).

Other artists have created visuals, posters, and paintings, in support of the movement. For example, Dwayne Bird (Cree from Peguis First Nation) created a poster series named the *Indigenous Rights Revolution*.[36] Pictures from this series, many of which show a Canadian flag with a hand holding up a feather in its centre, were transferred onto T-shirts. Lou-Ann Neel (Kwakwaka'wakw) transformed the Canadian flag by putting a traditional raven design inside the maple leaf. She also made the centre of the flag green and surrounded it with the "Idle no More" slogan; in the outer red blocks of the flag, she placed tree and mountain designs. Along the bottom of the flag are the words "Our Home on Native Land." Her designs have been reproduced on T-shirts, bags, and hats.

This movement has brought people of all ages together, standing in solidarity for rights, resisting colonization, and reasserting commitment to protecting the land of our ancestors. It has also played a part in creating a renewed sense of pride for some people. In his song supporting the Idle No More movement, Ojibwe hip-hop artist Plex sings, "The best day to be Native is now."[37]

Returning to the Teachings: Traditional Practices and Healing

As Mohawk scholar Patricia Monture-Angus teaches us, we need to know where we come from in order to move forward.[38] For far too long, Indigenous identities, cultures, and traditions have not been given proper recognition. Fortunately, many elders succeeded in retaining and preserving the foundations of Indigenous traditional cultures and knowledges, and many Indigenous peoples today are looking to the ways and teachings of our ancestors to provide part of the solution to the challenges and intergenerational trauma experienced by many of our peoples. In fact, some contend that Indigenous cultures, practices, and ways hold a key, if not *the* key, to the future survival of humankind.[39] According to distinguished Lakota Sioux youth-care expert Martin Brokenleg, the medicine for Indigenous peoples is found in traditional teachings. He contends that intergenerational trauma can be countered by following the traditional teachings.[40] For Brokenleg, returning to traditional childrearing practices is part of the answer because the focus should be on providing children and youth with a sense of belonging, giving them a purpose in life, empowering them to make decisions, and attending to their inborn thirst for learning and success.[41]

All peoples and nations have their own cultures and thus their own healing practices; there is not one "fixed" traditional Indigenous mode of healing.[42] Although appropriate methods will vary from nation to nation, traditions and practices of healing might include singing and drumming traditional songs, attending ceremonies, or role modelling.

Singing and drumming have been part of various Indigenous cultures since time immemorial.[43] Various Indigenous peoples throughout Turtle Island have referred to the drumbeat as the heartbeat of Mother Earth. Various drum groups meet together to drum and sing and to create safe places for many to share, practice, and, in some, cases relearn or reconnect with their culture. A research study examining Indigenous women's involvement in hand drumming linked traditional drumming with positive health factors and supported the idea that drawing on cultural traditions was strengthening and important.[44] The study described the experiences of Indigenous women from many nations who came together to drum in an urban northern Ontario community located on traditional Anishnaabe Ojibwe territory. It collected data through various methods, including a sharing circle, individual interviews, and journaling. The researcher and some of the co-researchers of the study were members of the Indigenous women's hand-drumming circle Waabishki Mkwaa (White Bear) Singers.

Qualitative data collected by and with the aid of this drum group found that Indigenous women's involvement in hand-drumming circles was linked with various health benefits: for example, it supported their physical, mental, emotional, and spiritual well-being and built on the existing strengths within their community. Through their experiences with hand drumming, women reported gaining a voice and a sense of holistic healing, empowerment, renewal, strength and *Mino-Bimaadiziwin* (meaning the "good life" in the Anishinaabe language). This last concept has existed and been promoted for centuries among various Indigenous peoples.[45]

Mino-Bimaadiziwin, living a "good life," requires a person to find balance between his or her emotional, spiritual, mental, and physical elements. The study found that hand-drumming practices supported all of these elements. For example, women talked about how drumming helped them with their self-confidence. The physical aspect of drumming increased physical energy and, at the same time, helped some to relax their bodies. The sounds of the drum helped to release tension. Drumming helped some women reduce stress, gain better clarity, and unclutter their minds of the busy schedules and daily pressures of life. Some even noted the pain-relieving effects of drumming. Drumming helped others deal with addictions; it was something positive to remember the next day, various women reported.

A medicine-wheel framework also evolved out of this study. Created by the researchers and participants of the drum group, this framework brought together everyone's perceptions on how drumming helps in life. It placed "culture" at the centre of the wheel and, in the four quadrants, listed mental, spiritual, emotional, and physical elements; surrounding all were social support networks.[46]

For some, being active in traditional drumming and singing and being a "drum carrier" mean that one acknowledges the responsibility that comes with carrying a drum. An aspect of this responsibility is abstaining from using any alcohol or drugs so as to have a clear mind and sober senses. The teachings of the Pow Wow (an Indigenous cultural celebration at which people gather to dance, pray, sing, and socialize) are similar. My Pow Wow dance mentor Shelly Hill, Mohawk from Six Nations in Ontario (Turtle Clan), shared that my participation in Pow Wow dancing is ceremonial, so, during this time, the use of drugs or alcohol is prohibited.

A research study that interviewed 381 urban Indigenous peoples in Edmonton in 2010 examined the role traditional culture plays in the protection against and resilience to both illicit and prescription drug use.[47] This study found that those who were engaged in traditional ways were less likely to use drugs. This finding might be explained by a related one reported by the study—that those engaged in their traditional culture had higher levels of self-esteem. Involvement in traditional culture was found to provide opportunities for people to interact with others who are involved in their culture and who have high esteem for themselves and for their Indigenous identities. Furthermore, the study concluded that "Aboriginal spiritual practices may provide a direct measure of protection against drug problems given they are often based on cultural teachings that promote abstinence from psychoactive substances or moderate use."[48]

Chief Darrell Bob also thinks that reviving traditional spiritual practices is necessary: "It's important for our people to come back to ceremony."[49] Anne Poonwassie and Ann Charter, experts in social work and counselling, published an article in the *Canadian Journal of Counselling* asserting that participation in ceremony helps people stay connected, or perhaps reconnect, to cultural roots.[50] Depending on the nation, traditional ceremonies might also include, pipe ceremonies, potlatches or giveaways, sweats, Sundances, storytelling, or sharing and talking circles. Poonwassie and Charter explain that ceremonies can help people establish social networks and connect to the natural environment. Many involve a cooperative effort in which people help others and are also helped in return. These types of ceremonies, as well the numerous spiritual traditions not mentioned here, also aid in confirming cultures and their coinciding values.

Poonwassie and Charter also assert that storytelling is a useful way of integrating and teaching cultural values. This practice is a non-competitive mode of information sharing. It helps to teach one how to listen. It reinforces the importance of respect. Often, stories have a lesson and, at the same time, share an important piece of history (be it current or ancestral). According to Stó:lō scholar Jo-ann Archibald, stories have energy and strength. They have a source of power that "feeds and revitalizes the mind, heart, body, and spirit in a holistic manner."[51] As she explains, a story challenges her to think and examine her emotional reactions in relation to plot and characters, to question and reflect on her behaviours and future actions, and to appreciate a story's connection to her spiritual nature.

Poonwassie and Charter also contend that sharing or talking circles are influential media for both healing and conveying values.[52] The circle is a place for learning and sharing stories or any other information. In these circles, no one is in a position of authority; everyone is equal. Usually, one person speaks at a time, as a talking piece is typically passed around the circle. Each person is given an opportunity to speak, but no one is forced to speak. Teachings that coincide with talking circles include respecting others while they are speaking by listening and giving others your full attention and vice versa. Thus, the circle incorporates as well as models respect.

Among Indigenous peoples, role modelling is also an influential method of educating and assisting, according to Poonwassie and Charter. Culture is made up of daily signals that happen within and help to define everyday human relations and interactions with the surrounding world. A powerful way to reinforce culture is through action, which serves to articulate the core values for new generations to grasp and follow. Poonwassie and Charter assert that positive behaviours and activities can be represented by positive role models, including elders, traditional healers or knowledge keepers, and healthy community members.

Indigenous-Specific Prevention Programming

Role modelling, talking circles, and other aspects of Indigenous cultures have also been incorporated into what are typically referred to as prevention programs. Prevention programs can include those targeting poor health or crime. Sometimes, programs that are set up to prevent poor health also play a role in reducing crime, and vice versa. For example, some crime prevention programs target alcohol or substance abuse, and these could reduce crime as well as poor health outcomes.

Generally, prevention programs can be defined as programs that first seek to identify the risk factors or root causes related to an undesirable outcome—such as crime or poor health—and then tackle these factors, in the hope that the undesirable outcome will not come to fruition. Often, these programs will also aim to enhance protective factors as well (see Chapter 8 for further descriptions of risk and protective factors). Some programs incorporate Indigenous cultural aspects, teachings, and knowledges. Some programs have also been designed specifically around Indigenous cultural values or traditions.

For example, the Warrior Spirit Walking Project (WSW) was based on both Indigenous values and psychological research. This program was funded through Canada's National Crime Prevention Centre for a period of four years, beginning in 2007, and was part of the broader Prince Albert Outreach Program, delivered by a not-for-profit organization of the same name dedicated to addressing the needs of high-risk youth in Prince Albert, Saskatchewan. WSW is an evidence-based crime prevention program that increases protective factors and reduces risk factors for Indigenous youth (males and females) aged 12 to 21 who are involved in gangs or at high risk of joining a gang.[53]

The program is based on Martin Brokenleg's "Circle of Courage" model for reclaiming youth at risk.[54] This model is based on Indigenous philosophies of childrearing and on ideas stemming from child psychology and resilience research. Brokenleg's rationale for using traditional childrearing practices to address contemporary issues is that our Indigenous ancestors knew how to raise children through challenging times—and we know we are living in challenging times because the symptoms of intergenerational trauma affecting our peoples today are momentous. Thus, we can again look to these methods that proved so effective and successful for our ancestors.[55] The key components of the model are rooted in the four central values found on the four points of the medicine wheel: belonging, mastery, independence, and generosity. Belonging represents the idea that every human being needs to have a sense of identity and be part of a social support network. Mastery refers to the need to be competent and to achieve personal goals, but it also means having *opportunities* to attain success and responsibility, to experience social recognition, to gain inner satisfaction, and, at the same time, to honour others who succeed. Independence is based on the idea that children must have opportunities to be independent and must be guided without interference, meaning that children must learn by doing, not by being instructed to do. Generosity means that children need to be taught to be unselfish and generous; they must develop a value system based on simplicity, generosity, and non-materialism.[56] Finally, all four components must be present for a person to be able to live in balance and harmony and have her or his circle of courage complete.

The primary aim of the Warrior Spirit Walking Project is to reduce Indigenous youth gang membership, affiliation, and future affiliation for those at risk of joining, as well as to reduce gang-related youth violence and crime.[57] The project consists of seven programming components: a cultural school, presentation team, youth activity centre, van outreach, court outreach, counselling and mediation in schools, and activity groups. For example, the cultural school—staffed by four teachers, four counsellors, and two elders—is designed specifically to enable high-risk Indigenous youth to complete high school training, earn high school credits, increase literary skills, increase life skills, receive employment training, and engage in cultural activities. In other words, it tackles the risk factors related to gang involvement, which include poor school performance, learning difficulties, and low attachment to school.[58]

The presentation team, another major program component, is a group of youth who have disengaged from gangs and now act as mentors to the youth in the program.[59] With staff supervision and support, they educate youth about the dangers of youth violence, bullying, and gang involvement through a variety of activities based on traditional cultural teachings, including school presentations, hip hop, rap, video productions, the sharing of personal stories, and recreational activities. The presentation team aims to tackle risk factors such as antisocial attitudes, aggression and violence, and low attachment to school.

An evaluation report on this project for the period of November 2007 to October 2009 showed promising results.[60] Using quantitative data analyses incorporating risk assessment surveys, researchers have shown that participants achieved reductions in overall levels of risk. Initial findings included a significant increase in attachment to teachers, with those who had been in the program for 18 months experiencing the highest increase. There was also a significant reduction in substance abuse among youth who had been in the program for 12 months. Additionally, researchers noted a reduction in levels of involvement in violent crime during the first six months of the program. Finally, youth were also found to be much more attached to the labour force, and there was a clear trend for youth to leave their gangs over time.

According to many researchers, crime prevention programs, such as the Warrior Spirit Walking Project, are promising alternatives to the standard system of crime control, which relies heavily on police, courts, and corrections.[61] Indeed, crime prevention programming has been pilot tested in Indigenous communities and has shown potential to reduce the risk factors associated with victimization and offending.[62] Even stronger evidence is provided by the many thriving Indigenous communities that had prevention measures automatically embedded in their everyday interactions for thousands of years. Although the exact structure and organization of the various nations would differ, they all had a strong commitment to family life, healthy and durable community bonds, and an emphasis on raising children in a culture of respect, familial support, and love.

Even though Indigenous peoples continue to be over-represented in the criminal justice system as both victims and those incarcerated, culturally safe programs emphasizing prevention are still not readily available to any large extent. The standard system, comprised of police, courts, and corrections, is still the primary means of crime control in Canada. Not surprisingly, these typical and Eurocentric modes of crime control and criminal justice application, which are embedded in the system, continue to receive substantial and sustained government funding, while other methods (e.g., crime prevention and healing initiatives) receive much less in the way of meaningful fiscal support.[63]

Canada does have a National Crime Prevention Centre (NCPC), which is a funding agency that allocates monies for pilot crime prevention programs throughout Canada. It funds many different projects, some of which are Indigenous-focused initiatives or have Indigenous cultural components (such as the Warrior Spirit Walking Project described previously). And the existence of Indigenous-specific prevention programs in Canada is a positive step. However, there are three major issues with the NCPC. First, all of the programs it funds are pilot programs, which means that they usually receive funds to operate for a period of only one to four years and then come to an end. Second, because the NCPC is primarily a funding agency, communities must produce and submit complex proposals to receive funding, and making these submissions could be difficult for the communities most in need of prevention programs. Expecting communities which experience high rates of victimization and incarceration to come up with evidence-based program ideas built on research and documented sources, develop a logic model and work plan, complete complex budget forms, and seek out letters of reference might be unrealistic, in some cases.

Finally, the NCPC has a small budget compared to those supporting standard crime control measures. During the NCPC's first three years of operation (1998–2000), it received $32 million per year as its total operating budget. It now receives about $70 million per year, more than double its original allocation. Yet when this $70 million is compared to federal expenditures on the criminal justice system, or to the amount spent on the criminal justice system as a whole, it is actually quite minimal. This $70 million is equivalent to 1.1 per cent of the federal expenditures on criminal justice, which is estimated to be about $6.18 billion. This includes $3 billion to federal policing and other RCMP expenditures in 2010,[64] $2.4 billion to corrections in 2010–11,[65] and $90 million to the courts in 2000–01.[66]

The Aboriginal Justice Strategy

Because of concern about the over-representation of Indigenous people within the criminal justice system, the federal government created the Aboriginal Justice Strategy (AJS).[67] This strategy started as a pilot project in 1991, and was originally named the Aboriginal Justice Initiative.[68] In 1996, it was expanded and renamed, and it has since continued to be renewed. The AJS provides funding through two streams, a community-based justice fund and a capacity building fund. The community-based justice fund, which was the first fund AJS offered, provides support for culturally relevant Indigenous justice programs, which are cost shared between provincial or territorial governments and Indigenous communities.[69] In 2007, the AJS was expanded to include funding for capacity building. This capacity building fund supports Indigenous communities to increase their knowledge and skills in order to create and administer community-based justice programs in the future. Funds are offered for training, data collection, fostering partnerships, conducting needs assessments, and other forms of capacity building.

In particular, the AJS funds programs that provide alternatives to the mainstream justice system, including various diversion or alternative measures programs, mediation, community sentencing, and community-court justice programs.[70] For instance, the Saddle Lake Restorative Justice Program is a youth and family-focused strategy that includes prevention, diversion, and reintegration programming.[71] It centres on identifying and tackling risk factors related to offending through awareness and education.

The AJS also funded the Mi'kmaq Customary Law Program offered in nine different Mi'kmaq communities in Nova Scotia. This program is rooted in traditional Mi'kmaw notions of holding wrongdoers accountable and achieving consensus. It provides three different types of circles: justice circles, healing circles, and sentencing circles. Justice circles are a pre- and post-charge diversion measure that typically includes victims, the wrongdoer, family members, and community peoples, who all work together to achieve consensus on an agreement that holds the wrongdoer accountable and seeks to make amends.[72] Once a consensus is reached, the charge is then withdrawn. Healing circles are also a pre- and post-charge diversion measure, but they focus on sharing the pain or trauma caused by wrongdoing. Sentencing circles are a post-conviction measure. After a person has been found guilty or charged in court, a judge may refer that person to a sentencing circle, which focuses on having the wrongdoer acknowledge the harm she or he might have caused and taking responsibility for harmful actions. It also enables anyone affected by the offence to play a role in making sentencing recommendations to the court.[73]

Two hundred and fourteen programs received AJS funding as of 2011–12, up from 100 as of 2006–07.[74] These programs can receive up to $500,000 a year in cost-shared funding. When AJS was first launched in 1996, it received $4.5 million per year as its total operating budget, which increased to $8.6 million a year by 2000–01. In 2011–12, its total budget rose to $17.5 million. Yet, like the NCPC budget, the AJS annual budget of $17.5 million is minimal in comparison to federal expenditures on the criminal justice system or to the cost of that system as a whole.

In 2010–11, an evaluation was completed by the Department of Justice (DOJ) on the Aboriginal Justice Strategy. Thirteen community-based justice programs were evaluated, including programs for family and civil mediation, community sentencing, and diversion.[75] Site visits were made, and 25 interviews were conducted with various key stakeholders, such as elders, police officers, program managers and staff, and program participants. One finding was that participants felt AJS programming contributed to an "increased sense of community safety" in 11 of the 13 communities evaluated. In one of the communities that did not feel safer as a consequence of AJS programming, people reported feeling fearful due to those released from prison being back in the community. In the other community, people had felt safe to begin with. Overall, as the DOJ noted, "while programs could have an impact on participants, some issues were beyond the scope of the AJS."[76]

Pre- and post-recidivism rates from 1998 through 2007 were also collected and examined as part of the AJS review. The rates of those who participated in AJS programs were compared to the rates of those who were referred to programs but never participated.[77] It was found that re-offending rates were "significantly lower" for program participants each year.[78]

Although AJS and NCPC programs are not an adequate solution to Indigenous over-representation in the criminal justice system, they are currently providing a Band-Aid for some peoples who are struggling with either causing or experiencing harms. That various aspects of Indigenous values, healing, or cultures are offered through some of these programs can be seen as constructive and valuable for those who have been pulled into colonial criminal justice processes and the cycle of harm they induce. Any success achieved through this cultural programming, offered from within the confines of the colonial state, perhaps stands to show how impactful and effective our cultures can be, even when bounded by colonial structures. Our cultures helped us thrive for thousands of years. With the advent of colonial disruption, they have been key to our survival in the face of murder, genocide, and deliberate attempts at eradication. Envision what Indigenous culturally based supports could do if they were not limited by and offered through colonial structures. It is no surprise that the DOJ's own evaluation admits that some issues are "beyond the scope of the AJS." As evidenced from the past 500 years, trying to "fit" Indigenous peoples into and under colonial structures and policies has neither reduced harm nor achieved balance.

In order to receive AJS funding, communities have to first meet the requirements of the DOJ, so the values driving the AJS are not rooted in traditional Indigenous ways of living and being—in harmony, balance, and respect. Rather, as its evaluations of funded programs show, the AJS has as key goals "efficiency and economy" and other outcomes that can be measured through "cost analysis."[79] Although individual programs may be rooted in an Indigenous community's value system, all programs have to be "approved" and siphoned through the DOJ's value system to be funded. They must reach the goals and respond to the priorities of the government *first.* Indigenous values, then, become secondary and must crowd under the umbrella of colonial structures and processes.

Thus, evaluations such as the one discussed here provide little information on the realities of these programs. I was alerted to this disconnect between official reports and community perceptions when I interviewed various community stakeholders in Winnipeg about Indigenous crime prevention programs. In my experience, program stakeholders usually have as a main priority trying to meet the demands of a government funding agency because they must struggle to keep programs afloat. Many program directors adjust their programs to fit the "wants" and priorities of the government in power at any given time. Ultimately, the bureaucratic structures and hoops Indigenous stakeholders have to jump through to deliver these programs engage our peoples in politics of distraction. They distract us from looking at and challenging the true source of this cycle of harm affecting our peoples, which is colonialism.

Indigenous-Specific Education Supports and Programming

Various educational supports and programs for Indigenous people exist at colleges and universities in Canada. Some have Indigenous resource centres that offer a space for Indigenous students to gather, connect with each other, and get educational support. These centres typically provide scholarship information and other resources, or they might host various workshops or cultural events. The University of Ottawa Aboriginal Resource Centre provides a culturally safe place for people to gather. The centre maintains an ongoing email list of Indigenous students and sends scholarship opportunities and other information to that list. Kwantlen Polytechnic University has an Aboriginal Gathering Place that houses the office of the First Nations Education Coordinator, who has an open-door policy and welcomes any Indigenous student. The university also runs an Indigenous student peer-to-peer tutoring program out of the Aboriginal Gathering Place.

The University of Alberta's Aboriginal Student Service Centre has a Smudge and Meditation Room, with specially installed ventilation for smudging. Medicines are provided for the students (and are picked yearly by the staff at the centre).[80] The university also provides on-the-go snacks for students who come through the centre, such as fruit or bannock. Once a month, the centre hosts a hot lunch for students. Elders, social workers, counsellors, and an academic advisor are also made available to students through the centre. Students can also access Indigenous student housing through the centre; the housing service provides secured residences for Indigenous students.

Brock University in Ontario offers Aboriginal student services. An elder is available on campus, and students are offered weekly lunches and a place to print documents, receive tutoring services, obtain a locker, and even make long distance phone calls (for those students far from home). Every summer, Brock also hosts a week-long camp for local Indigenous high school youth. Campers go north to reconnect with the land, explore traditional cultural roots, and learn about Indigenous histories. Various elders, Indigenous leaders, and other staff from the Brock Aboriginal Centre all attend to support the youth.

Saskatchewan is home to the First Nations University of Canada. This university, which was first established in 1976 as a college, has three campuses: Regina, Saskatoon, and Prince Albert (Northern Campus). It provides a culturally supportive environment that focuses on Indigenous knowledge. All courses taken are accredited by the University of Regina. All campuses offer students access to a male and female elder. Elders also work alongside

The Aboriginal Enriched Support Program at Carleton University: Geraldine King's Success Story

In its September 21, 2012, issue, *CAPITALWOMAN* magazine ran an article entitled "Aboriginal Issues: Discovering True Potential." Intended to acknowledge Indigenous women studying at post-secondary institutions in Ottawa, the article included the following story:

> Carleton University offers an Aboriginal Enriched Support Program (AESP). It is a one-year transition program for students who want to attend university but are experiencing barriers such as being out of school for a long time or not meeting entrance requirements. They get the support they need to hopefully succeed.
>
> Each of the universities and colleges in Ottawa have support systems and resource centres to help Aboriginal students. Here is where you'll find a lot of students with drive, ambition and determination to succeed—students like Geraldine King. She is the first person in her family to get a post-secondary education. She was born in a small First Nation in northwestern Ontario, didn't finish high school, had a baby when she was a teenager, worked for several years in Ottawa, and then realized she needed to go back to school. So she made the leap and is now in her third year studying Canadian Studies and History at Carleton. She works two to four jobs throughout the school year, and still maintains a perfect GPA. She says it feels like a whole new world of opportunities has opened up for her. And while not technically true, when Geraldine's son wrote her a Mother's Day poem that read "My mommy is the smartest person in her university," she said the fact that "this little person recognized my hard work; it was all I could ask for. I want to leave my son a legacy of academic excellence driven by Indigenous ways of knowing so he too can make his dreams a reality."
>
> Now Geraldine is doing so well that she was recently awarded the Ottawa Women's Canadian Club scholarship.

Since this article was published, Geraldine has graduated from Carleton University with a BA in Canadian Studies and a Minor in Indigenous Studies. She was on the Deans' Honour List every year of her degree. She went on to complete her MA in Indigenous Governance at the University of Victoria in British Columbia. Geraldine is also a published author and has won many scholarships and awards.

Source: Jennifer David, "Aboriginal Issues: Discovering True Potential." *CAPITAL WOMAN Magazine* 3 (September 21, 2012): 33. Excerpt reprinted with permission.

academic departments, providing students with knowledge of cultures, traditions, and teachings as they relate to various courses. See the textbox for an Indigenous-specific support program success story from Carleton University.

Indigenous Community-Based Organizations: Offering Programs by and for Indigenous Peoples

Many Indigenous community-based organizations across the country offer programming specific to Indigenous peoples. For example, Aboriginal Friendship Centres offer a variety of Indigenous-specific programs. These centres were not just created by Indigenous peoples; they are run by and for Indigenous peoples. In 2015, the National Association of Friendship Centres had 118 members, with centres operating across Canada.[81] These centres offer a variety of social programming initiatives for children, youth, and families, including sports, recreation, cultural education, teen parenting workshops, family violence intervention, family support programs, substance abuse intervention, and job skills training. Many friendship centres and other community-based Indigenous organizations provide programs that tackle the risk factors for crime and victimization that have been uncovered by criminological research. In other words, they offer programs that could reduce crime affecting Indigenous peoples.[82]

For example, the Seeing Oneself Program has as its primary focus reducing addictions to alcohol and other substances—as these addictions are risk factors cited as being highly correlated to victimization and offending.[83] The program is part of the Strong Heart Teaching Lodge, which operates out of the Indigenous, community-based Thunderbird House in Winnipeg. It targets youth and strives to provide them with a vision for their future through education and awareness, as well as through engaging them in traditional Indigenous teachings.

This program itself was modelled on an evidence-based program stemming from the work of psychology professor Nancy Comeau and her colleagues, the Nemi'simk Seeing Oneself intervention program.[84] This early alcohol misuse or abuse intervention initiative was developed and pilot tested with Indigenous youth from four schools in two Mi'kmaq communities in Nova Scotia. Interventions delivered through the program were cognitively behavioural in nature and culturally relevant, as they incorporated traditional Mi'kmaq knowledge and teachings. The evaluated interventions consisted of two 90-minute sessions.[85] These sessions provided interactive exercises and visual images and scenarios and were delivered using intervention manuals that were culturally relevant, based on information gathered in a preplanning stage from the youth in the actual community researchers were seeking to serve.

The evaluation of this intervention showed that, compared to pre-intervention, students who participated in the program drank less overall, engaged in fewer binge drinking episodes, had fewer alcohol-related problems, were more likely to abstain from alcohol use, and had also reduced their use of marijuana (a positive result that the study had not anticipated). A non-random control group had experienced no significant changes at the four-month post-intervention follow-up.[86]

The Seeing Oneself program developed by the Strong Heart Teaching Lodge also made interventions culturally relevant and specific to the Winnipeg community it was seeking to serve. During a planning stage, researchers conducted a thorough examination of this community and assessed the needs of the target population, including specific cultural requirements. They also performed an in-depth examination of the target population's various factors related to drinking behaviours.

This research was conducted through interviews (story sharing) with Indigenous youth and members of the community, including elders and others with local knowledge. The purpose was to understand more completely the needs of the target population in order to make the program as relevant as possible and to create facilitator program manuals specific to the target population, based on the consultations. Beyond developing valuable insights from community people, these interviews also sought to gain support and coordination from the community, given that a major aspect of this program is coordination among persons, organizations, and relevant agencies in the community.

This program aims to help youth understand why they are in their current situations. Achieving this aim involves teaching youth about residential school experiences, about the displacement and reallocation of their communities, and about how these harms have affected many Indigenous peoples today. This teaching endeavours to help youth understand why they and their families may now be faced with addictions and other associated issues. The importance placed on this goal of teaching youth about history and its after-effects is born out of the experiences of one program organizer, who once struggled with addictions himself. This man lived on the very streets of the neighbourhood where he subsequently implemented the program:

> I mean I used to live on the streets in this very neighbourhood before there was a Thunderbird House or an Aboriginal Centre, this was all dive bars and you know. And it wasn't until I began to understand many of the reasons

> how I wound up where I was, why I was feeling that anger, why I was feeling depressed, why I was using substances as a way to escape. And having the education and that awareness of recent historical events, unresolved historical events that helped me to see that, that put a light on in my head, cause then I was supposed to tackle something, I was actually able to see it, I was actually able to know the real issues as to why things were the way they were and I wasn't just doing a lot of blaming whether it was my own self, my own people or blaming other people, and blaming them. It put it into perspective so that I knew that by making these changes or focusing on where I could make change that's a big reason, that and going to the ceremonies for the first time that really helped support me to change my life to be you know get away from addictions and get away from violence and have a good family and do the work that I'm doing now and you know move into learn how to be lodge keeper, you know Sundance and sweat lodge keeper, I mean all these things, I mean it was a big influence as to why I changed.[87]

This program is premised on the idea that the current Westernized world view (dominant and mainly white) perpetuates the violence and crime affecting Indigenous peoples because it maintains a highly individualized and separated way of life that misses a holistic, collective approach to education, learning, and being. It is this holistic and collective approach that the program intends to reteach and bring back to the participants' families and communities. As the program director explains, Western society perpetuates an addictive logic due to the highly individualized lifestyle under which current Canadian society operates. The lack of connection with others and with the past caused by this extreme individualism fuels Indigenous people's addictive behaviours, according to program organizers, because it gives them no understanding of why they are in their current situations and, at the same time, leaves them with no source of collective support to address these situations.

Programs such as these offer promise for the future of our youth, and many programs are being delivered by people with a passion to make a difference. Unfortunately, Winnipeg's Seeing Oneself program faced barriers when trying to stay afloat, a common story. Receiving adequate and sustained funding is something that this preventative program and many others in Canada struggle with regularly. Many Indigenous organizations also face barriers in funding, as do other community-based organizations. For example, Aboriginal Friendship Centres have not received an increase in core funding since 1988.[88] In April 2014, centres were faced with cuts to this already limited core funding.[89] Additionally, Indigenous organizations compete for funding with other organizations and departments in order to maintain operations. Often, when organizations *do* manage to secure funds for programs, they receive support for only a certain period, typically for a year or three to four years (depending on the funder). This instability damages capacity. Many persons implementing this supportive programming are currently doing the best they can with the few resources and supports, using infrastructure that is in place and available.

Community Champions: Inspiring, Educating, and Making Change

According to Martin Brokenleg, Indigenous peoples are perfectly normal people who have lived through an abnormal history.[90] He further explains that intergenerational trauma gets stronger with every generation if we don't do our healing work. And it is past time to begin. Many recommendations made by many commissions and studies are waiting for action. The people, expertise, and passion needed to begin exist in Indigenous communities. We have many champions spearheading various programs and initiatives and raising awareness about the injustices facing Indigenous peoples in Canada.

One of these people is Michael Champagne. Michael is Cree, originally from Shamattawa First Nation in northern Manitoba. He grew up in the north end of Winnipeg, where he has lived and worked for most of his life.[91] As a child, he experienced poverty, relied on neighbourhood drop-in centres to eat, and also went through the child welfare system.[92] By the time he reached grade eight, he had been through 13 different schools in the north end. In school, he experienced bullying so severe that, by fourth grade, he felt hopeless and wanted to commit suicide. He says he knows what it is like to feel oppressed and hopeless.

But Michael turned all of this negativity into fuel for his work today. He has since learned about his traditions and about the beauty of this people, and he is proud of who he is and where he comes from. Michael naturally transformed into a community leader; he has earned a reputation as a positive force for change. He is the founder and organizer of Aboriginal Youth Opportunities (AYO!), which is a group of young people who are committed to fighting stereotypes through leadership—committed to reclaiming cultures and traditions. In Winnipeg, AYO! consists of several initiatives.[93] For instance, through a politics initiative, youth confront leaders on questions that matter to their community. The anti-violence initiative called "Meet Me at the Bell Tower" involves people rallying together to inspire change in the community and to speak out against violence. Michael continues to stay active in his community. He tells his story to empower youth and shares his passion for positive change. Youth such as Michael are a driving force in communities. As he states, "The young people know what is wrong and they know how to fix it."[94]

Gabrielle Fayant is another young Indigenous person rousing change in her community. She is Métis, originally from the Fishing Lake Métis Settlement in Alberta.[95] She tells of how she grew up in poverty and was surrounded by gangs, drugs, and alcohol, which became normal to her.[96] She did poorly in high school, eventually dropped out, and felt she had no hope for a better life. After the passing of her mother, she landed herself in the hospital for depression and alcohol on three separate occasions.

But now Gabrielle states that she is "proud to be alive" and notes that she is especially pleased to say that she is "happy." She says that "finding her cultural identity" was key to this change. Also important were the people who reached out to her and let her know that they believed in her. She explains that the Anishinaabe teachings about the seven fires helped her find her purpose and role in life.

Gabrielle is also pursuing postsecondary education; she is doing her psychology degree at Carleton University in Ottawa. She has become very active in giving back to youth in her community, a fact recognized at the prestigious 2015 Indspire awards where she was a recipient in the youth category. She is passionate about Indigenous rights, and this passion has inspired her involvement in many Indigenous organizations, committees, and events. For instance, she is the co-founder of a youth-led and youth-driven organization named the Assembly of Seven Generations (A7G), which seeks to empower youth to become leaders in their communities. She is also the program manager of an Indigenous youth program called ReachUp! North, which has formed a partnership with a Canadian international social enterprise called Digital Opportunity Trust (DOT) and supports Indigenous youth in becoming leaders of change through the balancing of technology with traditional cultures. As Gabrielle explains, this program creates a safe space for Indigenous youth to "take charge of their livelihoods through the use of technology."[97] For her, supporting Indigenous youth cultural programming is fundamental, as she declares "what is needed are solutions that include cultural learning from a youth-led, youth-driven perspective—A7G and DOT are doing just that."[98]

Candace Sutherland is another outstanding young Indigenous person making a major difference for Indigenous peoples. She is Métis from Bissett, Manitoba. Born into poverty, she remembers her family having to rely on the local food bank to put dinner on the table.[99] When her mother became institutionalized for mental health reasons, she and her two brothers came into the custody of her aunt and uncle.

It wasn't long until she discovered her love of running. By the time she was 12 years old, she was able to run 16 kilometres. During this time, her supportive aunt and uncle moved the family to Winnipeg so she could have better access to training facilities. Each day that she walked to the running track, Candace would pass a soup kitchen. Seeing the children lined up for food reminded her of her childhood, when her family also had to rely on support services for food. She then vowed that she would use her talents to make a difference.[100]

Candace has run in and organized several marathons to raise donations for Indigenous charities, food banks, and homelessness relief, and to help others in need of assistance. Her marathon advocacy and her charity and inspirational work were also recognized at the Indspire awards; in 2012, she was a recipient in the youth category. She has run in the Candace Sutherland Run (a marathon) each year since she was 12 years old. Through another race, the Run for the Hills marathon, she collects "turkey donations" to give to those in need of a thanksgiving meal.[101] At the age of 19, she became the first teen to run across Canada—her Vision4Hope Marathon raised over $2.6 million to support the Salvation Army, the Heart and Stroke Foundation, the Canadian Diabetes Association, and the Canadian Cancer Society. She explains that she chose these organizations because a lot of Indigenous peoples go through poverty and are affected by these diseases.[102] In addition to her fundraising efforts, Candace gives presentations to many northern Indigenous youth to empower them by sharing her story. She tells them, "Never give up on your dreams."[103]

Allan Downey is another young Indigenous person who went after his dreams and continues to inspire. He is from the Nak'azdli First Nation in British Columbia, but he grew up in Waterloo, Ontario. When he was young, he struggled in school. As he explains, "I wasn't always the best high school student."[104] For him, the sport of lacrosse became a "gateway."[105] He became exceptional in box lacrosse, which is a form of lacrosse played in a hockey arena. He did so well at this sport that he achieved a sports scholarship to Mercyhurst University in Erie, Pennsylvania. While at Mercyhurst he developed a passion for learning and an interest in history. He merged his love of learning and history with his passion for lacrosse and went on to get his master's and doctorate at the University of Waterloo, where he specialized in the history of lacrosse.

Allan has a strong desire to give back to Indigenous communities. He is a local advocate for Indigenous youth and speaks in Indigenous communities, where he promotes postsecondary education. He tells his story of initially struggling in school but following his dream, which made many opportunities open up for him. He shares with youth the mistakes he has made and the lessons he has learned. But his main message is about finding and following passion: "I tell them I was struggling and not always the best student, but that lacrosse opened the doors to so many opportunities. . . . But I remind them that it's not specifically about lacrosse. It's about finding your passion and following that passion and seeing where that will take you. Like me, you could be amazed at where you end up."[106]

His outreach work includes giving guest lectures at youth correctional facilities, where he uses his personal story to inspire others to find their path in life. He explains that "these are youths who have become disempowered. I try to reconnect with an important cultural element—lacrosse—as a way to look at bigger issues like setting goals and developing life skills."[107] He also shares cultural aspects of the game, as a way to give back traditional knowledge.[108]

Allan is also an Indigenous studies professor at McGill University, where he teaches core courses in the university's new Indigenous Studies Program. He says he is looking forward to a changing relationship between all Canadians and Indigenous peoples. As he sees it, "In order for this positive relationship change to take place we have to understand the roots of how that relationship has gone so sour."[109] He feels that there are great opportunities "to start bridging more Indigenous worldviews into our academic settings and into our cities, into our non-Indigenous communities so that greater understanding can take place."[110] This idea brings us back to where this book began. In order to achieve harmony, balance, and peaceful coexistence, education and awareness are the first steps all peoples in Canada must take. In order to talk about peace and harmony, the truth must first be revealed.

The individuals described in this section are acting on truths and advocating for change. They are just some of the outstanding Indigenous people who are educating, advocating for, inspiring, and healing the next generations of Indigenous youth. Champions such as these need worldwide support by all nations of peoples, including our settler brothers and sisters, new immigrants, and far-off friends. Conversations need to continue happening, and a true realization of history by all peoples residing in Turtle Island needs to take place.

Discussion Questions

1) Draw connections between history and the prophecies of the seven fires. Can you make links between where in history you have seen these various fires? Do you believe we are seeing a lighting of the eighth fire?
2) How and in what ways can we restructure the relationship between Indigenous peoples, governments, and non-Indigenous peoples in Turtle Island?

3) How and in what ways can we eliminate injustice and crime affecting Indigenous peoples in Canada?

Activities

1) Identify an Indigenous artist whose art is contributing to decolonization. Identify and explain the ways this artist is contributing to creating conversation around colonist discourses, is reversing the gaze, is active in resurgences against contemporary colonialism, or perhaps is reviving Indigenous traditions or culture.
2) Visit a local Indigenous community-based organization in your area. What types of programming does it offer? How and in what ways do its programs seek to have a positive effect on Indigenous peoples and communities today?
3) Watch the fourth episode of the CBC's 2012 documentary series *The 8th Fire*, "At the Crossroads" (available online at cbc.ca/8thfire). Consider and discuss the promise of Indigenous role models. What role can they play? How might they affect the lives of youth?
4) Write a letter to the prime minister outlining action you want to see happen in regards to Indigenous peoples in Canada and how and in what ways policies should be changed or eliminated.

Recommended Readings

Clouthard, Glen Sean. *Red Skin, White Masks: Rejecting the Colonial Politics of Recognition*. Minneapolis: University of Minnesota Press, 2014.

Guimond, Eric, Gail Guthrie Valaskakis, and Madeline Dion Stout, eds. *Restoring the Balance: First Nations Women, Community, and Culture*. Winnipeg: University of Manitoba Press, 2008.

Notes

Note to Instructors

1 Susan D. Dion, "Beyond the Three R's: Troubling Restitution, Reconciliation & Resurgence," the Fifth Annual William Waters Symposium on Urban Education, Native Canadian Centre of Toronto, Toronto, Ontario, April 17, 2013, http://www.youtube.com/watch?v=y5CRGqUw_5k (accessed November 25, 2013).

2 See Lynn Gehl, *Ally Bill of Responsibilities*, http://www.lynngehl.com/uploads/5/0/0/4/5004954/ally_bill_of_responsibilities_poster.pdf (accessed March 3, 2015).

3 Harsha Walia, "Decolonizing Together: Moving Beyond a Politics of Solidarity Towards a Practice of Decolonization," *Briarpatch Magazine*, January 1, 2012, http://briarpatchmagazine.com/articles/view/decolonizing-together (accessed March 3, 2015).

4 Seema Ahluwalia, personal email communication, November 27, 2013.

5 This is stated by Rita Kaur Dhamoon in Corey Snelgrove, Rita Kaur Dhamoon, and Jeff Corntassel, "Unsettling Settler Colonialism: The Discourse and Politics of Settlers, and Solidarity with Indigenous Nations," *Decolonization: Indigeneity, Education & Society* 3, no. 2 (2014): 1–32, 14.

6 Ibid., 14.

7 Ibid., 16–17.

8 Environics Research Group, *Final Report: 2008 National Benchmark Survey* (Ottawa: Environics Research Group, 2008), 13. This report was prepared for Indian Residential Schools Resolution Canada and the Truth and Reconciliation Commission.

9 Ibid., 16.

10 Ibid., 5.

11 Jeffrey S. Dennis, "Bridging Understandings: Anishinaabe and White Perspectives on the Residential School Apology and Prospects for Reconciliation," in *Reading Sociology*, 2nd edition, ed. Lorne Tepperman and Angela Kalyta, 257–62. (Don Mills, ON: Oxford University Press, 2012), 257.

12 Ibid., 258–59.

13 For example, the University of the Fraser Valley hosted a conference entitled "Indigenizing the Academy," August 26–28, 2012. See the final report of the conference: Ken Brealey, *Outcomes Report for the Indigenizing the Academy Conference* (Chilliwack, BC: University of the Fraser Valley, 2013), http://blogs.ufv.ca/indigenizingtheacademy/2013/10/10/outcomes-report-for-the-indigenizing-the-academy-conference-august-26-28-2012/ (accessed November 21, 2013).

14 For example, see *Destination 2020: The University of Ottawa's Strategic Plan*, http://www.uottawa.ca/about/sites/www.uottawa.ca.about/files/destination-2020-strategic-plan.pdf (accessed August 2012), 4; University of British Columbia,

Place and Promise: The UBC Plan Annual Report 2011/2012, http://strategicplan.ubc.ca/files/2009/08/2011-12-Place-and-Promise-Annual-Report-Final-June-2012.pdf (accessed December 16, 2012), 49–56. For UBC's most recent plan to promote Indigenous engagement, see its website: http://strategicplan.ubc.ca/the-plan/aboriginal-engagement/.

15 Memorial University of Newfoundland, *Strategic Plan Submission to the Department of Education, Government on Newfoundland and Labrador, April 1, 2008 to March 31, 2011*, http://www.mun.ca/ciap/Planning/MemorialStrategicPlan2008-11.pdf, 15.

16 University of Regina, mâmawohkamâtowin*: Our Work, Our People, Our Communities* [Strategic Plan 2009–2014], http://www.uregina.ca/strategic-plan/2009-14-strategic-plan/index.html.

17 See the University of Regina's website for its most recent strategic plan: http://www.uregina.ca/strategic-plan/.

18 For UBC's most recent plan to promote Indigenous engagement, see its website: http://strategicplan.ubc.ca/the-plan/aboriginal-engagement/.

19 For this argument, see Kathleen S. Berry, "Exploring the Authority of Whiteness in Education: An Auto-Ethnographic Journey," in *The Great White North? Exploring Whiteness, Privilege and Identity in Education*, ed. Paul R. Carr and Darren E. Lund, 13–26 (Rotterdam, Netherlands: Sense Publishers, 2007), 25; James Frideres, "Being White and Being Right: Critiquing Individual and Collective Privilege," in *The Great White North? Exploring Whiteness, Privilege and Identity in Education*, ed. Paul R. Carr and Darren E. Lund, 43–54 (Rotterdam, Netherlands: Sense Publishers, 2007), 45.

20 Quoted in Berry, "Exploring the Authority of Whiteness," 20–21.

21 Ibid., 19, 21.

22 Frideres, "Being White and Being Right," 46.

23 Frideres claims that "scalping" was "introduced by Europeans who wanted to eradicate Aboriginals"; see "Being White and Being Right" 46. Others claim the practice predated Columbus among some Indigenous peoples but was corrupted by settler goals of conquest.

24 Julie Caouette and Donald M. Taylor, "'Don't Blame Me for What My Ancestors Did': Understanding The Impact of Collective White Guilt," in *The Great White North? Exploring Whiteness, Privilege and Identity in Education*, ed. Paul R. Carr and Darren E. Lund, 89–104 (Rotterdam, Netherlands: Sense Publishers, 2007).

25 Lisa Monchalin and Olga Marques, "'Canada Under Attack from Within': Problematizing 'the Natives,' Governing Borders, and the Social Injustice of the Akwesasne Border Dispute," *American Indian Culture and Research Journal* 38, no. 4 (2014).

26 Taiaiake Alfred and Lana Lowe, *Warrior Societies in Contemporary Indigenous Communities* (Ipperwash, ON: Ipperwash Inquiry, 2005), 25.

27 Wenona Victor, "*Xexa:ls* and the Power of Transformation: The *Stó:lō*, Good Governance and Self-Determination" (PhD dissertation, Simon Fraser University, 2012), 2.

28 Rikia Saddy, *We Are Canada: A Very, Very Short History of Canada* (Vancouver: Red Leaf, 2012), 53.

29 Paulette Regan, *Unsettling the Settler Within: Indian Residential Schools, Truth Telling, and Reconciliation in Canada* (Vancouver: UBC Press, 2010), 54.

30 Coalition for the Advancement of Aboriginal Studies, *Learning About Walking in Beauty: Placing Aboriginal Perspectives in Canadian Classrooms* (Toronto: Canadian Race Relations Foundation, 2002), 103.

31 Coalition for the Advancement of Aboriginal Studies, *Learning About Walking in Beauty*, 129.

32 Susan D. Dion, *Our Place in the Circle: A Review of Métis Content in Ontario Faculties of Education* (Toronto: Métis Nation of Ontario, 2012), 6.

33 Ibid., 23.

34 Fyre Jean Graveline, *Circleworks: Transforming Eurocentric Consciousness* (Halifax: Fernwood Publishing, 1998), emphasis added.

35 Coalition for the Advancement of Aboriginal Studies, *Learning About Walking in Beauty*, 38. But see also, James (Sákéj) Youngblood Henderson, "Postcolonial Ghost Dancing: Diagnosing European Colonialism," in *Reclaiming Indigenous Voices and Vision*, ed. Marie Battiste, 57–76 (Vancouver: UBC Press, 2009), 59.

36 Patricia Monture-Angus, *Thunder in My Soul: A Mohawk Woman Speaks* (Halifax: Fernwood Publishing, 1995), 88.

37 Ibid., 62.

38 Ibid., 66.

39 Ibid., 32.

40 Regan, *Unsettling the Settler Within*, 33.

41 Ibid., 50. See also Seema Ahluwalia, *Supporting Aboriginal Literacy: A Guide for Decolonizing Curricula* (Surrey, BC: Kwantlen Polytechnic University, 2009), 4.

42 Megan Boler, and Michalinos Zembylas, "Discomforting Truths: The Emotional Terrain of Understanding Difference," in *Pedagogies of Difference: Rethinking Education for Social Change*, ed. Peter Pericles Trifonas, 107–30 (New York: Routledge Falmer, 2003), 107, 108.

43 Regan, *Unsettling the Settler Within*, 52.

44 Ahluwalia, *Supporting Aboriginal Literacy*, 9.

45 As Mohawk scholar Patricia Monture-Angus explains, the physical environments of university classrooms are not supportive learning environments. She notes how classrooms have a rigid setup, with fixed seating and rows. Professors are typically at the front of the room, sometimes behind podiums or up on a pedestal. She explains that universities offer an incomplete place to learn. Although they do involve education of the mind, they are not set up in a way that incorporates the education of "body, spirit and emotion"; see Patricia Monture-Angus, *Thunder in My Soul: A Mohawk Women Speaks* (Halifax: Fernwood Publishing, 1995), 83–84.

46 Margaret Kovach, *Indigenous Methodologies: Characteristics, Conversations, and Contexts* (Toronto: University of Toronto Press, 2009), 59.

47 Monture-Angus, *Thunder in My Soul*, 68.

48 Leanne Simpson, *Dancing on Our Turtle's Back: Stories of Nishnaabeg Re-Creation, Resurgence and a New Emergence* (Winnipeg: Arbeiter Ring Publishing, 2011), 49.

49 As quoted by J. Edward Chamberlin, *If This Is Your Land, Where are Your Stories: Finding Common Ground* (Toronto: Vintage, 2004), 79.

50 For practical advice, see the following books, the first by a Maori scholar and the second by a Nêhíyaw and Saulteaux scholar: Linda Tuhiwai Smith, *Decolonizing Methodologies: Research and Indigenous Peoples*, 2nd edition (London: Zed Books, 2012); Margaret Kovach, *Indigenous Methodologies: Characteristics, Conversations, and Contexts* (Toronto: University of Toronto Press, 2009).

Introduction and Purpose

1 Taiaiake Alfred, *Peace, Power, Righteousness: An Indigenous Manifesto*, 2nd edition (Don Mills, ON: Oxford University Press, 2009), 67.
2 Ibid., 66.
3 *Occupy Love*, DVD, directed by Velcrow Ripper (Vancouver: Fierce Love Films, 2013).
4 Alfred, *Peace, Power, Righteousness*, 167–68.
5 Vine Deloria, Jr., *Custer Died for Your Sins: An Indian Manifesto* (New York: Macmillan, 1969), 251–52.
6 As quoted in, *I AM: The Documentary*, DVD, directed by Tom Shadyac (Flying Eye Productions in association with Homemade Canvas Production, 2012).
7 Paulo Freire, *Pedagogy of the Oppressed* (New York: Continuum International Publishing Group, 1970), 125–26. This edition was reprinted in 1993, 2011, and 2012.
8 Mario Barrera, *Race and Class in the Southwest: A Theory of Racial Inequality* (Notre Dame, IN: University of Notre Dame Press, 1979), 193.
9 Arthur Manuel, "Colonial Oppression at Elsipogtog: Right to Self-Determination," *Last Real Indians*, http://lastrealindians.com/colonial-oppression-at-elsipogtog-right-to-self-determination-by-arthur-manuel/ (accessed March 24, 2014).
10 Taiaiake Alfred, "Beyond the Three R's: Troubling Restitution, Reconciliation & Resurgence," the Fifth Annual William Waters Symposium on Urban Education, Native Canadian Centre of Toronto, Toronto, Ontario, April 17, 2013, http://www.youtube.com/watch?v=y5CRGqUw_5k (accessed November 25, 2013).
11 Linda Tuhiwai Smith, *Decolonizing Methodologies: Research and Indigenous Peoples*, 2nd edition (London: Zed Books, 2012), 94–95.
12 Alfred, "Beyond the Three R's."
13 George Erasmus, "Address for the Launch of the Report of the Royal Commission on Aboriginal Peoples," *Publications: Aboriginal Affairs and Northern Development Canada*, http://www.aadnc-aandc.gc.ca/eng/ 1100100014639/1100100014640 (accessed November 27, 2013).
14 The use of the word "forefathers" is purposeful and alludes to European disregard of women's contributions.

Chapter 1

1 Mary Jane Norris, "Aboriginal Languages in Canada: Generational Perspectives on Language Maintenance, Loss, and Revitalization," in *Visions of the Heart: Canadian Aboriginal Issues*, 3rd edition, ed. David Long and Olive Patricia Dickason, 113–48 (Don Mills, ON: Oxford University Press, 2011), 113.
2 Lynda Gray, *First Nations 101: Tons of Stuff You Need to Know about First Nations People* (Vancouver: Adaawx Publishing, 2011), 162.
3 *Online Etymology Dictionary*, http://www.etymonline.com/index.php?allowed_in_frame=0&search=Ab&searchmode=none (accessed February 2, 2015); *Dictionary.com*, http://dictionary.reference.com/browse/ab- (accessed February 2, 2015).
4 Gray, *First Nations 101*, 162.

5 *Online Etymology Dictionary*, http://www.etymonline.com/index.php?allowed_in_frame=0&search=aboriginal&searchmode=none (accessed December 1, 2013).

6 Constitution Act, 1982, being Schedule B to the Canada Act, 1982 (UK), 1982, c. 11. at s. 35.

7 *Online Etymology Dictionary*, http://www.etymonline.com/index.php?term=native&allowed_in_frame=0 (accessed December 1, 2013); John Schertow, Ahniwanika, "Anishinabek Outlaw Term 'Aboriginal,'" *Intercontinental Cry*, June 30, 2008, https://intercontinentalcry.org/anishinabek-outlaw-term-aboriginal/ (accessed December 16, 2012).

8 *Online Etymology Dictionary*, http://www.etymonline.com/index.php?term=indigenous&allowed_in_frame=0 (accessed August 15, 2015).

9 Strategic Alliance of Broadcasting for Aboriginal Reflection, *Key Terminology Guidebook for Reporting on Aboriginal Topics*, http://www.sabar.ca/wp-content/uploads/2012/06/SABAR-Glossary-English-Final.pdf (accessed December 7, 2013), 5.

10 Schertow, "Anishinabek Outlaw Term 'Aboriginal.'"

11 Georges Sioui, *For An Amerindian Autohistory* (Montreal: McGill-Queen's University Press, 1992), 3.

12 Patricia Monture-Angus, *Thunder in My Soul: A Mohawk Woman Speaks* (Halifax: Fernwood Publishing, 1995), 2.

13 Schertow, "Anishinabek Outlaw Term 'Aboriginal.'"

14 Monture-Angus, *Thunder in My Soul*, 31.

15 Joan A. Lovisek, "Algonquins/Subarctic," in *Aboriginal Peoples of Canada: A Short Introduction*, ed. Paul Robert Magocsi, 98–128 (Toronto: University of Toronto Press, 2002), 102. *Nitassinan* is the term used by Innu peoples to describe the place they inhabit; it means "our land."

16 The terms "Naskapi" and "Montagnais" are still used to differentiate two of the three dialects of the Eastern Cree. The Naskapi dialect is used by the Schefferville and Natuashish Innu; the remaining Innu communities used the Montagnais dialect. For information on the naming of the Innu and Wendat peoples, see Lovisek, "Algonquins/Subarctic," 102.

17 Georges Sioui, *Histoires de Kanatha: Vues et Contées / Histories of Kanatha: Seen and Told,* (Ottawa: University of Ottawa Press, 2008), 151.

18 Constitution Act, 1982, being Schedule B to the Canada Act, 1982 (UK), 1982, c. 11. at s. 35.

19 Mary Jane Norris, "Aboriginal Peoples in Canada: Demographic and Linguistic Perspectives," in *Visions of the Heart: Canadian Aboriginal Issues*, 2nd ed., ed. David Long and Olive Patricia Dickason, 167–236 (Toronto: Harcourt Brace Canada, 2000), 168.

20 Statistics Canada, *2006 Census Dictionary* (Ottawa: Statistics Canada, 2008), http://www12.statcan.ca/census-recensement/2006/ref/dict/index-eng.cfm (accessed November 4, 2012).

21 Norris, "Aboriginal Peoples in Canada: Demographic," 168.

22 The Métis Nation of Saskatchewan, "Citizenship and Registry," http://www.mn-s.ca/pages/citizenship-and-registry.html (accessed November 13, 2013); The Métis Nation of Alberta, "Definition of Métis," http://www.albertametis.com/mnahome/mna-membership-definition.aspx (accessed November 13, 2013).

23 The Métis Nation of Alberta, "Definition of Métis."

24 Manitoba Metis Federation, *Who Are the Metis?*, http://www.mmf.mb.ca/who_are_the_metis.php (accessed November 13, 2013).
25 Sharon Stewart, *Louis Riel: Firebrand* (Toronto: Dundurn, 2007), 2.
26 Ibid., 67, 174.
27 Joesph Howard, *Strange Empire: Louis Riel and the Métis People* (Toronto: James Lorimer & Company, 1974), 367.
28 Arthur J. Ray refers to this as "Red River myopia, whereby Métis from other places receive little attention." See Arthur J. Ray, "Reflections on Métis and Fur Trade Social History in Canada," *American Indian Culture and Research Journal* 6, no. 2 (1982): 91–107.
29 These sentiments were expressed in discussions that followed Jean Teillet's presentation on Métis history at the Association for Canadian Studies and the Canadian Ethnic Association Joint Annual Conference: *Ethnicity, Governance and Social Justice: Linking Canada to the World*, Toronto, Ontario, November 6, 2010.
30 Lawrence J. Barkwell, Norman Fleury, and the Manitoba Métis Federation, *La Lawng—Michif Peekishkwewin: The Heritage Language of the Canadian Metis* (Winnipeg: Manitoba Metis Federation / Pemmican Publications, 2004), 6.
31 Chris Andersen, *"Métis" Race, Recognition, and the Struggle for Indigenous Peoplehood* (Vancouver: UBC Press, 2014), 11.
32 All quotations in this paragraph not attributed are from Andersen, *"Métis" Race, Recognition*, 24.
33 *R. v. Powley*, [2003] 2 S.C.R. 207, 2003 SCC 43, at para. 10.
34 Constitution Act, 1867 (UK), 30 & 31 Vict, c. 3, reprinted in RSC 1985, App II, No 5. At s.91(24); *Daniels v. Canada (Indian Affairs and Northern Development)*, 2013 FC 6, [2013] 2 F.C.R. 268, at para. 619.
35 Constitution Act, 1982, being Schedule B to the Canada Act, 1982 (UK), 1982, c. 11. at s. 35. Constitution Act, 1867 (UK), 30 & 31 Vict, c. 3, reprinted in RSC 1985, App II, No 5. at s.91(24).
36 Canadian Press, "Court of Appeal Upholds Landmark Ruling on Rights of Métis," *CBC News*, April 17, 2014, http://www.cbc.ca/news/aboriginal/court-of-appeal-upholds-landmark-ruling-on-rights-of-m%C3%A9tis-1.2613834 (accessed April 19, 2014).
37 Pamela D. Palmater, *Beyond Blood: Rethinking Indigenous Identity* (Saskatoon, SK: Purich Publishing, 2011), 21; Indian Act, R.S.C. 1985, c. I-5. at s. 4(1).
38 Inuit Tapiriit Kanatami (ITK), *Inuit Regions of Canada*, https://www.itk.ca/about-inuit/inuit-regions-canada (accessed February 2, 2015).
39 Statistics Canada, *Aboriginal Peoples in Canada in 2006: Inuit, Métis and First Nations 2006 Census: Findings*, Analysis Series (Ottawa, Statistics Canada, 2008).
40 Statistics Canada, *Aboriginal Peoples in Canada: First Nations People, Métis, and Inuit, National Household Survey, 2011* (Ottawa: Statistics Canada, 2013). This random sample survey of 4.5 million dwellings equals to slightly less than one-third (30 per cent) of private dwellings in 2011.
41 Statistics Canada, *NHS: Data Quality*, http://www12.statcan.gc.ca/NHS-ENM/2011/ref/about-apropos/nhs-enm_r005-eng.cfm (accessed November 29, 2013).
42 Statistics Canada, *Aboriginal Peoples in Canada: First Nations People, Métis, and Inuit, National Household Survey, 2011* (Ottawa: Statistics Canada, 2013), 6.
43 Statistics Canada, *Aboriginal Peoples in Canada in 2006.*

44 From 1996 to 2001, the fertility rate among all Canadian women was 1.5 children over a woman's lifetime, yet, for Indigenous women, the rate was 2.6. Inuit women are estimated to have about 3.4 children each, First Nations women about 2.9, and Métis about 2.2. For details see Vivian O'Donnell and Susan Wallace, *Women in Canada: A Gender-Based Statistical Report: First Nations, Métis and Inuit Women* (Ottawa: Statistics Canada, Ministry of Industry, 2011), 20.

45 Andrew J. Siggner, "The Challenge of Measuring the Demographic and Socio-Economic Conditions of the Urban Aboriginal Population," in *Not Strangers in These Parts: Urban Aboriginal Peoples*, ed. David Newhouse and Evelyn Peters, 119–30 (Ottawa: Policy Research Initiative, 2003), 119; Eric Guimond, "Fuzzy Definitions and Population Explosion: Changing Identities of Aboriginal Groups in Canada," in *Not Strangers in These Parts: Urban Aboriginal Peoples*, ed. David Newhouse and Evelyn Peters, 35–49 (Ottawa: Policy Research Initiative, 2003), 42; Norris, "Aboriginal Peoples in Canada: Demographic," 189.

46 Andrew J. Siggner and Rosalinda Costa, *Aboriginal Conditions in Census Metropolitan Areas, 1981–2001* (Ottawa: Statistics Canada, 2005), 11.

47 Palmater, *Beyond Blood*, 19.

48 Ibid., 29.

49 Ibid., 19.

50 Justice Murray Sinclair, "Rheal Brant Hall Lecture: Truth and Reconciliation" [public lecture], Carleton University, Ottawa, October 15, 2010.

51 Department of Indian Affairs and Northern Development, *Explanatory Paper: Proposed Amendments to the Indian Act Affecting Indian Registration* (Gatineau, QC: Department of Indian Affairs and Northern Development, 2010), 4.

52 Aboriginal Affairs and Northern Development, *Registered Indian Demography: Population, Household and Family Projections, 2004–2029* (Ottawa: Canadian Mortgage and Housing, 2004), https://www.aadnc-aandc.gc.ca/eng/1100100016838/1100100016855.

53 Ian F. Haney-López, "The Social Construction of Race: Some Observations on Illusion, Fabrication, and Choice," *Harvard Civil Rights–Civil Liberties Law Review* 29 (1994): 15–16, http://scholarship.law.berkeley.edu/facpubs/1815/ (accessed December 4, 2013).

54 Daniel N. Paul, *First Nations History: We Were Not the Savages—Collision between European and Native American Civilizations*, 3rd edition (Halifax: Fernwood, 2006), 7.

55 Haney-López, "The Social Construction of Race," 13.

56 As quoted in Lorelei Anne Lambert Colomeda, *Keepers of the Central Fire: Issues in Ecology for Indigenous Peoples* (Sudbury, MA: Jones and Bartlett Publishers, 1999), 5.

57 While doing my PhD at the University of Ottawa I had informal conversations with Professor George Sioui. In one of these conversations, I admitted to being self-conscious about my blue eyes, which is what began the conversation of how Wendat people and others would adopt Europeans into their nations.

58 For example, as described in the Navajo context, see Ellen McCullough-Brabson and Marilyn Help, *We'll Be in Your Mountains, We'll Be in Your Songs: A Navajo Woman Sings* (Albuquerque: University of New Mexico Press, 2001), 91.

59 As quoted by Lawrence Wright, "One Drop of Blood," in *Facing Difference: Race, Gender, and Mass Media*, ed. Shirley Biagi and Marilyn Kern-Foxworth, 227–36 (Thousand Oaks, CA: Pine Forge Press, 1997), 230.

60 Roland Chrisjohn and Sherri Young with Michael Maraun, *The Circle Game: Shadows and Substance in the Indian Residential School Experience in Canada* (Penticton: Theytus Books, 2006), 61. Duncan Scott, head of the Department of Indian Affairs from 1913 to 1932, made this public statement in 1920 and in reference to Bill-14. This bill was an amendment to the Indian Act which then allowed the federal government to enfranchise anyone it saw fit (enfranchisement meant losing "Indian" status); there was also a reinstatement of the government's right to impel attendance at residential schools.

61 Jennifer S.H. Brown, "Métis," *The Canadian Encyclopedia*, 2009, http://www.thecanadianencyclopedia.com/articles/metis (accessed December 27, 2012). This article was first published January 7, 2009 and last edited on March 4, 2015.

62 Palmater, *Beyond Blood*, 19.

63 Bonita Lawrence, *"Real" Indians and Others: Mixed Blood Urban Native Peoples and Indigenous Nationhood* (Lincoln: University of Nebraska Press, 2004), 7. See p. 38 for a discussion of how Canadian policy separates Indigenous peoples from their lands.

64 Harold Cardinal, *The Unjust Society* (Vancouver: Douglas & McIntyre, 1999).

65 Jeff J. Corntassel, "An Activist Posing as an Academic?" *American Indian Quarterly* 27, nos. 1 & 2 (2003), 164–65.

66 Jennifer David, "Aboriginal Issues: Discovering True Potential," *CAPITALWOMAN Magazine*, September 21, 2012, 33.

67 Ibid.

68 Sheila Carr-Stewart, "A Treaty Right to Education," *Canadian Journal of Education* 25, no. 2 (2001): 125–43, 125.

69 Quotations taken from Treaties 1–9 and 11 come from the following sources: *Treaties 1 and 2 Between Her Majesty The Queen and the Chippewa and Cree Indians of Manitoba and Country Adjacent with Adhesions*, transcribed from Edmond Cloutier, Queen's Printer and Controller of Stationery Ottawa, 1957 (Gatineau, QC: Aboriginal Affairs and Northern Development Canada), http://www.aadnc-aandc.gc.ca/eng/1100100028664/1100100028665 (accessed December 6, 2013); *Treaty 3 between Her Majesty the Queen and the Saulteaux Tribe of the Ojibbeway Indians at the Northwest Angle on the Lake of the Woods with Adhesions*, reprinted 1966 and 1978, transcribed from Roger Duhamel, Queen's Printer and Controller of Stationery, Ottawa, 1966 (Gatineau, QC: Aboriginal Affairs and Northern Development Canada), http://www.aadnc-aandc.gc.ca/eng/1100100028675/1100100028679 (accessed December 6, 2013); *Treaty No. 4 between Her Majesty the Queen and the Cree and Saulteaux Tribes of Indians at the Qu'appelle and Fort Ellice*, transcribed from Roger Duhamel, Queen's Printer and Controller of Stationery, Ottawa, 1966 (Gatineau, QC: Aboriginal Affairs and Northern Development Canada), http://www.aadnc-aandc.gc.ca/eng/1100100028689/1100100028690 (accessed December 6, 2013); *Treaty 5 between Her Majesty the Queen and the Saulteaux and Swampy Cree Tribes of Indians at Beren's River and Norway House with Adhesions*, transcribed from The Queen's Printer, Ottawa, 1969 (Gatineau, QC: Aboriginal Affairs and Northern Development Canada), http://www.aadnc-aandc.gc.ca/eng/1100100028699/1100100028700 (accessed December 6, 2013); *Copy of Treaty No. 6 between Her Majesty the Queen and the Plain and Wood Cree Indians and other Tribes of Indians at Fort Carlton, Fort Pitt and Battle River with Adhesions*, transcribed from Roger Duhamel, Queen's

Printer and Controller of Stationery, Ottawa, 1964 (Gatineau, QC: Aboriginal Affairs and Northern Development Canada), http://www.aadnc-aandc.gc.ca/eng/1100100028710/1100100028783 (accessed December 6, 2013); *Copy of Treaty and Supplementary Treaty No. 7 between Her Majesty the Queen and the Blackfeet and Other Indian Tribes, at the Blackfoot Crossing of Bow River and Fort Macleod*, reprinted from the edition of 1877 by Roger Duhamel, Queen's Printer and Controller of Stationery, Ottawa, 1966 (Gatineau, QC: Aboriginal Affairs and Northern Development Canada), http://www.aadnc-aandc.gc.ca/eng/1100100028793/1100100028803 (accessed December 6, 2013); *Treaty No. 8 Made June 21, 1899 and Adhesions, Reports, Etc.*, reprinted from file the 1899 edition by Roger Duhamel, Queen's Printer and Controller of Stationery, Ottawa, 1966 (Gatineau, QC: Aboriginal Affairs and Northern Development Canada), http://www.aadnc-aandc.gc.ca/eng/1100100028813/1100100028853 (accessed December 6, 2013); *The James Bay Treaty—Treaty No. 9 (Made in 1905 and 1906) and Adhesions Made in 1929 and 1930*, reprinted from the edition of 1931 by Roger Duhamel, Queen's Printer and Controller of Stationery, Ottawa, 1964 (Gatineau, QC: Aboriginal Affairs and Northern Development Canada), http://www.aadnc-aandc.gc.ca/eng/1100100028863/1100100028864 (accessed December 6, 2013); *Treaty No. 11 (June 27, 1921) and Adhesion (July 17, 1922) with Reports, etc.*, reprinted from the edition of 1926 by Edmond Cloutier, Queen's Printer and Controller of Stationery, Ottawa, 1957 (Gatineau, QC: Aboriginal Affairs and Northern Development Canada), http://www.aadnc-aandc.gc.ca/eng/1100100028916/1100100028947 (accessed December 6, 2013).

70 Carr-Stewart, "A Treaty Right to Education," 129.

71 *Treaty No. 10 and Reports of Commissioners,* reprinted from the edition of 1907 by Roger Duhamel, Queen's Printer and Controller of Stationery Ottawa, 1966 (Gatineau, QC: Aboriginal Affairs and Northern Development Canada), http://www.aadnc-aandc.gc.ca/eng/1100100028874/1100100028906 (accessed December 6, 2013).

72 United Nations, *The United Nations Declaration on the Rights of Indigenous Peoples* (Geneva: United Nations, 2008), 7.

73 Carr-Stewart, "A Treaty Right to Education," 132; Constitution Act, 1867 (UK), 30 & 31 Vict, c. 3, reprinted in RSC 1985, App II, No 5. at s. 91(24).

74 Carr-Stewart, "A Treaty Right to Education," 130.

75 Ibid., 130, 126.

76 Ibid., 131.

77 See *An Act to Amend and Consolidate the Laws Respecting Indians*, S.C. 1876, c.18 (39 Vict). at s. 2.

78 Carr-Stewart, "A Treaty Right to Education," 126.

79 Constitution Act, 1982, being Schedule B to the *Canada Act 1982* (UK), 1982, c. 11. at s. 35 (1).

80 Information in this paragraph on educational funding for First Nations is from Chiefs Assembly on Education, *Federal Funding for First Nations Schools* (Gatineau, QC: Palais des Congrès de Gatineau, 2012), http://www.afn.ca/uploads/files/events/fact_sheet-ccoe-8.pdf (accessed December 27, 2012).

81 Carr-Stewart, "A Treaty Right to Education," 130.

82 Dakshana Bascaramurty, "Note to Justin Bieber: There is No Free Gas for Aboriginals," *The Globe and Mail*, August, 3 2012, http://www.theglobeandmail.

com/news/national/note-to-justin-bieber-there-is-no-free-gas-for-aboriginals/article4461037/ (accessed December 18 2012).

83 Indian Act, RSC 1985, c. I-5. at s. 87.

84 CBC, "SOAP BOX: Wab Kinew on First Nations Stereotypes," *George Stroumboulopoulos Tonight*, November 24, 2012, http://www.cbc.ca/strombo/canada/soap-box-wab-kinew-on-first-nations-stereotypes.html. This clip is also available on YouTube: https://www.youtube.com/watch?v=GlkuRCXdu5A.

85 Assembly of First Nations, *The $9 Billion Myth Exposed: Why First Nations Poverty Endures*, http://www.crr.ca/divers-files/en/publications/reports/diversReports/mythExposed.pdf (accessed December 4, 2013).

86 The word "forefathers" is used purposefully, given European disregard of women's contributions.

87 For more details on the history described in this paragraph, see Lynda Gray, *First Nations 101: Tons of Stuff You Need to Know about First Nations People* (Vancouver: Adaawx Publishing, 2011), 8.

88 CBC, "SOAP BOX: Wab Kinew on First Nations Stereotypes."

89 George Santayana, *Reason in Common Sense: Vol. 1: The Life of Reason* (New York: Dover Publications, 1980), 284.

90 Data are from *Leadership Action Plan on First Nations Child Welfare* (Ottawa: Assembly of First Nations, 2006), http://www.turtleisland.org/healing/afncf.pdf (accessed December 19, 2012), 1.

91 Gray, *First Nations 101*, 7.

Chapter 2

1 Margaret Kovach, *Indigenous Methodologies: Characteristics, Conversations, and Contexts* (Toronto: University of Toronto Press, 2009), 163.

2 Duncan McCue, "Keynote Presentation," ACCC Symposium Serving Indigenous Learners and Communities, Vancouver, BC, December 2, 2013.

3 Jeannette Armstrong, "Sharing One's Skin," *Cultural Survival* 30, no. 4 (2006): 16–17, http://www.culturalsurvival.org/publications/cultural-survival-quarterly/canada/sharing-one-skin (accessed December 8, 2013).

4 Kovach, *Indigenous Methodologies*, 30.

5 Leroy Little Bear, "Jagged Worldviews Colliding," in *Reclaiming Indigenous Voices and Vision*, ed. Marie Battiste, 78–85 (Vancouver: UBC Press, 2009), 78.

6 The idea of the "health of the land, is the health of the people" has been cited in various other contexts before. For instance, this idea is expressed and further explained in: Brenda Parlee, Fikret Berkes, and the Teetl'it Gwich'in Renewable Resources Council, "Health of the Land, Health of the People: A Case Study on Gwich'in Berry Harvesting in Northern Canada," *EcoHealth*, 2 (2005): 127–37. The quote "what we do to the land, we do to ourselves" is a quote by American writer, poet, and environmental activist, Wendell Berry. Quoted in David R. Montgomery, *Dirt: Erosion of Civilizations* (Los Angeles: University of California Press, 2007), 1.

7 The Circle of Turtle Lodge, *Anishnabe 101* (Golden Lake, ON: The Circle of Turtle Lodge, 2010), 7.

8 Jack D. Forbes, *Columbus and Other Cannibals: The Wetiko Disease of Exploitation, Imperialism, and Terrorism* (New York: Autonomedia, 1992), 32.

9 Joseph M. Marshall III, *The Lakota Way: Stories and Lessons for Living* (New York: Viking Compass, 2001), 193–95.

10 Dawn Martin Hill, *Traditional Medicine in Contemporary Contexts: Protecting and Respecting Indigenous Knowledge and Medicine* (Ottawa: National Aboriginal Health Organization, 2003), 7.

11 Wenona Victor, "*Xexa:ls* and the Power of Transformation: The *Stó:lō*, Good Governance and Self-Determination" (PhD dissertation, Simon Fraser University, 2012), 19–20.

12 Lesley Malloch, "Indian Medicine, Indian Health: Study between Red and White Medicine," *Canadian Women Studies* 10, nos. 1 & 2 (1989): 105–113, 107.

13 Lynda Gray, *First Nations 101: Tons of Stuff You Need to Know about First Nations People* (Vancouver: Adaawx Publishing, 2011), 33.

14 Ibid.

15 Dr. Reg Crowshoe and Geoff Crow Eagle, *Piikani Blackfoot Teachings: Transcripts for Four Directions Teachings.com* (Toronto: Invert Media, 2006), http://www.fourdirectionsteachings.com/transcripts/blackfoot.pdf (accessed December 11, 2013), 2–3.

16 S.M Stiegelbauer, "What Is an Elder? What Do Elders Do? First Nations Elders as Teachers in Culture-Based Urban Organizations," *The Canadian Journal of Native Studies* 16, no. 1 (1996): 33–66, 39.

17 Walter Lightning, "Compassionate Mind: Implications of a Text Written by Elder Louis Sunchild," *Canadian Journal of Native Education* 19, no. 2 (1992): 215–53, as quoted in Jo-ann Archibald, *Indigenous Storywork: Educating the Heart, Mind, Body, and Spirit* (Vancouver: UBC Press, 2008), 13.

18 Georges E. Sioui, *Huron Wendat: The Heritage of the Circle* (Vancouver: UBC Press, 1999), 114.

19 Georges Sioui, *Histoires de Kanatha: Vues et Contées / Histories of Kanatha: Seen and Told* (Ottawa: University of Ottawa Press, 2008).

20 Ibid.; Vandana Shiva, "Forward: Cultural Diversity and the Politics of Knowledge," in *Indigenous Knowledges in Global Contexts: Multiple Readings of Our World*, ed. George J. Sefa Dei, Budd L. Hall, and Dorothy Goldin Rosenberg, vii–x (Toronto: University of Toronto Press, 2000).

21 Leroy Little Bear, "Jagged Worldviews Colliding," in *Reclaiming Indigenous Voices and Vision*, ed. Marie Battiste, 77–85 (Vancouver: UBC Press, 2009), 82.

22 Sioui, *Histoires de Kanatha*, 83.

23 This quotation and the material that follows comes from Crowshoe and Crow Eagle, *Piikani Blackfoot Teachings*, 3.

24 The term "white man" is being used so as not to change the perspective of the elders. This is the term they use, and its use is important to relay their perspective.

25 Crowshoe and Crow Eagle, *Piikani Blackfoot Teachings*, 4.

26 As quoted in Jacob Devaney, "Idle No More: Hints of a Global Super-Movement," *Huffington Post*, January 2, 2013, http://www.huffingtonpost.com/jacob-devaney/idle-no-more-the-beauty-o_b_2393053.html (accessed December 7, 2013).

27 Basil Johnston, *The Manitous: The Spiritual World of the Ojibway* (St. Paul: Minnesota Historical Society Press, 1995), 15.

28 David Newhouse, "Indigenous Knowledge in a Multicultural World," *Native Studies Review* 15, no. 2 (2004): 139–54, 144.

29 Ibid., 150.
30 Ibid., 153.
31 Kenneth Robinson, "Do Schools Kill Creativity?" *TED Talk* [Filmed February 2006], http://www.ted.com/talks/ken_robinson_says_schools_kill_creativity.html (accessed December 7, 2013).
32 David F. Peat, *Lighting the Seventh Fire—The Spiritual Ways, Healing and Science of the Native American* (New York: Carol Publishing Group, 1994), as quoted in Newhouse, "Indigenous Knowledge in a Multicultural World," 151.
33 Marlene Brant Castellano, "Updating Aboriginal Traditions of Knowledge," in *Indigenous Knowledges in Global Contexts: Multiple Readings of Our World*, ed. George J. Sefa Dei, Budd L. Hall, and Dorothy Goldin Rosenberg, 21–36 (Toronto: University of Toronto Press, 2000), 25; see page 30.
34 Margaret Kovach, *Indigenous Methodologies: Characteristics, Conversations, and Contexts* (Toronto: University of Toronto Press, 2009), 57, 117.
35 Ibid., 56.
36 Newhouse, "Indigenous Knowledge in a Multicultural World," 152.
37 Ibid., 144, 152.
38 Archibald, *Indigenous Storywork*, 1.
39 Castellano, "Updating Aboriginal Traditions of Knowledge."
40 Ibid.
41 CTV, "Aboriginal Video Game Puts Modern Twist on Tradition of Storytelling," *CTV News Montréal*, October 20, 2012, http://montreal.ctvnews.ca/aboriginal-video-game-puts-modern-twist-on-tradition-of-storytelling-1.1003880.
42 The Circle of Turtle Lodge, *Anishnabe 101*, 2.
43 For example, see *Anishnabe 101* by The Circle of Turtle Lodge, which teaches the philosophical ways of Anishinaabe peoples.
44 Many teachings outside of those included in this book exist; these come from many of the various different nations across Turtle Island, and some of these teachings have been put into writing. If you are interested in learning more, you are encouraged to seek out teachings from elders and knowledge keepers.
45 All quotations and information in this paragraph are from Edward Benton-Banai, *The Mishomis Book: The Voice of the Ojibway* (Minneapolis: University of Minnesota Press, 2010), 60–66.
46 For example, see David Bouchard and Dr. Joseph Martin, *Seven Sacred Teachings: Niizhwaaswi Gagiikwewin* (North Vancouver: More Than Words Publishers, 2009).
47 Crowshoe and Crow Eagle, *Piikani Blackfoot Teachings*, 1.
48 John G. Neihardt, *Black Elk Speaks: Being the Life Story of a Holy Man of the Oglala Sioux*, premier edition (Albany: State University of New York Press, 2008), 155–56.
49 Archibald, *Indigenous Storywork*, 11.
50 Georges Sioui, *For an Amerindian Autohistory* (Montreal: McGill-Queen's University Press, 1992), 8 and 11.
51 Sioui, *For an Amerindian Autohistory*, 10; Sharilyn Calliou, "Peacekeeping Actions at Home: A Medicine Wheel Model for a Peacekeeping Pedagogy," in *First Nations Education in Canada: The Circle Unfolds*, ed. Marie Battiste and Jean Barman, 47–72 (Vancouver: UBC Press, 1995), 51.

52 This and all quotations attributed to Mary Lee are from Mary Lee, *Cree (Nehiyawak) Teachings: Transcripts for Four Directions Teachings.com* (Toronto: Invert Media, 2006), http://www.fourdirectionsteachings.com/transcripts/cree.pdf (accessed December 11, 2013), 1.

53 Lillian Pitawanakwat, *Ojibwe/Powawatomi (Anishinabe) Teachings: Transcripts for Four Directions Teachings.com* (Toronto: Invert Media, 2006), http://www.fourdirectionsteachings.com/transcripts/ojibwe.pdf (accessed December 11, 2013), 1.

54 Lynn Gehl, *Anishinaabeg Stories: Featuring Petroglyphs, Petrographs, and Wampum Belts* (Southampton, ON: Ningwakwe Learning Press, 2012), 48.

55 Calliou, "Peacekeeping Actions at Home," 52 for the first quote, and page 53 for the second.

56 Sioui, *For an Amerindian Autohistory*, 10.

57 Benton-Banai, *The Mishomis Book*, 63.

58 Margaret Kovach, *Indigenous Methodologies: Characteristics, Conversations, and Contexts* (Toronto: University of Toronto Press, 2009), 127.

59 Dee Brown, *Bury My Heart at Wounded Knee: An Indian History of the American West* (New York: Holt, Rinehart & Winston, 1970), 311.

60 Joseph M. Marshall III, *The Lakota Way: Stories and Lessons for Living* (New York: Viking Compass, 2001), 9–10, 18.

61 Evan S. Connell, *Son of the Morning Star: Custer and the Little Bighorn* (New York: North Star Press, 1984), 72.

62 The Circle of Turtle Lodge, *Anishnabe 101*, 3.

63 Kovach, *Indigenous Methodologies*, 102–03.

64 Ibid., 110; see also page 98 for discussion of this protocol.

65 Patricia Monture-Angus, *Thunder in My Soul: A Mohawk Women Speaks* (Halifax: Fernwood Publishing, 1995), 86.

66 The Circle of Turtle Lodge, *Anishnabe 101*, 3.

Chapter 3

1 Pamela Williamson and John A. Roberts, *First Nations People*, 2nd edition (Toronto: Emond Montgomery Publications, 2004), 182.

2 John L. Steckley and Bryan D. Cummins, *Full Circle: Canada's First Nations* (Toronto: Pearson, Prentice Hall, 2008), 234.

3 Some Indigenous people consider North America as Turtle Island—not all. For example, there are Indigenous people in the West and in northern areas of Canada who do not identify with calling the land Turtle Island.

4 See Leanne Simpson, *Dancing on Our Turtle's Back: Stories of Nishnaabeg Re-Creation, Resurgence, and a New Emergence* (Winnipeg: Arbeiter Ring Publishing, 2011), 35–39 for the Nishnaabeg creation story as told to her by Edna Manitowabi.

5 Tom Porter, *Mohawk (Haudenosaunee) Teachings: Transcripts for Four Directions Teachings.com* (Toronto: Invert Media, 2006), 1–2, http://www.fourdirectionsteachings.com/transcripts/mohawk.pdf (accessed December 11, 2013).

6 See Thomas King, *The Truth about Stories: A Native Narrative* (Minneapolis: University of Minnesota Press, 2005).

7 Dr. Reg Crowshoe and Geoff Crow Eagle, *Piikani Blackfoot Teachings: Transcripts for Four Directions Teachings.com* (Toronto: Invert Media, 2006), 3, http://www.fourdirectionsteachings.com/transcripts/blackfoot.pdf (accessed December 11, 2013).
8 Lynda Gray, *First Nations 101: Tons of Stuff You Need to Know about First Nations People* (Vancouver: Adaawx Publishing, 2011), 30.
9 Leroy Little Bear, "Jagged Worldviews Colliding," in *Reclaiming Indigenous Voices and Vision*, ed. Marie Battiste, 77–85 (Vancouver: UBC Press, 2009), 84.
10 Daniel N. Paul, *First Nations History: We Were Not the Savages—Collision between European and Native American Civilizations*, 3rd edition (Halifax: Fernwood, 2006), 18.
11 Taiaiake Alfred, *Peace, Power, Righteousness: An Indigenous Manifesto*, 2nd edition (Don Mills, ON: Oxford University Press, 2009), 45; see page 51 for information that follows.
12 Gray, *First Nations 101*, 30.
13 Menno Boldt, *Surviving as Indians: The Challenge of Self-Government* (Toronto: University of Toronto Press, 1993), 119.
14 Michael Harkin, "Whales, Chiefs, and Giants: An Exploration into Nuu-Chah-Nulth Political Thought," *Ethnology* 37, no. 4 (1998): 317–32.
15 Ibid., 328; see also page 317 for the significance of the whale.
16 Sarah Eppler Janda, *Beloved Women: The Political Lives of LaDonna Harris and Wilma Mankiller* (DeKalb: Northern Illinois University Press, 2007), 147.
17 Boldt, *Surviving as Indians*, 119.
18 Leslie Jane McMillian, "Koqqwaja'ltimk: Mi'kmaq Legal Consciousness" (PhD dissertation, University of British Columbia, 2002), 39; please note that the word "chief" is part of colonial language and is used here to reflect the language of sources.
19 John S. Milloy, *The Plains Cree: Trade, Diplomacy, and War, 1790 to 1870* (Winnipeg: The University of Manitoba Press, 1988), 77.
20 Earle H. Waugh, *Dissonant Worlds: Roger Vandersteene among the Cree* (Waterloo, ON: Wilfrid Laurier Press, 1996), 66.
21 Harkin, "Whales, Chiefs, and Giants," 324.
22 Sioui, *Huron Wendat*, 89–90.
23 Ibid., 129.
24 Christie Jefferson, *Conquest by Law* (Ottawa: Solicitor General of Canada, 1994), 26.
25 Sioui, *Huron Wendat*, 129; Bruce G. Trigger, *The Huron: Farmers of the North*, 2nd edition (New York: Holt, Rinehart and Winston, 1990), 82.
26 Sioui, *Huron Wendat*, 132; see also page 129 for the other information in this paragraph.
27 Alan D. McMillan and Eldon Yellowhorn, *First Peoples in Canada* (Vancouver: Douglas & McIntyre, 2004), 155; Jefferson, *Conquest by Law*, 47.
28 Jefferson, *Conquest by Law*, 47.
29 Ibid., 48; Thomas C. Mails, *Dog Soldiers, Bear Men & Buffalo Women* (Englewood Cliffs, NJ: Prentice Hall, 1973), 85.
30 All information in this paragraph is from *Unlocking Aboriginal Justice: Alternative Dispute Resolution for the Gitksan and Wet'suwet'en People*, proposal to the BC Ministry of the Attorney General prepared by the Gitksan-Wet'suwet'en Education Society, Smithers Indian Friendship Centre, and Upper Skeena Counselling and Legal Assistance Society, March 20, 1989, 15–17.

31 See *Unlocking Aboriginal Justice*, 15–17 for information on this governance system.
32 Crowshoe and Crow Eagle, *Piikani Blackfoot Teachings*.
33 Wenona Victor, "*Xexa:ls* and the Power of Transformation: The *Stó:lō*, Good Governance and Self-Determination" (PhD dissertation, Simon Fraser University, 2012), 245–46.
34 Ibid., 55.
35 See ibid., 246–49 for the effects of colonial legislation and Stó:lō resistance.
36 See ibid., 247, 249 for a discussion of this and information in the following two paragraphs.
37 Ibid., 285–86.
38 Ibid., 287.
39 Alfred, *Peace, Power, Righteousness*, 25.
40 Ibid., 11, 50.
41 Gerald Taiaiake Alfred, "Colonialism and State Dependency," *Journal of Aboriginal Health* 5, no. 2 (2009): 42–60, 44.
42 Alfred, *Peace, Power, Righteousness*, 29; see also pages 26 and 53.
43 Ibid., 5.
44 Theresa McCarthy, "De'ni:s nisa'sgao'de?: Haudenosaunee Clans and the Reconstruction of Traditional Haudenosaunee Identity, Citizenship, and Nationhood," *American Indian Culture and Research Journal* 34, no. 2 (2010): 81–101, 81.
45 Jefferson, *Conquest by Law*, 34.
46 "Neighbours of the Onondaga Nation: Understanding Haudenosaunee Culture," article reprinted from www.sixnations.org, the official website of the Haudenosaunee Confederacy, on the Syracuse Peace Council website: http://www.peacecouncil.net/noon/understanding-haudenosaunee-culture (accessed July 9, 2015).
47 Patricia Monture-Angus, *Thunder in My Soul: A Mohawk Woman Speaks* (Halifax: Fernwood Publishing, 1995), 32.
48 Alfred, *Peace, Power, Righteousness*, 126.
49 Ibid., 126; quotations taken from this page, but see also page 125.
50 Haudenosaunee Confederacy: The League of Nations, *The Great Law of Peace* (Ohsweken, ON: Haudenosaunee Development Institute), http://www.haudenosauneeconfederacy.com/greatlawofpeace.html (accessed January 20, 2013).
51 The four external Haudenosaunee reviewers include Kaherakwas Donna Goodleaf (EdD), executive director, Kanien'kehá:ka Onkwawén:na Raotitióhkwa Language and Cultural Center, Kahnawake Mohawk Nation Territory via Québec; Teiowisonte Tommy Dear, graphic artist, illustrator, and cultural liaison for the Kanien'kehá:ka Onkwawén:na Raotitióhkwa Language and Cultural Center, Kahnawake Mohawk Nation Territory via Québec; Perry Ground (Onondaga, Turtle Clan), project coordinator, Native American Resource Center, Rochester City School District; and Faithkeeper to the Cattaraugus Seneca Nation G. Peter Jemison (Seneca, Heron Clan), site manager, Ganondagan State Historic Site (Victor, NY). Reviewers from the museum included one Haudenosaunee person and four additional people, two of them from other First Nations: Stephanie Betancourt (Seneca), Clare Cuddy, Gaetana De Gennaro (Tohono O'odham), Edwin Schupan (Muscogee), and Shawn Termin. There were two editors from the museum, and these included one Haudenosaunee person, Alexandra Harris, and Tim Johnson (Mohawk). National Museum of the American Indian,

Haudenosaunee Guide for Educators (Washington, DC: National Museum of the American Indian, Smithsonian Institution, Education Office, 2009), 21.

52 National Museum of the American Indian, *Haudenosaunee Guide*, 2.

53 The Dish with One Spoon, *The Great Law—The White Roots of Peace* [YouTube documentary], January 4, 2012 http://www.youtube.com/watch?v=NVcuO9uwJ3E (accessed December 15, 2013).

54 See Sotsisowah, "Thoughts of Peace: The Great Law," in *Basic Call to Consciousness*, ed. Akwesasne Notes, 31–40 (Summertown: Native Voices, 1981) for the interpretation that follows.

55 Ibid., 34.

56 See National Museum of the American Indian, *Haudenosaunee Guide for Educators*, 2, for the interpretation that follows.

57 For information of the Haudenosaunee governance structure, see National Museum of the American Indian, *Haudenosaunee Guide for Educators*, 3–4.

58 Doug George-Kanentiio, *Iroquois Culture & Commentary* (Santa Fe, CA: Clear Light Publishers, 2000), 96.

59 National Museum of the American Indian, *Haudenosaunee Guide for Educators*, 3–4.

60 Gray, *First Nations 101*, 31.

61 National Museum of the American Indian, *Haudenosaunee Guide for Educators*, 2.

62 United States Congress, *Concurrent Resolution to Acknowledge the Contribution of the Iroquois Confederacy of Nations*, 100th Cong., 2nd sess., H. Con. Res. 331, October 5, 1998, http://www.senate.gov/reference/resources/pdf/hconres331.pdf (accessed December 15, 2013).

63 Gray, *First Nations 101*, 31.

64 Bruce E. Johansen, "Native American Ideas of Governance and the United States Constitution," *Indigenous People Today: Living in Two Worlds* 14, no. 6 (June 2009): 12–15, see page 15, http://iipdigital.usembassy.gov/media/pdf/ejs/0609.pdf.

65 Sotsisowah, "Thoughts of Peace: The Great Law."

66 National Museum of the American Indian, *Haudenosaunee Guide for Educators*, 3.

67 McCarthy, "De'ni:s nisa'sgao'de?" 81.

68 Deborah Doxtator, "What Happened to the Iroquois Clans? A Study of Clans in Three Nineteenth-Century Rotinonhsyonni Communities" (PhD dissertation, University of Western Ontario, 1996), 6, quoted in McCarthy, "De'ni:s nisa'sgao'de?" 85.

69 Ibid.

70 Chief Thomas, interview by Theresa McCarthy, Six Nations of Grand River, August 13, 1997, quoted in McCarthy, "De'ni:s nisa'sgao'de?" 85.

71 Lottie Keye, conversation with Theresa McCarthy, Hamilton Regional Indian Centre, Hamilton, ON, January 16, 2001, quoted in McCarthy, "De'ni:s nisa'sgao'de?" 85.

72 For this story, see Chief Thomas, interview by Theresa McCarthy, Six Nations of Grand River, August 13, 1997, quoted in McCarthy, "De'ni:s nisa'sgao'de?" 86–87.

73 McCarthy, "De'ni:s nisa'sgao'de?" 86; emphasis in original.

74 Ibid., 87; the following discussion draws on McCarthy.

75 For the following discussion on clans and marriage, see Haudenosaunee Confederacy: The League of Nations, *Clan System* (Ohsweken, ON: Haudenosaunee Development Institute), http://www.haudenosauneeconfederacy.com/clansystem.html (accessed January 21, 2013).

76 Martha Montour, "Iroquois Women's Rights with Respect to Matrimonial Property on Indian Reserves," in *Racism, Colonialism, and Indigeneity in Canada*, ed. Martin J. Cannon and Lina Sunseri, 80–86 (Don Mills, ON: Oxford University Press, 2011), 81.

77 For information that follows about adoption into the Haudenosaunee, see Haudenosaunee Confederacy: The League of Nations, *Adoption* (Ohsweken, ON: Haudenosaunee Development Institute), http://www.haudenosauneeconfederacy.com/adoption.html (accessed January 21, 2013).

78 Haudenosaunee Confederacy, *Clan System*.

79 Sino General (Cayuga Nation, Wolf Clan), personal communication, Kwantlen Polytechnic University, Surrey, British Columbia, April 25, 2013.

80 Robert Yazzie, "Healing as Justice: The Navajo Response to Crime," in *Justice as Healing: Indigenous Ways*, ed. Wanda D. McCaslin, 121–33 (St. Paul, MN: Living Justice Press, 2005), 122.

81 Aboriginal Justice Implementation Commission, *Report of the Aboriginal Justice Inquiry of Manitoba*, vol. 1, *The Justice System and Aboriginal People* (Winnipeg: Manitoba Government, 1999), http://www.ajic.mb.ca/volume.html (accessed December 17, 2012). The previous sections focus on the Haudenosaunee system of justice for two reasons. First, it is one of the systems about which information has been shared widely in writing. Second, I was raised in Haudenosaunee and Neutral traditional territory in the Niagara Region, and I want to acknowledge, learn about, and honour the territory in which I grew up and have been a guest for so many years.

82 Leroy Little Bear, "Jagged Worldviews Colliding," 79.

83 "Unlocking Aboriginal Justice: Alternative Dispute Resolution for the Gitksan and Wet'suwet'en People, A Proposal to the BC Ministry of the Attorney General by Gitksan-Wet'suwet'en Education Society, Smithers Indian Friendship Centre, and Upper Skeena Counselling and Legal Assistance Society, March 20, 1989, 14–15.

84 Paul, *First Nations History: We Were Not the Savages*, 7.

85 Taiaiake Alfred, *On His Indigenous Manifesto* [YouTube video], March 1, 2012, https://www.youtube.com/watch?v=fT9WKzZgB9I (accessed December 19, 2013).

86 Alfred, *On His Indigenous Manifesto*.

87 Ross Gordon Green, *Justice in Aboriginal Communities: Sentencing Alternatives* (Saskatoon, SK: Purich Publishing, 1999), 30–31.

88 Robert Yazzie, "Indigenous Peoples and Postcolonial Colonialism," in *Reclaiming Indigenous Voices and Vision*, ed. Marie Battiste, 39–49 (Vancouver: UBC Press, 2009), 43.

89 Paul, *First Nations History: We Were Not the Savages*, 9.

90 Ibid.

91 John G. Hansen, "Countering Imperial Justice: The Implications of a Cree Response to Crime," *Indigenous Policy Journal* 23, no. 1 (2012): 1–16; see page 4, http://www.indigenouspolicy.org/index.php/ipj/article/view/47/106.

92 This explanation of Western justice was given to me by Haida Elder Woody Morrison in several conversations in 2014. He also outlined it during a presentation he gave to my CRIM 4240 "Aboriginal Peoples and Justice" class, Kwantlen Polytechnic University, Surrey, British Columbia, May 20, 2014.

93 Hansen, "Countering Imperial Justice," 1.
94 Ibid., 2.
95 Ibid., 8.
96 Ibid., 9, 14.
97 Ibid., 13.
98 Jefferson, *Conquest by Law*, 20; Green, *Justice in Aboriginal Communities*, 30–31.
99 Jefferson, *Conquest by Law*, 65.
100 Paul H. Carlson, *The Plains Indians* (College Station: Texas A&M University Press, 1998), 75.
101 Steckley and Cummins, *Full Circle*, 234.
102 Little Bear, "Jagged Worldviews Colliding," 84.
103 For more on responses to crime in Inuit communities, see Andreas Tomaszewski, "Inuit Customary Law Meets Criminal Law in Nunavut—What's the Status Ten Years Afte r?" *LawNow* 34, no. 1 (2009): 18–21, 19; Andreas E. Tomaszewski, "'AlterNative' Approaches to Criminal Justice: John Braithwaite's Theory of Reintegrative Shaming Revisited," *Critical Criminology* 8, no. 2 (1997):105–18, 106.
104 Menno Wiebe, *Native Culture and Canadian Law: A Cultural Look at Native People and the Canadian Justice System* (Kingston: Queen's Theological College, 1984), 8, as cited in Aboriginal Justice Implementation Commission, *Report of the Aboriginal Justice Inquiry: Volume 1: The Justice System and Aboriginal People* (Winnipeg: Aboriginal Justice Implementation Commission, 1999). See Chapter 2, Aboriginal Concepts of Justice http://www.ajic.mb.ca/volumel/chapter2.html (accessed October 3, 2015).
105 Carlson, *The Plains Indians*, 75.
106 Tomaszewski, "'AlterNative' Approaches to Criminal Justice," 107.
107 Jane Richardson, *Law and Status Among the Kiowa Indians* (New York: J. J. Augustin, 1940), quoted in Andrea Smith, *Conquest: Sexual Violence and American Indian Genocide* (Cambridge, MA: South End Press, 2005), 19.
108 Lillian Alice Ackerman, *A Necessary Balance: Gender and Power among Indians of the Columbia Plateau* (Norman: University of Oklahoma Press, 2003), 93–94.
109 See Aboriginal Justice Implementation Commission, *Report of the Aboriginal Justice Inquiry* for information in this and the preceding sentence.
110 Williamson and Roberts, *First Nations People*, 182–83.
111 Marrianne Jones, director, *Tetzan Biny: The Disappearance of Fish Lake: Part 1*, SAMAQAN: Water Stories Series 1 (Winnipeg: Aboriginal Peoples Television Network, 2010). Video is available from Moving Images Distribution, http://movingimages.ca/store/products.php?samaqan_tetzan_biny_disappearance_fish_lake&osCsid=102da1179f9e080ee85dcbd1c0bab6af.
112 Emma LaRocque, "Re-examining Culturally Appropriate Models in Criminal Justice Applications," in *Aboriginal Treaty Rights in Canada*, ed. Micheal Asch, 75–96 (Vancouver: UBC Press, 2002), 84.
113 Alice B. Kehoe, "Blackfoot Persons," in *Women and Power in Native North America*, ed. Laura Frances Klein and Lillian Alice Ackerman, 113–25 (Norman: University of Oklahoma Press, 1995), 120.
114 Ibid., 116.
115 As quoted in Hansen, "Countering Imperial Justice," 6.

116 Ackerman, *A Necessary Balance*, 93.
117 Tehanetorens (Ray Fadden), *Roots of the Iroquois* (Summertown, TN: Native Voices, 2000), 58.
118 Carlson, *The Plains Indians*, 82.
119 Ibid., 75.
120 Ibid., 75.
121 Ibid., 48–49.
122 For information on Haudenosaunee responses to murder, see Jefferson, *Conquest by Law*, 22–23.
123 Peter Hessel, *The Algonkin Tribe* (Arnprior, ON: Kichesippi Books, 1987), 40.
124 Andrea Smith, *Conquest: Sexual Violence and the American Indian Genocide* (Cambridge, MA: South End Press, 2005), 19.
125 Hessel, *The Algonkin Tribe*, 40.
126 Tom Holm, "Patriots and Pawns: State Use of American Indians in the Military and the Process of Nativization in the United States," in *The State of Native America: Genocide, Colonization, and Resistance*, ed. M. Annette Jaimes, 345–70 (Boston: South End Press, 1992), quoted in Smith, *Conquest*, 19.
127 Sioui, *For an Amerindian Autohistory*, 26.
128 Paul, *First Nations History: We Were Not the Savages*, 28.
129 Sioui, *For an Amerindian Autohistory*, 42.
130 Ronald Wright, *Stolen Continents: Conquest and Resistance in the Americas* (Toronto: Penguin Canada, 2003), 248–49.

Chapter 4

1 Cora Voyageur, "Female First Nations Chiefs and the Colonial Legacy in Canada," *American Indian Culture and Research Journal* 35, no. 3 (2011): 59–78, 59.
2 Lisa Monchalin, "Canadian Aboriginal Peoples Victimization, Offending, and Its Prevention," *Crime Prevention and Community Safety: An International Journal* 12, no. 2 (2010): 119–39, 124; Junius P. Rodriguez, *The Historical Encyclopedia of World Slavery*, 2 (Santa Barbara, CA: ABC-CLIO Inc., 1997), 469.
3 Rodriguez, *The Historical Encyclopedia of World Slavery*, 2: 469; Jérémie Gilbert, *Indigenous Peoples' Land Rights under International Law: From Victims to Actors* (New York: Transnational Publishers, 2006), 5.
4 Sharon Helen Venne, *Our Elders Understand Our Rights: Evolving International Law Regarding Indigenous People* (Penticton, BC: Theytus Books, 1999), 2–3.
5 Georges E. Sioui, *For an Amerindian Autohistory* (Montreal: McGill-Queen's University Press, 1992), 3.
6 Venne, *Our Elders Understand Our Rights*, 4.
7 Alexander VI, "Inter Caetera," *Papal Encyclicals Online*, http://www.papalencyclicals.net/Alex06/alex06inter.htm.
8 Robert A. Williams, *The American Indian in Western Legal Thought: The Discourses of Conquest* (New York: Oxford University Press, 1993), 80, quoted in Venne, *Our Elders Understand Our Rights*, 4. For other information on these early rulings, see Venne, *Our Elders Understand Our Rights*, 3–4, and Gilbert, *Indigenous Peoples' Land Rights*, 5–9.
9 For more on the doctrine of discovery and its legacy, see Venne, *Our Elders Understand Our Rights*, 4; Robert J. Miller, "The Doctrine of Discovery in

American Indian Law," *Idaho Law Review* 42, no. 1 (2005): 8–21, see p. 2; Robert J. Miller, *Native America, Discovered and Conquered: Thomas Jefferson, Lewis & Clark, and Manifest Destiny* (Westport, CT: Praeger, 2006), 1.

10 Michael Asch, "From Terra Nullius to Affirmation: Reconciling Aboriginal Rights with the Canadian Constitution," *Canadian Journal of Law and Society* 17, no. 2 (2002): 23–39, 24.

11 David E. Stannard, *American Holocaust: The Conquest of the New World* (New York: Oxford University Press, 1992).

12 Robert R. Berkhofer Jr., *The White Man's Indian: Images of the American Indian from Columbus to Present* (New York: Random House Vintage Books, 1978), 120.

13 Miller, *Native America, Discovered and Conquered*, 1.

14 Berkhofer Jr., *The White Man's Indian*, 9–23.

15 Tracey Lindberg, "The Doctrine of Discovery in Canada," in *Discovering Indigenous Lands: The Doctrine of Discovery in the English Colonies*, ed. Robert J Miller, Jacinta Ruru, Larissa Behrendt, and Tracey Lindberg, 89–125 (New York: Oxford University Press, 2010); Tracey Lindberg, "Contemporary Canadian Resonance of an Imperial Doctrine," in *Discovering Indigenous Lands: The Doctrine of Discovery in the English Colonies*, ed. Robert J. Miller, Jacinta Ruru, Larissa Behrendt, and Tracey Lindberg, 125–70 (New York: Oxford University Press, 2010).

16 General Assembly on United Nations Res. 1514, 15 UN Supplement 16, 66, quoted in Patrick Macklem, *Indigenous Difference and the Constitution of Canada* (Toronto: University of Toronto Press, 2001), 36.

17 Jeff Corntassel, "Towards Sustainable Self-Determination: Rethinking the Contemporary Indigenous-Rights Discourse," *Alternatives* 33 (2008), 108. For the salt-water thesis, see S. James Anaya, *Indigenous Peoples in International Law*, 2nd edition (New York: Oxford University Press, 2000); Macklem, *Indigenous Difference and the Constitution of Canada*, 36; Glen T. Morris, "International Law and Politics: Towards a Right to Self-Determination for Indigenous People," in *The State of Native America: Genocide, Colonization, and Resistance*, ed. M. Annette Jaimes, 55–86 (Cambridge, MA: South End Press, 1992), 74.

18 Brian Slattery, "The Land Rights of Indigenous Canadian Peoples, as Affected by the Crown's Acquisition of the Territory" (PhD dissertation, University of Oxford, 1979), 10–11.

19 Ibid., 10–11.

20 Ibid., 11.

21 Asch, "From Terra Nullius to Affirmation," 24.

22 Miller, *Native America: Discovered and Conquered*, 1.

23 Mary L. Caldbick, "Locke's Doctrine of Property and the Dispossession of the Passamaquoddy" (MA thesis, University of New Brunswick, 1997).

24 James (Sákéj) Youngblood Henderson, Marjorie L. Benson, and Isobel M. Findlay, *Aboriginal Tenure in the Constitution of Canada* (Scarborough, ON: Carswell, 2000), 257–58; Thomas Hobbes, *Leviathan* [1651] (Chicago: Encyclopaedia Britannica, 1952), 85.

25 Youngblood Henderson, Benson, and Findlay, *Aboriginal Tenure*, 258; Hobbes, *Leviathan*, 87–88.

26 James (Sákéj) Youngblood Henderson, "The Context of the State of Nature," in *Reclaiming Indigenous Voices and Vision*, ed. Marie Battiste, 11–38 (Vancouver: UBC Press, 2009), 19; Youngblood Henderson, Benson, and Findlay, *Aboriginal Tenure*, 259.

27 Youngblood Henderson, Benson, and Findlay, *Aboriginal Tenure*, 260.
28 Youngblood Henderson, "The Context of the State of Nature," 17.
29 Ibid.; Thomas Hobbes, *Leviathan, or the Matter, Forme & Power of a Commonwealth, Ecclesiasticall and Civill*, ed. A. R. Waller (Cambridge: Cambridge University Press, 1904), 84.
30 Youngblood Henderson, "The Context of the State of Nature," 17.
31 See Barbara Arneil, *John Locke and America: The Defence of English Colonialism* (Oxford: Clarendon Press, 1996), especially Chapter 2, "Colonialism and Natural Law."
32 Youngblood Henderson, "The Context of the State of Nature," 17.
33 See ibid., 20–21 for information in this paragraph.
34 Hugo Grotius, *On the Law of War and Peace* (Indianapolis: Bobbs-Merrill, 1925), 44.
35 Gregory Younging, "Inheriting the History and Acknowledging the Present Reality of Colonization," paper presented at Kwantlen Polytechnic University's Weaving Together: Healing, Education, and Reconciliation Week, Kwantlen Polytechnic University, Surrey, BC, September 20, 2013.
36 John Locke, *The Second Treatise of Government*, in *John Locke: Two Treatises of Government*, ed. Peter Laslett (Cambridge: Cambridge University Press, 1960), section 45.
37 Locke, *Second Treatise of Government*, section 26.
38 Ibid., section 32.
39 Shiri Pasternak, "Empty Lands and Raw Seeds: From the Doctrines of Discovery to Patents on Life," *Cadrages* 33 (June/August 2007), http://www.omics-ethics.org/observatoire/cadrages/cadr2007/c_no33_07/cai_no33_07_01.html.
40 Ibid.
41 Barbara Arneil, "Trade, Plantations, and Property: John Locke and the Economic Defense of Colonialism," *The Journal of the History of Ideas* 55, no. 4 (1994): 591–609, 592.
42 Pasternak, "Empty Lands and Raw Seeds."
43 Arneil, "Trade, Plantations, and Property," 603.
44 Most material about the dispossession of the Passamaquoddy has been taken from Caldbick, "Locke's Doctrine of Property and the Dispossession of the Passamaquoddy."
45 Caldbick, "Locke's Doctrine of Property," 121.
46 James Tully, "Rediscovering America: The Two Treaties and Aboriginal Rights," in *An Approach to Political Philosophy: Locke in Contexts*, 137–76 (Cambridge: Cambridge University Press, 1993), see especially pages 139–40; Caldbick, "Locke's Doctrine of Property."
47 James Tully, *Strange Multiplicity: Constitutionalism in an Age of Diversity*, (New York: Cambridge University Press, 1995), 72.
48 See Tully, "Rediscovering America," 139 for this and the following.
49 Ibid.; Gilbert, *Indigenous Peoples' Land Rights*, 24.
50 Caldbick, "Locke's Doctrine of Property."
51 Jack D. Forbes, *Columbus and Other Cannibals: The* Wétiko *Disease of Exploitation, Imperialism, and Terrorism* (New York: Autonomedia, 1992), 32; other material in this paragraph on the *wétiko* psychosis is taken from pages 32–34 and 55 in this source.
52 Erica-Irene Daes, "Prologue: The Experience of Colonization around the World," in *Reclaiming Indigenous Voice and Vision*, ed. Marie Battiste, 3–8 (Vancouver: UBC Press, 2009), 4.

53 Ronnie Martin told me this in one of our many conversations that took place when I lived in Ottawa between 2006 and 2011.

54 Barbara-Helen Hill, *Shaking the Rattle: Healing the Trauma of Colonization* (Penticton, BC: Theytus Books, 1995), 8.

55 Chief Dan George, *My Heart Soars* (Surrey, BC: Hancock House Publishing, 1989).

56 Francis Parkman, *The Conspiracy of Pontiac and the Indian War after Conquest of Canada*, 6th edition, vol. 2 (Boston: Little Brown and Company, 1870), 39–40.

57 Camilla Townsend, ed., *American Indian History: A Documentary Reader* (New York: John Wiley & Sons, 2009), 78. This note was enclosed in a letter to Colonel Henry Bouquet at Carlisle, PA, and was written July 7, 1763 in response to Pontiac's powerful resistance to British settlement.

58 Townsend, *American Indian History*, 79. Note: some claim that Bouquet's response reads as follows: "I will try to inoculate the bastards with Some Blankets that may fall in their Hands, and take Care not to get the disease myself." Given the overt racism of the rest of Bouquet's communication, this interpretation may well be correct.

59 The small pox quotation and the one about using dogs to hunt Indigenous peoples took place during Pontiac's War. We should remember that official letters and documents likely do not record the extent of the genocidal policies actually used against Indigenous peoples.

60 Parkman, *The Conspiracy of Pontiac*, 41.

61 Louis M. Waddell, ed., *The Papers of Henry Bouquet* (Harrisburg: The Pennsylvania Historical and Museum Commission, 1994), 304–05.

62 All quotations related to the three forms of colonialism have been taken from the lecture given by Michael Yellow Bird, "Decolonizing the Mind: Healing Through Neurodecolonization and Mindfulness," lecture, Multicultural Center SMSU, Portland State University, Portland, Oregon, January 24, 2014, http://www.indigenousfoodsystems.org/content/decolonizing-mind-talk-dr-michael-yellowbird (accessed July 15, 2015).

63 Daes, "Prologue," 6; Forbes, *Columbus and Other Cannibals*.

64 Hill, *Shaking the Rattle*, 8.

65 Youngblood Henderson, Benson, and Findlay, *Aboriginal Tenure*, 257.

66 Daes, "Prologue," 7.

67 Forbes, *Columbus and Other Cannibals*, 69.

68 Daes, "Prologue," 7.

69 Youngblood Henderson, "The Context of the State of Nature," 11.

70 Youngblood Henderson, Benson, and Findlay, *Aboriginal Tenure*, 261; see also pages 257–63 for more on these subjects.

71 See Youngblood Henderson, "The Context of the State of Nature," 27, 29 for more on this choice and on Locke's "treaty commonwealth."

72 Youngblood Henderson, Benson, and Findlay, *Aboriginal Tenure*, 274.

73 Brian Rice and Anna Snyder, "Reconciliation in the Context of a Settler Society: Healing the Legacy of Colonialism in Canada," in *From Truth to Reconciliation Transforming the Legacy of Residential Schools*, ed. Marlene Brant Castellano, Linda Archibald, and Mike DeGagné, 47–62 (Ottawa: The Aboriginal Healing Foundation, 2008), 49.

74 Taiaiake Alfred and Jeff Corntassel, "Being Indigenous: Resurgences against Contemporary Colonialism," *Government and Opposition* 40, no. 4 (2005): 597–614, 601.

75 Youngblood Henderson, Benson, and Findlay, *Aboriginal Tenure*, 257.

76 Edward Said, *Orientalism* (New York: Vintage Books, 1979), 7.

77 Daniel N. Paul, *First Nations History: We Were Not the Savages—Collision between European and Native American Civilizations*, 3rd edition (Halifax: Fernwood, 2006), 9.

78 Luther Standing Bear, *Land of the Spotted Eagle* (Lincoln: University of Nebraska Press, 1978), 227, as quoted in Forbes, *Columbus and Other Cannibals*, 108.

79 Berkhofer Jr., *The White Man's Indian*, 76.

80 Alfred and Corntassel, "Being Indigenous," 597–98.

81 John Leonard Taylor, "Canada's Northwest Indian Policy in the 1870s: Traditional Premises and Necessary Innovations," in *The Spirit of the Alberta Indian Treaties* (Third edition), ed. Richard T. Price, (Edmonton: University of Alberta Press, 2014), 6.

82 Frances Henry, Carol Tator, Winston Mattis, and Tim Rees, *The Colour of Democracy: Racism in Canadian Society*, 2nd edition (Toronto: Harcourt Brace & Company, 2000), 56.

83 Ibid., 56.

84 As quoted in Robert McMillian Jr., *The Mentality of Racist White America Is the Mentality of Black America* (Bloomington, IN: Xlibris Corporation, 2010), 19.

85 Thomas King, *The Inconvenient Indian: A Curious Account of Native People in North America* (New York: Doubleday Canada, 2012), xv.

86 United Nations Development Programme, *The Human Development Report 2011—Sustainability and Equality: A Better Future For All* (New York: UNDP, 2011).

87 Martin Cooke, Francis Mitrou, David Lawrence, Eric Guimond, and Dan Beavon, "Indigenous Well-Being in Four Countries: An Application of UNDP's Human Development Index to Indigenous Peoples in Australia, Canada, New Zealand, and the United States," *BMC International Health and Human Rights* 7, no. 9 (2007), http://www.biomedcentral.com/content/pdf/1472-698X-7-9.pdf.

88 Bonita Lawrence, "Gender, Race, and the Regulation of Native Identity in Canada and the United States: An Overview," *Hypatia* 18, no. 2 (2003): 3–31, 9.

89 Ibid., 9.

90 Lawrence, "Gender, Race, and the Regulation of Native Identity," 9; *An Act to Amend and Consolidate the Laws Respecting Indians*, S.C. 1876, c.18 (39 Vict). at s. 3.

91 Ibid., 3.

92 Ibid., 5.

93 Alfred and Corntassel, "Being Indigenous," 598–600; Constitution Act, 1982, being Schedule B to the Canada Act, 1982 (UK), 1982, c. 11. at s. 35 (2).

94 Alfred and Corntassel, "Being Indigenous," 600.

95 I use the word "forefathers" intentionally to reference European disregard of women's contributions.

96 Lisa Monchalin, "Reducing Crime Affecting Urban Aboriginal People: The Potential for Effective Solutions in Winnipeg" (PhD dissertation, University of Ottawa, 2012), 199.

97 Yazzie, "Indigenous Peoples and Postcolonial Colonialism," 46.

98 James Frideres, "Being White and Being Right: Critiquing Individual and Collective Privilege," in *The Great White North? Exploring Whiteness, Privilege and Identity in Education*, ed. Paul R. Carr and Darren E. Lund, 43–56 (Rotterdam, Netherlands: Sense Publishers, 2007), 44.

99 Ibid., 43, 45.

100 These points are quoted directly from Susan D. Dion, "(Re)telling to Disrupt: Aboriginal People and Stories of Canadian History," *Journal of the Canadian Association for Curriculum Studies* 2, no. 1 (2004): 55–76, 57–58.

101 Dion, "(Re)telling to Disrupt," 58.

Chapter 5

1 Aboriginal Justice Implementation Commission, *Report of the Aboriginal Justice Inquiry of Manitoba*, vol. 1, *The Justice System and Aboriginal People* (Winnipeg: Manitoba Government, 1999), http://www.ajic.mb.ca/volume.html (accessed December 17, 2012); Lynn Gehl, *Anishinaabeg Stories: Featuring Petroglyphs, Petrographs, and Wampum Belts* (Southampton, ON: Ningwakwe Learning Press, 2012), 36.

2 In 1996, Barbara Mann and Jerry Fields of the University of Toledo combined Indigenous oral tradition with academic expertise and archaeological data to make the case that the Great Law of Peace was ratified in 1142 by the Haudenosaunee, see Bruce Elliott Johansen, *The Encyclopedia of Native American Legal Tradition* (Westport, CT: Greenwood Publishing, 1998), 157.

3 George F. G. Stanley, "As Long as the Sun Shines and Water Flows: An Historical Comment," in *As Long as the Sun Shines and Water Flows: A Reader in Canadian Native Studies*, ed. Ian A. L. Getty and Antoine S. Lussier, 1–28 (Vancouver: UBC Press, 2000), 11.

4 Aboriginal Justice Implementation Commission, *Report of the Aboriginal Justice Inquiry of Manitoba*. (Winnipeg: Aboriginal Justice Implementation Commission, 1999).

5 Anishinabek Nation, *Robinson-Huron Treaty Rights: 1850 and Today* (North Bay: Union of Ontario Indians, n.d.), 4, 6.

6 David T. McNab, "Sovereignty, Treaties and Trade in the Bkejwanong Territory," *The Journal of Aboriginal and Economic Development* 3, no. 2 (2003): 52–66, 55.

7 J. R. Miller, *Compact, Contract, Covenant: Aboriginal Treaty-Making in Canada* (Toronto: University of Toronto Press, 2009), 70.

8 Menno Boldt, *Surviving as Indians: The Challenge of Self-Government* (Toronto: University of Toronto Press, 1993), 3–4.

9 *The Invisible Nation*, DVD, directed by Richard Dejardins and Robert Monderie (Ottawa: National Film Board of Canada, 2007).

10 John Borrows, "Wampum at Niagara: The Royal Proclamation, Canadian Legal History, and Self-Government," in *Aboriginal Treaty Rights in Canada*, ed. Michael Asch, 155–72 (Vancouver: UBC Press, 2002), 155.

11 Borrows, "Wampum at Niagara," 171.

12 For text of the Royal Proclamation, see "250th Anniversary of the Royal Proclamation of 1763," *Aboriginal History in Canada* from the AANDC website: https://www.aadnc-aandc.gc.ca/eng/1370355181092/1370355203645#a6; See Borrows, "Wampum at Niagara," 159–61 for other material in this section.

13 Borrows, "Wampum at Niagara," 161.

14 Lynn Gehl, *Indigenous Knowledge, Symbolic Literacy and the 1764 Treaty at Niagara* (Ottawa: Federation for the Humanities and Social Sciences), http://www.ideas-idees.ca/blog/indigenous-knowledge-symbolic-literacy-and-1764-treaty-niagara (accessed January 11, 2013); Lynn Gehl, *The Truth that Wampum Tells: My Debwewin on the Algonquin Land Claims Process* (Black Point, NS: Fernwood Publishing, 2014), 33.

15 John Ralston Saul, *A Fair Country: Telling Truths about Canada* (Toronto: Viking Canada, 2008), 69.

16 Gehl, *Indigenous Knowledge, Symbolic Literacy.*

17 See Borrows, "Wampum at Niagara," 161–62 for more on wampum belts.

18 Bruce Morito, "The Rule of Law and Aboriginal Rights: The Case of the Chippewas of Nawash," *Canadian Journal of Native Studies* 19, no. 2 (1999): 263–88, 265.

19 Borrows, "Wampum at Niagara," 162.

20 For more on how the meeting was arranged see Gehl, *Indigenous Knowledge, Symbolic Literacy*; James (Sákéj) Youngblood Henderson, Marjorie L. Benson, and Isobel M. Findlay, *Aboriginal Tenure in the Constitution of Canada* (Scarborough, ON: Carswell, 2000), 154; and Borrows, "Wampum at Niagara," 162.

21 Borrows, "Wampum at Niagara," 162.

22 Ibid., 162; Miller, "Compact, Contract, Covenant," 72.

23 Gehl, *Indigenous Knowledge, Symbolic Literacy.*

24 McNab, "Sovereignty, Treaties and Trade in the Bkejwanong Territory," 55.

25 Borrows, "Wampum at Niagara," 163.

26 Morito, "The Rule of Law and Aboriginal Rights," 265; Gehl, *Indigenous Knowledge, Symbolic Literacy*; Borrows, "Wampum at Niagara," 163; Saul, *A Fair Country*, 69; Miller, *Compact, Contract, Covenant*, 72.

27 Borrows, "Wampum at Niagara," 163.

28 Gehl, *Indigenous Knowledge, Symbolic Literacy.*

29 For more on these belts, see Bonita Lawrence, *Fractured Homeland: Federal Recognition and Algonquin Identity in Ontario* (Vancouver: UBC Press, 2012), 33; Gehl, *Indigenous Knowledge, Symbolic Literacy*; and Gehl, *The Truth that Wampum Tells*, 60. Much of the following is drawn from these sources.

30 Borrows, "Wampum at Niagara," 163.

31 Lawrence, *Fractured Homeland*, 33.

32 Gehl, *The Truth that Wampum Tells*, 54; Kathryn V. Muller, "The Two 'Mystery' Belts of Grand River: A Biography of the Two Row Wampum and the Friendship Belt," *American Indian Quarterly* 31, no. 1 (2007), 129–64, 129.

33 The quotation is from Gehl, *Indigenous Knowledge, Symbolic Literacy*; for the meaning of the Two-Row Wampum Belt, see Mohawk Council of Akwesasne, "The Kaswentha (Two Row Wampum)," http://www.akwesasne.ca/node/118 (accessed July 20, 2015) and Morito, "The Rule of Law and Aboriginal Rights," 265, 276.

34 Gehl, *Indigenous Knowledge, Symbolic Literacy.*

35 See Borrows, "Wampum at Niagara," 168–69 for information in this paragraph.

36 Muller, "The Two 'Mystery' Belts of Grand River," 135.

37 Ibid., 136.

38 Borrows, "Wampum at Niagara," 169–70.

39 Ibid., 164.

40 Ibid.

41 David T. McNab, "The Waters of Bkejwanong and the Treaty Making Process," in *Earth, Water, Air and Fire: Studies in Canadian Ethnohistory*, ed. David T. McNab, 35–63 (Waterloo, ON: Wilfrid Laurier University Press, 1998), 43.

42 Taiaiake Alfred, *Peace, Power, Righteousness: An Indigenous Manifesto*, 2nd edition (Don Mills, ON: Oxford University Press, 2009), 82.

43 Ibid., 79.

44 Ibid., 80.

45 Ibid., 76.

46 Ibid., 76.

47 John Douglas Belshaw, *Canadian History: Pre-Confederation*, (Vancouver: BC Open Textbook Project, 2015), 136, http://opentextbc.ca/preconfederation/ (accessed December 3, 2015); Cynthia C. Wesley-Esquimaux and Magdalena Smolewski, *Historic Trauma and Aboriginal Healing*, (Ottawa: The Aboriginal Healing Foundation, 2004), iii.

48 Ted Palys, "Considerations for Achieving 'Aboriginal Justice' in Canada," paper presented at the annual meetings of the Western Association of Sociology and Anthropology, Simon Fraser University, Vancouver, 1993, http://www.sfu.ca/~palys/WASA93.pdf (accessed November 28, 2014).

49 Gehl, *The Truth that Wampum Tells*, 55.

50 Boldt, *Surviving as Indians*, 275.

51 BC Treaty Commission, *Why Treaties? A Legal Perspective* (Vancouver: BC Treaty Commission, 2008), 3.

52 Ibid., 3.

53 Boldt, *Surviving as Indians*, 275.

54 Treaties and Historical Research Centre, P.R.E. Group, Indian and Northern Affairs, *The Historical Development of the Indian Act* (Ottawa: Indian and Northern Affairs, 1978), 4.

55 Gehl, *The Truth that Wampum Tells*, 91.

56 Chief Joe Mathias and Gary R. Yabsley, "Conspiracy of Legislation: The Suppression of Indian Rights in Canada," *BC Studies* 89 (1991): 34–47; see p. 35.

57 Ibid.

58 Ibid.

59 For general information on the numbered treaties, see Menno Boldt, *Surviving as Indians: The Challenge of Self-Government* (Toronto: University of Toronto Press, 1993), 274; Daschuk, *Clearing the Plains*, 79; and John Leonard Taylor, "Canada's Northwest Indian Policy in the 1870s: Traditional Premises and Necessary Innovations," in *The Spirit of the Alberta Indian Treaties*, 3rd edition, ed. Richard T. Price, 3–7 (Edmonton: University of Alberta Press, 2014), 3.

60 Daschuk, *Clearing the Plains*, 79.

61 Derek Whitehouse, "The Numbered Treaties: Similar Means to Dichotomous Ends," *Past Imperfect* 3 (1994): 35–45, 32.

62 Daschuk, *Clearing the Plains*, 79.

63 For more on this view, see Whitehouse, "The Numbered Treaties," 26, 32.

64 Thomas Isaac and Kristyn Annis, *Treaty Rights in the Historic Treaties of Canada* (Saskatoon: Native Law Centre, University of Saskatchewan, 2010), 57.

65 Isaac and Annis, *Treaty Rights in the Historic Treaties*, 57; Aimée Craft, *Breathing Life into the Stone Fort Treaty: An Anishinabe Understanding of Treaty One* (Saskatoon, SK: Purich Publishing, 2013), 115–18.

66 Alexander Morris, the government treaty negotiator who renegotiated Treaty 1 and 2, admitted as much. See page 126 in Alexander Morris, *The Treaties of Canada with the Indians of Manitoba and the North-West Territories Including Negotiations on Which They are Based, and Other Information Relating Thereto* (Toronto: Willing & Williamson, 1880), https://archive.org/details/cihm_14955 (accessed February 24, 2015), which states the following: "When Treaties, Numbers One and Two, were made, certain verbal promises were unfortunately made to the Indians, which were not included in the written text of the treaties, nor recognized or referred to, when these Treaties were ratified by the Privy Council. This, naturally, led to misunderstanding with the Indians, and to widespread dissatisfaction among them."

67 Morris, *The Treaties of Canada*, 126–42; John Leonard Taylor, "Two Views on the Meaning of Treaties Six and Seven," in *The Spirit of the Alberta Indian Treaties*, 3rd edition, ed. Richard T. Price, 9–45 (Edmonton: University of Alberta Press, 2014), 14.

68 Isaac and Annis, *Treaty Rights in the Historic Treaties of Canada*, 57.

69 Ibid., 57; Taylor, "Two Views on the Meaning of Treaties Six and Seven," 15.

70 Craft, *Breathing Life into the Stone Fort Treaty*, 11.

71 Ibid., 111.

72 Ibid.

73 Taylor, "Canada's Northwest Indian Policy," 6.

74 Ibid.

75 Isaac and Annis, *Treaty Rights in the Historic Treaties of Canada*, 58.

76 For more on Treaty 3, 4, and 5, see Isaac and Annis, *Treaty Rights in the Historic Treaties of Canada*, 59–61. The following discussion draws on this source.

77 Nishnawbe Aski Nation, *Treaty No. 5 History*, http://www.nan.on.ca/article/treaty-no5-history-418.asp (accessed February 22, 2015).

78 Isaac and Annis, *Treaty Rights*, 61.

79 Taylor, "Two Views on the Meaning of Treaties Six and Seven," 10.

80 Laurel Sefton MacDowell, *An Environmental History of Canada* (Vancouver: UBC Press, 2012), 35.

81 Paul Hatcher and Nick Battery, *Biological Diversity: Exploiters and Exploited* (Chinchester, UK: Wiley-Blackwell, 2011), 399; Andrew C. Isenberg, *The Destruction of the Bison: An Environmental History, 1750–1920* (Cambridge: Cambridge University Press, 2000), 158–59.

82 Andrew C. Isenberg, "The Wild and the Tamed: Indians Euroamericans, and the Destruction of the Bison," in *Animals in Human Histories: The Mirror of Nature and Culture*, ed. Mary Henninger-Voss, 115–43 (Rochester, NY: University of Rochester Press, 2002), 132.

83 Ibid., 134.

84 Sylvia A. Johnson and Alice Aamodt, *Wolf Pack: Tracking Wolves in the Wild* (Minneapolis: Lerner Publishing Group, 1985), 76.

85 Quoted in Hatcher and Battery, *Biological Diversity*, 399. See also the following for more on poisoning wolves and its environmental effects: Isenberg, *The Destruction of the Bison*, 159; Isenberg, "The Wild and the Tamed," 134; and Johnson and Aamodt, *Wolf Pack*, 76.

86 Dan Flores, *The Natural West: Environmental History in the Great Plains and Rocky Mountains* (Norman: University of Oklahoma Press, 2001), 66.

87 Whitehouse, "The Numbered Treaties," 31.

88 Peter Erasmus and Henry Thompson, *Buffalo Days and Nights* (Calgary: Fifth House Publishers, 1999), 249.

89 Whitehorse, "The Numbered Treaties," 39.
90 Sharon Venne, "Understanding Treaty 6: An Indigenous Perspective," in *Aboriginal and Treaty Rights in Canada: Essays on Law, Equality, and Respect for Difference*, ed. Michael Asch, 173–207 (Vancouver: UBC Press, 2002), 194.
91 Ibid., 199; Isaac and Annis, *Treaty Rights in the Historic Treaties of Canada*, 62.
92 Venne, "Understanding Treaty 6," 200.
93 Isaac and Annis, *Treaty Rights in the Historic Treaties of Canada*, 63.
94 Venne, "Understanding Treaty 6," 199.
95 For more on these treaty violations, see ibid., 201.
96 *Copy of Treaty No. 6 between Her Majesty the Queen and the Plain and Wood Cree Indians and other Tribes of Indians at Fort Carlton, Fort Pitt and Battle River with Adhesions* (Ottawa: Roger Duhamel, Queen's Printer, 1964), https://www.aadnc-aandc.gc.ca/eng/1100100028710/1100100028783; see also Venne, "Understanding Treaty 6,"192.
97 Ibid.
98 Whitehorse, "The Numbered Treaties," 31.
99 Treaty 7 Elders and Tribal Council with Walter Hildebrandt, Sarah Carter, and Dorothy First Rider, *The True Spirit and Original Intent of Treaty 7* (Montreal: McGill-Queen's University Press, 1996), xiii.
100 Whitehouse, "The Numbered Treaties," 32.
101 Isaac and Annis, *Treaty Rights in the Historic Treaties of Canada*, 63; Treaty 7 Elders et al., *The True Spirit and Original Intent of Treaty 7*, 240.
102 Treaty 7 Elders et al., *The True Spirit and Original Intent of Treaty 7*, viii.
103 Ibid., 24; see also xi.
104 Ibid., xi, 144.
105 Ibid., xi–xii, 134.
106 On starvation as a fact and policy, see Treaty 7 Elders et al., *The True Spirit and Original Intent of Treaty 7*, 162; Daschuk, *Clearing the Plains*, 123.
107 Canada, Parliament, House of Commons, *Debates*, 4th Parl., 4th sess., April 16, 1882; see also Daschuk, *Clearing the Plains*, 123.
108 Aboriginal Affairs and Northern Development Canada, *Treaty Texts—Treaty No. 8*, https://www.aadnc-aandc.gc.ca/eng/1100100028813/1100100028853 (accessed February 24, 2015).
109 Sheldon Cardinal, "The Spirit and Intent of Treaty Eight: A Sagaw Eeniw Perspective" (Masters thesis: University of Saskatchewan, 2001), 16–17.
110 Ibid., 17–18.
111 Ibid., 23–24.
112 Ibid., 27.
113 Ibid., 31; Richard Daniel, "The Spirit and Terms of Treaty Eight," in *The Spirit of the Alberta Indian Treaties*, 3rd edition, ed. Richard T. Price, 46–96 (Edmonton: University of Alberta Press, 2014), 93.
114 Cardinal, "The Spirit and Intent of Treaty Eight," 32.
115 Ibid., 97.
116 Ibid., 39–40.
117 For more on these last numbered treaties, see Isaac and Annis, *Treaty Rights in the Historic Treaties of Canada*, 70–71.
118 Richard T. Price, "Introduction," in *The Spirit of the Alberta Indian Treaties*, 3rd edition, ed. Richard T. Price, ix–xv (Edmonton: University of Alberta Press, 2014), xii.

Chapter 6

1 An Act to Amend and Consolidate the Laws Respecting Indians, S.C. 1876, c. 18 (39 Vict.). at s. 4.

2 Sharon Venne, "Understanding Treaty 6: An Indigenous Perspective," in *Aboriginal and Treaty Rights in Canada: Essays on Law, Equality, and Respect for Difference*, ed. Michael Asch, 173–207 (Vancouver: UBC Press, 2002), 197. Much of the following, including quotations, originates in Venne's essay.

3 Ibid. *Copy of Treaty No. 6 between Her Majesty the Queen and the Plain and Wood Cree Indians and other Tribes of Indians at Fort Carlton, Fort Pitt and Battle River, with Adhesions* (Ottawa: Roger Duhamel, Queen's Printer, 1964), https://www.aadnc-aandc.gc.ca/eng/1100100028710/1100100028783#chp1.

4 This speech was recorded by Peter Erasmus, an eyewitness to the signing of Treaty 6, but see also Richard Price, *The Spirit of the Alberta Treaties* (Edmonton: University of Alberta Press, 1999), 19.

5 Michèle DuCharme, "The Segregation of Native People in Canada: Voluntary or Compulsory?" *Currents* (Summer 1986): 3–4. DuCharme's work informs much of this paragraph.

6 Erin Hanson, *Indian Reserves* (Vancouver: Indigenous Foundations UBC, n.d.), http://indigenousfoundations.arts.ubc.ca/home/government-policy/reserves.html?type=123&filename=Reserves.pdf (accessed February 3, 2013), 2.

7 Wendy Moss and Elaine Gardner-O'Toole, *Aboriginal People: History of Discriminatory Laws* (Ottawa: Library of Parliament of Canada, Law and Government Division: 1991), http://publications.gc.ca/Collection-R/LoPBdP/BP/bp175-e.htm#2 (accessed February 4, 2013). See the section entitled "Restricted Right to Sell Agricultural Products."

8 Victor Satzewich, "Indian Agents and the 'Indian Problem' in Canada in 1946: Reconsidering the Theory of Coercive Tutelage," *The Canadian Journal of Native Studies* 17, no. 2 (1997): 227–57, 230.

9 Steckley and Cummins, *Full Circle*, 124.

10 For a synopsis of the powers of Indian agents, see Satzewich, "Indian Agents and the 'Indian Problem,'" 231. Other useful sources are F. Laurie Barron, "The Indian Pass System in the Canadian West, 1882–1935," *Prairie Forum* 13, no. 1 (1988); James Miller, *Shingwauk's Vision: A History of Residential Schools* (Toronto: University of Toronto Press, 1996); Kathleen Pettipas, *Severing the Ties that Bind* (Winnipeg: University of Manitoba Press, 1994); Vic Satzewich, "Where's the Beef?: Cattle Killing, Rations Policy and First Nations 'Criminality' in Southern Alberta, 1892–1895," *Journal of Historical Sociology* 9 (1996): 188–212; and Vic Satzewich and Linda Mahood, "Indian Affairs and Band Governance: Deposing Indian Chiefs in Western Canada," *Canadian Ethnic Studies* 26 (1994), 40–58.

11 Unless otherwise specified, the information on the pass system that follows is from Barron, "The Indian Pass System in the Canadian West," 25–26.

12 R. Douglas Francis, Richard Jones, and Donald B. Smith, *Journeys: A History of Canada*, 2nd edition (Toronto: Nelson Education, 2010), 168.

13 Olive Patricia Dickason, *Canada's First Nations: A History of Founding Peoples from Earliest Times*, 3rd edition (Don Mills, ON: Oxford University Press, 2002), 228.

14 For details regarding the implementation of this act, see E. Brian Titley, *A Narrow Vision: Duncan Campbell Scott and the Administration of Indian Affairs in Canada*

(Vancouver: UBC Press, 1986), 4; Dickason, *Canada's First Nations*, 228–29. The subsequent discussion draws on these authors.

15 On the assimilative policy of enfranchisement, see Titley, *A Narrow Vision*, 4.

16 Ibid. I draw on Titley's work through the following discussion.

17 Indian and Northern Affairs Canada, *A History of Indian and Northern Affairs Canada* (Gatineau, QC: Indian and Northern Affairs Canada, n.d.) http://www.aadnc-aandc.gc.ca/DAM/DAM-INTER-HQ/STAGING/texte-text/ap_htmc_inaclivr_1314920729809_eng.pdf (accessed February 3, 2013), 7.

18 Aboriginal Affairs and Northern Development Canada, *First Nations in Canada* http://www.aadnc-aandc.gc.ca/eng/1307460755710/1307460872523 (accessed February 2, 2013).

19 Constitution Act 1867 (UK), 30 & 31 Vict., ch. 3, reprinted in R.S.C. 1985, app ii, no 5, s. 91(24).

20 Dickason, *Canada's First Nations*, 237. Constitution Act 1867 (UK), 30 & 31 Vict., ch. 3, reprinted in R.S.C. 1985, app ii, no 5, s. 91(24).

21 An Act for the Gradual Enfranchisement of Indians, the Better Management of Indian Affairs, and to Extend the Provisions of the Act 31st Victoria, 1869 S.C., 32–33 Vict., c. 6. Available from Aboriginal Affairs and Northern Development Canada: http://www.aadnc-aandc.gc.ca/DAM/DAM-INTER-HQ/STAGING/texte-text/a69c6_1100100010205_eng.pdf (accessed February 2, 2013).

22 Ibid., ch. 6, s. 4.

23 Ibid., ch. 6, s. 10.

24 Canada, Department of the Secretary of the State for the Provinces, *Report of the Indian Branch of the Department of the Secretary of State for the Provinces* (Ottawa: I. B. Taylor, 1872), 4; see also, Lori Henry, *Dancing Through History: In Search of Stories That Define Canada* (Vancouver: Dancing Traveller Publishing, 2012), 111.

25 Dickason, *Canada's First Nations*, 263.

26 Cora Voyageur, "Female First Nations Chiefs and the Colonial Legacy in Canada," *American Indian Culture and Research Journal* 35, no. 3 (2011): 59–78, 59.

27 D. Laird, *Report of the Department of the Interior for the Year Ended 30th June, 1875* (Ottawa: Department of the Interior, 1876), xii–xiii.

28 Bonita Lawrence, *"Real" Indians and Others*, 31–32.

29 Dickason, *Canada's First Nations*, 263–64.

30 Voyageur, "Female First Nations Chiefs," 60.

31 Patricia Monture-Angus, *Thunder in My Soul: A Mohawk Woman Speaks* (Halifax: Fernwood Publishing, 1995), 136.

32 See Yvonne Boyer, "First Nations Women's Contributions to Culture and Community through Canadian Law," in *Restoring the Balance: First Nations Women, Community, and Culture*, ed. Gail Guthrie Valaskakis, Madeleine Dion Stout, and Eric Guimond, 69–96 (Winnipeg: University of Manitoba Press, 2009), 85, 95.

33 This discussion is informed by ibid., 95.

34 Indigenous Bar Association in Canada, *Position Paper on Bill C-3—Gender Equity in Indian Registration Act* (Ottawa: IBA, 2010). This paper was submitted to the Senate Committee on Human Rights on December 6, 2010.

35 Pamela D. Palmater, *Beyond Blood: Rethinking Indigenous Identity* (Saskatoon, SK: Purich Publishing, 2011), 18–19.

36 Thomas King, *The Truth about Stories: A Native Narrative* (Minneapolis: University of Minnesota Press, 2005), 143–44.

37 Both quotations are from ibid., 144.
38 Palmater, *Beyond Blood*, 47.
39 Ibid.
40 Dickason, *Canada's First Nations*, 264.
41 The amendments enabling municipalities access to the ownership or control of First Nations lands were also referred to as the "Oliver Act," after the politician and journalist Frank Oliver.
42 Dickason, *Canada's First Nations*, 217.
43 Ibid.
44 Mathias and Yabsley, "Conspiracy of Legislation," 38.
45 Olthuis, Kleer, Townshed LLP, *Aboriginal Law Handbook*, 4th edition (Toronto: Thomson Reuters Canada), 205–07.
46 Ibid., 207.
47 Both quotations are from ibid., 205; see also 207.
48 Moss and Gardner-O'Toole, Law and Government Division, *Aboriginal People: History of Discriminatory Laws*. Much of the detail subsequently discussed here appears in the section entitled "Liquor Offences."
49 Dickason, *Canada's First Nations*, 265–66.
50 Mathias and Yabsley, "Conspiracy of Legislation," 37–38; see especially 38 for other details presented here.
51 Dickason, *Canada's First Nations*, 266.
52 Henry, *Dancing Through History*, 112.
53 Quoted in Mathias and Yabsley, "Conspiracy of Legislation," 37–38.
54 Dale Turner, *This Is Not a Peace Pipe: Towards a Critical Indigenous Philosophy* (Toronto: University of Toronto Press, 2006), 12. Much of the detail presented in subsequent paragraphs comes from Turner.
55 Turner, *This is Not a Peace Pipe*, 19; Department of Indian Affairs and Northern Development, *Statement of Government of Canada on Indian Policy, 1969* (Ottawa: Department of Indian Affairs and Northern Development, 1969), http://www.aadnc-aandc.gc.ca/DAM/DAM-INTER-HQ/STAGING/texte-text/cp1969_1100100010190_eng.pdf (accessed February 15, 2013), 1. NB: Page references may not correspond to the document made available online, which has been converted for effective digital display. Because of this conversion, the original 13-page White Paper will probably have fewer or more pages depending upon the digital display.
56 Turner, *This Is Not a Peace Pipe*, 19.
57 Department of Indian Affairs and Northern Development, *Statement of Government of Canada on Indian Policy, 1969*, 13.
58 Ibid., 18.
59 See Turner, *This Is Not a Peace Pipe*, 16, 21 for all information in this paragraph.
60 Ibid.
61 For this and the previous sentence, see Robert Robson, "The Indian Act: A Northern Manitoba Perspective," *Canadian Journal of Native Studies* 11, no. 2 (1991): 295–331, 301.
62 Harold Cardinal, *The Unjust Society* (Vancouver: Douglas & McIntyre, 1999).
63 Harry B. Hawthorn, ed., *A Survey of the Contemporary Indians of Canada: Economic, Political, Educational Needs and Policies*, 2 vols. (Ottawa: Indian Affairs Branch, 1966), 1: 6.
64 Ibid., 1: 13.

65 Alan, Cairns, *Citizens Plus: Aboriginal Peoples and the Canadian State* (Vancouver: UBC Press, 2000), 12.

66 Indian Chiefs of Alberta, *Citizens Plus* (Edmonton: Indian Association of Alberta, 1970).

67 Pauline Comeau and Aldo Santin, *The First Canadians: A Profile of Canada's Native People Today* (Toronto: James Lorimer & Company, 1995), 10.

68 Ibid., 10.

69 Dr. Joseph Gosnell (President, Nisga'a Tribal Council), Evidence before the Standing Committee on Aboriginal Affairs and Northern Development, Thursday, November 4, 1999, section 0915, http://www.parl.gc.ca/HousePublications/Publication.aspx?DocId=1039765&Language=E.

Chapter 7

1 Richard A. Enns, "But What Is The Object of Educating These Children, If It Costs Their Lives to Educate Them?: Federal Indian Education Policy in Western Canada in the Late 1800s," *Journal of Canadian Studies* 43, no. 3 (2009): 101–23, 105.

2 Davin, Nicholas F., *Report on Industrial Schools for Indians and Half-Breeds* (Ottawa: CIHM, 1879), https://archive.org/details/cihm_03651, 1.

3 Ibid., 10.

4 Ibid., 12.

5 Enns, "But What Is The Object of Educating These Children," 105.

6 Celia Haig-Brown, *Resistance and Renewal: Surviving the Indian Residential School* (Vancouver: Arsenal Pulp Press, 1991), 30.

7 Suzanne Stewart, "Family Counseling as Decolonization: Exploring an Indigenous Social-Constructivist Approach in Clinical Practice," *First Peoples Child & Family Review*, 4, no. 1, 68.

8 Richard Henry Pratt, *Battlefield and Classroom: Four Decades with the American Indian 1867–1904*, ed. Robert M. Utley (Norman: University of Oklahoma Press, 2003).

9 Paulette Fairbanks Molin, *"Training the Hand, The Head, and The Heart": Indian Education at Hampton Institute* (Minneapolis: Minnesota History/Minnesota Historical Society, 1988), http://collections.mnhs.org/MNHistory Magazine/articles/51/v51i03p082-098.pdf (accessed May 9, 2014), 84.

10 Brad D. Lookingbill, *War Dance at Fort Marion: Plains Indian War Prisoners* (Norman: University of Oklahoma Press, 2006), 62.

11 Robert L. Brunhouse, "The Founding of the Carlisle Indian School," *Pennsylvania History* 6, no. 2 (1939): 72–85, 75; Robert, A. Trennert, "From Carlisle to Phoenix: The Rise and Fall of the Indian Outing System, 1878–1930," *Pacific Historical Review* 52, no. 3 (1983): 267–91, 270.

12 Trennert, "From Carlisle to Phoenix," 270.

13 R. H. Pratt, "Report of Training-School at Carlisle, Pennsylvania," in *Fifty-Ninth Annual Report of the Commissioner of Indian Affairs to the Secretary of the Interior*, 308–14 (Washington, DC: Government Printing Office, 1890), 308.

14 This and the previous sentence draw on Brunhouse, "The Founding of the Carlisle Indian School," 73.

15 O'Connor and O'Neal, *Dark Legacy*, 18; Klaus Frantz, *Indian Reservations in the United States: Territory, Sovereignty, and Socioeconomic Change* (Chicago: University of Chicago Press, 1999), 17.

16 O'Connor and O'Neal, *Dark Legacy*, 18.

17 Evelyn Nakano Glenn, *Forced to Care: Coercion and Caregiving in America* (Cambridge, MA: Harvard University Press, 2010), 50.

18 Nakano Glenn, *Forced to Care*, 50; Mary A. Stout, *Native American Boarding Schools: Landmarks of the American Mosaic* (Santa Barbara, CA: ABC-CLIO, 2012), 138.

19 Kathie Marie Bowker, "The Boarding School Legacy: Ten Contemporary Lakota Women Tell Their Stories" (PhD dissertation, Montana State University, Bozeman, Montana, 2007), 4. The subsequent sentence draws on Bowker also.

20 O'Connor and O'Neal, *Dark Legacy*, 19. The remainder of this section draws on information presented by O'Connor and O'Neal.

21 Ibid., 20.

22 Quoted in Madeleine Dion Stout and Gregory Kipling, *Aboriginal People, Resilience, and the Residential School Legacy* (Ottawa: The Aboriginal Healing Foundation, 2003), 30.

23 Georges Erasmus, "Notes on the History of the Indian Residential School System in Canada," paper prepared for the conference *The Tragic Legacy of Residential Schools: Is Reconciliation Possible?*, hosted by the Assembly of First Nations and the University of Calgary, Calgary, March 12–13, 2004, 3. For more on the residential schools in Canada, see Helen Cote and Wendy Schissel, "Damaged Children and Broken Spirits: A Residential School Survivor's Story," in *Marginality and Condemnation*, ed. Carolyn Brooks and Bernard Schissel, 175–92 (Halifax: Fernwood, 2002), 177.

24 Suzanne Fournier and Ernie Crey, "'Killing the Indian in the Child': Four Centuries of Church-Run Schools," in *The Indigenous Experience: Global Perspectives*, ed. Roger CA Maaka and Chris Anderson, 141–49 (Toronto: Canadian Scholars' Press, 2006), 143.

25 Justice Murray Sinclair, "Rheal Brant Hall Lecture: Truth and Reconciliation," public lecture, Carleton University, Ottawa, October 15, 2010.

26 See Truth and Reconciliation Commission of Canada, *What We Have Learned: Principles of Truth and Reconciliation* (Ottawa: Truth and Reconciliation Commission of Canada, 2015), 32–33; Fred Kelly, "Confession of a Born Again Pagan," in *From Truth to Reconciliation Transforming the Legacy of Residential Schools*, ed. Marlene Brant Castellano, Linda Archibald and Mike DeGagné, 11–41 (Ottawa: The Aboriginal Healing Foundation, 2008), 23.

27 Elizabeth Furniss, *The Victims of Benevolence: The Dark Legacy of the Williams Lake Residential School* (Vancouver: Arsenal Pulp Press, 1995), 108.

28 Kelly, "Confession of a Born Again Pagan," 24.

29 Laurence J. Kirmayer, Gregory M. Brass, Tara Holton, Ken Paul, Cori Simpson, and Caroline Tait, *Suicide among Aboriginal People in Canada* (Ottawa: The Aboriginal Healing Foundation, 2007), 68.

30 Canada, Department of Indian Affairs, *Annual Report of the Department of Indian Affairs for the Year Ended 31st December 1889* (Ottawa: Brown Chamberlin, 1890), 169.

31 Canada, Parliament, House of Commons, *Debates*, 7th Parliament, 3rd session, vol. 1, March 9, 1893, 2106, http://parl.canadiana.ca/view/oop.debates_HOC0703_07.

32 Barbara-Helen Hill, *Shaking the Rattle: Healing the Trauma of Colonization* (Penticton, BC: Theytus Books, 1995), 13. For the following sentence, see Furniss, *The Victims of Benevolence: The Dark Legacy of the Williams Lake Residential School* (Vancouver: Arsenal Pulp Press, 1995), 31.
33 Dickason, *Canada's First Nations*, 315.
34 The sources for the following information are: Fournier and Crey, "Killing the Indian in the Child," 148; Suzanne Fournier and Ernie Crey, *Stolen from Our Embrace: The Abduction of First Nations Children and Restoration of Aboriginal Communities* (Vancouver: Douglas & McIntyre Ltd, 1997), 57; Kelly, "Confession of a Born Again Pagan," 24.
35 John S. Milloy, *A National Crime: The Canadian Government and the Residential School System 1879 to 1986* (Winnipeg: The University of Manitoba Press, 1999), 298; Kelly, "Confession of a Born Again Pagan," 24; Cote and Schissel, "Damaged Children and Broken Spirits," 177; Deborah Chansonneuve, *Addictive Behaviours among Aboriginal People in Canada* (Ottawa: The Aboriginal Healing Foundation, 2007), 11; Raymond R. Corrado and Irwin M. Cohen, *Mental Health Profiles for a Sample of British Columbia's Aboriginal Survivors of the Canadian Residential School System* (Ottawa: The Aboriginal Healing Foundation, 2004), 41: Agnes Grant, *No End of Grief: Indian Residential Schools in Canada* (Winnipeg: Pemmican Publications, 1996), 225–31.
36 Milloy, *A National Crime*, 298.
37 Fournier and Crey, "'Killing the Indian in the Child,'" 141–42.
38 About the various rules and punishments discussed in the following paragraph, see, in order, Haig-Brown, *Resistance and Renewal: Surviving the Indian Residential School* (Vancouver: Arsenal Pulp Press, 1991), 83; Andrea Smith, *Conquest: Sexual Violence and American Indian Genocide* (Cambridge, MA: South End Press, 2005), 40; Fournier and Crey, *Stolen from Our Embrace*, 59; Roland Chrisjohn and Sherri Young with Michael Maraun, *The Circle Game: Shadows and Substance in the Indian Residential School Experience in Canada* (Penticton, BC: Theytus Books, 2006), 49; Chansonneuve, *Addictive Behaviours*, 11.
39 Fournier and Crey, "'Killing the Indian in the Child,'" 148.
40 For the crimes discussed here, see, in order, Chrisjohn and Young with Maraun, *The Circle Game, 49*; Smith, *Conquest: Sexual*, 40; and Chansonneuve, *Addictive Behaviours*, 11.
41 O'Connor and O'Neal, *Dark Legacy*, 27.
42 Kirmayer et al., *Suicide among Aboriginal People*, 65.
43 Milloy, *A National Crime*, 259.
44 The details presented here about the poor health at residential schools are drawn from Furniss, *The Victims of Benevolence*, 28–29; and Smith, *Conquest*, 9.
45 Peter Henderson Bryce, *Report on the Indian Schools of Manitoba and the North-West Territories* (Ottawa: Government Printing Bureau, 1907), 15.
46 Ibid., 17.
47 Ibid., 18.
48 Ibid.
49 These details are presented in Canadian Paediatric Society, *Peter Henderson Bryce, M.D. Award for Excellence in Public Health Advocacy for First Nations, Metis, and Inuit Children and Youth: Award Summary, Criteria and Nomination Form*,

http://www.cps.ca/awards/BryceAward.pdf (accessed December 29, 2014), 2; for more about Bryce, see Adam J. Green, "Humanitarian M.D.: Dr. Peter Bryce's Contributions to Canadian Federal Native and Immigration Policy, 1904–1921" (MA thesis, Queens University, 1999).

50 The Onion Lake resident is quoted in Milloy, *A National Crime*, 109; the second quote also comes from this source. For hunger in residential schools more generally, see the same source, 109–27.

51 Ian Mosby, "Administering Colonial Science: Nutrition Research and Human Biomedical Experimentation in Aboriginal Communities and Residential Schools, 1942–1952," *Social History* 46, no. 91 (2013): 145–72, 171.

52 Ibid., 161.

53 Ibid., 148. The following paragraph, including quotations, borrows from Mosby's article, especially pp. 147–48, 162–63, 171.

54 Ibid., 168.

55 Chrisjohn and Young with Maraun, "The Circle Game," 77.

56 As quoted in William P. Quigley, *Ending Poverty as We Know It: Guaranteeing a Right to a Job at a Living Wage* (Philadelphia: Temple University Press, 2003), 8.

57 For the remainder of this paragraph, see Chrisjohn and Young with Maraun, *The Circle Game*, especially pages 60–61.

58 Raphael Lemkin, *Axis Rule in Occupied Europe* (Concord, NH: Carnegie Endowment for International Peace and Rumford Press, 1944; Clark, NJ: The Lawbook Exchange, 2008), 79. Citations refer to the 2008 reprint.

59 Quoted in Chrisjohn and Young with Maraun, *The Circle Game*, 61.

60 Lemkin, "Axis Rule in Occupied Europe," 79.

61 Dominion of Canada, *Annual Report of the Department of Indian Affairs for the Year Ended 30th June 1896* (Ottawa: S.E. Dawson, Printer to the Queen's Most Excellent Majesty, 1897), in the *Sessional Papers of the Dominion of Canada*, vol. 11, 2nd sess. 8th Parliament, sess. 1897.

62 Milloy, *A National Crime*, 3.

63 O'Connor and O'Neal, *Dark Legacy*, 27.

64 Susan Lazaruk, "77-Year-Old Pedophile Sentenced to 11 Years," *Windspeaker* 13, no. 2 (1995): 3. Details of the case come from Lazaruk's article.

65 Fournier and Crey, *Stolen from Our Embrace*, 66–67, quoted in O'Connor and O'Neal, *Dark Legacy*, 25.

66 Lazaruk, "77-Year-Old Pedophile Sentenced to 11 Years."

67 Hannah Spray, "Dorm Supervisor Guilty of Molesting Boys," *The Star Phoenix*, November 6 2013, http://www.theinquiry.ca/wordpress/misc/prominent-non-clerical-catholics-charged-sued-or-accused/leroux-paul-leroux/dorm-supervisor-guilty-of-molesting-boys/.

68 Dave Deibert, and Hannah Spray, "Leroux's Sentence for Molesting Boys Increased to 8 Years," *The Star Phoenix*, May 6, 2015, http://www.thestarphoenix.com/news/Leroux+sentence+molesting+boys+increased+years/11032593/story.html.

69 Aboriginal Affairs and Northern Development Canada, *Backgrounder—Indian Residential Schools Settlement Agreement* (Gatineau, QC: Aboriginal Affairs and Northern Development Canada, 2008). All details about the IRSSA are taken from this source.

70 Justice Murray Sinclair, "Rheal Brant Hall Lecture: Truth and Reconciliation."

71 For more on the TRC, see AANDC, *Backgrounder—Indian Residential Schools Settlement Agreement*; and the TRC website: www.trc.ca.

72 Paulette Regan, *Unsettling the Settler Within: Indian Residential Schools, Truth Telling, and Reconciliation in Canada* (Vancouver: UBC Press, 2010), 7. I draw on Regan for other details presented in this paragraph.

73 Truth and Reconciliation Commission, "TRC Releases Calls to Action to Begin Reconciliation," *Truth and Reconciliation Commission of Canada: Press Release*, June 2, 2015, http://www.trc.ca/websites/trcinstitution/File/TRCReportPressRelease(1).pdf (accessed August 6, 2015).

74 APTN National News, "Watch Prime Minister Trudeau's Address to the AFN's Special Chiefs Assembly here," *APTN National News*, December 8, 2015, http://aptn.ca/news/2015/12/08/watch-prime-minister-trudeaus-address-to-the-afns-special-chiefs-assembly-here/ (accessed December 8, 2015).

75 AANDC, *Backgrounder—Indian Residential Schools Settlement Agreement*. This is the source for other information about the AHF presented here.

76 Daniel Schwartz, "Truth and Reconciliation Commission: By the Numbers," *CBC News*, June 2, 2015, http://www.cbc.ca/news/aboriginal/truth-and-reconciliation-commission-by-the-numbers-1.3096185.

77 O'Connor and O'Neal, *Dark Legacy*, 27–28.

78 Canadian Conference of Catholic Bishops, *Apology on Residential Schools by the Catholic Church*, http://www.cccb.ca/site/eng/media-room/files/2630-apology-on-residential-schools-by-the-catholic-church (accessed August 20, 2015).

79 The Aboriginal Healing Foundation, *Response, Responsibility and Renewal: Canada's Truth and Reconciliation Journey* (Ottawa: The Aboriginal Healing Foundation, 2009), 375.

80 The Aboriginal Healing Foundation, *Response, Responsibility and Renewal*, 383.

81 Stephen Harper, "Prime Minister Stephen Harper's Statement of Apology," *CBC News*, June 11, 2008, http://www.cbc.ca/news/canada/prime-minister-stephen-harper-s-statement-of-apology-1.734250.

82 On this issue and for other information in this paragraph, see O'Connor and O'Neal, *Dark Legacy*, 29–31.

83 On the issue of the intergenerational trauma induced by residential schools, see Rosalyn Ing, "Canada's Indian Residential Schools and Their Impacts on Mothering," in "*Until Our Hearts Are on the Ground": Aboriginal Mothering, Oppression, Resistance and Rebirth*, ed. D. Mermee Lavell-Harvard and Jeannette Corbiere Lavell, 157–72 (Toronto: Demeter Press, 2006), 158. I draw on Ing's work in the subsequent paragraph.

84 Fournier and Crey, *Stolen from Our Embrace*, 82.

85 Chansonneuve, *Addictive Behaviours*, 20.

86 Grant, *No End of Grief*, 229.

87 Royal Commission on Aboriginal Peoples, *Bridging the Cultural Divide: A Report on Aboriginal People and Criminal Justice in Canada* (Ottawa: Minister of Supply and Services Canada, 1996), 370–80.

88 Ibid., 379.

89 Amy Bombay, Kimberly Matheson, and Hymie Anisman, "The Impact of Stressors on Second Generation Indian Residential School Survivors," *Transcultural Psychiatry* 48, no. 4 (2011): 367–91, 367.

90 Chansonneuve, *Addictive Behaviours*, 12.

91 See, for example, David Farrington and Brandon Welsh, *Saving Children from a Life of Crime: Early Risk Factors and Effective Interventions* (New York: Oxford University Press, 2007).

92 Ingrid Söchting, Raymond Corrado, Irwin M. Cohen, Robert G. Ley, and Charles Brasfield, "Traumatic Pasts in Canadian Aboriginal People: Further Support for a Complex Trauma Conceptualization?" *BC Medical Journal* 49, no. 6 (2007): 320–26, 323–24.

93 Corrado, and Cohen, *Mental Health Profiles*, 46.

94 Judy Atkinson, *Trauma Trails: Recreating Song Lines: The Transgenerational Effects of Trauma in Indigenous Australia* (North Melborne: Spinifex Press, 2002) as cited by Elizabeth Comack, Lawrence Deane, Larry Morrissette, and Jim Silver, *"Indians Wear Red" Colonialism, Resistance, and Aboriginal Street Gangs* (Blackpoint, NS: Fernwood Publishing, 2013), 38.

95 Ibid., 52.

96 Ibid., 92.

97 Maria Yellow Horse Brave Heart, *Welcome to Takini's Historical Trauma*, http://www.historicaltrauma.com/ (accessed February 19, 2015).

98 Maria Yellow Horse Brave Heart, "The Historical Trauma Response among Natives and Its Relationship with Substance Abuse: A Lakota Illustration," *Journal of Psychoactive Drugs* 35, no. 1 (2003): 7–13, 8.

99 Ibid. For other information discussed here, including quotes, see the same source, 7–8.

100 For example, see Cynthia C. Wesley-Esquimaux and Magdalena Smolewski, *Historic Trauma and Aboriginal Healing* (Ottawa: The Aboriginal Healing Foundation, 2004); Deborah Chansonneuve, *Reclaiming Connections: Understanding Residential School Trauma among Aboriginal People* (Ottawa: The Aboriginal Healing Foundation, 2005); Söchting et al., "Traumatic Pasts in Canadian Aboriginal People"; Beverley Jacobs and Andreas J. Williams, "Legacy of Residential Schools: Missing and Murdered Aboriginal Women," in *From Truth to Reconciliation Transforming the Legacy of Residential Schools*, ed. Marlene Brant Castellano, Linda Archibald, and Mike DeGagné, 119–40 (Ottawa: The Aboriginal Healing Foundation, 2008).

101 See Chansonneuve, *Reclaiming Connections*, 43–48, 50–53; Söchting et al., "Traumatic Pasts in Canadian Aboriginal People"; Jacobs and Williams, "Legacy of Residential Schools," 126; Wesley-Esquimaux and Smolewski, *Historic Trauma and Aboriginal Healing*; Bombay, Matheson, and Anisman, "The Impact of Stressors on Second Generation Indian Residential School Survivors."

Chapter 8

1 Samuel Perreault, "Violent Victimization of Aboriginal People in the Canadian Provinces, 2009," *Juristat* 30, no. 44 (2011): 1–35; Samuel Perreault, "Admissions to Adult Correctional Services in Canada, 2011/2012," *Juristat* 34, no. 1 (2014).

2 Samuel Perreault, *The Incarceration of Aboriginal People in Adult Correctional Services* (Ottawa: Canadian Centre for Justice Statistics, 2009), 9.

3 Samuel Perreault, "Admissions to Adult Correctional Services in Canada, 2011/2012."

4 Office of the Correctional Investigator, *Spirit Matters: Aboriginal People and the Corrections and Conditional Release Act* (Ottawa: Office of the Correctional Investigator, 2012), 11.

5 Correctional Investigator of Canada, *Annual Report of the Office of the Correctional Investigator, 2012–2013* (Ottawa: Her Majesty the Queen in Right of Canada, 2013), 31.

6 Correctional Investigator of Canada, *Annual Report of the Office of the Correctional Investigator, 2013–2014* (Ottawa: Her Majesty the Queen in the Right of Canada, 2014), 44.

7 See, for example, Wendy Chan and Dorothy Chunn, *Racialization, Crime, and Criminal Justice in Canada* (Toronto: University of Toronto Press, 2014), 12.

8 Jonathan Rudin, "Aboriginal Peoples and the Criminal Justice System," background paper prepared for the Ipperwash Inquiry, 2005, http://www.archives.gov.on.ca/en/e_records/ipperwash/policy_part/research/pdf/Rudin.pdf, 26.

9 Research Working Group of the Task Force on Race and the Criminal Justice System, "Preliminary Report on Race and Washington's Criminal Justice System," *Washington Law Review* 87, no. 1 (2012), 1–49, 9. This source supplies other ideas communicated in this paragraph.

10 CBC, "Aboriginal Corrections Report Finds 'Systemic Discrimination,'" *CBC News*, March 7, 2013, http://www.cbc.ca/news/politics/aboriginal-corrections-report-finds-systemic-discrimination-1.1338498.

11 Patricia Monture-Angus, *Thunder in My Soul: A Mohawk Women Speaks* (Halifax: Fernwood Publishing, 1995), 178.

12 Samuel Perreault, *Violent Victimization of Aboriginal People in the Canadian Provinces, 2009* (Ottawa: Canadian Centre for Justice Statistics, 2011).

13 Leah Mulligan and Zoran Miladinovic, *Homicide in Canada 2014* (Ottawa: Canadian Centre for Justice Statistics, 2015), 16.

14 Perreault, *Violent Victimization of Aboriginal People*, 7.

15 Ibid.

16 This paragraph, including the quote, draws on Monture-Angus, *Thunder in My Soul*, 170.

17 See Jodi-Anne Brzozowski, Andrea Taylor-Butts, and Sara Johnson, *Victimization and Offending Among the Aboriginal Population in Canada* (Ottawa: Canadian Centre for Justice Statistics, 2006); Carol La Prairie, *Seen but not Heard: Native People in the Inner City* (Ottawa: Department of Justice, 1994); Carol La Prairie, *Dimensions of Aboriginal Over-Representation in Correctional Institutions and Implications for Crime Prevention* (Ottawa: Aboriginal Peoples Collection, Solicitor General of Canada, 1992); Carol La Prairie, "Aboriginal Over-Representation in the Criminal Justice System: A Tale of Nine Cities," *Canadian Journal of Criminology* 44, no. 2 (2002): 181–208.

18 See Lisa Monchalin, "Reducing Crime Affecting Urban Aboriginal People: The Potential for Effective Solutions in Winnipeg" (PhD dissertation, University of Ottawa, 2012), 47–50 for an overview of risk factors derived from research studies.

19 Ann S. Masten, J. Cutuli, Janette E. Herbers, and Marie-Gabrielle Reed, "Resilience in Development," in *Oxford Handbook of Positive Psychology*, 2nd

ed., ed. C. R. Snyder and Shane J. Lopez, 117–31 (New York: Oxford University Press, 2009), 118.

20 Madeleine Dion Stout and Gregory Kipling, *Aboriginal People, Resilience and the Residential School Legacy* (Ottawa: The Aboriginal Healing Foundation, 2003), v. Dion Stout and Kipling's work provides much of the detail subsequently presented.

21 For example see, World Health Organization, *Preventing Violence: A Guide to Implementing the Recommendations of the World Report on Violence and Health* (Geneva: WHO, 2004); this source uses these categories to outline the different levels of risk factors.

22 Richard F. Catalano and J. David Hawkins, "The Social Development Model: A Theory of Anti-Social Behaviour," in *Delinquency and Crime*, ed. J. David Hawkins, 149–98 (Cambridge: Cambridge University Press, 1996).

23 Richard F. Catalano, J. David Hawkins, Rick Kosterman, Robert Abbott, and Karl G. Hill, "Preventing Adolescent Health-Risk Behaviors by Strengthening Protection During Childhood," *Archives of Pediatrics Adolescent Medicine* 153, no. 3 (1999): 226–34.

24 Robert J. Sampson and W. Byron Groves, "Community Structure and Crime: Testing Social Disorganization Theory," *American Journal of Sociology* 94, no. 4 (1989): 774–802.

25 Robin T. Fitzgerald and Peter J. Carrington, "The Neighbourhood Context of Urban Aboriginal Crime," *The Canadian Journal of Criminology and Criminal Justice* 50, no. 5 (2008): 523–57; Cathleen Knotsch and Dianne Kinnon, *If Not Now . . . When: Addressing the Ongoing Inuit Housing Crisis in Canada* (Ottawa: National Aboriginal Health Organization, 2011), 28; La Prairie, *Dimensions of Aboriginal Over-Representation*; La Prairie, "Aboriginal Over-Representation in the Criminal Justice System"; Charlotte Loppie Reading and Fred Wien, *Health Inequalities and Social Determinants of Aboriginal Peoples' Health* (Prince George, BC: National Collaborating Centre for Aboriginal Health, 2009), 3; J. Reading, *The Crisis of Chronic Disease Among Aboriginal Peoples: A Challenge for Public Health, Population Health, and Social Policy* (Victoria, BC: Centre for Aboriginal Health Research, 2009), 13.

26 As quoted by Gabor Maté, *In The Realm of Hungry Ghosts: Close Encounters with Addiction* (Toronto: Vintage Books, 2012), 196.

27 Ibid.

28 Ibid., 198.

29 Chalsa M. Loo, "Density, Crowding, and Preschool Children," in *Human Response to Crowding*, ed. A. Baum and Y. M. Epstain, 371–88 (Hillsdale, NJ: Lawrence Erlbaum, 1978); Chalsa M. Loo, "The Effects of Spatial Density on the Social Behavior of Children," *Journal of Applied Social Psychology* 2, no. 4 (1972): 372–81; Mason Durie, "Understanding Health and Illness: Research at the Interface Between Science and Indigenous Knowledge," *International Journal of Epidemiology* 33, no. 2 (2004): 1138–43.

30 Maria E. Parente and Joseph L. Mahoney, "Residential Mobility and Exposure to Neighborhood Crime: Risks For Young Children's Aggression," *Journal of Community Psychology* 37, no. 5 (2009): 559–78, 559–60.

31 Robert J. Sampson and Stephen W. Raudenbush, "Systematic Social Observation of Public Spaces: A New Look at Disorder in Urban Neighborhoods," *American Journal of Sociology* 105, no. 3 (1999): 603–51.

32 Robin T. Fitzgerald and Peter J. Carrington, "The Neighbourhood Context of Urban Aboriginal Crime," *The Canadian Journal of Criminology and Criminal Justice* 50, no. 5 (2008): 523–57.
33 Jeffrey Reiman, *The Rich Get Richer and the Poor Get Prison: Ideology, Class, and Criminal Justice* (Boston: Allyn and Bacon, 2007).
34 Reiman, *The Rich Get Richer*, 183.
35 Statistics Canada, *2001 Census: Analysis Series Aboriginal Peoples of Canada—A Demographic Profile* (Ottawa: Minister of Industry, 2003), 11.
36 Statistics Canada, *Aboriginal Peoples in Canada in 2006: Inuit, Métis, and First Nations 2006 Census Findings* (Ottawa: Minister of Industry, 2008), http://www12.statcan.ca/census-recensement/2006/as-sa/97-558/pdf/97-558-XIE2006001.pdf (accessed February 19, 2013); Statistics Canada, *2001 Census: Analysis Series Aboriginal Peoples of Canada.*
37 Jim Silver, with Joan Hay, Parvin Ghorayshi, Darlene Klyne, Peter Gorzen, Cyril Keeper, Michael Mackenzie, and Freeman Simard, *In Their Own Voices: Building Urban Aboriginal Communities* (Halifax: Fernwood Publishing, 2006), 16–17.
38 Ibid., 17.
39 These numbers and percentages are derived from a Statistics Canada custom tabulation based on 2001 census data, cited by Tom Carter, *Planning for Newcomers in Winnipeg's Inner. City* (Winnipeg: Metropolis, 2009), 1.
40 In 2006, 11 per cent of Indigenous people were living in homes with more than one person per room, which is down from 17 per cent in 1996, according to Statistics Canada.
41 Statistics Canada, *Aboriginal Peoples in Canada in 2006*, 16.
42 See the following documentary films for examples, *Third World Canada*, DVD, directed by Andrée Cazabon (Ottawa: Productions Cazabon, 2010); *The Invisible Nation*, DVD, directed by Richard Dejardins and Robert Monderie (Ottawa: The National Film Board of Canada, 2007); *The People of the Kattawapiskak River*, DVD, directed by Alanis Obomsawin (Ottawa: The National Film Board of Canada, 2012).
43 For the details of the situation discussed here, see *The People of the Kattawapiskak River.*
44 *Attawapiskat First Nation v. Canada*, 2012 FC 948.
45 For this crisis in Kashechewan, see Heather Scoffield, "Neighbouring Reserve to Attawapiskat Narrowly Avoids Fuel, Housing Crisis," *Globe and Mail*, December 2 2012, http://www.theglobeandmail.com/news/national/neighbouring-reserve-to-attawapiskat-narrowly-avoids-fuel-housing-crisis/article5899087/ (accessed February 17, 2013); the quotation is also from this article.
46 Andrea Harden and Holly Levallient, *Boiling Point! Six Community Profiles of the Water Crisis Facing First Nations within Canada* (Ottawa: The Polaris Institute, 2008), 6.
47 Canadian Centre for Policy Alternatives, *A Budget for the Rest of Us: Alternative Federal Budget 2012* (Ottawa: Canadian Centre for Policy Alternatives, 2012), 37–38.
48 These details are presented in Assembly of First Nations, *AFN Supports Pikangikum First Nation's Call for New Water Supply System: State of Emergency Issued Over Lack of Clean Drinking Water*, April 19, 2011, http://www.afn.ca/index.php/en/news-media/latest-news/afn-supports-pikangikum-first-nations-call-for-new-water-supply-system (accessed February 17, 2013).
49 Harden and Levallient, *Boiling Point! Six Community Profiles*, 13.

50 This information is drawn from ibid., 13.

51 Northwestern Health Unit, "Inspection Report on the Pikangikum Water and Sewage Systems," prepared for the Pikangikum First Nation by the Northwestern Health Unit, September 2006, http://www.turtleisland.org/healing/pikangikum06a.pdf (accessed August 3, 2015).

52 Leslie Young, "First Nations Enduring Decade-old Boil Water Advisories," *Global News*, January 20, 2012, http://globalnews.ca/news/202047/first-nations-enduring-decade-old-boil-water-advisories/ (accessed July 30, 2015).

53 Jody Porter, "Pikangikum First Nation Water Aid Stalled by Limited Power Supply," *CBC News*, February 24, 2015, http://www.cbc.ca/news/canada/thunder-bay/pikangikum-first-nation-water-aid-stalled-by-limited-power-supply-1.2968295.

54 Tara Carman, "Warnings Prompt Metro Vancouver-Area Bands to Improve Water Quality on First Nations Reserves [sic]: Semiahmoo Band Has Been Testing its Own Water Since 1996," *Vancouver Sun*, January 16, 2013, http://www.vancouversun.com/news/Warnings+prompt+Metro+Vancouver+area+bands+improve+water/7830173/story.html (accessed February 17, 2013).

55 Leslie Young, "First Nations Enduring."

56 CBC, "Ottawa-area Reserve Still Waiting for Clean Tap Water," *CBC News*, February 20, 2006, http://www.cbc.ca/news/canada/ottawa/ottawa-area-reserve-still-waiting-for-clean-tap-water-1.620131. .

57 Harden and Levallient, *Boiling Point! Six Community Profiles*, 8.

58 See the "Environmental Health" section of the First Nations Health Authority website for up-to-date information (http://www.fnha.ca/what-we-do/environmental-health) for British Columbia. Health Canada provides statistics on drinking water advisories in First Nation communities for the rest of Canada.

59 T. Kue Young, Jeff Reading, Brenda Elias, and John D. O'Neil, "Type 2 Diabetes Mellitus in Canada's First Nations: Status of an Epidemic in Progress," *Canadian Medical Association Journal* 163, no. 5 (2000): 561–66.

60 Michael Tjepkema, *The Health of the Off-Reserve Aboriginal Population* (Ottawa: Statistics Canada, 2002), 3; Public Health Agency of Canada, *2011 Diabetes in Canada: Facts and Figures from a Public Health Perspective* (Ottawa, Public Health Agency of Canada, 2011), 92.

61 Susan J. Whiting and Michelle L. Mackenzie, "Assessing the Changing Diet of Indigenous Peoples," *Nutrition Reviews* 56, no. 8 (1998): 248–50; S. S. Anand, S. Yusuf, R. Jacobs, A. D. Davis, Q. Yi, H. Gerstein, P. A. Montague, and E. Lonn, "Risk Factors, Atherosclerosis, and Cardiovascular Disease Among Aboriginal People in Canada: The Study of Health Assessment and Risk Evaluation in Aboriginal Peoples (SHARE-AP)," *Lancet* 358, no. 9288 (2001): 1147–53; Andrea M. Kriska, Anthony J. G. Hanley, Stewart B. Harris, and Bernard Zinman, "Physical Activity, Physical Fitness, and Insulin and Glucose Concentrations in an Isolated Native Canadian Population Experiencing Rapid Lifestyle Change," *Diabetes Care* 24, no. 10 (2001): 1787–92.

62 H. L. MacMillan, A. B. MacMillan, D. R. Offord, and J. L. Dingle, "Aboriginal Health," *Canadian Medical Association Journal* 155, no. 11 (1996): 1569–78; Statistics Canada, "Introduction," in *The Health Divide—How the Sexes Differ*, special issue, *Health Reports* 12, no. 3 (2001): 9–10; Indian and Northern Affairs Canada, *Comparison of Social Conditions, 1991 and 1996: Registered Indians, Registered Indians Living On Reserve and the Total Population of Canada* (Ottawa: Indian Affairs and

Northern Development Canada, 2000), quoted by Michael Tjepkema, *The Health of the Off-Reserve Aboriginal Population* (Ottawa: Statistics Canada, 2002), 1.

63 Louise Elliott, "Ontario Native Suicide Rate One of the Highest in World, Expert Says," *Canadian Press*, November 27, 2000, http://www.hartford-hwp.com/archives/41/353.html.

64 Laurence J. Kirmayer, Gregory M. Brass, Tara Holton, Ken Paul, Cori Simpson, and Caroline Tait, *Suicide Among Aboriginal People in Canada* (Ottawa: The Aboriginal Healing Foundation, 2007), 1; see also, Laurence Kirmayer, Cori Simpson, and Margaret Cargo, "Healing Traditions: Culture, Community and Mental Health Promotion with Canadian Aboriginal Peoples," *Australasian Psychiatry* 11 (2003): S15–S23.

65 Michael J. Kral, *Contagion, Mimesis, Internalization: A Cultural Model of Suicide* (Champaign: University of Illinois at Urbana-Champaign, 2011), 8. Available at http://www.inter-disciplinary.net/wp-content/uploads/2011/10/kralspaper.pdf (accessed February 18, 2013).

66 Kral, *Contagion, Mimesis*, 8.

67 Michael J. Chandler and Christopher E. Lalonde, "Cultural Continuity as a Hedge Against Suicide in Canada's First Nations," *Transcultural Psychiatry* 35, no. 2 (1998): 191–219.

68 Darcey Hallett, Michael J. Chandler, and Christopher E. Lalonde, "Aboriginal Language Knowledge and Youth Suicide," *Cognitive Development* 22, no. 3 (2007): 392–99, 393.

69 Laurence J. Kirmayer, Sarah-Louise Fraser, Virginia Fauras, and Rob Whitley, *Current Approaches to Aboriginal Youth Suicide Prevention* (Montreal: Jewish General Hospital, 2009), 13.

70 Ibid., 19.

71 Iris Wagman Borowsky, Michael D. Resnick, Marjorie Ireland, and Robert W. Blum, "Suicide Attempts Among American Indian and Alaska Native Youth: Risk and Protective Factors," *Archives of Pediatrics and Adolescent Medicine* 153, no. 6 (1999): 573–80; Paul Kettl and Edward O. Bixler, "Alcohol and Suicide in Alaska Natives," *American Indian and Alaska Native Mental Health Research* 5, no. 2 (1993): 34–45; J. Paul Seale, Sylvia Shellenberger, and John Spence, "Alcohol Problems in Alaska Natives: Lessons from the Inuit," *American Indian & Alaskan Native Mental Health Research: The Journal of the National Center* 13, no. 1 (2006): 1–30, 2.

72 Kirmayer, Fraser, Fauras, and Whitley, *Current Approaches*, 15.

73 See Royal Commission on Aboriginal Peoples, *Bridging the Cultural Divide: A Report on Aboriginal People and Criminal Justice in Canada* (Ottawa: Supply and Services Canada, 1996). This report came to this conclusion after examining several studies.

74 Health Canada, *A Statistical Profile on the Health of First Nations in Canada: Determinants of Health, 1999–2003* (Ottawa: Minister of Health Canada, 2009), 22, http://www.hc-sc.gc.ca/fniah-spnia/alt_formats/fnihb-dgspni/pdf/pubs/aborig-autoch/2009-stats-profil-eng.pdf (accessed February 18, 2013).

75 Statistics Canada, *Select Health Indicators of First Nations People Living Off Reserve, Métis and Inuit* (Ottawa: Statistics Canada, 2011), http://www.statcan.gc.ca/pub/82-624-x/2013001/article/11763-eng.htm.

76 The Health Canada report *A Statistical Profile* is cited by Tjepkema, *The Health of the Off-Reserve Aboriginal Population*, 8.

77 Health Canada, *A Statistical Profile*, iv.

78 Statistics Canada, *Select Health Indicators of First Nations* (2011).

79 Health Canada, *A Statistical Profile*, 22.

80 C. Lavallee and C. Bourgault, "The Health of Cree, Inuit and Southern Québec Women: Similarities and Differences," *Canadian Journal of Public Health* 9, no. 3 (2000): 212–16.

81 World Health Organization, *Violence Prevention: The Evidence—Overview* (Geneva: WHO, 2009), 46.

82 Ibid., 47.

83 Chansonneuve, *Addictive Behaviours*.

84 CBC, "Politicians Weight in on Gas Sniffing in Natuashish," *CBC News*, September 21, 2012, http://www.cbc.ca/news/canada/newfoundland-labrador/politicians-weigh-in-on-gas-sniffing-in-natuashish-1.1146972 (accessed February 18, 2013).

85 Aušra Burns, "Moving and Moving Forward: Mushuau Innu Relocation from Davis Inlet to Natuashish," *Acadiensis* 35, no. 2 (Spring 2006): 64–84.

86 Myriam Denov and Kathryn Campbell, "Casualties of Aboriginal Displacement in Canada: Children at Risk Among the Innu of Labrador," *Refuge* 20, no. 2 (2002): 21–33, see especially 21–25.

87 Ibid., 24. Denov and Campbell's article provides much of the detail for the subsequent discussion.

88 Bruce K. Alexander, *The Roots of Addiction in Free Market Society* (Vancouver: Canadian Centre for Policy Alternatives, 2001), 13, 14. I draw on this source for the next two sentences.

89 Chansonneuve, *Addictive Behaviours*, 28.

90 Gabor Maté, *In The Realm of Hungry Ghosts: Close Encounters with Addiction* (Canada: Vintage Books, 2012).

91 Ibid., 192.

92 Gabor Maté, "Dr. Gabor Maté on the Stress-Disease Connection, Addiction and the Destruction of American Childhood," *Democracy Now: A Daily Independent Global News Hour*, December 25, 2012, http://www.democracynow.org/2012/12/25/dr_gabor_mat_on_the_stress (accessed April 8, 2013).

93 Robert J. Sampson and John H. Laub, *Crime in the Making: Pathways and Turning Points Through Life* (Cambridge, MA: Harvard University Press, 1993), 147.

94 The cities involved were San Antonio (TX), Philadelphia (PA), Milwaukee (WI), Saginaw (MI), and Oklahoma City (OK); the project began in September 1989.

95 Details about the program are taken from Andrew Hahn, Tom Leavitt, and Paul Aaron, *Evaluation of the Quantum Opportunities Program (QOP) Did the Program Work?* (Waltham: Brandeis University, 1994), see especially 6–15.

96 As well as the study's report itself, see Peter W. Greenwood, Karyn E. Model, Peter C. Rydell, and James Chiesa, *Diverting Children from a Life of Crime: Measuring Costs and Benefit* (Santa Monica, CA: RAND, 1996).

97 Hahn, Leavitt, and Aaron, "Evaluation of the Quantum Opportunities," 15.

98 Irvin Waller, *Less Law, More Order: The Truth about Reducing Crime* (Ancaster, ON: Manor House Publishing, 2008), 29.

99 Daniel Wilson and David MacDonald, *The Income Gap Between Aboriginal Peoples and the Rest of Canada* (Ottawa: Canadian Centre for Policy Alternatives, 2010), 15.

100 Jason Gilmore, *Trends in Dropout Rates and the Labour Market Outcomes of Young Dropouts* (Ottawa: Labour Statistics Division, Statistics Canada, 2010).

101 This information comes directly from Assembly of First Nations, "Fact Sheet—Quality of Life of First Nations, June 2011," http://www.afn.ca/uploads/files/factsheets/quality_of_life_final_fe.pdf (accessed February 18, 2013).

102 Wilson and MacDonald, *The Income Gap*, 17.

103 Ibid., 15.

104 Statistics Canada, *The Educational Attainment of Aboriginal Peoples in Canada: National Household Survey, 2011* (Ottawa: Statistics Canada, 2013), 4–5, http://www12.statcan.gc.ca/nhs-enm/2011/as-sa/99-012-x/99-012-x2011003_3-eng.pdf.

105 Cindy Blackstock, *Jordan & Shannen: First Nations Children Demand that the Canadian Government Stop Racially Discriminating Against Them* (Ottawa: First Nations Child and Family Caring Society, 2011), 8, http://www.fncaringsociety.ca/sites/default/files/Canada_FNCCaringSocietyofCanada_CRC61.pdf (accessed February 18, 2013).

106 Ibid., 8.

107 Provincial Advocate for Children and Youth, *Our Dreams Matter Too: First Nations Children's Rights, Lives, and Education—An Alternate Report from the Shannen's Dream Campaign*, report given to the United Nations Committee on the Rights of the Child on the occasion of Canada's 3rd and 4th periodic reviews (Toronto: Office of the Provincial Advocate for Children and Youth, 2011), 78, http://www2.ohchr.org/english/bodies/crc/docs/ngos/Canada_ShannensDreamCampaign_CRC61_en.pdf (accessed November 30, 2013).

108 Ibid., 14; some reports have the spill at over 50,000 litres of diesel fuel; see Provincial Advocate for Children and Youth, *Our Dreams Matter Too*, 8.

109 Blackstock, *Jordan & Shannen*, 8.

110 Provincial Advocate for Children and Youth, *Our Dreams Matter Too*, 11–14.

111 Jessica Young, "Attawapiskat Outrage Grows," *The Daily Press*, April 15, 2009, http://www.timminspress.com/2009/04/15/attawapiskat-outrage-grows (accessed November 30, 2013).

112 CBC, "Attawapiskat Names Long-Awaited School 'Kattawapiskak,'" *CBC News*, August 27, 2014, http://www.cbc.ca/news/canada/sudbury/attawapiskat-names-long-awaited-school-kattawapiskak-1.2748073 (accessed August 2, 2015).

113 This and the following paragraph's details, including the quote, are found in Blackstock, *Jordan & Shannen*, 7.

114 Assembly of First Nations, "Fact Sheet—Quality of Life of First Nations, June 2011," http://www.afn.ca/uploads/files/factsheets/quality_of_life_final_fe.pdf.

115 Blackstock, *Jordan & Shannen*, 7.

116 Statistics for Winnipeg are from Statistics Canada, *2006 Aboriginal Population Profile for Winnipeg* (Ottawa: Minister of Industry, 2010), http://www.statcan.gc.ca/pub/89-638-x/2010003/article/11082-eng.pdf (accessed February 19, 2013); Statistics Canada, *Aboriginal Peoples in Canada in 2006: Inuit, Métis and First Nations, 2006 Census* (Ottawa: Minister of Industry, 2008), http://www12.statcan.ca/census-recensement/2006/as-sa/97-558/pdf/97-558-XIE2006001.pdf (accessed February 19, 2013).

117 Jim Silver and Kathy Mallett with Janice Greene and Freeman Simard, *Aboriginal Education in Winnipeg Inner City High Schools* (Winnipeg: Canadian Centre for Policy Alternatives–Manitoba, 2002); for the following material on textbooks, see 26.

118 Coalition for the Advancement of Aboriginal Studies, *Learning About Walking in*

Beauty: Placing Aboriginal Perspectives in Canadian Classrooms (Toronto: Canadian Race Relations Foundation, 2002), 103.

119 Ibid., 129.

120 Ibid., 103.

121 Ibid., 128.

122 Ibid., 38; James (Sákéj) Youngblood Henderson, "Postcolonial Ghost Dancing: Diagnosing European Colonialism," in *Reclaiming Indigenous Voices and Vision*, ed. Marie Battiste, 57–76 (Vancouver: UBC Press, 2009), 59.

123 Monture-Angus, *Thunder in My Soul*, 79.

124 Coalition for the Advancement of Aboriginal Studies, *Learning About Walking in Beauty*, 2.

125 Monture-Angus, *Thunder in My Soul*, 88.

126 Coalition for the Advancement of Aboriginal Studies, *Learning About Walking in Beauty*, 15.

127 Vancouver School Board, *Aboriginal Focus School*, http://www.vsb.bc.ca/aboriginal-school (accessed March 13, 2014).

128 John Woods, "Winnipeg School Division Adds Ojibway, Cree, Spanish, French Programs," *Winnipeg Free Press*, December 8, 2015, http://www.winnipegfreepress.com/local/Winnipeg-School-Division-adds-Ojibway-Cree-Spanish-French-programs-360911701.html (accessed December 8, 2015).

129 The details of this paragraph, including the quote, can be found in Coalition for the Advancement of Aboriginal Studies, *Learning About Walking in Beauty*, 15, 16.

130 Juha Mikkonen and Dennis Raphael, *Social Determinants of Health: The Canadian Facts* (Toronto: York University School of Health Policy and Management, 2010), http://www.thecanadianfacts.org/The_Canadian_Facts.pdf (accessed February 18, 2013).

131 Dana Mitra, *Pennsylvania's Best Investment: The Social and Economic Benefits of Public Education* (Philadelphia: Education Law Centre, 2011).

132 Evelyne Bougie, Karen Kelly-Scott, and Paula Arriagada, *The Education and Employment Experiences of First Nations People Living Off Reserve, Inuit, and Métis*. (Ottawa: Statistics Canada, 2013).

133 Aboriginal Affairs and Northern Development Canada, "Fact Sheet: 2006 Census Aboriginal Demographics," http://www.aadnc-aandc.gc.ca/eng/1100100016377/1100100016378 (accessed March 23, 2014).

134 For data on Aboriginal and non-Aboriginal employment and income, see Wilson and MacDonald, *The Income Gap*, 3.

135 Canadian Council on Social Development, *Unequal Access: A Canadian Profile of Racial Differences in Education, Employment and Income* (Toronto: Canadian Race Relations Foundation, 2000), see especially 3, 35–36 for information in this paragraph.

136 Statistics Canada, *2001* Census, 9.

137 Rolf Loeber and David P. Farrington, "Young Children Who Commit Crime: Epidemiology, Developmental Origins, Risk Factors, Early Interventions, and Policy Implications," *Development and Psychopathology* 12, no. 4 (2000): 737–62.

138 Maté, *In the Realm of Hungry Ghosts*, 188.

139 Ibid., 191.

140 Ibid., 191, 198.

141 Ibid., 191.

142 Five hundred women were invited to participate and 400 enrolled; details of the study mentioned here are from David L. Olds, Charles R. Henderson Jr., Harriet J. Kitzman, John J. Eckenrode, Robert E. Cole, and Robert C. Tatelbaum, "Prenatal and Infancy Home Visitation by Nurses: Recent Findings," *The Future of Children* 9, no. 1 (1999): 44–65, 49, 53.

143 High risk was defined as the mothers being unmarried, adolescent, or poor.

144 At the 15-year follow-up, assessments were completed on 324 participants, representing 81 per cent of the original random sample, as well as 87 per cent of the families in which there were no fetal, maternal, or child deaths. For more on follow-up, see Olds et al., "Prenatal and Infancy Home Visitation," 53–54.

145 Olds et al., "Prenatal and Infancy Home Visitation," 44; Irvin Waller, *Less Law, More Order: The Truth About Reducing Crime* (Ancaster, ON: Manor House Publishing, 2008), 26.

146 Olds et al., "Prenatal and Infancy Home Visitation," 44.

147 As well as the study, see Lynn A. Karoly, Peter W. Greenwood, Susan S. Everingham, Jill Houbé, M. Rebecca Kilburn, C. Peter Rydell, Matthew Sanders, and James Chiesa, *Investing in Our Children: What We Know and Don't Know about the Costs and Benefits of Early Childhood Interventions* (Santa Monica, CA: RAND, 1998), 32.

148 Julie Savignac, *Families, Youth, and Delinquency: The State of Knowledge, and Family-Based Juvenile Delinquency Prevention Programs* (Ottawa: National Crime Prevention Centre, 2009).

149 Indian Act, RSC 1985, c I-5. at s. 88.

150 For this paragraph, I have drawn on Lynda Gray, *First Nations 101: Tons of Stuff You Need to Know about First Nations People* (Vancouver: Adaawx Publishing, 2011), 65–66.

151 Raven Sinclair, "Identity Lost and Found: Lessons from the Sixties Scoop," *First Peoples Child & Family Review* 3, no. 1 (2007): 65–82, 65–66.

152 Marlyn Bennett, Cindy Blackstock, and Richard De La Ronde, *A Literature Review and Annotated Bibliography on Aspects of Aboriginal Child Welfare in Canada*, 2nd edition (Ottawa: First Nations Child and Family Caring Society, 2005), 22.

153 Patrick Johnston, *Aboriginal Children and the Child Welfare System* (Toronto: Canadian Council on Social Development, 1983).

154 For the quote and subsequent details, see Sinclair, "Identity Lost and Found," 66.

155 For abuses see, Bennett, Blackstock, De La Ronde, *A Literature Review and Annotated Bibliography on Aspects of Aboriginal Child Welfare in Canada*, 19–20.

156 Ibid., 20.

157 See Christine Smith (McFarlane), "A Legacy of Canadian Child Care: Surviving the Sixties Scoop," *Briarpatch Magazine*, September 1, 2013, https://briarpatchmagazine.com/articles/view/a-legacy-of-canadian-child-care for her full story.

158 Sinclair, "Identity Lost and Found," 67.

159 Cindy Blackstock, John Loxlely, Tara Prakash, and Fred Wien, *Wen:de: We Are Coming to the Light of Day* (Ottawa: First Nations Child and Family Caring Society of Canada, 2005).

160 Assembly of First Nations, *Leadership Action Plan on First Nations Child Welfare* (Ottawa: Assembly of First Nations, 2006), 1, http://www.turtleisland.org/

healing/afncf.pdf (accessed December 19, 2012); Assembly of First Nations, "Fact Sheet—Child Welfare, October 2013," http://www.afn.ca/uploads/files/13-02-23_fact_sheet_-_child_welfare_updated_fe.pdf.

161 Blackstock, *Jordan & Shannen*, 4.

162 Native Women's Association of Canada, *Special Submission to the Expert Mechanism on the Rights of Indigenous Peoples (EMRIP) on Access to Justice for Aboriginal Women in Canada*, March 10 (Ottawa: NWAC, 2014), 5.

163 Indian and Northern Affairs Canada, *Evaluation of the First Nations Child and Family Service Program* (Gatineau, QC: Indian and Northern Affairs Canada, Department of Audit and Evaluation Branch, 2007), 35, http://www.aadnc-aandc.gc.ca/DAM/DAM-INTER-HQ/STAGING/texte-text/aev_pubs_ev_06-07_1332356163901_eng.pdf (accessed January 16, 2013).

164 Mark Totten, "Preventing Aboriginal Youth Gang Involvement in Canada: A Gendered Approach," paper prepared for the Aboriginal Policy Research Conference, Ottawa, March 2009, 8, http://www.turtleisland.org/resources/gangsnwac09.pdf (accessed January 16).

165 This and the following sentence are informed by Mark E. Courtney, Amy Dworsky, Adam Brown, Colleen Cary, Kara Love, and Vanessa Vorhies, *Midwest Evaluation of the Adult Functioning of Former Foster Youth: Outcomes at Age 26* (Chicago: Chaplin Hall at the University of Chicago, 2011).

166 Many of the details of this paragraph come from Cindy Blackstock, "The Canadian Human Rights Tribunal on First Nations Child Welfare: Why If Canada Wins, Equality and Justice Lose," *Child and Youth Services Review* 33, no. 1 (2011): 187–94.

167 Indspire, *Cindy Blackstock*, https://indspire.ca/laureate/cindy-blackstock/ (accessed March 17, 2015).

168 First Nations Child and Family Caring Society of Canada, *I Am Witness: Canadian Human Rights Tribunal Hearing, Final Arguments*, http://www.fncaringsociety.ca/final-arguments (accessed March 17, 2015).

169 Statistics Canada, *Aboriginal Peoples in Canada: First Nations People, Métis, and Inuit—National Household Survey, 2011* (Ottawa: Statistics Canada, 2013), 14.

170 Shannon Brennan, *Police-Reported Crime Statistics in Canada, 2011* (Ottawa: Ministry of Industry, 2012), 20.

171 Public Safety Canada, *Corrections and Conditional Release Statistical Overview: Annual Report 2012* (Ottawa: Public Safety Canada, 2012), 43.

172 Brennan, *Police-Reported Crime*, 20.

173 Michael Shader, *Risk Factors for Delinquency: An Overview* (Rockville, MD: US Department of Justice, 2004).

174 Laurence Steinberg, "A Social Neuroscience Perspective on Adolescent Risk-Taking," *Developmental Review* 28, no. 1 (2008): 78–106.

175 Employment and Social Development Canada, *Canadians in Context— Aboriginal Population*, http://well-being.esdc.gc.ca/misme-iowb/.3ndic.1t.4r@-eng.jsp?iid=36 (accessed August 2, 2015); Vivian O'Donnell and Susan Wallace, *Women in Canada: A Gender-Based Statistical Report: First Nations, Métis and Inuit Women* (Ottawa: Statistics Canada, Ministry of Industry, 2011), 20.

176 Statistics Canada, *Aboriginal Peoples in Canada in 2006*, 14.

177 Ibid.

178 Linda Goyette, "Still Waiting in Attawapiskat," *Canadian Geographic*, December

2010. http://www.canadiangeographic.ca/magazine/dec10/attawapiskat.asp (accessed February 18, 2013).

179 Statistics Canada, *Aboriginal Peoples in Canada in 2006*, 14.

180 Goyette, "Still Waiting in Attawapiskat."

181 Ron Melchers, "Aboriginal Peoples Experiences with Crime and Criminal Justice," Presentation to CRIM 3322 Aboriginal Peoples and Justice, University of Ottawa, February 4, 2011.

182 Julian Roberts and Ronald Melchers, "The Incarceration of Aboriginal Offenders: Trends from 1978 to 2001," *Canadian Journal of Criminology and Criminal Justice* 45, no. 2 (2003): 211–43.

183 Office of the Correctional Investigator, *Spirit Matters: Aboriginal People and the Corrections and Conditional Release Act* (Ottawa: Office of the Correctional Investigator, 2012), 11.

184 Pauktuutit Inuit Women of Canada, *National Strategy to Prevent Abuse in Inuit Communities and Sharing Knowledge, Sharing Wisdom: A Guide to the National Strategy* (Ottawa: Pauktuutit Inuit Women of Canada, 2006), 3.

185 Ibid.

186 This study used a variety of research techniques, including participant observation; survey instruments; and open-ended, ethnographic-style interviews. Initial data collection began in 1990 at the Regional Psychiatric Centre in Saskatoon, where researchers conducted participant observation and ethnographic interviews with 30 people who were incarcerated. Research continued through to 1994, when an additional phase was implemented that involved interviewing 249 Indigenous incarcerated persons at the Saskatchewan Penitentiary and Riverbend institutions in Prince Albert and the Stony Mountain Penitentiary and Rockwood Institution in Winnipeg; for these details and more, see James B. Waldram, *The Way of the Pipe: Aboriginal Spirituality and Symbolic Healing in Canadian Prisons* (Peterborough, ON: Broadview Press, 1997), xi, 45–46.

187 Elizabeth Comack, Lawrence Deane, Larry Morrissette, and Jim Silver, *If You Want to Change Violence in the "Hood," You Have to Change the "Hood": Violence and Street Gangs in Winnipeg's Inner City* (Winnipeg: Canadian Centre for Policy Alternatives, 2009), 14, http://www.policyalternatives.ca/sites/default/files/uploads/publications/Manitoba_Pubs/2009/Violence_and_Street_Gangs_091009.pdf (accessed January 17, 2013).

188 Ibid., 5.

Chapter 9

1 The report in question is Shannon Brennan, *Violent Victimization of Aboriginal Women in the Canadian Provinces, 2009* (Ottawa: Statistics Canada, 2011), 7.

2 The information presented here can be found in Brennan, *Violent Victimization*, 10.

3 Human Rights Watch, *Those Who Take Us Away: Abusive Policing and Failures in Protection of Indigenous Women and Girls in Northern British Columbia, Canada* (New York: Human Rights Watch, 2013), 25.

4 Amnesty International, *Stolen Sisters: A Human Rights Response to Discrimination and Violence Against Indigenous Women in Canada* (Ottawa: Amnesty International, 2004), 23.

5 Mulligan and Miladinovic, *Homicide in Canada 2014*, 16.
6 Native Women's Association of Canada, *What Their Stories Tell Us: Research Findings from the Sisters in Spirit Initiative* (Ohsweken, ON: Native Women's Association of Canada, 2010), 29.
7 Samuel Perreault, *The Incarceration of Aboriginal People in Adult Correctional Services* (Ottawa: Statistics Canada, 2009), 9.
8 Public Safety Canada, *Corrections and Conditional Release Statistical Overview: Annual Report 2012* (Ottawa: Public Safety Canada, 2012), 53.
9 Samuel Perreault, "Admissions to Adult Correctional Services in Canada, 2011/2012," *Juristat* 34, no. 1 (2014).
10 Native Women's Association of Canada, *Research Findings, Policy Challenges, and Lessons Learned: NWAC's Sisters in Spirit Initiative* (Ottawa: Native Women's Association of Canada, 2007), 3.
11 Kay Givens McGowan, "Weeping for the Lost Matriarchy," in *Daughters of Mother Earth: The Wisdom of Native American Women*, ed. Barbara Alice Mann, 53–68 (Westport, CT: Praeger Publishers, 2006); Georges Sioui, *Histoires de Kanatha: Vues et Contées / Histories of Kanatha: Seen and Told* (Ottawa: University of Ottawa Press, 2008), 138.
12 Royal Commission on Aboriginal Peoples, *Bridging the Cultural Divide: A Report on Aboriginal People and Criminal Justice in Canada* (Ottawa: Supply and Services Canada, 1996); Bruce E. Johansen, "Native American Ideas of Governance and the United States Constitution," *Indigenous People Today: Living in Two Worlds* 14, no. 6 (June 2009): 12–15, see page 15, http://iipdigital.usembassy.gov/media/pdf/ejs/0609.pdf.
13 Sarah Eppler Janda, *Beloved Women: The Political Lives of LaDonna Harris and Wilma Mankiller* (DeKalb: Northern Illinois University Press, 2007), 170.
14 Andrea Smith, *Conquest: Sexual Violence and the American Indian Genocide* (Cambridge, MA: South End Press, 2005), 18; Sarah Eppler Janda, *Beloved Women*, 172.
15 Smith, *Conquest*, 18.
16 William Leete Stone, *Life of Joseph Brant, Thayendanegea*, 2 vols. (Albany, NY: J. Munsell, 1865), 1: 404.
17 Daniel N. Paul, *First Nations History: We Were Not the Savages—Collision between European and Native American Civilizations*, 3rd edition (Halifax: Fernwood, 2006), 24.
18 Smith, *Conquest*, 19; Paul, *First Nations History*, 24.
19 Jack D. Forbes, *Columbus and Other Cannibals: The Wetiko Disease of Exploitation, Imperialism, and Terrorism* (New York: Autonomedia, 1992), 40–41.
20 Ibid., 41.
21 Native Women's Association of Canada, *Research Findings*, 3.
22 Barbara-Helen Hill, *Shaking the Rattle: Healing the Trauma of Colonization* (Penticton, BC: Theytus Books, 1995), 12.
23 Emma LaRocque, *Violence in Aboriginal Communities* (Ottawa: National Clearinghouse on Family Violence, 1994).
24 Emma LaRocque, written presentation to the Aboriginal Justice Inquiry hearings, February 5, 1990, quoted in Alexandra (Sandi) Pierce, "'Sexual Savages': Christian Stereotypes and Violence Against North America's Native Women," in *Religion and Men's Violence Against Women*, ed. Andy J. Johnson, 63–98 (New York: Springer, 2015), 79.

25 LaRocque, *Violence in Aboriginal Communities.*
26 Andrea Smith, "Sexual Violence as a Tool of Genocide," in *Racism, Colonialism, and Indigeneity in Canada*, ed. Martin J. Cannon and Lina Sunseri, 252–62 (Don Mills, ON: Oxford University Press, 2011), 253.
27 Laura Tohe, "Ciphering the Images of Indian Women in Popular Culture," presentation at the 14th Annual Conference of the American Indian Studies Association, Tempe, Arizona, February 7, 2013.
28 Adrienne Keene, "Nudie Neon Indians and the Sexualization of Native Women," *Native Appropriations: Examining Representations of Indigenous Peoples*, July 17, 2010, http://nativeappropriations.com/category/neon-indian (accessed May 7, 2014).
29 Kim Shuck, "Say Hau to Native American Barbie," in *Cultural Representation in Native America*, ed. Andrew Jolivétte (Lanham, MD: AltaMira Press, 2006), 36.
30 Lisa Monchalin, "The Continued Struggle, Sexualization and Subjugation of Native Women: Deconstructing Pop Culture Depictions," Aboriginal Gathering Place Lecture Series, Kwantlen Polytechnic University, Surrey, BC, March 1, 2012.
31 See the following writings by Adrienne Keene (Cherokee Nation) for exceptional and significant discussions on racism and the inappropriateness of "Indian" Halloween costumes: Adrienne Keene, "Halloween Costume Shopping: A Sampling of Racism for Sale," *Native Appropriations: Examining Representations of Indigenous Peoples*, October 27, 2011, http://nativeappropriations.com/2011/10/halloween-costume-shopping-a-sampling-of-the-racism-for-sale.html (accessed May 7, 2014); Keene, "Nudie Neon Indians."
32 *Collins English Dictionary: Complete and Unabridged*, 10th edition (London: William Collins and Sons, 2009).
33 Herbert C. Kelman, "Violence Without Moral Restraint: Reflections on the Dehumanization of Victims and Victimizers," *Journal of Social Issues* 29, no. 4 (1973): 25–61.
34 Tohe, "Ciphering the Images of Indian Women."
35 Keene, "Halloween Costume Shopping."
36 For the statistics in this paragraph, see Native Women's Association of Canada, *What Their Stories Tell Us*, 18, 20, 23, 24.
37 See Maryanne Pearce, "An Awkward Silence: Missing and Murdered Vulnerable Women and the Canadian Justice System," (PhD dissertation, University of Ottawa, 2013), 10–11, 20–23 for this quote and other information about the project presented here.
38 The statistics in this paragraph are from Royal Canadian Mounted Police, *Missing and Murdered Aboriginal Women: A National Operational Overview* (Ottawa: Her Majesty the Queen in Right of Canada, 2014), 7–9.
39 Human Rights Watch, *Those Who Take Us Away*, 7. According to Human Rights Watch, this statistic is based on an estimate from the Native Women's Association of Canada.
40 James Anaya, *Statement Upon Conclusion of the Visit to Canada*, October 15, 2013, http://www.unsr.jamesanaya.org/statements/statement-upon-conclusion-of-the-visit-to-canada (accessed December 28, 2013).
41 Smith, "Sexual Violence as a Tool of Genocide," 258; Amnesty International, *Stolen Sisters*.
42 Native Women's Association of Canada, *What Their Stories Tell Us*, 27.

43 Laurie Odjick, "A Letter from Laurie Odjick, March 8, 2009," *Justice for Missing and Murdered Indigenous Women*, http://www.missingjustice.ca/a-letter-from-laurie-odjick/.

44 CTV, "Fugitive Feline Captured, Heading to Québec Zoo," *CTV News*, May 1, 2008, http://www.ctvnews.ca/fugitive-feline-captured-heading-to-Québec-zoo-1.292729 (accessed January 15, 2013).

45 Ellen Gabriel, "Justice pour les victimes issues des communautés autochtones: deux poids, deux mesures?" Presentation at the 5e Colloque Plaidoyer-Victimes Au Cœur des Droits, Montreal, Québec, October 29, 2009.

46 Stephen Harper, "Speech from the Throne to Open the Third Session, Fortieth Parliament of Canada," March 3, 2010, Ottawa, Ontario, http://www.parl.gc.ca/Parlinfo/Documents/ThroneSpeech/40-3-e.html (accessed December 1 2013).

47 Department of Justice, *Government of Canada Takes Concrete Action Regarding Missing and Murdered Aboriginal Women* (Ottawa: Department of Justice, 2010), http://news.gc.ca/web/article-en.do?nid=569819.

48 Native Women's Association of Canada, "NWAC Responds to $10M Announcement from the Department of Justice Canada," *Native Women's Association of Canada Press Release*, November 9, 2010, http://www.sawcc.sk.ca/pdf/PressRelease_9November2010_NWACrespondsto10Mannouncement.pdf.

49 Voices–Voix, "Sisters in Spirit—What Happened," *Documentation Project*, http://voices-voix.ca/en/facts/profile/sisters-spirit.

50 The Honourable Wally T. Oppal, QC Commissioner, *Forsaken: Report of the Missing Women Commission If Inquiry Executive Summary* (British Columbia: Library and Archives Canada, 2012), 134–35; Rudy Kelly, "Free Buses Proposed for Highway of Tears," *Raven's Eye* 10, no. 3 (2006), http://www.ammsa.com/publications/ravens-eye/free-buses-proposed-highway-tears-0 (accessed February 27, 2013).

51 This paragraph draws on Deborah Chansonneuve, *Reclaiming Connections: Understanding Residential School Trauma Among Aboriginal People* (Ottawa: The Aboriginal Healing Foundation, 2005), 63.

52 Ibid., 63.

53 RCMP in BC, *Project E-Pana*, http://bc.cb.rcmp-grc.gc.ca/ViewPage.action?siteNodeId=1525&languageId=1&contentId=-1 (accessed February 27, 2013). Information in the following sentence is also from this source.

54 Human Rights Watch, *Those Who Take Us Away*, 37.

55 Jonathan Hayward, "Highway of Tears: Arrest of Bobby Jack Fowler Prompts Emotional Plea From Family of Murdered Woman," *The Star*, September 27, 2012. http://www.thestar.com/news/canada/article/1262959—highway-of-tears-arrest-of-bobby-jack-fowler-prompts-emotional-plea-of-murdered-woman (accessed January 15, 2013).

56 Human Rights Watch, *Those Who Take Us Away*, 19.

57 The Vancouver Province, "Aboriginal Leader Slams Ex-Judge's Parole Bid," *Canada.com*, September 12, 2007, http://www.canada.com/theprovince/news/story.html?id=11c1cbd9-765e-45a5-9ac2-fe2a78146064 (accessed February 27, 2013).

58 The details of these stories are found in Human Rights Watch, *Those Who Take Us Away*, 31, 32.

59 Ibid., 32.

60 Information in this paragraph is taken from ibid., 59–60.
61 Ibid., 33.
62 Ibid., 33–34.
63 Ibid., 34.
64 Ibid., 34.
65 This paragraph draws on ibid., 50–51, 53.
66 For these and other details mentioned in this paragraph, see ibid., 57–62.
67 These were sentiments expressed in 2012. The location and exact date of communication are not being disclosed in order to protect the identity of the officer.
68 CBC, "RCMP Says Force Is Changing after Sexual Harassment Allegations," *CBC News*, November 8, 2012, http://www.cbc.ca/news/canada/british-columbia/rcmp-says-force-is-changing-after-sexual-harassment-allegations-1.1270973.
69 Jeff Nagel, "RCMP Abuse Lawsuit Gets Underway," *Surrey North Delta Leader*, August 2, 2012.
70 CBC, "RCMP Says Force Is Changing."
71 Human Rights Watch, *Those Who Take Us Away*, 42.
72 Ibid., 10.
73 Ibid.
74 According to Geraldine Pratt, 39 of the 67 missing women were Indigenous, quoted in Yasmin Jiwani and Mary Lynn Young, "Missing and Murdered Women: Reproducing Marginality in News Discourse," *Canadian Journal of Communication* 31, no. 4 (2006): 895–917, 898.
75 O'Connor and O'Neal, *Dark Legacy*, 61.
76 James Keller, "Missing Women Inquiry: Bias Against Pickton's Victims Led to Police Failures, Indifference," *Huffington Post*, December, 17, 2012, http://www.huffingtonpost.ca/2012/12/17/missing-women-inquiry-report-families_n_2314069.html (accessed February 27, 2013).
77 Jiwani and Young, "Missing and Murdered Women," 897.
78 These two sentences, including the quote, follow O'Connor and O'Neal, *Dark Legacy*, 63; Frank Larue, "The Legacy of the Robert Pickton Trial," *First Nations Drum*, February 3, 2008, http://www.firstnationsdrum.com/2008/02/the-legacy-of-the-robert-pickton-trial/ (accessed May 7, 2014).
79 Beverly A. Pitman, "Re-mediating the Spaces of Reality Television: *America's Most Wanted* and the Case of Vancouver's Missing Women," *Environment and Planning A* 34 (2002): 167–84, 176–77.
80 O'Connor and O'Neal, *Dark Legacy*, 64.
81 Ibid., 66–67; Pearce, "An Awkward Silence," 375.
82 Wally T. Oppal, *Forsaken: The Report of the Missing Women Commission of Inquiry—Executive Summary* (Vancouver: Missing Women Commission of Inquiry, November 19, 2012), 69; Pearce, "An Awkward Silence," 377.
83 O'Connor and O'Neal, *Dark Legacy*, 67.
84 Sean Devlin, "A Working Girl's Nightmare: The Murdered and Missing Women of Skid Row," *First Nations Drum*, December 26, 2000, http://www.firstnationsdrum.com/2000/12/a-working-girls-nightmare-the-murdered-and-missing-women-of-skid-row/.
85 Wally T. Oppal, *Forsaken: The Report of the Missing Women Commission of Inquiry—Volume IIA* (Vancouver: Missing Women Commission of Inquiry, November 19, 2012), 102–05.

86 Wally T. Oppal, *Forsaken: The Report of the Missing Women Commission of Inquiry—Volume I* (Vancouver: Missing Women Commission of Inquiry, November 19, 2012), 33.

87 The Royal Canadian Mounted Police, *Missing and Murdered Aboriginal Persons*, http://www.rcmp-grc.gc.ca/aboriginal-autochtone/mmaw-fada-eng.htm (accessed February 26, 2013).

88 Oppal, *Forsaken: Volume IIB*, 91.

89 RCMP, *Missing and Murdered*; Oppal, *Forsaken: Executive Summary*, 14.

90 Oppal, *Forsaken: Executive Summary*, 66–79.

91 Jiwani and Young, "Missing and Murdered Women," 896.

92 Canadian Press, "Robert Pickton Won't Face 20 Remaining Murder Charges," *CTV News*, August 4, 2010, http://www.ctvnews.ca/robert-pickton-won-t-face-20-remaining-murder-charges-1.539024.

93 Keller, "Missing Women Inquiry."

94 For the recommendations, including those in the two foregoing sentences, see Oppal, *Forsaken: Executive Summary*, 160–69.

95 Union of BC Indian Chiefs, "Community & Advocacy Groups Respond to Missing Women Commission of Inquiry's Final Report," *Joint News Release*, December 17, 2012, http://ubcic.bc.ca/News_Releases/UBCICNews1217 1202.html#axzz2MBYScCRZ (accessed February 28, 2013).

96 Anaya, *Statement Upon Conclusion*.

97 Special Committee on Violence Against Indigenous Women, *Invisible Women—A Call to Action: A Report on Missing and Murdered Indigenous Women in Canada*, Canada, House of Commons, March 2014, 41st Parliament, Second Session.

98 Carolyn Bennett, "So Sad. . . . Today the Hugely Disappointing Report from the Special Parliamentary Committee on Violence Against Indigenous Women Was Tabled," Carolyn Bennett, MP Blog, March 7, 2014, http://carolynbennett.liberal.ca/blog/sad-today-hugely-disappointing-report-special-parlimentary-committee-violence-indigenous-women-tabled/ (accessed March 12, 2014).

99 Native Women's Association of Canada, "NWAC Disappointed Once Again by Report Released by Special Parliamentary Committee on VAIW," *Native Women's Association of Canada Press Release*, March 7, 2014, http://nwac.virtustructure.com/2014/03/nwac-disappointed-once-again-by-report-released-by-special-parliamentary-committee-on-vaiw/.

100 Assembly of First Nations, "Assembly of First Nations Says Special Committee Report Disappoints Victims and Families of Missing and Murdered Women and Girls and Calls on Government to Take Real Action: National Indigenous Leaders to Meet Monday to Plan Action," *AFN News Release*, March 7, 2014, http://www.afn.ca/index.php/en/news-media/latest-news/assembly-of-first-nations-says-special-committee-report-disappoints-vi (accessed March 12, 2014).

101 Special Committee on Violence Against Indigenous Women, *Invisible Women*, 13.

102 Native Women's Association of Canada, "NWAC Disappointed Once Again."

103 Special Committee on Violence Against Indigenous Women, *Invisible Women*, 39.

104 Devon Black, "A National Tragedy Lands in a Bucket of Whitewash," *iPolitics*, March 10, 2014, http://www.ipolitics.ca/2014/03/10/a-national-tragedy-lands-in-a-bucket-of-whitewash/ (accessed March 12, 2014).

105 Native Women's Association of Canada, "NWAC Disappointed Once Again."

106 CBC, "Loretta Saunders Homicide Sparks Call by Native Group for Public Inquiry," *CBC News*, February 26, 2014, http://www.cbc.ca/news/canada/nova-scotia/loretta-saunders-homicide-sparks-call-by-native-group-for-public-inquiry-1.2552572 (accessed March 12, 2014).

107 Assembly of First Nations, "Nova Scotia Native Women's Association Media Advisory—Memorial and Rally for Loretta Saunders to be held on Parliament Hill on Wednesday, March 5," *AFN News Release*, http://www.afn.ca/index.php/en/news-media/latest-news/nova-scotia-native-womens-association-media-advisory-memorial-and-rall (accessed March 12, 2014).

108 CBC, "Loretta Saunders Homicide Sparks Call."

109 Native Women's Association of Canada, "NWAC Disappointed Once Again."

110 Susana Mas, "Tempers Flare on Eve of Report into Missing and Murdered Aboriginal Women," *CBC News*, March 6, 2014, http://www.cbc.ca/news/politics/tempers-flare-on-eve-of-report-into-missing-and-murdered-aboriginal-women-1.2561475 (accessed March 12, 2014).

111 CBC, "Native Rights Lawyer Backs Inquiry into Murdered Aboriginal Women," *CBC News*, March 11, 2014, http://www.cbc.ca/news/canada/nova-scotia/native-rights-lawyer-backs-inquiry-into-murdered-aboriginal-women-1.2568267 (accessed March 12, 2014).

112 Chinta Puxley, "Volunteers to Dredge Red River Again to Find Missing, Murdered Women," *Toronto Star*, April 5, 2015, http://www.thestar.com/news/canada/2015/04/05/volunteers-to-dredge-red-river-again-to-find-missing-murdered-women.html (accessed August 12, 2015).

113 CBC, "Tina Fontaine Death Renews Call for Inquiry into Missing Women," *CBC News*, August 19, 2014, http://www.cbc.ca/news/canada/manitoba/tina-fontaine-death-renews-calls-for-inquiry-into-missing-women-1.2740749 (accessed August 12, 2015).

114 For information in this paragraph, see the following: *Missing and Murdered Indigenous Women and Girls*, Trudeau Election Platform (Ottawa: Liberal Party of Canada, 2015), https://www.liberal.ca/realchange/missing-and-murdered-indigenous-women-and-girls/ (accessed December 4, 2015); Office of the Prime Minister, *Minister of Indigenous and Northern Affairs Mandate Letter* (Ottawa: Office of the Prime Minister, 2015) http://pm.gc.ca/eng/minister-indigenous-and-northern-affairs-mandate-letter (accessed December 4, 2015); Office of the Prime Minister, *The Honourable Jody Wilson-Raybould* (Ottawa: Office of the Prime Minister, 2015) http://pm.gc.ca/eng/minister/honourable-jody-wilson-raybould (accessed December 4, 2015).

115 For information in this paragraph, see the following: Tiar Wilson "Indigenous Affairs Minister Begins 'Pre-Inquiry Engagements' with Families of MMIW," *CBC News*, November 18, 2015, http://www.cbc.ca/news/aboriginal/indigenous-affairs-minister-begins-pre-inquiry-engagements-with-families-of-mmiw-1.3323527 (accessed December 4, 2015); APTN National News, "Watch Prime Minister Trudeau's Address"; APTN National News, "Trudeau Government Releases Details on First Phase of National Inquiry into MMIW," *APTN National News*, December 8, 2015, http://aptn.ca/news/2015/12/08/trudeau-government-releases-details-on-first-phase-of-national-inquiry-into-mmiw/ (accessed December 8, 2015).

Chapter 10

1 J. S. Frideres and R. R. Gadacz, *Aboriginal Peoples in Canada: Contemporary Conflicts*, 6th edition (Toronto: Prentice Hall, 2001), 9.
2 *St. Catherines Milling and Lumber Company v. the Queen* (1887), 13 S.C.R. 577, at 596–97.
3 Canadian Charter of Rights and Freedoms, s 2, Part I of the Constitution Act, 1982, being Schedule B to the Canada Act 1982 (UK), 1982, c 11 at s. 25.
4 Erin Hanson, "Constitution Act, 1982 Section 35," *Indigenous Foundations*, http://indigenousfoundations.arts.ubc.ca/home/government-policy/ constitution-act-1982-section-35.html (accessed February 6, 2015).
5 Constitution Act, 1982, being Schedule B to the *Canada Act 1982* (UK), 1982, c 11 at s. 35.
6 *Calder et al. v. Attorney-General of British Columbia* [1973] S.C.R. 313.
7 BC Treaty Commission, *Why Treaties? A Legal Perspective* (Vancouver: BC Treaty Commission, 2008), 6.
8 *R v. Sparrow*, [1990] 1 S.C.R. 1075.
9 Ibid., 1075, 1076.
10 Ibid., 1075, at para 70.
11 Ibid., 1075, 1008.
12 *R. v. Van der Peet,* [1996] 2 S.C.R. 507, 509.
13 Ibid., 507, at paras 48–74.
14 *R. v. Gladstone*, [1996] 2 S.C.R. 723.
15 Ibid; Douglas C. Harris, "Territoriality, Aboriginal Rights, and the Heiltsuk Spawn-On-Kelp Fishery," *UBC Law Review* 34 (2000): 195–238, 198.
16 *R. v. Gladstone*, [1996] 2 S.C.R. 723, at para 20.
17 *R. v. N.T.C. Smokehouse Ltd.*, [1996] 2 S.C.R. 672.
18 Ibid., 672, at para 26.
19 *Delgamuukw v. British Columbia*, [1997] 3 S.C.R. 1010.
20 Ibid; BC Treaty Commission, *Why Treaties? A Legal Perspective* (Vancouver: BC Treaty Commission, 2008), 8.
21 Bonita Lawrence, *Fractured Homeland: Federal Recognition and Algonquin Identity in Ontario* (Vancouver: UBC Press, 2012), 60.
22 Brian Thom, "Aboriginal Rights and Title in Canada After *Delgamuukw*: Part One, Oral Traditions and Anthropological Evidence in the Courtroom," *Native Studies Review* 14, no. 1 (2001): 1–26, 4.
23 *Delgamuukw*, 1010, at para 84.
24 Ibid., 1010.
25 Thom, "Aboriginal Rights and Title in Canada After *Delgamuukw*," 4.
26 *Delgamuukw*, 1010, at para 86.
27 Much of the information presented in this paragraph is taken from Thom, "Aboriginal Rights and Title in Canada After *Delgamuukw*," 5, 6; Lawrence, *Fractured Homeland*, 61.
28 *R. v. Sioui,* [1990] 1 S.C.R. 1025. *R. v. Marshall,* [1999] 3 S.C.R. 533.
29 Peter Kulchyski, *Unjust Relations: Aboriginal Rights in Canadian Courts* (Toronto: Oxford University Press, 1994), 182.
30 Ibid.

31 Peter Kulchyski, "A Step Back: The Nisichawayasihk Cree Nation and the Wuskwatim Project," in *Power Struggles: Hydro Development and First Nations in Manitoba and Québec*, ed. Thibault Martin, Steven M. Hoffman, 129–44 (Winnipeg: University of Manitoba Press, 2008), 132.
32 *Sioui*, 1025.
33 Ibid.
34 Ibid., 1025; Kulchyski, "A Step Back," 132.
35 Most of the details of this paragraph, including the quote, are from *Marshall*, 533; Kulchyski, "A Step Back," 132.
36 *Marshall*, 533; Mahmud Jamal, "Treaty Interpretation after *R. v. Marshall*; *R. v. Bernard*," *Supreme Court Law Review* 34 (2006): 443–63, 445.
37 Jamal, "Treaty Interpretation," 445.
38 *Marshall*, 533; *Sioui*, 1025; Kulchyski, "A Step Back," 132.
39 *R. v. Marshall (No 2)* [1999] 3 S.C.R. 533, page 535.
40 Ibid.
41 Olthuis, Kleer, Townshed LLP, *Aboriginal Law Handbook*, 4th edition (Toronto: Thomson Reuters Canada, 2012), 12.
42 *R. v. Badger*, [1996] 1 S.C.R. 771, at para 41.
43 The details presented in the following paragraph are from Olthuis, Kleer, Townshed LLP, "*Aboriginal Law Handbook*," 11.
44 *Haida Nation v. British Columbia (Minister of Forests)*, [2004] SCC 73; *Taku River Tlingit First Nation v. British Columbia (Project Assessment Director)*, [2004] SCC 74; *Mikisew Cree First Nation v. Canada (Minister of Canadian Heritage)*, [2005] 3 S.C.R. 388; *Beckman v. Little Salmon/Carmacks First Nation*, [2010] 3 S.C.R. 103.
45 *Haida Nation*, 73.
46 Ibid., 73, at para 16 and 10.
47 Ibid., 73, at para 4.
48 *Taku River Tlingit First Nation*, 74.
49 Ibid., 74, at para 46.
50 *Mikisew Cree First Nation* 388, at para 3.
51 Ibid.
52 Ibid., 388, at para 4.
53 Council of Yukon First Nations, "Little Salmon Carmacks First Nation," http://cyfn.ca/nations/little-salmon-carmacks-first-nation/ (accessed February 5, 2015).
54 *Little Salmon/Carmacks First Nation*, 103.
55 Ibid., 103, at para 1.
56 Ibid., 103, at para 202, 203, and 204.
57 *Tsilhqot'in Nation v. British Columbia*, 2014 SCC 44; *Grassy Narrows First Nation v. Ontario (Natural Resources)*, 2014 SCC 48.
58 Sean Fine, "Supreme Court Expands Land-Title Rights in Unanimous Ruling," *Globe and Mail*, June 26, 2014, http://www.theglobeandmail.com/news/national/supreme-court-expands-aboriginal-title-rights-in-unanimous-ruling/article19347252/ (accessed February 5, 2015).
59 *Tsilhqot'in Nation*, 44.
60 Ibid., 44, at para 153.
61 Ibid., 44, at para 73.
62 Ibid., 44, at para 76.
63 *Grassy Narrows First Nation*, 48.

64 Ibid., 48, 53.

65 Patrick Macklem, *Indigenous Difference and the Constitution of Canada* (Toronto: University of Toronto Press, 2001), 170.

66 For the details presented here and in the subsequent paragraph, see *R. v. Van der Peet*, [1996] 2 S.C.R. 507, at para 49; Jennifer E. Dalton, "Aboriginal Self-Determination in Canada: Protections Afforded by the Judiciary and Government," *Canadian Journal of Law & Society* 21, no. 1 (2006): 11–37, 16.

67 *Delgamuukw*, 1010, at para 186, quoting *Van der* Peet, 507, at para 31; *Haida Nation*, 511, at para 17.

68 Arthur Manuel, "Colonial Oppression at Elsipogtog: Right to Self-Determination," *Last Real Indians*, http://lastrealindians.com/colonial-oppression-at-elsipogtog-right-to-self-determination-by-arthur-manuel/ (accessed March 24, 2014).

69 John Borrows, "Sovereignty's Alchemy: An Analysis of *Delgamuukw*," *Osgoode Hall Law Journal* 37, no. 3 (1999): 537–96, 537.

70 Patricia Monture-Angus, *Thunder in my Soul: A Mohawk Woman Speaks* (Halifax: Fernwood Publishing, 1995), 81.

71 Taiaiake Alfred, *Peace, Power, Righteousness: An Indigenous Manifesto*, 2nd edition (Don Mills, ON: Oxford University Press, 2009), 146.

72 Ibid., 146.

73 The two previous sentences are informed by ibid., 146–47.

74 Dalton's heritage is so complex that it could not be detailed in a parenthetical comment. She is of Scottish, English, French-Canadian, Mohawk of Six Nations, Métis, and Innu (Montagnais) ancestry. Dalton, "Aboriginal Self-Determination in Canada," 21; *Delgamuukw*, 1010.

75 Dalton, "Aboriginal Self-Determination in Canada," 21; *Delgamuukw*, 1010, at para 161.

76 Jeff Corntassel and Cheryl Bryce, "Practicing Sustainable Self-Determination: Indigenous Approaches to Cultural Restoration and Revitalization," *The Brown Journal of World Affairs* 18, no. 2 (2012): 151–62, 152. The following sentences draw on this source.

77 Richard Woodbury, "Historical Tsilhqot'in: What the Court Decision Really Means for First Nations People," *The Aboriginal Business Report*, February 2015, 44–46.

78 *Tsilhqot'in Nation*, 44, at para 30.

79 Ibid., 44, at para 50.

80 Russell Diabo, "The Tsilhqot'in Decision and Canada's First Nations Termination Policies," *New Socialist Webzine*, January 13, 2015, http://www.newsocialist.org/782-the-tsilhqot-in-decision-and-canada-s-first-nations-termination-policies (accessed February 5, 2015).

81 Ibid.

82 Monture-Angus, *Thunder in My Soul*, 69.

83 Corntassel and Bryce, "Practicing Sustainable Self-Determination," 153.

84 *Kanehsatake 270 Years of Resistance*, DVD, directed by Alanis Obomsawin (Ottawa: The National Film Board of Canada, 1993).

85 Geoffrey York and Loreen Pindera, *People of the Pines: The Warriors and the Legacy of Oka* (Toronto: Little, Brown & Company, 1991), 44–45.

86 Harry Swain, *Oka: A Political Crisis and Its Legacy* (Vancouver: Douglas & McIntyre, 2010), 69.

87 York and Pindera, *People of the Pines*, 44.
88 Swain, *Oka*, 71.
89 Olthuis, Kleer, Townshed LLP, *Aboriginal Law Handbook*, 15.
90 The details here are largely drawn from Swain, *Oka*, 60, 80.
91 Ibid., 81.
92 The documentary film *Kanehsatake 270 Years of Resistance* gave this explanation.
93 Sidney B. Linden, "Primer on Aboriginal Occupations," in *Report of the Ipperwash Inquiry: Volume 2, Policy Analysis* (Toronto: Queen's Printer for Ontario, 2007), 15–41; see page 36.
94 Swain, *Oka*, 134.
95 *Kanehsatake 270 Years of Resistance*; Zig Zag, "Oka Crisis, 1990," *Warrior Publications*, https://warriorpublications.wordpress.com/2014/06/11/oka-crisis-1990/.
96 Linda Pertusati, *In Defense of Mohawk Land: Ethnopolitical Conflict in Native North America* (New York: SUNY Press, 1997), 107.
97 Andrea Smith, *Conquest: Sexual Violence and the American Indian Genocide* (Cambridge, MA: South End Press, 2005), 28.
98 The preceding paragraph draws on York and Pindera, *People of the Pines*, 405.
99 "Revisiting the Pines: Oka's Legacy," *WC Native News*, July 10, 2015, http://westcoastnativenews.com/revisiting-the-pines-okas-legacy/.
100 For details of this story, see Musqueam Indian Band, "c̓əsnaʔəm," http://www.musqueam.bc.ca/c̓əsnaʔəm (accessed January 27, 2013) and *c̓əsnaʔəm: The City Before the City*, http://www.thecitybeforethecity.com/ (accessed February 4, 2015). The information in the remainder of this section is largely drawn from these sources.
101 CBC, "Ancient Musqueam Village, Burial Site Saved in Vancouver," *CBC News*, October 3, 2013, http://www.cbc.ca/news/canada/british-columbia/ancient-musqueam-village-burial-site-saved-in-vancouver-1.1875969.
102 Andrea Harden and Holly Levallient, *Boiling Point! Six Community Profiles of the Water Crisis Facing First Nations within Canada* (Ottawa: The Polaris Institute, 2008).
103 Elizabeth Comack, Lawrence Deane, Larry Morrissette, and Jim Silver, *"Indians Wear Red": Colonialism, Resistance, and Aboriginal Street Gangs* (Blackpoint, NS: Fernwood Publishing, 2013), 36.
104 Constitution Act, 1982, being Schedule B to the Canada Act 1982 (UK), 1982, c. 11 at s. 35.
105 Patrick Brethour, "Why Is Cancer Sweeping Tiny Fort Chipewyan?" *Globe and Mail*, May 22, 2006.
106 Shannon Montgomery, "Those Touched by Cancer on Alberta Reserve Tell Their Stories at Legislature," *Tar Sands Watch*, March 1, 2008, http://www.tarsandswatch.org/those-touched-cancer-alberta-reserve-tell-their-stories-legislature.
107 Harden and Levallient, *Boiling Point! Six Community Profiles*, 17.
108 Kevin P. Timoney, *A Study of Water and Sediment Quality as Related to Public Health Issues, Fort Chipewyan, Alberta* (Sherwood Park, AB: Treeline Ecological Research, 2007), http://www.ualberta.ca/~swfc/images/fc-final-report-revised-dec2007.pdf. For the details of the study communicated in the following discussion, see in particular from this source pages 4 and 13–14.

109 Kevin P. Timoney and Peter Lee, "Does the Alberta Tar Sands Industry Pollute? The Scientific Evidence," *The Open Conservation Biology Journal* 3 (2009): 65–81. From this source, see in particular pages 67, 74, and 78. The details given here are from this source.

110 Dawn Walton, "Alberta Researchers Receive Apology for Attack on Oil Sands Study, Calgary" *Globe and Mail*, June 21 2010, http://www.theglobeandmail.com/news/national/alberta-researchers-receive-apology-for-attack-on-oil-sands-study/article4322540/ (accessed March 1, 2013).

111 Walton, "Alberta Researchers Receive Apology."

112 For both sides of the story, see Ontario Chamber of Commerce, "Ring of Fire: The Ring of Fire Is One of the Most Promising Mining Opportunities in a Generation," *Ontario Chamber of Commerce: Key Issues*, http://www.occ.ca/advocacy/ring-of-fire/ (accessed February 6, 2015); Josh Hjartarson, Liam McGuinty, and Scott Boutilier, with Eva Majernikova, *Beneath the Surface: Uncovering the Economic Potential of Ontario's Ring of Fire* (Toronto: Ontario Chamber of Commerce, 2014); Chief Peter Moonias, "A New Deal for First Nations and the North," Open Letter from the Neskantaga First Nation, June 12, 2012, http://neskantaga.com/images/NFNNewDeal.pdf (accessed February 6, 2015).

113 Bill C-45, A Second Act to Implement Certain Provisions of the Budget Tabled in Parliament on March 29, 2012 and Other Measures, 1st sess., 41 Parliament, 2011–2012.

114 As well as Bill C-45, see the Navigable Waters Protection Act, R.S.C., 1985, c. N-22.

115 As well as Bill C-45, see Ecojustice, *Legal Backgrounder: Bill C-45 and the Navigable Waters Protection Act (RSC 1985, C N-22)* (Vancouver: Ecojustice, 2012), http://foca.on.ca/wp-content/uploads/2014/06/Ecojustice_Legal_Backgrounder_NWPA_changes_Fall_2012-1.pdf (accessed January 3, 2014), 7.

116 Grace Li Xiu Woo, *Canada's Democratic Deficit and Idle No More* (Vancouver: Lawyers Rights Watch Canada, 2013), http://www.lrwc.org/ws/wp-content/uploads/2013/04/Arctic-Review-LRWC2.pdf (accessed January 3, 2014); Ecojustice, *Legal Backgrounder: Bill C-45*, 7.

117 Ecojustice, *Legal Backgrounder: Bill C-45*, 2 and 7.

118 See Bill C-45, 204.

119 Chief Terrance J. Paul and Chief Gerard Julian, Letter to Honourable Stephen Harper, Honourable Joe Oliver, Honourable Peter Kent, Honourable Keith Ashfield, Honourable Diane Findley, and Premier Darrell Dexter, from the Kwilmu'kw Maw-klusuaqn Negotiation Office, Mi'kmaq Rights Initiative, December 18, 2012, http://mikmaqrights.com/uploads/PMLetter.pdf (accessed March 4, 2013).

120 Constitution Act, 1982, being Schedule B to the Canada Act 1982 (UK), 1982, c 11 at s. 35.

121 Dennis Bevington, *Bill C-45: Jobs and Growth Act (Omnibus Budget Bill) Implication for Canada's North* (Yellowknife: Office of Dennis Bevington, Member of Parliament for the Western Artic, March 2013), http://www.dennisbevington.ca/pdfs/en/2013/Bill_C-45_Final_Report_English.pdf (accessed May 8, 2014), 23.

122 Bill C-45, 208.

123 Ibid., 227.

124 The Governor in Council (GIC) is an appointment "made by the Governor General, on the advice of the Queen's Privy Council for Canada (i.e., the Cabinet)." Government of Canada, *Governor in Council Appointment Process Overview*, http://appointments-nominations.gc.ca/prsnt.asp?page=Process&lang=eng (accessed February 6, 2015).

125 Bill C-45, 227.

126 Janyce McGregor, "22 Changes in the Budget Bill Fine Print," *CBC News*, October 26, 2012, http://www.cbc.ca/news/politics/22-changes-in-the-budget-bill-fine-print-1.1233481 (accessed August 31, 2015).

127 Linda Hoang, "Hundreds of First Nations, Métis, Rally against Bill C-45," *CTV News Edmonton*, December 10, 2012, http://edmonton.ctvnews.ca/hundreds-of-first-nations-m%C3%A9tis-rally-against-bill-c-45-1.1073796 (accessed February 6, 2015).

128 Bill C-45, 227–28.

129 These ideas were expressed by Pamela Palmater throughout various news interviews and public speaking events from December 2012 and January 2013.

130 Ibid.

131 *Save the Fraser Declaration*, http://savethefraser.ca/.

132 There are also other very offensive bills that were introduced by the Harper government. Here are some that have become law: Bill C-10, which became the Safe Streets and Communities Act, S.C. 2012; Bill C-27, which became the First Nations Financial Transparency Act, S.C. 2013; Bill C-428, which became the Indian Act Amendment and Replacement Act, S.C. 2014; Bill S-6, which became the First Nations Elections Act, S.C. 2014; and Bill S-2, which became the Family Homes on Reserves and Matrimonial Interests or Rights Act, S.C. 2013, c. 20.

133 David Suzuki Foundation, *Bill C-38: What You Need to Know* (Vancouver: David Suzuki Foundation, 2012), http://www.davidsuzuki.org/publications/downloads/2012/C-38%20factsheet.pdf (accessed February 6, 2015).

134 The previous three sentences are drawn from information in Leanne Simpson, "Think Chief Spence Is on a 'Liquid Diet'? I Think You're Ignorant," *Huffington Post*, January 20, 2013, http://www.huffingtonpost.ca/leanne-simpson/fish-broth-chief-spence_b_2517450.html (accessed March 4, 2013).

135 These sentiments were expressed by Pamela Palmater during the Idle No More Unity Walk in Windsor, Ontario, January 16, 2013. Palmater's speech "Harper Is Not Above the Law" is available from her website: http://www.pampalmater.com/category/idle-no-more/.

136 Doug Bedard (Plex), "No More Feat. Lase (Official Video)," *YouTube*, posted January 28, 2013, http://www.youtube.com/watch?v=u9FXdVnweok.

137 Drezus, "Red Winter (Official Video)," *YouTube*, posted January 11, 2013, https://www.youtube.com/watch?v=VEc3ZYqj5Fw.

138 Sino General (Chief Rock), personal communication. These sentiments were expressed through several conversations throughout 2011 to 2013, on Coast Salish Territories, primarily in the territories that include Kwantlen, Katzie, Semiahmoo, Tsawwassen and Musqueam.

Chapter 11

1 For information in this paragraph, see Specific Claims Tribunal Canada, *History—A Brief History of Specific Claims Prior to the Passage of Bill C-30: The Specific Claims Tribunal Act* (Ottawa: Specific Claims Tribunal, 2011), http://www.sct-trp.ca/hist/hist_e.htm (accessed February 9, 2015).

2 Peter Kulchyski, "A Step Back: The Nisichawayasihk Cree Nation and the Wuskwatim Project," in *Power Struggles: Hydro Development and First Nations in Manitoba and Québec*, ed. Thibault Martin, Steven M. Hoffman, 129–44 (Winnipeg: University of Manitoba Press, 2008), 275.

3 Minister of Aboriginal Affairs and Northern Development, *2008–2010 Nunavut Implementation Panel: Annual Report* (Ottawa: Minister of Aboriginal Affairs and Northern Development, 2011), https://www.aadnc-aandc.gc.ca/eng/1351178274391/1351178318963 (accessed February 9, 2015).

4 Aboriginal Affairs and Northern Development Canada, *Indian Specific Claims Commission*, http://www.aadnc-aandc.gc.ca/eng/1100100011078/1100100011079 (accessed February 9, 2015). The following sentences reference this source as well.

5 Ibid.; Indian and Northern Affairs Canada, *Specific Claims: Justice At Last* (Ottawa: Minister of Indian Affairs and Northern Development and Federal Interlocutor for Métis and Non-Status Indians, 2007), 8–10.

6 Aboriginal Affairs and Northern Development Canada, *Indian Specific Claims Commission*.

7 Specific Claims Tribunal Act (S.C. 2008, c. 22); Indian and Northern Affairs Canada, *Specific Claims: Justice At Last*, 3.

8 Information about the Tribunal in this and the subsequent paragraph can be found in Specific Claims Tribunal Canada, *Welcome to the Specific Claims Tribunal* [homepage], http://www.sct-trp.ca/hom/index_e.htm (accessed February 9, 2015).

9 Justice Harry A. Slade, *Annual Report For Presentation to the Honourable Bernard Valcourt Minister of Aboriginal Affairs and Northern Development Canada* (Ottawa: Specific Claims Tribunal, September 30, 2014), 2, http://www.sct-trp.ca/pdf/Annual%20Report%202014.pdf (accessed February 9, 2015).

10 See the "Claims" and "SCT Decisions" sections of the Specific Claims Tribunal Canada website: http://www.sct-trp.ca/hom/index_e.htm.

11 Aboriginal Affairs and Northern Development Canada, *Comprehensive Claims*, https://www.aadnc-aandc.gc.ca/eng/1100100030577/1100100030578 (accessed February 9, 2015).

12 Mary C. Hurley, *Settling Comprehensive Land Claims* (Ottawa: Library of Parliament, 2009), 2, http://www.parl.gc.ca/Content/LOP/ResearchPublications/prb0916-e.pdf (accessed February 9, 2015).

13 Department of Indian Affairs and Northern Development, *Comprehensive Land Claims Policy* (Ottawa: Department of Indian Affairs and Northern Development 1986); Hurley, *Settling Comprehensive Land Claims*, 2.

14 Indian and Northern Affairs Canada, *Federal Policy for the Settlement of Native Claims* (Ottawa: Ministry of Indian Affairs and Northern Development, 1998), 11.

15 Hurley, *Settling Comprehensive Land Claims*, 2.

16 Ibid.
17 Minister of Indian Affairs and Northern Development, *The Government of Canada's Approach to Implementation of the Inherent Right and the Negotiation of Aboriginal Self-Government* (Ottawa: Minister of Indian Affairs and Northern Development, 1995), http://www.aadnc-aandc.gc.ca/eng/1100100031843/1100100031844#PartI (accessed February 9, 2015).
18 Hurley, *Settling Comprehensive Land Claims*, 2.
19 The remainder of this paragraph draws on Shiri Pasternak and Russ Diabo, "Harper v. First Nations: The Assimilation Agenda," *IdleNoMore* [post], October 23, 2014, http://www.idlenomore.ca/harper_v_first_nations_the_assimilation_agenda (accessed February 9, 2014).
20 For the details in this and the subsequent sentence, see Indian and Northern Affairs Canada, *Resolving Aboriginal Claims: A Practical Guide to Canadian Experiences* (Ottawa: Minister of Public Works and Government Services Canada, 2003), 13.
21 Aboriginal Affairs and Northern Development Canada, *Renewing the Comprehensive Land Claims Policy: Towards a Framework for Addressing Section 35 Aboriginal Rights* (Ottawa: Her Majesty the Queen in right of Canada, represented by the Minister of Aboriginal Affairs and Northern Development, 2014), 18–19.
22 *Tsilhqot'in Nation v. British Columbia*, 2014 SCC 44.
23 Aboriginal Affairs and Northern Development Canada, *Renewing the Comprehensive Land Claims Policy*, cover page.
24 *Tsilhqot'in Nation*, 44.
25 The remainder of this paragraph draws on Pasternak and Diabo, "Harper v. First Nations."
26 Aboriginal Affairs and Northern Development Canada, *Renewing the Comprehensive Land Claims Policy*; see section "A Note on the Text."
27 Douglas R. Eyford, *Forging Partnerships Building Relationships: Aboriginal Canadians and Energy Development* (Ottawa: Her Majesty the Queen in Right of Canada, represented by the Minister of Natural Resources, 2013), 2.
28 Ibid., 52.
29 Pasternak and Diabo, "Harper v. First Nations"; Aboriginal Affairs and Northern Development Canada, *Renewing the Comprehensive Land Claims Policy*, see section "A Note on the Text."
30 Aboriginal Affairs and Northern Development Canada, *Renewing the Comprehensive Land Claims Policy*, 6; Eyford, *Forging Partnerships*, 32.
31 Aboriginal Affairs and Northern Development Canada, *Renewing the Comprehensive Land Claims Policy*, 6.
32 Ibid., 6–7.
33 Ibid., 8.
34 *R. v. Sparrow*, [1990] 1 S.C.R. 1075; *R. v. Van der Peet,* [1996] 2 S.C.R. 507.
35 Aboriginal Affairs and Northern Development Canada, *Renewing the Comprehensive Land Claims Policy*, 11.
36 Ibid., 15.
37 Indian and Northern Affairs Canada, *Resolving Aboriginal Claims*, 18.
38 Aboriginal Affairs and Northern Development Canada, *Comprehensive Claims.*
39 Indian and Northern Affairs Canada, *Resolving Aboriginal Claims*, 18.

40 Office of the Treaty Commissioner, *Treaties and The Law: Information Backgrounder* (Public Legal Education Association of Saskatchewan, 2007), 14, http://docs.plea.org/pdf/TreatiesAndTheLawInformationBackgrounder.pdf (accessed January 2, 2015).

41 Menno Boldt, *Surviving as Indians: The Challenge of Self-Government* (Toronto: University of Toronto Press, 1993), 278.

42 This and the next sentence reference Inuit Tapiriit Kanatami (ITK), *James Bay and Northern Québec Agreement Signed*, https://www.itk.ca/historical-event/james-bay-and-northern-Québec-agreement-signed (accessed February 8, 2015).

43 Evelyn J. Peters, "Native People and the Environmental Regime in the James Bay and Northern Québec Agreement," *Arctic* 52, no. 4 (1999): 395–410, 396; Miranda Lynn Dyck, "The Recognition of Indigenous Rights during the Red Power Movement" (MA thesis, Carleton University, 2011), 75.

44 For the foregoing sentences, see Peters, "Native People and the Environmental Regime," 396; ITK, *James Bay and Northern Québec Agreement Signed.*

45 These details can be found in Lynn Dyck, "The Recognition of Indigenous Rights," 64.

46 ITK, *James Bay and Northern Québec Agreement Signed.*

47 Ibid.; Boyce Richardson, *Strangers Devour the Land: Revised Edition* (White River Junction, VT: Chelsea Green Publishing, 2008).

48 The foregoing sentences draw on ITK, *James Bay and Northern Québec Agreement Signed*; Peters, "Native People and the Environmental Regime," 396.

49 This paragraph draws on information in Boldt, *Surviving as Indians*, 276.

50 For the details of this paragraph, see Grand Council of the Crees, "Section 8, Sovereign Injustice—Grand Council of the Crees: Relevance of the James Bay and Northern Québec Agreement," *Québec Relations,* http://www.gcc.ca/archive/article.php?id=131 (accessed January 27, 2013).

51 Ibid.

52 Ibid.

53 A. C. Hamilton, *Canada and Aboriginal Peoples: A New Partnership* (Ottawa: Minister of Public Works and Government Services, 1995), 11–12; see also Grand Council of the Crees, "Section 8, Sovereign Injustice."

54 This sentence and the previous paragraph draw on Grand Council of the Crees, "Section 8, Sovereign Injustice."

55 Richardson, *Strangers Devour the Land* supplies the details of the next four sentences.

56 Matthew Coon-Come, "Self-Determination an Inherent Right of Indigenous Peoples [speech given January 1992]," in *Canadian Speeches: Issues of the Day* 5, no. 9 (1992): 13.

57 *Delgamuukw v. British Columbia*, [1997] 3 S.C.R. 1010.

58 BC Treaty Commission, "Negotiation Support Funding: Fact Sheet," *About Us: Quick Facts*, http://www.bctreaty.net/files/pdf_documents/funding_fact_sheet.pdf.

59 Taiaiake Alfred, *Peace, Power, Righteousness: An Indigenous Manifesto*, 2nd edition (Don Mills, ON: Oxford University Press, 2009), 144–45.

60 Taiaiake Alfred, "Deconstructing the British Columbia Treaty Process," *Balayi: Culture, Law and Colonialism* 3 (2001): 37–65, 39–40.

61 Ibid., 40.

62 British Columbia Treaty Commission, *Pathways to Change: BC Treaty Commission Annual Report, 2013* (Vancouver: BC Treaty Commission, 2013), 25.

63 Darrell Bob, Chief, Xaxl'ip Nation, personal communication, Tsleil-Waututh Nation Community Centre, December 22, 2012.

64 Hurley, *Settling Comprehensive Land Claims*, 6–7; Keith Crowe, "Comprehensive Land Claims: Modern Treaties," *Canadian Encyclopedia*, February 27, 2015, http://www.thecanadianencyclopedia.ca/en/article/comprehensive-land-claims-modern-treaties/.

65 Richard LeBourdais (Honorary Chief, Secwepemc citizen of the Shuswap Nation), "Presentation in Short Course 1: Aboriginal Awareness, Community and Mineral Exploration," Westin Bayshore, Vancouver, January 25, 2013. In a further personal communication with Honorary Chief Richard LeBourdais, he explained that, when discussing treaty-process options with government officials during the beginnings of this process, he questioned the officials, saying that there surely must be another option and way to move forward. He said he did not want to enter into this process and risk having his community possibly end up in debt.

66 Darrell Bob, Chief, Xaxl'ip Nation and Robert Shintah, Chief, Ts'kw'aylaxw, personal communication, Tsleil-Waututh Nation Community Centre, December 22, 2012. NB: Unless otherwise stated, all quotations attributed to these two individuals are from this personal communication.

67 The First Nations of British Columbia, the Government of British Columbia, and the Government of Canada, *The Report of the British Columbia Claims Task Force*, June 28, 1991.

68 BC Treaty Commission, "Six Stages: Policies and Procedures," *Negotiations*, http://www.bctreaty.net/files/sixstages.php.

69 Aboriginal Affairs and Northern Development Canada, *Renewing the Comprehensive Land Claims Policy*, 20.

70 While he was the leader of the Opposition in the British Columbia legislature, Gordon Campbell, along with two of his Liberal colleagues, launched a British Columbia Supreme Court case that challenged the constitutional validity of the Aboriginal self-government provisions of the Nisga'a Treaty. Known as the *Campbell v. British Columbia* case, it affirmed that the self-government provisions of the Nisga'a Treaty are constitutionally valid. Justice Williamson rejected the arguments made by Campbell and his associates and asserted that First Nations have an inherent right to self-government protected by section 35 of the Constitution Act, 1982. Kent McNeil, *The Jurisdiction of Inherent Right Aboriginal Governments* (Ottawa: National Centre for First Nations Governance, October 11, 2007), 15, http://fngovernance.org/ncfng_research/kent_mcneil.pdf (accessed January 2, 2015); *Campbell v. British Columbia*, [2000] 4 C.N.L.R 1 (B.C.S.C.).

71 Shintah, personal communication, December 22, 2012.

72 Arthur Manuel, "Idle? Know More! A Public Panel on Indigenous Issues," *YouTube*, posted January 22, 2013, https://www.youtube.com/watch?v=WkD0MpiiSow.

73 Shintah, personal communication, December 22, 2012.

74 Arthur Manuel, "The Tsilhqot'in Decision and Indigenous Self-Determination," *The New Socialist Webzine*, January 25, 2015. http://www.newsocialist.org/

785-the-tsilhqot-in-decision-and-indigenous-self-determination (accessed February 8, 2015).

75 Manuel, "Idle? Know More!"

76 Ibid.

77 Bob, personal communication, December 22, 2012.

78 For more on this story, see Alan Hanna, "Crown—First Nations Relationships: A Comparative Analysis of the Tsawwassen Final Agreement and Tsilhqot'in v. British Columbia" (MA thesis, University of Victoria, 2009), 73–77. The details given subsequently are drawn from this source. The quote occurs on page 73.

79 Ibid., 74.

80 Ibid.

81 Kim Baird (former Chief of Tsawwassen First Nation), personal communication, Tsawwassen First Nation Head Office, February 1, 2013. All quotations and information attributed to Baird in this chapter are from this communication, unless otherwise specified.

82 Baird, personal communication, February 1, 2013.

83 Tsawwassen First Nation, *Making History, Tsawwassen First Nation: First Urban Treaty in Modern-Day British Columbia* (Tsawwassen: Tsawwassen First Nation, 2007), http://www.tsawwassenfirstnation.com/pdfs/TFN-About/Treaty/071015_Chief_Baird_Speech.pdf (accessed April 15, 2014).

84 Carol Hilton, "Landmark Land Settlement: Canada's First Modern, Urban Treaty Gives Tsawwassen First Nation Control of Its Land and the Chance at a Prosperous Future—Q&A: Grand Chief Stewart Phillip," *Canadian Geographic*, April 7, 2008. http://www.canadiangeographic.ca/magazine/apr08/indepth/phillip.asp (accessed April 15, 2014); Baird, personal communication, February 1, 2013.

85 Baird, personal communication, February 1, 2013.

86 *The Vancouver Province*, "Riled Semiahmoo Aims to Block Tsawwassen Treaty," *Canada.com*, July 24, 2007 http://www.canada.com/story_print.html?id=969e360f-fafa-40a7-b66d-5b3ebec7402f&sponsor= (accessed April 17, 2014).

87 Terri Theodore, "Native Band Objects to Treaty Settlement," *Globe and Mail*, July 5, 2007, http://www.theglobeandmail.com/news/national/native-band-objects-to-treaty-settlement/article688822/.

88 *Cook v. The Minister of Aboriginal Relations and Reconciliation*, 2007 BCSC 1722.

89 Constitution Act, 1867 (UK), 30 & 31 Vict, c 3, reprinted in RSC 1985, App II, No 5 at s. 91(24).

90 Constitution Act, 1982, being Schedule B to the Canada Act, 1982 (UK), 1982, c 11 at s. 35.

91 Baird, personal communication, February 1, 2013.

92 Ibid.

93 Union of British Columbia Indian Chiefs, *Tsawwassen Final Agreement: One Down, Hundreds More to Go* (Kamloops: Union of British Columbia Indian Chiefs, 2007), http://ubcic.bc.ca/files/PDF/UBCICPress_TFNAgreement_072507.pdf.

94 Ibid., i.

95 Ibid., 2.

96 Ibid.

97 Hilton, "Landmark Land Settlement."

98 Tsawwassen First Nation, Canada, and British Columbia, *Tsawwassen First Nation Final Agreement* (Vancouver: Indian and Northern Affairs Canada, British Columbia Region, 2007), 23, http://www2.gov.bc.ca/gov/content/environment/natural-resource-stewardship/consulting-with-first-nations/first-nations-negotiations/first-nations-a-z-listing/tsawwassen-first-nation (accessed April 15, 2014); Hanna, "Crown—First Nations Relationships," 80.

99 Tsawwassen First Nation, Canada, and British Columbia, *Tsawwassen First Nation Final Agreement*, 75.

100 Hanna, "Crown—First Nations Relationships," 82.

101 Tsawwassen First Nation, Canada, and British Columbia, *Tsawwassen First Nation Final Agreement,* 2.

102 *Van der Peet*, 507.

103 Graham Hingangaroa Smith, "Indigenous Struggle for the Transformation of Education and Schooling," keynote address to the Alaskan Federation of Natives (AFN) Convention, Anchorage, Alaska, October 2003, http://www.kaupapamaori.com/assets/indigenous_struggle.pdf.

104 Waziyatawin and Michael Yellow Bird, "Introduction: Decolonizing Our Minds and Actions," in *For Indigenous Eyes Only: A Decolonization Handbook*, ed. Waziyatawin and Michael Yellow Bird, 1–14 (Santa Fe, NM: School for Advanced Research Press, 2012), 5.

105 Gerald Taiaiake Alfred, "Colonialism and State Dependency," *Journal of Aboriginal Health* 5, no. 5 (2009): 42–60, 44, as quoted in Jeff Corntassel, "Living in a Longer Now: Moving Beyond the State-Centric System," in *For Indigenous Eyes Only: A Decolonization Handbook*, ed. Waziyatawin and Michael Yellow Bird, 85–98 (Santa Fe, NM: School for Advanced Research Press, 2012), 91–92.

106 Corntassel, "Living in a Longer Now," 92.

107 BC Treaty Commission, *Tsawwassen Embraces Self Government as the Way Forward*, http://www.bctreaty.ca/files/pdf_documents/homepage-treaty-web-articles/Tsawwassen-embraces-self-government-as-way-forward_FINAL.pdf (accessed April 17, 2014). NB: Other information about development around the Tsawwassen Nation was taken from this fact sheet.

108 Hilton, "Landmark Land Settlement."

109 Union of British Columbia Indian Chiefs, *Tsawwassen Final Agreement.*

110 Heinmot Tooyalakekt (Chief Joseph), "Chief Joseph's Own Story," in *Eyewitnesses to the Indian Wars, 1865–1890: The Wars For the Pacific Northwest*, ed. Peter Cozzens, 300–315 (Mechanicsburg, PA: Stackpole Books, 2002) 304.

111 Hilton, "Landmark Land Settlement."

112 Hanna, "Crown—First Nations Relationships," 81.

113 Ibid., 76.

114 Ibid., 81.

115 George Edward Ellis, *The Red Man and the White Man in North America from Its Discovery to the Present Time* (Boston: Little Brown and Company, 1882), 615.

116 Union of British Columbia Indian Chiefs, *Tsawwassen Final Agreement*, 3.

117 Ibid., 7.

Chapter 12

1 Marrianne Jones, director, *Tetzan Biny: The Disappearance of Fish Lake: Part 1*, SAMAQAN: Water Stories Series 1 (Winnipeg: Aboriginal Peoples Television Network, 2010). Video is available from Moving Images Distribution, http://movingimages.ca/store/products.php?samaqan_tetzan_biny_disappearance_fish_lake&osCsid=102da1179f9e080ee85dcbd1c0bab6af.

2 As quoted in Steve Taylor, *Back to Sanity: Healing the Madness of our Minds* (London: Hay House, 2012), 110.

3 Stephen Harper, *Statement by the Prime Minister of Canada in Cartagena, Columbia*, April 14, 2012, http://www.pm.gc.ca/eng/node/24935 (accessed May 7, 2014).

4 Brian McLeod, personal communication, Thunderbird House, Winnipeg, October 22, 2009; see also, Linda Tuhiwai Smith, *Decolonizing Methodologies: Research and Indigenous Peoples* (London: Zed Books, 1999), 20.

5 Ibid.

6 Jeffrey Reiman, *The Rich Get Richer and the Poor Get Prison: Ideology, Class, and Criminal Justice* (Boston: Allyn and Bacon, 2007).

7 Ibid., 4.

8 Ibid.

9 Both of the foregoing sentences draw on ibid., 183.

10 Ibid., 4.

11 Nils Christie, *Crime Control as Industry* (New York: Taylor & Francis Group, 2000), 13.

12 Georges Sioui, *Histoires de Kanatha: Vues et Contées / Histories of Kanatha: Seen and Told* (Ottawa: University of Ottawa Press, 2008), 83.

13 This and the next sentence reference Taylor, *Back to Sanity*, 81–82.

14 *Two Worlds Colliding*, DVD, directed by Tasha Hubbard (Ottawa: The National Film Board of Canada, 2004). See this DVD for details of this story.

15 David H. Wright, *Report of the Commission of Inquiry: Into Matters Relating to the Death of Neil Stonechild* (Regina: Ministry of Justice, Government of Saskatchewan, October 2004), 1.

16 For these two sentences, see ibid., 1, 35.

17 Ibid., 1.

18 Ibid., 151.

19 Ibid., 25.

20 Ibid.

21 Ibid., 176.

22 Ibid., 204.

23 Ibid., 193–94.

24 Joyce Green, "From Stonechild to Social Cohesion: Anti-Racist Challenges for Saskatchewan," paper presented to the Canadian Political Science Association: Theory, Policy and Pedagogy of Decolonization, University of Western Ontario, London, ON, June 2–4, 2005, http://www.cpsa-acsp.ca/papers-2005/Greene.pdf (accessed May 11, 2014), 1.

25 *Two Worlds Colliding*, DVD.

26 Elizabeth Comack, *Racialized Policing: Aboriginal Peoples' Encounters with the Police* (Halifax: Fernwood Publishing, 2012), 118.

27 Wright, *Report of the Commission of Inquiry*, 126.
28 John Steckley, *Learning from the Past: Five Cases of Aboriginal Justice* (Whitby, ON: deSitterPublications, 2013), 152.
29 Comack, *Racialized Policing*, 118.
30 John L. Steckley and Bryan D. Cummins, *Full Circle: Canada's First Nations* (Toronto: Pearson, 2008), 230.
31 Steckley, *Learning from the Past*, 152.
32 Ibid.
33 *Two Worlds Colliding*, DVD.
34 Steckley, *Learning from the Past*, 151–52.
35 Comack, *Racialized Policing*, 120; Steckley and Cummins, *Full Circle*, 230.
36 Steckley, *Learning from the Past*, 15.
37 Comack, *Racialized Policing*, 124.
38 DeNeen L. Brown, "Left for Dead in a Saskatchewan Winter," *The Washington Post*, November 22, 2003, http://web.archive.org/web/20050915100829/http://msnbc.msn.com/id/3540725/.
39 For more on this program, see Bryan D. Cummins and John L. Steckley *Aboriginal Policing: A Canadian Perspective* (Toronto: Pearson Education Canada, 2003), 20–21. Details reported here are found in this source.
40 Indian and Northern Affairs, *Report of Task Force: Policing on Reserves* (Ottawa: Indian and Northern Affairs, January 8, 1973), 9. See also, Jayne Seagrave, *Introduction to Policing in Canada* (Scarborough, ON: Prentice Hall, 2007), 255.
41 This and the following sentence draw on E.J. Dickson-Gilmore and Carol LaPrairie, *Will the Circle Be Unbroken? Aboriginal Communities, Restorative Justice, and the Challenges of Conflict and Change* (Toronto: University of Toronto Press, 2005), 70.
42 Jayne Seagrave, *Introduction to Policing in Canada* (Scarborough, ON: Prentice Hall, 1997), 256.
43 C.T. Griffiths and J.C. Yerbury, "Natives and Criminal Justice Policy: The Case of Native Policing," *Canadian Journal of Criminology* 26, no. 2 (April 1984): 147–60; see also, Seagrave, *Introduction to Policing in Canada*, 256.
44 Julie Jars, *Inventory of Aboriginal Policing Programs in Canada* (Ottawa: Ministry of the Solicitor General, 1992), quoted in Seagrave, *Introduction to Policing in Canada*, 256.
45 For the details of this paragraph, see Dickson-Gilmore and LaPrairie, *Will the Circle Be Unbroken?*, 68, 71.
46 This paragraph draws on Mylène Jaccoud, "La justice pénale et les Autochtones: D'une justice imposée au transfert de pouvoirs," *Revue canadienne Droit et Société*, 17, no. 2 (2003): 107–21, 116–17.
47 For this and the following sentence, see Rémi Savard, "Les peuples américains et le système judiciaire canadien: Spéléologie d'un trou de mémoire," *Revue canadienne Droit et Société* 17, no. 2 (2003): 123–48.
48 Robynne Neugebauer, "First Nations People and Law Enforcement: Community Perspectives on Police Response," in *Interrogating Social Justice: Politics, Culture and Identity*, ed. Marilyn Corsianos and Kelly Amanda Train, 247–69 (Toronto: Canadian Scholars Press, 1999).
49 Carol La Prairie, *Seen but not Heard: Native People in the Inner City* (Ottawa: Department of Justice, 1994).

50 Manitoba Aboriginal Justice Inquiry, *The Justice System and Aboriginal People* (Winnipeg: The Aboriginal Justice Implementation Commission, 1999), chapter 16, http://www.ajic.mb.ca/volumel/chapter16.html#1.
51 Manitoba Aboriginal Justice Inquiry, *The Justice System and Aboriginal People.*
52 Ibid.
53 Barbara Perry, "Nobody Trusts Them! Under- and Over-Policing Native American Communities," *Critical Criminology* 14, no. 4 (2006): 411–44.
54 Although, in the case of *R. v. Wells*, the Supreme Court opined that "the more violent and serious the offence, the more likely as a practical matter that the appropriate sentence will not differ as between Aboriginal and non-Aboriginal offenders."
55 Although the case involved two defendants, it is cited under the name of only one: *R. v. Ipeelee*, 2012 SCC 13.
56 The Honourable Judge Cunliffe Barnette (retired), Public Lecture, at *Gladue Growing Pains: Racial Sentencing Discounts or Emancipation from Racial Sentencing?* Allard Hall, Franklin Lew Forum, University of British Columbia, Vancouver, March 20, 2013.
57 Jonathan Rudin, *A Court of Our Own: More on the Gladue Courts* (Toronto: ALST, 2006), http://www.nanlegal.on.ca/upload/documents/legal-articles/a-court-of-our-own---more-on-gladue-courts.pdf.
58 Pamela Shields, public lecture presented at *Gladue Growing Pains: Racial Sentencing Discounts or Emancipation from Racial Sentencing?* Allard Hall, Franklin Lew Forum, University of British Columbia, Vancouver, March 20, 2013.
59 The details provided in this section, including quotations, are taken from Kent Roach and Jonathan Rudin, "Gladue: The Judicial and Political Reception of a Promising Decision," *Canadian Journal of Criminology* 42, no. 3 (July 2000): 355–88, 369.
60 See for other information in this paragraph, Roach and Rudin, "Gladue: The Judicial and Political Reception," 369–71.
61 *R. v. Proulx* [2000] 1 S.C.R. 61.
62 Roach and Rudin, "Gladue: The Judicial and Political Reception," 372.
63 See for other information in this paragraph, ibid., 371.
64 Ibid., 357.
65 Office of the Correctional Investigator, *Spirit Matters: Aboriginal People and the Corrections and Conditional Release Act* (Ottawa: Office of the Correctional Investigator, 2012), 4.
66 For details of this report, including those presented here, see ibid., 3–5.
67 Ibid., 25.
68 Ibid., 12. Emphasis added.
69 Joseph C. Johnston, *Aboriginal Offender Survey: Case Files and Interview Sample* (Ottawa: Research Branch, Correctional Services Canada, 1997). Johnston studied approximately 50 per cent of Indigenous people who were in federal custody by reviewing their files, executing face-to-face interviews, and researching their criminal history data obtained through the Canadian Police Information Centre.
70 Doug Heckbert and Douglas Turkington, *Turning Points: A Study of the Factors Related to the Successful Reintegration of Aboriginal Offenders* (Ottawa: Correctional Service of Canada, 2001), 3.
71 Jeff Latimer and Laura Casey Foss, *A One-Day Snapshot of Aboriginal Youth in Custody Across Canada: Phase II* (Ottawa: Research and Statistics Division, Department of Justice Canada, 2004), 22. This study had two parts to its data collection: the

"sharing circle" method and the "snap shot" method. This study also revealed that the high incarceration rate of Indigenous youth is likely related to a series of interrelated factors, such as high rates of poverty and substance abuse.

72 James B. Waldram, *The Way of the Pipe: Aboriginal Spirituality and Symbolic Healing in Canadian Prisons* (Peterborough, ON: Broadview Press, 1997), 136–40.

73 The preceding sentences draw on ibid., 140.

74 Rupert Ross, *Dancing with a Ghost: Exploring Aboriginal Reality* (Toronto: Penguin Canada, 2006).

75 The source for this paragraph is ibid., 15.

76 This and the previous sentence draw on ibid., 16.

77 Ibid.

78 Ibid., 20.

79 Ibid., 36.

80 Ibid., 38–39.

81 Waldram, *The Way of the Pipe*, 144–45.

82 For information and quotations related to this case, including those presented here, see ibid., 34–35.

83 For information and quotations related to this case, including what is presented here, see ibid., 36.

84 Ross, *Dancing with a Ghost*, 41.

85 The preceding two sentences draw on ibid., 42.

86 Canadian Resource Centre for Victims of Crime, *Restorative Justice in Canada: What Victims Should Know* (Ottawa: Canadian Resource Centre for Victims of Crime, 2011), http://www.crcvc.ca/docs/restjust.pdf (accessed December 20, 2012).

87 The information in this paragraph comes from ibid.

88 Jo-Anne Wemmers and Marisa Canuto, *Victims Experiences with, Expectations and Perceptions of Restorative Justice: A Critical Review of the Literature* (Ottawa: Department of Justice Canada, 2002).

89 Frank Iacobucci, *First Nations Representation on Ontario Juries: Report of the Independent Review Conducted by the Honourable Frank Iacobucci* (Toronto: Office of the Attorney General, February 2013), 1.

90 The quote and previous sentence are from ibid., 4.

91 Ibid.

92 Ibid., 4–5.

93 Ibid., 5.

94 Ibid., 6.

95 Hadley Friedland, *Accessing Justice and Reconciliation—IBA Accessing Justice and Reconciliation Project: Final Report* (Victoria, BC: Indigenous Law Research Unit, February 4, 2014), http://indigenousbar.ca/indigenouslaw/wp-content/uploads/2013/04/iba_ajr_final_report.pdf (accessed February 13, 2015). The subsequent details are also located in this source; see especially page 8.

96 Ibid., 8.

97 Ibid.

98 Ibid., 10.

99 Chris Andersen, "Governing Aboriginal Justice in Canada: Constructing Responsible Individuals and Communities Through Tradition," *Crime Law and Social Change* 31, no. 4 (1999): 303–26, 304.

100 Ibid., 314.

101 Rudin, "Aboriginal Justice and Restorative Justice," 97–98.
102 Ibid., 97.
103 Robert Koopmans, "Sentencing Circle a First for Kamloops," *Kamloops Daily News*, September 20, 2012, http://www.kamloopsnews.ca/article/20120920/KAMLOOPS0101/120929989/-1/kamloops/sentencing-circle-a-first-for-kamloops (accessed December 17, 2012).
104 Jonathon Rudin, "Aboriginal Justice and Restorative Justice," in *New Directions in Restorative Justice: Issues, Practice, Evaluation*, ed. Elizabeth Elliot and Robert M. Gordon, 89–114 (Portland, OR: Willan Publishing, 2005); Julian Roberts and Carol La Prairie, "Sentencing Circles: Some Unanswered Questions," *Criminal Law Quarterly* 39 (August 1996): 69–83.
105 Emma LaRocque, Re-examining Culturally Appropriate Models in Criminal Justice Applications, in *Aboriginal Treaty Rights in Canada*, ed. Micheal Asch, 75–96 (Vancouver: UBC Press, 2002), 76.
106 Ibid., 83.
107 Ibid., 82.
108 Ibid.
109 Ibid.
110 Friedland, *Accessing Justice and Reconciliation*, 17.
111 John Borrows, *Canada's Indigenous Constitution* (Toronto: University of Toronto Press, 2010), 283.

Chapter 13

1 *The 8th Fire: Aboriginal Peoples, Canada & the Way Forward*, DVD, directed by Ryszard Hunka (Canadian Broadcasting Corporation, 2012). This idea was explained by host Wab Kinew at the very beginning of the first episode, "Indigenous in the City."
2 The Circle of Turtle Lodge, *Anishnabe 101* (Golden Lake, ON: The Circle of Turtle Lodge, 2010), 10–12. The story is drawn from this source.
3 Edward Benton-Banai, "The Seven Fires," *The Mishomis Book* (Minneapolis: University of Minnesota Press, 2010), 89. Also see this source for details of the story.
4 The Circle of Turtle Lodge, *Anishnabe 101*, 11.
5 Ibid., 12.
6 Benton-Banai, "The Seven Fires," 93.
7 Gregory Younging, "The Rhetoric and the Reality," Aboriginal Gathering Place Lecture Series, Kwantlen Polytechnic University, Surrey, BC, March 21, 2013.
8 Olthuis, Kleer, Townshed LLP, *Aboriginal Law Handbook*, 4th edition (Toronto: Thomson Reuters Canada, 2012), 15.
9 Younging, "The Rhetoric and the Reality."
10 United Nations, *United Nations Declaration on the Rights of Indigenous Peoples* (New York: UN, 2007), http://www.un.org/esa/socdev/unpfii/documents/DRIPS_en.pdf. See in particular articles 33 and 31.
11 Andy Radia, "AFN Runner-up Pam Palmater Accuses PM of Trying to Break up Communities," *Yahoo News Canada*, December 27, 2012, http://ca.news.yahoo.com/blogs/canada-politics/yahoo-exclusive-afn-runner-pam-palmater-accuses-pm-144833734.html (accessed March 25, 2013).

12 APTN National News, "Watch Prime Minister Trudeau's Address."
13 Harsha Walia, "Decolonizing Together: Moving Beyond a Politics of Solidarity Towards a Practice of Decolonization," *Briarpatch Magazine*, January 1, 2012, http://briarpatchmagazine.com/articles/view/decolonizing-together (accessed March 3, 2015).
14 Gerald Taiaiake Alfred, "Colonialism and State Dependency," *Journal of Aboriginal Health* 5, no. 5 (2009): 42–60, 44.
15 Michael Yellow Bird, *Indigenous Social Work* (Aldershot, UK: Ashgate, 2008), as cited from Michael Yellow Bird, "Decolonizing the Mind: Healing Through Neurodecolonization and Mindfulness," lecture delivered at the Multicultural Center SMSU, Portland State University, Portland, OR, January 24, 2014, available from http://www.indigenousfoodsystems.org/content/decolonizing-mind-talk-dr-michael-yellowbird (accessed April 3, 2014). All quotations attributed to Michael Yellow Bird in this section are from this lecture unless otherwise specified.
16 Leanne Simpson, *Dancing on Our Turtle's Back: Stories of Nishnaabeg Re-Creation, Resurgence and a New Emergence* (Winnipeg: Arbeiter Ring Publishing, 2011), 21.
17 Ibid., 21–22.
18 Truth and Reconciliation Commission of Canada, *Our Mandate*, http://www.trc.ca/websites/trcinstitution/index.php?p=7.
19 Ibid., 1.
20 Justice Murray Sinclair, "Rheal Brant Hall Lecture: Truth and Reconciliation," public lecture, Carleton University, Ottawa, October 15, 2010.
21 Ibid.
22 Sino General, (Cayuga Nation, Wolf Clan), personal communication, Kwantlen Polytechnic University, Surrey, BC, April 25, 2013.
23 Martin J. Cannon and Lina Sunseri, "Conclusion," in *Racism, Colonialism, and Indigeneity in Canada*, ed. Martin J. Cannon and Lina Sunseri, 263–72 (Don Mills, ON: Oxford University Press, 2011), 263.
24 Jeff Corntassel, "Re-Envisioning Resurgence: Indigenous Pathways to Decolonization and Sustainable Self-Determination," *Decolonization: Indigeneity, Education & Society* 1, no. 1 (2012): 86–101, 93.
25 This paragraph draws on Simpson, *Dancing on Our Turtle's Back*, 22–23.
26 This paragraph draws on Corntassel, "Re-Envisioning Resurgence", notably pages 89 and 90; also see Simpson, *Dancing on Our Turtle's Back*; Taiaiake Alfred, *Wasáse: Indigenous Pathways of Action and Freedom* (Toronto: University of Toronto Press, 2009), 151.
27 Bear Witness, DJ Shub (Dan General), and Dee Jay NDN (Ian Campeau), personal communication, Skwachays Healing Lodge Gallery, Vancouver Native Housing Complex, Vancouver, November 10, 2012. All quotations attributed to these individuals are from this communication unless otherwise specified.
28 "Episode 1: Indigenous in the City," *The 8th Fire: Aboriginal Peoples, Canada & the Way Forward*, DVD, directed by Ryszard Hunka (Canadian Broadcasting Corporation, 2012). All quotations attributed to Monkman are taken from this documentary unless otherwise indicated; the discussion here draws on this source.
29 Musée Huron-Wendat, *La Loi sur les Indiens Revisitée—The Indian Act Revisited* (Wendaké, QC: Musée Huron-Wendat, 2009).

30 Sino General (Chief Rock), personal communication. These sentiments were expressed through several conversations from 2011 to 2013 that took place throughout Coast Salish territories.

31 Inez Jasper, *Biography*, http://inezjasper.com/bio/ (accessed December 7, 2014).

32 MTV, *Rebel Music: Native America*, https://www.facebook.com/video.php?v=10152456634446701&set=vb.7245371700&type=3&theater (accessed December 7, 2014).

33 Inez Jasper, "Dancin' on the Run [2013]," *YouTube*, https://www.youtube.com/watch?v=QgOluBcedw0 (accessed December 7, 2014).

34 Inez Jasper, quoted in an interview by Christina Rose, "She's a Rebel! Inez Jasper Can't Wait for Today's 'Rebel Music' Premiere (4 PM ET)," *Indian Country Today Media Network*, November 13, 2014, http://indiancountrytodaymedianetwork.com/2014/11/13/shes-rebel-inez-jasper-cant-wait-todays-rebel-music-premiere-4-pm-et-157823 (accessed December 7, 2014).

35 Manitoba Metis Federation, *Louis Riel Quotes*, http://www.mmf.mb.ca/louis_riel_quotes.php (accessed May 8, 2014).

36 Jesse Ferreras, "Idle No More Art: Posters Promote a Revolution," *Huffpost British Columbia*, January 19, 2013, http://www.huffingtonpost.ca/2013/01/19/idle-no-more-art-posters_n_2499292.html (accessed May 8, 2014). See this article for more on the art of Lou-Ann Neel and Dwayne Bird; additional information in this paragraph is taken from this source.

37 Plex (Doug Bedard), "No More feat. Lase (Official Video) [2013]," *YouTube*, http://www.youtube.com/watch?v=u9FXdVnweok (accessed January 29, 2013).

38 Patricia Monture-Angus, *Thunder in My Soul: A Mohawk Women Speaks* (Halifax: Fernwood Publishing, 1995).

39 Joseph E. Couture, "The Role of Native Elders: Emergent Issues," in *Visions of the Heart: Canadian Aboriginal Issues*, ed. David Long and Olive Patricia Dickason, 31–48 (Scarborough, ON: Thomson Nelson, 1998), 31.

40 Martin Brokenleg, "Spiritual Restoration among Native Peoples," lecture hosted by The Spirit of the Children Society, Douglas College, New Westminster, BC, April 20, 2013. (Dr. Brokenleg is a member of the Rosebud Sioux Tribe practicing the culture of his Lakota people.)

41 Larry K. Brendtro, Martin Brokenleg, and Steven Van Bockern, *Reclaiming Youth at Risk: Our Hope for the Future*, revised edition (Bloomington, IN: Solution Tree Press, 2002).

42 Anne Poonwassie and Ann Charter, "An Aboriginal Worldview of Helping: Empowering Approaches," *Canadian Journal of Counselling* 35, no. 1 (2001): 63–73, 67.

43 This paragraph draws on Ghislaine Goudreau, Cora Weber-Pillwax, Sheila Cote-Meek, Helen Madill, and Stan Wilson, "Hand Drumming: Health-Promoting Experiences of Aboriginal Women from a Northern Ontario Urban Community," *Journal of Aboriginal Health* 4, no. 1 (2008): 72–83, 73–75.

44 Ibid.

45 Ibid., 73.

46 Ibid., 76.

47 Cheryl Currie, T. Cameron Wild, Donald P. Schopflocher, Lory Laing, and Paul Veugelers, "Illicit and Prescription Drug Problems among Urban Aboriginal Adults in Canada: The Role of Traditional Culture in Protection and Resilience," *Social Science & Medicine* 88 (July 2013): 1–9.

48 Ibid., 6.

49 Darrell Bob, Chief, Xaxl'ip Nation, personal communication, Tsleil-Waututh Nation Community Centre, December 22, 2012.

50 The remainder of this paragraph draws on Poonwassie and Charter, "An Aboriginal Worldview of Helping," 68.

51 This quote and the following sentence are drawn from Jo-ann Archibald, *Indigenous Storywork: Educating the Heart, Mind, Body, and Spirit* (Vancouver: UBC Press, 2008), 85.

52 The remainder of this section is informed by Poonwassie and Charter, "An Aboriginal Worldview of Helping," 67.

53 Mark Totten and Sharon Dunn, *Annual Evaluation Report for the Prince Albert Outreach Program Inc. Youth Alliance Against Gang Violence Project* (Toronto: Totten and Associates, February 15, 2010), 5.

54 Ibid., 11; Brendtro, Brokenleg, and Van Bockern, *Reclaiming Youth at Risk.*

55 Brokenleg, "Spiritual Restoration among Native Peoples."

56 See Brendtro, Brokenleg, and Van Bockern, *Reclaiming Youth at Risk*, 52–53, for the description of these four values.

57 Totten and Dunn, *Annual Evaluation Report*, 2010.

58 Mark Totten and Sharon Dunn, *Annual Evaluation Report for the Prince Albert Outreach Program Inc. Youth Alliance Against Gang Violence Project* (Gatineau: Totten and Associates, February 20, 2009), 57.

59 The details of this paragraph are from ibid., 10, 57.

60 For this paragraph, see Totten and Dunn, *Annual Evaluation Report*, 2010, especially page 39.

61 For example, see Irvin Waller, *Less Law, More Order: The Truth About Reducing Crime* (Ancaster, ON: Manor House Publishing, 2008).

62 For example, see Mark Totten, "Preventing Aboriginal Youth Gang Involvement in Canada: A Gendered Approach," paper prepared for the Aboriginal Policy Research Conference, Ottawa, March 2009; Lisa Monchalin, "Canadian Aboriginal Peoples Victimization, Offending, and Its Prevention," *Crime Prevention and Community Safety: An International Journal* 12, no. 2 (2010): 119–39, 119–32.

63 Lisa Monchalin, "Pourquoi pas la prévention du crime? Une perspective canadienne," *Criminologie* 42, no. 1 (2009): 115–42.

64 Marta Burczycka, *Police Resources in Canada, 2010* (Ottawa: Statistics Canada, 2010), 19.

65 Public Safety Canada, *Corrections and Conditional Release Statistical Overview: Annual Report 2012* (Ottawa: Public Safety Canada, 2012), 21.

66 Andrea Taylor-Butts, "Justice Spending in Canada 2000/01," *Juristat* 22, no. 11 (2002), 7.

67 Department of Justice Canada, *Aboriginal Justice Strategy Evaluation* (Ottawa: Department of Justice, 2011), ii.

68 Department of Justice Canada, *Aboriginal Justice Strategy Mid-Term Evaluation* (Ottawa: Department of Justice, 2010), i.

69 See the following for information on the program: Department of Justice Canada, *Aboriginal Justice Strategy Mid-Term Evaluation*, i-ii.

70 Department of Justice Canada, *Aboriginal Justice Strategy Evaluation*, 5.

71 Department of Justice Canada, *Location of Aboriginal Justice Strategy Programs in Canada*, http://www.justice.gc.ca/eng/fund-fina/acf-fca/ajs-sja/cf-pc/location-emplace/ab.html (accessed November 27, 2014).

72 Mi'Kmaw Legal Support Network, *Mi'Kmaq Customary Law Program*, http://www.mlsn.ca/index.php?cont=customary-law-program (accessed November 27, 2014).

73 Ibid.

74 For statistics related to these programs, see Department of Justice Canada, *Aboriginal Justice Strategy Evaluation*, 5, 11.

75 Ibid., 13–14.

76 Quotation is on page 37, but see for other details of this evaluation, Department of Justice Canada, *Aboriginal Justice Strategy Evaluation*, 36–37.

77 Ibid., 15.

78 Ibid., 74.

79 Ibid., 42.

80 Shana Dion, Director of Aboriginal Student Services Centre, personal communication, University of Alberta, September 26, 2013.

81 For information on the number and location of centres, see the National Association of Friendship Centre's website, http://nafc.ca/en/friendship-centres/.

82 See Lisa Monchalin, "Reducing Crime Affecting Urban Aboriginal People: The Potential for Effective Solutions in Winnipeg" (PhD dissertation, University of Ottawa, 2012).

83 Sources that outline the correlation between alcohol and crime are, for example, Nicole P. Yuan, Mary P. Koss, Mona Polacca and David Goldman, "Risk Factors for Physical Assault and Rape among Six Native American Tribes," *Journal of Interpersonal Violence* 21, no. 12 (2006): 1566–90; Jodi-Anne Brzozowski, Andrea Taylor-Butts, and Sara Johnson, "Victimization and Offending Among the Aboriginal Population in Canada," *Juristat* 26, no. 3 (2006): 1–23.

84 M. Nancy Comeau, Sherry H. Stewart, Christopher Mushquash, David Wojcik, Cheryl Bartlett, Murdena Marshall, Jerry Young, and Doreen Stevens, "Community Collaboration in Developing a Culturally Relevant Alcohol Abuse Early Intervention Program for First Nation Youth," *OCAS Journal* 49, no. 1 (2005), 39–46.

85 Christopher J. Mushquash, M. Nancy Comeau, and Sherry H. Stewart, "An Alcohol Abuse Early Intervention Approach with Mi'kmaq Adolescents," *First Peoples Child & Family Review* 3, no. 1 (2007): 17–26, 20.

86 This paragraph is informed by ibid., 21.

87 Monchalin, "Reducing Crime Affecting Urban Aboriginal People," 220.

88 National Association of Friendship Centres, *Business Case for the Long Term Sustainability of Friendship Centres* (Ottawa: The National Association of Friendship Centres and The Department of Canadian Heritage, 2009), 8; on March 28, 2012, funding for friendship centres was transferred from the Department of Canadian Heritage to Aboriginal Affairs and Northern Development Canada (now Indigenous and Northerm Affairs Canada).

89 Annette Morgan, "BC Friendship Centres Facing Funding Crisis," *News Release of the BC Association of Aboriginal Friendship Centres*, March 10, 2014, http://www.bcaafc.com/newsandevents (accessed May 11, 2014).

90 Brokenleg, "Spiritual Restoration among Native Peoples."

91 Colleen Simard, "The Seventh Fire GENERATION: How Young Aboriginals see the Present and Future," *Winnipeg Free Press*, September 20, 2009, http://www.winnipegfreepress.com/arts-and-life/life/the-seventh-fire-generation-59930162.html (accessed February 14, 2015).

92 Wab Kinew, director, "Dispatch: Michael Champagne," *8th Fire Dispatches*, http://www.cbc.ca/8thfire/2012/03/michael-champagne.html (accessed February 14, 2015); Michael Champagne, "TEDxManitoba—Michael Champagne: Oppression to Opportunity [2012]," *YouTube*, https://www.youtube.com/watch?v=pXJOQYxxV2Y (accessed February 14, 2015). All material attributed to Michael Champagne is from these two sources, unless otherwise specified.

93 Aboriginal Youth Opportunities (AYO!), *Michael Champagne, Organizer*, http://www.ayomovement.com/michael.html (accessed February 14, 2015).

94 Champagne, "TEDxManitoba."

95 Gabrielle Fayant, "Gabrielle Fayant: Native Youth Claim Their Future through Technology," *Globe and Mail*, February 9, 2015, http://www.theglobeandmail.com/globe-debate/gabrielle-fayant-native-youth-claim-their-future-through-technology/article22856060/ (accessed February 16, 2015); Assembly of Se7en Generations, "The Team: Gabrielle Fayant," https://a7g.dotrust.org/about/team/ (accessed February 16, 2015).

96 Fayant, "Gabrielle Fayant: Native Youth Claim their Future"; Centre for Aboriginal Culture and Education, "Gabrielle Fayant," http://carleton.ca/aboriginal/resources/cuaboriginal-student-profiles/gabrielle-fayant/ (accessed February 16, 2015). See these two sources for the details presented here about Fayant's life and story.

97 Fayant, "Gabrielle Fayant: Native Youth Claim their Future."

98 Ibid.

99 Craig and Marc Kielburger, "Let's Hear It for Positive Aboriginal Role Models," *Globe and Mail*, June 25, 2012, http://www.theglobeandmail.com/life/giving/lets-hear-it-for-positive-aboriginal-role-models/article4369264/ (accessed February 16, 2015).

100 This paragraph draws on ibid.

101 Indspire, "Candace Sutherland," *Indspire Laureates*, https://indspire.ca/laureate/candace-sutherland/ (accessed February 16, 2015).

102 Indspire "Candace Sutherland: 2012 Award Laureate—Youth [2013]," *YouTube*, https://www.youtube.com/watch?v=kHo8aObc2PU&feature=youtu.be (accessed February 16, 2015).

103 Indspire, "Candace Sutherland," *Indspire Laureates*.

104 LaurierVideo "Laurier Inspiring Lives: Allan Downey, PhD Candidate in History [2013]," *YouTube*, https://www.youtube.com/watch?v=UkKMLdB8lW0 (accessed February 16, 2015).

105 Neale McDevitt, "Allan Downey: Using Lacrosse to Teach, Inspire and Heal," *McGill Reporter*, September 15, 2015, http://publications.mcgill.ca/reporter/2014/09/allan-downey-using-lacrosse-to-teach-inspire-and-heal/ (accessed February 16, 2015).

106 Ibid.

107 Ibid.

108 LaurierVideo "Laurier Inspiring Lives: Allan Downey."

109 McDevitt, "Allan Downey."

110 Ibid.

Index